Practicing Responsible Tourism

INTERNATIONAL CASE STUDIES IN TOURISM PLANNING,
POLICY, AND DEVELOPMENT

Edited by

Lynn C. Harrison
Winston Husbands

Ryerson Polytechnic University
Toronto, Ontario, Canada

JOHN WILEY & SONS, INC.

New York | Chichester | Brisbane | Toronto | Singapore

This text is printed on acid-free paper.

Copyright © 1996 by John Wiley & Sons, Inc.

All rights reserved. Published simultaneously in Canada.

No part of this publication may be reproduced, stored in a retrieval system or transmitted
in any form or by any means, electronic, mechanical, photocopying, recording, scanning
or otherwise, except as permitted under Sections 107 or 108 of the 1976 United States
Copyright Act, without either the prior written permission of the Publisher, or
authorization through payment of the appropriate per-copy fee to the Copyright
Clearance Center, 222 Rosewood Drive, Danvers, MA 01923, (978) 750-8400, fax
(978) 750-4470. Requests to the Publisher for permission should be addressed to the
Permissions Department, John Wiley & Sons, Inc., 111 River Street, Hoboken, NJ 07030,
(201) 748-6011, fax (201) 748-6008, E-Mail: PERMREQ@WILEY.COM.

To order books or for customer service please, call 1(800)-CALL-WILEY (225-5945).

This publication is designed to provide accurate and
authoritative information in regard to the subject
matter covered. It is sold with the understanding that
the publisher is not engaged in rendering legal, accounting,
or other professional services. If legal advice or other
expert assistance is required, the services of a competent
professional person should be sought.

Library of Congress Cataloging in Publication Data:
Harrison, Lynn (Lynn C.)
     Practicing responsible tourism: international case studies in
tourism planning, policy, and development / Lynn Harrison, Winston
Husbands.
     p.   cm.
     Includes bibliographical references.
     ISBN 0-471-12236-X (cloth : alk. paper)
     1. Tourist trade.   I. Husbands, Winston.   II. Title.
G155.A1H364   1996
338.4'791—dc20   98-14316

10 9 8 7

Contents

Acknowledgments

Many people from around the world generously assisted the editors in preparing this book.

At the start of the project, Bryce Aguiton and Jacqueline Clarke, our former students, helped us identify and contact prospective contributors.

Our perspectives on the tourism knowledge base and tourism-related career opportunities were developed from a research project carried out by several former fourth-year students: Michal Cahlon, Lisa Holzwarth, Karlene Jaikaran, Wendy MacInnis, Miranda Townsend, and Michele Vaughan-Greig.

The case studies benefited from the insights and comments of our review panel. The panel, which reviewed each chapter anonymously, comprised the following tourism researchers and educators: Dan Fesenmaier (University of Illinois), Harry French (Canadian Tourism Research Institute), Alison Gill (Simon Fraser University), Simon Milne (McGill University), Douglas Pearce (University of Canterbury), Gord Phillips (Economic Planning Group of Canada), Jane Siegel (Longwoods International), Bill Siegel (Longwoods International), Stephen L.J. Smith (University of Waterloo), and Paul Wilkinson (York University).

During the final stages of preparation, additional comments and suggestions were received from alumni and second- to fourth-year students from the School of Hospitality and Tourism Management, Ryerson Polytechnic University, who undertook a review of the chapters from the audience's perspective: Michael Bower, Chris Clarke, Murray Dickson, Sue Dalmage, Peta-Gaye Gordon, Gail Kulczycki, Louis Loranger, Angelina McMayo, Megan Meltzer, Melissa Otto, and Suzan Trabert.

We drew on the word processing skills of Ruth Andrews, Rikki Durbin, and Vira Kozlowsky during the preliminary formatting of the initial manuscripts, in addition to Sheila Thompson's expertise with database and graphics software.

We also thank the respective authors for their wholehearted support throughout the various phases of the project. Their kind words of encouragement and good humor throughout the process were much appreciated.

We thank Claire Thompson, Maria Colletti, and Donna Conte of John Wiley & Sons for their trust, patience, and enthusiasm.

Finally, but not least, we extend our appreciation to our respective families, friends, and colleagues who stood by us. Ross and Bryan Harrison, and Kambili and Aman Husbands, we hope that the lessons and examples presented in this volume of case studies take us one step closer to practicing responsible tourism so that you might one day experience the wonders of the world's many tourist destinations.

Our work in the book was supported in part by a grant from the Faculty of Business, Ryerson Polytechnic University.

Contributors

Australia and New Zealand

Lisa Bourke, Lecturer, Department of Psychology and Sociology, James Cook University, Townsville.

Michael V. Conlin (B.A., M.B.A., and L.I.B., University of Western Ontario; Ph.D. candidate, University of Buckingham), Dean, Australian International Hotel School, Australian Capital Territory.

Derrin Davis (B.Ag. Ec., M.Sc.), Senior Lecturer in Resource Economics, Centre for Coastal Management, Southern Cross University, New South Wales.

C. Michael Hall (Ph.D.), Professor of Tourism and Services Management, Victoria University of Wellington, New Zealand.

Vicki Harriott (B.Sc., M.Sc., Ph.D.), Senior Lecturer in Marine Biology, Centre for Coastal Management, Southern Cross University, New South Wales.

Bob McKercher, Senior Lecturer and Course Coordinator, Tourism Management Program, Charles Sturt University, New South Wales.

Canada

Liz Addison, President, Addison Consulting Services Inc., Toronto, Ontario.

Richard W. Butler [B.A. (Honors), University of Nottingham; Ph.D., University of Glasgow], Professor, Department of Geography, University of Western Ontario, London, Ontario.

Sally Davidson (M.A., M.C.P., M.C.I.P.), Principal, Blackstone Corporation, Resource Management and Tourism Consultants, Toronto, Ontario.

Douglas Hainsworth (Masters of Community and Regional Planning, University of British Columbia), Researcher, Centre for Tourism Policy and Research, Simon Fraser University, British Columbia.

Lynn C. Harrison [B.Sc. (Psychology), University of Toronto; M.B.A., York University], Professor of Tourism, Marketing, and Research, School of Hospitality and Tourism Management, Ryerson Polytechnic University, Toronto, Ontario.

K. Michael Haywood, Professor and Director, School of Hotel and Food Administration, University of Guelph, Ontario.

Winston Husbands [Ph.D.(Geography of Tourism), University of Western Ontario], Research Coordinator, Daily Bread Food Bank, Toronto, Ontario.

Marion Joppe [Ph.D. (Law and Economics), Centre des Hautes Etudes Touristiques, Aix-en-Provence, France), Assistant Professor of Tourism, School of Hospitality and Tourism Management, Ryerson Polytechnic University, Toronto, Ontario.

Barbara Lamb (B.E.S., M.Sc.), Principal, Blackstone Corporation, Resource Management and Tourism Consultants, Toronto, Ontario.

Julie Paul, Senior Consultant, ARA Consulting Group Inc., Vancouver, British Columbia.

Laurel J. Reid [B.Sc. (Communications/Marketing), Syracuse University; Masters of Communications Studies, University of Calgary; Ph.D. (Parks, Recreation, and Tourism Management), Clemson University], Associate Professor, Department of Recreation and Leisure Studies, Brock University, Ontario.

David Russell [B.A. (Economics), Carleton University; M.C.P. (City Planning), University of Pennsylvania], Partner, ARA Consulting Group Inc., Vancouver, British Columbia.

Geoffrey Wall (Ph.D.), Professor, Geography and Recreation and Leisure Studies, University of Waterloo, Ontario.

Paul F. Wilkinson [B.A. (Geography), York University; M.A. and Ph.D. (Geography), University of Toronto], Professor, Faculty of Environmental Studies and Graduate Programme in Geography, York University, Toronto, Ontario.

Peter W. Williams (Ph.D.), Director, Centre For Tourism Policy and Research, Simon Fraser University, British Columbia.

Caribbean

Wrenford Ferrance, former Parks Commissioner, Nelson's Dockyard National Park, Antigua and Barbuda.

Jean Stewart Holder [M.V.O., B.A., M.A., D.P.S.A., Harrison College (Barbados), Oxford University, University of Toronto], Secretary General, Caribbean Tourism Organization, Barbados.

Ann Marie Martin, Parks Commissioner, Nelson's Dockyard National Park, Antigua and Barbuda.

United Kingdom and Other Europe

Alison J. Beeho, Visiting Lecturer in Tourism Management and Postgraduate Researcher, Queen Margaret College, Edinburgh.

Stephen W. Boyd [B.A. (Honors), The Queen's University of Belfast; M.A., University of Saskatchewan; Ph.D., University of Western Ontario], Division of Geography, Faculty of Sciences, Staffordshire University, Stoke-on-Trent.

Clodagh Cunningham, Research Officer, Centre for Development Studies, University College Galway, Ireland.

Karl Donert (M.Sc., Imperial College, London), Senior Lecturer in Geography, Liverpool Hope University College, Liverpool.

Kerry B. Godfrey [B.Sc. (Honors), University of Victoria; M.Sc., University of Surrey; Ph.D., Oxford Brookes University], Senior Lecturer in Tourism Development, School of Planning, Oxford Brookes University, Oxford.

Michael J. Keane (Ph.D.), Senior Lecturer, Centre for Development Studies and the Department of Economics, University College Galway, Ireland.

Mary S. Klemm (graduate of London and Sheffield Hallam Universities), Lecturer in Tourism Management, Bradford University, Bradford.

Duncan Light (Ph.D., University of Wales, Swansea), Lecturer in Geography, Liverpool Hope University College, Liverpool.

Maria A. Mart'n-Quir—s (graduate in Psychology, University of Granada; M.B.A., Bradford University), Consultant, Plan Excel, Granada, Spain.

Micheál S. Ó Cinnéide (Ph.D.), Chair, Social Sciences Research Centre and Associate Professor of Geography, Centre for Development Studies, University College Galway, Ireland.

Richard C. Prentice (Ph.D.), Professor of Tourism and Director of Research, Hospitality and Tourism, Queen Margaret College, Edinburgh.

Christoph Stadel (Ph.D.), Professor of Geography, University of Salzburg, Austria.

Javier Vazquez-Illa (B.Sc., Madrid; M.P.A., Cornell University), General Manager, Arnedillo Spa and Hotels, Spain.

United States

Russell A. Bell (B.A., Washington & Jefferson College; M.S. and Ph.D., Kansas State University), Associate Professor of Marketing, Cornell School of Hotel Administration, Ithaca, New York.

John Cunningham (Master of Tourism and Ph.D. candidate, The George Washington University), Graduate Assistant, International Institute of Tourism Studies, The George Washington University, Washington, D.C.

Donald Hawkins, founder of the Tourism Studies Program, The George Washington University, Washington, D.C.

Jill Knowles-Lankford (M.L.A., M.U.P., University of Oregon), Lecturer, Recreation and Leisure Science Program, University of Hawaii.

Samuel V. Lankford (M.U.P., Ph.D., University of Oregon), Associate Professor and Director, Recreation and Leisure Science Program and Member, Graduate Faculty of the Travel Industry Management School, University of Hawaii.

A.E. Luloff, Professor of Rural Sociology, Department of Agricultural Economics and Rural Sociology, The Pennsylvania State University.

Robert M. O'Halloran (Ph.D.), Associate Professor, School of Hotel, Restaurant, and Tourism Management, Daniels College of Business, University of Denver, Colorado.

David C. Povey (M.R.P., Ph.D., Cornell University), Professor and Graduate Coordinator, Urban and Regional Planning Program, Department of Planning, Public Policy, and Management, University of Oregon.

Susan Irish Stewart (Ph.D., Michigan State University), Research Social Scientist, USDA Forest Service, North Central Experimental Station, Evanston, Illinois.

Daniel J. Stynes, Professor, Department of Park, Recreation, and Tourism Resources, Michigan State University.

Laurel J. Walsh [B.Sc. (Honors), University of Massachusetts at Amherst], Vice-President, International Strategies, Boston, Massachusetts.

Practicing Responsible Tourism

1

Practicing Responsible Tourism

UNDERSTANDING TOURISM TODAY TO PREPARE FOR TOMORROW

Winston Husbands
Lynn C. Harrison

❡ | K E Y   L E A R N I N G   P O I N T S

- To fully grasp the dynamics of the tourism system, and even to manage effectively the respective microlevel components, a body of knowledge that reflects the international reach of the industry and the interdisciplinary nature of decision making within the industry is required.

- Responsible tourism is *not* a tourism product or brand. It represents a way of *doing* tourism planning, policy, and development to ensure that benefits are optimally distributed among impacted populations, governments, tourists, and investors.

- The implementation of responsible tourism practices requires strong leadership and involves ways of managing tourism resources to achieve optimum benefits for the different communities of interest.

- Responsible tourism acknowledges that there is a place for well-conceived ecotourism products. However, it also recognizes that, drawing on experience, foresight, and new techniques, mass tourism itself can be practiced in ways that minimize and mitigate its obvious disbenefits.

INTRODUCTION

The tourism industry is truly international in scope. Not only does it involve a large-scale movement of people and money in which all countries participate, but changes in one part of the international tourism system reverberate throughout the system as well. Therefore, to fully grasp the dynamics of the system, and even to manage effectively the respective national, regional, state/provincial, municipal, or community components, students and their mentors, researchers, consultants, planners, and managers require a body of knowledge that reflects (1) the international reach of the industry and (2) the interdisciplinary nature of decision making within the industry.

Such knowledge is especially crucial in view of the continually rising demand for tourism, the corresponding expansion of tourism infrastructure and development of new

1

products, and the highly competitive nature of the industry. Taking all these factors into consideration, the case studies in this volume represent a critique of trends in tourism planning, policy, and development and, at the same time, offer a prescriptive view of contemporary tourism.

By definition, case studies examine specific instances of particular issues. Consequently, the cases presented are concerned with the practical implications of issues and decision making in tourism planning, policy, and development. In every instance, however, the authors locate their specific issue (or family of issues) in an appropriate conceptual framework. Hence, the case studies examine the theory *and* the practice of responsible tourism planning, policy, and development.

The case studies provide an indication of the degree to which responsible tourism practices are recognized and instituted. Although many are aware of the underlying principles, it is evident that practicing responsible tourism involves more than simply having the desire to do so. Responsible tourism represents a way of *doing* tourism planning, policy, and development to ensure that benefits are optimally distributed among impacted populations, governments, tourists, and investors. Furthermore, responsible tourism practices require strong leadership and involve ways of managing tourism resources to achieve optimum benefits for the different communities of interest. In short, responsible tourism *is not* a tourism product or brand. It is a way of *doing* tourism.

In the remainder of this introductory chapter, a context for the case studies is established and a rationale for practicing responsible tourism is developed. First, patterns of growth in international tourism since the early 1960s are discussed. Next, it is suggested that, given the persistent and rapid growth of tourism, it is important to derive a framework and a set of practices to ensure that expectations are met without imperiling the physical or social resource base. Third, the knowledge base of tourism studies and the implications for practicing responsible tourism are examined. This is followed by a discussion of tourism careers and tourism education in view of necessary changes in the industry.

INTERNATIONAL TOURISM GROWTH TRENDS SINCE THE 1960s

The international tourism industry has grown rapidly since the early 1960s. Moreover, projections to the year 2010 indicate that the industry will continue to grow, albeit less quickly than previously (see Table 1.1). For example, world international tourist arrivals grew at an average annual rate of 8.4 percent from 1962 to 1972, but they are expected to grow by 4 percent per year from 1992 to the year 2000 and by 3.6 percent annually from 2000 to 2010. On the whole, world arrivals data from 1962 to 1992 show that relatively prolonged and numerous episodes of rapid growth (1962–1967, 1968–1973, 1976–1979, and 1986–1990) were interrupted by short periods of stagnation (1980–1982 and 1990–1991).

Worldwide, the general trend in the growth of arrivals is reflected in receipts and, to a lesser degree, accommodation. Calculations based on data published by the World Tourism Organization (WTO) (1992, 1994) show that international tourism receipts increased at an average annual rate of 11.7 percent during the period from 1982 to 1992. Receipts per tourist nearly doubled during this period, from approximately US$340 to

TABLE 1.1
Growth in International Tourist Arrivals Since
1962

Year	Arrivals	Average Annual Growth Rate (%)
1962	81,329,000	—
1972	181,851,000	8.4
1982	286,780,000	4.7
1992	481,463,000	5.3
2000	660,000,000	4.0
2010	940,000,000	3.6

Sources: Arrivals from WTO (1992, 1994) and Jaura (1994).

US$618. Meanwhile, the supply of accommodation (i.e., rooms in hotels and similar establishments) grew more modestly at 2 percent per year.

Although all world regions experienced growth in international arrivals between 1982 and 1992, there was a redistribution of international arrivals among the regions (see Table 1.2). Asia and Oceania experienced the highest growth rates. Together, these two regions increased their share of international arrivals from approximately 11 percent in 1982 to slightly more than 15 percent in 1992. On the other hand, Europe's share of international arrivals declined.

Some subregions achieved particularly impressive growth (see Table 1.3). International arrivals in Southern Africa grew by 17 percent annually from 1988 to 1992, although North Africa still accounted for approximately half of all international arrivals in Africa in 1992. In the Americas, North America accounted for the largest share of arrivals in 1992 (about 70 percent), but the fastest growth occurred in Central America. In Asia, East Asia captured the largest share of arrivals in 1992 (slightly more than 20

TABLE 1.2
International Tourist Arrivals by World Region, 1982 and 1992

World Region	Arrivals		Average Annual Growth (%)	Share of Arrivals	
	1982	1992		1982 (%)	1992 (%)
Africa	9,375,000	17,471,000	6.4	3.3	3.6
Americas	50,799,000	101,137,000	7.1	17.7	21.0
Asia	29,301,000	66,953,000	8.6	10.2	13.9
Europe	195,222,000	290,219,000	4.0	68.1	60.3
Oceania	2,083,000	5,785,000	10.8	0.7	1.2

Source: Arrivals from WTO (1992, 1994).

TABLE 1.3
Highest Subregional Growth in International Tourist Arrivals per World Region,
1988 and 1992

	Arrivals		Average Annual Growth Rate (%)
World Subregion	**1988**	**1992**	
Southern Africa	1,379,000	2,583,000	17.0
Central America	1,426,000	2,400,000	13.9
Micronesia (Oceania)	847,000	1,402,000	13.4
Southeast Asia	14,662,000	21,498,000	10.0
Central/East Europe	37,663,000	49,118,000	6.9

Source: Arrivals from WTO (1994).

percent), but arrivals in Southeast Asia grew more rapidly than in the other Asian subregions. Australia and New Zealand together accounted for more than 60 percent of international arrivals in Oceania in 1992. However, Micronesia recorded the highest growth rate in this region between 1988 and 1992.

GROWTH TRENDS IN PERSPECTIVE

Unlike other types of resources, tourism resources are highly ubiquitous. Consequently, the international tourism industry is very competitive. Within this competitive environment, virtually every country aims to rapidly increase the magnitude of its tourism industry, thereby capturing as much market share for a particular type of product and earning as much foreign exchange as possible. For example, in Asia, the first half of 1992 brought increases in tourist arrivals of about 20 percent in Indonesia and Singapore, and over 8 percent in the Philippines, compared to the previous year. Malaysia alone was expecting to attract 7 million visitors in 1994 (Makabenta, 1992).

Jordan, in the Middle East, attracted 21,000 visitors in 1989, but received that many from Germany alone in 1993 (Jaura, 1994). Normally, the Middle East accounts for less than 2 percent of international arrivals. However, in the wake of the Gulf War and with a gradual resolution of outstanding political problems in the region, several Middle Eastern countries are planning for a vastly expanded tourism industry.

Caribbean countries, many of whom depend economically on tourism, are being urged by the World Bank to adapt to the new global economic environment by intensifying their reliance on international tourism[1] (Lobe, 1994). According to the World Bank, the region's economic outlook will not be particularly promising without more tourism. In the first place, foreign aid to the region has fallen since the early 1980s, without any indication that previous levels can be regained in the future. Second, it is expected that the North American Free Trade Agreement (NAFTA), instituted in 1993, will adversely affect export income throughout the region. Furthermore, Caribbean banana producers are experiencing a gradual reduction in preferential access to the European market, which translates into a corresponding loss of income.

In Africa, especially sub-Saharan Africa, growth in tourism is particularly crucial for future economic health. Africa generally accounts for less than 4 percent of world arrivals and about 2 percent of world receipts, most of which are concentrated in North Africa. However, given the difficult economic situation prevailing throughout the continent, a rapid improvement in the tourism sector would indeed be helpful. The WTO projects arrivals should grow by 7 percent annually in Southern and Eastern Africa and by 5 percent annually throughout Africa as a whole between 1994 and the year 2000 (Jaura, 1995).

Postapartheid South Africa is a striking example of the hopes that countries attach to tourism, particularly given that tourism everywhere is relatively labor-intensive. South Africa also offers tremendous and outstanding diversity in scenery and wildlife. Therefore, logically, the South African government has accorded a high priority to tourism as it attempts to restructure and improve the country's economy. This much has been stated by Nelson Mandela himself, the country's president (Travel Show Indaba, 1995). Consequently, the South African Tourist Board (SATOUR) aims to attract one million international visitors to the country by 1996, with expected earnings of US$2.6 billion (compared to US$800 million in 1992), and create 200,000 additional jobs by the year 2000 (Koch, 1994).

Clearly, in conventional economic terms, the outlook for global tourism appears very promising due to increasing demand and the fact that some countries appear to need substantial tourism earnings over the short and medium term. However, it is widely acknowledged that conventional tourism is capable of destroying its own resource base. Hence, even the casual observer may question whether tourism is sustainable on the scale suggested by past trends and projected for the future.

RESPONSIBLE TOURISM

The authors in this volume attempt, in various ways, to raise the profile of responsible tourism. As mentioned previously, the term responsible tourism does not refer to a brand or type of tourism. Rather, the term encompasses a framework and a set of practices that chart a sensible course between the fuzziness of ecotourism and the well-known negative externalities associated with conventional mass tourism. The basic point of responsible tourism is that there is a place for well-conceived ecotourism products, but that, drawing on experience, foresight, and new techniques, mass tourism itself can be practiced in ways that minimize and mitigate its obvious disbenefits. Product development, policy, planning, and marketing can all be instituted in ways to ensure that tourists, host populations, and investors reap the long-term benefits of a vibrant and healthy tourism industry.

The expert opinions (such as those represented by the authors in this volume) concerning responsible tourism resonate among host populations as well. Evidence suggests that even though host populations want the economic benefits generated by tourism, they are unimpressed by the environmental degradation and undue social disruption that often accompany mass tourism. In Hawaii, only one-fifth of respondents to an opinion survey in the early 1980s agreed that the economic gains from tourism were more important than environmental protection (Liu et al., 1987). In fact, a considerable proportion of respondents believed that tourism had contributed to ecological degradation in Hawaii.

In Sri Lanka, the government was forced in 1994 to cancel a large resort development after protests by a broad cross section of Sri Lankan society. The proposed development, which included a golf course, a horse-racing facility, and a casino hotel, would have virtually destroyed coconut production over a considerable area (Wanigasundera, 1994). Similarly, in Barbados, the government bowed to public opposition in 1993–1994 against a proposal to develop more golf courses as a means of boosting the country's tourism industry (Martindale, 1994). Barbados' water supply is entirely rain-fed, and the present supply is barely enough to meet the demand.

The examples just cited all refer to local or national issues, but impacted populations are also mobilizing internationally to oppose the threats posed by mass tourism. For example, in 1995 a joint meeting of three service workers' organizations held in Penang, Malaysia,[2] adopted a resolution urging workers and their unions throughout Asia and elsewhere to actively oppose tourism-related prostitution, especially child sex tourism (Tourism Service Workers' Seminar, 1995). Certainly, these examples of community reaction to the excesses of conventional tourism suggest that community involvement in tourism development ought to be a hallmark of responsible tourism.

Still, there are limits to the sort of public support for responsible tourism outlined above. First, responses to the Hawaiian opinion survey discussed earlier also suggested that people attached a higher value to their standard of living than to environmental protection. Second, it is fairly obvious that the level of popular support for responsible tourism practices depends on the immediate economic outlook. Third, it is also likely that public and professional debates about the consequences and future of tourism really concern individual projects rather than the overall process or content of tourism development.

For sure, these are some of the dilemmas now facing South African tourism authorities. Indeed, bearing in mind the legacy of apartheid in South Africa, it is difficult to argue without proposing sound alternatives that the country's democratically elected government should eschew rapid tourism growth when, in conventional economic terms, rapid tourism growth is the worldwide norm and appears to have been successful in generating a measure of economic benefit elsewhere. At this stage in the debate about responsible tourism, the chapters to follow contribute to the search for reasoned alternatives to conventional tourism practices and modes of development.

PATTERNS IN THE TOURISM KNOWLEDGE BASE

Due to the international reach and significance of tourism, researchers, consultants, and industry decision makers must continually communicate and access knowledge about the industry beyond their geographical community and immediate specialization. This communication will ensure that they have access to a knowledge base necessary for enhancing the industry and their own professional practice. In particular, today's students must keep abreast of the issues, tools, and techniques appropriate to forging responsible tourism in the future. What, then, is the state of the current knowledge base?

This question can be answered in several ways. However, to utilize efficiently the resources at hand, trends in themes appearing in three widely read and available professional journals were examined. A data base of 473 articles published between 1988 and

1994 in the *Annals of Tourism Research* (48.2 percent), the *Journal of Travel Research* (23.9 percent), and *Tourism Management* (27.9 percent)[3] was compiled. Each article was coded with two keywords (or, in some cases, key phrases) to signify the two main themes or issues addressed in each article. Keywords were derived from some combination of the title, the abstract, or the keywords published with the article (usually accompanying the abstract).

The initial large number of different keywords was reduced to a smaller number of core keywords by grouping those that described similar issues (e.g., "airline transportation" and "rail transportation" were grouped as "transportation") and eliminating keywords with fewer than three occurrences. It was assumed that keywords occurring less than three times represented issues that are marginal to the substantive knowledge base elaborated in the three journals. The process of grouping and eliminating keywords reduced the initial number of core keywords to 29. This method of creating core keywords meant that some articles retained only one associated keyword.[4]

The frequency of core keywords (i.e., the number of articles associated with each keyword) is listed in Table 1.4. "Tourism impacts" was the most frequent theme in the resulting knowledge base, representing 13.2 percent of all core keyword occurrences. "Sustainable tourism" (which includes "green," "responsible," and other related names) accounted for 4.3 percent of all keyword occurrences. As expected (based on the distribu-

TABLE 1.4
Frequency of Core Keywords Describing Articles Published in Three Journals

Keyword	Number of Articles	Percent of Total Occurrences	Keyword	Number of Articles	Percent of Total Occurrences
Accommodation	15	3.4	Religion	7	1.6
Attractions	4	0.9	Research	25	5.7
Culture	16	3.6	Residents	16	3.6
Demand	13	2.9	Resorts	11	2.5
Destinations	20	4.5	Rural	9	2.0
Expenditure	7	1.6	Segmentation	13	2.9
Forecasting	13	2.9	Service	7	1.6
History	10	2.3	Souvenirs	10	2.3
Information centers	6	1.4	Sustainable tourism[a]	19	4.3
Information technology	11	2.5	Theme parks	6	1.4
International	16	3.6	Tourism development	33	7.5
Life (resort) cycle	8	1.8	Tourism education	7	1.6
Marketing	27	6.1	Tourism impacts	58	13.2
Planning	31	7.0	Transportation	19	4.3
Politics	4	0.9	Total	441	99.9[b]

[a] Does not include occurrences of the keyword in the June 1991 edition of *Tourism Management*.

[b] Total adds to less than 100 percent due to rounding.

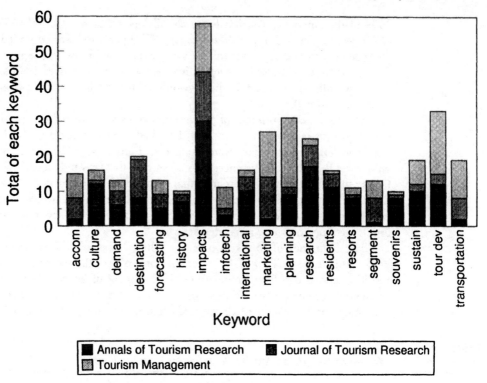

Figure 1.1
Frequency of core keywords by journal source.

tion of total articles among the three journals), articles published in the *Annals of Tourism Research* accounted for most of the core keyword occurrences, followed by *Tourism Management*, and the *Journal of Travel Research* (see Figure 1.1).

Figure 1.2 shows the percentage of occurrences for each core keyword arranged by journal source and compares this to each journal's proportion of the total core keyword occurrences. Patterns of specialization among the three journals emerge. The *Annals* specializes in studies dealing with culture, history, impacts, international tourism, research/methodology issues, resident populations, resorts, souvenirs and souvenir trade (including art and crafts), and sustainable tourism. The *Journal of Travel Research* appears to specialize in studies of accommodation, destinations, marketing, and segmentation. Finally, *Tourism Management* appears to focus on studies of accommodation, information technology, marketing, planning, tourism development, and transportation.

These patterns provide a synopsis of the issues and themes in the tourism knowledge base, but they are not conclusive. The three journals included here are perhaps the most widely read peer-reviewed outlets for tourism research, but they are not the only ones. Moreover, it may be argued that the keywords used are not necessarily the most efficient or effective representation of the themes and issues covered in the professional tourism literature. Nevertheless, the data do provide a consistent interpretation of the current tourism knowledge base. Students may find this interpretation useful for research pur-

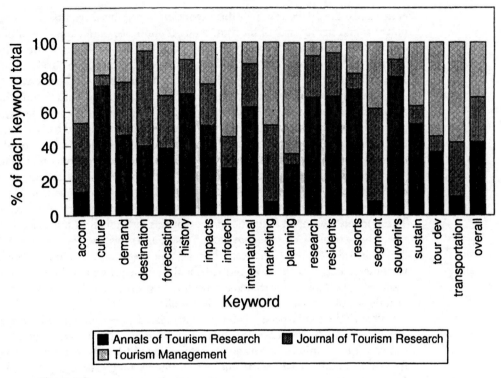

Figure 1.2
Keywords as a percentage of total occurrences in each journal (total for each journal = 100 percent).

poses by having a reasonable idea of the range and distribution of the core issues, including their most likely published sources.

As far as responsible tourism is concerned, even in the most widely read, professional peer-reviewed journals, although numerous articles examine issues relating to tourism's impacts, there is a relative paucity of articles that specifically examine "responsible tourism" issues. Ultimately, from a research perspective, most of the themes in the knowledge base are in some way important to generating a framework for responsible tourism and an appreciation of responsible tourism practices. However, only a limited number of articles broach the subject squarely, either as critique or in a prescriptive sense. It is hoped that the current volume will contribute to overcoming this lacuna by providing students with a theoretical and practical appreciation of concepts, issues, tools, and techniques from the vantage point of responsible tourism.

TOURISM-RELATED CAREER PROSPECTS

Tourism research and tourism studies are still somewhat marginal to the subject matter of accepted disciplines and fields of inquiry in most universities (Shaw and Williams 1994, p. 243). Nevertheless, university tourism programs and specializations have proliferated since the 1970s. Though this expansion is perhaps driven by the huge economic potential and significance of tourism, many economists, politicians, and others generally do not take tourism as seriously as they do other sectors of production. In any case, tourism is still a labor-intensive industry attracted by cheap, relatively unskilled labor. This means that the demand for highly educated workers is relatively low.

Tourism also suffers from the fact that the education and skills required for fulfilling a professional role in the industry are derivative. Tourism is a topic of study, not a disciplinary specialization. As yet, there is no theoretical or conceptual basis to tourism studies that definitively sets it apart from other areas and topics of study in the social sciences or business management or that effectively distinguishes tourism from other industries.

These issues are important to university students specializing in tourism studies. Accordingly, in 1995, several upper-level students in Ryerson's School of Hospitality and Tourism Management were required to write a research paper on careers in tourism. The students developed a questionnaire that was distributed to university-based tourism researchers, public sector tourism professionals, and private sector consultants in Canada, the United States, the Caribbean, Europe, and Australia. The questionnaire solicited responses concerning the availability, benefits, and requirements for tourism-related professional opportunities for students expecting to graduate in the near future with a four-year degree or a specialization in tourism studies.

One of the major benefits of a tourism-related career identified by respondents was the opportunity to influence this huge and expanding but relatively poorly understood industry (i.e., to influence new areas of study, identify trends, make improvements). The force of this response was borne out by respondents' observations that tourism still suffers from people's failure to recognize sufficiently the economic significance of tourism compared to other industries.

Moreover, even though a majority of respondents indicated that postsecondary education is now more important for a career in tourism than five years previously and that educational requirements will become more rigorous in the future (see Table 1.5), over one-third of respondents indicated that tourism is not a recognized field of study.

It appears, therefore, that tourism can present rewarding career opportunities because

TABLE 1.5
Preparing for a Career in Tourism: Advice from the "Experts"

Develop communication and listening skills

Gain a broad base of experience . . . take advantage of opportunities to "open doors" through volunteer activities

Obtain a post-secondary education . . . masters degrees are becoming more important

Be prepared to start at the "bottom" and work hard

Start developing your network of industry contacts now . . . join associations

Develop proficiency in a second language

Keep current with technological advances

Be prepared for teamwork

Be flexible and show initiative

of the magnitude of the industry and the ongoing development of new tourism products. However, relative to other industries and areas of study, the career importance of tourism suffers from society's failure to appreciate fully the social and economic significance of the industry. Certainly, the combination of globalized markets and production systems, widespread and heightened environmental awareness, and increased interest in community well-being consequent to economic restructuring, when set against the background of persistent worldwide growth in the tourism industry, suggests that tourism is now perhaps more crucial to the livelihood of communities, regions, and nations than it had been previously.

Responsible tourism is strategically located at the intersection of globalization, the environment, and community development. If this is indeed the case, tourism-related careers should become increasingly attractive and the demand for tourism education should increase. In a practical sense, tourism education can fulfill this promise by generating a body of enlightened knowledge and well-conceived practices that address the tension between community well-being; sensible environmental stewardship, and the sense of dislocation that globalization is capable of fostering.

CONTENT AND ORGANIZATION OF THE BOOK

Content The chapters in this book present current analyses of contemporary tourism issues in the United States, Canada, the Caribbean, Europe, and the Asia-Pacific area. The case studies are written by experienced tourism researchers and consultants who bring their experience and expertise to bear on the subject matter. Therefore, students should derive a comprehensive, issues-oriented understanding of tourism in the late 1980s and early 1990s, as well as an understanding of likely trends in tourism planning, policy, and development around the world during the next decade.

The case studies are also evaluations of various tools, techniques, and strategies that decision makers have used or may use to resolve planning, policy, and development issues. From this perspective, the book conveys a practical understanding of tourism worldwide. Though the case studies were written with the needs of undergraduates in mind, the content is broadly appealing to graduate students, researchers, and consultants.

This case studies book has also been conceived as a vehicle for improving critical thinking among students specializing in tourism studies. Critical thinking is indispensable to the major tourism-related career paths normally available to graduates, whether in universities, government, or the private sector. The case studies are instrumental to effective tourism education because they simultaneously introduce the conceptual and theoretical foundations of tourism activity *and* contextualize this knowledge in a practical way by applying it in "real world" situations.

The case studies examine various issues, concepts, techniques, and tools important to the present and future of tourism. Each is preceded by a short list of "key learning points" and followed by a list of "problem solving and discussion activities," both written by the respective authors at the request of, and with input from, the editors. The key learning points draw students' attention to important lessons contained in the case studies. The problem solving and discussion activities enhance students' grasp of the substantive case study material by requiring students, in the role of decision makers or researchers, to critically examine the concepts, issues, tools, and techniques, as well as to apply them (sometimes in situations and settings other than those specifically addressed in the case studies).

Organization All the case studies address tourism development to some extent. However, the sequence of the chapters follows six themes, beginning with case studies that address tourism development, planning, and policy more generally, and ending with studies that examine special interest products or markets.

The first eight chapters (Chapters 2–9) carve a fairly broad view of planning, policy, and development issues. Wilkinson (and, to a lesser extent, Wall) examines some implications of the product (destination) life cycle for planning and policy. Wall focuses on the importance and likely outcome of tourism planning by comparing two destinations with obvious differences in the level of tourism planning. Godfrey analyzes one of the common pitfalls of effective tourism planning, namely, the potential contradiction between economic goals and political imperatives, and discusses how this apparent contradiction may be resolved. Conlin, Haywood and Walsh, Klemm and Martín-Quirós, and Holder all address destination planning and policy as a response to changes in market demand or power structures and the need for destinations to remain viable over the long run. Similarly, Keane et al. examine issues affecting how impacted communities, especially in small islands, may plan and manage an expanding tourism industry to ensure that the physical and cultural resource base is reasonably protected.

The next four chapters (Chapters 10–13) turn to the economic role of tourism. Donert and Light and Russell et al. focus on tourism's role in national, regional, and local economic regeneration. Stynes and Stewart discuss impact assessment and measure the local and regional impact of a resort development, while Lamb and Davidson examine how transportation may facilitate tourism development and integrate tourism into the regional or national economy.

Community attitudes and community involvement in the tourism development process are addressed in the case studies by Bourke and Luloff, Addison, Joppe, and Lankford et al. (Chapters 14–17). These authors argue on behalf of local initiative and community consultation in developing and planning tourism initiatives. However, Bourke and Luloff add that destinations are successful according to their level of participation readiness. These case studies demonstrate how consultation may be accomplished and offer lessons for improving community input in decision making.

Tourism development is, among all else, a political process. This theme is examined by Hawkins and Cunningham and by Hall (Chapters 18 and 19). Both chapters focus on large-scale projects to demonstrate how various communities and interest groups often disagree on the necessity, objectives, and process of developing large-scale projects. Both indicate that consensus is not always achieved and that the fate of tourism projects is sometimes a test of political power and mobilization by different segments of society or different interest groups.

The next six chapters (Chapters 20–25) emphasize techniques for identifying and making inventories of tourism resources, as well as techniques for product development and management. Boyd and Butler discuss the application and usefulness of geographic information systems (GIS) for identifying the locational feasibility of ecotourism. GIS approaches are also discussed by Williams et al., who focus more generally on techniques for inventorying natural resources to identify locations for tourism development and to ensure that conflicts between tourism and other land uses are minimized.

Both Davis and Harriott and Stadel examine tourism development in the context of protected areas (marine and terrestrial). They identify approaches that attempt to resolve the competing, and sometimes contradictory, objectives of tourism development and protected areas. Beeho and Prentice elaborate a technique for incorporating visitor experiences into product planning and development. O'Halloran draws attention to a multiagency approach to developing and managing naturally occurring tourism resources where the relevant features of the physical landscape fall under the jurisdiction of several government agencies.

The final three chapters (Chapters 26–28) present special interest topics. McKercher shows how and why destinations may exploit an existing or potential visitor base—in this case, the relatively neglected VFR (visiting friends and relatives) market. Reid examines the marketing of special events and festivals in the context of optimizing economic benefits. Finally, Bell and Vazquez-Illa discuss the changing nature of spa tourism, focusing on a dilemma facing the management of a spa hotel in Spain.

CONCLUSION

Continued growth of the global tourism industry into the twenty-first century will likely be accompanied by important changes in the nature of tourism itself. These changes include the development of new products and destinations, as well as an expansion in the magnitude and scope of the tourism knowledge base. Likewise, both the demand for tourism-related education and the opportunities for tourism-related careers will grow. However, new ways of managing will probably be required to accommodate the industry's continued quantitative growth, the development of new products, the emergence of new destinations, and ongoing changes in the global economy. For these reasons, the theme of responsible tourism, in which local communities, governments, tourists, and investors all have a stake, is particularly timely and appropriate. The issues, concepts, strategies, tools, and techniques discussed contribute to a more thorough understanding of tourism today and in the future.

ACKNOWLEDGMENTS

The authors express their gratitude to the following students, past and present, for their untiring efforts in compiling some of the background materials referred to in this chapter: Michal Cahlon, Lisa Holzwarth, Karlene Jaikaran, Wendy MacInnis, Mary Sekeres, Miranda Townsend, and Michele Vaughan-Greig.

NOTES

1. See Chapter 8 for additional discussion pertaining to tourism in the Caribbean region.
2. The three workers' organizations were the International Transport Workers Federation (ITF), the International Union of Food, Agricultural, Hotel, Restaurant, Catering and Allied Workers' Associations (IUF), and the International Federation of Commercial, Clerical, Professional and Technical Employees (FIET).

3. There were no articles from *Tourism Management* in 1991 (this is important because the June 1991 edition had a series of articles that specifically addressed the topic of responsible tourism); articles from the *Journal of Travel Research* begin in 1991.
4. Some articles only had one keyword because, in grouping related keywords, both of the original keywords may have been placed in the same category (e.g., an article coded as "air transportation" and "rail transportation" was coded as "transportation" only).

REFERENCES

Jaura, R. 1994. Tourism-environment: developing countries seek the right balance. InterPress Third World News Service (IPS). IGC Electronic Conference (ips.english), March.

Jaura, R. 1995. Africa-tourism: sizeable growth predicted in the next five years. IPS. IGC Electronic Conference (africa.news), March.

Koch, E. 1994. South Africa-economy: tourism—a new window of opportunity. IPS. IGC Electronic Conference (ips.english), June.

Liu, J., P. Sheldon, and T. Var. 1987. Resident perception of the environmental impacts of tourism, *Annals of Tourism Research*, 14, 17–37.

Lobe, J. 1994. Caribbean-finance: tourism, services best hope, says World Bank. IPS, IGC Electronic Conference (reg.carib), May.

Makabenta, L. 1992. Environment: tourism joins ecological bandwagon. IPS. IGC Electronic Conference (gen.travel), September.

Martindale, C. 1994. Barbados-water: drought drying up support for golf courses. IPS. IGC Electronic Conference (reg.carib), May.

Shaw, G. and A. Williams. 1994. *Critical Issues in Tourism*. Oxford: Blackwell.

Tourism Service Workers' Seminar. 1995. Resolution on prostitution, *Contours*, 7(2), 6.

Travel Show Indaba. 1995. *Southern African Tourism Update*, June (http://www.pix.za/business/travel/tourism/past.html).

Wanigasundera, M. 1994. Coconuts beat off plans for a tourist complex. Panos Features. IGC Electronic Conference (panos.news).

World Tourism Organization (WTO). 1992. *Yearbook of Tourism Statistics*, 1(44). Madrid.

World Tourism Organization (WTO). 1994. *Compendium of Tourism Statistics, 1988–1992*, 14th ed. Madrid.

⚡ | PROBLEM SOLVING AND DISCUSSION ACTIVITIES

1. What is responsible tourism? How many definitions of responsible tourism can you find in the literature? What challenges do definitional issues pose for encouraging managers to understand the philosophy and practice responsible tourism?
2. Conduct a review of the literature to identify factors that have contributed to the need to practice responsible tourism. What implications do these factors have with respect to the responsibilities that you will assume as a future leader, manager, researcher, planner, developer, or educator in the tourism industry? Identify several positions/jobs in the industry that are of interest to you and explain how your roles and responsibilities in the next decade might differ from those of a person who held such a position in the 1980s.
3. To what extent are responsible tourism philosophies and practices currently embraced by host populations, governments, tourists, investors, and developers?

What is required to encourage widespread adoption of responsible tourism practices within the international tourism industry?

4. What can you be doing today to prepare yourself to be an advocate and practitioner of responsible tourism in the future? What skills, knowledge, experience, and attitudes should you be honing? How can these be acquired?

5. Select two areas in the world where you would like to work. Use secondary source materials to identify past and projected growth of tourism in each area. What implications do these data have for the opportunities and challenges relevant in these two areas—and, therefore, for the nature of priorities—for managing tourism in each of these areas in the future?

6. Is tourism sustainable on the scale suggested by past trends and projections for the future? Why or why not? What are the implications of this given the increasing importance being accorded tourism throughout the world as an economic generator?

2

Graphical Images of the Commonwealth Caribbean

THE TOURIST AREA CYCLE OF EVOLUTION

 *Paul F. Wilkinson*

✎ | K E Y   L E A R N I N G   P O I N T S

- The tourist area cycle of evolution may be used either as a descriptive, explanatory, or heuristic tool. It describes both the differences between destinations and the differences in the length, shape, and pattern of change within a particular destination over time as it passes through the stages of the cycle; it explains relationships between variables; and it presents the possibility of framing significant questions raised by alternative measures of tourism.
- Simple measures of tourism (e.g., tourist arrivals, total visitor expenditures) have limited utility in that they mask the complexity of tourism and tourists.
- Graphical images are powerful research and learning tools that allow researchers to see other pictures and patterns of data and, therefore, facilitate their ability to test alternative hypotheses easily and quickly.

INTRODUCTION

Based on the concept of the product life cycle, the tourist area cycle of evolution has been the focus of much discussion since it was first proposed by Butler (1980) and later elaborated by other authors. The life cycle has been used in marketing to describe the evolution of a product as it passes through the stages of introduction, maturity, and decline. Most applications of the concept, however, utilize very simple measures (e.g., total visitor arrivals) that provide only a description of the development of tourist destinations.

It is suggested in this chapter that a very different image of the evolution of tourism in a particular destination is presented if other more complex measures are examined (e.g., particular types of arrivals such as stayover visitors, indices of change, number of tourist nights, current and real visitor expenditures). It is argued that, while description is extremely important, the cycle concept also has potential utility as an explanatory and heuristic tool.

The chapter begins with a discussion of the background to the concept and then focuses on three different models of the cycle, followed by an overview of problems associated with the concept. It then shows how the concept was used to select six case studies in the Commonwealth Caribbean (Dominica, Anguilla, St. Lucia, Cayman Islands, Barbados, and the Bahamas) for a larger research project examining the role of tourism policy and planning in national development of island microstates (Wilkinson, 1996). Data from these case studies are then used to present graphical images of the cycle (using microcomputer spreadsheet software) in an attempt to show the utility of the cycle concept in descriptive, explanatory, and heuristic terms.

Such graphical images assist in describing both the differences between destinations and the differences in the length, shape, and pattern of change within a particular destination over time as it passes through the stages of the cycle. They can help to explain relationships between variables, such as the number of visitors of different types and their varying levels of expenditures, or the differences between current and real expenditures. They also have heuristic value in helping to frame significant questions through alternative measures such as indices of change.

THE LIFE CYCLE CONCEPT: CONTEMPORARY PERSPECTIVES AND ISSUES

Rooted in theories of the population dynamics of species and diffusion of innovations or change over space (Hannan and Freeman, 1977; Haywood, 1990; Lambkin and Day, 1989), the product life cycle has been used in marketing to describe the evolution of a product as it passes through the stages of introduction, maturity, and decline (Cooper, 1993, p. 146) or a "birth to death" cycle (Cooper, 1994, p. 340). The concept, however, has been the focus of much debate in marketing. In its favor has been the well-documented progression of sales of various goods and services. In contrast are arguments about the lack of operational validity and its tautological nature rendering it devoid of explanatory power (Brown, 1987; Cooper, 1994; Hunt, 1976).

The life cycle concept has been employed in tourism research to explain destination area development (Goodall, 1992; Pearce, 1989). In the first application of the life cycle concept to tourism, Butler (1980, p. 5) noted that:

> There can be little doubt that tourist areas are dynamic, that they evolve and change over time. This evolution is brought about by a variety of factors, including changes in the preferences and needs of visitors, the gradual deterioration and possible replacement of the physical plant and facilities, and the change (or even disappearance) of the original natural and cultural attractions which were responsible for the initial popularity of the area.

Butler (1980, p. 6) compared this pattern of change in the number of tourists visiting an area to the concept of the product life cycle "whereby sales of a product proceed slowly at first, experience a rapid growth, stabilize, and subsequently decline; in other words, a basic asymptotic (S-shaped) curve is followed" (see Figure 2.1). Rather than viewing it as a simplistic geometric analogy of visitor numbers, Cooper (1994, p. 342) argues that the life cycle concept provides the following:

> . . . a useful framework for analysis of the growth of destinations [and] the interplay between markets and physical development, [as well as] allows historical examination of the factors that

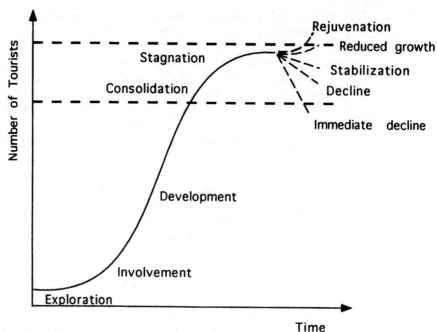

Figure 2.1
Butler's model of the tourist area cycle of evolution. (From Butler, 1980.)

lead to turning points in a destination's development and the characteristics and leadership styles at each particular stage of the destination's evolution.

Cooper (1994, p. 346) goes so far as to assert that the explanatory power of the life cycle provides the "seeds of a generalised theory of tourism."

Tourism researchers have explored the use of the concept in terms of both theory and application in a wide variety of tourism settings. Nevertheless, as will be seen in subsequent discussion, the concept is not without problems and criticism.

Three Models of the Tourist Area Cycle of Evolution

BUTLER'S TOURIST AREA CYCLE OF EVOLUTION   Butler (1980) described a hypothetical tourist area cycle of evolution consisting of six stages:

1. *Exploration*: A small number of "explorers" (Cohen, 1972) makes individual travel arrangements and follows irregular visiting patterns. No specific facilities are provided for tourists.
2. *Involvement*: As numbers of visitors increase and assume some regularity, some local residents begin to provide facilities for visitors.
3. *Development*: This stage reflects a well-developed "institutionalized" (Cohen, 1972) tourist market area and is shaped in part by advertising in tourist generating areas. Local involvement and control of development decline rapidly, being replaced by larger, more elaborate, and more up-to-date facilities provided by external organizations.
4. *Consolidation*: The rate of increase in the number of visitors declines, but a major part of the area's economy is tied to tourism.
5. *Stagnation*: The peak number of visitors has been reached, and capacity levels for

many variables (e.g., water supply, available labor, costs of infrastructure) have been reached or exceeded, with attendant environmental, social, and economic problems.

6. *Decline/Rejuvenation:* The area may not be able to compete with new destinations and thus will face a declining market, both spatially and numerically. On the other hand, there may be an increase in tourists if major efforts are made to add built attractions or to take advantage of previously untapped natural resources. A third possibility is a complete change in function (Agarwall, 1994).

The life cycle concept outlines both the physical development of a destination and its market evolution as changing provision of facilities and access is matched by an evolving clientele in both quantitative and qualitative terms (Cooper, 1993, p. 147). As such, Cooper (1994, p. 342) argues that the theories of *market segmentation* and the *diffusion of innovations* (Plog, 1991) can be linked with the cycle concept (Cooper, 1992):

> The resort can be thought of as an "innovation" which is progressively adopted initially by the more "adventurous" tourists in the early stages to be replaced by "laggards" or more conservative tourists as the resort moves into the later stages of the cycle. Of course, the development of an increasingly standardised resort product over time will progressively appeal to low risk-taking . . . visitors who prefer the security this provides. In other words successive waves of different numbers and types of tourists with distinctive preferences, motivations and desires populate the resort at each stage of the life cycle.

In this way, the concept can be seen as having potential for assisting in marketing and planning.

Referring to Butler's model, various authors have argued that particular tourist destinations have experienced the cycle—for example, Atlantic City (Stansfield, 1978); Grand Isle, Louisiana (Meyer-Arendt, 1985); Isle of Man (Cooper and Jackson, 1989); the Laurentians, Québec (Lundgren, 1982); Malta (Oglethorpe, 1984); Mexico (Butler, 1980); the Northwest Territories, Canada (Keller, 1987); Paradise Island, the Bahamas (Debbage, 1991); and Vancouver Island, British Columbia (Nelson and Wall, 1986). Cooper (1994, p. 340) provides an important caveat, however, that not all destinations go through all stages of the cycle. For example, access and physical conditions may dictate that some regions (e.g., parts of Antarctica, Latin America, and the Canadian Arctic) never pass beyond the exploration stage (Goodall, 1992).

LUNDBERG'S SIX-PHASE MODEL OF TOURISM DEVELOPMENT Lundberg (1980) developed a somewhat similar six-phase model of tourism development:

1. Government incentives for development, promiscuous location of projects, no identification of land qualities requiring protection, and highly optimistic feasibilities.
2. Short-run success (i.e., a halcyon period for all concerned that may last from 5 to 10 years).
3. The beginning of the awareness of some realities (e.g., less economic impact than anticipated, labor unrest, local resistance, and environmental degradation).
4. A tourism recession resulting from overbuilding, high labor costs, and a backlash against poor service.
5. The exposure of even deeper difficulty (e.g., local conflict, erosion of natural and

cultural resources, and further decline in the popularity of the area among visitors).

6. A reflective phase in which investors, developers, managers, local society, and political leadership reassess the entire tourism development pattern and wish they had planned.

This model has attracted less attention than Butler's, perhaps because it presents a more pessimistic and deterministic view, with little hope being held out at the end for recovery. This is important because the most significant phases of both of these models are the later stages of the cycle, given their implications for tourism in general and for the planning and arrangement of particular tourist areas. As Butler (1980, p. 10) argued:

> The assumption that tourist areas will always remain tourist areas and be attractive to tourists appears to be implicit in tourism planning. Public and private agencies alike rarely, if ever, refer to the anticipated life span of a tourist area or its attractions. Rather, because tourism has shown an, as yet, unlimited potential for growth, despite economic recessions, it is taken for granted that numbers of visitors will continue to increase. The fallacy of this assumption can be seen in the experience of older tourist areas, such as those of southern Ontario, over the past two decades.

Similarly, the later phases of Lundberg's model suggest that, after tourism has begun to decline and serious structural problems are recognized, planners and decision makers will realize that much of the situation is attributable to lack of planning and might take the opportunity to reassess how they are going to deal with the future.

DE ALBUQUERQUE AND MCELROY'S THREE-STAGE TOURISM GROWTH PROCESS In the context of the Caribbean, de Albuquerque and McElroy (1992, p. 620) developed a version of Butler's model that postulated three clearly identifiable stages in the tourism growth process (see Figure 2.2).

The characteristics of each stage are as follows:

1. *Emergence or initial discovery:* A slow and irregular stream of long-staying explorers who seek pristine and exotic natural surroundings and unusual cultural experiences and tend to be satisfied with modest lodging/eating facilities. This low-density, environmentally benign phase is typified by small-scale local entrepreneurial participation and resident–visitor interaction. Often lacking major airport and harbor infrastructure, such quiet destinations frequently become retirement hideaways for North Americans and Europeans.

2. *Transition to rapid expansion:* Rapid change, increased foreign investment and control, and rising international visibility is reflected in expanded transport facilities, large-scale hotels, liberal hotel tax incentives, and aggressive visitor promotion. Marked winter seasonality often spawns summer specialty tourism substyles based on unique natural amenities (e.g., fishing, scuba diving, sailboarding, sailing). The one-day cruise ship passenger trade may be significant.

3. *Maturity:* The mass market mature destination is characterized by the dominance of tourism in the economy, growth stagnation, short-stay visitors with a taste for familiar, international chain hotels and restaurants, high densities and crowding that alter the visitor experience and disturb the host population, and the substitution of artificial attractions (e.g., casino gambling, duty-free shopping, golf courses) for de-

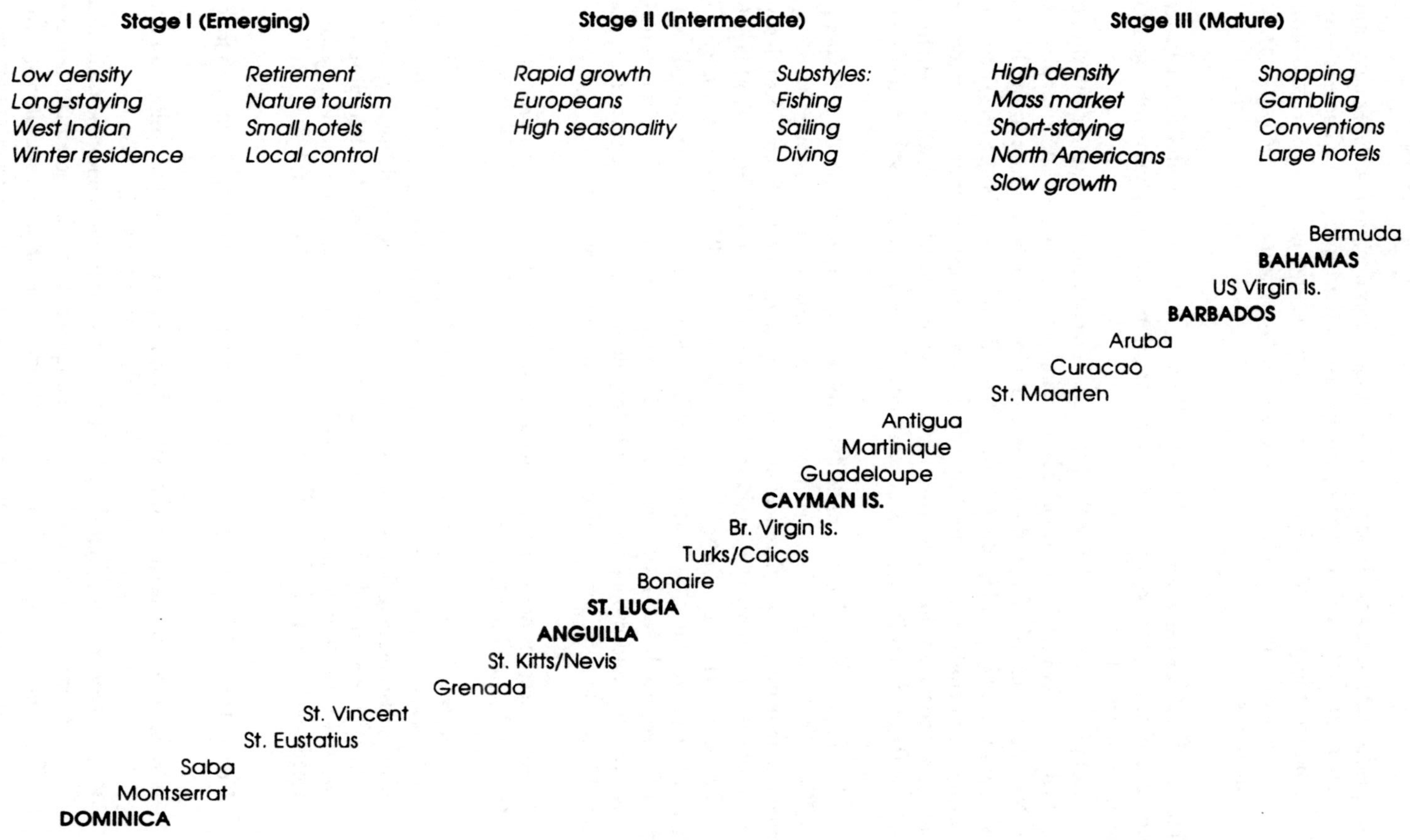

Stage I (Emerging)

Low density
Long-staying
West Indian
Winter residence

Retirement
Nature tourism
Small hotels
Local control

Stage II (Intermediate)

Rapid growth
Europeans
High seasonality

Substyles:
Fishing
Sailing
Diving

Stage III (Mature)

High density
Mass market
Short-staying
North Americans
Slow growth

Shopping
Gambling
Conventions
Large hotels

DOMINICA
Montserrat
Saba

St. Eustatius
St. Vincent

Grenada
St. Kitts/Nevis
ANGUILLA
ST. LUCIA

Bonaire
Turks/Caicos
Br. Virgin Is.
CAYMAN IS.
Guadeloupe
Martinique
Antigua

St. Maarten
Curacao
Aruba

BARBADOS
US Virgin Is.
BAHAMAS
Bermuda

Source: de Albuquerque and McElroy 1992

Figure 2.2
de Albuquerque and McElroy's Caribbean small island tourism stages and styles. Note: The destinations featured in **bold face** represent the case study areas. (From de Albuquerque and McElroy, 1992.)

graded natural assets. Resident–visitor resource competition becomes commonplace, and local cultural identity and participation in tourism decline. There is some environmental impact mitigation, but most of the energy goes into intensive advertising for high-volume visitors (e.g., conventions, cruise ships, packaged charters, and all-inclusives).

This model is basically compatible with Butler's, but it has greater detail in terms of impacts, changes in types of tourists (e.g., cruise passengers), seasonality, and government involvement.

Noting that the only test of the life cycle model in the Caribbean context published by that time[1] involved four small islands (Antigua, Aruba, St. Lucia, and the United States Virgin Islands) and confirmed an evolutionary fit "at least up to the later stages" (Wilkinson, 1987, p. 144), de Albuquerque and McElroy (1992, p. 623) classified 23 Caribbean microstates into the three stages based on examination of a wide range of data (e.g., characteristics of tourists such as origins, lifestyles, activities, length of stay, seasonality, and density, types of accommodation, patterns of growth, and degree of local control).

Arguing that the life cycle model has strong policy implications, de Albuquerque and McElroy (1992, p. 630) believed that tourism tends to move through these dynamic stages, despite the many differences among the islands, with the Stage Three destinations of the late 1980s having been in Stage Two in the 1960s and 1970s and in Stage One in the 1950s. Similarly, the Stage Two islands of the late 1980s were just emerging on the tourist horizon in the 1960s and 1970s. While implications are most immediate for late Stage Three islands faced with stagnation of the tourism sector and environmental problems, this dynamic model also suggests that destinations in the earlier stages need to consider ways to avoid serious medium- and long-term problems.

Problems with the Cycle Concept

The cycle concept is not without limitations. In the context of tourism research, Cooper (1993, p. 149) noted the following:

> Opponents of the cycle argue that, to date, empirical studies simply demonstrate that the shape of the curve varies depending upon supply factors (rate of development, access, government policy and competing destinations) and factors on the demand side (such as the changing nature of clientele) as the destination's market evolves hand in hand with supply-side developments. Clearly this demonstrates that the life cycle is destination-specific. Each stage varies in length and the curve displays different shapes and patterns (Hovinen, 1981).

Cooper (1993, 1994) discusses the main problems of the cycle concept as follows:

- *A focus on a single sector or product*: This is in contrast to the multisector approach taken by economic development models (Goodall, 1992).
- *Identifying turning points in the curve*: Several indicators could be used, including growth rate of visits, level of visits compared to market potential, percentage of first-time visitors, number of competitors, levels of prices and profits, advertising and price elasticity, and emergence of destinations that meet customer needs more effectively (Day, 1981; Doyle, 1976; Haywood, 1986; Rink and Swan, 1979).

- *Identifying stages:* A variety of possible shapes of the curve and of acceleration/ delay due to external factors make it difficult to identify the stage reached by a destination, although this can be achieved by plotting the rate of change of visitor numbers, visitor expenditure, type of tourist, market share, or profitability. However, Jones and Lockwood (1990, p. 7) argued that shape is less relevant than different types of growth (slow, medium, high, constant, declining).
- *Differing lengths:* The length of each stage, and of the cycle itself, is variable depending on the nature of the destination (e.g., new or well established). Furthermore, there is a variety of types of cycles [e.g., a scalloped pattern where a sequence of developments at the destination prompts a revival of visitor arrivals (Buttle, 1986)].
- *Level of aggregation and geographical scale:* The unit of analysis is crucial because the cycle for each country comprises a mosaic of resorts and tourist areas (which, in turn, contain cycles for hotels, theme parks, etc.), with each element perhaps being at a different stage in the cycle (Brownlie, 1985; Kotler, 1980; Rink and Swan, 1979).

Nevertheless, Cooper (1993, p. 156) argued that the life cycle concept does have utility as a descriptive tool because it integrates the disparate factors involved in developing a destination (e.g., demand, supply, organization, investment, scale, impact, planning). He did, however, raise the question as to whether the concept can be used as a prescriptive tool, a use that Butler's original conceptualization did not envisage. Accurate forecasting requires the ability to isolate and predict the forces driving a system (Onkvisit and Shaw, 1986), the use of strict assumptions (e.g., a constraint on long-run growth, an asymptotic diffusion curve, homogeneity of customers), and no explicit consideration of marketing decisions or the competition (Cooper, 1993, p. 150).

Moreover, successful forecasting demands long runs of visitor arrival data to provide stable parameter estimates (Brownlie, 1985). These are lacking for most types of destinations (Butler, 1980). Commonly, only island destinations are able to provide such data sets because all arrivals pass through a very small number of ports of entry, usually a single airport or a single harbor, thus facilitating the gathering of entry and exit data (Cooper, 1993, p. 150). Towner (1994, p. 724) also notes that the absence of consistent and accurate data raises questions about the degree of *post hoc* reasoning involved in the use of such models. Yet, retrospective studies have shown that many destinations fit the life cycle model (Cooper, 1994, p. 344).

Cooper (1993, p. 156) argued that sceptics, therefore, believe:

> . . . the cycle, at best, can assist general trend projections rather than causal forecasts. In terms of its use for strategic planning, some argue that rather than being an independent guide for strategy, or forecasting, the cycle is simply an outworking of management decisions and heavily dependent on external factors such as competition, the development of new destinations, swings in consumer taste, government legislation and regional policy (Dhalla and Yuspeh, 1976).

For this reason, therefore, no attempt is made in this chapter to use the concept as a forecasting tool. Instead, it is analyzed in terms of its heuristic utility in understanding trend projection.

In emphasizing its strength for integration, Cooper (1993, pp. 156–157) concluded that the life cycle concept:

> . . . provides tourism researchers with a glimmer of the elusive unifying concept or generalization of tourism. The life cycle approach has, therefore, much to offer tourism researchers and rather less to offer the tourist practitioner. Its logical and intuitive appeal deserves greater attention among tourism researchers, who should not be swayed by those who criticize the life cycle for its lack of operational value. By regarding destinations as dependent upon the actions of managers, the tourist industry and their markets, the life cycle provides an integrating medium for the study of tourism, a promising vehicle for future research, and a frame of reference for emergent themes in tourism, such as sustainable tourism.

Thus, despite some weaknesses, the life cycle concept does have utility as a measure against which to compare the development of tourist destinations and as an organizing framework (Cooper, 1994, p. 345) or heuristic framework for understanding destination development.

CASE STUDY SELECTION

While many parts of the world have come to depend economically to a very great extent on tourism, one region where tourism dominates much of the economy is the Caribbean.[2] In 1970 there were 4.24 million stayover arrivals in the Caribbean, while in 1993 there were 13.3 million. This represents an increase of 213 percent in just over two decades.

It has been estimated that tourist expenditures accounted for 25 percent of the region's exports in 1988 (EEC, 1990, p. 54) and approximately 420,000 jobs or between 8 percent and 10 percent of total employment in 1990 (Mather and Todd, 1993, p. i). With visitor expenditures in the region in 1993 estimated at US$11.1 billion (CTO, 1994), "there is probably no other region in the world in which tourism as a source of income, employment, hard currency earnings and economic growth has greater importance than in the Caribbean" (Mather and Todd, 1993, p. 11).

Clearly, there are too many states in the Caribbean for an analysis of all of them (see Figure 2.3). The islands of the Commonwealth Caribbean (i.e., islands that historically have been administered by Great Britain) were chosen for several reasons related mainly to the need for conceptual equivalence and equivalence of measurement (Warwick and Osherson, 1973), especially in cross-cultural studies (Pearce, 1993, p. 30). Similarities include (1) government structures, policy, and planning based on that of Great Britain, (2) English as the language of government and business, (3) mainly stable social and political climates that are conducive to tourism, (4) open economies that have the potential to receive tourists from any other nation, and (5) various internal regional ties.

Despite these commonalities, there is a great deal of variation among these islands. Ten are independent nations (Antigua and Barbuda, the Bahamas, Barbados, Dominica, Grenada, Jamaica, St. Kitts and Nevis, St. Lucia, St. Vincent and the Grenadines, and Trinidad and Tobago), while five are colonies or dependent territories (Anguilla, British Virgin Islands, Cayman Islands, Montserrat, and the Turks and Caicos).

The islands range in population from approximately 9000 inhabitants (Anguilla) to

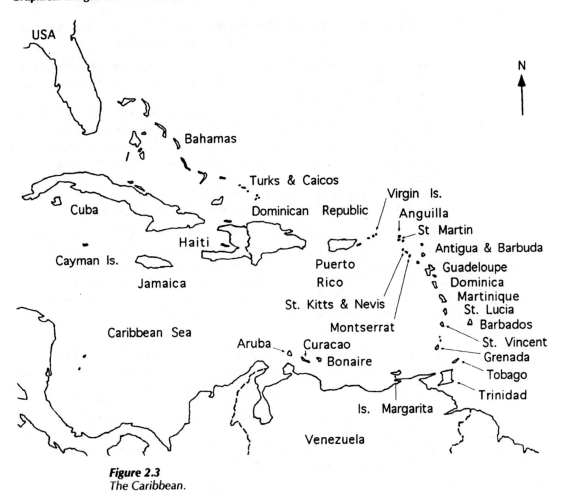

Figure 2.3
The Caribbean.

2.5 million (Jamaica); in area from approximately 35 square miles (91 square kilometers; Anguilla) to 5445 square miles (13,941 square kilometers; the Bahamas); in number of stayover tourist arrivals (1993) from about 36,700 (Anguilla) to just under 1.5 million (the Bahamas); in total visitor expenditures (1993) from US$15.2 million (Montserrat) to US$1304.0 million (the Bahamas); and in number of hotel rooms (1993) from 710 (Montserrat) to 13,521 (the Bahamas). Nevertheless, for all of them, tourism is the major economic sector, with visitor expenditures as a percentage of gross domestic product (GDP) ranging from 25 percent (Jamaica, Montserrat) to 75 percent (British Virgin Islands) (CTO, 1994). Clearly, these are "tourist islands."

For reasons related to the availability of research funding, the case studies were selected in two phases. For the first phase (undertaken in 1987), a trend analysis of basic tourism statistics focusing on stayover arrivals and visitor expenditures in the previous decade in the Commonwealth Caribbean was completed to compare the patterns to the models formulated by Butler and Lundberg, but particularly the former (Wilkinson, 1990). The goal was to select a maximum of four case studies, with the selection representing as wide a range as possible of the types of tourism development. The four island states chosen and their respective stages on Butler's model were as follows:

- *Dominica:* This island had low but fluctuating levels of tourism, followed in recent years by growth, with tourism being only a minor component of the national economy (Stage Two—Involvement).
- *Anguilla:* This island experienced almost continuous dramatic growth, with tourism coming to dominate the economy (early Stage Three—Development).
- *St. Lucia:* Following serious declines in the early 1980s, this island evidenced continuous growth, with tourism becoming a major economic sector (Stage Four—Consolidation).
- *Barbados:* Fluctuations were experienced, but tourism levels at the end of the period were similar to those at the beginning (Stage Five—Decline).

In the second phase, two additional case studies were selected. The intention was to broaden the range of types of patterns along the cycle's curve. At that time, McElroy and de Albuquerque (1989) had presented their model [later published as de Albuquerque and McElroy (1992)]. While this model used a wider range of data than in the selection of the first four case studies, those islands appeared to fit approximately similar locations as suggested earlier. Two states were chosen as filling out the range of stages of development:

- *Cayman Islands:* Rapid growth to high levels, with tourism being a major force in the economy and a sector characterized by large-scale development, aggressive marketing, niche marketing (scuba diving), and a major cruise ship presence (late Stage Two—Transition in de Albuquerque and McElroy's model).
- *Bahamas:* A mass market destination, with tourism dominating the economy, growth stagnation, short average lengths of stay, international hotel chains, high densities, casinos, packaged charters, cruise ships (late Stage Three—Maturity in de Albuquerque and McElroy's model).

Therefore, the six case studies, are located in the following order on de Albuquerque and McElroy's model: Dominica in the early phases of Stage One; Anguilla, St. Lucia, and Cayman Islands in successive phases of Stage Two; and Barbados and Bahamas in the late phases of Stage Three. Basic information on the nature of the tourism sector in each of the destinations is presented in Table 2.1 [for a detailed analysis, see Wilkinson (1996)].

GRAPHICAL IMAGES OF THE CYCLE

Although the analysis presented in this chapter was developed using a particular microcomputer spreadsheet software (Excel 5.0 for Windows), any major spreadsheet package could be used. However, recent versions of this type of software are needed to provide sophisticated graphical output with a minimum of effort.

The data were collected from a wide range of published and unpublished sources, most notably the Caribbean Tourism Organization (CTO) and the governments of the case study islands, and consist of time series data in common definitions, formats, and measures. Although, in some cases, reliable data are available from earlier dates, a com-

TABLE 2.1

Characteristics of the Tourism Sector in the Case Study Areas

Statistics[a]	Dominica	Anguilla	St. Lucia	Cayman Islands	Barbados	Bahamas
Area (square kilometers)	750	91	616	260	431	13,941
Population (thousands)	72.9	9.0	142.0	26.8	263.5	269.0
Gross domestic product (GDP)(US$ millions)	185.0	56.5	433.0	670	1385.3	3059.1
Annual growth in GDP (%)	2.6	7.5	6.6	4.4	(4.2)	2.0
Per capita GDP (US$ thousands)	2.5	6.3	3.1	22.7	5.3	11.4
Exports of goods and services (US$ millions)	54.6	NA[b]	130	470.4	768	2487.3
Labor force (thousands)	25	3.0	43.8	15.7	120.9	127.4
Employment rate (%)	85.0	95.0	95.0	93.0	77.0	84.0
Stayover tourists (thousands)	51.9	36.7	194.1	287.3	396.0	1488.7
Excursionists (thousands)	5.6	73.7	6.5	NA	NA	146.2
Cruise passengers (thousands)	87.8	0.0	154.4	605.7	428.6	2047.0
Total visitors (thousands)	145.3	110.4	355.1	892.3	824.6	3681.9
Top three stayover markets (%)	French West Indies (28.1) US (15.9) UK (9.0)	US (64.9) Caribbean (17.2) UK (5.3)	US (29.0) UK (25.3) Caribbean (23.5)	US (80.9) Caribbean (5.8) UK (4.2)	US (28.5) UK (25.3) Canada (12.4)	US (81.2) Europe (8.9) Canada (6.5)
Number of tourist rooms	757	978	2919	3453	5580	13,521
Average length of stay (nights)	7.8	10.3	10.6	4.9	11.2	5.8
Tourist nights (thousands)	404.8	378.0	2057.5	1407.8	4435.2	8634.5
Number of hotel rooms Mean	23	27	88	72	70	125
Range	5–76	6–98	5–256	4–306	7–288	5–1550
Visitor expenditures (US$ millions)	33.2	43.3	221	258.5	528.0	1304.0
Direct jobs in tourism	409	1064	3413	1252	7215	12,263

[a] 1993 or latest year.
[b] NA, not available.

27

mon starting point of 1980 is used most frequently. It is suggested that this is adequate to meet Brownlie's (1985) concern about using sufficiently long runs of data to give stable parameter estimates. Space limitations do not permit the inclusion of the extensive data set or the lengthy bibliography related to the data, both of which are detailed in Wilkinson (1996).

Because the original data are amenable to statistical analysis, they could be represented by linear regression equations and r^2 statistics.[3] Such statistics may have both utility and meaning to the researcher with strong quantitative research skills, but they are unlikely to be either useful or meaningful to many students, planners, policy makers, or the lay public. Instead, graphical representations of the data are useful heuristic devices that can aid many people to gain, literally, a picture that represents what otherwise might for them be a meaningless set of statistics. They also have the advantage of providing output that can quickly be created (with a high degree of graphic quality) and compared across a variety of case studies, variables, or measures of those variables.

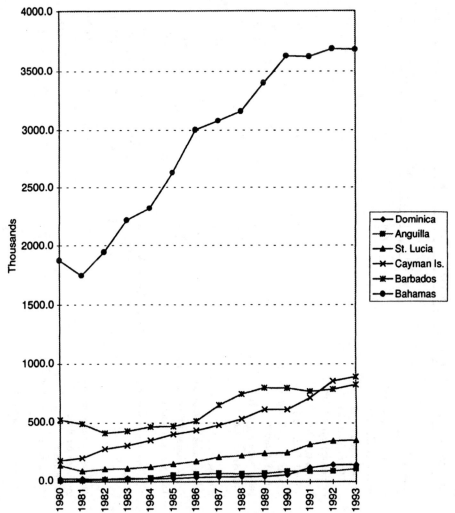

Figure 2.4
Total visitor arrivals,
1980–1993.

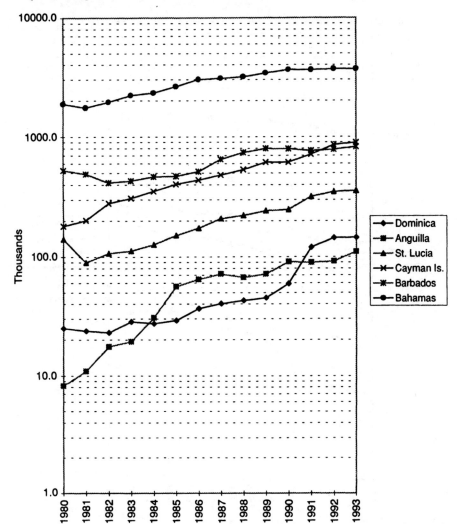

Figure 2.5
Total visitor arrivals
(semilogarithmic),
1980–1993.

A Sample The most common data used in a discussion of the life cycle concept are simple numbers
Presentation of visitors (i.e., an aggregate of stayover tourists, cruise passengers, and excursionists).
Figure 2.4 illustrates total visitor arrivals for the six destinations. It appears to give a clear
picture: Dominica and Anguilla are very minor destinations with slow growth; St. Lucia
and the Cayman Islands are both larger and growing faster; Barbados is still larger but has
had fluctuations and seems to have plateaued; and, finally, the Bahamas is very large and
growing dramatically. These patterns clearly demonstrate the location of the destinations
on de Albuquerque and McElroy's model and reinforce Jones and Lockwood's (1990,
p. 7) argument that type of growth is more relevant than shape.

Part of this picture is a function of the widely varying absolute sizes of the numbers
involved. Using a semilogarithmic[4] presentation that places more emphasis on relative
growth than on absolute numbers, Figure 2.5 presents a somewhat different picture,
notably for the largest and smallest destinations. The growth for Dominica and Anguilla
appears more dramatic, but is less so for the Bahamas.

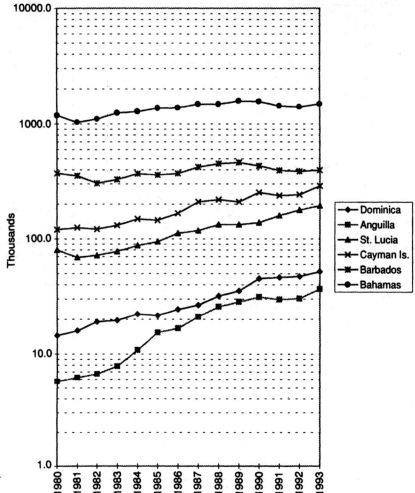

Figure 2.6
Stayover visitors, 1980–1993.

A very different image emerges when total visitor arrival statistics are disaggregated into types of visitors. Obviously, all the destinations have stayover arrivals[5] but the mix of stayover arrivals, cruise passengers,[6] and excursionists[7] varies greatly. Anguilla, for example, had 110,400 total visitors in 1993, consisting of 36,700 stayover arrivals (33.2 percent of total visitors), 73,700 excursionists (66.8 percent), and no cruise passengers. On the other hand, the Bahamas had 3,681,900 total visitors, consisting of 1,488,700 stayover arrivals (40.4 percent of total visitors), 146,200 excursionists (4.0 percent), and 2,047,000 cruise passengers (55.6 percent).

Using a semilogarithmic scale, again because of the wide absolute ranges between countries, Figure 2.6 shows different patterns for stayover arrivals than for total visitors: less dramatic growth for some countries with a strong cruise passenger sector (e.g., the Bahamas), but more even growth for others once the effects of excursionists (e.g., Anguilla) or cruise passengers (e.g., Dominica) are eliminated.

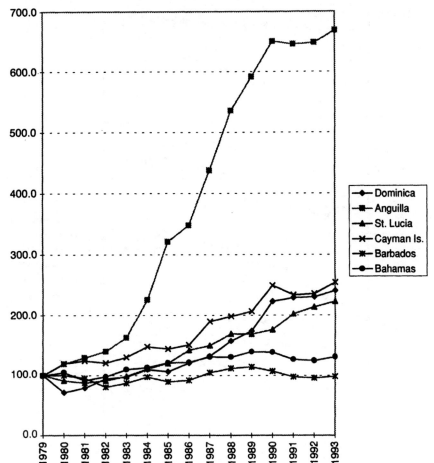

Figure 2.7
Index of change
(1979 = 100.0) in stayover
visitors, 1980–1993.

One reason for disaggregating types of arrivals is to uncover varying impacts (i.e., social, economic, and biophysical). Several thousand cruise passengers arriving *en masse* in a port (usually a small city or a town) clearly have a very different social impact (e.g., congestion, demand for taxis or guides) per day than do the same number of stayover visitors spending the day in a hotel on a beach outside of town. The latter, however, requires more electricity and water per capita. The average stayover visitor also probably spends much more money over the course of one or two weeks (and possibly even more money for every day of the stay) than does a cruise passenger during a six-hour visit. Unfortunately, data are not available to measure and demonstrate such patterns directly.

Figures 2.4, 2.5, and 2.6 represent absolute numbers of visitors (i.e., plotting the actual numbers of people). As noted earlier, one of the problems with the cycle concept focuses on the need to emphasize turning points in the curve, suggesting that relative change is more important than absolute numbers. Figure 2.7 demonstrates an index of change in stayover visitors (calculated by adding consecutively the percentage change in the number of stayover visitors from the previous year, with 1979 as a base year equaling

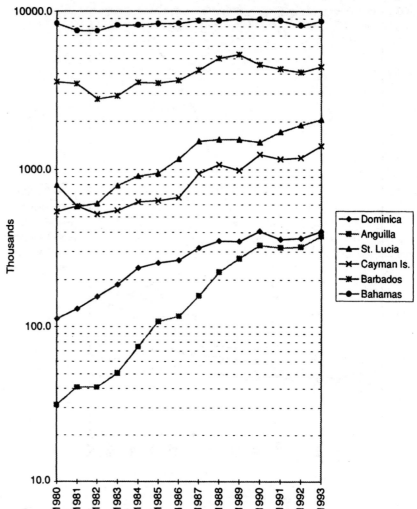

Figure 2.8
*Annual tourist nights,
1980–1993.*

100.0). This figure identifies Anguilla as by far the leader in growth, followed by the Cayman Islands, Dominica, and St. Lucia. The two largest destinations from the perspective of absolute numbers, the Bahamas and Barbados, appear as being stagnant and even declining in terms of growth.

Thus far, the data for stayover visitors focus only on the absolute number of people entering a country. They do not deal with their average length of stay (LOS) in the country. There are considerable differences among these destinations in LOS (e.g., 10.6 nights for St. Lucia in 1993, compared to 5.8 for the Bahamas). Such differences are important in terms of impacts; *ceteris paribus*, the longer a visitor stays in a country, the greater the local economic impact is likely to be. Figure 2.8 converts the number of stayover visitors into annual tourist nights using average length of stay. Clearly, the Bahamas and Barbados have stagnated, while the others show stronger growth.

As noted earlier, expenditure statistics that can accurately disaggregate the patterns of

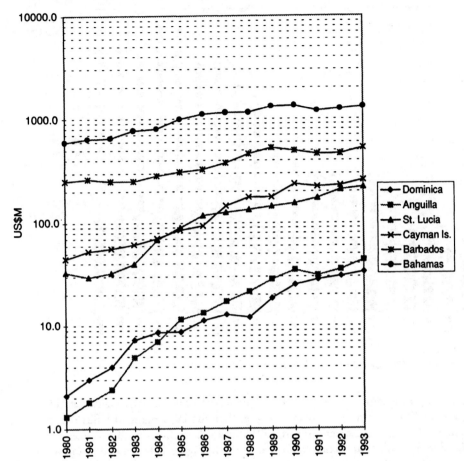

Figure 2.9
Total tourist expenditure (current), 1980–1993.

different types of visitors are not available. Figure 2.9, however, illustrates that the pattern of total tourist expenditures (in current US$ millions)[8] is very similar to that presented in Figure 2.4 for total visitor arrivals.

Analysis of the figures presented thus far has been subjective. It is possible to include statistical analyses on the figures for each of the six destinations, but they would then become visually very cluttered. Therefore, it is useful to switch to an examination of a particular destination. The Bahamas is used for two reasons. First, reliable data on visitor numbers, visitor expenditures, and the country's consumer price index (CPI) exist dating back to 1971. Second, the data present clear differences between current and real patterns.

Figure 2.10 illustrates the dramatic difference between current and real total visitor expenditures, with the latter using the CPI as an inflation factor. In real terms, the Bahamas is only slightly better off in 1993 than it was in 1971 in total visitor expenditures, with total real visitor expenditures of US$442.0 million having increased only 59.2 percent from US$277.7 million. This pattern is both visually and statistically more apparent when the linear regression line and equation are considered.

The picture of stagnation is even more apparent in Figure 2.11, which shows that

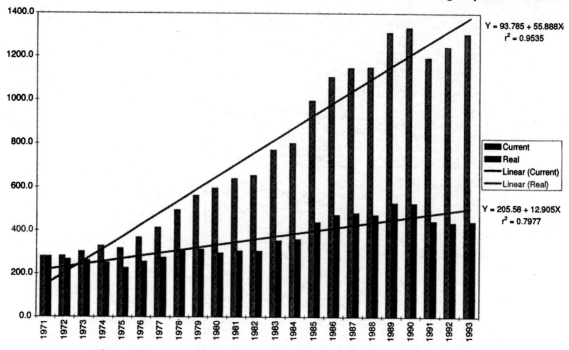

Figure 2.10
Bahamas: Visitor expenditure (US$ millions), 1971–1993.

total visitor expenditure per capita of local population has virtually plateaued. The 1993 figure of US$1643 is only 2.9 percent higher than the 1971 figure of US$1596 (note the dramatic decrease in expenditure in 1991 due to disruptions in global tourist patterns related to the Gulf War). The reason is apparent in Figure 2.12. In contrast to the seemingly positive picture of increasing total visitor arrivals presented in Figures 2.2 and 2.3, the problem is that expenditure per visitor declined 26.7 percent in real terms from US$1897 in 1971 to US$1201 in 1993. Data are not available to separate expenditures by type of visitor, but this average decline per visitor is believed to be directly related to the rapidly expanding numbers of cruise passengers who, quite simply, appear to have little positive economic impact on the Bahamas.

The statistics presented may provide little information to anyone but a skilled statistician. Similarly, the mass of data used to develop these figures tends to mask trends, particularly when simplistic measures such as total visitor arrivals or current expenditures are the only ones used. In contrast, the graphical images present pictures that might startle a potential investor, a local businessperson, or a local politician and raise provocative questions.

For example, how much longer can the Bahamas expect to experience such dramatic growth in cruise passenger numbers? What happens to the economy when total visitor expenditure starts to decrease as inflation surpasses growth? Did no one foresee that Bahamian tourism has long been stagnant? Is a "crash" imminent? What, if anything, can be done to reverse the trends? These are important questions for a country such as the Bahamas where visitor expenditures represent an extremely high proportion of GDP (40.7 percent in 1992).

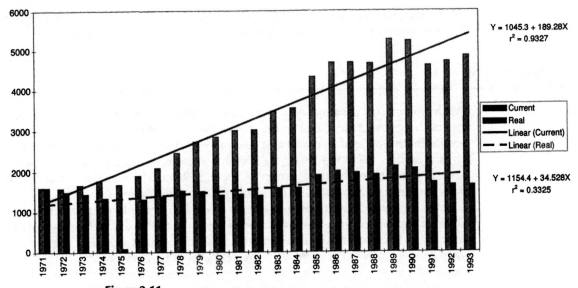

Figure 2.11
Bahamas: Visitor expenditure (US$) per capita of local population, 1971–1993.

Although space does not permit the provision of additional examples, further extensions to the analysis presented in this chapter are possible. For example, the measures employed in Figures 2.10, 2.11, and 2.12 could be presented comparatively for the six case studies. Moreover, as indicated by the questions proposed above for the Bahamas, this type of analysis can also suggest other avenues of research (e.g., analysis of tourism

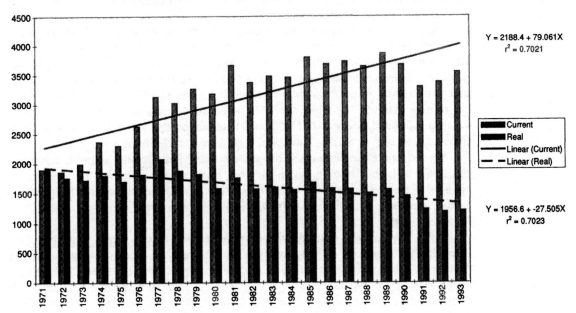

Figure 2.12
Bahamas: Expenditure (US$) per visitor, 1971–1993.

policies and plans that have shaped the current situation). Finally, it could also suggest that other types of data (e.g., expenditures by types of visitors) should be collected.

CONCLUSION

Clearly, tourism is a dynamic industry with destinations often undergoing dramatic patterns of change over time. Based on the product life cycle, which is used in marketing to describe the evolution of a product as it passes through the stages of introduction, maturity, and decline, the tourist area cycle of evolution has been described as providing the "seeds of a generalised theory of tourism" (Cooper, 1994, p. 346) because of its analytical utility concerning the dynamics of the growth of tourist destinations.

Most frequently, research on the cycle has focused on elementary graphical representations of such simple measures as numbers of total visitors or amounts of total visitor expenditures in current terms. This approach, however, does not accurately represent the complexity of tourism. For example, using aggregate visitor numbers does not take into account the varying social, economic, and biophysical impacts of different types of visitors, such as stayover tourists, cruise passengers, and excursionists. Similarly, using total expenditures in current terms masks the real value of such expenditures and true rates of change in expenditures.

The availability of powerful microcomputer spreadsheets, however, presents the researcher with an analytical method that can not only quickly provide quality graphical and statistical output, but also can facilitate the development of alternative measures of tourism such as indices of change. This enhances the use of the cycle concept not only as a descriptive tool, but also as explanatory and heuristic tools. Using a variety of data on Dominica, Anguilla, St. Lucia, Cayman Islands, Barbados, and the Bahamas, this chapter has demonstrated these three uses of the cycle concept.

First, the cycle concept clearly is useful as a descriptive tool. As Hovinen (1981) suggested, the images of the tourist cycle presented in this chapter demonstrate that each stage in the cycle varies in length, and the curve displays different shapes and patterns. There is, however, consistency within a particular destination in terms of length, shape, and pattern when different variables are used. In Cooper's (1993, 1994) terms, therefore, the turning points in the curve appear to be constant across variables. This appears to confirm Jones and Lockwood's (1990, p. 7) contention that shape is less relevant than different types of growth (slow, medium, high, constant, declining).

Second, the examples suggest the cycle concept has potential utility not just as a descriptive tool, but also as an explanatory tool. For example, if accurate data on expenditures by type of visitor were available, the relationship between the stagnant expenditure picture presented for the Bahamas and the increasing number of cruise passengers would be much clearer.

Third, the graphical examples demonstrate that the use of a variety of measures can be applied to the concept of the tourist cycle, and the results can be used to raise questions that have important implications for tourist destinations. Simple numbers of tourists or expenditures are useful only as a beginning step in comparing destinations and should be supplemented by other measures, such as indices of change. Similarly, the use of data such as current visitor expenditures is extremely misleading when medium- to long-term trends are examined. In contrast, alternative measures (e.g., indices of change, per capita figures, trend analysis), particularly when graphically portrayed, have heuristic utility in that they provide vehicles for the framing of significant questions about both the past and future of tourist destinations.

In conclusion, the life cycle concept is an extremely useful measure of the development of tourist destinations in descriptive, explanatory, and heuristic terms. Portrayed graphically using microcomputer spreadsheet software, the concept becomes a very powerful research and teaching tool.

ACKNOWLEDGMENTS

Appreciation is extended to the Social Sciences and Humanities Research Council of Canada for its support. Microsoft Excel 5.0 is a registered trademark of Microsoft Corporation.

NOTES

1. While Weaver's work on Dominica (1991) and Grand Cayman (1990) and Debbage's work on the Bahamas (1991), all of which employed the life cycle concept, had appeared just prior to the publication of de Albuquerque and McElroy's 1992 paper, the latter's research had actually been completed earlier and presented in McElroy and de Albuquerque (1989).
2. See Chapter 8 for a comprehensive overview of tourism in the Caribbean region.
3. A linear regression equation describes the relation between two variables (Jackson, 1988). The general form of the equation is $Y = a + b(X)$, where Y is the dependent variable (e.g., total number of visitors in a given year), X is the independent variable (e.g., time measured in years), a is a constant that identifies the point at which the regression line crosses the Y (vertical) axis, and b refers to the slope of the regression line that best describes the relation between the variables (in terms of the vertical deviations of the points above the line equalling the vertical deviations below the line). The correlation coefficient (r) is a measure of the strength of the association between the two variables, ranging from $+1$ to -1; r^2 is the measure of the amount of variation in the dependent variable that is explained by the independent variable and is frequently expressed as a percentage. In Figure 2.10, for example, the linear regression formula $Y = 55.888X + 93.785$ describes a regression line that shows the relationship between the amount of visitor expenditure (in US\$ millions) in the Bahamas between 1971 and 1993; with $r^2 = 0.9535$, this line measures 95.35 percent of the variation in that expenditure over that time period.
4. In a semilogarithmic presentation, the values of dependent variable Y (e.g., total number of visitors) are represented by a logarithmically scaled axis in which each major division of the axis represents ten times the value of the previous major division. This type of scale is useful when plotting series of data with wide variations in magnitude. It can also reveal, for example, that a series of data that seemingly are increasing in a steady progression might have a rate of growth that is actually decreasing (e.g., note the differences between Figures 2.4 and 2.5 for Dominica). The presentation is semilogarithmic because the independent variable (e.g., time measured in years) is represented on the X axis by a standard scale in which each major division represents an equal value (i.e., one year).
5. Stayover arrivals are visitors who spend more than 24 hours in the country.
6. Cruise passengers are visitors who reside on a cruise ship for a week or two, visiting numerous destinations for short periods of time, usually only a few hours.
7. Excursionists are visitors who are stayover arrivals in one country and travel by air or boat to another country for a short period of time.

8. Because a variety of currencies is used in the Caribbean, data are usually presented in United States dollar equivalents.

REFERENCES

Agarwall, S. 1994. The life cycle approach and south coast resorts. In C. Cooper and A. Lockwood (eds.), *Progress in Tourism, Recreation and Hospitality Management*, Vol. 5. Chichester: John Wiley & Sons, pp. 194–208.

Brown, S. 1987. Institutional change in retailing: a review and synthesis, *European Journal of Marketing*, 21(6), 5–36.

Brownlie, D. 1985. Strategic marketing concepts and models, *Journal of Marketing Management*, 1, 157–194.

Butler, R.W. 1980. The concept of a tourist area cycle of evolution: implications for management of resources, *Canadian Geographer*, (24)1, 5–12.

Buttle, F. 1986. *Hotel and Food Service Marketing*. London: Holt.

Caribbean Tourism Organization (CTO). 1994. *Caribbean Tourism Statistical Report 1993*. St. Michael, Barbados: CTO.

Cohen, E. 1972. Towards a sociology of international tourism, *Social Research*, 39, 164–182.

Cooper, C.P. 1992. The life cycle concept and strategic planning for coastal resorts, *Built Environment*, (18)1, 57–66.

Cooper, C.P. 1993. The life cycle concept and tourism. In P. Johnson and B. Thomas (eds.), *Choice and Demand in Tourism*. London: Mansell, pp. 145–160.

Cooper, C.P. 1994. The destination life cycle: an update. In A.V. Seaton (ed.), *Tourism: The State of the Art*. Chichester: John Wiley & Sons, pp. 340–346.

Cooper, C.P. and S. Jackson. 1989. Destination life cycle: the Isle of Man case study, *Annals of Tourism Research*, 16(3), 377–398.

Day, G.S. 1981. The product life cycle: analysis and applications issues, *Journal of Marketing*, 45(1), 60–67.

de Albuquerque, K. and J. McElroy. 1992. Caribbean small-island tourism styles and sustainable strategies, *Environmental Management*, 16(5), 619–632.

Debbage, K.G. 1991. Spatial behavior in a Bahamian resort, *Annals of Tourism Research*, 18(2), 251–268.

Dhalla, N.K. and S. Yuspeh. 1976. Forget the product life cycle concept, *Harvard Business Review*, 54, 102–110.

Doyle, P. 1976. The realities of the product life cycle, *Quarterly Review of Marketing*, 1(1), 1–6.

European Economic Community (EEC). 1990. *The Courier*, Vol. 122. Brussels: EEC, pp. 50–86.

Goodall, B. 1992. Coastal resorts: development and redevelopment, *Built Environment*, 18(1), 5–11.

Hannan, M.T. and J. Freeman. 1977. The population ecology of organizations, *American Journal of Sociology*, 82(5), 929–964.

Haywood, K.M. 1986. Can the tourist area life cycle be made operational? *Tourism Management*, 7, 154–167.

Haywood, K. M. 1990. Resort cycles: a commentary. Association of American Geographers. Toronto, 20–22 April.

Hovinen, G.R. 1981. A tourist cycle in Lancaster County, *Tourism Management*, 7, 154–167.

Hunt, S.D. 1976. *Marketing Theory: Conceptual Foundations of Research in Marketing.* Columbus, Ohio: Grid.

Jackson, W. 1988. *Research Methods: Rules for Survey Design and Analysis.* Scarborough, Ontario: Prentice-Hall.

Jones, P. and A. Lockwood. 1990. *Productivity and the Product Life Cycle in Hospitality Firms.* Contemporary Hospitality Management Conference, Bournemouth.

Keller, C.P. 1987. Stages of peripheral tourism development: Canada's Northwest Territories, *Tourism Management*, 8(1), 20–32.

Kotler, P. 1980. *Principles of Marketing*, 3rd ed. Englewood Cliffs, NJ: Prentice–Hall.

Lambkin, M. and G.S. Day. 1989. Evolutionary processes in competitive markets: beyond the product life cycle, *Journal of Marketing*, 53(1), 4–20.

Lundberg, D.E. 1980. *The Tourist Business.* Boston: Cahners Books.

Lundgren, J.O.J. 1982. The development of tourist accommodation in the Montreal Laurentians. In G. Wall and J. Marsh (eds.), *Recreational Land Use: Perspectives on its Evolution in Canada*. Ottawa: Carleton University Press, pp. 175–189.

Mather, S. and G. Todd. 1993. *Tourism in the Caribbean*, Special Report No. 455. London: EIU.

McElroy, J. and K. de Albuquerque. 1989. *Tourism Styles and Policy Response in the Open Economy-Closed Environment Context.* Conference on Economics and the Environment, CCA, Bridgetown, Barbados, 6–8 November.

Meyer-Arendt, K.J. 1985. The Grand Isle, Louisiana resort cycle, *Annals of Tourism Research*, (12)3, 449–466.

Nelson, R. and G. Wall. 1986. Transport and accommodation: changing interrelationships on Vancouver Island, *Annals of Tourism Research*, 13(2), 239–260.

Oglethorpe, M. 1984. Tourism in Malta: a crisis of dependence, *Leisure Studies*, 3, 147–162.

Onkvisit, S. and J.J. Shaw. 1986. Competition and product management: can the product life cycle help? *Business Horizons*, 29, 51–62.

Pearce, D.G. 1989. *Tourist Development.* London: Longman, Harlow.

Pearce, D.G. 1993. Comparative studies in tourism research. In D.G. Pearce and R.W. Butler (eds.), *Tourism Research: Critiques and Challenges.* London and New York: Routledge, in association with the International Academy for the Study of Tourism, pp. 20–35.

Plog, S.C. 1991. *Leisure Travel: Making It a Growth Market Again!* New York: John Wiley & Sons.

Rink, D.R. and J.E. Swan. 1979. Product life cycle research: literature review, *Journal of Business Research*, 78, 219–242.

Stansfield, C.A. 1978. Atlantic City and the resort cycle: background to the legalization of gambling, *Annals of Tourism Research*, 5(2), 238–351.

Towner, J. 1994. Tourism history: past, present and future. In A.V. Seaton (ed.), *Tourism: The State of the Art.* Chichester: John Wiley & Sons, pp. 721–728.

Warwick, D.P. and S. Osherson. 1973. *Comparative Research Methods.* Englewood Cliffs, NJ: Prentice–Hall.

Weaver, D.B. 1990. Grand Cayman Island and the resort cycle concept, *Journal of Travel Research*, 29(2), 9–15.

Weaver, D.B. 1991. Alternative to mass tourism in Dominica, *Annals of Tourism Research*, 18, 414–432.

Wilkinson, P.F. 1987. Tourism in small island nations: a fragile dependency, *Leisure Studies*, 6(2), 127–146.

Wilkinson, P.F. 1990. Tourism and integrated national development: the case of the Caribbean. In P.F. Wilkinson and W.C. Found (eds.), *Resource Analysis Research in Developing Countries: The Experience of Ontario Geographers*, Toronto: Faculty of Environmental Studies, York University, pp. 83–97.

Wilkinson, P.F. 1996. *Tourism Policy and Planning: Case Studies from the Commonwealth Caribbean*. Elmsford, NY: Cognizant Communications.

¶ | PROBLEM SOLVING AND DISCUSSION ACTIVITIES

1. Develop a set of tourist destination data involving a variety of traditional measures (e.g., total visitor arrivals) covering at least 10 years for one or more destinations. Describe the patterns that these data suggest.

2. Using a microcomputer spreadsheet package, analyze these measures with both statistical (e.g., simple linear regression) and graphical tools. Compare the patterns suggested with those determined in the first exercise above.

3. Develop alternative measures of the cycle (e.g., indices of change) for these data. Again, compare the patterns suggested with the earlier analyses.

4. Prepare analyses for the five other case study areas using the measures employed in Figures 2.10, 2.11, and 2.12. Compare these results to those evidenced for the Bahamas. What implications do these findings have for tourism's contribution to the economic well-being of these islands?

5. Although the life cycle was not designed as a predictive tool, test the concept as a predictive tool to determine whether, for example, by using data ending several years ago, the resulting trend lines accurately predict the figures for the current period. Then, use the entire data set and create a trend line 5 and 10 years into the future. Discuss whether the life cycle has utility as a predictive tool.

6. Select one of the destinations featured in this chapter and conduct secondary source investigations to determine what policies and plans were in place over time. Comment on whether the government appears to have been taking a proactive role in planning and controlling the evolution of the tourism sector.

3

One Name, Two Destinations

PLANNED AND UNPLANNED COASTAL RESORTS IN INDONESIA

 *Geoffrey Wall*

¶ | K E Y   L E A R N I N G   P O I N T S

- Different types of tourism are likely to have very different consequences for host communities, making it difficult to generalize concerning the impacts of tourism.
- The impact of tourism varies according to the nature of the host population. Therefore, it is important to understand who gains and who loses, not only whether the benefits are likely to exceed the costs.
- Planning is a political process that empowers some and disadvantages others, often strengthening the position of the powerful and further undermining the position of the weak.
- Economic, environmental, and social impacts are not discrete phenomena, but are intertwined in complex ways.
- It is seldom possible to maximize benefits and minimize costs at the same time. Rather, trade-offs are involved and steps should be taken to identify and mitigate negative impacts.

INTRODUCTION

Kuta is the name of two coastal resorts in Indonesia. Both have tropical climates and attractive beaches. However, they differ considerably in other ways. The most well known and well established of the two is Kuta, Bali, which, with a minimum of planning, has grown into a major international tourist destination since the 1970s. In contrast, Kuta, Lombok is an emerging resort that is currently under construction following the formulation of a detailed plan.

A comparison of the two resorts permits discussion of such issues as planning, accessibility, scale of development, involvement of local people, the role of culture, and maintenance of environmental quality. In particular, it is shown that, in the absence of planning, local people have found ways to become involved in, and benefit from, tourism development in Kuta, Bali but at the cost of a degraded environment. In contrast, planned resort development in Kuta, Lombok is likely to protect environmental quality, but there may be little opportunity for local people to benefit from the development, and some will be displaced and disadvantaged by the construction of a resort enclave.

TOURISM PLANNING: CONTEMPORARY PERSPECTIVES AND ISSUES

Tourism development in most capitalist countries of the so-called developed western world is strongly influenced by private and corporate decisions. National governments, while they may determine such matters as airline routes and visa requirements, usually emphasize marketing rather than the planning of tourism. At the local level, tourism development generally has to conform to processes that are designed to regulate developments of all kinds, such as zoning systems, building permits, and environmental impact assessments. Thus, in the western world, public sector planning specifically for tourism is often rudimentary.

In contrast, governments often play a major role in all aspects of tourism in developing nations. Not only are they responsible for the marketing and regulation of tourism and for encouraging and facilitating the training of an appropriate labor force, they may also be major investors in tourism. Where there is little experience with tourism and access to capital is limited, governments may take the initiative to attract experienced developers and international capital. To reassure potential developers of the security of their investments, it is necessary to have a vision for the destination that is being developed. Hence, plans are created to guide the development, often with the assistance of consultants from the developed world. Thus, tourism planning is often undertaken in a more comprehensive manner in the developing than in the developed world.

There is a vast literature on principles of planning, and there is a substantial literature on tourism planning. Much of the latter adopts a normative perspective, indicating how plans should be formulated.[1] However, there are extremely few studies of actual tourism processes, of how tourism plans are actually created, and of the consequences of those plans for the people who are affected by them. There is a substantial gap between the theory and practice of tourism planning.

Planning is not a dispassionate process. Moreover, not all of those who are impacted by tourism are able to influence the planning agenda or contribute to the formulation of plans. Nonetheless, the decisions that are made influence the allocation of resources and, ultimately, largely determine who gains and who loses from the resulting tourism. Thus, tourism development is a political process involving differential access to power and control (Britton, 1991; Hall, 1994). The presence or absence of plans, the content of plans, and whether plans are actually implemented have far-reaching implications for the character of tourism that occurs, including trade-offs between the economic, environmental, and social consequences of development as well as the extent to which residents are able to become involved in tourism as it evolves in their community.[2]

Many residents of destination areas support tourism development because they want change. They want higher incomes, more jobs, and greater opportunities for their children. However, they may not want the other modifications to their community that tourism may bring, such as environmental modifications and changes to the social structure and distribution of power. Economic, environmental, and social consequences of tourism are not distinct impact categories. They are closely intertwined. Furthermore, and unfortunately, it is seldom possible to maximize benefits and to minimize costs at the same time. Thus, in all forms of development, there are likely to be winners and losers, as well as a need for trade-offs and compromise. Ideally, the planning process should promote equity as well as growth. However, any type of tourism development is likely to favor the interests of some groups as opposed to others.

The purpose of this comparative study is to describe tourism and tourism planning in Kuta, Bali and Kuta, Lombok. Although they are both coastal locations with attractive beaches, their experiences have been, and will continue to be, very different. Before embarking upon a comparison of tourism planning in these two areas, it is important to provide an overview of tourism in Indonesia as well as describe Bali and Lombok, which constitute the contexts of the two sites. A more extensive comparative discussion of Bali and Lombok is available in Wall (1996b).

TOURISM IN INDONESIA

Indonesia is a large and varied country with a rich potential to provide a diversity of tourism experiences. The Indonesian archipelago consists of over 1500 tropical islands that are inhabited by more than 300 ethnic groups who speak approximately 250 languages (Wall, 1996a). The country's tourist attractions cover a wide spectrum and include the following:

- *Natural features* such as beaches, volcanoes, coral reefs, forests, and endemic plant and animal species.
- *Cultural attractions* based on music, dance, crafts, and textiles.
- *Historic monuments* such as the UNESCO (United Nations Economic and Social Council) World Heritage sites at Borobudor and Prambanan.
- *Humanized landscapes*, including cascading rice fields and picturesque villages.

If planned and managed appropriately, these attractions could provide experiences to satisfy many tastes.

At the same time, a growing population already in excess of 180 million and great regional differences in lifestyles and standards of living present immense development challenges. Declining oil revenues forced the government of Indonesia to seek other sources of foreign exchange. Hence, as indicated in the growing prominence given to tourism in successive *Repelitas* (five-year development plans), the government has turned increasingly to tourism to meet this need. In 1994 tourism was third behind forestry and textiles as a non-oil earner of foreign exchange (Directorate General of Tourism, 1994).

Tourism has grown very rapidly in Indonesia since the 1970s (Oppermann, 1992; Wall, 1996a). In 1969 there were only 86,100 international visitors. This increased to 501,430 in 1979 and to 1,625,965 in 1989. By 1994 there were 4,006,312 international arrivals, representing an increase of 17.7 percent over the previous year. However, the distribution of visitors within Indonesia is very uneven, with approximately one-quarter of international arrivals entering the country in each of Jakarta (the capital) and Bali.

TABLE 3.1
Number of International Tourists,[a] 1984–1990

Year	Indonesia	Bali	West Nusa Tenggara
1984	701,000	189,000	7,100
1985	749,000	211,000	8,800
1986	825,000	243,000	13,600
1987	1,060,000	309,000	25,700
1988	1,301,000	360,000	44,800
1989	1,626,000	436,000	56,100
1990	2,177,000	490,000	107,200
Average Annual Growth (%)	20.8	17.2	57.2

[a] These figures report *direct* arrivals only. Indirect arrivals and domestic vistation are not included.

Sources: Picard (1992, p. 56); Dinas Pariwisata Daerah Tingkat I (1993, p. 9).

Approximately one-half of all international visitor-nights are spent in Bali. As a tropical country sitting astride the equator and attracting visitors from both hemispheres, seasonality in visits, although present, is less marked in Indonesia than in many other countries. An impression of the number of international tourists visiting Indonesia, Bali, and West Nusa Tenggara, of which Lombok is a part, can be gained from Table 3.1.

The data for Bali greatly underestimate the number of foreign visitors because they only include direct arrivals, thereby excluding visitors who entered Indonesia elsewhere. Furthermore, the data do not include domestic tourists. Although accurate statistics on domestic tourism are not available, it is believed that domestic visitors may equal the number of international tourists in both Bali and Nusa Tenggara.[3] It is safe to say that the observations of recent rapid growth and uneven distribution also apply to the domestic market.

In its initial years, tourism in Indonesia grew in an unplanned manner. However, increasingly, tourism development has been, and is being, guided through formal plans with considerable involvement of the national government, international funding agencies, and outside experts (Wall and Dibnah, 1992). A national tourism strategy was completed in 1992 and in 1995 steps were being taken to formulate a national tourism plan (Directorate General of Tourism, 1994). Some provinces, especially Bali, have been the focus of a number of tourism planning initiatives, whereas others have yet to receive similar detailed attention. In recognition of the fact that provinces often do not constitute good units for tourism planning, there is also a move to focus upon tourism regions that may not conform to provincial boundaries.

Dating from approximately 1970, Kuta, Bali was the first Indonesian coastal tourist resort to achieve an international reputation (see Figure 3.1). It developed without the benefit of restrictions or plans and, although it has since been the subject of a number of planning initiatives, it still bears the marks of its unplanned origins and growth. Kuta, Lombok, on the other hand, is the site of an emerging planned resort (see Figure 3.2).

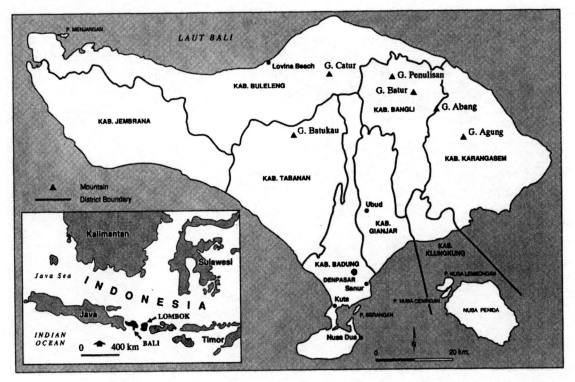

Figure 3.1
Location of Bali.

Although some tourists currently visit Kuta, Lombok, visitation volumes are limited. However, the area is designated for resort development (at the time of this writing in 1995, building was about to commence).

BALI AND LOMBOK

Bali and Lombok are adjacent islands located in the south-center of Indonesia (see Figure 3.1). Of comparable size and population, they are separated by the Lombok Strait and sandwiched between the Java Sea to the north and the Indian Ocean to the south. Bali supports a population of approximately 2.8 million on its 2185 square miles (5600 square kilometers), whereas Lombok has about 2.4 million people living on 2120 square miles (5435 square kilometers). At roughly 1280 people per square mile (500 people per square kilometer), these are high population densities. Both have volcanic cores and attractive coastlines, but they differ in many other ways. Bali is a province of Indonesia, whereas Lombok, along with Sumbawa, is part of the neighboring province of West Nusa Tenggara. Bali is relatively well watered and is more productive agriculturally than Lombok. Standards of living are generally lower in Lombok than in Bali.

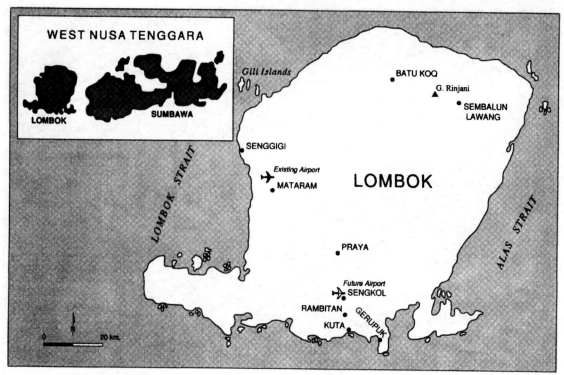

Figure 3.2
Location of Lombok.

While the majority of the population of Indonesia is Moslem, more than 90 percent of the population of Bali is Hindu. Balinese Hinduism has evolved in a distinctive manner over the centuries (Budihardjo, 1986; Covarrubias, 1937; Eiseman, 1988, 1990; Lansing, 1991). Each family compound has a temple in the corner nearest to Mount Agung, the home of the gods. Each village has three major temples. There are also temples in the rice fields. Offerings are made three times each day in most households and businesses. Ceremonies and festivals abound and have become major tourist attractions. The tolerant Balinese have become accustomed to sharing their celebrations with outsiders. In fact, cremations are advertised as tourist attractions in the resorts. There is a rich tradition of music and dance, much of which was, and still is, performed for the gods as well as for the tourists, and many skilled painters, carvers, and silversmiths ply their trades.

The unique Balinese culture and its religious and cultural expressions attracted the attention of western artists and anthropologists who came to document and interpret Balinese cultural activities and experiences (Picard, 1992; Vickers, 1989). Their reports and publications drew attention to "the last paradise" and "the land of morning calm." These exotic images were reinforced by film. Thus, even before the onset of mass tourism and the advertising of packaged holidays, Bali was viewed and publicized as a very special place that was worth visiting "before it is too late." This image has been retained to the present. In most markets, Bali has a much stronger image than Indonesia, the country of which it is a part.

Although there is a Balinese Hindu minority in Lombok, the great majority of the population of Lombok are Sasaks who are devotees of Islam. In addition, there is a minority of Wetu Telu who mix aspects of Islam with animism and ancestor worship. These cultures have their own architectural, ceremonial, and artistic expressions that are of intrinsic interest to outsiders. Indeed, Sasak architectural styles are incorporated into hotel designs, Lombok weaving and pottery make excellent souvenirs, and interesting folk carvings are available for purchase. However, most outsiders would agree that Lombok lifestyles and cultural expressions are generally less colorful than those found in profusion in Bali. Lombok has received much less attention from western artists and anthropologists than Bali.

Bali and Lombok are at very different stages of tourism development. Lombok is in a somewhat similar situation to that of Bali prior to the arrival of mass tourism in the 1970s (Butler, 1980). In 1990, there were 1,850,000 visitors (direct, indirect, and domestic) to Bali (of whom approximately 60 percent were foreign tourists) compared with only 56,000 visitors to Lombok in 1991 (of whom approximately 80 percent were foreign tourists) (Hassall and Associates, 1992a; Sofreavia et al., 1993). Differences in the volume of tourist traffic are also reflected in the volume and types of tourism infrastructure. For example, in 1992 more than half of Indonesia's five-star hotels (13 of 23) were located in Bali. In contrast, West Nusa Tenggara had no five-star hotels (the highest rated hotel was the three-star Sheraton Senggigi in Lombok).

A corollary of this is that a much larger proportion of accommodation in Lombok than in Bali is in small unclassified establishments, although such accommodation is also a very important component of the commercial accommodation supply in Bali because it affords a different type of experience from that gained by staying in a five-star hotel. Differences in hotel provision are complemented by differences in other aspects of supply. For example, Bali has far more licensed tourist guides (in 1992 Bali had 1046, whereas West Nusa Tenggara had 113) as well as a greater number of travel bureaus (in 1992 Bali had 111, whereas West Nusa Tenggara had 37) (Directorate General of Tourism, 1994).

Variations in supply confirm the earlier comment that, although in close juxtaposition, the two locations are at very different stages of tourism development. In the terminology of Butler,[4] Bali is probably towards the end of the development, or even the consolidation stage, whereas Lombok is in the involvement or early development stage (Butler, 1980). In both cases, Butler's cycle is difficult to apply without modification because foreign investment and planning initiatives have taken place in the early stages of tourism development.

Therefore, in spite of superficial similarities, for physical, cultural, and stage of development reasons, the tourist experiences available in Lombok are somewhat different from those to be found in Bali. Bali provides a mix of sea–sun–sand and cultural tourism offerings with its attractive landscapes being partially a result of human activities, particularly *sawah* (irrigated rice fields). Lombok also offers sea–sun–sand vacations (although in a less developed setting than is available in the major resorts of Bali) in addition to relatively natural landscapes suitable for various forms of adventure tourism and ecotourism.[5] For the purposes of this chapter, the important point to note is that Kuta, Bali and Kuta, Lombok have evolved, and continue to evolve, in very different tourism contexts.

KUTA, BALI

Located on the south coast, Kuta, Bali's most noted assets are its beach, including waves that are ideal for surfing, and a magnificent sunset. It has been famous as a tourist resort for several decades, particularly among a young, adventurous clientele. Tourists began arriving in small numbers in the late 1960s. At that time, Kuta had only one hotel, the Kuta Beach, which was founded in 1955 as a successor to one of the same name that opened in 1935 but closed in 1942 with the arrival of the Japanese (Mabbett, 1985). The first guidebooks did not appear until the early 1970s. In 1970, the airport located close to Kuta was expanded, permitting the arrival of jet planes. Almost immediately the era of mass tourism began.

The first major tourism planning initiative in Bali was the *Bali Tourism Study*, which was undertaken by SCETO, a consortium of French consultants, with support from the United Nations Development Programme (UNDP) and the World Bank (SCETO, 1971; Wall and Dibnah, 1992). The 1971 report recommended the concentration of tourism in the south of the island and the construction of a major five-star hotel complex, called Nusa Dua, to the south of Kuta. In recognition of the unplanned, small-scale developments that existed, Kuta was expected to continue to grow on the basis of *losmen* or homestays, which are similar to western bed-and-breakfast establishments. No five-star hotels were to be permitted in Kuta, in part to try to direct such investments to Nusa Dua.

Losmen have proliferated and have been joined by restaurants, souvenir shops, bars, and discothèques, all of which have grown very rapidly in an unplanned, haphazard manner (Hussey, 1986, 1989). In recent years, the small establishments have also been joined by star rated hotels, some of which have been built on narrow lanes that are difficult to access with tourist buses.

Desa adat (customary village) Kuta is the village in which tourism originated. However, *kawasan* (designated tourism area) Kuta consists of 10 *desa adat*, all but two of which have been considerably influenced by tourism. Tourism development extends north through the *desas* of Legian and Seminyak and, increasingly, into Canggu, as well as south into Jimbaran and Tuban, thereby creating a large, urbanized resort area (see Figure 3.3).

The data that follow are for *desa adat* Kuta alone, where the most dense development exists and, therefore, are extremely conservative since they do not include the recent rapid growth in adjacent *desas*. Furthermore, much activity is in the informal sector which tends to be undercounted in official statistics (Cukier and Wall, 1994). The data are taken mostly from the *Bali Tourism Management Project* (1992a,b).

The resident population of *desa* Kuta is approximately 15,000, but this rises to well above 50,000 if the neighboring areas of *kawasan* Kuta are included. A survey undertaken by the *Bali Tourism Management Project* (1992a) indicated that, in *desa* Kuta alone, there were 600 accommodation establishments that offered 10,873 rooms. Of these, 8.5 percent were star rated (51 properties with a total of 4858 rooms), 42.8 percent were *melati* (not star rated; 257 properties with a total of 4332 rooms), and the remainder were

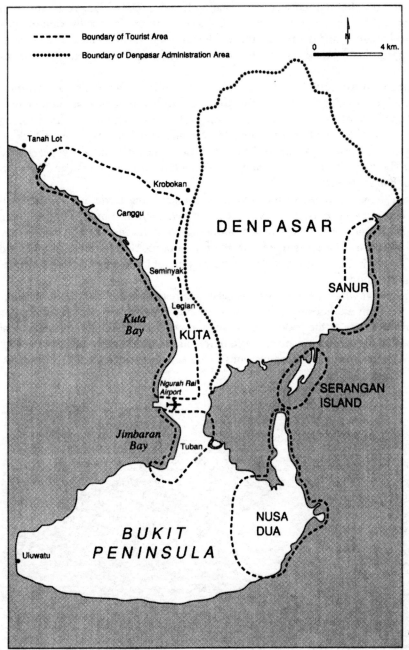

Boundary of Tourist Area
Boundary of Denpasar Administration Area

N

0   4 km.

Tanah Lot

Krobokan

Canggu

DENPASAR

Seminyak

Kuta Bay

Legian

KUTA

SANUR

Ngurah Rai Airport

SERANGAN ISLAND

Jimbaran Bay

Tuban

NUSA DUA

BUKIT PENINSULA

Uluwatu

Figure 3.3
Kuta, Bali.

mostly *losmen*. In addition, there were 447 restaurants with a total of 9511 seats, although 56.4 percent of these businesses (252 operations) were *warungs* (food stalls) catering primarily to local residents and domestic tourists. The same report enumerated 352 souvenir outlets (many in the informal sector), 107 taxi businesses, and seven tourist bus companies.

This urban tourism complex (see Figure 3.4) has evolved in an unplanned manner, in a traditional pattern of streets and landholdings, and with a substantial amount of local investment and local participation in business and profits (although this may be changing slowly because outside investors, including McDonald's and Kentucky Fried Chicken, are moving in). The result is a vibrant, hedonistic atmosphere that initially appears to be at odds with the policy of *pariwisata budaya* (cultural tourism) and the slogan "Tourism for Bali, not Bali for tourism."

Although there is a considerable amount of money being made and a substantial proportion of it remains in local hands, these gains have their own price. Parking is at a premium and, in spite of the introduction of one-way road systems, traffic congestion is the normal situation. The air is filled with the fumes of motorcycles, cars, trucks, and buses, and the environment is inundated with a mixture of traffic noises, canned music, and invitations to buy.

The traditional village architecture has been greatly modified to accommodate tourists. Since the Balinese housing compound is usually oriented towards Mount Agung (regarded as the abode of the gods, it is the highest point of the island) and individual structures within the compound are arranged in relation to each other in accordance with the tenets of Balinese cosmology, conversions to tourist accommodation and restaurants,

Figure 3.4
View of Kuta, Bali.

as well as associated modifications of orientation and spatial relationships, may have adverse cultural and religious consequences (Budihardjo, 1986; Sulistyawati, 1989; Wall and Long, 1996).

Following rain, particularly in the wet season, the streets flood because the sewers are unable to cope. Care must be taken in walking the sidewalks because of the gaping holes that are ready to engulf the unwary pedestrian. Although municipal piped water is available, because of the costs, many people use wells that may become contaminated as population density increases. Declining ground water levels are resulting in the intrusion of salt water (Rahmi, 1992). Extension of the airport runway may even be contributing to beach erosion.

Nonetheless, Kuta continues to grow. Immigrants from other parts of Bali and elsewhere in Indonesia are attracted by the economic opportunities. The result is that in 1992 only 80.2 percent of residents of *desa* Kuta were Hindu. There was a substantial Islamic minority (11.8 percent), with most of the remainder being either Christian or Buddhist (Bali Tourism Management Project, 1992a).

In spite of the evidence of crass commercialism and slowly changing ethnic and religious compositions, tradition lives on in Kuta. Religious and ceremonial activities are still very much alive, and *gamelan* (gong orchestras) and traditional dances are still performed (both for the gods and for tourists). Temple maintenance is less of a problem than in the past given that a number of the *desas* have rented out communal land. The income from rentals is more than sufficient to cover expenses (Bali Tourism Management Project, 1992a).

Benefiting from the magnificent beach and proximity to an international airport and in the absence of firm planning guidelines, local entrepreneurs cater successfully to an international tourism clientele. Although the culture has proven to be surprisingly resilient, the environment has been severely degraded. This could have negative consequences for both residents and tourists. A recent study indicated that 20 percent of international tourists claimed that they became sick while in Bali, with the proportions rising to 28 percent of Australians and almost one-third of Americans (Bali Tourism Management Project, 1992b). Prudence would suggest a need to upgrade basic infrastructure. However, this cannot be easily achieved by individual investors.

KUTA, LOMBOK

Kuta, Lombok is an attractive coastal area in the south of Lombok and, according to the Periplus travel guide, offers "the best view in Lombok" (Muller, 1991) (see Figure 3.5). It is located in one of the poorest areas on the island, which is itself generally poorer than most of Bali. Lombok lacks an international airport, although this is about to change. The drive from the domestic airport to Kuta takes several hours along poor, dusty roads. At present, the small number of overnight tourists stay in a few cottages and eat at one of several basic restaurants that are clustered along the road at the back of the beach.

A number of strategic planning exercises have recognized Kuta's tourism potential, but little development has taken place. In 1981, a tourism plan for Nusa Tenggara was completed with support from the World Tourism Organization (WTO) and the United Nations Development Programme (UNDP) (1981). Although the potential of Kuta was

Figure 3.5
View of Kuta,
Lombok.

acknowledged, Lombok was just one among a number of islands in the archipelago that received consideration. In 1986, the WTO and the UNDP undertook a village tourism development program for Nusa Tenggara, and Kuta was identified for resort development. In 1987, a more detailed tourism development plan was undertaken for Nusa Tenggara by Japanese consultants (JCP Inc., 1987). With respect to Lombok, both strengths (especially beaches) and weaknesses (particularly transportation) were identified. Phased resort development was suggested, commencing with Putri Nyale beach (Kuta, Lombok) on the south coast.

Nusa Dua, to the south of Kuta, Bali, is the model that Kuta, Lombok will follow. Nusa Dua is a planned luxury resort near the southern tip of Bali that has evolved under the guidance of the Bali Tourism Development Corporation. This state-controlled corporation draws up site contracts and acts with considerable independence. The resort was built in an area with limited agricultural capabilities, and a conscious effort was made to minimize possible adverse effects on Balinese lifestyles by isolating developments from the main settlements of the island. The first hotel in Nusa Dua opened in 1983. Luxury accommodations with associated facilities such as manicured gardens, a golf course, conference facilities, and exclusive shopping have been developed. A total of nine four- and five-star hotels has been completed, and it is likely that timeshare villas and condominiums will be added (Hassall and Associates, 1992b).

Care has been taken in Nusa Dua to maintain the environment at a high quality. Sewage lagoons were built, and waste water is recycled onto the golf course. Also, a hotel and catering training school were incorporated in an attempt to upgrade the skills and increase the participation of local people. Nusa Dua is often touted as one of the best examples (if not the best) of resort development in Asia (Inskeep, 1991; Inskeep and Kallenberger, 1992). However, rumors exist that water pressures are reduced in Denpasar (the main city of Bali) in the morning so that tourists can have showers, and local entrepreneurs who would like to sell items to tourists have been excluded and pushed back behind walls and fences. Thus, environmental quality has been achieved partly at the cost of local participation. Yet, an evaluation of the impact of Nusa Dua on the neighboring village of Tanjung Benoa indicated that, although there have been both winners and losers, the infrastructure in the village has been greatly improved (Lihou-Perry, 1992).

As will occur in a number of other places in Indonesia, Kuta, Lombok will be the recipient of a similar resort developed under the guidance of a development corporation (Engineering Consulting Firms Association, Japan, 1992). The Putri Nyale Resort in Kuta is being developed by the Lombok Tourism Development Corporation, a company formed jointly by PT Rajawali Wira Bhakti Utama and the provincial government of West Nusa Tenggara.

The Lombok Tourism Development Corporation administers 1235 acres (500 hectares) on the south coast of the island. The area includes five beaches but is lacking in infrastructure. It will require the development of all services, including electricity, transportation, telecommunications, sewage system, and water treatment and distribution. Lots have been set aside for seven five- and four-star hotels and eight three- and two-star hotels comprising a total of 9000 rooms. In addition, it is expected that there will be 72 villas, 300 condominium units, two 18-hole golf courses, and a marina for 50 boats (Engineering Consulting Firms Association, Japan, 1992). Infrastructure construction began in April 1992.

When the author visited the site in 1992, an office building had been constructed, an area had been fenced off, and some local residents had been displaced and their houses razed. This situation has become the subject of an uncomplimentary video prepared by an American group (Realize Empowerment Productions, 1993). However, studies have been undertaken in an attempt to identify ways in which residents of Gerupuk, a neighboring fishing community, can obtain benefits from their proximity to the development (Direktorat Jenderal Cipta Karya, 1993).

A joint venture agreement for the development and management of the initial hotel on the site was made early in 1995 between Rajawali and Accor Asia Pacific, a new company bearing the name PT Istana Putri Manadalika. This is a new partnership and, unlike Rajawali's four other hotels in Indonesia that have ties to ITT Sheraton, the new resort is linked to Novotel. It will be the eighth Accor Novotel hotel in Indonesia, all of which have four-star ratings. The hotel will be built on a five-acre (two-hectare) site at an estimated cost of between US$8 and US$9 million. Scheduled to open in mid-1996, it will consist of 60 rooms in two- and three-story buildings plus bungalows (Anonymous, 1995).

The lack of direct international flights and the presence of Bali as a formidable intervening opportunity mean that Lombok is currently a secondary destination for many visitors. However, the situation in Lombok could change rapidly and radically given the plans in place for the construction of a new airport in Sengkol, near Praya, in the center of the island (Sofreavia et al., 1993). Lombok is poised for takeoff. It is expected that completion of an international airport will result in rapid growth in tourism similar to that which occurred in Bali. At present, the lack of such an airport is a constraint to tourism development, and the uncertainty concerning airport construction is tending to foster more speculation than real investment.

CONCLUSION

This chapter has compared tourism in Kuta, Bali and Kuta, Lombok, Indonesia from the perspective of the differing cultural contexts and development status of the two islands. While both are coastal resorts, they differ in most other respects. In large part, this is because the former is more developed than the latter. However, it is also due to the fact that Kuta, Bali has evolved with limited planning direction whereas Kuta, Lombok is evolving as a planned resort.

Bali has been an intervening opportunity with respect to Lombok given that international visitors must pass through Bali to access Lombok. With a location virtually adjacent to an international airport on an island with a strong international image, Kuta, Bali was an early developer in Indonesian tourism. In contrast, Lombok still does not have an international airport, and Kuta is distant from the domestic airport. In fact, resort and airport development have constituted a "chicken-egg" problem in Lombok. Entrepreneurs have been unwilling to make commitments to build hotels in the absence of an international airport. On the other hand, there has been a reluctance to upgrade the airport in the absence of a demonstrable market.

Lombok does not possess as clear an image as Bali, although that may be changing slowly as awareness of its natural attributes increases and concern is raised over the intensity of tourism development in Bali. Relative inaccessibility and lack of an international image have protected Kuta, Lombok from the excesses that have occurred in Kuta, Bali. Nonetheless, at the same time, residents of Kuta, Lombok have not obtained the economic benefits from tourism that have accrued in Bali.

In the absence of firm planning guidelines and, in some cases, with a failure to implement the regulations that exist, tourism development has taken place rapidly but haphazardly in Kuta, Bali. As a result, the environment appears to be suffering many adverse consequences. In contrast, detailed planning is likely to ensure that the environment is protected in Kuta, Lombok, although there will be difficult challenges in providing an adequate water supply in a relatively remote and dry area if substantial development occurs along the southern coast of the island. Moreover, unless ways are found to involve local people in meaningful ways, they may not benefit from the tourism development that is occurring, literally in some cases, on their doorsteps.

ACKNOWLEDGMENTS

This chapter has benefited greatly from participation in the *Bali Sustainable Development Project* that was part of the University Consortium on the Environment funded by the Canadian International Development Agency. Special thanks are due to Ms. Wiendu Nuryanti for providing access to many of the documents that have been used, as well as for her efforts to keep the author current with the rapid evolution of Indonesian tourism.

NOTES

1. See Chapters 4–6, 9, and 28 for overviews of the tourism planning process.
2. See Chapters 5, 9, 11, 12, and 14–19 for additional discussion and examples concerning community attitudes and community involvement in the tourism planning and development processes.

3. It is estimated that *total* visitation to Bali in 1990 was over 1.8 million if direct arrivals, indirect arrivals, and domestic visitors are included.
4. See Chapters 2, 5, 7, and 28 for additional discussion relating to the role and application of life cycle models.
5. See Chapters 11, 15, and 20 for more comprehensive discussions pertaining to ecotourism.

REFERENCES

Anonymous. 1995. Rajawali-Accor tie-up for Novotel Lombok, *Travel Indonesia*, April 17.

Bali Tourism Management Project. 1992a. *Final Report, Volume 8, Part Two: Main 1992 Establishment Census of Kuta, Sanur, Ubud and Sukawati*. Denpasar: United Nations Development Programme and the Government of Indonesia.

Bali Tourism Management Project. 1992b. *Final Report, Volume 7, Annex 1: Bali Visitor Survey 1992*. Denpasar: United Nations Development Programme and the Government of Indonesia.

Britton, S.G. 1991. Tourism, capital and places: towards a critical geography of tourism, *Environment and Planning D: Society and Space*, 9(4), 451–478.

Budihardjo, E. 1986. *Architectural Conservation in Bali*. Vogyakarta: Gadjah Mada University Press.

Butler, R.W. 1980. The concept of a tourist area cycle of evolution: applications for management of resources, *Canadian Geographer*, 24(1), 5–12.

Covarrubias, M. 1937 (1986 reprint). *Island of Bali*. London: KPI Limited.

Cukier, J. and G. Wall. 1994. Informal tourism employment: vendors in Bali, Indonesia, *Tourism Management*, 15(6), 464–467.

Dinas Pariwisata Daerah Tingkat I. 1993. *Analisis Pasar Wisata Nusa Tenggara Barat 1993*. Mataram.

Directorate General of Tourism (DGT). 1994. *Tourism Data and Statistics 1993*. Jakarta: DGT, Directorate of Marketing.

Directorate General of Tourism and United Nations Development Programme, Tourism Sector Programming and Policy Development. 1992. *National Tourism Strategy*. Jakarta: Government of Indonesia.

Direktorat Jenderal Cipta Karya, Direktorat Perumahan, Bagian Perencanaan Teknik dan Pengelolaan Data Perumahan Rakyat. 1993. *Penataan Permukiman Dan Perumahan Nelyan Pada Pengembangan Kawasan Pariwisata Di Pulau Lombok, Nusa Tenggara Barat* (Arrangements of the Fishing Settlement and Housing in Developing a Tourist Resort in Lombok, West Nusa Tenggara).

Eiseman, F.B. 1988. *Bali, Sekala and Niskala: Essays on Religion, Ritual and Art*. Berkeley: Periplus Editions.

Eiseman, F.B. 1990. *Bali, Sekala and Niskala: Essays on Society, Tradition and Craft*. Berkeley: Periplus Editions.

Engineering Consulting Firms Association, Japan. 1992. *Preliminary Study for Tourism Clusters Development Project in Indonesia* (mimeo).

Hall, C.M. 1994. *Tourism and Politics: Policy, Power and Place*. Chichester: John Wiley & Sons.

Hassall and Associates. 1992a. *The Tourism Sector: Comprehensive Tourism Development Plan for Bali*, Annex 3. Denpasar.

Hassall and Associates. 1992b. *Comprehensive Tourism Development Plan for Bali, Volume II: The Fifteen Designated Tourist Areas*. Denpasar.

Hussey, A. 1986. *Resources for Development, Tourism and Small Scale Indigenous Enterprise in Bali*. Unpublished PhD thesis. Honolulu: University of Hawaii.

Hussey, A. 1989. Tourism in a Balinese village, *Geographical Review*, 79, 311–325.

Inskeep, E. 1991. *Tourism Planning: An Integrated and Sustainable Development Approach*. New York: Van Nostrand Reinhold.

Inskeep, E. and M. Kallenberger. 1992. *An Integrated Approach to Resort Development*. Madrid: World Tourism Organization.

JCP Inc. 1987. *Tourism Development Planning Study for Nusa Tenggara*. Jakarta: United Nations Development Programme, World Tourism Organization, and Directorate General of Tourism.

Lansing, J.S. 1991. *Priests and Programmers: Technologies of Power in the Engineered Landscape of Bali*. Princeton: Princeton University Press.

Lihou-Perry, C. 1992. *Resort Enclaves and Sustainable Development: A Balinese Example*. Unpublished Masters thesis. Waterloo, Ontario: University of Waterloo.

Mabbett, H. 1985. *The Balinese*. Wellington, N.Z: January Books.

Muller, K. 1991. *East of Bali From Lombok to Timor*. Berkeley: Periplus Editions.

Oppermann, M. 1992. Regional aspects of the Indonesian tourist industry, *Indonesian Journal of Geography*, 22(63), 31–44.

Picard, M. 1992. *Bali: Tourisme culturel et culture touristique*. Paris: L'Harmattan.

Rahmi, D. 1992. *Integrated Development for Spatial Water Supply and Sanitation Systems in the Tourism Area of Kuta, Bali, Indonesia*. Unpublished Masters thesis. Waterloo, Ontario: University of Waterloo.

Realize Empowerment Productions. 1993. *The Lombok Controversy* (video).

SCETO. 1971. *Bali Tourism Study* (6 vols.). Paris: SCETO.

Sofreavia, PT Asana Wirasata Setia and PT Desigras. 1993. *Feasibilty Study for Airport Development in Lombok*. Jakarta: Government of the Republic of Indonesia, Ministry of Communications, and Directorate General of Air Communications.

Sulistyawati. 1989. *The Balinese Home, Factors That Influence Change in Its Architecture*. Unpublished Master's thesis. Yogyakarta: Gadjah Mada University.

Vickers, A. 1989. *Bali: A Paradise Created*. Berkeley: Periplus Editions.

Wall, G. 1996a. Indonesia: the impact of regionalization. In F. Go and C. Jenkins (eds.), *Tourism and Development in Asia and Australasia*. London: Mansell.

Wall, G. 1996b. Bali and Lombok: a comparative study. In D. Drakakis-Smith and D. Lockhart (eds.), *Island Tourism: Problems and Prospects*. London: Mansell.

Wall, G. and S. Dibnah. 1992. The changing status of tourism in Bali, Indonesia, *Progress in Tourism, Recreation and Hospitality Management*, 4, 120–130.

Wall, G. and V. Long. 1996. Balinese 'homestays', an indigenous response to tourism opportunities. In R. Butler and T. Hinch (eds.), *Tourism and Native Peoples*. London: Routledge.

World Tourism Organization and United Nations Development Programme. 1981. *Nusa Tenggara Tourism Development Plan*. Jakarta: Republic of Indonesia.

World Tourism Organization and United Nations Development Programme. 1987. *Village Tourism Development Programme for Nusa Tenggara*. Madrid: WTO.

Further Reading

The most comprehensive and up-to-date document on Bali is:

Martopo, S. and B. Mitchell. 1995. *Bali: Balancing Environment, Economy and Culture*. Waterloo: Department of Geography, Publication Series No. 44, University of Waterloo.

For discussions of the influence of tourism on Balinese culture see:

Cohen, M. 1994. God and mammon: luxury resort triggers outcry over Bali's future, *Far Eastern Economic Review*, 157(21), 28–34.

McKean, P. 1989. Towards a theoretical analysis of tourism: economic dualism and cultural involution in Bali. In V. Smith (ed.), *Hosts and Guests: The Anthropology of Tourism*, 2nd ed. Philadelphia: University of Pennsylvania Press, pp. 119–138.

Noronha, R. 1976. Paradise reviewed: tourism in Bali. In E. de Kadt (ed.), *Tourism: Passport to Development?* Oxford: Oxford University Press, pp. 177–204.

Picard, M. 1990. 'Kebalian orang Bali': tourism and the uses of 'Balinese culture' in new order Indonesia, *Review of Indonesian and Malaysian Affairs*, 24, 1–38.

For examination of differing scales of development and their consequences with reference to Bali see:

Jenkins, C. 1982. The effects of scale in tourism projects in developing countries, *Annals of Tourism Research*, 9(2), 229–249.

Long, V. and G. Wall. 1995. Small-scale tourism development in Bali. In M.V. Conlin and T. Baum, (eds.), *Island Tourism: Management Principles and Practice*. Chichester: John Wiley & Sons, pp. 237–257.

Rodenburg, E. 1980. The effects of scale in economic development: tourism in Bali, *Annals of Tourism Research*, 7(2), 177–196.

⚡ | PROBLEM SOLVING AND DISCUSSION ACTIVITIES

1. How do the impacts of tourism vary with the stage of tourism development?
2. What are the advantages and disadvantages of (a) large-scale versus small-scale tourism developments and (b) concentration versus dispersal of tourists?
3. Who are the major beneficiaries of tourism planning? Why?
4. Discuss the role of accessibility for tourism development. Does improved accessibility always enhance the competitive position of tourism businesses?
5. What types of tourism development are most likely to benefit the residents of destination areas? What can be done to facilitate the involvement of local people in tourism?
6. Tourism is sometimes considered to be a form of neocolonialism. Do you agree with this? Why or why not?
7. Are the differences in the manifestations of tourism in developed and developing countries differences of degree or differences of kind?
8. What future steps should be taken in Kuta, Bali and in Kuta, Lombok to facilitate the ongoing evolution of tourism in each of these destinations in a responsible manner?
9. Assess the status of tourism planning in your country or community. Is it oriented to responsible tourism planning principles and practices?
10. Comment on the following statement: "In recognition of the fact that provinces often do not constitute good units for tourism planning, there is a move to focus upon tourism regions that may not conform to provincial boundaries." To what extent is this statement relevant in the context of your country?

4

Towards Sustainability?

TOURISM IN THE REPUBLIC OF CYPRUS

 *Kerry B. Godfrey*

✦ | K E Y   L E A R N I N G   P O I N T S

- Planning for sustainable tourism development is not simply about developing new environmentally friendly products, but about trying to make all aspects of the industry more resource conscious.

- Tourism has often been developed for its economic potential. Although governments may wish to mitigate negative social or environmental impacts, political considerations sometimes take a backseat to the economic driving force.

- There are many different factors that impinge upon the success of tourism development in any location (e.g., war, civil disruption, the power of foreign investors, and changing consumer tastes). Often these are not within the control of the destination.

- Despite government policy and legislation, the power of external agents (e.g., air carriers, tour operators, charter operations, foreign investors) to dictate the scale and style of development can be overwhelming.

- Many governments are now preparing what they perceive to be sustainable tourism development plans and policies. These alone, however, will not ensure success without full implementation and enforcement of rules and regulations designed to limit potential problems.

- Tourism is but one of several useful industries that can aid economic growth and diversification. Therefore, it should never be planned or developed in isolation from other aspects of socioeconomic development or at the neglect of other industries.

INTRODUCTION

The concept of sustainable tourism development has ostensibly caught the attention of both government and industry. Yet, what this means in practice is not always clear. Common phrasing and terminology such as "appropriate," "responsible," and "alternative" have been used interchangeably to describe this new industry paradigm. To some, sustainable tourism development is all about new "green" products or "ecofriendly" tourists; to others it is a guiding principle to which all tourism should aspire. This chapter briefly examines this debate, describing key concepts of planning for sustainable tourism development and highlighting critical differences between planning new sustainable "products" (often small-scale initiatives in rural environments) and planning for a more sustainable "industry" as a whole (applying such techniques as development restrictions and fiscal restraint policies).

Following the Turkish invasion of Cyprus in 1974 and subsequent loss of territory and tourism infrastructure, the newly formed republic pursued rapid tourism development. The speed and concentration of this development have led to some undesirable impacts, particularly along coastal areas. Recently, however, the government has taken steps to slow down development and to adopt a more informed and planned approach, including the formulation of a new *Town and Country Planning Law* (1990) and national tourism strategy (1990). Using Cyprus, this chapter examines two recent projects that have tried to apply sustainable development principles to their tourism planning activity.

The first, the Alternative Rural Tourism Initiative, was conceived to draw visitors into the hill resorts in an attempt to stimulate local economies and relieve some of the pressure exerted on the overdeveloped coastal areas. The second, a new development program in the Akamas Peninsula, was launched to help establish the island's first national park and offer an opportunity to this last "wilderness" area to regenerate economically through the development of so-called new mild forms of tourism.

This chapter demonstrates, however, that despite all the government's good intentions, it has not been tourism per se that has caused problems in the past, but rather the lack of enforcement of existing rules and regulations designed to guide the development of tourism along a more sustainable path.

SUSTAINABLE DEVELOPMENT AND TOURISM PLANNING: CONTEMPORARY PERSPECTIVES AND ISSUES

Recognition of the Need for Sustainable Tourism Development

Tourism planning[1] has evolved through a number of stages during the latter half of the twentieth century, more or less in response to the global increase in visitor numbers. Originally, facilitating travel was the primary concern, often focusing on tourism promotion. Subsequently, policies broadened to include spatial planning, but the emphasis remained on maximizing economic development (Getz, 1986). While government and industry continued their active support of tourism development, they did so in relative isolation, virtually excluding any cost recognition. Little attention was paid to the more qualitative and less tangible socioeconomic and environmental impacts.

Recently, this singular emphasis on economics has come under closer scrutiny, with increasing evidence highlighting tourism's adverse effects. The awakening of a global environmental conscience, spurred on by pollution and the loss of pristine resources, has begun to change the once conventional wisdom. Ever since the World Commission on Environment and Development (WCED, 1987), "sustainability" has become the order of the day, and many now argue that without a significant change towards a more sustainable approach to development, severe damage to cultural and natural resources will accelerate (Globe '90). If this is allowed to continue, the very resources upon which tourism is based will be lost.

In reply, both government and industry have ostensibly begun to develop policies that dictate the scale, location, and management of tourism, based not only on economic considerations but also on social and environmental concerns as well—all in the name of sustainable tourism development. Yet, while tourism development may have entered a new phase of sensibility, with many tolerant in principle or even actively supportive of the concept, this has generally been without a full understanding of its meaning or its implications for planning and development activity (Butler, 1989; Godfrey, 1993; Wheeller, 1991, 1992).

Tourism and Sustainable Development
The WCED described sustainable development simply as paths of human progress that satisfy the needs and aspirations of present generations without compromising the ability of future generations to meet their needs (WCED, 1987). The concept challenges the conventional wisdom behind economic growth and seeks to shift the debate away from "development versus conservation" to "development in harmony with the environment." It puts emphasis on meeting the basic needs of society's poorer members, cultural sensitivity, and "grassroots" participation in the development process, and it also looks to a general improvement in the quality of life of all people (Barbier, 1987). Nonetheless, what this means in practice is not always apparent and, given that one is attempting to describe environmental, economic, social, and political features of an ongoing development process, obvious problems emerge (Barbier, 1987; Cocklin, 1989; Lindner, 1989; Taylor, 1991).

Sustainability is essentially about resource management. It recognizes that if the earth's resources are used, this will inevitably bring about some form of change, with the objective being to manage this change within acceptable limits.[2] However, how this will actually be achieved remains the subject of much discussion, and what may have appeared simple at first becomes more complex and controversial upon closer inspection. Despite this problem, sustainability has achieved buzzword status (in spite of numerous definitions and points of view[3]) in virtually all areas of discussion concerning economic activity and the environment. The tourism industry has not been immune to this trend, and while the WCED report does not actually mention tourism, this concept has seemingly been endorsed as the new ideal to arrest the industry's damaging effects.

The idea of sustainable tourism development has achieved virtual global endorsement as the new industry paradigm since the late 1980s. However, this has been achieved at the expense of almost becoming a platitude. Ironically, it is this aspect of universal acceptance that casts doubts on the validity of the concept, representing both its strength and weakness as the new environmental ethos. As a strength, sustainability has become a general issue and represents a catalyst for change, but as a weakness, it is used by both governments and industry to justify or legitimize current activities and policies.

Much of the confusion surrounding sustainable tourism development is based primarily on the preoccupation of some to avoid the mass tourism label which "functions in this context as a repulsive point of reference" (Cazes, 1989, p. 123). In trying to be different, common phrasing and synonyms such as soft (Kariel, 1989; Krippendorf, 1982), postindustrial (SEEDS, 1989), alternative (Gonsalves and Holden, 1985), responsible

(WTO, 1990), appropriate (Singh et al., 1989), green (Bramwell, 1991), rural (Lane, 1989, 1990), low impact (Lillywhite and Lillywhite, 1991), eco- (Boo, 1990), and nature-based (Fennell and Eagles, 1990) have all been applied. To some, sustainable tourism development is all about new products or market segments. To others, it is a process of development, while to still others it represents a guiding principle to which all tourism should aspire.[4]

Thus, like the general concept of sustainable development, what is really meant by sustainable tourism development is also the subject of some discussion.[5] While there exists a number of definitions, the key objectives and rationale underpinning these many different terms have been similar and generally can be placed within one of two broad schools of thought (Godfrey, 1993). One school tends to support sustainability as representing an alternative to, or replacement of, conventional (evil) mass tourism with new (good) green products (the *product approach*). The other argues that mass tourism is inevitable due to sheer tourist demand, and what is needed is a way to make all tourism more sustainable (the *industry approach*).

Much of what has transpired in the literature exemplifies the product approach, resulting in an examination of "either-or" choices, particularly in rural European environments (e.g., Krippendorf, 1982; Lane, 1988, 1990). Frequent reference is made to issues concerning concentration versus dispersion of development, the scale of development (small versus large), degree of control and ownership (local versus foreign), rate of development (slow versus rapid), types of tourists (high spend versus low spend), and the type of interaction taking place within the destination area (hosts and guests versus tourist anonymity) (see Table 4.1).

Alternatively, the industry approach suggests that, while there is nothing intrinsically wrong with the development of new small-scale "green" products, this alone fails to address a number of inherent aspects of tourism such as its diversity, scale, and ownership, none of which operates in isolation (see Godfrey, 1993). Instead it is suggested that while there are many positive qualities associated with the product approach that are endorsed by the industrywide view, this somewhat shallow comparison between new green products as good and different from traditional or conventional holidays is naive and misleading (e.g., Butler, 1989; Wheeller, 1991, 1992). They argue that the real value of this softer outlook does not lie in replacing mass tourism, which it could not in any case, but rather in helping to "reform the tourist establishment and mass tourism from within" (Cohen, 1989, p. 138).

Key points of the industry approach suggest planning for sustainable tourism requires development to take place within the context of all local socioeconomic development and be considered as an element of land use planning alongside other development options. Its long-term goal is to enable a comprehensive development process where products draw from and add to the quality of local resources based on a sound understanding of market demand and motivations. It should also communicate with and involve the local population in planning and management decisions,[6] while offering a fair distribution of the benefits and costs among tourism businesses, promoters, and the host community.

These principles, however, are not necessarily new and have been promoted since the early 1980s (see Globe '90; IPU, 1989; WTO, 1980, 1982, 1985). As Taylor (1991) suggests, despite this "new" thinking, little has actually been done to come to grips with

TABLE 4.1
Product Approach: Elements of Sustainable versus Nonsustainable Tourism Development

Hard, Mass, Nonsustainable	Soft, Green, Sustainable, Alternative, Rural
General Concepts	
Rapid development	Slow development
Uncontrolled	Controlled
Without scale	In scale
Short term	Long term
Quantitative	Qualitative
Remote control	Local control
Growth	Development
Development Strategies	
Development without planning	First plan, then develop
Project-led schemes	Concept-led schemes
District level planning	Coordination of district plans
Concentration on "honey pots"	Fine landscapes preserved
New building and bed capacity	Pressures and benefits diffused
Development by outsiders	Local developers
Employees imported	Employment based on local potential
Urban architecture	Vernacular architecture
Tourist Behavior	
Mass tourism: high-volume trips	Singles, families, friends: low-volume travel
Little or no mental preparation	Some mental preparation
Little time	Much time
No foreign language	Language training
Shopping	Bring present
Nosy	Tactful
Loud	Quiet
Unlikely to return	Repeat visits

Sources: Adapted from Krippendorf (1982) and Lane (1989, 1990).

the problems and develop practical and acceptable solutions. The fundamental problem has been the lack of ability or willingness to undertake both qualitative and structural changes in the way tourism is planned and managed overall (see Table 4.2).

While precise definition may remain somewhat elusive between these two broad views, the general concept suggests that sustainable tourism development is essentially an issue of tourism asset management, where development activity guarantees the integrity

TABLE 4.2
Industry Approach: Key Elements of Planning for Sustainable Tourism Development

Comprehensive	Social, environmental, economic, and political implications are fully analyzed and understood as part of a holistic approach to planning.
Iterative and dynamic	Planning is continuous, responds to changing circumstances, and able to make adjustments within the context of an adopted policy and strategy.
Systematic	Possible impacts are assessed with actions set to counter negative effects; examines visitor demands and motivations, combining these with local capacities to develop products that enhance the integrity of local resources.
Integrative	Planning and management places tourism within the wider socioeconomic and land use planning process of the destination, so decisions taken with influence over tourism are fully considered and understood.
Community-oriented	Communicates with and involves the local community in planning and management activity, where all those affected have a structured opportunity to put their views forward; also encourages maximum participation of residents in the supply of tourism services.
Renewable	Manages tourism as a renewable industry where natural and cultural resources maintain their integrity for continued and future use; limits to acceptable change and the capacity to absorb tourism become primary objectives of all tourism planning; encourages products which draw from and enhance the integrity of local resources.
Goal-oriented and implementable	Clear recognition of what tourism development can realistically achieve through policy; development strategy and action programs are specifically adapted to achieve tangible goals; offers a fair distribution of the benefits and costs among tourism businesses, promoters, and the host community now and in the future.

Sources: Adapted from Globe '90 (1990), Godfrey (1993), Inskeep (1991), and IPU (1989).

of the resource on which the industry is based, while maintaining economic viability (Godfrey, 1994). Both demand and supply components of tourism are balanced within a framework of maintaining social and environmental objectives (Inskeep, 1991). Therefore, planning for sustainable tourism development is not an end in itself, but rather one of several tools of national and local resource management. In a broader context, this suggests that tourism planning should be undertaken with the understanding that it is not a unique or isolated procedure, but an interdependent function of a wider and permanent socioeconomic development process.

The purpose of this chapter is to explore issues associated with the application of sustainable tourism development principles using the island of Cyprus to highlight some of the problems of defining and interpreting the concept. In the early 1990s, following several years of excessive development and concomitant damage to the resource base, the Cypriot government took steps to slow down the growth of its tourism industry. By taking a more informed and planned approach, the government hoped to achieve "sustainable tourism development."

Data and other source information on Cyprus presented in this chapter were collected primarily via secondary source investigations of published material and other reports, supplemented by a study visit to the island in June 1994. The author was a delegate to the 18th Meeting of Experts on Human Settlements Problems in Southern Europe of the United Nations Economic Commission for Europe (UNECE). The primary theme of discussion was concerned with the problems and prospects of planning for a more sustainable tourism industry in countries of the Mediterranean region (see Godfrey, 1994, 1995).

Following the presentation of background information pertaining to the location of Cyprus, its economic situation, and the evolution of its tourism industry, two pilot projects (the Alternative Rural Tourism Initiative and the Akamas Peninsula) which attempted to apply sustainable tourism principles are outlined. From these two pilot projects, more insight into the principal differences between planning new sustainable "products" and planning for a more sustainable "industry" as a whole may be gained. In addition, issues associated with achieving a balance between political and economic objectives are illustrated.

CYPRUS: LOCATIONAL CONTEXT AND BACKGROUND

The Mediterranean island of Cyprus, covering approximately 3600 square miles (9250 square kilometers), lies approximately 40 miles (65 kilometers) south of Turkey and 60 miles (95 kilometers) west of Syria. It has three distinct physiographic regions: (1) the Kyrenian Mountains in the north, (2) the Mesaoria Plain in the center which merges with fertile coastal plains to the southeast, and (3) the Troodos Massif in the central-south, which occupies about one-half of the island and is dominated by the country's highest peak, Mount Olympus (6400 feet; 1950 meters) (see Figure 4.1). Its 485-mile (780-kilometer) coastline is indented and rocky, particularly in the south and southwest where the Troodos Mountains reach the sea, and it also boasts long sandy beaches adjoining the coastal strip.

With a typical Mediterranean climate that is strongly affected by its two mountain systems, summers are hot and dry, while winters (October to March) tend to be wet and temperate. The daily maximum temperature reaches 97°F (36°C), while the average daily minimum is 70°F (21°C). Precipitation varies, with most rain falling on southwestern slopes exposed to the sea (approximately 40 inches or 1000 millimeters per year). Elevations above 3280 feet (1000 meters) receive snow in the winter, and a ski hill operates on Mount Olympus. The Mesaoria Plain is much drier, receiving only about 15 inches (370 millimeters) of precipitation per year. All rivers on the island are dry for at least part of the year.

Cyprus has been colonized, occupied, or dominated by virtually all who have held power in the region. In 1878, the British were the last to assume control through an agreement reached with Turkey. Independence from Britain was achieved only in 1960. Prior to independence, settlement was predominantly rural, with over 600 villages but only six main towns (Famagusta, Kyrenia, Nicosia, Limassol, Larnaca, and Paphos). Landholdings were (and still are) fragmented and dispersed under traditional laws of inheritance. Today, Greeks and Turks are the two main ethnic communities in the Cypriot population. Of the 720,000 estimated inhabitants (1994), approximately 80 percent are of Greek origin and just under 20 percent are descendants of the Ottoman Turks, with the remainder comprised of Armenians, Arabs, and Europeans.

Following independence, Cyprus was underdeveloped, with a distinct lack of em-

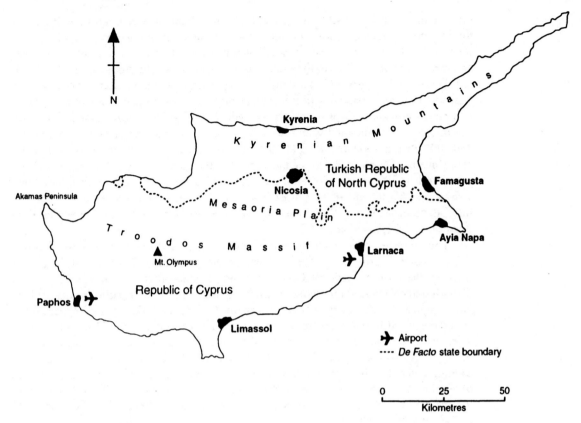

Figure 4.1
Location of Cyprus.

ployment opportunities. While agriculture was the largest industry (nearly half the island's workers), it accounted for less than 25 percent of the gross domestic product (GDP). Manufacturing represented only 10 percent and mining a further 12 percent of GDP. Imports were equal to 50 percent of the island's GNP (gross national product).

Faced with the serious task of restructuring the economy, the government established a series of five-year plans aimed at full utilization of its productive resources, rapid and balanced economic growth and regional development, a sound balance of payments, full employment, and improved social services and quality of life (Andronicou, 1979). However, Cyprus was not an industrial society. It had little water, and mineral reserves were modest. Consequently, in common with many other Mediterranean countries, the government chose tourism as one of the main sectors in its economic development program.

HISTORICAL OVERVIEW OF TOURISM ACTIVITY IN CYPRUS

In 1960 Cypriot tourism was relatively undeveloped, with only 21,000 visitor arrivals and 4000 beds, nearly half of which were located in the Troodos hill resorts. The five coastal towns (Kyrenia, Famagusta, Limassol, Larnaca, and Paphos) accounted for less than one-third of all tourist beds, with the remainder in the capital, Nicosia. To support growth, the government established a series of economic measures to encourage rapid development of hotels in prime coastal areas. Policy was consistently aimed at attracting high- and middle-income visitors to the exclusion of mass tourism (Andronicou, 1979, 1983).

The Cyprus Tourism Organisation (CTO), a semigovernmental agency, was established in 1969 and charged with full responsibility for tourism development and promotion aimed at making Cyprus competitive with other Mediterranean resorts. The result was dramatic. International visitor arrivals rose by an average of 21 percent per year to 250,000 between 1960 and 1973 (a 1090 percent increase overall compared to 175 percent globally). Development was concentrated in the coastal areas of Kyrenia and Famagusta, and by 1973 these two resort areas accounted for 73 percent of all international arrivals and 65 percent of all tourist beds. In contrast, Larnaca and Paphos attracted little attention, with only three hotels in the three- to four-star categories between them (Ioannides, 1992; Lockhart, 1993).

The success of tourism, its pattern of development, and the volume of international arrivals changed abruptly in 1974. Following a successful *coup d'état* against the government by the Cypriot National Guard (pursuing *Énosis*—that is, Union with Greece), Turkish soldiers invaded the island, claiming to invoke the 1960 tripartite *Treaty of Guarantee* (signed at independence between Britain, Greece, and Turkey) and effectively dividing the island in half.[7] The direct result was a loss of 37 percent of Cypriot territory to Turkish control, along with 50 percent of the island's manufacturing capacity and two-thirds of its main agricultural areas. More importantly for tourism, 50 percent of all catering and entertainment facilities, 82 percent of all accommodation, and 96 percent of new hotels under construction (Andronicou, 1979) were lost to the Turks. In addition, the main international airport at Nicosia was closed to commercial traffic, and visitor arrivals seriously declined.

Cypriot tourism faced a potential collapse that represented a serious blow to the government's attempts to restructure the economy. In response, the new Greek–Cypriot government (of the south) instigated a series of emergency economic action plans designed to reestablish the southern part of the island as a major tourist destination. To maximize tourism development potential, a number of new measures were established, including the relaxation of planning controls, development easements, economic and fiscal incentives, and tax benefits (CTO, 1994). Large sections of the coast were zoned for tourism purposes, and a new international airport was built at Larnaca. Although the conflict had an immediate effect on visitor arrivals, this was comparatively short-lived. Visitor numbers slumped to 47,000 in 1975, but reached 172,000 by 1976. By 1979 visitor arrivals surpassed preinvasion levels. Growth rates were dramatic and faster than in any other Mediterranean destination.

Cyprus was becoming a "sun lust" destination for visitors from Central and Northern Europe. Mass charter tourism brought visitors principally from the United Kingdom, Sweden, and (West) Germany to the Cypriot Mediterranean coastline. Despite the government's intentions for regionally balanced economic development, great emphasis was placed on building in coastal areas to meet the demand, mainly in places with very little previous experience with tourism. Mass coastal tourism was taking over, with the Troodos resorts providing only a minor counterbalance to the vast growth in tourist beds and visitor arrivals along the coast (Lockhart, 1993).

While the rate of growth had effectively fueled the country's economic recovery, there was a price to pay. Architectural pollution, ribbon development, traffic congestion, litter, water pollution, and increased noise levels were evident in and around resort areas, primarily due to a lack of investment in infrastructure and the absence of adequate planning and regulation (CTO, 1994).

Consequently, the government established a new set of incentives and regulations in the early 1980s to bring development under control. Three key objectives for tourism were to underpin its approach:

- Continued growth of tourism's contribution to GDP.
- Protection of the environmental and cultural qualities of Cyprus.
- Attraction of higher-spending tourists.

A special fund and investment incentives were established, particularly for priority projects in the hill resorts such as the development of five-star hotels, tourist villages,[8] and camping facilities to encourage development away from the beach areas. Legislation was again amended to establish greater control over the planning process, with new emphasis placed on environmental protection and the design and character of buildings. Local development plans were introduced to take into account local resource availability and act as the basis for all future development activity. Finally, the CTO redoubled its efforts to promote the island as a prestige destination for middle- and upper-income tourists, whom they believed were least likely to cause stress and strain on the traditional culture and the environment (Andronicou, 1986).

To some, these new measures and policy decisions were regarded as landmarks for the CTO and were seen as a first step towards rational balanced development. The main purpose was to curtail the rate of growth of new hotels, place greater emphasis on improving the current product, and shift demand away from the coast. Initially, the new measures were effective and new hotel development applications fell from 120 in 1982 to 17 in 1985 (Andronicou, 1986; Ioannides, 1992).

However, the reprieve was short-lived, and throughout the 1980s the average annual increase in visitor arrivals attained preconflict levels, rising to 1.4 million by 1988 (up by 700 percent from 1976 whereas, globally, international arrivals rose by only 83 percent). Tourism's contribution to the GNP in Cyprus rose from 6 percent in 1983 to 8.3 percent in 1988. At the same time, average length of stay declined with a corresponding increase in inclusive tours (ITs) from the United Kingdom and Western Europe.

Again, contrary to the government's efforts to push growth into the hill resorts, almost all new development took place in coastal areas with a shift to self-catering hotel apartments. Ayia Napa, once described as a "sleepy village but now *turbo-garish*" (Wickers, 1994), accounted for 34 percent of all tourist beds. In fact, 90 percent of all tourist beds in southern Cyprus could be found along its 185-mile (295-kilometer) coastline (CTO, 1994).

The resultant tenfold expansion in the supply of accommodations represented a major shift in the spatial distribution of tourism and began to seriously undermine the CTO's efforts to portray the island as a quality destination (Gillmor, 1989). Tourist enclaves in Paphos, Limassol, and Larnaca, lacking adequate resort infrastructure (i.e., sewage disposal, pedestrian areas, landscaped open space, street furniture, and parking), were becoming "placeless, could be anywhere" resorts.

Extensive exploitation of the coastal zone and a singular tourist market (i.e., the sun and sea mass market from Northern Europe) suggested that tourism was becoming a monoactivity, assuming the role of pacemaker in the island's economy at the expense of agriculture and other industry (CTO, 1994). While the sun, sand, and sea image plus the comparatively low costs of goods and services were still evident, the CTO began to recognize that, unless they could upgrade the island's infrastructure and achieve a wider spread of facilities, they might experience some difficulty in maintaining their share of the quality tourist market.

CONTEMPORARY DEVELOPMENT AND PLANNING OF TOURISM IN CYPRUS

Once again, the government and CTO began to rethink their strategy, and in 1988, with the help of the World Tourism Organization (WTO), a comprehensive tourism development plan for Cyprus was prepared (see WTO, 1994a, b). The new plan proposed a much wider analysis of economic, environmental, and social issues in the planning stage. Like previous strategies (of the government and CTO), the United Nations Development Programme (UNDP)/WTO plan suggested controlled growth through consolidation of the product in existing areas and environmental improvements. This, supposedly, would provide much greater diversity in facilities and activities as well as product improvement to attract higher-spending visitors and lengthen the tourist season.

Successful implementation depended on the government's ability to regulate the quantity, type, and location of development through a combination of institutional structures, incentives, and disincentives promoting the development of complementary products and infrastructure (WTO, 1994a, b). Subsequently, in fear of the island becoming a massive tourist camp, the government took its most decisive actions to date. A temporary moratorium was placed on all further tourism development in June 1989, not just to arrest the rate of growth in the industry but to give the government and the CTO time to prepare a new policy for the industry (CTO, 1994). The moratorium was lifted in December 1990 with the enactment of a new *Town and Country Planning Law* and national tourism strategy.

The *Town and Country Planning Law* (1990) was designed to provide a new legal framework for the preparation and implementation of comprehensive land use development plans at three levels: (1) townwide plans in urban areas, (2) policy statements for rural and countryside areas, and (3) small-area detailed plans within rural or urban areas. The primary objective for all development plans was to restrain the growth of the industry in congested areas and govern the location and scale of development in other areas. The new law essentially represented a series of development control measures that placed restrictions on new development such as building height and appearance, protected culturally significant structures and areas, and accorded greater attention to detail on the setting and site context (see Table 4.3).

Critical aims of the national tourism strategy (1990), on the other hand, were to improve and diversify the current tourism product. It also sought to encourage new forms of tourism that would build on a region's cultural and natural assets. Based on the creation of broad regulatory measures, the strategy focused on directing both the quality and quantity of new development and, where possible, diverting investment into ancillary facilities and improved infrastructure.

Specific elements placed restrictions on minimum plot size for new hotels, encour-

TABLE 4.3
Tourism Elements of the Town and Country Planning Law (1990), Republic of Cyprus

1. All new developments were restricted to much lower densities (plot ratios, height restrictions, and required open space) than previous development. Policies concerning product quality and environmental content also aimed to limit the quantity of provision of facilities in different areas.

2. Esthetic control of building style, materials used, and site to reflect the environmental and social context of the setting.

3. Detailed area/site studies focused on landscaping, infrastructure provision, beach quality and access, and other basic infrastructure.

4. Preservation, protection, and enhancement of cultural heritage through the use of preservation orders and protective zoning (buffer zones).

5. Town center renewal schemes sought to reestablish functional neighborhoods and encouraged traditional leisure activities in the central business district. In rural areas, the creation of "listed building" status would help to maintain the cultural context of structures used for tourism purposes.

6. Protection of the natural environment through the creation of nature reserves, areas of outstanding natural beauty (AONBs), and a national park.

Source: Cyprus Tourism Organisation (1994).

aged development of supplementary facilities (e.g., golf courses), established capacity standards for beach quality, and continued to promote the image of a quality destination through the development of new small-scale tourist facilities and attractions in rural locations (see Table 4.4).

The new law and strategy were designed to encourage a more sustainable tourism industry that took account of environmental tolerance and avoided economic disruption in other sectors of the economy (CTO, 1994). To test their applicability and demonstrate a new resolve to mitigate the negative effects of tourism on the island, two pilot projects were established: (1) the Alternative Rural Tourism Initiative and (2) tourism development in the Akamas Peninsula (including the Laona Project).

The Alternative Rural Tourism Initiative The rural tourism initiative, launched by the CTO in 1991, was designed to (1) provide tourist accommodation and facilities in 50 hill settlements, (2) attract visitors away from the coast, and (3) help stimulate village economies. Its main activities concentrated on the renovation and conversion of traditional small-scale buildings to some form of tourist use such as accommodation, catering, crafts, or exhibition space. The program had six broad objectives (Katsouris, 1994):

1. To revitalize rural communities through tourism, not as an economic substitute but rather as a supplement to local income in an attempt to reduce out-migration to coastal areas and abroad.
2. To restore village settings (e.g., traditional architecture, street scenes, public space, and points of interest), thereby retaining a "sense of place" and enhancing the quality of life for residents (and quality of experience for tourists).
3. To enable suppliers of village accommodation and catering facilities to attain CTO ratings and classification. The financial assistance program and product quality monitoring program implemented by the CTO were critical in this regard.

TABLE 4.4
Main Provisions of the National Tourism Strategy (1990), Republic of Cyprus

1. Enforcement of a moratorium on tourism development in municipal areas not yet covered by a local plan.

2. Designation of two broad zones, urban and rural, in coastal areas. Desired types and minimum sizes for new tourism enterprises defined.

3. Increased land requirements for new facilities to promote a better quality of accommodation and service: 222,000 square feet (20,000 square meters) for hotels, 166,500 square feet (15,000 square meters) for tourist villages, and 111,000 square feet (10,000 square meters) for tourist villas.

4. Implementation of a special policy within development boundaries of some coastal areas that permitted a wider range of establishments such as small family units that do not conform to the new general restrictions of plot size.

5. Use traditional buildings for tourist use, with controls placed on the extension of existing establishments that do not conform to the current national tourism strategy.

6. Discouragement of hotel apartments and their replacement with tourist villages.

7. Exploration of opportunities for developing tourism in hill resorts and village settlements.

8. Improvement of hotel occupancy through an extension of the tourist season and possibilities of winter tourism because of the temperate climate.

9. Correct the current regional imbalance in tourism distribution through easements and other incentives.

10. Encourage development and classification of "luxury villas" for tourists in the form of village clusters that cater exclusively to tourist family needs of the highest order with private facilities such as tennis courts and swimming pools.

Source: Cyprus Tourism Organisation (1994).

4. To develop a cooperative marketing and promotions campaign with project participants and village authorities and to establish a central bookings and information office. This was critical for establishing quality standards and avoiding loss of control to large tour operators.

5. To provide technical advice and guidance to local craftsmen on the restoration of traditional forms of architecture, thereby enchancing local awareness of the value of cultural heritage and its role in tourism.

6. To coordinate potential visitor activities and attractions on a regional basis in an attempt to establish the identity of different village clusters, including the development and promotion of local festivals, archaeology, flora and fauna, arts and crafts, and winemaking.

By the end of 1994, the CTO considered this initiative to be successful in terms of the restoration and renovation of facilities without the influence of speculative development. In addition, the program has led to an enhanced awareness by Cypriots in both rural and urban settings of the intrinsic value of cultural heritage (Katsouris, 1994). However, success in terms of actual investment and subsequent returns from tourism activity remains uncertain because the full program has yet to be launched in the tourist market and the total supply of properties and facilities is incomplete.

Tourism
Development
in the Akamas
Peninsula

The second and related program emerging from the new law and strategy focused on the Akamas Peninsula in the west, which is the last "unspoiled wilderness" of Cyprus and is relatively isolated from the rest of the country (see Figure 4.2). Formed by a series of raised terraces carved with deep ravines and canyons, the Akamas region is different from many other parts of southern Cyprus. Beaches and coves form its northern flank, with sand dunes and long sandy beaches on the southwest. It hosts over 60 different vegetation types, and it supports 168 species of birds plus numerous reptiles and insects. It is an important breeding ground for the rare Griffon vulture, and the Lara and Toxeutra beaches on its western flank are breeding grounds for the endangered green and logger-head turtles. In addition, its cultural heritage includes Neolithic, Hellenistic, Roman, and Byzantine remains, as well as the mythical baths of Aphrodite.

Following the 1974 conflict, the Akamas area was effectively cut off from the capital and the island's only international airport. The subsequent 20 years have witnessed a declining economy and depopulation on a more pronounced scale than other regions of the country (DTPH, 1994). Most of the Akamas (Laona) villages have been affected by declining employment opportunities, low agricultural productivity (due to poor soils and lack of water), and a general scarcity of retail shops, medical care, clubs, and community associations. The majority of its buildings are in a poor state of repair (DTPH, 1994).

Development of the peninsula is now at the center of a passionate debate. Given the extent of overdevelopment in other parts of the island, it is not surprising that this area has recently come under the scrutiny of developers. While conservationists call for a more sensitive approach to development, developers—and, in particular, members of the local community—want their share of the "economic miracle" that has been experienced elsewhere on the island.

Given the pressure of development and the experience of past mistakes, the government decided to act. In 1988, a local plan was prepared for the greater Akamas region. Strict zoning regulations were enacted which became part of the *Countryside Policy*, established under the new planning law. Four elements of the local plan are specifically related to tourism (DTPH, 1994):

1. The first national park on Cyprus should be established on the peninsula, with an emphasis on nature conservation and landscape preservation. Park use should conform to the International Union for the Conservation of Nature[9] (IUCN) recommendations of inspirational, educational, cultural, and recreational purposes. By mid-1995, this suggestion had been accepted in principle, but it remains a politically sensitive issue with strong lobbies, both for and against, that have delayed a final decision.

2. A scheme of fiscal and investment incentives designed to aid Laona villages in the regeneration of their communities, similar to the rural tourism initiative in the hill resorts, should be developed.

3. Specific programs should be initiated to conserve and protect various ecosystems in the area which may not fall within the proposed park boundaries, but which are equally significant to the ecology and context of the region. This has resulted in the cancellation of a tourism development zone planned for Lara Bay (the green turtle breeding grounds) and, indirectly, in the continued protection of the last refuge of the Mediterranean mouflon (a species of wild sheep believed to be unique to Cyprus).

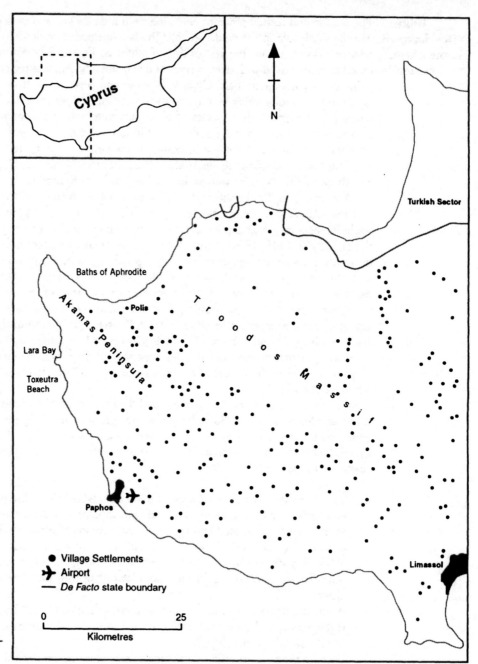

Figure 4.2
The Akamas Peninsula, Cyprus: Laona and hill villages.

4. New "mild forms of tourism" should be developed on the peninsula. An approach similar to the "rural tourism initiative" would be most appropriate. The Laona Project,[10] proposed by the environmental organization Friends of the Earth, and promoted as "green tourism" was believed to be "a good alternative to mass tourism, which had destroyed other areas of the island" (DTPH, 1994).

Although the government and CTO recognize that these actions will not bring about dramatic changes in the short term, they believe that they will help to limit tourism development to levels compatible with available resources and lead to a general improvement in product quality. Both the government and CTO believe that their planning and management initiatives, based on the promotion of new "mild forms" of tourism, will provide for a more sustainable form of economic development. "Existing traditional village houses and small family hotels and other supporting facilities will provide the necessary impetus for the envisaged sustainable tourism development" (DTPH, 1994, p. 6).

While acknowledging that it may take years of effort and investment, and prove both politically and economically unyielding, the CTO believes that only by taking a long-term view will they be able to "prevent total and terminal frustration of all investment in tourism which is the inevitable result of over-exploitation of the human and natural resource of the country" (CTO, 1994, p. 10).

THE FUTURE OF TOURISM IN CYPRUS: TOWARDS SUSTAINABILITY?

Many of the changes in Cypriot tourism planning and development, particularly since the late 1980s, are claimed to represent "an interesting example of formulating future development strategies for sustainable tourism in an already substantially developed and successful tourist destination . . . " (WTO, 1994b, p. 120). However, while such actions as the promotion of "agrotourism" and the rural tourism program are socially and environmentally sensitive in their approach, they are more appropriately considered as product diversification or "quality enhancement" initiatives.

Although these small-scale products are to be developed as part of a local industry, they will do little to mitigate the effects of the estimated two million visitor arrivals in 1994 (CTO, 1994). Modification of the planning law and its application, particularly in the Akamas Peninsula, are more significant for the nation as a whole. Yet this, too, may have little effect on controlling the impact of tourism. While, on paper, the introduction of stronger development control policies recognizes the failure of past actions, this alone may not bring about a more sustainable industry.

The development and growth of tourism is influenced by a number of different local and global factors that are neither absolutely predictable nor necessarily controllable. In Cyprus these have included the effects of war and civil disruption, the power of foreign operators,[11] and the tastes and preferences of tourists themselves. While war may have had a very obvious impact, with rapid development pursued to provide an adequate resupply of accommodation, the effects of the latter two have become most evident today.

During the island's early stage of development, most tourists arrived on the national airline, Cyprus Airways. Through price mechanisms and restrictions on the number of available aircraft, the government was able to influence both the quantity and quality of island visitors, essentially to their advantage. During the late 1970s and 1980s, however, the introduction of more efficient aircraft, the growth of charter operations, and the development of less expensive all-inclusive packaged holidays have seen this position substantially eroded. While the government has some control over the frequency of charter flights, it has little or no power to affect prices because charter operations are not subject to the same bilateral agreements as scheduled services (WTO, 1994a).

The growth of charter airlines, particularly foreign-owned, has also placed external operators in a dominant market position where they are able to negotiate lower prices and force income levels down. In addition, most operators do not have a long-term commitment to the country, since they do not generally own the island's hotels (Andronicou, 1986). Similarly, as current practice suggests, once visitors have become disenchanted with product quality and diversity, they may simply move on to less mature but unspoiled areas in competing countries.

Thus, while the tourism sector in Cyprus has generally benefited from increased charter traffic and total gross earnings have continued to rise, average expenditure has stagnated and declined partly due to prepaid inclusive holidays and a general market shift in Europe towards inexpensive self-catering accommodation (Ioannides, 1992). Although the new tourism strategy may seek to attract higher-spending visitors and encourage a greater variety of products in the interest of economic sustainability, the influence of external agents such as charter airlines, foreign operators, and tourist motivation may forestall their effects. This serves to highlight the imbalance between political objectives and economic clout, particularly where tourism forms a major element of the nation's economy.

A second aspect of determining the effectiveness of new policies concerns the government's willingness and/or ability to enforce regulations and implement strategy. While planners hope that they will be better able to protect the industry's competitive ability through new development control legislation and product diversification (DTPH, 1994), past experience in Cyprus suggests otherwise. Since the 1960s, the state has claimed to have been an active player in the island's tourism development, not through intensified state controls but through encouragement of the private sector (Andronicou, 1979). Yet, while the government and the CTO may have established policies and legislation to direct development along desired paths, the pressure, trends, and pace of development soon outstripped the planning process.

The failure of these initiatives was primarily because economic intervention through incentives and disincentives had a limited effect given that (1) the prevailing free market approach allowed for alternative means of finance (DTPH, 1994), (2) local governments were not technically or professionally prepared to deal with the speed and level of development (Andronicou, 1979), and (3) adequate regional planning guidance and comprehensive programs to encourage development away from the coast were not developed (CTO, 1994). Therefore, despite claims that "there were adequate controls at the national level" (Andronicou, 1979, p. 264) and that a development policy was designed with the intention of excluding mass tourism, legislation can only set the framework for development control. The problem lies in the way in which authorities actually define and enforce their national objectives.

Finally, whether new small-scale developments will prove environmentally sustainable and not mirror the typical development cycle of other parts of the island depends, to a large extent, on whether the authorities can learn from past experience. The CTO is determined not to allow speculative development in the Akamas or other rural areas, and it is conscious that excessive development may simply transplant coastal problems to rural areas. It has been recommended that restrictive measures should be established to control bed provision in already congested resorts, but restrictions should be relaxed in other rural and coastal areas that currently have only minimal development (such as the Polis region on the north edge of the Akamas Peninsula). Here, it is suggested that a preferential locational policy should be reinforced with additional incentives (CTO, 1994).

However, most problems evident in other parts of the island have resulted from relaxed planning provisions and offering significant development incentives to invite investment in favor of expedience. If new developments are to maintain their intended character and not evolve into a mass tourism complex as evidenced elsewhere in Cyprus, then past mistakes must be carefully analyzed to avoid repeating them and to maintain the integrity of the nation's last "wilderness" area.

CONCLUSION

While the problems associated with tourism in Cyprus are said to be the result of mass tourism in the coastal areas, the primary response has been to propose new small-scale development in the countryside. However, as in other aspects of economic development and resource exploitation, it has not been tourism per se that is causing the problems. Rather, unplanned and mismanaged tourism that lacks policy direction and comprehensive development strategies represents the root cause (Gunn, 1991; Mill and Morrison, 1985).

The current economic and spatial imbalance may not necessarily be the fault of mass tourism but, rather, a lack of planning and development control foresight. It could be suggested that these actions are more an attempt to tackle the consequence of past inaction than one to address the cause. However, whatever the response, the true sustainability of these actions will not be determined in the immediate future. True to the concept, the validity of sustainable tourism will only really be measured through the course of time.

ACKNOWLEDGMENTS

The author would like to thank Rob Woodward, Oxford Brookes University, for his assistance in producing the maps that appear in this chapter.

NOTES

1. See Chapters 3, 5, 6, 9, and 28 for additional discussion on the tourism planning process.
2. See Chapter 22 for further discussion relating to limits of acceptable change.
3. John Pezzey (1989) found over 60 definitions of, or commentaries on, sustainable development and related concepts. The bias and tone of these definitions are often dependent on the background of the writer. See Chapters 5, 7, 8, 17, 18, 22, and 23 for additional discussion relating to sustainable tourism development principles.
4. Personal communication with Professor Geoffrey Wall, University of Waterloo, 1992.

5. Richard Butler (1994, p. 29) suggests that there is a difference between *sustainable tourism* and *sustainable development in the context of tourism*. The former, he suggests, is tourism in a form that can maintain its viability in an area for an indefinite period of time. The latter, he argues, is tourism that is developed and maintained in an area (community, environment) in such a manner, and at such a scale, that it remains viable over an indefinite period *and* does not degrade or alter the environment (human and physical) in which it exists to such a degree that it prohibits the successful development and well-being of other activities and processes. While, theoretically, this may or may not be correct, in practice both government and industry are unable or unwilling to differentiate between the two. When referring to sustainable tourism, anything from new "green" products to new tourism development control policies, and anything in between, are the focus of their discussions. Therefore, this chapter does not seek to separate the two but, rather, refers to the parallel concepts of a "product" versus an "industry" approach to sustainable tourism development.

6. See Chapters 5, 9, 11, 12, and 14–19 for additional discussion and examples concerning community attitudes and involvement in the tourism planning and development processes.

7. For further information and opposing points of view on this issue see Denktash (1982) and Vanezis (1977).

8. A "tourist village" is a cluster of small houses/villas designed to cater to tourist family needs, providing self-contained, self-catering facilities. The development of "luxury villas" could possibly include private swimming pools and tennis courts.

9. See Chapter 23 for additional discussion of the International Union for the Conservation of Nature categories. Also note, this organization is now known as the World Conservation Union.

10. The Laona Project (n.d.) was designed to offer local people the technical and financial assistance to enable them to restore properties that can be used for visitor accommodation and associated small-scale industry. "Mild" forms of tourism are described in this project as agro-tourism, the encouragement of small family run hotels, walking and hiking, scientific tourism (university students and special interest field work such as archaeological and nature studies), and the opportunity to experience traditional Cypriot culture.

11. See Chapter 7 for additional discussion relating to the role of international tour operators in destination development.

REFERENCES

Andronicou, A. 1979. Tourism in Cyprus. In E. de Kadt (ed.), *Tourism—Passport to Development?* Oxford: Oxford University Press, pp. 237–264.

Andronicou, A. 1983. Selecting and planning for tourists—the case of Cyprus, *Tourism Management*, 4 (September), 209–211.

Andronicou, A. 1986. Cyprus—management of the tourist sector, *Tourism Management*, 7(2), 127–129.

Barbier, E.B. 1987. The concept of sustainable economic development, *Environmental Conservation*, 14(2), 101–110.

Boo, E. 1990. *Ecotourism: Potential and Pitfalls*. Washington, D.C.: World Wildlife Fund.

Bramwell, B. 1991. Sustainability and rural tourism policy in Britain, *Tourism Recreation Research*, 16(2), 49–51.

Butler, R.W. 1989. Alternative tourism: pious hope or trojan horse? *World Leisure and Recreation*, Winter, 9–17.

Butler, R.W. 1994. Tourism—an evolutionary perspective. In J.G. Nelson, R. Butler, and G.

Wall (eds.), *Tourism and Sustainable Development: Monitoring, Planning, Managing*, Department of Geography Publications Series Number 37. Ontario, Canada: University of Waterloo, pp. 26–43.

Cazes, G.H. 1989. Alternative tourism: reflections on an ambiguous concept. In T.V. Singh et al. (eds.), *Towards Appropriate Tourism: The Case of Developing Countries*, European University Studies, Series X, Vol. 11. Frankfurt am Main: Peter Lang, pp. 117–126.

Cocklin, C.R. 1989. Methodological problems of evaluating sustainability, *Environmental Conservation*, 16(4), 343–351.

Cohen, E. 1989. Alternative tourism—a critique. In Singh et al. (eds.), *Towards Appropriate Tourism: The Case of Developing Countries*, European University Studies, Series X, Vol. 11. Frankfurt am Main: Peter Lang, pp. 127–142.

Cyprus Tourism Organisation (CTO). 1994. *Tourism Development, Planning and Sustainability*. Paper presented by the Cyprus Tourism Organisation, Nicosia, Cyprus (CTO) at the United Nations Economic and Social Council, Economic Commission for Europe, Committee on Human Settlements, 18th Meeting of Experts on Human Settlements Problems in Southern Europe. Nicosia, Cyprus, 6–8 June.

Denktash, R.R. 1982. *The Cyprus Triangle*. London: Allen and Unwin.

Department of Town Planning and Housing (DTPH). 1994. *The Akamas Peninsula: Tourism, Sustainability and Conservation Management*. A paper presented by DTPH, at the United Nations Economic and Social Council, Economic Commission for Europe, Committee on Human Settlements, 18th Meeting of Experts on Human Settlements Problems in Southern Europe, Nicosia. Cyprus, 6–8 June.

Fennell, D.A. and P.F.J. Eagles. 1990. Ecotourism in Costa Rica: a conceptual framework, *Journal of Parks and Recreation Association*, 8(1), 23–34.

Getz, D. 1986. Models in tourism planning: towards integration of theory and practice, *Tourism Management*, 17 (March), 21–32.

Gillmor, D.A. 1989. Recent tourism development in Cyprus, *Geography*, 74(3), 262–265.

Globe '90. 1990. *An Action Strategy for Sustainable Tourism Development*. Tourism Stream Action Strategy Committee, Global Opportunities for Business and Environment (Globe '90) Conference. Vancouver, Canada, 19–23 March.

Godfrey, K.B. 1993. *Tourism and Sustainable Development: Towards a Community Framework*. Unpublished PhD dissertation. School of Planning, Oxford Brookes University.

Godfrey, K.B. 1994. *Sustainable Tourism—What Is It Really?* Address to the 18th Meeting of Experts on Human Settlements Problems in Southern Europe, United Nations Economic and Social Council, Economic Commission for Europe, Committee on Human Settlements. Nicosia, Cyprus, 6–8 June.

Godfrey, K.B. 1995. Planning for sustainable tourism development in Mediterranean countries, *Journal of Sustainable Tourism*, 3(1), 55–58.

Gonsalves, P. and P. Holden (eds.). 1985. *Alternative Tourism: A Resource Book*. Bangkok: Ecumenical Coalition on Third World Tourism.

Gunn, C.A. 1991. Sustainable Development: A Reachable Tourism Objective. Conference Proceedings of the TTRA Canadian Chapter, *Tourism–Environment–Sustainable Development: An Agenda for Research*. Hull, Quebec, 27–29 October, pp. 15–20.

Inskeep, E. 1991. *Tourism Planning: An Integrated and Sustainable Development Approach*. London: Chapman and Hall.

Inter-Parliamentary Union (IPU). 1989. *The Hague Declaration on Tourism*. Inter-Parliamentary Union and the World Tourism Organization.

Ioannides, D. 1992. Tourism development agents: the Cypriot resort cycle, *Annals of Tourism Research*, 19(4), 711–731.

Kariel, H.G. 1989. Tourism and development: perplexity or panacea? *Journal of Travel Research*, 28 (Summer), 2–6.

Katsouris, P. 1994. *The Development of Rural Tourism in Cyprus: An Alternative Form of Tourism.* Paper presented at the United Nations Economic and Social Council, Economic Commission for Europe, Committee on Human Settlements, 18th Meeting of Experts on Human Settlements Problems in Southern Europe. Nicosia, Cyprus, 6–8 June.

Krippendorf, J. 1982. Towards new tourism policies: the importance of environmental and sociocultural factors, *Tourism Management*, 3(3), 135–148.

Lane, B. 1988. What is Rural Tourism? Paper presented at the 1988 Countryside Recreation Conference, *Changing Land Use and Recreation*. Churchill Hall, Bristol University, 21–22 September, pp. 60–63.

Lane, B. 1989. The future of rural tourism, *Insights* (English Tourist Board), D5.1–5.6.

Lane, B. 1990. Developing Sustainable Rural Tourism. Paper presented at the Irish National Planning Conference, *Planning and Tourism in Harmony*. Newmarket on Fergus, County Clare, April.

Laona Project. (n.d.). *A Green Alternative to Mass Tourism.* The Laona Project Office, Limassol, Cyprus.

Lillywhite, M. and L. Lillywhite. 1991. Low impact tourism. In D.E. Hawkins and J.R. Brent Ritchie (eds.), *World Travel and Tourism Review: Indicators, Trends and Forecasts*, Vol. 1. Oxford, UK: C.A.B. International, pp. 162–169.

Lindner, W. 1989. Preface, *Journal of SID*, 2(3), 3.

Lockhart, D. 1993. Tourism and politics: the example of Cyprus. In D. Lockhart, D. Drakakis-Smith, and J. Schembri (eds.), *The Development Process in Small Island States*. London: Routledge, pp. 228–246.

Mill, R.C. and A.M. Morrison. 1985. *The Tourism System—An Introductory Text*. London: Prentice–Hall International (U.K.).

Pezzey, J. 1989. *Definitions of Sustainability*, Discussion Paper No. 9. University of Colorado: Institute of Behavioral Sciences.

Singh, T.V., H.L. Theuns, and F.M. Go (eds.). 1989. *Towards Appropriate Tourism: The Case of Developing Countries*. European University Studies, Series X, Vol. 11. Frankfurt am Main: Peter Lang.

South East Economic Development Strategy (SEEDS). 1989. *The Last Resort: Tourism, Tourist Employment and Post-Tourism in the South East*. Stevenage, Herts.

Taylor, G.D. 1991. Tourism and Sustainability—Impossible Dream or Essential Objective? Conference Proceedings of the TTRA Canadian Chapter, *Tourism–Environment–Sustainable Development: An Agenda for Research*. Hull, Quebec, 27–29 October, pp. 27–29.

Vanezis, P.N. 1977. *Cyprus: The Unfinished Agony*. London: Abelard–Schuman.

Wheeller, B. 1991. Tourism's troubled times: responsible tourism is not the answer, *Tourism Management*, 12 (June), 91–96.

Wheeller, B. 1992. Eco or ego tourism, new wave tourism—a short critique, *Insights*, May, D41–D44.

Wickers, D. 1994. Cyprus: an island guide, *The Mail on Sunday*, 38–39.

World Commission on Environment and Development (WCED). 1987. *Our Common Future*. Oxford: Oxford University Press.

World Tourism Organization (WTO). 1980. *Manila Declaration on World Tourism*. World Tourism Conference, Manila, Philippines, 27 September–10 October.

World Tourism Organization (WTO). 1982. *WTO/UNEP Joint Declaration*.

World Tourism Organization (WTO). 1985. *Tourism Bill of Rights and Tourist Code Adopted in Sofia*.

World Tourism Organization (WTO). 1990. *Seminar on "Alternative" Tourism: Introductory Report (SEM/ALG/89/IR) and Seminar on "Alternative" Tourism: Final Report (SEM/ALG/89/FR)*. Held in Tamanrasset, Algeria, 26–30 November, 1989. Madrid: WTO.

World Tourism Organization (WTO). 1994a. *Aviation and Tourism Policies: Balancing the Benefits*. A WTO Publication. London: Routledge.

World Tourism Organization (WTO). 1994b. *National and Regional Tourism Planning: Methodologies and Case Studies*. A WTO Publication. London: Routledge.

ℊ | PROBLEM SOLVING AND DISCUSSION ACTIVITIES

1. How effective is land use planning for developing sustainable tourism?

2. What role(s) do foreign tour operators and charter airlines play in the development of tourism? What steps could be taken to make tour operators more responsive to the social and environmental consequences of tourism activity in destination countries? What problems might be encountered when trying to implement these steps? What might be the consequences if strict controls were enacted on foreign tour operators and charter airlines?

3. Why do governments often fail to enforce tourism policies and plans developed to safeguard the environment? What can be done to change this situation?

4. Given the comment concerning recent government actions in Cyprus as addressing the "effect" of tourism problems and not the "cause," what other actions will be necessary to ensure a more sustainable future for the island's tourism industry? Ensure that you include a discussion relating to the apparent disregard of existing coastal tourism problems.

5. Select one of the six broad objectives associated with the Alternative Rural Tourism Initiative and provide recommendations for achieving such an objective. Identify opportunities and challenges that could affect the satisfaction of the selected objective.

6. Undertake a critical analysis of other tourism products and destinations promoting a sustainable theme, and determine whether these are promotional gimmicks, product diversification/repositioning, or real attempts at developing a more sustainable tourism industry.

5

Revitalizing Bermuda

TOURISM POLICY PLANNING IN A MATURE ISLAND DESTINATION

 *Michael V. Conlin*

♪ | K E Y   L E A R N I N G   P O I N T S

- Planning must be an ongoing and flexible activity if a tourist destination is to remain competitive in the international marketplace.
- Macrolevel planning concerns itself with the growth of tourist destinations as geographic, political, and social units. With the growing intensity of international competition, planning must consider the full range of issues associated with tourism development and adopt an integrated approach.
- The political environment has a direct impact on tourism planning and development in that it affects whether controls, policies, and regulations are implemented *and* enforced.
- The destination life cycle model, although not a totally accurate predictor of development and its consequences, indicates that destinations must be constantly aware of the dangers of unplanned growth, particularly at the maturation or saturation point of the cycle. What a destination does at this stage may signal either decline or rejuvenation.
- Tourism planning must be community-based, especially in areas such as small island destinations where the population is considered to be a major part of the tourism product. Involving the community has consequences for policy adoption and implementation. Inclusion of the community carries a responsibility for increased communication between policy-making bodies and the public.

INTRODUCTION

Located in the Atlantic Ocean some 575 miles (925 kilometers) east of North Carolina (USA), Bermuda has long been considered to be one of the world's premiere island tourist destinations. It has a relatively long tradition of tourism activity dating from the late 1800s, and tourism now represents a major and fiscally successful component of the country's economic activity.

Bermuda's tourism industry is somewhat unique: (1) It is generally considered as a positive model of tourism development from both an economic and an environmental perspective, and (2) its market position is possibly as narrowly defined as any international tourist destination in the world. However, notwithstanding the long-term success of its tourism industry, Bermuda experienced a significant deterioration of its visitor count beginning in the early 1990s that has had a serious impact on the country as a whole.

In 1992, in response to this downturn, the country entered into a process of reassessing its market position and product profile that touched upon a range of important tourism planning issues, including the implications of the product life cycle for mature destinations, the role of public participation in the planning process, and the role of the public and private sectors in the planning and management of the tourism product. This chapter discusses these and other issues. Specifically, this chapter includes the following:

- A discussion of some of the current theories and concepts in tourism planning, including integrated tourism planning, the destination life cycle, and community-based planning.
- A brief history of the growth and profile of tourism in Bermuda from the 1890s through to 1994 and the policies that have contributed to its narrow market niche, controlled development, and relatively benign impact.
- A detailed description of Bermuda's process of reassessing its tourism product, including the strengths and weaknesses that were identified and the range of recommendations for addressing the downturn.
- An opportunity to consider the implications of various alternatives for future tourism growth, including new products, national tourism awareness strategies, and public and private sector cooperation in national tourism planning.

Although the focus is on Bermuda's tourism industry, a number of the issues have application to most small island destinations and, indeed, most regional resort-style tourism products.

DESTINATION PLANNING APPROACHES AND MODELS: CONTEMPORARY PERSPECTIVES AND ISSUES

Tourism has become one of the world's largest industries and continues to grow.[1] Tourism has also undergone dramatic changes as technological advances and personal wealth have resulted in the development of new destinations and more informed consumers with greater choice and higher expectations. As a result, the tourism industry has become highly complex and globally competitive. This has created a need for sophisticated planning and management. The following discussion presents a review of some of the theoretical considerations—planning, destination life cycle, and community involvement—that have become popular within the tourism industry.

Tourism Planning Planning[2] within the tourism industry takes place at both the microlevel and the macrolevel. The microlevel involves planning that specific operators undertake when determining the feasibility of their business activities. To a large extent, this is essentially strategic planning[3] of a corporate nature and is basically similar to corporate planning in

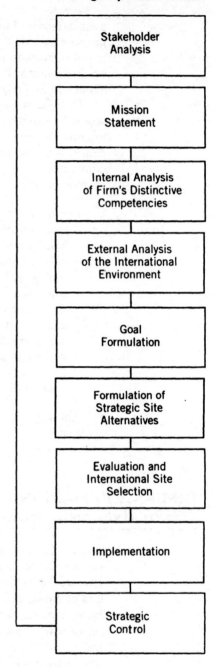

Figure 5.1
*International strategic management and goal planning model.
(From Hoffman and Schneiderjans, 1990, p. 179;* Courtesy of
the *International Journal of Hospitality Management.)*

other industries. Corporate planning models generally follow a common structure. Figure
5.1 presents a strategic planning model synthesized by Hoffman and Schniederjans (1990,
pp. 178–179) from the strategic planning literature. The model is based on the goal of
matching an organization's strengths with the market opportunities presented by a changing external environment. This model was designed to provide a systematic approach to

the assessment of growth alternatives for lodging corporations at various sites. In common with all strategic planning activity, the model seeks to align the firm's recommended action with its strengths and guard against the uncertainties of the external environment.

Macrolevel planning in the tourism industry, on the other hand, is concerned with the growth of destinations as geographic, political, and social units, be they countries, states, provinces, or regions. Traditionally, tourism planning activity at this level focused on regional and local issues relating to land use and the physical development of destinations (Helber, 1995, p. 106). Gravel (1979) described these early planning efforts as being "nonintegrated" (i.e., highly market- or site-specific).

Increasingly, however, concerns about economic survival, sustainable development,[4] and acceptable levels of environmental and social impact[5] have resulted in a recognition of the need to plan for the development of entire tourism industries within the context of global markets. Gravel argued that there was a process of maturation of tourism planning and that, in the mid-1960s, tourism planning began to take a more macro perspective, recognizing the wider environment of tourism development. He labeled this an "integrated" approach.

It is now more common for economic issues such as market position, product value, and destination image, along with environmental and community impacts, to be dominant concerns of tourism planning. This more elaborate form of planning recognizes not only the pressures of the marketplace but also the impact of tourism on the host, and not just in economic terms but also in social and environmental terms. Support for this position is widespread. As asserted by Mathieson and Wall (1982, p. 45), "Tourism will only flourish given the appropriate conditions. It is an industry which, like any other industry, requires sophisticated planning and organization if its full potential is to be realized."

Past failure to plan for tourism is all too obvious to the experienced traveler (Conlin and Baum, 1995, p. 6). Many islands are particularly susceptible to the consequences of poor planning given their small size and the relatively greater impact that tourism can have on their development (Stonich et al., 1995). Increasingly, the failure to plan will not simply be a cosmetic issue but a more fundamental economic, ecological, and social concern.

Macrolevel tourism planning is particularly concerned with the manipulation of controllable variables within a destination's tourism industry (i.e., infrastructure, market position, product development, and promotion) to achieve goals that the political and social community set within the context of a rapidly changing global marketplace. This has been described by Mathieson and Wall (1982, p. 46) as follows:

> . . . the ability of destinations to compete globally depends upon the four following conditions:
> 1. The mixture, quality, and price of the facilities and services being offered.
> 2. The existence of a skilled and experienced organizational body.
> 3. The geographical location of the destination area in relation to the main tourist generating regions, and the ability of these destinations to capitalize on the advantages of being well located, or to ameliorate the disadvantages of being poorly located.
> 4. The nature and origin of financial investment.

This description underscores the necessity for successful tourism planning to match product, price, location, and management expertise with the market and its expectations in a way that will attract investment. Increasingly, this must be done with the needs of the host community[6] as a major focal point.

The Destination Life Cycle Theory of Tourism Development

Considerable research has been conducted into the application of the traditional marketing management theory of the product life cycle to the tourism industry. The product life cycle is rooted in the development of post–World War II marketing theory and has been a staple of marketing management ever since. Although it has been criticized for not explaining the many exceptions that one finds to the theory, for the most part ". . . the life-cycle concept has proved to be a sound planning tool when properly used" (Patton, 1968, p. 329).

The product life cycle continues to play an important role in marketing management, including applications to the hospitality industry. Indeed, Morrison lists the product life cycle as one of the "seven core principles of marketing" (Morrison, 1989, p. 15), describing the concept as follows (1989, p. 17):

> The Product Life Cycle idea suggests all hospitality and travel services pass through four predictable stages: (1) introduction, (2) growth, (3) maturity, and (4) decline. Marketing approaches need to be modified with each stage. Avoiding a decline is the key to long-term survival. Atlantic City, New Jersey is a great example of a travel destination that went through one life cycle (from a fashionable to a rather seedy seaside resort) and then got a completely new lease on life as an exciting gambling destination.

The notion of modifying one's approach to changing situations brought on by the stages of the product life cycle, when applied to tourist destinations, is called *the destination life cycle theory*.[7] One of the first proponents of the theory suggested that a destination's life cycle consists of six stages: exploration, involvement, development, consolidation, stagnation, and decline or rejuvenation (Butler, 1980). Figure 2.1 illustrates Butler's model, which has remained the mainstay of destination life cycle discussion in the tourism field.

More recent investigators, including de Albuquerque and McElroy (1992, p. 620), have tended to simplify the model, arguing in favor of a three-phase model consisting of ". . . (1) emergence or initial discovery, (2) followed by the transition to rapid expansion, and (3) culminating in maturity as defined by visitor saturation." While admitting the destination life cycle model has received little empirical testing, de Albuquerque and McElroy nonetheless cite examples of situations where the model has proven useful in predicting tourism growth in small islands (Wilkinson, 1987). Their own analysis suggests that tourism development on many Caribbean islands also follows the destination life cycle in a general sense.

Bermuda, for example, exhibits greater-than-predicted levels of visitor density (141 daily visitors per square kilometer compared with 66 for other mature destinations) and hotel density (78 rooms per square kilometer compared with five and three for destinations at the transition and emergence phases, respectively) (de Albuquerque and McElroy, 1992, p. 625).

The model has come under serious criticism, however, particularly in the area of its operationalization. For example, Haywood (1986, p. 167) argued:

> . . . tourism planners need to look beyond the tourist area life cycle concept if they are searching for meaningful insights as to how to manage a tourist area as it evolves . . . ; the product

life cycle can be misleading and force marketers and planners to discontinue their products prematurely when they enter a decline stage. . . . If tourism area planners and managers are to be more effective, they must broaden their thinking about tourist area evolution, and how it can best be managed given the economic, political and other forces that shape it.

Notwithstanding this criticism, Haywood (1986, pp. 162–164) suggested four strategies that flow from the model as it applies to destinations approaching the decline stage, and which are aimed at extending the life of a tourism area: (1) promoting more frequent use among current users, (2) developing more varied use among current users, (3) creating new uses, and (4) finding new users by expanding the market. Haywood (1986) also recommended that market share data be incorporated into the destination life cycle model to provide planners with a more comprehensive picture of a destination's position within changing, competitive tourism markets.

The destination life cycle model would seem to provide some assistance to planners if treated with a degree of caution. It is clearly not a totally accurate predictor of development and its consequences. However, it does indicate that destinations must be constantly aware of the dangers of unplanned growth, particularly at the maturation or saturation point of the cycle. What a destination does at this stage may well signal either decline or rejuvenation.

Community-Inclusive Tourism Planning

With growing concern about the environmental and social impacts of tourism, planning has become more integrated (Gravel, 1979) and has matured to the point where it must consider the impact of tourism development on a number of constituencies, not just organizational or site-specific economic sectors. Perhaps the most innovative consequence of this maturation of planning has been a call for the inclusion of host communities in the planning process.

As the Bermuda example described later demonstrates, the inclusion of a wide range of stakeholders within the planning process has its costs in terms of potentially longer time horizons and an increased possibility of conflict and uncertainty. However, others have argued that this is not necessarily so, stating that " . . . if the public and private groups are given the chance to participate at an early stage there is sufficient consensus of opinion to permit broadly based planning objectives" (Murphy, 1985, p. 172). Murphy's (1980, p. 366) research identified:

. . . the willingness of the residents to participate and their ability to develop rational and practical options. This confirms that tourism planning need not remain the realm of the expert alone; given the chance, the public can provide a useful input into the decision-making process.

The call for more inclusive planning is widespread in tourism planning circles and has even taken advantage of developments in computer-aided decision support technology. The University of Calgary's Group Decision Support Laboratory, for example, has been used by different groups affected by tourism planning in Calgary (Canada) to reach consensus among the various affected constituencies on acceptable planning objectives. Other forms of decision-making innovations, including brainstorming, focus groups, and Delphi surveys, are also used to bring issues of concern among affected constituencies to the forefront of debate about tourism development and facilitate the identification of acceptable solutions. Murphy (1985, p. 176) summarized this movement to inclusion and its advantages as follows:

> Public opinion and political power must be courted and won if the industry is to continue to rely on government support and community assets for its survival and success. By stressing the community and systems aspects of tourism it becomes apparent that this activity is now inter-woven into the social, economic, and environmental aspects of all communities, whether or not they are major destinations. Under these circumstances, tourism can be integrated into general planning procedures of all communities and become coordinated with facility developments in the physical and social fabric of destination areas.

In the case of small island nations, the advantages of community participation are significant. By seeking and including the input of those whose lives are perhaps most affected by tourism planning decisions, a destination gains the support of the community for the outcomes of the planning activity. In this way, the tourism product is enhanced by the presence of a host population who, in varying degrees, is sympathetic to the objective of the industry and, hopefully, will enthusiastically endorse it. Given that the host community is either, by design or default, an integral part of the actual tourism product on many small island resort destinations, the support of the community may well be a fundamental key to success.

BERMUDA TOURISM

Bermuda is commonly thought of and referred to as a single island. It is also commonly believed to be part of the Caribbean region. However, the reality is that Bermuda is composed of over 100 islands, tightly grouped in a "fish hook" shape, that lie approximately 1000 miles (1610 kilometers) north of the Bahamas. Bermuda sits 575 miles (925 kilometers) east of Cape Hatteras, North Carolina. The Gulf Stream runs between the mainland and the islands, giving them a semitropical climate. Because of the Gulf Stream, Bermuda has the most northerly coral reefs in the world. The island is approximately 22 miles (35 kilometers) from end to end.

Bermuda is a British Dependent Territory (or colony) but has enjoyed self-government since 1620, just 11 years after it was accidentally settled by the British when a fleet bound for the new Virginia colony in America was wrecked on its reefs. This event was immortalized by Shakespeare in *The Tempest*. The population hovers around 60,000 persons and is approximately 40 percent white and 60 percent black.

Bermuda enjoys one of the highest standards of living in the world, with a per capita employment income of just over US$30,000 (1992). There are no taxes in Bermuda, and the island is considered to be the reinsurance capital of the world. The international business sector represents about half of the island's economy. Tourism represents the other half.

Development of Bermuda's Tourism Industry Tourism began in Bermuda in the second half of the nineteenth century and started to realize its full potential with the visit in the second half of the century by Princess Louise, the wife of the Governor General of Canada and one of Queen Victoria's daughters. Publicity over her visit, along with the island's developing reputation as a destination for people of means, resulted in the launching of Bermuda, notwithstanding the difficulty most travelers experienced in reaching the island. Mark Twain perhaps put it best when he reportedly said " . . . Bermuda is Paradise, but you have to go through Hell to get to it" (Zuill, 1973). A winter sea voyage across the Gulf Stream between the North American mainland and Bermuda was no "holiday" and, indeed, the modern day cruise business to Bermuda does not operate in the winter months.

The main response to this increased tourist activity was the opening of the Princess Hotel in 1885 (in honor of Princess Louise). This marked the first significant investment in facilities to house and cater to visitors. Originally offering 100 rooms, the hotel quickly became the center for Bermudian society. The tourist season then was during the winter, and it was not for another 25 years that the first major tourism facility was constructed on one of Bermuda's beaches. The Elbow Beach Hotel, which opened just prior to World War I, marked the first time that consideration was given to those assets that have formed the foundation for Bermuda tourism for the past half century—namely, sun, sand, and surf.

In 1920 an English shipping company, Furness Withy & Co., opened the Bermudiana Hotel in Hamilton (the capital) and, within several years, developed the Castle Harbor Hotel and Mid-Ocean Club, both in the prestigious Tucker's Town area of St. George's Parish. These properties marked an early stage of vertical integration of tourism products (i.e., the company owned and operated both the means of transportation for visitors coming to the island and the accommodation and amenities when they arrived).

Another event of pivotal significance occurred in 1938 when Pan American Airways and Imperial Airways (the predecessor of B.O.A.C. and British Airways) began flying boat service to the island. With the building of the airstrip by the United States Navy during the war, Bermuda was well equipped following World War II to enter the age of air travel. This was to have a dramatic effect on the number of visitor arrivals to Bermuda.

In 1920, 13,327 people visited Bermuda. This number had almost tripled to 46,463 by 1930. In 1937, total visitor arrivals numbered 82,815 (Zuill, 1973). By 1951, with the advent of regular air service, Bermuda surpassed the arrivals level achieved in 1937, with a total of 92,066 visitors, 62 percent of whom arrived by air. Table 5.1 provides visitor arrival data for the period 1949 through 1979. The data clearly show the ascendancy of air travel throughout the 1950s to the point where regular visitor arrivals by sea virtually ceased by the mid-1960s. Today, air travel forms the transportation foundation for the island's tourism industry. The data also indicate the rapid rise in the popularity of cruise visitors to Bermuda, which represented almost one-quarter of all arrivals in 1979.

Characteristics of Bermuda's Contemporary Tourism Industry

The development of tourism in Bermuda following World War II has been characterized by a number of distinct features, particularly the initial rapid growth of the industry and a "conservative" tourism policy. These and related issues are discussed below.

RAPID GROWTH OF THE INDUSTRY As shown in Table 5.1, tourist arrivals in Bermuda during the period from 1949 to 1979 grew tenfold (or at an average annual rate of 8.3 percent from 54,899 to 599,145). Three trends became evident during this period: (1) the increase in air arrivals from 28,258 (51.5 percent) in 1949 to 458,095 (76.5 percent) in 1979 (average annual increase of 9.7 percent), (2) the increase in cruise ship arrivals from 3410 (6.2 percent) in 1949 to 140,364 (23.4 percent) in 1979 (average annual increase of

TABLE 5.1
Bermuda Tourism: Historical Picture of Visitor Arrivals, 1949–1979

Year	Air (%)	Ship (%)	Cruise (%)	Total
1949	51.5	42.3	6.2	54,899
1950	55.5	39.2	5.4	67,816
1951	62.1	25.8	12.1	92,066
1952	61.7	27.0	11.4	93,066
1953	63.4	23.3	13.3	103,501
1954	64.1	21.9	14.1	106,804
1955	67.6	19.1	13.3	110,651
1956	68.9	18.2	12.9	109,131
1957	71.3	13.4	15.2	120,984
1958	70.7	12.2	17.1	130,821
1959	67.9	9.0	23.1	142,330
1960	65.6	7.9	26.5	151,406
1961	66.4	6.1	27.5	170,622
1962	64.4	4.8	30.9	192,802
1963	65.0	4.4	30.6	204,181
1964	73.0	3.8	23.2	188,992
1965	76.0	2.7	21.2	237,782
1966	80.0	2.0	18.0	256,772
1967	83.7	0.6	15.7	281,167
1968	80.1	0.6	19.3	331,379
1969	75.3	0.5	24.2	370,920
1970	77.6	0.3	22.1	388,914
1971	77.1	0.2	22.7	412,947
1972	80.4	0.3	19.3	420,950
1973	82.3	0.2	17.6	467,256
1974	79.0	0.2	20.8	531,568
1975	80.4	0.1	19.4	512,124
1976	80.4	0.1	19.5	558,874
1977	76.7	0.3	23.0	572,855
1978	76.0	0.1	23.9	551,466
1979	76.5	0.1	23.4	599,145
Average annual growth (%)	9.7	(11.5)	13.2	8.3

Note: Numbers may not total 100 percent due to rounding.
Source: Bermuda Department of Tourism (1991).

13.2 percent), and (3) the decrease in arrivals by ship from 23,231 (42.3 percent) in 1949 to 686 (0.1 percent) by 1979 (average annual decrease of 11.5 percent).

During the 1980s, tourism continued to be a dominant factor in the island's economy. Although this period saw several swings, arrivals continued to be strong (see Table 5.2). In 1980, arrivals reached a new high of 609,556 followed by five years in which arrivals remained below the 600,000 level, with 1984 representing the lowest level in this period at 528,871. This was a period of recession in North America and was also marked by labor unrest in Bermuda that directly affected the tourism industry.

In 1987, another record was reached with 631,314 arrivals, but between then and 1992 the total declined. This decline has generally been attributed to the effects of a declining economy in North America, the Gulf War in 1990–1991, and other factors relating to the changing international tourism market. In particular, there was general concern about the price–value relationship of a Bermuda holiday. For example, the average high-season rack rate for two persons with meals at one of Bermuda's large properties in 1994 was approximately US$400 per night. Although other upscale destinations have similar or higher rates, many in the travel industry believe Bermuda is too highly priced.

CONSERVATIVE TOURISM POLICY During the 1960s and 1970s, Bermuda continued to promote itself as an upscale resort destination (Riley, 1991). As a result of numerous studies, policies were adopted to preserve this image. For example, that cliché of upscale destination planning, prohibition on the use of internally lit signs, has always been a hallmark of planning in Bermuda. This level of conservatism also extended to the exclusion of international franchise operations. There are, for example, no McDonald's restaurants on the island. These policies continue to be the cornerstone of the island's tourism policy.

Moratorium on Development Bermuda was one of the first destinations to realize the danger of uncontrolled growth. Consequently, the island has limited tourism growth through a moratorium on the construction of new hotels and the creation of a ceiling of 10,000 bed spaces. This policy is enforced through a phasing scheme that respects the ceiling and allocates available space to the stronger properties that maintain high standards.

The policy has been overruled on two occasions. In the late 1970s, the government gave Bermuda College permission to construct a 64-room resort hotel on the island's south shore. Named the Stonington Beach Hotel, the property is adjacent to the College's Hotel School and serves as the training facility for students in hospitality programs. The government also agreed in 1989 to allow the Ritz–Carlton group to construct a 400-room resort property, also on the south shore. It was believed that the island's tourism industry could benefit from a new world class facility given the perceived steady deterioration of the industry's existing physical plant. However, the deteriorating financial condition of the industry worldwide and the continuing objections of local residents caused the project to be postponed indefinitely.

Notwithstanding the above exceptions, the policy of controlling growth in tourist accommodation continues to be in effect. The overall emphasis of tourism policy is on strengthening existing properties and improving occupancy.

Hotel Grading Policy The emphasis on controlled, upscale development was further strengthened by the introduction of the Department of Tourism's hotel grading plan in

TABLE 5.2
Bermuda Tourism: Distribution of Total Visitor Arrivals by Month, 1980–1989

Month	1980 (%)	1981 (%)	1982 (%)	1983 (%)	1984 (%)	1985 (%)	1986 (%)	1987 (%)	1988 (%)	1989 (%)
January	2.0	2.2	1.5	1.9	1.8	1.6	1.4	1.6	1.9	1.7
February	4.1	3.9	2.8	3.4	2.9	2.7	2.7	2.9	2.6	2.9
March	7.8	7.8	5.9	6.8	6.4	6.2	5.8	6.1	5.9	5.7
April	8.6	11.0	10.6	8.8	9.6	8.7	7.5	7.9	7.2	7.6
May	12.2	9.8	14.3	13.0	12.9	12.5	11.7	13.0	13.1	12.5
June	11.0	11.9	12.2	12.3	11.6	13.1	12.8	13.0	12.9	12.9
July	10.1	11.0	12.2	11.9	11.8	12.9	13.8	13.2	13.5	12.8
August	11.6	12.0	11.9	13.3	12.7	13.9	14.0	13.3	14.1	13.5
September	11.2	10.4	9.9	10.3	11.4	11.2	11.0	11.3	11.0	10.4
October	11.0	10.5	10.2	9.6	10.2	9.3	10.4	9.7	9.6	10.6
November	7.2	6.7	5.8	6.1	5.7	5.1	5.8	5.3	5.2	5.6
December	3.2	2.8	2.7	2.7	3.0	2.8	3.2	2.8	3.0	3.7
Total	609,556	535,246	544,466	567,710	528,871	549,590	591,913	631,314	585,218	549,595

Note: Numbers may not total 100 percent due to rounding.
Source: Bermuda Department of Tourism (1991).

90

1988. Under this plan, properties are required to meet high standards of cleanliness and attractiveness and to offer defined levels of amenities to ensure the renewal of their operating licenses.

Timeshare Development Policy The conservative approach is further mirrored by the country's policy with respect to timesharing properties. During the 1980s, two hotel properties received permission to convert to timesharing, and permission was granted in 1981 to York–Hannover, the Canadian developer, to construct a timesharing resort in the Town of St. George. However, a moratorium has since been placed on further development of timeshare properties until the government can assess timesharing's role as a tourism product.

This policy is contrary to that of many other island resort destinations that have embraced the timesharing concept (not always with positive results). In this sense, the policy is an indicator of the control Bermuda exercises over both innovative and traditional development.

Cruise Ship Policy As indicated earlier, cruise ship arrivals have played a major part in Bermuda's tourism industry since its inception. Prior to 1994 this segment reached its high point in 1988, when arrivals totaled 158,368. However, hoteliers' concerns about overcrowding and the related impact on the island's image resulted in Bermuda adopting yet another restrictive policy in 1988. This policy limited cruise ship arrivals to 120,000 during the high season (May to October) and allowed only four scheduled cruise ships weekly between Monday and Friday. It also permitted up to 12 additional occasional callers.

The rationale was to reduce pressure on Bermuda's tourism infrastructure and to maintain the image of the island as an upscale destination (Riley, 1991). To further bolster these objectives, visits were only awarded to upmarket cruise operators (e.g., the Royal Viking Line, Chandris Celebrity Cruises, Royal Caribbean, and Norwegian Cruise Lines).

In 1989, the year the restrictive policy took effect, cruise ship arrivals fell to 131,322. In 1990, they fell below the 120,000 ceiling, totaling only 113,000. As a result of this decrease and the general deterioration in the tourism industry in Bermuda, the government raised its ceiling in the early 1990s to 150,000. The relaxing of the policy was designed to offset the drop in air arrivals that had been evidenced since the 1987 visitor arrival record.

This policy and its recent amendments again underscore the extent to which the maintenance of a narrow market approach forms the basis of Bermuda tourism. Policies are flexible, striving always for a balance between arrivals and profitability. The focus is always on extracting the maximum return from the least number of visitors, thereby respecting the environment, its natural resources, and the people of Bermuda.

NARROWLY DEFINED MARKET NICHE Bermuda has achieved its goals in terms of the type of tourist attracted. The emphasis on controlled development, a flexible approach aimed at maximizing profitability as opposed to numbers of arrivals, and concern for the maintenance of the product and the country's infrastructure have resulted in a very narrowly defined market.

By far, the majority of visitors to Bermuda (both air and cruise) come from the United States. In 1980, arrivals from the United States accounted for 86.4 percent of air and 93.6 percent of cruise ship visitors. The corresponding numbers in 1989 were 84.0 percent and 93.2 percent, respectively. Overall, Americans accounted for 87.9 percent of visitors in 1980 and 86.2 percent in 1989. The regional origin of American visitors is marked by a high degree of concentration. In 1980, 81.0 percent came from the Mid-Atlantic and North–East regions. In 1989, visitors from these two regions still accounted for 74.5 percent of the American total. The South–East region increased from 6.1 percent to 10.9 percent of the total during this period (Bermuda Department of Tourism, 1991, Tables 2 and 7).

Bermuda's visitors tend to be older than visitors to other islands. In 1980, 47.5 percent of visitors were 40 years of age or older. By 1989, this had grown to 55.7 percent (Bermuda Department of Tourism, 1991, Table 10), partly due to the decline in younger visitors from the United States during the annual spring break. Prior to the mid-1980s, Bermuda could expect over 10,000 students to visit each year, but recently this market segment has generated less than 4000 visitors annually. While not significant in absolute terms, the long-term implications of not establishing early linkages with the affluent, young college market segment may be substantial.

That there is a shift to Bermuda becoming a summer destination is born out by data presented in Table 5.2. The majority of tourists visit during the period from May through August. In spite of continuing attempts to promote the shoulder and off seasons, little success has been achieved.

Bermuda is attracting more educated visitors. In 1980, 50 percent of air arrivals had graduated from college. This rose to 70 percent by 1989. Indeed, 34 percent of visitors in 1989 had completed some postgraduate education (Bermuda Department of Tourism, 1991, Table 21). Moreover, consistent with its upscale image and corresponding levels of accommodation and amenities, Bermuda visitors enjoy substantial incomes. In 1989, 72 percent of visitors reported family incomes in excess of US$40,000 annually, with close to one-third (32 percent) reporting annual family incomes in excess of US$75,000. In the same year, 74 percent of visitors reported having white collar occupations, while only 9 percent considered themselves to be blue collar workers. Of these, most described themselves as working in service or craft areas (Bermuda Department of Tourism, 1991, Table 23).

THE SITUATION IN THE EARLY 1990s

As Bermuda's tourism industry moved into the 1990s, it was characterized by a sense of complacency, a reluctance to innovate, a decreasing level of service quality, and a deteriorating physical plant. Particularly relevant to the future growth of the industry and its ability to adapt to changing consumer demands in the 1990s was the generally held belief that the island was a unique destination and without competition. Industry performance through the early 1990s, however, did not support this view. Total visitors to Bermuda declined by close to 6 percent in 1990–1991 (from 547,500 in 1990 to 514,900 in 1991) (see Table 5.3). The largest decrease was in air arrivals (who tend to be hotel-based visitors), which fell from 434,900 in 1990 to 386,700 in 1991. This 11.1 percent decrease

TABLE 5.3
Bermuda Tourism: Visitor Arrivals and Expenditures, 1990–1994

Year	Arrivals (Thousands)						Expenditures (US$ millions)					
	Air	Percent	Cruise	Percent	Total		Air	Percent	Cruise	Percent	Total
1990	434.9	79.4	112.6	20.6	547.5		467.9	95.5	22.2	4.5	490.1
1991	386.7	75.1	128.2	24.9	514.9		423.9	93.0	31.7	7.0	455.6
1992	375.2	74.1	131.0	25.9	506.2		410.5	92.7	32.5	7.3	443.0
1993	412.4	72.8	153.9	27.2	566.3		NA[a]		NA		NA
1994	415.9	70.6	172.8	29.4	588.7		NA		NA		NA

[a] NA, not available.

Sources: Commission on Competitiveness Final Report (1994 p. 48); *Bermuda in Perspective* (January 1994, February 1995).

was particularly devasting since air arrivals or the hotel-based visitor represented a significantly higher daily average expenditure (US$225) compared to cruise visitors (US$70) (Commission on Competitiveness, 1994, p. 54).

Although the decline slowed in 1992, air arrivals or hotel-based visitors evidenced a further decrease of almost 3 percent, or 11,500 visitors. Notwithstanding a slight increase in cruise visitors, the overall visitor total for 1992 was 506,200, the lowest level experienced since 1973. The direct impact was a decline of almost 10 percent in total tourist expenditures during the first two years of the 1990s, from US$490.1 million in 1990 to US$443.0 million in 1992.

By the middle of 1992, the island's tourism authorities recognized that Bermuda's tourism industry was not immune to the international economic climate or, indeed, to the changes that were taking place in the global tourism marketplace. The downturn made residents aware of just how dependent the country had become on the well-being of the tourism industry. The unemployment caused by the downturn was reflected in government policy to scale down the levels of expatriate employment on the island. This had a negative impact on the residential rental market, a traditional source of investment for many Bermudians. Thus, the whole economic life of the island was negatively affected.

THE COMMISSION ON COMPETITIVENESS

The government's response in 1992 was the creation of the Commission on Competitiveness, which was charged with examining the island's two main economic sectors, tourism and international business. In addition, the commission was responsible for exploring new areas of economic activity in an attempt to lower the country's reliance on a narrowly based economic foundation. The mandate of the commission reflected a broad concern about national economic well-being in a rapidly changing international marketplace (Commission on Competitiveness, 1994, p. 4):

> The Commission's mandate originated from concern over the economic performance of Bermuda during the 1980s and early 1990s amid signs that Bermuda's competitiveness was trailing other countries and jeopardizing . . . standard of living. The mandate also recognized the tremendous changes which were taking place outside of Bermuda and the impact these changes were having on Bermuda's traditional sources of foreign exchange revenues.

Figure 5.2 shows the organization of the commission. The Tourism Planning Committee was charged with examining the island's tourism industry. The composition of this committee, which comprised representatives from the tourism industry, the public sector, education, and international business, reflected an understanding by the island's leaders that the country's two main economic activities were interdependent, and indeed synergistic. Its chairperson was a prominent banker. In this way, the committee had linkages with all major stakeholder groups in the island's tourism industry and its economic partners in the country's overall economy.

Consistent with this integrated approach to planning, the committee decided to employ an inclusive process. Given the small size of Bermuda and the pervasiveness of the

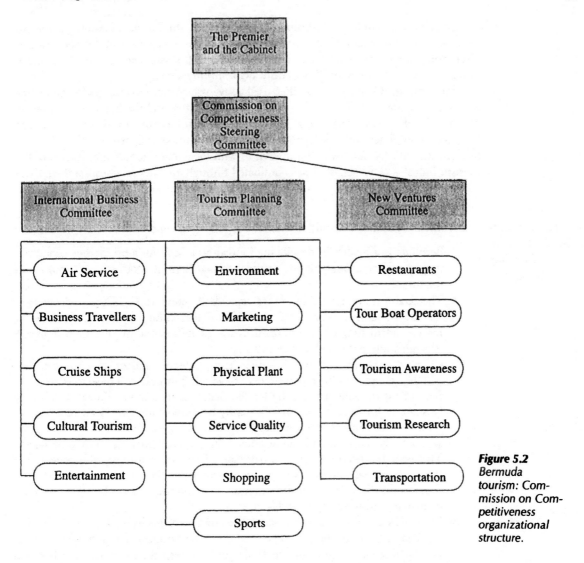

Figure 5.2
Bermuda tourism: Commission on Competitiveness organizational structure.

tourism industry in island life, the general population was considered to be an important part of the tourist experience, and the support of the community was considered essential. As Haywood (1988, p. 105) observed:

> . . . in the way tourism is planned . . . the underlying theme is a call to include a greater degree of public participation. The rationale is as follows: the positive and negative aspects of tourism (economic, social and ecological) have their most profound impact in and on host communities. Whenever tourism activity is concentrated in time and space, builds rapidly, dominates a local economy, disrupts community life, endangers the environment, and ignores community input, the seeds of discontent are sown. Whenever the residents' thresholds of tolerance for tourism and tourists are exceeded, host–tourist encounters sour, and the industry has a tendency to peak, fade and self-destruct.

To achieve a high level of community involvement, the Tourism Planning Committee created 16 task forces under the leadership of prominent local stakeholders. At any given time, this structure resulted in approximately 120 persons being actively involved in the process of examination. It was truly a community activity.

The Tourism Planning Committee used a seven-stage planning model for its investigation (see Figure 5.3). Within this model, the committee and the task forces utilized a number of techniques for soliciting information and opinion from a wide cross section of the population. These included public forums, focus groups with senior stakeholders in the tourism industry, and over 100 interviews with local and international leaders of the tourism industry. This activity was coordinated through an external consultant who was funded through the Tourism Planning Committee chairperson's bank.

The Findings of the Tourism Planning Committee

The Tourism Planning Committee reached the following conclusions:

- Bermuda is a model for developing tourism as a basis for a prosperous economy. Its past success should provide confidence that Bermuda tourism can improve in the future.
- The economy and quality of life are dependent upon tourism. Current declines in tourism are serious and will not correct themselves without concerted effort. Nothing can adequately replace tourism in the island's economy, not even a greatly expanded international business sector.
- Changes in world tourism, including new products, choices, and competition, will dictate many of the circumstances to which Bermuda will have to adapt.
- Bermuda is dependent upon the United States for its tourism market. It is losing its share of this market, and not primarily because of the American economy or international conflicts such as the Gulf War. The American market cannot be satisfactorily replaced with some other source market such as Europe or Japan. This issue has been the focus of national debate between those who believe that the decrease was due primarily to the downturn of the American economy and those who believe that there are structural issues in the industry brought on by the changing tourism industry worldwide.
- Bermuda's essential tourism product (the large hotels) is losing business. This has resulted in losses in jobs, income, and domestic business. Large hotels have not been profitable as a group since 1987 and have seen their occupancies drop, on average, from 68.0 percent in 1987 to 55.9 percent in 1992 (Commission on Competitiveness, 1994, p. 62).
- The cruise ship visitor cannot replace the stayover visitor for economic impact on the island.
- Seasonality is a problem. Although its pattern has not changed significantly in recent years, it appears worse because all tourism has declined.
- There are concerns about the lack of awareness and appreciation for tourism. Some Bermudians do not appreciate or respect the need to accommodate tourists on the island.
- Management–labor problems exacerbate issues of hotel profitability, labor recruitment, costs, and respect for the industry.
- Bermuda has major deficiencies relating to the product, information, and access

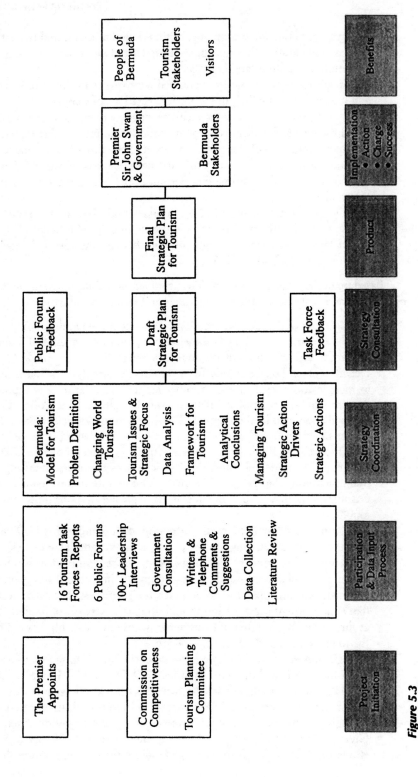

Figure 5.3
Bermuda tourism: Strategic reassessment planning process. (Source: LDR International in Commission on Competitiveness Final Report, 1994. Courtesy of the Tourism Planning Committee of the Commission on Competitiveness.)

with respect to providing shopping, dining, entertainment, and recreational experiences to the tourist. Bermuda has not capitalized on its natural resources, marine environment, culture, and heritage.

- Bermuda's tourism product is overpriced compared with some of its competitors, and it does not satisfy the price–value expectations of visitors.
- Bermuda's problems are not the result of inadequate marketing or promotion, but rather the result of inadequate product policies and price–value issues.
- Bermuda's source market is small, exclusive, and affluent. This market is targeted by much of Bermuda's competition, including destinations in the United States. It is no longer valid to assume that Bermuda does not have serious competition for this market niche.
- Bermuda must accept the need for fundamental change. It cannot dictate the terms of world tourism. This will require significant investment of resources and effort. There are no simple, single, or quick fixes for improving the tourism industry in Bermuda (Conlin, 1995, pp. 198–199).

Based upon these conclusions, the Tourism Planning Committee made the following recommendations aimed at rejuvenating the island's tourism industry:

- Management of the tourism industry must place more emphasis on product policy and development through a comprehensive planning process that incorporates input from various sectors of the industry. Suggestions were made to expand the Department of Tourism's role from one that is essentially a marketing function to include some level of responsibility for strategic planning and product policy determination and implementation. The formation of a Policy Coordination Council appointed by the premier, Tourism Action Councils representing various sectors of the industry, and a Tourism Education Council to coordinate education, training, and tourism awareness activities was recommended. The Tourism Planning Committee also presented various options for restructuring the department, including the QUANGO concept (Quasi-Autonomous Non-Governmental Organization) that would provide it with greater responsibility and more autonomy.
- The tourism product (i.e., events, accommodation and eating facilities, transportation, amenities, retailing, public places, and recreational activities) requires enhancement. The Tourism Planning Committee recommended the creation of the Bermuda Development Fund to attract domestic investment and to provide capital for small business operators to enhance their services. They also recommended that enhancement coordination should utilize the services of national bodies such as the Bermuda Chamber of Commerce, whose membership has a direct stake in the improvement of the tourism industry.
- Recognizing that poor management–labor relations relating to wages and workers' rights have bedeviled the industry since the 1970s, a Task Force on Employment should be created to depolarize the two sides through the greater dissemination of information, education, and development of innovative human resource strategies including worker empowerment, involvement, and recognition schemes.
- Given the importance of large hotels to the continued viability of the industry, efforts must be made to improve profitability through expanding the season by

developing innovative packages that reflect emerging trends (i.e., cultural tourism and ecotourism). Cost structures should be reviewed within the context of Bermuda's highly oligopolistic economy, and relief should be sought to allow the hotels to become more competitive.

- Recognizing the relationship between price–value perceptions and repeat visitation, value-added strategies including the offering of a greater range of no-cost or sponsored activities were recommended. Again, the need for a review of the island's cost structures to bring costs more in line with competing destinations was emphasized.

- In its adoption of an inclusive planning process, the Tourism Planning Committee recognized the fundamental role the population plays in determining the quality of the product and the level of service provided for tourists. Accordingly, creation of a Tourism Education Council was recommended to facilitate education and human resource development within the industry and also to encourage development of national programs of certification and recognition, all of which were considered to be critical to enhancing the perceptions the population has of the industry and its value as a career choice.

- Although the superior reputation of the island for marketing was acknowledged, it was recommended that greater use be made of data base marketing techniques and cooperative advertising. Ongoing research into emerging niches was recommended to provide a basis for determining market opportunities that would fit with Bermuda's resources (Conlin, 1995, pp. 199–200).

The final stage saw the Tourism Planning Committee present these findings and recommendations to the government. The report also contained recommended timelines for implementation of the recommendations, and it identified local organizations and people who should be responsible for implementation and ongoing management.

POSTSCRIPT

The government did not act on the Tourism Planning Committee's report immediately. Given the underlying debate between the economic cyclists and structuralists, it is not surprising that its adoption and implementation have been slow. In part, this reflects the interdependency of the tourism industry with other economic sectors in Bermuda. A wide range of recommendations relating to the international business sector, along with proposals for new economic activity in general, must be considered when evaluating recommendations specific to tourism. Consequently, the process of adoption is slow and involves trade-offs between competing interests. Inevitably, in a small island community like Bermuda, wide-ranging recommendations that would create fundamental changes in how the tourism industry is planned and managed would encounter political opposition as well.

In the meantime, in early 1994 the industry believed that the worst was over and that tourism would experience a resurgence. Early data suggested that visitor arrivals were increasing. However, this was not to be the case. Notwithstanding the early optimism, as Table 5.3 indicates, total arrivals in 1994 were 588,700, a 4 percent increase over 1993's total of 566,300. Perhaps indicative of some of the changes taking place in the resort industry, the increase in 1994 was primarily in cruise arrivals. While cruise arrivals increased 12.3 percent from 153,944 in 1993 to 172,865 in 1994, the corresponding increase for conventional arrivals was only 0.8 percent.

The news was not all bad. The 1994 Conde Nast Traveler "Gold List" Poll ranked three of Bermuda's hotels—The Southampton Princess, The Princess, and The Elbow Beach Hotel—among the top 50 tropical resorts in the world. In the Caribbean tropical resort category, another seven Bermuda hotels ranked in the top 50, including Bermuda College's training facility, The Stonington Beach Hotel. Interestingly, in the price–value category of the poll, Bermuda came out ahead in the Caribbean tropical resort category, with the island's most expensive property, Horizons, being less expensive than 35 other properties in the category (*Bermuda Sun*, 1994, p. 3).

Nonetheless, many questions remain. How is Bermuda going to plan for the future development of its tourism industry given the continuing stagnation in conventional arrivals? How is it going to proceed with the management of its industry? Will it adopt a more inclusive planning process as other destinations have done? Who will make these decisions?

NOTES

1. See Chapter 1 for a more detailed discussion on growth in international tourism.
2. See Chapters 3, 4, 6, 9, and 28 for additional overviews of the toursim planning process.
3. See Chapters 6, 24, 26, and 28 for additional discussion regarding strategic planning, situation analysis, and SWOT analysis.
4. See Chapters 4, 7, 8, 17, 18, 22, and 23 for additional discussion regarding sustainable tourism and sustainable tourism development.
5. See Chapters 9, 22, and 23 for detailed discussions on the carrying capacity concept and limits of acceptable change.
6. See Chapters 9, 11, 12, and 14–19 for further discussion regarding community attitudes, community-based planning, and public consultation processes.
7. See Chapters 2, 3, 7, and 28 for further discussion and examples of the tourist area cycle of evolution.

REFERENCES

Bermuda Department of Tourism. 1991. A *Statistical Review of the Years 1980–1989*.

Bermuda Department of Tourism. 1994. *Bermuda in Perspective*. January 27.

Bermuda Department of Tourism. 1995. *Bermuda in Perspective*. February 2.

Bermuda Sun, December 30, 1994.

Butler, R. 1980. The concept of the tourist area cycle of evolution: implications for management of resources, *Canadian Geographer*, 24(1), 5–12.

Commission on Competitiveness, Final Report. 1994. Available through the Centre for Tourism Research and Innovation, Bermuda College, P.O. Box DV356, Devonshire DV BX, Bermuda.

Conlin, M.V. 1995. Rejuvenation planning for island tourism: the Bermuda example. In M.V. Conlin and T. Baum (eds.), *Island Tourism: Management Principles and Practice*. Chichester, UK: John Wiley & Sons, pp. 181–202.

Conlin, M.V. and T. Baum. 1995. Island tourism: an introduction. In M.V. Conlin and T. Baum (eds.), *Island Tourism: Management Principles and Practice*. Chichester, UK: John Wiley & Sons, pp. 3–13.

de Albuquerque, K. and J.L. McElroy. 1992. Caribbean small-island tourism styles and sustainable strategies, *Environmental Management*, 16(5), 619–632.

Gravel, J. 1979. Tourism and recreational planning: a methodological approach to the valuation and calibration of tourism activities. In W.T. Perks and I.M. Robinson (eds.), *Urban and Regional Planning in a Federal State: The Canadian Experience*. Stroudsburg, Pennsylvania: Dowden, Hutchinson & Ross, pp. 122–134.

Haywood, K.M. 1986. Can the tourist-area life cycle be made operational? *Tourism Management*, September, 154–167.

Haywood, K.M. 1988. Responsible and responsive tourism planning in the community, *Tourism Management*, June, 105–118.

Helber, L.E. 1995. Redeveloping mature resorts in new markets. In M. V. Conlin and T. Baum (eds.), *Island Tourism: Management Principles and Practice*. Chichester, UK: John Wiley & Sons, pp. 105–113.

Hoffman, J.J. and M.J. Schniederjans. 1990. An international strategic management/goal programming model for structuring global expansion decisions in the hospitality industry: the case of Eastern Europe, *International Journal of Hospitality Management*, 9(3), 175–190.

Mathieson, A. and G. Wall. 1982. *Tourism: Economic, Physical and Social Impacts*. London: Longman.

Morrison, A.M. 1989. *Hospitality and Travel Marketing*. Albany, New York: Delmar Publishers.

Murphy, P.E. 1980. Perceptions and preferences of decision-making groups in tourist centers: a guide to planning strategy. In D.E. Hawkins, E.L. Shafer, and J.M. Rovelstad (eds.), *Tourism Planning and Development Issues*. Washington, D.C.: George Washington University Press, pp. 356–367.

Murphy, P.E. 1985. *Tourism: A Community Approach*. New York: Routledge.

Patton, A. 1968. Top management's stake in the product life cycle. In S. H. Britt and H. W. Boyd, Jr. (eds.), *Marketing Management and Administrative Action*. New York: McGraw-Hill, pp. 321–331.

Riley, C.W. 1991. Controlling growth while maintaining your customer base. *Proceedings of the 22nd Travel and Tourism Research Association Conference*, Long Beach, California, pp. 65–73.

Stonich, S.C., J.H. Sorensen, and A. Hundt. 1995. Ethnicity, class, and gender in tourism development: the case of the Bay Islands, Honduras, *Journal of Sustainable Tourism*, 3(1), 1–28.

Wilkinson, P. 1987. Tourism in small island nations: a fragile dependence, *Leisure Studies*, 6, 153–177.

Zuill, W.S. 1973. *The Story of Bermuda and Her People*. London: Macmillan Education Ltd.

¶ | PROBLEM SOLVING AND DISCUSSION ACTIVITIES

1. Select three countries that exhibit a heavy dependence on tourism and determine the existence and nature of controls relating to the growth of the tourism industry in each of these nations. Based on the social, political, economic, and ecological characteristics of these countries, prepare a critique of the policies in place (or lack thereof) in each country.

2. What are strengths and weaknesses of the community participation process that was implemented in Bermuda? What challenges impact the implementation of a community-inclusive planning process? What could be done to maximize community input in Bermuda in the future?

3. Conduct a review of the literature to trace the evolution and current status of developing and implementing national tourism awareness strategies. What factors can render such programs effective or ineffective?

4. What are advantages and disadvantages of pursuing a narrow-approach to defining the market such as is the case in Bermuda? What recommendations would you offer to Bermuda with respect to its market development in the future?

5. Prioritize the Tourism Planning Committee's recommendations for addressing the challenges Bermuda faces as a tourist destination and provide a justification for your suggestions.

6. One of the challenges Bermuda faces involves dealing with seasonal patterns in visitation. Undertake a review of secondary sources to determine how other destinations have addressed seasonality problems. What are some of the difficulties that any destination might face in attempting to smooth out seasonal patterns in visitation? What should Bermuda do?

7. It was suggested that Bermuda should consider value-added strategies to enhance the relationship between price–value perceptions and repeat visitation. Identify some examples of value-added strategies that might be considered on Bermuda.

8. How should Bermuda plan for the future development of its tourism industry given the continuing stagnation in conventional arrivals? Are the recommendations outlined by the Tourism Planning Committee sufficient to address the challenges? Why or why not? How should Bermuda proceed with the management of its industry? Who should make these decisions?

6

Strategic Tourism Planning in Fiji

AN OXYMORON OR PROVIDING FOR COHERENCE
IN DECISION MAKING?

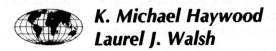

K. Michael Haywood
Laurel J. Walsh

⚡|KEY LEARNING POINTS

- Tourism and tourism development are prone to fluctuation, randomness, and unpredictability. Tourism can cohere to a more predictable form, but this requires the presence of guiding visions, rules to shape behavior, and strong organizational values.

- Strategic planning focuses on determining the future and how to get there. A major goal is to balance external uncontrollable factors and internal controllable factors in an effort to capitalize on opportunities and obviate threats.

- The values and expectations of the leadership as well as the ethics of the society and other aspects of social and corporate responsibility must be considered when formulating strategic plans.

- Strategy formulation is an immensely complex process that must be informed, responsive, and integrative. It must be directed at helping people and organizations to maintain focus, rather than attempting hands-on control.

INTRODUCTION

International tourism is one of the most important and fastest growing aspects of global trade. However, in many regions, supply is growing more rapidly than demand, thereby creating an intensely competitive marketplace. Although tourism has been embraced by both developed and developing countries as a means to stimulate the economy, generate employment opportunities, and assist with infrastructure development, questions about whether tourism's benefits are being optimized are becoming more common.

Governments and communities have begun to recognize that tourism has broader implications than simply economic. Political, sociocultural, and ecological considerations can no longer be looked upon as secondary issues. Consequently, governments and communities are beginning to play more active roles in affecting the evolution of tourism industries. More than the existence of interesting natural and cultural resources is required for success in the tourism industry.

This chapter suggests that conventional master planning is no longer sufficient to enable tourist destinations to maintain a strong market and competitive presence. A new attitude toward strategic planning is suggested—one that acknowledges the importance of informed decision making, yet also recognizes that the competitive environment is not static and, therefore, encourages responsiveness and flexibility.

A discussion of tourism in Fiji highlights factors (internal and external) that influence the evolution of tourism. In the early history of the Pacific, Fiji was considered the crossroads of ancient voyagers between Melanesia, Micronesia, and Polynesia. Today, Fiji is still considered as the hub of travel in the South Pacific. Yet, tourism within this archipelago of islands appears to be experiencing challenges relating to access, competition, infrastructure/superstructure, and social pressures. Indeed, visitor numbers in the early 1990s have declined.

Following a discussion of strategic planning approaches, information relating to tourism in Fiji in the late 1980s and early 1990s that was synthesized from various travel publications and planning documents is presented. The chapter concludes with a hypothetical scenario around which the problem solving and discussion activities are constructed. This chapter differs somewhat from others in that the authors provide a general description of a situation rather than illustrate effective or ineffective strategic planning processes.

STRATEGIC APPROACHES TO TOURISM PLANNING: CONTEMPORARY PERSPECTIVES AND ISSUES

The traditional strategic planning model derives from a SWOT analysis[1] (analysis of strengths, weaknesses, opportunities, and threats) and is founded on the belief that the "heart" of strategy formulation involves defining the "fit" between internal and external factors. Strategy is developed subsequent to identifying (1) threats and opportunities arising from external uncontrollable environments (i.e., market, competitive, economic, sociocultural, technological, political, ecological) and (2) strengths and weaknesses of the tourism organization, the natural and cultural resources, and the communities and businesses providing the tourism experience (Heath and Wall, 1992).

Whereas exogenous factors create conditions that affect market and competitive positioning, the internal environment has implications for whether the organization and the destination are equipped to seize opportunities and mitigate threats (Heath and Wall, 1992). The extent to which strengths and weaknesses constrain or positively affect ability to counter threats and/or capitalize on opportunities is central to the formulation of strategic plans (Heath and Wall, 1992). The values and expectations of the leadership as well as the ethics of the society and other aspects of social and corporate responsibility should also be taken into consideration. Figure 6.1 provides an overview of a strategic planning framework.

Strategic planning as a ritualized, rational, and formal process has come under attack (Mintzberg, 1994). The failures of strategic planning have been catastrophic at times and

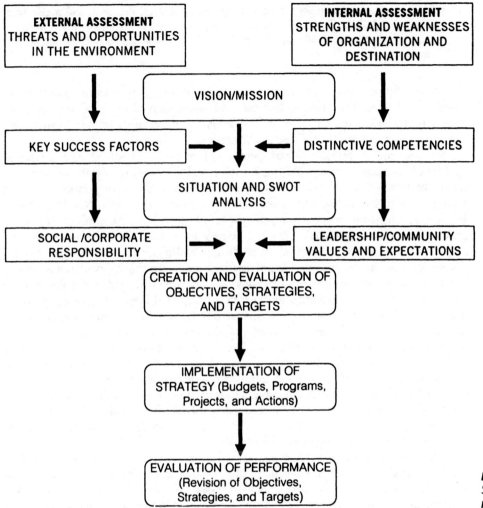

Figure 6.1
Strategic tourism planning model.

litter the organizational landscape. Why? First, the planning process is highly political. Second, the objective detachment that characterizes most planning can undermine commitment to the strategic planning process. Third, the tendency toward conservatism and an obsession with control often breed a climate of conformity and inflexibility that favors incremental and generic change focused on the short run. The most fundamental criticism is that strategic planning is an oxymoron. Strategy cannot be planned because planning is about analysis whereas strategy is about synthesis (Mintzberg, 1994). As Langley (1988) noted:

> Formal strategic planning and strategic planners do not make strategic decisions. People and organizations make strategic decisions and sometimes they use strategic planning as a discipline within which to do this, or seem to do this. Strategic planning supplies a forum for announc-

ing, setting, negotiating, rationalizing and legitimizing strategic decisions, and it also offers means for controlling their implementation. These roles are as important if not more important than the more usually noted role of providing information to improve the content of strategy.

Strategy formulation is an immensely complex process that must be informed, responsive, and integrative. The skills, time, and inclinations of planners must be combined with the authority, information, and flexibility of managers so that organizations and destinations can master the present and preempt the future.

From a tourism organization's perspective, this means that tremendous effort should be devoted to selecting appropriate target markets and determining how the organization can make best use of its unique competencies. From a long-term perspective, effort should be redirected to determining the future and, more importantly, how to get there. While the strategic intent of many organizations is to provide for the needs of customers, achieve functional area compliance, and manage for results, planning necessitates reshaping organizations to compete more effectively, finding new and bolder ways of conducting business, and rethinking ways of discovering and creating an exhilarating future.

With numerous tourism organizations working somewhat independently of each other, the importance of planning for tourism on a regional level has assumed increased importance. There are disparate concerns relating to how to (1) create interesting and attractive destinations, (2) generate visitation from appropriate visitor segments, (3) adjust the flow, timing, and duration of stays to correspond to seasonal, business, and leisure cycles, (4) facilitate the development and enhancement of attractions, accommodations, and amenities, (5) satisfy access and infrastructure requirements, (6) encourage investment and provision of a stable environment for businesses, (7) sustain the natural, cultural, and built environments, (8) enhance the quality of life for people who reside in the destinations, and (9) enhance the quality of experience for those who wish simply to experience the essence of the places themselves.

The type and amount of planning, as well as the people involved, vary depending on the availability of market intelligence, political agendas, the desire to cooperate, dispositions toward planning, the importance accorded to updating existing plans, and/or whether an imbalance between long-range planning and immediate project planning has been recognized.

The notion that tourism planning at a regional level needs to be considered from a strategic perspective is quite recent. It results from recognizing that destinations have certain characteristics that determine visitor interest and that something can be gained from responding to the changes in the external environment. For example, given the dynamics of the social, political, economic, and physical environment, no longer is it expected that the future will mirror much of the past or present. Turbulence, uncertainty, and surprise require a different approach to planning and management. Previous planning approaches that could be built on assumptions of general stability and continuity no longer suffice.

The very pace of change poses challenges to planning. Technology, particularly communications technology, has caused an acceleration in many dimensions of life, as well as recognition of the interdependence of organizations. Hence, organizations and communities must identify and create partnerships. Adaptability and versatility are at a premium. Systematically developing and carefully assessing alternative courses of action become important features of the planning process. It is now perhaps more important to have contingency plans rather than a fixed master plan, regardless of how well developed or inspiring it may be.

Corporate decisions on profit targets, market share objectives, and revenue expectations made in distant urban centers around the world have direct effects on the scale and level of tourism activity. Understanding the emerging external development trends and translating these into localized implications are now key activities in tourism planning. Knowledge is at a premium and has assumed strategic importance.

Complex cross-impacts create challenges for the development of tourism. Increasingly, there appears to be cynicism regarding the effectiveness of political representatives. Regional interests, consumer and environmental lobbies, aboriginal interests, and other special interest groups tend to circumvent, if not supplant, the conventional geographically placed constituency and its elected representatives. These developments, combined with new demographic realities, a move away from material greed to a more quality-conscious consumer, and a decoupling of employment expansion from growth in production (through more efficient product and management techniques), underscore a need to plan and manage differently.

These cursory comments on tourism planning and the need to formulate strategy in a responsive and integrative way suggest that a strategic approach to planning should (1) provide for course correction, contingency, and tactical maneuverability, (2) clarify options, (3) assess and allow for risk, (4) provide coherence for decision making, (5) systematically identify control points and leverage, (6) integrate decisions across levels and functions, (7) provide opportunities for more systematic organizational and community development, (8) highlight the need for managing performance, and (9) foster team building.

In contrast to traditional tourism "master" planning, the more strategic approach should (1) focus more on alternatives or options, (2) recognize planning as a subset of management, (3) assess capacity to act, (4) make fewer assumptions about actors, activities, protocols, and other means as constraints, (5) place more emphasis on key or pivotal decisions and choices, (6) insist that people in key roles and functions pay attention to the agenda associated with answering questions such as "what type of community and quality of life are desired" and "what type of tourism is desired," (7) concentrate on issues that bring a commitment to develop a game plan, (8) identify stakeholders and ensure their involvement, and (9) create a change process and management orientation.

As an economic, social, and quintessential human activity, tourism is idolized for its benefits as well as chastised for its costs. In reality, it is always a mixture of both and, consequently, engenders "love–hate" factions, whether at an organizational or a community level. The typical response is to interfere, stabilize, and shore things up. In other words, bring in the strategic planners to develop a strategic plan and control tourism!

What should be obvious is that tourism and tourism development have always been prone to fluctuation, randomness, and unpredictability. This is tourism's natural state. It is virtually impossible to state with certainty what is going to happen next. Tourism can cohere to a more predictable form, but this requires the presence of self-referential principles: guiding visions, strong organizational values, and rules to shape behavior.

The strategic planning approach succeeds by helping people to maintain focus, rather than attempting hands-on control. In this way, the flexibility and responsiveness that tourism organizations crave can be provided. The key to successful strategic planning is to shape organizations and communities through concepts, not elaborate rules and structures.

The remainder of this chapter presents background relating to tourism in Fiji and the circumstances influencing the need for strategic planning initiatives.

FIJI: LOCATIONAL CONTEXT AND BACKGROUND

Location Fiji is located in the South Pacific approximately 1875 miles (3000 kilometers) east of Australia and about 1200 miles (1930 kilometers) south of the equator (see Figure 6.2a). The Fiji archipelago comprises over 320 islands (7100 square miles; 18,330 square kilometers), 105 of which are uninhabitable. Each island is quite distinctive. The two largest are Viti Levu and Vanua Levu (see Figure 6.2b), both of which are extinct volcanoes that arise abruptly from the sea.

Fiji has thousands of streams and rivers, the largest being the Kioa River on Viti Levu, which is navigable for 80 miles (130 kilometers). Mount Victoria, also on Viti Levu, is the country's highest peak (4430 feet; 1350 meters). The Great Sea Reef is located between Viti Levu and Vanua Levu. The Astrolabe Reef, south of Viti Levu, offers spectacular coral reefs and diving. Another reef extends for 19 miles (30 kilometers) off Taveuni.

Climate Fiji enjoys a South Sea tropical climate. Maximum summer temperatures (January, February) average 86°F (30°C), with a mean minimum of 73°F (23°C). The winter average maximum (July, August) is 79°F (26°C) and the mean minimum is 68°F (20°C). Temperatures are much cooler in the interior uplands of the larger islands. A cooling trade wind blows from the east–south–east for most of the year.

The People Fiji's population is about 780,000 people (1993), 50 percent of whom are of mixed Poly-
and the nesian and Melanesian ancestry (native Fijians) and 46 percent are Indian. The remain-
Culture der are Chinese, Asian, and European. Approximately 90 percent of Fiji's population is rural, mostly confined to the principal islands of Viti Levu, Vanua Levu, Taveuni, and Ovalau. Suva (Viti Levu), the capital, had a population of over 80,000 in the early 1990s.

English is the official language. Fijian and Hindustani are the next most common languages, although Chinese and Urdu are also spoken. Most native Fijians are Christian (Methodist and Roman Catholic), while the majority of Indo-Fijians are Hindu. A strictly fundamentalist Methodist version of Christianity is enshrined in and informs the Fijian constitution. Muslims comprise about 10 percent of the population.

Local people respect and strive to sustain tradition. Customs govern every aspect of life, whether it be the building of a house or manner of dress. One ritual involves the presentation of a *tabua* (sperm whale tooth) at births, deaths, marriages, and state and provincial functions. Traditional Fijian society is based on the principles of village or communal life where obligations and rewards are shared equally. If someone asks *kerekere* (please may I have a favor), it is socially unacceptable to refuse. Approximately 83 percent

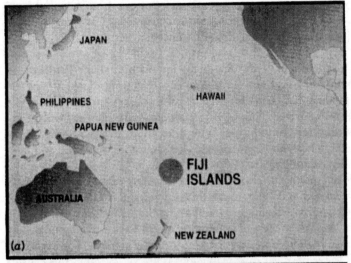

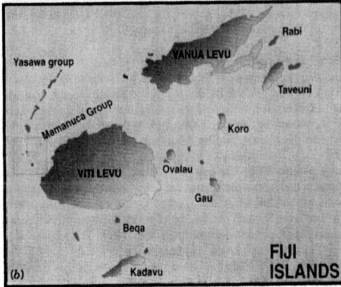

Figure 6.2a
Fiji's location. (Courtesy of Fiji Visitor Bureau.)
Figure 6.2b
Main islands of the Fiji archipelago. (Courtesy of Fiji Visitor Bureau.)

of the land is owned by Fijians as communal property and may not be leased without the consent of the Native Land Trust Board, the government agency responsible for administering leases of native land. A village is led by a hereditary chief (a *Ratu*). Tourists cannot visit a Fijian village unless invited and accompanied.

Another ritual involves the drinking of *kava* [also known as *yaqona* (pronounced "yang gona") or grog]. *Kava* is the pulverized root of a pepper plant that is mixed with water and, when consumed, produces a mildly intoxicating effect. *Kava* is prepared whenever there is a special occasion, but it is also drunk when people meet socially.

Those taking part in a *yaqona* ceremony dress in *masi* (cloth made from a special bark) decorated with green leaves. It is tradition for visitors to local villages to bring a kilo of *kava* to present to the chief (the act of giving this gift is known as *sevusevu*).

The Economy   Fiji's economy is largely agricultural, with sugar being the main product. Tourism and agriculture comprise about 90 percent of Fiji's foreign export earnings. Copra, once the second most important product, has been overtaken by gold, fish, and timber. Low-grade copper deposits have been discovered, although it is not clear whether they will be exploited. There are a number of light industrial enterprises producing goods such as cement, paint, cigarettes, biscuits, flour, nails, barbed wire, furniture, matches, and footwear, mainly for domestic consumption.

The government is attempting to attract manufacturers for export by offering tax incentives. Textiles have started to develop under this regime, and it is hoped that shipping services (repair yards and boat building) as well as the timber industry will develop along the same lines. In the past, trade and commerce in Fiji have been dominated by the Indian population, many of whom are now trying to leave the country. The expiration in 1991 of many Indian leases on sugar cane plantations is one of several factors causing unease. Fiji's largest trading partners are Australia, New Zealand, the United States, and the United Kingdom.

History and   The indigenous islanders were first introduced to Europeans in the mid-seventeenth cen-
Government   tury when traders, missionaries, and shipwrecked sailors came to the area. As the rivalry of the European imperial powers spread in the Pacific during the late nineteenth century, Fiji fell under British control. The British brought in a large number of workers from India to develop a plantation economy. By the 1960s, Indian descendants formed the majority of the community on the islands, leading to social tensions between them and the indigenous Fijians.

Indians won a majority parliament for the first time in the elections of 1987. This triggered an army *coup d'état* to ensure the preservation of native Fijian rights. There was an interim military government, pending a new constitution. Constitutional reforms were discussed and approved by the Great Council of Chiefs comprising the hereditary leaders. Negotiations involving leaders of all parties began in September 1987. The results led to another coup at the end of that month and several key aides were removed.

With the governor resigning, the foundation was set for Fiji to withdraw from the Commonwealth. A large-scale emigration, particularly from the Indian community, could have ill effects on the economy. A new constitution allowing for a bicameral legislature comprising a 70-seat house of representatives and a senate of chiefs with 34 appointed members came into force in July 1990. The seats in the house are divided along ethnic lines, with 37 seats elected by native Fijians, 27 by Indians, and the remainder by others. Today, Fiji is a republic.

TRANSPORTATION AND TOURISM RESOURCES

Transportation   Fiji is accessible from most parts of the world (see Figure 6.2a and Table 6.1) by either Air Pacific (the local airline) or Air New Zealand, Qantas, and Polynesian Airlines. Nadi

TABLE 6.1
Fiji's Proximity to Major Markets

Origin Market Area	Flying Time to Nadi Airport (Hours)
Vancouver, B.C. (Canada)	12.0
San Francisco, California	11.0
Los Angeles, California	11.0
Tokyo, Japan	6.0
Hawaii	6.0
Melbourne, Australia	4.5
Sydney, Australia	4.0
Brisbane, Australia	3.8
Auckland, New Zealand	3.0
Cook Islands	2.0

International Airport (pronounced "nan dee") on Viti Levu is the gateway for international travelers. One implication of Fiji's strategically important location is the promotion of regional tour packages using Fiji as a hub.

The reduction in airline capacity on North American routes is a serious problem not only for Fiji but also for the region as a whole, since Fiji is the gateway for the redistribution of visitors to other island countries. The withdrawal of Continental Airlines (due largely to a dispute with Australian authorities and Qantas) and Canadian Airlines has resulted in reduced seat capacity and the loss of promotional and sales support. Restoration and maintenance of withdrawn schedules and capacity are vital.

Fiji boasts an extensive network of air routes, boats, and bus and taxi services to facilitate movement within and between islands. All the major rental car companies are represented, with most maintaining offices at Nadi International Airport or in the urban centers of Suva and Lautoka.

Accommodations The number of visitor accommodations has grown from approximately 523 rooms in 1960 to 4365 rooms in 1990 (125 accommodation facilities). By 1992–1993, there were at least 128 properties concentrated primarily on Viti Levu, Vanua Levu, Taveuni, and Ovalau (see Table 6.2). Much of the growth in the accommodations sector occurred in the early 1970s. Only one major new hotel, the Hyatt Regency on the Coral Coast (Viti Levu), was built between 1974 and 1986. Fiji's hotels are primarily small-scale operations typically located on the outer islands, or budget hotels on the main islands. The chain-affiliated resorts (e.g., Hyatt, Sheraton, Travelodge, Raffles, Regent) target upscale and mid-market international visitors. Independent North American visitors tend to select such resorts. The average annual occupancy hovers around the 50 percent mark or lower.

During the period from 1988 to 1990, around 16 new resorts were developed. These mainly small resorts located on the islands off Viti Levu cater to the middle and luxury market segments. Two vacant hotel properties were reopened during this period, and some major upgrading and expansion work has been undertaken at existing resorts. In

TABLE 6.2
Distribution of Hotel Properties in Fiji in the Early 1990s

Area	Main Island(s)	Number of Properties	Percent of Total
Nadi	Viti Levu	32	25.0
Lautoka Area	Viti Levu	9	7.0
Nadi Offshore	Mamanuca and Yasawa	14	10.9
Coral Coast	Viti Levu	17	13.3
Pacific Harbour	Viti Levu	5	3.9
Outer Islands	Ovalau	12	9.4
Northern	Vanau Levu, Taveuni, Laucala, Qamea, Matagi, Kaimbu	17	13.3
Suva	Viti Levu	13	10.2
Other Offshore	Kadavu, Beqa, Kaibu	9	7.0
Total		128	100.0

Sources: Adapted from various Fiji Islands visitor guides and tour operator brochures.

total, these developments increased the supply of accommodations by approximately 600 rooms. There is need to update a large portion of Fiji's lodging facilities.

It is estimated that 1200 additional, mainly upscale, hotel rooms are required to accommodate the anticipated increase in visitor levels in the medium term (for planning purposes an 8 percent growth in arrivals is forecast). Investment proposals valued at F$1200 million (US$800 to US$900 million) and involving more than 8000 rooms have been put forward by the private sector and approved by government. While not all will be implemented, a doubling of existing capacity is possible in the medium term.

Although the tourism industry remains concentrated in western Viti Levu and the surrounding offshore islands, there is also an expanding base for the industry around Savusavu (on Vanua Levu) and nearby Taveuni. There is scope for dispersion of the industry to spread benefits to a wider portion of the population.

Attractions Fiji's islands are islands of legends: Captain James Cook, William Bligh (after whom the islands were initially named), pirates, adventurers, sandalwood traders, *beche de mer* seekers, mercenaries, beachcombers, settlers, and civil wars.

Attractions are concentrated on Viti Levu. Among the most commonly promoted attractions are Nadi Town, Momi Bay Gun Site, Garden of the Sleeping Giant, the markets (located in every urban center including Nadi, Suva, Lautoka, and Sigatoka), the Fiji Museum in Thurston Gardens, the Cultural Centre and Marketplace, Orchid Island, Emperor Goldmine, and Kula Bird Park.

Fiji is a popular destination for fishing (about a dozen gamefishing operators), sailing (at least a dozen cruise and charter companies), and scuba diving (at least 20 operators). Dangerous reef waves prevent surfing. Various small cruise boats offer one- to three-day package tours to the outer islands. Whitewater rafting, jetboating, trekking, horseback riding, river rafting, and sightseeing tours are also available.

Fiji's climate is ideal for golf, an activity that is especially popular among Fijians and Japanese visitors. There are a number of courses (two 18-hole and numerous 9-hole). Upgrading to international standards would contribute to positioning Fiji in the upscale golf tourism market.

Fiji also stages various festivals: Fiji Day, the Sugar Festival (Lautoka in September), and the Hibiscus Festival (Suva in August). The Indian holiday for Divali coincides with the Hindu festival of lights. Visitors may not, however, appreciate the elaborate symbolism of the ritual codes that are suggestive of ethnic antagonism between Indians and Fijians.

Only about 17 percent of visitors in 1990 participated in organized island tours. This may be attributable to a combination of lack of overall marketing, limited tourist spending power, and lack of developed activities. There is consensus that more activities should be developed. Fiji has potential for festivals, events, marine life exhibits, and built attractions that will enhance the destination and encourage higher visitor spending. Some progress is being made (Bouma and Waikatakata national parks, Motoruki Inland Tours, Tavinin Hill fortification). Attention is also being paid to duty-free shopping (e.g., duties on major items sold by the trade were reduced in the 1991 budget).

Dining and Entertainment International cuisine is available but local Fijian and Indian cooking prevails. *Magiti* (banquet) Fijian fare is usually prepared in a *lovo* (an oven in the ground consisting of stones heated over a period of several hours by a fire of hardwood). The food, such as pork, chicken, fish, and various native root crops (*dalo* and *kumala*), is placed on hot stones wrapped in leaves, covered with additional layers of banana leaves, and then covered with earth to allow the food to cook slowly.

Local beers, wines, and distilled products are also available. Major hotels and resorts usually have entertainment in the evening and there are a number of night clubs, especially in Suva. Most of Fiji's social life, however, is in private clubs. Visitors can obtain temporary membership through hotels.

Meke (the occasion to sing and dance) is an important feature of the Fijian experience. All *meke* tell a story and are usually performed by large groups of people in colorful costumes. The repertoire varies from village to village. Vigorous club and spear dances depict past heroic actions, victories in war, and threats against enemies. There are also sitting and standing posture dances that are usually performed by women. Musical accompaniment and rhythm is provided by other performers who tell the story in song and keep the beat with hollow bamboo (the end is struck on the ground to produce a booming sound) and wooden *lali* (slit drums).

TOURISM INDUSTRY PERFORMANCE

Tourism is one of Fiji's two main industries, accounting for around 12 percent of gross domestic product (GDP) and 25 percent of foreign exchange earnings. It provides employment, directly and indirectly, for an estimated 20,000 people. An overview of tourism performance in the international tourism arena, the East Asia and Pacific region, and in Fiji is presented below.

International Tourism The East Asia and Pacific region experienced the largest gains in global tourist arrivals and receipts during the last decade. Its share of international tourist arrivals rose from 7 percent in 1980 to 19.9 percent in 1990, whereas its share of tourist receipts increased from 7.3 percent to 15.9 percent during this period (WTO, 1992).

Assuming sustained economic development and an absence of conflict and acts of terrorism, global international tourist arrivals of 515 million and 637 million are forecast for 1995 and 2005, respectively. Global international tourism receipts (at 1989 value) are projected to increase by 8 percent per annum, reaching more than US$527 billion by the year 2000. Regions recording higher than average growth of arrivals are likely to be Asia/ Oceania, the Americas, and Africa. While Europe's share of international arrivals is forecast to fall from 62 percent in 1989 to 53 percent by the year 2000, Asia/Oceania's share of international tourist arrivals is forecast to rise from 14.7 percent to 21.9 percent during this period. Asia/Oceania's share of global tourist receipts is likely to be even more significant, rising from 19.5 percent in 1989 to 30.5 percent in 2000 (WTO, 1991).

Tourism Performance in the East Asia and Pacific Region From 1970 to 1990, arrivals into the East Asia and Pacific region (EAP) more than quadrupled and receipts rose by a factor of nearly seven. Strong growth in the 1980s was interrupted by only two dips reflecting (1) the world recession during the early 1980s and (2) political events in China in 1989. EAP tourist arrivals increased 4.8 percent between 1989 and 1990 to 46.5 million, while tourist receipts increased 12.6 percent to US$36.5 billion (WTO, 1991). This growth was believed to be due to (1) recovery of travel to China and Hong Kong during the second half of 1990, (2) sustained business and holiday travel to and within the region, (3) an increased number of inbound visitors to Japan despite the strength of the yen, (4) outbound travel from Japan to Asian countries, and (5) creative promotion and advertising activities by all countries of the region in major generating markets.

Table 6.3 summarizes data for each of the EAP countries in 1989 and compares average annual growth rates for tourist arrivals and receipts between 1985 and 1989.

Some interesting points to note include the following:

- Countries generating the highest volumes of tourist arrivals are concentrated in Eastern and Southeastern Asia. Although Fiji reported the highest visitor arrivals within Melanesia, it ranked sixteenth overall in the region. Of the 20 countries with populations of less than 100,000, Fiji ranked fifth in terms of visitor arrivals, behind Macau, Brunei, the Mariana Islands, and Guam.
- The Marshall Islands, the Mariana Islands, and Indonesia reported the highest average annual growth in tourist arrivals between 1985 and 1989. Within Melanesia, only New Caledonia and Papua (New Guinea) evidenced growth rates within the top ten. Fiji ranked twenty-fourth overall in the region.
- The top ten tourism earners were located in Eastern Asia, Southeastern Asia, and Australia/New Zealand. Fiji ranked fourteenth overall in the region.
- The highest average annual growth rates for tourist receipts between 1985 and 1989 were evidenced in Korea, Australia, and Thailand. Melanesia, New Caledo-

TABLE 6.3
Tourism in the East Asia and Pacific Region, 1989

Countries	Population (Millions)	Tourist Arrivals	Average Growth 1985–1989 Arrivals %	Tourism Receipts (US$ Millions)	Average Growth 1985–1989 Receipts %	Tourism Receipts as Percent of GNP	Average Length of Stay (Nights)	Average Daily Spending (US$)	Number of Rooms	Occupancy Percent
Melanesia										
Fiji	0.74	251,000	2.4	189	6.5	16.24	8	94.12	3,725	48
New Caledonia	0.16	82,000	12.8	112	24.2	12.95	16	85.36	1,667	61
Papua, New Guinea	3.80	49,000	13.0	21	20.4	0.61	2	214.28	1,912	—
Solomon Islands	0.32	10,000	(4.5)	6	18.9	3.41	12	50.00	292	—
Vanuatu	0.15	24,000	(1.0)	19	—	14.96	13	60.90	464	40
Eastern Asia										
China	1,119.70	9,361,000	7.0	1,861	17.4	0.45	2	99.40	267,505	57
Hong Kong	5.76	5,361,000	12.3	4,595	26.6	7.29	3	285.71	27,031	79
Japan	123.12	2,676,000	6.2	3,143	28.9	0.11	13	90.35	206,802	71
Republic of Korea	42.38	2,728,000	17.8	3,558	45.9	1.69	5	260.70	36,211	62
Macau	0.45	1,008,000	8.1	—	—	—	1	—	4,808	75
Mongolia	2.09	237,000	2.2	—	—	—	—	—	550	—
Southeastern Asia										
Brunei	0.25	600,000	10.8	32	13.9	1.05	—	—	587	—
Indonesia	179.14	1,626,000	21.4	1,628	31.3	1.83	11	91.02	105,709	48
Lao People's Democratic Republic	3.87	25,000	(3.6)	—	—	—	—	—	—	—
Malaysia	16.96	3,954,000	7.8	839	7.8	2.35	4	53.05	43,149	55
Philippines	60.10	1,076,000	9.3	1,465	10.2	3.33	12	113.48	13,911	76
Singapore	2.68	4,397,000	12.6	2,907	15.0	10.06	3	220.38	23,948	86
Thailand	55.45	4,810,000	18.5	3,754	33.8	5.71	7	111.49	148,153	—
Viet Nam	65.88	167,000	7.1	59	22.7	0.85	5	70.66	7,477	—

TABLE 6.3
Tourism in the East Asia and Pacific Region, 1989 (Continued)

Countries	Population (Millions)	Tourist Arrivals	Average Growth 1985–1989 Arrivals %	Tourism Receipts (US$ Millions)	Average Growth 1985–1989 Receipts %	Tourism Receipts as Percent of GNP	Average Length of Stay (Nights)	Average Daily Spending (US$)	Number of Rooms	Occupancy Percent
Australia/New Zealand										
Australia	16.81	2,080,000	16.1	3,435	34.1	1.27	30	55.05	145,914	53
New Zealand	3.31	901,000	7.7	1,005	24.9	2.57	21	53.11	39,330	56
Micronesia										
Guam	0.12	310,000	(4.8)	605	27.2	80.67	4	487.90	4,000	84
Kiribati	0.07	3,000	—	1	—	1.96	—	—	—	—
Mariana Islands	0.02	334,000	23.8	261	21.2	—	3	260.48	1,824	71
Marshall Islands	0.34	7,000	36.8	—	—	—	—	—	74	—
Pohnpei	0.03	3,000	—	—	—	—	—	—	—	—
Truk State	0.04	4,000	—	—	—	—	—	—	—	—
Yap State	0.01	1,000	—	—	—	—	—	—	—	—
Polynesia										
American Samoa	0.04	47,000	11.9	9	6.5	4.11	—	—	282	58
Cook Islands	0.02	33,000	3.3	22	10.0	—	9	74.07	678	65
French Polynesia	0.19	140,000	3.5	157	12.5	5.41	9	124.60	2,824	51
Niue	0.01	1,000	(15.9)	—	—	—	—	—	—	—
Samoa	0.16	55,000	9.0	17	24.8	16.45	—	—	400	—
Tonga	0.12	21,000	10.7	9	15.8	8.82	—	—	445	55
Tuvalu	0.01	1,000	—	—	—	—	—	—	—	—

Note: — indicates that data are not available.
Source: WTO (1992).

nia, Papua (New Guinea), and the Solomon Islands all exhibited strong growth rates, whereas Fiji was tied for last place in the region with American Samoa.

- With few exceptions, tourism appears to be most important to countries with populations under 100,000 people. Fiji ranked third overall behind Guam and Samoa in terms of the percentage of GNP generated through tourism activity. Almost 81 percent of Guam's GNP is generated by tourism.
- The longest stays were reported in Australia and New Zealand. The next highest stays were in Melanesia (New Caledonia and Vanuatu) and Japan. Fiji was eleventh overall in the region.
- Guam, Hong Kong, and Korea generated the highest average daily spending per arrival. Papua (New Guinea) is the only Melanesian country within the top ten for this variable. Fiji ranked eleventh overall in the EAP, a higher ranking than was achieved with respect to overall receipts.
- The accommodations supply is concentrated in Eastern Asia, Southeastern Asia, and Australia and New Zealand. Although Fiji boasts the largest accommodations supply in Melanesia, it ranks fifteenth overall in the EAP region.
- The highest occupancy percentages were reported in Singapore, Guam, and Hong Kong. Fiji was tied for second last place with Indonesia. Only Vanuatu (Melanesia) reported lower occupancy rates than the former two destinations.

Tourism Performance in Fiji Mass tourism did not develop in Fiji until the late 1960s. However, tourism experienced rapid growth as visitor arrivals rose from 15,000 in 1960 to 110,000 in 1970, 190,000 in 1980, and 278,996 in 1990. Nevertheless, Fiji experienced slumps in tourism in the mid-1970s due to the global energy crisis and in 1983 and 1985, attributable to cyclones and Fiji's dollar appreciation over the Australian currency, and (3) in 1987, due to political unrest. The forecast for 1991 pointed to another shortfall, with just under 260,000 arrivals, due mostly to the global recession (see Table 6.4).

The mode of transportation used for accessing Fiji was relatively steady between 1988 and 1991. Virtually all of Fiji's tourists arrived by plane. When total visitor arrivals are considered (i.e., including cruise ship passengers), air arrivals represented slightly under 90 percent. Interestingly, the cruise ship market was nowhere as large as it was in 1985 when 69,433 cruise passengers arrived. Most cruise ship passengers stay two to three days. Total visitor receipts from international tourism amounted to F$335.9 million in 1990, representing a 126 percent increase from 1987. However, a decline of 8.4 percent in visitor receipts was projected for 1991.

Fiji does not appear to demonstrate the marked seasonality that is evidenced in some "tropical island" destinations (see Table 6.5). Interestingly, the period which North Americans and Europeans would refer to as "summer" consistently accounted for between 28 percent and 29 percent of total visitation. In the years following the coup in 1987, the third and fourth quarters generated higher levels of visitation than did the first and second quarters.

Throughout the period between 1987 and 1991, Australians and Americans represented the two primary geographic targets (see Table 6.6). However, the share of total visitors to Fiji generated by these two countries has declined. Although visitation from Australia grew in absolute terms in 1991 compared with 1987, Americans evidenced a dramatic decrease. Canada's share of total Fiji visitors has also declined. Growth markets appear to be Japan, the United Kingdom, New Zealand, and Other Europe.

TABLE 6.4
Visitation to Fiji, 1987–1991

Year	Tourist Arrivals			Cruise Ship Visitor Arrivals	Total Visitor Arrivals	Total Earnings (F$ Millions)
	Air	Sea	Total			
1987	186,587	3,279	189,866	32,564	222,430	148.4
1988	204,675	3,480	208,155	19,991	228,146	186.5
1989	245,596	4,969	250,565	30,932	281,497	295.1
1990	275,306	3,690	278,996	27,874	306,870	335.9
1991 (est.)	255,100	4,000	259,100	27,300	286,400	310.0
Average annual growth (%)	8.1	5.1	8.1	(4.3)	6.5	20.2

Source: Bureau of Statistics, Fiji (1992); Tourism Council of the South Pacific (1992).

AUSTRALIA AND NEW ZEALAND Visitation from Australia, Fiji's primary target and generally a long-stay market (average of 10–11 days), exhibited steady growth between 1987 and 1989, peaking in 1990 with 103,535 visitors. A 16 percent decrease from Australia was estimated between 1990 and 1991. In contrast, the New Zealand market showed continuous growth throughout this period, although the rate of growth appeared to be slowing. New Zealand was consistently Fiji's third most important source of visitation between 1988 and 1991.

TABLE 6.5
Seasonal Distribution of Visitation to Fiji, 1987–1990

Month	1987	Percent of Total[a]	1988	Percent of Total[a]	1989	Percent of Total[a]	1990	Percent of Total[a]
January	21,734	11.4	13,939	6.7	19,642	7.8	21,075	7.6
February	19,355	10.2	12,915	6.2	15,748	6.3	18,410	6.6
March	21,328	11.2	16,429	7.9	19,514	7.8	20,519	7.4
April	22,066	11.6	14,870	7.1	17,613	7.0	21,312	7.6
May	13,203	7.0	13,391	6.4	16,581	6.6	19,626	7.0
June	5,120	2.7	16,302	7.8	21,159	8.4	22,346	8.0
July	15,166	8.0	19,687	9.5	23,751	9.5	27,490	9.9
August	20,762	10.9	19,316	9.3	25,108	10.0	27,823	10.0
September	17,991	9.5	20,217	9.7	24,206	9.7	25,733	9.2
October	10,037	5.3	21,123	10.1	22,741	9.1	25,780	9.2
November	9,990	5.3	19,002	9.1	21,695	8.7	24,678	8.8
December	13,164	6.9	20,964	10.1	22,771	9.1	24,204	8.7
Total	189,916	100.0	208,155	99.9	250,529	100.0	278,996	100.0

[a] Numbers may not total 100 percent due to rounding.
Sources: Bureau of Statistics, Fiji (1992); Tourism Council of the South Pacific (1992).

TABLE 6.6
Visitation from Major Market Areas, 1987–1991

Market	1987 (%)	1988 (%)	1989 (%)	1990 (%)	1991(est.) (%)	Percent Change 1987–1991
Australia	34.4	36.2	38.7	37.1	33.4	32.4
New Zealand	8.5	10.3	11.2	10.5	11.8	88.9
United States	24.8	20.2	13.7	13.2	12.3	(32.4)
Canada	8.9	8.1	6.6	6.6	5.9	(9.6)
United Kingdom	4.5	4.1	4.6	6.0	6.4	93.9
Other Europe	7.8	9.8	9.5	9.8	10.1	78.0
Japan	2.9	1.6	5.5	7.7	10.7	406.6
Pacific Islands	5.9	6.8	7.2	6.3	6.2	44.4
Other Countries	2.4	2.8	2.9	2.7	3.2	82.6
Total	189,866	208,155	250,565	278,996	259,100	36.5

Note 1: Cruise ship passenger arrivals not included.
Note 2: Numbers may not total 100 percent due to rounding.
Sources: Bureau of Statistics, Fiji (1992); Tourism Council of the South Pacific (1992).

The growth potential of these traditional short-haul markets is not particularly remarkable because Fiji has already achieved considerable penetration. As Australians and New Zealanders discover other destinations, growth will be slow and accomplished only through tough, competitive action. "Aussies" and "Kiwis" have an in-depth awareness of Fiji due to proximity and marketing by wholesalers and other travel intermediaries. They are also extremely price-sensitive and have high multiple-occupancy levels.

CANADA AND THE UNITED STATES   The North American market appears to be in decline. The American market is a mature one. Tourists visit Fiji on multicountry group package tours, and they demand a high quality of accommodations and services similar to those in Hawaii. Average length of stay is short (five to seven days). Although the United States was consistently Fiji's second most important source of tourists throughout the period, New Zealand and Japan are gaining. Fiji's success in the American market is believed to be tied to growth in visitors from the United States to New Zealand. Visitation from Canada was consistent throughout the period, with the greatest increase evidenced between 1989 and 1990. The decline in Canadian visitors in 1991 is believed to have resulted, in large part, from the withdrawal of Canadian Airlines from the region.

EUROPE   The United Kingdom, Germany, and Sweden are the primary European target markets. Although the United Kingdom exhibited overall growth between 1987 and 1991, visitation from this market in 1991 is estimated to have decreased slightly, by 1.6 percent. It is believed that Canadian Airlines' withdrawal may have influenced visitation from the United Kingdom. In 1990, it was estimated that approximately 19 percent of visitors from the United Kingdom arrived on this carrier. Thailand, Hong Kong, Singapore, Australia, and New Zealand are the primary destinations in this region for Germans. Air New Zealand is the primary carrier for this market segment.

JAPAN The Japanese market appears to be increasing, although the pattern of growth needs to be examined cautiously. Japan suspended and withdrew airline services to Fiji after the *coup d'état*. The scope for attracting stopover traffic is quite limited because of the largely single-destination, short-duration travel patterns (4–5 days) that characterize this market. Moreover, it has been reported that Fiji lacks the amenities and standards considered essential by this market. Nonetheless, the fact that neighboring destinations in the Pacific receive a substantial and growing volume of Japanese visitors suggests there is some potential within this geographic market.

FIJI'S TOURISM INDUSTRY: HOW IT WORKS

An industry as large and important as tourism must be well organized and coordinated to function efficiently. From the middle of the 1970s, the government has taken an active interest in tourism, providing incentives to interested parties and formulating regulations to ensure proper functioning. As the needs of the industry have changed, so have the regulations. The government has begun to show concern about the impact of tourism on Fiji's society. Hence, the development of tourism ventures has been limited to carefully chosen areas of the country, with the main locality designated for hotel and resort development running from Navua to the western centers of Nadi and Lautoka on Viti Levu.

Investors have shown interest in developing other areas and islands such as Kadavu. The government, however, always tries to seek approval from local inhabitants[2] before allowing hotel and resort construction in these areas. Priority is always given to local landowners who wish to develop tourism ventures, financed with assistance from the Fiji Development Bank and the Ministry of Tourism (e.g., Hotel Aid Assistance). Local landowners of Monasavu, for instance, formed Naboubuco Landowners Enterprise Ltd. to develop a mountain resort at Koroni-O.

Structure of the Industry Figure 6.3 provides an overview of the structure of the tourism industry. Established by government ordinance, the Fiji Tourist Commission (FTC) consists of the minister responsible for tourism and two other ministers appointed by the prime minister. Its main role is to establish broad policies to guide the entire tourism industry. As set out by the Fiji Tourist Commission Act in 1978, the FTC's mandate is to encourage and develop the Fiji tourism industry, taking into account at all times the cultures and customs of the people of Fiji.

The role of the minister of tourism (a combined portfolio with Civil Aviation and Energy) is to determine specific policies for the tourism industry, including civil aviation and bilateral air agreements, in consultation with the FTC and the Fiji National Tourism Association (FNTA). The minister of tourism also works with the Hotel Licensing Board

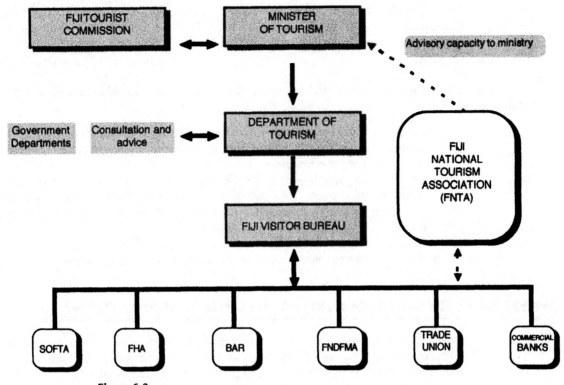

Figure 6.3
Structure of Fiji's tourism industry. (Courtesy of Fiji Visitor Bureau.)

and the director of the Department of Tourism on matters relating to the issuing of licenses to build hotels and resorts.

Reporting directly to the minister of tourism, the Department of Tourism (DOT) coordinates and implements policies handed down from the decision-making bodies. It also conducts research aimed at improving the operation of the tourism industry, including the development of education and training programs for all levels of personnel.

The Fiji Visitors Bureau (FVB) is a statutory body headed by a general manager. Its primary role is to promote and market Fiji, mainly in Australia, New Zealand, the United States, and Japan. Directly under the FVB are the sector organizations, including (1) the Society of Fiji Travel Agents (SOFTA), (2) the Fiji Hotel Association (FHA) comprising independent hotel owners, (3) the Board of Airline Representatives (BAR) from government and other airlines, (4) the Fiji National Duty Free Merchants Association (FNDFMA) consisting of independent merchants, (5) trade unions for hotel employees, and (6) commercial banks.

Each sector appoints two representatives to sit on the FNTA, which works in an advisory capacity to the minister of tourism. Membership in any of the six sector organizations is not compulsory. In this way, an avenue is provided for the voice of even the ordinary worker at the policy-making level. Also part of the FNTA are the town clerk, a chairperson, and a secretary. The goal of the FNTA is to create better conditions and improve the tourism industry as a whole. At present, however, it is not as effective as it could be.

Tourism The following tourism objectives were outlined in the Ninth Development Plan (1986–
Objectives 1991):

- Ensure tourism is in harmony with national development policies.
- Increase the use of agricultural and other produce in hotels to enhance linkages with the rest of the economy.
- Provide more opportunities for local entrepreneurs to invest in hotels and related industries and to employ local people at the senior and middle management levels.
- Encourage small-scale secondary activity of local entrepreneurs by providing basic infrastructure, physical resources, and credit.
- Increase tourism awareness levels among locals and visitors.
- Ensure that adverse effects on local customs and cultures are avoided.

WHERE DOES FIJI GO FROM HERE?: A HYPOTHETICAL SITUATION [3]

Teresa Lauder (Knowlton Mathieson Consultants, Auckland, New Zealand) received a letter from Stephan Somfich [Executive Vice President, International Finance Corporation (IFC)–World Bank, Washington, DC] indicating that approval had been given to proceed with Phases 1 and 2 of the tourism assessment and strategic recommendations for the Fiji Islands.

The timing could not have been worse. Teresa's firm had just been awarded two other major contracts for tourism studies within the South Pacific region. Time pressures would require her to assign responsibility for the IFC–World Bank contract to a junior partner, Colin Brookes. He was the only person in the office sufficiently knowledgeable about conducting strategic assessments. The World Bank was a high-profile client and, as Teresa had learned from others, difficult to please. Moreover, they were demanding a fast turnaround. Mr. Somfich requested a debriefing in six weeks. The IFC had agreed to assist the South Pacific islands with investment and had chosen Fiji as a pilot. To guide the allocation of funds, the IFC believed that it would be necessary to assess tourism opportunities and create a strategy for development not only in Fiji but in the region as a whole. [4]

The Minister for Tourism, Civil Aviation, and Energy had expressed his position regarding the project in a prior conversation with Teresa:

Local supplies of capital are insufficient to meet total capital requirements. Whether Fiji can achieve its tourism targets will depend on the ability of the country to attract foreign capital. That is why we approached the World Bank. But, they were adamant that the needs of the region as a whole be evaluated. Luckily they have decided to start with us. We will gain some leverage as a result.

I know what you are thinking. We are a member of the Tourism Council of the South Pacific (TCSP) but I am not convinced their focus on regional tourism promotion (reiterated by the World Bank) is necessary or that we would benefit. Almost 60 percent of the registered international tourist arrivals are recorded in Fiji. Do we need to cooperate with competitive regional destinations?

The nuances of satisfying various stakeholders troubled Teresa. She emphasized to Colin how important it was to develop a comprehensive strategic assessment of the Fijian tourist industry:

> Since the 1980s, with the decline of sugar prices, Fiji's tourism industry has assumed increasing importance to the economy. In 1986, the spending associated with 260,000 visitors accounted for 14 percent of GDP. The Ninth Development Plan targeted 400,000 visitors by 1990, but political upheavals in 1987 scotched that objective. Visitor arrivals and the value of their gross expenditures dropped precipitously. By 1990, actual arrivals only amounted to 279,000.
>
> Then, in 1991, a decline of 7 percent was experienced as total overseas tourist arrivals fell to 259,100. Total overseas visitor-days in Fiji during 1991 were recorded at 2.21 million, a drop of 157,000 or 6.6 percent compared to 1990. Average length of stay declined slightly from 8.8 days in 1990 to 8.7 days in 1991. Provisional estimates by the Bureau of Statistics place total earnings from tourism in 1991 at F$310.0 million, down F$25.9 million, or close to 8 percent, from 1990.
>
> Obviously a recovery is going to be contingent on finding a long term solution to political problems. But, Fiji is beset by other difficulties. In the past, declines in tourism have been attributed to both the effects of cyclones and the appreciation of the Fiji currency over the Australian dollar. In the future, longer range aircraft, especially between the United States and Australia/New Zealand, will be tempted to overfly Fiji. Then, of course, there is the issue of the environment vis-à-vis further tourism infrastructure expansion.
>
> Quite a number of Fiji's hotels, resorts, and attractions are not up to international standards and, although Fijians are very hospitable, there is growing concern that tourism has caused an increased incidence of alcoholism, drug addiction, traffic congestion, and crime. I mention these points to encourage you to consider the complexities of island tourism.

Teresa indicated that she would set aside a few hours on the following Monday to meet with Colin and discuss the details of the project. She asked Colin to come prepared to discuss (1) current issues, underlying constraints, challenges, and opportunities that the Fijian visitor industry needs to address and (2) a framework that concentrates on the components as well as the procedures for developing a thorough strategic assessment.

Colin reassured Teresa that he was up to the task. But, as she left his office, he began to wonder. Was the traditional strategic planning model appropriate in this situation? Could he produce a document that would assist all stakeholders in developing strategies that could master the present and preempt the future?

NOTES

1. See Chapters 5, 24, 26, and 28 for additional discussion on situation analysis, SWOT analysis, and strategic planning.
2. See Chapters 5, 9, 11, 12, and 14–19 for additional discussion of community attitudes and community involvement in the tourism planning and development processes.
3. Although the scenario presented is hypothetical, the statistics and information relating to tourism are based on actual data.
4. See Chapter 8 for discussion of regional cooperation strategies in the Caribbean.

REFERENCES

Bureau of Statistics. 1992. *Tourism Statistics, Fiji*.

Heath, E. and G. Wall. 1992. *Marketing Tourism Destinations: A Strategic Planning Approach*. New York: John Wiley & Sons.

Langley, A. 1988. The roles of formal strategic planning, *Long Range Planning*, 21(3), 48.

Mintzberg, H. 1994. *The Rise and Fall of Strategic Planning*. New York: The Free Press.

Tourism Council of the South Pacific. 1992. *South Pacific Regional Tourism Statistics*.

World Tourism Organization. 1992. *Tourism Trends Worldwide and in Europe, 1950–1990*. Madrid: WTO.

Reference was also made to various Fiji visitor guides, including the *Fiji Islands Travel Guide* (1990–1991 and 1992–1993), *Fiji Calling* (Vol. 1, First Half 1993 and Vol. 2, 1993–1994), and Brendan Tours and Tapa Tours brochures for Fiji (1994–1995).

♪ | PROBLEM SOLVING AND DISCUSSION ACTIVITIES

1. Provide evidence to support or refute the following statements: (a) planning approaches built on assumptions of general stability and continuity no longer suffice and (b) having contingency plans is more important than having a fixed master plan regardless of how well developed it is.

2. What are current issues, constraints, challenges, and opportunities that the Fijian tourism industry must address? Organize your response so that both positive and negative internal and external factors are clearly delineated and the implications of each factor are presented. What criteria should be used to prioritize the various issues? Identify the components of the strategic planning process that should be initiated within Fiji.

3. How can Fiji's ability to act and respond to circumstances affecting its market and competitive position be assessed? What criteria should be used to make such a determination?

4. What role should traditions and customs play in Fiji's tourism product offering? What protections appear to exist to preserve the culture? What risks does Fiji face with respect to sustaining its culture and traditions as tourism grows? What proactive measures can be put in place to mitigate such risks? Provide evidence to support your answers based on the experiences of other destinations.

5. What may prevent Fiji from attaining its goal of minimizing leakage? To what extent is Fiji's apparent reliance on foreign capital consistent with the goal of minimizing leakage? What can be done to optimize the realization of this goal given the apparent reality of the situation?

6. Although Fiji is strategically located to act as a hub for the promotion of regional South Pacific tour packages, the tourism minister appears to believe that regional cooperation is not important. What are the pros and cons of regional cooperation from Fiji's perspective? With which other countries should Fiji initiate partnerships? Why? How should Fiji be positioned within such a package (i.e., in terms of product offerings and benefits, length of stay, placement during the trip)? Justify your response.

7. Who would the stakeholders be in negotiations initiated to restore airline sched-

ules and capacity to Fiji? What are the interests of the various stakeholder groups? How might Fiji most effectively achieve its goal of enhancing air access?

8. What are potential costs and benefits associated with dispersing tourism more widely throughout Fiji? What is required to determine where and how much tourism should be developed on various islands? What information is required to determine whether the outlying islands should be positioned as destinations in their own right or as part of a multi-island Fiji package (which may or may not involve overnight stays)?

9. Conduct a competitor analysis to determine the potential market position of Fiji in the golf tourism market. Who are the strongest competitors? What factors are likely to enhance or detract from Fiji's ability to penetrate this market?

10. What role might festivals and special events play in Fiji's tourism industry? What has been the experience of other destinations with respect to using festivals and special events as demand generators? Select at least two other destinations and highlight lessons that Fiji can learn from them.

11. What short-term and long-term steps can be taken in Fiji to increase visitor interest in activities and attractions located outside resort or hotel complexes? Should Fiji encourage such exploration as part of organized island tours or as activities to be engaged in by independent traveler parties? Justify your response highlighting advantages and disadvantages of each.

12. Discuss strengths and weaknesses of the organizational structure of Fiji's tourism industry. Identify factors that might be detracting from the effectiveness of the Fiji National Tourism Association based on problems common to tourism associations worldwide.

7

Changing the Balance of Power

TOUR OPERATORS AND TOURISM SUPPLIERS IN THE SPANISH TOURISM INDUSTRY

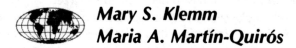

Mary S. Klemm
Maria A. Martín-Quirós

𝔤 | K E Y   L E A R N I N G   P O I N T S

- Tourist destinations develop because of their attractiveness and accessibility to particular origin markets. International tour operators, because of their marketing and selling expertise as well as their access to consumers in the generating countries, play a vital role in the development of many tourist destinations.

- The pressure on newly emerging destinations to cater to the mass market can lead to a decline in the quality of tourism resources and experiences available after just a few years. To prevent this, tourism development and market growth must be controlled.

- International tour operators are generally large companies that, because of their size and control of distribution channels, can strongly influence decisions relating to pricing structures and product offerings. Long-term detrimental effects may result when the interests of tour operators differ from those of the suppliers. Tourism suppliers must work together to reduce their dependence on, and strengthen their negotiating power with, tour operators.

- It is important to develop the management and marketing skill base of tourism suppliers in any destination area. This is particularly relevant to improving the quality of exisiting tourist services, creating new products, and strengthening promotional efforts aimed at repositioning a mature or declining tourism industry.

INTRODUCTION

Since the 1970s Spain has been transformed into a prosperous and democratic nation that, in 1993, became a full member of the European Union (EU). Tourism has been an important element in Spain's economic growth and remains a vital industry, accounting for 9 percent of gross domestic product (GDP), 30 percent of export earnings, and 11

126

percent of employment in the 1990s. However, the tourism industry, like the country, has changed considerably since the death of General Franco in 1976. The liberalization of many aspects of the Spanish economy and society has led to increased standards of living and foreign travel by Spaniards. A greater number of inbound tourists is now required to restore the balance of the travel trade account.

Between 1986 and 1991 the Spanish economy grew faster than any other national economy within the EU. Increases in wages and social security protection introduced by the socialist government led to higher costs for tourism businesses. By the mid-1980s Spain was no longer an inexpensive destination and, therefore, had to appeal to a more discerning tourist on the basis of quality and variety. To capture new markets, as well as retain existing ones, Spain has had to develop a new image as a tourist destination and develop a wider range of tourism products. Moreover, it has been necessary to develop a stronger, more integrated, and more independent home industry to act as a counterbalance to the power of large international tour operators and hotel chains.

The development of Spanish tourism is examined in this chapter in the context of tourist destination life cycle models. The ways in which the nature of tourism demand and the fragmented structure of the Spanish tourism industry have led to a dependence on international tour operators are discussed. This is followed by an overview of the policies formulated to reduce that dependence, including the government-inspired strategy to change the image of Spain and encourage the development of products for different market segments. Also considered is the devolution of tourism to regional communities, which has encouraged investments in improving the quality of infrastructure and tourism products at the regional level. Finally, as an illustration of the entrepreneurial spirit in the Spanish tourism industry, the birth of an independent marketing organization on the Catalonian Costa Brava in northeast Spain is described.

DESTINATION LIFE CYCLES, TOUR OPERATORS, AND SUSTAINABLE TOURISM DEVELOPMENT: CONTEMPORARY PERSPECTIVES AND ISSUES

Destination Life Cycles   Observers such as Butler (1980) believe that tourist areas rise and fall in popularity following a life cycle similar to that of other products.[1] Despite difficulties associated with their application (Haywood, 1986), life cycle models can be used to understand the development process in some of the Spanish resorts, especially when there has been a *laissez-faire* approach to planning (Pearce, 1989).

The concept of the resort life cycle is useful because it generates an understanding of why resorts decline and, therefore, how to avoid decline. Wolfe (1983) suggests that an increase in visitor numbers beyond the carrying capacity[2] of the area leads to negative environmental effects and a reduction in the quality of the tourist experience. The resort becomes unfashionable, declines in popularity, and requires a new impetus to retain the interest of tourists and tour companies. Rejuvenation has been successfully achieved in some of the cold water resorts of Northern Europe (e.g., Brighton, the United Kingdom and Deauville, France) through investment in the physical fabric of the resorts and by repositioning them as short break destinations (Diamond, 1990).

The Life Cycle An analysis of tourist psychology can also help to explain the rise and decline of resorts.
and Plog's (1973) hypothesis is that destination areas rise and fall in popularity according to the
Psychographic psychographic characteristics of the groups to which they appeal. This research, originally
Segmentation conducted among American travelers, identified two psychologically opposite types of
tourists: allocentrics and psychocentrics (see Figure 7.1a).

The allocentric is a confident and adventurous tourist who welcomes challenge, new
experiences, foreign environments, and "going it alone." By contrast, the psychocentric
tourist seeks familiar and safe surroundings, tends to lack confidence in a strange environment, and prefers to be entertained and looked after. Plog suggested that tourists were
normally distributed along a continuum, with the majority in the midcentric category
(i.e., most tourists are looking for new experiences, but also require a framework of security and familiarity).

In the early stage of the destination life cycle a new resort appeals to the allocentric
group, the explorers. As the area becomes better known, develops good transport links,
and is promoted by tour operators, the allocentrics are replaced by a much larger number
of midcentrics. It is at this stage that the resort reaches the height of its popularity. This

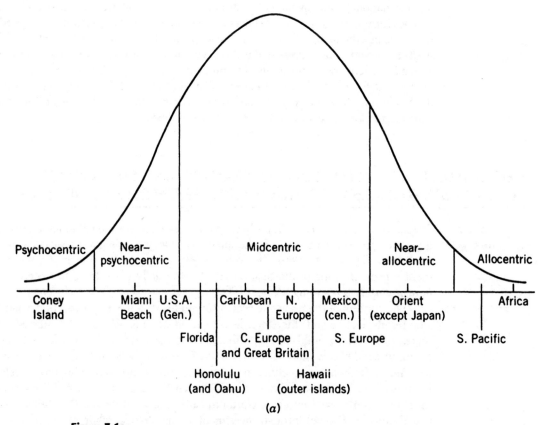

Figure 7.1a
*Plog's destination life cycle for American tourists. (Plog, 1973 as presented in Mill and Mor-
rison, 1992. Courtesy of Prentice-Hall, Inc.)*

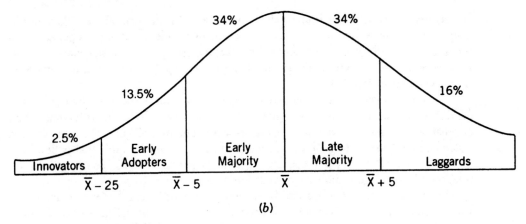

34%   34%

13.5%   16%

2.5%

| Innovators | Early Adopters | Early Majority | Late Majority | Laggards |

$\overline{X} - 25$ $\overline{X} - 5$ $\overline{X}$ $\overline{X} + 5$

(b)

Figure 7.1b
Roger's diffusion of innovation model. (Rogers, 1962 as presented in Mill and Morrison, 1992. Courtesy of Prentice-Hall, Inc.)

can be likened to the maturity phase of the product life cycle. After some years as a mass market destination, the resort loses its appeal to the midcentrics, perhaps because it has lost much of its original and unique character or because new and competing destinations have emerged (Cooper, 1990). In the decline stage the resort appeals to psychocentrics who not only generate lower volumes of visitation but often also spend less. Competition to fill excess capacity leads to a reduction in prices. Consequently, businesses lose income and are unable to reinvest in their product.

Everett Rogers' diffusion of innovation model (1962) suggests a similar pattern of rise and decline (see Figure 7.1b). In this model the explorers and allocentrics are the innovators, but a difference is found in the later stages of the cycle where the laggards (similar to Plog's psychocentrics) represent a sizable group.

An important message of these life cycle and segmentation models is that tourist destinations contain the seeds of their own decline. One of the seeds of this destruction is the volatility of tourism demand and the fickle nature of consumer tastes. Another important factor is the role of powerful tour operators, airlines, and international hotel chains, each of which provides a vital link between the destination and its customers.

Role of Tour Operators International tour companies[3] assemble the essential elements of the tourism product (i.e., transport, accommodation, and resort services) in the form of an inclusive or package tour, and they offer these to the customer through a travel agent or retailer. The package tour business has expanded steadily since the 1950s, encouraged by the growth of charter flights. In the United Kingdom in the 1980s, for example, approximatley 10 million package tours were sold annually. In areas such as Northern Europe and Japan, package tours dominate travel. In other areas, such as Southern Europe and the United States, inclusive tours have a lower market share. Shaw and Williams (1994, p. 115) suggested that "in some respects the geography of tour company operations is the geography of dependency relationships."

Tour operators are generally based in the tourist-generating area. However, most of the services they contract are from smaller enterprises in the destination area. Their dominant position derives from the fact that they are buying under conditions of perfect competition but are selling under conditions approaching oligopoly. Tour operators use their knowledge of the market to design products to suit specific demographic and psychographic market segments.

The tour operators' marketing and selling expertise, not to mention their control of the distribution channels, is vital to many destination areas. However, with competition based almost entirely on price, large operators seek economies of scale. The result is often a standardized product (e.g., "lakes and mountains" or "summer sun") that is devoid of nationality or local context and appeals to a wide range of customers. To maximize revenue, most large tour operators target midcentrics or psychocentrics.

The need to commit substantial funds up to two years before the level of demand is known, coupled with the volatility of demand, renders tour operating a risky business. Unexpected events (e.g., an international crisis like the Gulf War or a change in the weather) can cause demand to collapse overnight. Negative publicity or industrial disputes in the transport industry, which are a regular feature of the European summer, can also have devastating effects on demand.

Due to the frontloading of costs, tour operators must sell a substantial number of holidays just to break even. Given that holidays are "perishable," there is a temptation to reduce prices below cost if it appears that the breakeven point will not be reached and the survival of the company is threatened. These structural and economic factors result in intense price competition among tour operators in tourist origin markets which, in turn, places pressure on the suppliers of services in the destination to reduce their prices.

Sustainable Tourism Development Sustainable development[4] was defined by the World Commission on Environment and Development (1987) as growth that brings benefits to people today without damaging resources or prospects for future generations. A declining tourist destination is not sustainable; that is, it is not providing jobs for the current generation, resources are wasted, and environments are damaged for the future. Sustainable tourism development (and avoidance of decline) can only be achieved through planning (Mill and Morrison, 1992). A *laissez-faire* approach may result in visitation levels that exceed the carrying capacity of an area. Consequently, valuable natural environments (e.g., the shoreline) may be polluted.

The role of marketing in sustainability has received little attention. To ensure that a destination is sustainable from a marketing perspective, its appeal and image should be capable of adaptation over time. Just as an industrial company should maintain a range of products, destinations should not become too dependent on one type of tourism product and should appeal to a variety of market segments.

EVOLUTION OF SPANISH TOURISM

Growth of Spanish Tourism Spain has a tradition in tourism dating back to the pilgrimages of the Middle Ages. In the nineteenth century it was famous for spas[5] and aristocratic resorts in the cooler areas. In the 1930s it became popular with artists and writers such as Ernest Hemingway. Mass tourism began to develop in the 1960s (see Figure 7.2). By the 1990s Spain ranked third

Millions of visitors

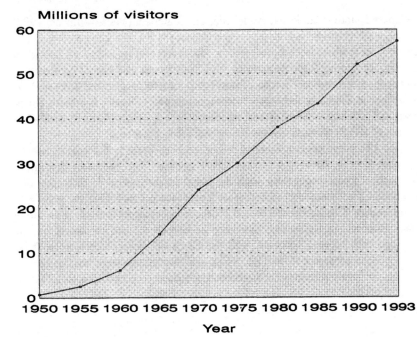

Figure 7.2
*Foreign visitors to Spain:
1950–1993. (Adapted from
General de Turismo, 1993.)*

in the world in terms of tourist arrivals, receiving 8 percent of world tourist arrivals (57 million visitors) in 1993 (Plazas Garbine, 1994) and generating 7 percent of world tourists receipts.

The reasons for this remarkable growth include (1) Spain's proximity to the large tourist-generating areas of Northern Europe, (2) its warm and sunny climate, and (3) the relatively low cost of living and accommodations in Spain until the late 1980s.

Approximately 80 percent of visitors to Spain in 1993 were from other EU countries. Most parts of Spain are within two hours flying time from countries in Northern Europe, such as Germany, Great Britain, the Netherlands, and Scandinavia that have cold climates, large industrial cities, and wealthy populations with paid holidays. The northern Spanish resorts can be reached by car in approximately 15 hours from Frankfurt or Brussels. Good communications within Europe also means that Spain is able to reach this market with its various promotional tools.

A warm and sunny climate, with average temperatures of 54°F (12°C) in winter and 75°F (24°C) in summer on the Mediterranean coast, renders Spain an attractive destination. The Canary Islands, located off the coast of West Africa but part of Spain, have a subtropical climate and temperatures ranging from 64°F to 75°F (18°C to 24°C) year round. Mainland Spain has 3725 miles (6000 kilometers) of beaches, including the Costa Brava, Costa Blanca, and Costa del Sol. Indeed, the sun and beach are the major attractions for approximately 80 percent of visitors to Spain.

The coasts and islands are the most popular tourist destinations in Spain. Approximately 85 percent of hotel capacity is concentrated in only five of Spain's 17 regions: the

Balearic and Canary islands, Catalonia, Andalusia, and Valencia (Martín-Quirós, 1992) (see Figure 7.3).

Although tourism tends to be concentrated on the coast, the interior does provide a variety of scenery, including high mountains and both green and desert landscapes. Spain's distinct and ancient culture is also of interest to tourists (e.g., attractions such as the Alhambra Palace in Granada and many historic towns and villages). Northern Europeans are drawn to Spain's colorful traditions and festivals (e.g., Holy Week in Seville) as well as by its store of artistic treasures in the Prado and other museums.

Until the late 1980s the general level of prices, and particularly the cost of hotels, was lower in Spain than in the rest of Europe. This attracted tour operators that could offer inclusive tours at lower prices than could be found in competing destinations such as France and Italy. The lower cost of living in Spain was an incentive for people to purchase second homes. During the 1970s and 1980s, housing developments grew along the Mediterranean coast. In particular, extensive developments can be found on the Costa Blanca, especially around Alicante, and the Costa del Sol, which was built up almost all the way from Malaga to Gibraltar. Villas and apartments were built as second and, in some cases, retirement homes for Northern Europeans, mainly Germans, Dutch,

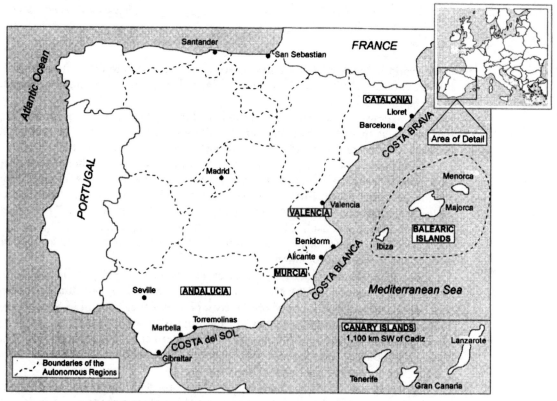

Figure 7.3
Spain: The tourist areas.

and British. The building boom associated with tourism was a stimulus to the economy, which grew rapidly in the 1980s (e.g., GDP increase of 3.3 percent per year) (Hooper, 1995).

Visitors to Spain An analysis of visitors to Spain by country of origin in 1991 shows that a large percentage (41.7 percent) came from the neighboring countries of France (22.37 percent) and Portugal (19.4 percent), but many of these were only day visitors. Figure 7.4 indicates that the Spanish hotel trade is highly dependent on British and German visitors. In 1990 over half of overnight stays were generated by visitors from these two countries.

In terms of trends in visitor flows, the number of visitors from Italy and Japan is increasing, whereas Spain's share of the American market is stagnating. The flow from Latin America is steady. Spain is the main entry point to Europe for Latin Americans.

Most tourists visiting Spain do not stay in hotels. They tend to rent villas and apartments, stay in second homes (of which Spain has over a million), or stay in timesharing developments (of which there are over 200,000 units). This ownership pattern has contributed to considerable loyalty to the country as a tourist destination. When hotels are used, 75 percent of visitors stay in properties that are graded three star or less, thus firmly positioning Spain as a middle market destination. Tourists in Spain in 1991 spent an average of $512 per person per trip, or a little under the world average of $581 (Albert-Piñole, 1993).

Dependence on Tour Operators The number of tourists visiting Spain doubled between 1970 and 1990. Much of this growth was in inclusive tours, with British and German companies being the most significant. A study in 1986 (Drexl and Agel, 1987) indicated that, with packages worth DM11 billion (around US$7 billion in 1995 dollars) having been sold in the 1980s, the German inclusive tour business was the largest in the world. A study by Fitch (1987)

% of all visitors   % of hotel overnight stays

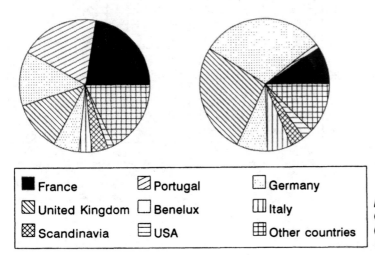

■ France	▨ Portugal	▢ Germany
◩ United Kingdom	▢ Benelux	▥ Italy
▨ Scandinavia	▤ USA	▦ Other countries

Figure 7.4
Origin of visitors to Spain, 1990.
(Adapted from General de Turismo, 1990.)

showed that 70 percent of British tourists to Spain were on a package holiday (see Figure 7.5).

Although the European package tour business has many small operators offering special interest holidays, the mass market is dominated by a few large companies. In the 1980s, 40 percent of the German outbound inclusive tour market was in the hands of only three companies. The outbound package tour market in the United Kingdom is even more concentrated, with over 50 percent of business in the hands of two companies, Thompson and Airtours, both with access to major travel agency chains that offer discounts for selling the holidays of the parent company. The extent of vertical integration between tour operators and travel agents led to a British government investigation in 1993 following accusations of unfair competition and a limitation of consumer choice (Office of Fair Trading, 1994).

Because tour companies, with their travel agent and airline partners, dominated the distribution channels in Germany and Great Britain, Spanish tourism providers found it very difficult to reach the customer independent of the tour operators. Consequently, during the crucial development phase of the Spanish tourism industry in the 1970s and 1980s, hotel proprietors and other tourism providers became highly reliant on interna-

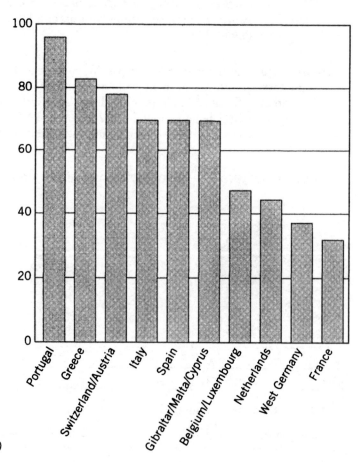

Figure 7.5
Market share of inclusive tours in the main holiday destinations of UK residents. (Adapted from Fitch, 1987, as presented in Shaw and Williams, 1994, p. 112. Courtesy of Blackwell Publishers.)

tional tour companies. The power of these companies, based primarily on their size and purchasing power, was much greater than that of the mostly small and independent businesses in the Spanish tourism industry. As suggested earlier, the economics of tour companies results in volume buying of undifferentiated products at the lowest possible cost. Moreover, tour operators' system of subcontracting transport and accommodation makes it more economical for them to concentrate on a few resorts.

Evidence of the power of concentrated buying by tour companies is shown in a study of hotels in Portugal, Greece, and Spain (cited in Urry, 1990) in which British tour operators obtained the lowest prices in 39 of the 57 hotels surveyed. The imbalance in the subcontracting system between the small local businesses in Spain and the oligopolistic tour operators led to what has been called a "tourist neocolonialism which allowed a mass arrival of foreigners, but generated business conditions which in the long term proved negative for Spanish companies" (Albert-Piñole, 1993).

THE CRISIS OF 1990

The number of foreign visitors to Spain fell for the first time in 1989, and then again in 1990, albeit only slightly (see Table 7.1). Following the long period of growth in the 1970s and 1980s, coupled with unemployment at 20 percent and industrial unrest (Hooper, 1995), this was perceived to represent a crisis in Spain's tourism industry.

Major players in the Spanish tourism industry recognized that dependence on certain origin markets (i.e., the United Kingdom and Germany) and reliance on "sun and sand" holidays made them vulnerable not only to tour operators, but also to fluctuations in the tourists' home economies and changes in consumers' tastes. For example, the doubling of the mortgage rate in the United Kingdom in 1989–1990 drastically reduced consumers' disposable income.

Moreover, Spain experienced an 80 percent increase in overall tourist prices between 1983 and 1990 (El Turismo Español en Cifras, 1991). The rising value of the *peseta*

TABLE 7.1
Foreign Visitors to Spain, 1986–1993

Year	Number of Visitors (Millions)	Percent Change
1986	47.3	
1987	50.5	6.8
1988	54.2	7.2
1989	54.1	(0.2)
1990	52.0	(3.8)
1991	53.5	2.8
1992	55.3	3.4
1993	57.3	3.6

Source: Secretaria General de Turismo (1993).

(whose value against the pound sterling increased by 30 percent beween 1986 and 1992) and increases in pay for Spanish workers, particularly hotel staff, were critical factors in this regard. The resulting decrease in demand in 1989–1990 was greatest for the two-week seaside holiday. Tour operators, seeking a lower-cost "sun and sand" product, found this in Turkey and Greece. Given its higher tourist prices, Spain was now positioned in a different market. However, the product (or rather that which the tour operators were offering) did not match the higher expectations of the tourists that Spain needed to attract in the 1990s.

The Life Cycle and Spanish Resorts France and Barke (1992) documented the passage of Torremolinos in Southern Spain (see Figure 7.3) through the stages of the life cycle. This archetypal Costa del Sol resort evolved from a small fishing village with only a few adventurous visitors in the 1960s to an intensively developed resort receiving many thousands of package tourists in the 1980s. During this 20-year period most of the local inhabitants left their traditional occupations to seek tourism-related employment and then moved outside the original village to "make way" for hotels, bars, and other tourism businesses.

A feature of Butler's (1980) model is the loss of local control in the development phase during which ownership of property is transferred from local people to large hotel and finance companies that can supply the necessary level of investment and expertise for large-scale developments. This occurred in Torremolinos and other mass market resorts, such as Benidorm and Lloret de Mar (see Figure 7.3), where large high-rise developments grew to dominate the original villages.

It is not surprising that owners of coastal land that had been virtually valueless before the growth of tourism were prepared to sell to the highest bidder (Hooper, 1995). The seafront was the most desirable location for tour companies and property developers. Hence, high-rise blocks were built close together to accommodate as many tourists as near to the sea as possible. Planning regulations, which would have had the effect of spacing out development and creating a more pleasing environment, took second place to commercial considerations (Pearce, 1989).

By the mid-1980s Torremolinos, like several other resorts on the Spanish Costas and the Balearic Island of Majorca (see Figure 7.3), had become a mass market tourist destination serving Northern Europeans. Management and control of demand passed to international tour companies with access to and understanding of the consumers in their home countries. Thus, the allocentrics who followed in the footsteps of the writers and travelers between the two world wars were replaced by increasingly psychocentric tourists looking for familiar food and surroundings. Some of the resorts began to lose their Spanish character, serving English and German food to the accompaniment of music and televised sports from the home country. A considerable number of tourism businesses, especially the bars, were taken over by expatriates.

By 1989 the Costa del Sol resorts were facing a leveling and, in some cases, a decline in demand (i.e., they were entering the consolidation or even the stagnation phase). However, it is not possible to be precise about the turning point of the cycle because the model is a descriptive rather than a prescriptive tool. Discussions with hotel managers and other tourism professionals in the Costa del Sol in 1992 conveyed a feeling of demoralization in the face of declining demand. The persistence of tour operators in retaining inexpensive "sun and sand" tourism forced hoteliers to cut costs and offer a level of quality that they were not happy with. However, because tour operators controlled access to the customer and operated as a "cartel" in the resorts, individual hotel owners were in weak negotiating positions.

To strengthen their negotiating stance, some hotel owners attempted to join forces to present a united front, mainly to resist price cuts but also to gain access to the higher spending tourist. At the time, they were not successful in maintaining the alliance. There was an underlying fear that they would be forced into becoming hotel management subsidiaries for tour operators. Spanish hoteliers also feared a direct takeover by foreign hotel chains such as Holiday Inn or Forte, that were expanding their network in Spain. Foreign ownership is a very sensitive issue in Spain.

Not all Spanish resorts faced a decline in the early 1990s. In some Costa Brava resorts, the town councils exerted more control to prevent overcrowding and high-rise developments (Priestley, 1986 in Pearce, 1989). Other parts of the coast escaped the building boom because, like the northern areas of Majorca, they were less accessible. Nonetheless, it is important to understand the process by which the power of tour operators contributed to a downturn of some Spanish resort areas. Although other factors (e.g., rising prices in Spain and lower disposable income in the origin markets) played a role, there is no doubt that pressure from tour operators led to overcrowded resorts in the growth phase. This, in turn, resulted in a reduction in the quality of the tourism product and environment and, in the next phases of the cycle, difficulty in adapting the tourism product to rejuvenate the resort in the way described by Butler (1980).

The Problem of Fragmentation Most companies in the Spanish tourism industry are small, particularly in the hotel sector where family businesses predominate. Spain has around 4200 hotels (and an equivalent number of registered guest houses), approximately 60 percent of which are independently owned. Hotel chains tend to be small and based in one region. Only three of these chains have more than 50 hotels: Grupo Sol Melia (120 hotels), Hoteles Husa (77 hotels), and the state-owned Paradores Nacional de Turismo (83 hotels) (Gonzales, 1994). The fragmentation of the domestic tourism industry is shown by the lack of vertical links between hotels, transport companies, travel agencies, and other tourist businesses.

The dominance of small businesses makes it difficult to develop greater autonomy and bargaining power vis-à-vis powerful foreign tour operators such as Thompson (the United Kingdom) and Touristik Union International (TUI, Germany). Foreign tourism businesses in Spain are more integrated. They own hotels, charter airlines, transport companies, and travel agencies (Concentration y Asociacionismo Empresarial en el Sector Turistic, 1989). For example, German tour operators (i.e., TUI and NUR) in Majorca offer hotel accommodation through their subsidiaries Iberotel and Royaltur. Drexl and Agel (1987) noted that the number of beds offered through this system was larger than the total accommodation capacity of Greece.

Spanish authorities believed that the greater economic power of foreign companies enabled them to determine the nature of the Spanish tourism product, limiting it to "sun and sand" as opposed to promoting other aspects of Spain (Martín-Quirós, 1992). Although foreign companies dominate Spain's distribution channels in the United Kingdom and Germany, this is less of an issue in France, Italy, and the United States.

ADDRESSING THE CHALLENGES

Tourism will continue to be an important industry in Spain. However, new sources of competition have emerged within Europe (e.g., Eastern Europe) as well as from further afield, which have created a number of challenges. The first challenge was the need to reposition Spain as a destination that offers not only sun and sand to the mass package holiday tourist, but a much greater variety of tourism products. Cultural/city tourism, business tourism, sport and adventure tourism, and leisure and short-stay tourism were believed to represent opportunities in this regard. These "products," which more accurately reflect the diversity of Spain's scenery, culture, and heritage, would appeal to new international customers as well as the growing domestic market.

The second challenge involved expanding the distribution channels to reduce Spain's dependence on large tour operators and other intermediaries when introducing the new products. Action was also required to promote cooperation and consolidation within the Spanish tourism industry and to encourage the development of management and marketing skills. The Spanish Ministry for Trade, Industry and Tourism, headed by the General Secretary for Tourism (GST), was charged with responsibility for creating a more sustainable tourism industry. Research into the structure of the Spanish tourism industry, its markets, and the perceptions and images of Spain in the minds of tourists confirmed (1) the overdependence on certain markets and products and (2) the need to develop and promote an image that better reflected the vitality and variety of modern Spain.

The Marketing Plan for Spanish Tourism   The plan to reposition Spain was begun in 1983 by Turespana, the promotional office under the GST. The first task was to create a logo that represented the essential elements of Spain's attractiveness (i.e., its unique value proposition). Juan Miro's sun, with the word *España* taken from the logo of the 1982 World Cup, was selected. Red, yellow, black, and green were chosen to reflect the sunshine, the Spanish flag, and the green of nature. This was important in the development of Spain as a tourist brand.[6]

The next stage involved development of a promotional campaign highlighting the diversity of Spanish tourism. Advertisements showing historic towns and villages, dramatic scenery with castles, interesting cuisine, colorful festivals, and sporting activities were featured with the caption "Spain, everything under the sun" and were placed in newspapers and magazines in important tourist origin markets. Well-known images of Spain such as flamenco dancing, bullfighting, and crowded beaches were avoided. By 1988, 800 million *pesetas* (around US$6 million in 1995 dollars) had been invested in this advertising campaign.

Two major international events[7] were held in Spain in 1992: the Olympic Games in Barcelona and EXPO in Seville. To create a more contemporary image and reposition Spain, Turespana launched a new promotional campaign featuring the slogan, "Spain, Passion for Life" (see Figure 7.6). The campaign stressed the creativity and dynamism of modern Spain as well as the passion, style, and vitality of its people. The goal was to differentiate Spain from its competitors and appeal to more demanding and higher spending tourists. The visual images in this campaign conveyed physical and intellectual activity through art, sport, nature, cuisine, and imagination. The advertising message was designed to appeal to allocentrics looking for challenge and adventure.

Today's specials include Art, Ballet, Theatre, Music, Sports, Concerts and Exhibitions.

In Madrid, you don't need a good food guide. Starting at the Puerta del Sol and eating your way outwards, you'll encounter a bewildering variety of tapas bars, comedores and restaurants. • And your fellow drivers will be more than happy to mark your card for between-meals activities. • Perhaps a little classical music or world class rock or jazz? Or maybe the colour of international theatre or ballet is more to your palate? Then there's the all pervading art of the capital, from the Prado to the plazas. • With good reason, the world is coming to eat at Madrid's table. • And you are strongly advised to join the party.

Passion
for life.

For further information please contact your travel agent. The Spanish Tourist Office. 57 St. James's Street. London SW1A 1LD.
Telex: 888138. Prestel: 46047. For replies please send legible address label.

*Figure 7.6
Sample advertise-
ment from the
"Passion of
Spain" cam-
paign. (Courtesy
of Secretaria Gen-
eral de Turismo.
Turespaña.)*

TABLE 7.2
Advertising Budget for the "Passion for Spain"
Campaign Allocated by Geographic Market, 1992

Country	Budget (Spanish Pesetas, Millions)
Germany	350
Britain	250
France	250
Italy	190
Japan	125
Other markets	399
Spain (local)	2
Total	1566

Source: Martín-Quirós, personal communication with the office of the General Secretary for Tourism (1992).

Media budget allocations by geographic market area in 1992 are presented in Table 7.2. The campaign, which allocated 60 percent of the budget to magazines, 20 percent to newspapers, and 20 percent to television, was successful in gaining positive exposure of Spain in Northern Europe. For example, the *Daily Telegraph*, a national newspaper in the United Kingdom, carried a free three-part color guide to "the Spain other people will never discover" in the spring of 1992. The campaign was well-timed and journalists drew on these materials to prepare press reports on EXPO and the Olympics.

The Growth of Regional Autonomy The constitution of 1978, which established Spain as a democracy, set up 17 autonomous regions each with its own elected government and administration. Considerable powers were devolved to these regions, notably responsibility for the development and administration of tourism. The regions are subdivided into municipalities, otherwise known as *town councils*, that undertake local promotion and run the local tourist offices. Thus, there are three levels of official administration for tourism in Spain, headed by the central government in Madrid, which is responsible for promoting Spain as a whole and the development of infrastructure. The empowerment of the regions, their greater role in tourism policy formulation, and cooperation among local businesses and neighboring towns have strengthened the Spanish tourism industry at the local level.

Regions that receive the most tourists (e.g., Catalonia, Valencia, the Balearic Islands) have developed their own tourism plans (Fayos Solá, 1992). For example, seafront improvements including demolition of buildings to widen the beach and promenade, planting palm trees, and enhancing the esthetics of the central resort area occurred in Magalluf on the Balearic island of Majorca in 1992–1993 (BBC, 1993).

Lloret de Mar, on the Catalonian Costa Brava, launched a major program of public works and private initiatives in 1991, including investment in a marina, a conference center, botanical gardens, and restoration of the old town. These repositioning initiatives resulted in improvements to the quality of the tourist environment, thereby enabling the resort, which had been seen as the archetypal mass package tour destination, to appeal to a broader market (the slogan was "Lloret, quality of life").

Reducing the Role of Tour Operators—An Example Both the central and regional governments encouraged Spanish companies to assert greater control over their own industry[8] by reducing dependence on foreign tour operators, increasing marketing and management skill levels, and overcoming local rivalries through pooling expertise. One example of this was the establishment of an independent marketing organization in Catalonia in 1991. Catalonia is a large triangular-shaped region in the northeast of Spain that includes a long stretch of coastline known as the Costa Brava (which is translated as "the rugged coast") (see Figure 7.3). It has many well-established resorts, such as Tossa and Lloret de Mar. The city of Barcelona is located in this region. Catalonia, which receives around 20 percent of foreign visitors to Spain, has depended heavily on British and German tour operators.

The members of the hotel marketing organization, called the Costa Brava Centre, were 26 small (under 150 rooms), locally owned, independent, and mostly family-owned hotels on the northern part of the Costa Brava. The group began marketing in 1992 using a four-language brochure and a purpose-built communications center for direct booking by computer reservation. The brochure contained information on local cultural and sporting activities that reflected the Catalan heritage of the area. The target market was mobile independent travelers from France, Spain, Germany, Italy, and to a lesser extent, the United Kingdom.

The hotels, which represented a distinctly local character, differed in the degree of luxury (ranging from one to five stars) and in their location (some were on the coast while others were inland). This presented a challenge in that the hotels were not a single brand and the office staff needed to develop expertise in guiding enquirers to the right product. The group was also a purchasing organization, enabling its members to obtain supplies at more favorable rates than they could achieve individually.

The establishment of the group and its communications center involved considerable investment, both financially and in terms of business risk for the members. Prior to joining the organization they could rely on tour operators to fill their hotels, particularly in the low season. This was no longer the case.

In 1993 the group moved into the short holiday market by offering themed packages in the spring and autumn (e.g., hiking, sailing, golf, and gastronomic weekends). Developing such packages is the norm for tour companies, but it was an important step forward for a group of independent businesses and former rivals. For example, persuading local restaurants to join forces for a gastronomic weekend holiday was a major hurdle. In the words of one of the founding members, "the Centre has made us think beyond our own petty rivalries to work together to control our own industry."

This small, but interesting, venture represented a new independent and cooperative spirit in Spain. One measure of success was that overall bookings for the group increased threefold in 1993 compared to 1992. However, by 1994 a new demand pattern was emerging, with a larger percentage of tourists coming from the Spanish market, particularly from the nearby city of Barcelona. This demand is highly seasonal. Moreover, access to the international market remains a problem. Some hotels in the group have linked up with smaller independent tour operators in Northern Europe, but this cannot provide the "shop window" mass package that tour operators have at their disposal through their vertically integrated travel agencies.

CONCLUSION

This chapter has documented the growth of Spanish tourism and has shown how knowledge of certain aspects of tourism theory can enhance understanding of this process. Some Spanish resorts have declined in the way predicted by the the destination life cycle, but others have been rejuvenated through reinvestment and repositioning to appeal to new markets.

This chapter has also demonstrated (1) the important role of tour operators in selling a destination and (2) the long-term risks inherent in allowing tour operators to dominate the relationship between the destination and the tourists and to determine the image of the receiving country in international markets. Recent marketing campaigns have been successful in projecting a more diverse image of Spain and its tourist offerings. The image building was undoubtedly assisted by the international publicity and acclaim resulting from EXPO and the Olympic Games in 1992.

In terms of strengthening the role of Spanish companies in tourism, government initiatives and the greater power of the autonomous regions have had some effect in improving the business climate and infrastructure. However, considerable structural difficulties in the development of an independent home industry remain, especially given the prevalence of small businesses and local rivalry. Many are still reliant on international tour operators, although others, as the example from the Costa Brava has shown, have been able to reduce that dependence.

The underlying strengths of the Spanish tourism industry based on its climate, scenery, and culture, together with its proximity to the major tourist origin markets, has meant that the number of visitors has continued to grow despite the dip in demand in the early 1990s.

ACKNOWLEDGMENT

We would like to acknowledge the assistance of Bertrand Hallé (President, Costa Brava Hotels) in the preparation of this case study.

NOTES

1. See Chapters 2, 3, 5, and 28 for additional discussion of life cycle models.
2. See Chapters 9, 22, and 23 for further discussion of carrying capacity and limits of acceptable change.
3. See Chapter 4 for additional discussion of the role of international tour operators.
4. See Chapters 4, 5, 8, 17, 18, 22, and 23 for additional discussion on sustainable tourism and sustainable tourism development philosophies and concepts.
5. See Chapter 28 for an overview of the evolution of Spain's spa industry.
6. Branding is a marketing strategy that is well established in consumer markets, but it is still relatively undeveloped for tourist markets (see Parkinson et al., 1993).
7. See Chapters 19 and 27 for additional discussion relating to the roles of hallmark events and festivals in tourism.

8. See Chapters 9 and 15 for further discussion of issues pertaining to balancing power structures within the tourism industry.

REFERENCES

Albert-Piñole, I. 1993. Tourism in Spain. In W. Pompl and P. Lavery (eds.), *Tourism in Europe*. Oxford, UK: C.A.B. International, pp. 242–261.

British Broadcasting Corporation (BBC). 1993. Radio 4, *Breakaway*, 1 May.

Butler, R.W. 1980. The concept of a tourist area cycle of evolution: implications for the management of resources, *Canadian Geographer*, 24(1), 5–12.

Concentracion y Asociacionismo Empresarial en el Sector Turistic. 1989. Study undertaken in 1988 with the assistance of Doxa S.A. *Estudios Turisticos*, Vol. 103.

Cooper, C.P. 1990. *The Life Cycle Concept and Tourism*. Paper presented at Tourism Research into the 1990s conference, University of Durham.

Diamond, N.P. 1990. A *Strategy for Cold Water Resorts into the Year 2000*. Unpublished MSc thesis. Surrey, UK: University of Surrey.

Drexl, C. and P. Agel. 1987. Tour operators in West Germany, *Travel & Tourism Analyst*. London: Economist Intelligence Unit.

El Turismo Español en Cifras. 1991. *Estudios Turisticos*, Vol. 113, Dirección General de la Politica Turistica.

Fayos Solá, E. 1992. A strategic outlook for regional tourism policy: the white paper on Valencian tourism, *Tourism Management*, 13(1), 45–49.

Fitch, A. 1987. Tourism in the UK, *Travel & Tourism Analyst*. London: Economist Intelligence Unit.

France, L. and M. Barke. 1992. *Torremolinos: The Evolution of a Resort*. Tourism in Europe 1992 Conference, Durham, UK, July.

Gonzales, G. 1994. Las Grandes cadenas apuestas por la calidad, *Cinco Dias*, 25 March, 107.

Haywood, K.M. 1986. Can the tourist area life cycle be made operational? *Tourism Management*, 7, 154–167.

Hooper, J. 1995. *The New Spaniards*. Harmondsworth, UK: Penguin Books.

Martín-Quirós, M.A. 1992. *Spain's Branding Strategy*. Unpublished MBA dissertation. Bradford, UK: University of Bradford.

Mill, R.C. and A.M. Morrison. 1992. *The Tourism System*, 2nd ed. Upper Saddle River, NJ: Prentice-Hall International.

Office of Fair Trading. 1994. Press Release 37/94, *Decision on the Travel Industry*. Announced 11 August, London.

Parkinson, S., M.A. Martín, and L. Parkinson. 1993. A *Passion for Life: The Development of Spain as an International Tourist Board*. Proceedings from 22nd EMAC Conference, Vol II, ESADE, Barcelona.

Pearce, D. 1989. *Tourist Development*, 2nd ed. London: Longman, Harlow.

Plazas Garbine. 1994. El major año de toda la historia será 1994, *Cinco Dias*, 25 April, Dirección General de la Politica Turistica.

Plog, S.C. 1973. Why destination areas rise and fall in popularity, *Cornell Hotel and Restaurant Association Quarterly*, November, 13–16.

Rogers, Everett M. 1962. *Diffusion of Innovation*. New York: Free Press of Glencoe.

Secretaria General de Turismo. 1990. Libro Blanco del Turismo Español, Madrid.

Secretaria General de Turismo. 1993. Libro Blanco del Turismo Español, Madrid.

Shaw, G. and A.M. Williams. 1994. *Critical Issues in Tourism: A Geographical Perspective*. Oxford: Blackwell.

Urry, J. 1990. *The Tourist Gaze: Leisure and Travel in Contemporary Societies*. London: Sage.

Wolfe, R.I. 1983. Recreational travel, the new migration revisited, *Ontario Geography*, 19, 103–124.

World Commission on Environment and Development. 1987. *Our Common Future* (known as the Brundtland Report). Oxford: Oxford University Press.

ℊ | PROBLEM SOLVING AND DISCUSSION ACTIVITIES

1. How and why has Spain been able to maintain its position as one of the world's major tourist destinations?

2. Identify and examine the positive and negative effects of international tour companies in the development of tourism in Spain.

3. For any region with which you are familiar, discuss the role international tour companies have played in the evolution of tourism. Has this role changed in recent years, or are changes to the role likely? Why or why not?

4. What can the members of the Costa Brava Centre do to address some of the issues that still remain with respect to enhancing the position of their region in the international tourism marketplace?

5. Outline challenges that a destination might face when attempting to reposition itself in the international tourism marketplace. Identify two examples of international tourist destinations that have successfully achieved this objective and delineate factors that likely contributed to their success.

6. Is Butler's tourist area cycle of evolution relevant to the part of the world in which you live?

8

Maintaining Competitiveness in a New World Order

REGIONAL SOLUTIONS TO CARIBBEAN TOURISM SUSTAINABILITY PROBLEMS

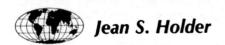 *Jean S. Holder*

ℊ | KEY LEARNING POINTS

- Tourism sustainability is often addressed from an environmental perspective (e.g., carrying capacity, solid and liquid waste disposal, coastal pollution and erosion, water quality, deforestation, air pollution, and the protection of natural assets). Less frequently this is coupled with sociocultural concerns. However, to be sustainable, Caribbean tourism must also be profitable, competitive, safe, acceptable, and under Caribbean management and control.

- Global strategic alliances created under the New World Order (i.e., as a consequence of globalized markets) have endorsed the philosophies of "survival of the fittest" and "marginalization of the weak." The processes of deregulation, liberalization, free trade, privatization, and consolidation cannot be taken in a vacuum as inherently good. They have obvious advantages, but they are reactions to past problems caused by bureaucratic overregulation, state control, and protectionism through tariff and nontariff barriers to trade.

- There are cases where some regulation is required, some protection is desirable, and some limits to privatization and other processes must be set, either to protect the weak or because the benefits of a particular process have produced greater negative effects than positive results. Caribbean tourism-dependent states must develop alliances among themselves to provide the critical mass required to compete in a world of giants that have developed ground rules in their own interest.

- Short-term solutions which cede total control of key industries to foreign companies will ultimately lead to problems worse than those solved.

INTRODUCTION

The Caribbean region, comprised largely of small island states, developed a comparative advantage in tourism during the 1960s to 1980s that permitted a relatively high standard of living for Caribbean people. The base of the economy in some states was broadened by the addition of financial and other related services. In others, there had already been some diversification through the production and export of primary products to old and new colonial powers. A few of the larger states with oil and bauxite resources and/or populations large enough to support an industrial sector were, for a while, at the top of the table of developing states.

Worldwide dramatic geopolitical and economic changes in the 1990s have threatened the future of, or diminished the earnings from, the export of crops and manufactured items, thereby creating a growing dependence on tourism in the Caribbean. At least in the short term, the economic survival of the Caribbean would seem to depend on creating a sustainable tourism industry. However, this sustainability is threatened by potential negative environmental impacts, escalating competition, an unprofitable hotel sector, loss of control over air access, significant levels of crime in some destinations, and the failure of local populations to benefit from the increased jobs and wealth likely to flow from better development of linkages between tourism and other economic sectors.

By aggregating resources to tackle problems that are regional in scope, functional cooperation, both among the states and at other public and private sector levels, seems to be the key to future economic survival because it can lead to the creation of a competitive force.

This chapter examines the implications of the factors outlined above for the sustainability of tourism in the Caribbean. Following the presentation of background information on tourism in the region, this chapter provides an overview of a regional approach to addressing the challenges. Two main arguments underlie the strategic approach as outlined: (1) Preservation of the environment, though a necessary condition, is not sufficient for the sustainability of the tourism industry in the Caribbean, and (2) given the small size and other geographical and economic realities of the majority of Caribbean states, dealing successfully with the frame conditions is best achieved through the formation of partnerships. The countries of focus are the 32 states that are members of the Caribbean Tourism Organization (CTO).

TOURISM SUSTAINABILITY AND COOPERATION IN THE TOURISM INDUSTRY: CONTEMPORARY PERSPECTIVES AND ISSUES

Tourism has often been described as an industry that destroys the resources on which it depends for its very existence. Much of the discussion on sustainability[1] has correctly been focused on the negative impacts that growing numbers of visitors and the provision of facilities for them have had on the marine and land resources (both natural and built). In many parts of the world, tourism seems to be suffering from its own success.

The World Travel and Tourism Environment Review (WTTERC) quotes the *Financial Times* of January 9, 1993 as describing the Mediterranean Sea, a major tourism area, as a "diluted sewer":

The Mediterranean Basin is home to 130 million people and is visited by 100 million tourists annually. Jointly these generate two billion tons of sewage of which roughly 30 percent is treated. The remainder is discharged into the sea untreated and contaminates the area with little room to escape. The result? Only 4 percent of shellfish from the area are considered fit for human consumption and periodic increases in algae are to be expected.

The executive director of the Coral Reef Alliance (based in the United States), speaking on World Oceans Day 1995, said:

> . . . at the current rate of destruction, up to 70 percent of the world's coral reefs may be killed within our lifetime. Of the 234,320 square miles of coral reefs worldwide, ten percent are already destroyed beyond recovery; 30 percent face a similar fate in the next 20 years. Destruction of the reefs would mean the extinction of thousands of marine species and elimination of the primary source of food, employment, and income for millions of people.

The dangers are greatest when the countries involved are small islands with fragile social and ecological systems. Solutions posed speak to determining carrying capacity,[2] introducing and promoting environmental education, and establishing regulatory systems that reward preventative action and punish infringement of established codes and conventions (Holder, 1988). This chapter takes a more comprehensive look at the factors that affect the sustainability of tourism in the Caribbean region (see Figure 2.3), particularly the 32 members of the Caribbean Tourism Organization (CTO).

Sustainable development is a concept that marries two often conflicting ideas: development and sustainability. Development has traditionally been defined in terms of growth—that is, higher gross domestic product (GDP), more construction, more houses, more of everything. On the other hand, sustainability, which connotes survival, involves achieving a balance, and balance often requires moderation and control. Sustainable development, therefore, is about balancing growth through the use and conservation of resources such that those resources remain intact and available for succeeding generations. Governments, particularly in small countries, are frequently subjected to pressure from developers to choose unrestrained development (growth) over planned, careful, and modest growth.

The CTO has defined tourism as an environmentally dependent industry (Holder, 1988) in that its core resources are the natural and built environments of the tourist destination. To these may be added sociocultural and historic assets. Together these comprise the tourism product. The hotel room is simply a base from which tourists experience the destination's assets (Holder, 1988). Any industry that manages its resources in such a manner that they become depleted (especially when they are nonrenewable) must inevitably self-destruct. It is, therefore, a necessary condition of tourism's sustainability (in the sense of its survival) that the environmental and sociocultural resources comprising the product are not destroyed in the process of the tourism development activity itself.

This chapter argues that preservation of the environment, though a necessary condition, is not a sufficient condition for the sustainability of tourism in the Caribbean. Other factors that supply the frame conditions within which tourism in the region will succeed or fail must be present. "Sustainable tourism development," which has been defined in terms of preserving tourism's core resources, is contrasted with "sustainable tourism," which is defined in terms of the additional factors needed to ensure its success. The distinction is elaborated elsewhere (e.g., Butler, 1994).

This chapter also argues that, given the small size and other geographical and economic realities of the majority of Caribbean states, dealing successfully with the frame conditions is best achieved through the formulation of partnerships—that is, partnerships between the tourism public and private sectors and partnerships among the states that comprise the region.

The need for partnership between government and the private sector derives from the nature of tourism itself. The country is, in the broadest sense, the tourism product; it is the country as a product that is offered by the government (Holder, 1992). For tourism to work well, the physical offer of the hotel plant and other facilities must be complemented by the country's infrastructure, public services, and public utilities. The attitudes of private sector service personnel must be complemented by those of front-line public sector officials at ports, airports, and elsewhere.

Governments must market the destination if the hotel advertising campaign is to have its fullest impact in global marketplaces. Government's research and statistics, and its tracking of global trends, provide a background against which private sector plans can be developed. Government policies can either facilitate or frustrate business development. Public sector–private sector integrated approaches to marketing the destination create a focus and rationalization of resources. Only governments can establish and enforce environmental quality standards that the entire society must observe. In brief, government is responsible for maintaining the rails along which the private sector drives the train (Holder, 1992).

Owen (1992) argued for the cooperative approach as follows:

> If the public sector and the private sector in any country, or in any group of nations sharing close political or economic interests, cannot combine effectively to promote tourism, the potential of this burgeoning industry will not be realized or may be realized only at the cost of, say, the product's quality (and long term profitability) or the host community's environment and way of life.

This view, expressed with respect to European countries, has even more relevance when applied to the Caribbean because it is populated largely by microstates with limited resources, must deal with major conglomerates, and competes with large developed states and megablocs of states. Strategic alliances among Caribbean states working within the CTO, national hotel associations working within the Caribbean Hotel Association (CHA), and alliances between the CTO and the CHA have created a formula for public sector–private sector and regional cooperation that is being held as "best practice" for the rest of the world (Owen, 1992). The Pacific Asia Travel Association (PATA) and the European Travel Commission (ETC) provide other examples.

THE CARIBBEAN REGION AND TOURISM

The Caribbean region is said to be the world's most tourism-dependent region, relying as it does on tourism for approximately 25 percent of its export earnings (compared to a world average of about 7 percent; WTO, 1990). Tourism development, which began in a few states such as Cuba, Jamaica, Bahamas, Bermuda, and Barbados in the 1940s and 1950s, spread rapidly across the region after the demise of the Cuban tourism industry following the Cuban revolution in 1959. By the mid-1990s, regardless of size or level of economic development, there was not a single Caribbean state that had not ranked tourism either as *the* priority for economic development or as being among the priorities.

Several Caribbean states, in varying stages of structural adjustment, perceive tourism to be capable of addressing their two most pressing problems of scarce foreign reserves and unacceptably high levels of unemployment. In spite of an undeserved reputation for fickleness, tourism has shown remarkable resilience since the mid- to late 1970s in the face of two major energy crises, a number of recessions, and the Gulf War in 1991.

Caribbean tourism has consistently outperformed international tourism, growing 83.4 percent between 1983 and 1993 (cf. international tourist arrivals 70.9 percent), and 26.8 percent from 1988 to 1993 (cf. international tourist arrivals 24.4 percent). From 1970 through 1993, Caribbean stayover tourist arrivals grew by 217 percent, or at an average annual rate of 5.1 percent (CTO, 1993). In 1993, visitors spent an estimated US$11.145 billion, or 11.6 percent more than in 1992 (see Table 8.1). Direct and indirect employment in Caribbean states (excluding Mexico) in 1993 was estimated at 500,000. Stayover tourist arrivals were close to 13.3 million (see Table 8.2), and cruise passenger arrivals were just under 8.9 million (see Table 8.3).

Predictions are that the Caribbean's dependence on tourism will become even greater. This is a function of the reality that tourism has become the world's fastest growing industry (WTTC, 1995), as well as the fact that several of the Caribbean's other economic sectors are either in decline or threatened.[3]

ECONOMIC HISTORY AND STRUCTURE OF THE CARIBBEAN REGION

The Caribbean region is comprised of 40 states, 29 of which are islands. Nonisland nations include Mexico; the Central American states of Guatemala, Honduras, Belize, El Salvador, Nicaragua, Costa Rica, and Panama; and the South American states of Colombia, Guyana, Suriname, and Venezuela. The term *Caribbean region* is used, although a number of states are not touched by the Caribbean Sea. The Bahamas, Guyana, and Suriname are located in the Atlantic Ocean but are part of the Caribbean Community (CARICOM). El Salvador, which is in Central America, has only a Pacific coastline. However, these four countries are situated close to the Caribbean Sea and share a socioeconomic and political history with the states in, or bordering on, the Caribbean Sea.

Fourteen of the 29 island states have populations under 100,000 persons, and an additional ten have populations under 500,000 (see Table 8.4). Seventeen of the islands have a land area less than 195 square miles (500 square kilometers). If Mexico, Venezuela, Cuba, the Dominican Republic, and Haiti are excluded, the Caribbean might be described as comprising a large number of tiny states that are poorly endowed with the kind of resources traditionally associated with industrial development. Many are also geographically isolated from one another.

The region had been balkanized, first by the major European metropolitan colonial powers of England, France, Spain, and Holland and later by the United States, into four

TABLE 8.1
Estimates of Visitor Expenditure[a], 1989–1993

Country	1989	1990	1991	1992	1993
Anguilla[b]	28.1	34.6	30.8	35.2	43.3
Antigua and Barbuda	267.1	298.2	314.0	329.0	372.1[c]
Aruba[d]	309.8	353.4	400.5	442.4	463.9
Bahamas	1,310.0	1,332.9	1,192.7	1,243.5	1,304.0
Barbados	527.8	493.5	459.7	462.5	528.0
Belize	78.9	91.4	94.5	64.7	71.6
Bermuda	450.8	490.1	456.0	443.0[b]	504.5
Bonaire[d]	13.4	17.7	24.0	26.7	27.8[c]
British Virgin Islands	124.7	132.1	109.4	109.4[e]	122.0[c]
Cayman Islands[f]	177.4	235.7	222.3	229.6	258.5
Cuba	204.0	243.4	387.4	567.0	720.0
Curacao	98.0	238.4[f]	232.2	234.2	241.2
Dominica	18.5	25.0	28.1	30.3	33.2
Dominican Republic[b,d]	818.4	899.5	877.5	1,054.8	1,233.8
Grenada	30.8	37.5	41.7	42.3	48.1
Guadeloupe[b]	203.3	197.1	233.6	269.0	369.8
Guyana[b]	28.1	26.8	30.3	31.2	36.4[c]
Haiti	46.0	46.0	46.0	46.0	46.0
Jamaica	593.0	740.0	764.0	850.0[b]	950.0
Martinique	272.3	240.0	254.6	281.6	331.5
Montserrat[b]	9.1	7.2	9.9	13.6	15.2
Puerto Rico[b,g]	1,234.5	1,367.0	1,435.7	1,520.0	1,629.1
St. Kitts and Nevis[b]	52.5	57.7	67.5	67.2	76.6
St. Lucia	144.6	153.8	173.4	207.9	221.0
St. Maarten[d,h]	260.3	315.5	309.9	340.1	376.4[c]
St. Vincent and the Grenadines	50.5	56.0	53.0	52.7	54.5
Suriname	7.8	10.7	10.7	10.7	10.7
Trinidad and Tobago	84.5	94.7	100.9	109.2	82.0
Turks and Caicos Islands	39.3	36.5	50.1	47.8	53.0
US Virgin Islands[b]	625.1	704.9	750.3	826.6	921.2
Total	8,108.6	8,977.3	9,160.7	9,988.2	11,145.4

[a] US$ millions, at current prices.
[b] Revised.
[c] Provisional.
[d] Central Bank estimates.
[e] CTO estimate.
[f] New series.
[g] Fiscal years.
[h] Includes estimates for Saba and St. Eustatius.

Note: The three destinations presented in italics are not CTO members. Other CTO members not identified in the table are Mexico, St. Barts, St. Martin, Saba, St. Eustatius, and Venezuela.

Sources: National Tourism Offices and CTO estimates.

TABLE 8.2
Stayover Tourist Arrivals in the Caribbean, 1989–1993

Country	1989 (Thousands)	1990 (Thousands)	1991 (Thousands)	1992 (Thousands)	1993 (Thousands)	Percent Change 1992–1993
Bahamas	1,575.1	1,561.6	1,427.0	1,398.9	1,488.7	6.4
Bermuda	416.0	432.7	385.3	373.5	412.5	10.4
OECS Countries	573.6	619.5	649.7	688.7	755.6	9.7
Antigua and Barbuda	198.0	205.7	204.7	217.9	249.4	14.5
Dominica	35.2	45.1	46.3	47.0	51.9	10.4
Grenada	68.6	82.0	85.0	87.6	93.9	7.2
Montserrat	17.0[a]	18.7	19.2	17.3[b]	21.0	21.4
St. Kitts and Nevis	72.1	75.7	83.9	88.3	88.6	0.3
St. Lucia	132.8	138.4	159.0	177.5	194.1	9.4
St. Vincent and the Grenadines	49.9	53.9	51.6	53.1	56.7	6.8
Other Commonwealths	2,071.7	2,233.8	2,204.8	2,176.6[c]	2,605.3	19.8[c]
Anguilla	28.4	31.2	29.7	30.4	36.7	20.7
Barbados	461.3	432.1	394.2	385.5	396.0	2.7
Belize	172.8	216.4	215.4	247.3	284.5	15.0
British Virgin Islands	175.8	160.0	136.4	NA[h]	200.2	—
Cayman Islands	209.7	253.2	237.4	241.8	287.3	18.8
Guyana	67.4	64.2	72.8	74.9	107.1	43.0
Jamaica	714.8	840.8	844.6	909.0	978.7	7.7
Trinidad and Tobago	194.2	194.0	219.7	234.7	248.0	5.7
Turks and Caicos Islands	47.3	41.9	54.6	52.0	66.8	28.5
Dutch West Indies	1,095.2	1,264.8	1,327.0	1,406.0	1,386.0	(1.4)
Aruba	344.3	432.8	501.3	541.7	562.0	3.7
Bonaire	37.2	41.3	49.5	50.6	55.1	8.9
Curacao	193.0	207.7	205.6	206.9	214.1	3.5
Saba[d]	10.6	11.7	13.4	25.2[f]	25.1	(0.4)
St. Eustatius[e]	6.4	6.6	9.2	12.9	9.5	(26.4)
St. Maarten	503.7	564.7	548.0	568.7	520.2	(8.5)
French West Indies	595.7	569.9	685.6	661.2	819.1	23.9
Guadeloupe	284.0	288.4	370.5	340.5	452.7	33.0
Martinique	311.7	281.5	315.1	320.7	366.4	14.2
US Territories	2,893.8	3,022.2	3,083.3	3,127.1	3,417.8	9.3
Puerto Rico[g]	2,443.8	2,559.7	2,613.0	2,639.8	2,856.6	8.2
US Virgin Islands	450.0[b]	462.5[b]	470.3[b]	487.3	561.2	15.2

TABLE 8.2
Stayover Tourist Arrivals in the Caribbean, 1989–1993 (Continued)

Country	1989 (Thousands)	1990 (Thousands)	1991 (Thousands)	1992 (Thousands)	1993 (Thousands)	Percent Change 1992–1993
Other Countries	1,869.0	2,018.8	1,990.8	2,134.4	2,413.1	13.1
Cuba	326.3	340.3	424.0	460.6	544.1	18.1
Dominican Republic	1,400.0[b]	1,530.0	1,416.8[b]	1,523.8	1,719.0	12.8
Haiti[a]	122.0	120.0	120.0	120.0	120.0	—
Suriname	20.7	28.5	30.0[a]	30.0[a]	30.0[a]	—
Total	11,090.1	11,723.3	11,753.5	11,965.4[c]	13,298.1	11.1[c]

[a] CTO estimate.
[b] Revised.
[c] Does not include BVI stayover visitors.
[d] Air arrivals, including excursionists.
[e] Excluding Antilleans.
[f] New series.
[g] Fiscal years (July–June).
[h] NA, not available.

Note: The three destinations presented in italics are not CTO members. Other CTO members not identified in the table are Mexico, St. Barts, St. Martin, and Venezuela.

distinct language groups of largely primary producers catering to the needs of different "mother countries." The English, French, Spanish, Dutch, and American dependencies practiced a culture of isolationism in respect of each other and, with few exceptions, existed in a state of dependence supported by preference systems and protected markets in the mother country and/or by "grants in aid" that subsidized inadequate local budgets.

Until the arrival of tourism, many of these states survived on the export of sugar and products like rum, coffee, bananas, spices, cotton, and tobacco. Others, like Aruba and Curacao, that were not major primary producers depended on the economic activity of oil refineries located by metropolitan companies in their states. A few, including Guyana and Jamaica (with bauxite) and Trinidad and Tobago (with oil and gas deposits), were able to achieve a significant level of economic diversification and even develop a respectable industrial sector.

However, even these advantages have been threatened by world economic developments, thereby creating a greater shift to tourism than was earlier thought desirable. For many residents, emigration to the mother country during the colonial period provided an economic safety valve when existing economic activity failed to provide adequate employment opportunities. This possibility, in most cases, no longer exists, since citizens of those states that achieved independence lost the right of automatic entry to live and work in the metropolitan countries of which they had been colonial territories.

Tourism development was a natural option for a region that is endowed with an almost perfect warm climate year round, myriad white sand beaches, clean air and clear unpolluted waters, a variegated tropical landscape, and a built environment that reflects

TABLE 8.3
Cruise Passenger Arrivals, 1989–1993

Country	1989 (Thousands)	1990 (Thousands)	1991 (Thousands)	1992 (Thousands)	1993 (Thousands)	Percent Change 1992–1993
Antigua and Barbuda	208.0	227.3	255.6	250.2	238.4	(4.7)
Aruba	70.3	130.0	133.2	216.6	251.1	15.9
Bahamas[a]	1,644.6	1,853.9	2,020.0	2,139.4	2,047.0	(4.3)
Barbados	337.1	362.6	372.1	399.7	428.6	7.2
Bermuda[b]	131.3	112.6	128.2	131.0	153.9	17.5
Bonaire	7.0	4.5	12.5	28.2	17.4	(38.3)
British Virgin Islands	71.6	95.1	78.9	87.6	85.8	(2.0)
Cayman Islands	403.9	361.7	474.7	613.5	605.7	(1.3)
Curacao	117.3	158.6	156.6	160.1	182.9	14.2
Dominica	7.3	6.8	65.0	89.8	87.8	(2.2)
Dominican Republic[c]	100.0	50.0[d]	50.0[d]	50.0[d]	50.0[d]	—
Grenada	120.7	183.2	196.1	195.9	200.1	2.1
Guadeloupe[e]	86.3	130.0	282.4	245.7	262.5	6.8
Jamaica	444.1	385.8	490.5	649.5	629.6	(3.1)
Martinique	368.2	421.3	417.0	398.9	428.7	7.5
Montserrat[c]	NA[f]	NA	NA	4.5	10.0	122.2
Puerto Rico	800.1	892.9	994.9	1,019.2	968.1	(5.0)
St. Kitts and Nevis	36.6	33.9	52.8	74.0	83.1	12.3
St. Lucia	104.3	101.9	152.8	164.9	154.4	(6.4)
St. Maarten	472.0	515.0	502.2	469.7	659.9	40.5
St. Vincent and the Grenadines	49.7[g]	78.6	87.6	63.4	69.3	9.3
Trinidad and Tobago	16.5[h]	32.4	31.7	26.9	32.6	21.2
US Virgin Islands[a]	1,062.6	1,119.6	1,221.1	1,277.3	1,208.7	(5.4)
Total[i]	6,710.0	7,450.0	8,150.0	8,780.0	8,880.0	1.1

[a] At first port of entry only.

[b] Excludes sea/air arrivals.

[c] All sea arrivals.

[d] CTO Estimate.

[e] Port of Guadeloupe only (excludes arrivals at St. Barts).

[f] NA, not available.

[g] Data incomplete due to fire.

[h] Revised.

[i] Includes estimates for missing data.

Note 1: Total cruise passenger arrivals as given above represent the sum of arrivals at individual destinations. However, because most cruise ships stop at more than one destination this figure is considerably larger than the number of cruise passengers visiting the region.

Note 2: The two destinations presented in italics are not CTO members.

Source: Section 3 of the 1993 Caribbean Tourism Report and CTO estimates.

TABLE 8.4
Midyear Population Estimates, 1989–1993

Country	1989 (Thousands)	1990 (Thousands)	1991 (Thousands)	1992 (Thousands)	1993 (Thousands)
Anguilla	8.4	8.7	9.0	9.0[a]	9.0
Antigua and Barbuda	65.0	65.0	66.0	66.0	66.0
Aruba	61.5	64.6	64.7	71.2	71.2
Bahamas	249.0	255.0	259.0	264.0	269.0
Barbados	259.8	260.6	261.6	262.8	263.5
Belize	184.5	189.0	194.0	199.0	205.0
Bermuda	59.1	59.6	58.5	58.8	59.0
Bonaire	10.8	11.0	11.0	11.1	11.1
British Virgin Islands	14.3	16.6	17.0	17.5	18.0
Cayman Islands	24.7	25.7	26.5	28.5	30.0
Cuba	10,503.0	10,608.0	10,709.0	10,808.0	10,900.0
Curacao	147.7	145.8	145.3	144.1	144.0
Dominica	71.7	71.4	71.2	71.6	72.9
Dominican Republic	7,007.0	7,168.0	7,333.0	7,471.0	7,624.0
Grenada	105.8	107.1	94.8	95.4	96.0
Guadeloupe	384.0	390.0	396.0	400.0	405.0
Guyana	753.1	749.9	739.6	760.0	768.0
Haiti	6,361.8	6,486.0	6,619.0	6,754.0	6,893.0
Jamaica	2,363.5	2,403.0	2,425.2	2,448.0	2,470.0
Martinique	354.4	359.6	359.6	359.6	360.0
Mexico	76,600.0	81,200.0	82,900.0	84,600.0	86,400.0
Montserrat	11.9	11.0	11.0	11.0	10.0
Puerto Rico	3,497.0	3,528.0	3,549.0	3,579.0	3,621.0
Saba	1.1	1.1	1.1	1.1	1.1
St. Eustatius	1.9	1.7	1.8	1.8	1.9
St. Kitts and Nevis	42.0	41.9	41.0	41.0	41.0
St. Lucia	132.2	134.1	136.0	138.2	139.9
St. Maarten	29.8	31.7	32.6	32.2	33.0
St. Vincent and the Grenadines	114.3	115.7	107.6	108.9	109.4
Suriname	400.8	402.5	404.0	405.5	405.1
Trinidad and Tobago	1,213.2	1,227.4	1,237.0	1,252.0	1,260.0
Turks and Caicos Islands	12.0	12.4	12.6	12.8	13.0
US Virgin Islands	108.9	104.8	106.0	107.5	109.0
Venezuela	18,872.0	19,321.0	19,787.0	20,249.0	20,712.0

[a] Population census 1992.

Note: The three destinations presented in italics are not CTO members.

Sources: UNECLAC, IBRD, CDB, and Country Document.

the cultural diversity resulting from the historic meeting of Europeans, Africans, Asians, and Americans. The process was accelerated by social legislation in metropolitan countries that provided holidays with pay and technological developments in air transportation that made long-haul travel both swift and affordable (Savignac, 1994).

Caribbean stayover tourist arrivals grew from 4.2 million in 1970 to approximately 13.3 million in 1993 (CTO, 1993). The Caribbean has also become the world's premiere cruise tourism destination (EIU, 1992). In 1994, according to the Cruise Line International Association (CLIA), 19.1 million bed-days, or 54.9 percent of total worldwide capacity, were assigned to the Caribbean and Bermuda (CLIA, 1994). Between 1989 and 1993, total cruise passenger visits to the Caribbean increased by 32.3 percent (see Table 8.3).

The 1960s were good years for the Caribbean. Tourism prospered, and export agriculture enjoyed protected markets at guaranteed prices. A number of English-speaking Commonwealth Caribbean states followed the example of Puerto Rico by inviting foreign companies to establish light industries for reexport based on an offer of prolonged tax holidays, an educated work force, and a low-wage bill.

However, several factors emerged in the 1970s and 1980s to "destroy this dream," including energy crises and attendant economic recessions, the contraction of the business of foreign investors as tax holidays ran out, increased wages caused by inflation and union activity, widespread competition both from within the guaranteed markets for products such as sugar and from other sources (e.g., from Central American dollar bananas), and competition for manufactured goods from the countries of the Pacific Rim. By the 1990s, tourism had become the major earner of foreign exchange in the majority of Caribbean states and, in a number of cases, visitor expenditure surpassed earnings from all other merchandise exports combined (see Tables 8.5 and 8.6).

Burdened by the need to service massive long-term external debt, a number of countries were either in structural adjustment programs with the International Monetary Fund (IMF) or seemed in danger of so entering. Between 1984 and 1990 Barbados' debt grew from approximately US$399 million to US$531 million, Jamaica's from US$2071 million to just over US$4152 million, and Antigua and Barbuda's from US$54 million to about US$268 million. Trinidad and Tobago's debt increased from US$1299 million in 1985 to US$2520 million in 1990 (CTO, 1993). Increasingly, the burden of servicing this debt and paying for greater amounts of imports was being shifted to the tourism industry, which was challenged to increase its foreign exchange earnings.

FACTORS AFFECTING THE CARIBBEAN REGION IN THE 1990s

The 1990s have witnessed the culmination of a worldwide process that is proceeding at several levels which will further marginalize the Caribbean's agricultural and manufacturing sectors. At a global level, the world's most developed and rich nations are creating trade agreements that will further reduce the status of Third World countries as trading partners unless special transitional arrangements are made. With the admission of Austria, Finland, and Sweden to the European Union (EU) on January 1, 1995, the EU's population expanded from 348 million to 370 million (40 percent more than the United

TABLE 8.5
Ratio of Visitor Expenditure to Merchandise Exports, 1989–1993

Country	1989	1990	1991	1992	1993
Anguilla	75.95	93.51	83.24	47.57	NA
Antigua and Barbuda	NA[a]	17.86	NA	NA	NA
Aruba	2.88	2.63	2.05	1.55	1.74
Bahamas	0.51	0.51	NA	NA	NA
Barbados	2.82	2.34	2.26	2.34	2.90
Belize	0.63	0.69	0.75	0.46	0.54
Bermuda	9.02	8.20	9.31	5.26	14.29
Bonaire	2.69	4.59	3.80	1.58	NA
British Virgin Islands	NA	40.03	NA	NA	NA
Cayman Islands	69.57	62.52	73.13	51.02	NA
Cuba	0.04	NA	NA	NA	NA
Curacao	0.07	0.13	NA	NA	NA
Dominica	0.41	0.45	0.52	0.56	0.65
Dominican Republic	0.89	1.22	1.33	1.79	NA
Grenada	1.10	1.41	1.80	2.12	2.36
Guyana	0.13	0.12	0.12	0.09	0.09
Haiti	0.31	0.29	0.38	1.12	NA
Jamaica	0.67	0.72	1.24	0.78	1.22
Martinique	1.40	0.88	1.18	1.09	NA
Montserrat	7.22	4.86	4.76	8.61	6.70
Puerto Rico	0.08	0.07	0.07	0.07	0.08
St. Kitts and Nevis	1.84	2.09	2.45	2.34	NA
St. Lucia	1.39	1.28	1.58	1.67	2.06
St. Vincent and the Grenadines	0.68	0.68	0.79	0.67	NA
Suriname	0.01	0.02	0.03	0.03	NA
Trinidad and Tobago	0.06	0.05	0.05	0.06	0.06
Turks and Caicos Islands	NA	9.13	NA	NA	NA
US Virgin Islands	NA	0.25	3.36	NA	NA
Venezuela	0.03	0.02	NA	NA	NA

[a] NA, not available.

Note: The three destinations presented in italics are not CTO members.

Source: Calculated from Tables 54 and 61 of the *1993 Caribbean Tourism Statistical Report*.

TABLE 8.6
Visitor Expenditure and Merchandise Exports Compared (Selected Countries), 1984 and 1991

Country	1984		1991	
	Visitor Expenditure (US$ Millions)	Total Merchandise Exports (US$ Millions)	Visitor Expenditure (US$ Millions)	Total Merchandise Exports (US$ Millions)
Barbados	284.2	394.0	459.7	203.4
Jamaica	406.6	687.9	764.0	613.5
St. Kitts and Nevis	24.2	20.1	67.5	27.5
US Virgin Islands	434.0	3,974.6	750.3	2,518.4

States and 64 percent more than Japan) and its gross domestic product increased by 7 percent (EU, 1995).

The North American Free Trade Agreement (NAFTA) between Canada, Mexico, and the United States has created a monolithic trading bloc in the American hemisphere. The General Agreement on Trade and Tariffs (GATT), signed in 1994, has capped all these developments, each of which sends the message that the New World Order is about a regime of deregulation, privatization, and liberalization in which developing states cannot expect the protection of traditional preference arrangements for their products and, therefore, must seek sources of government revenue other than those gained by tariffs.

Geoffrey Barrett, Acting Head of the Unit of Trade and Tourism Development of the European Union's Directorate General for Development, speaking at the midterm meeting of Lomé IV in Barbados in December 1994, described the Lomé Convention as an ambitious accord between developing and developed countries in terms of both geographic scope and the extent of the preferences (Barrett, 1994). He also stated that the agreement had failed to promote trade between the ACP (Africa, the Caribbean, and the Pacific) and the community and to accelerate the growth of trade between the partners.

Barrett argued that in 1975 the ACP percentage of EU trade had been 7.4 percent but that by 1991 it had slipped to 4 percent. He claimed that, during the same period, developing countries not party to the Lomé Convention, and not benefiting from preferences, had done much better. Barrett called for enhanced competitiveness, appropriate economic policies, and a central role for the private sector. He criticized overvalued exchange rates and foreign exchange rationing and suggested that there is no alternative to streamlining, simplification, and uniformity of measures affecting imports and that there might be no alternative to gradually reducing high levels of protection to make domestic production more competitive.

The creation of international trading blocs has been paralleled by a process of globalization in which major national companies are "gobbling" each other up and "scrambling" to gain a foothold around the globe by forming alliances and partnerships with major operations in other countries (Holder, 1991). This has been fueled by national deregulation and privatization. Perhaps one of the best examples is the airline industry. Carriers operate in a global marketplace and need market relationships, equity interest, and mergers to be competitive. A few large carriers own and control the computer reservation systems which, for some, have become more profitable than carrying passengers (e.g., Sabre at AMR, American Airlines' parent company).

Like developing states, the smaller airline companies have become clients of the larger ones. Small developing states have the option to leave the airline business, thereby freeing up the skies to competition from a wide range of external companies. This would remove concerns that the restrictive practices of these states alienate foreign carriers and that the costs involved in protecting and subsidizing state-owned carriers may actually exceed the foreign exchange generated by the tourism industry. However, the validity of the latter must be questioned in cases where state-owned carriers are bought and controlled by Caribbean entrepreneurs. National and state are not synonymous. Privately owned carriers receive no government subsidy.

Much of the advice to small primary producers to be more efficient and competitive is unrealistic. There is always room for greater efficiency. However, given the lack of economies of scale in the Caribbean and the cost of production due to factors that are difficult to change radically, the removal of special arrangements is nothing short of a call to leave the arena (e.g., without special assistance Caribbean sugar cannot compete with European beet sugar nor can Caribbean bananas compete with dollar bananas from Central America).

As was demonstrated in 1994 in its opposition to America and Guatemala's attempts at GATT to frustrate the extension of the Lomé preference arrangements for Caribbean bananas, the Caribbean answer involves a "system" wherein common interests combine forces to achieve mutual objectives. Caribbean countries must determine how to best use their foreign services to achieve economic ends. Any call for the Caribbean to leave its air access entirely in the hands of foreign companies must be seen as a hostile act, inimical to the industry's sustainability.

SUSTAINING CARIBBEAN TOURISM

Local and foreign companies as well as Caribbean governments have invested substantially in the tourism industry. The World Travel and Tourism Council (WTTC, 1995) estimates that economic activity associated with travel and tourism represents 78.2 percent of capital investment in the Caribbean and 31.5 percent of gross domestic product (GDP), as well as being responsible for US$7 billion in tax revenues. Why there is a need to sustain tourism activity in the sense of maintaining it as an economic sector within the Caribbean is clearly articulated in such statistics.

What follows is an attempt to delineate the factors or conditions that are both necessary *and* sufficient for guaranteeing the survival of Caribbean tourism. In essence, sustaining Caribbean tourism depends on the region's ability to do the following:

- Maintain product quality (with special emphasis on environmental resources defined as the core resources of the tourism product).
- Ensure profitability.
- Promote the region effectively.
- Provide air access at competitive rates from major tourist markets.
- Provide a secure environment for the industry in terms of (1) the personal safety of visitors and (2) generating acceptance of tourism among the local population.

- Strengthen linkages between tourism and other economic sectors.
- Combine regional efforts to create a competitive force.

While it is difficult to establish a priority ranking among the factors, pride of place would have to be given to environmental factors as being the core resources of the tourism product. The need for regional cooperation is defined with respect to each of the other factors as they are discussed.

Product Quality Without underestimating the importance of good service and the need for accommodations, food and beverage facilities, and attractions that provide good value, the product quality issue is fundamentally one of maintaining the natural environment of the Caribbean. A recent poll of 450,000 American consumers by the Caribbean Coalition for Tourism (CCT) confirmed that the primary reasons for choosing the Caribbean as a vacation destination are related to its environment (warm and equable climate, beautiful beaches, clean air, pure water, and tropical vegetation). Factors associated with the diversity of the product came a distant second.

Given the small size of most Caribbean islands, the daily operation (and waste disposal needs) of 161,000 hotel rooms and 19.1 million bed-days on cruise ships that together cater to over 22 million visitors per year (CTO, 1994) pose considerable threats to the environment. One cruise ship alone is estimated to generate approximately 7.2 tons of waste per day (Simmons, 1994).

Concerned about reports that cruise ships were illegally dumping ship-generated waste in the Caribbean Sea, the CTO commissioned a study, *The Impact of Tourism on the Marine Environment,* in 1994. It was found that the cruise line industry (stung by a negative environmental image and operating against the background of strict legislation in the United States) had already begun to put its house in order (Simmons, 1994). Old ships were being refitted, and new ships were being built with state-of-the-art processing facilities for treating waste. Steps were being taken to recycle waste and to reduce the volume of disposable materials brought on board.

Nonetheless, this still left the problem of the disposal of ship-generated waste by ships when calling at ports. The legal options include transportation of the waste to local landfills or incineration on land (most probably at the port). Many Caribbean nations are struggling to dispose of locally generated waste. Hence, few are prepared to deal with additional waste from ships. Moreover, there is little evidence that routine inspections of the waste received are carried out. Some countries refuse to accept waste, thereby intensifying the problem for the next port of call. In the 1990s, questions are being raised about the negative pollution impacts of the incineration process itself.

The study's major discovery, however, had nothing to do with cruise ships. A survey of 68 hotels and resorts in the Eastern Caribbean revealed that "compliance with the basic effluent criteria . . . was generally poor, and that it is common practice for many of these hotels to dispose of their effluent at sea" (Simmons, 1994). The study concluded that "these practices are impacting negatively on the marine environment (corals, seagrass beds, mangroves, and fishing resources, all of which are considered to be economically and environmentally necessary for the viability of the region's fishing resources)" (Simmons, 1994).

Legislative provisions to control effluent discharge are weak or nonexistent, as is the enforcement capacity of agencies responsible for monitoring and enforcing the legislation. In addition, there is no regional consensus on appropriate sewage/waste water effluent and coastal sanitary water criteria (Simmons, 1994).

It is clear that environmentally insensitive practices by the tourism sector, together with the monumental problems small islands face in managing solid and liquid waste from their own populations, are beginning to pose serious threats to the tourism industry. It is even clearer that the Caribbean environment is indivisible, and there is a need to adopt a unified and regional approach to the management of environmental resources, including biodiversity measures and monitoring environmental quality. A Caribbean-specific environmental convention that consults the specific geographic arrangements of the region is required. To be signed by all Caribbean states, it should provide for preventative action, education, regulation, penalties, and user fees to finance proper waste management. Ultimately, if predictions for growth to 937 million international tourists in the global tourism industry by the year 2010 (WTO, 1990) are fulfilled, setting some limits to tourism expansion in the smaller Caribbean states will be necessary.

Profitability   To survive as a business, tourism must be profitable. However, profitability must be sought in harmony with environmentally and socially acceptable standards. This should be non-negotiable (Shafer, 1995). Profitable businesses pay taxes, employ people, earn foreign exchange, and provide surpluses for reinvestment. In the Caribbean context, however, tourism has to do much more. It must earn sufficient foreign exchange to meet an import bill for a region that imports most of what it consumes. Unlike other economic sectors, tourism enjoys no form of tariff protection. It must, and does, compete directly with other international tourist destinations and, therefore, has to survive on the basis of product quality and efficiency.

According to Pannell Kerr Forster (PKF) (1993), lodging establishments in the Caribbean generate the highest rates per available room of any region in the world, yet yield the lowest net income. This points to basic structural weaknesses. A major contributor to hotels' profitability problems is the burden of taxes and duties, which has actually increased as other sectors have become less able to contribute to government revenue. Hotelier Gordon Seale of Barbados stated that "In the land based captive hotel industry, a number of items attract a combination of duties and taxes that will often double the price of the item required. For example, a simple drinking glass in some islands attracts combined duties and taxes of 120 percent" (Seale, 1994).

In contrast, although cruise lines operate more than 50 percent of their berths in the Caribbean, they are "moving assets" and, therefore, far less subject to government control and taxation. This dispute, which has been a source of bitter hostility between the two tourism subsectors during the first half of the 1990s, was intensified by the cruise lines' successful resistance against the imposition of a region-wide minimum per passenger tax of US$10 proposed by the Organization of Eastern Caribbean States (OECS) and the Caribbean Community (CARICOM). A few states already charge US$10 per passenger or more, but the majority charge less (see Table 8.7).

The high cost of labor and utilities, massive importation of goods and services due to weak intersectoral linkages, high payments to intermediaries in the distribution system, and low productivity due to inadequate training facilities are among other factors contributing to the unprofitability of hotels.

The solutions, once more, point to regional approaches. Caribbean governments must agree to develop a common concept of the tourism industry as an export sector, as

TABLE 8.7
Cruise Passenger Taxes (as of March 1995)

Country	Passenger Tax (US$ per Manifested Passenger)	
Antigua and Barbuda	6.00	
Anguilla	3.50	
Aruba	3.00	(less if more than 50,000 pax annually)
Bahamas	15.00	
Barbados	6.00	
Belize	20.00	
Bermuda	60.00	
Bonaire	under review	
British Virgin Islands	7.00	
Cayman Islands	6.25	
Curacao	3.50	
Dominica	5.00	
Grenada	2.00	
Guadeloupe	1.85	
Jamaica		
Ocho Rios	13.00	($15.00 from October 1995)
Other Ports	12.00	($13.50 from January 1996; $15.00 from January 1997)
Martinique	—	
Mexico (Cozumel)	3.00	
Montserrat	3.00	(if 10 or more calls/year or 500 or more pax/ship or Montserrat is the only destination)
Puerto Rico	8.56	
St. Lucia	5.00	(until September 1997)
St. Kitts and Nevis	5.00	(less if more than 12,000 pax annually or call between May 1 and October 31)
St. Maarten	—	(introduction of tax under consideration)
St. Vincent and the Grenadines	10.00	(for vessels with more than 150 pax)
Trinidad and Tobago	10.00	
US Virgin Islands	4.00	

Note: Bermuda is not a member of the CTO.

well as to provide a regime of incentives that enhances its ability to operate profitably. To the extent possible and, in an effort to reduce the import bill, these incentives should be tied to increased local or regional purchases.

A region so dependent on tourism must have access to quality tourism training at all levels within the region itself. The cost of operating and staffing appropriate training institutions must be shared by the region as a whole. Efforts by the University of the West Indies (UWI) in the 1990s to upgrade its Tourism and Hotel Management Centre in the Bahamas are most welcome and much overdue. CHA, CTO, and UWI agreed on a strategic alliance in June 1995, the objective being to rationalize tourism training, institutions, and qualifications throughout the region.

To reduce control of the hotel inventory by tour operators,[4] sales representatives, and other intermediaries, the Caribbean hotel sector has created the Caribbean Hotel Reservation and Management Systems (CHARMS). This system enables the travel agency, and even the client, to more easily reserve accommodation directly with hoteliers who, with the use of personal computers, can better monitor and control the sales of rooms. No one Caribbean country in isolation can negotiate from a position of strength with international tour operators who set the price. The growing success of CHARMS is one more example of the need for a regional approach.

There can be little doubt that recognition of the importance of the CHA and its programs has brought Caribbean hotels into an action-oriented federation, where problems are addressed and solutions sought on a regional basis. Cooperative arrangements with CTO, especially in marketing and research, are beginning to address the promotional and data base needs of the hotel sector. The results of a CTO hotel study completed by PKF in 1995 presented important information that will serve as the basis for an action plan to address some of the structural problems.

Regional Promotion The good news for the Caribbean is that world tourism growth has been spectacular, and more of the same is projected for the future (WTO, 1990). International tourists grew from 25 million in 1950 to 500 million in 1993, or at an average annual rate of 7 percent for 43 years (CTO, 1993). International tourism receipts, which grew from US$2 billion in 1950 to US$304 billion in 1993, now represent approximately 8.4 percent of world exports, leading crude petroleum and petroleum products (6.5 percent), passenger road vehicles and their parts (5.6 percent), and electronic equipment (4.5 percent) (WTO, 1990; WTTC, 1995). Global tourist arrivals are projected to grow to 660 million by 2000 and 937 million by 2010.

The forecast for the Caribbean is for 19 million stayover visitors by 2000 and 30 million by 2010 (CTO, 1993). However, these projections can be realized only if the Caribbean succeeds in having its voice heard amid the growing clamor in the marketplace. Many of the developed countries, formerly seen by the developing world as tourist-generating countries, are now treating the industry as an economic priority and are seeking to achieve a travel balance in their favor. For example, the hosting of a Western Hemispheric tourism ministerial conference in October 1993 and the national presidential tourism conference in October 1995 confirms America's seriousness of purpose in focusing on increasing both domestic and international tourism. Achievement of such goals could come at the expense of the Caribbean region.

Growing technological innovations in tourism marketing are also likely to place developing states at a disadvantage. There is a rapid movement into a world of computerized data bases and electronic directories that are capable of presenting (in a digital format) all travel directories, brochures, and promotional material now in print, as well as transaction processing systems and dedicated telecommunications networks. These systems provide easy access to complex information, search out products and services on demand, send messages, request additional information or brochures, process reservations, and track activity.

This new technological world is clearly not one in which tiny states with limited resources, acting in isolation, can make a serious impact. The marketing of Caribbean tourism involves the outlay of millions of dollars of scarce foreign exchange from both the public and private sectors to cover the costs associated with maintaining individual overseas tourism promotion offices, hiring advertising and public relations agencies, and general marketing and promotions expenditures. Promotion by Caribbean national tourism organizations alone reached US$250 million in 1993 (CTO, 1993). However, except for a few countries that have significant budgets, it is doubtful that individual states are getting the "bang for the buck" that an aggregated sum of US$250 million could buy in the marketplace, both for the region and for its component states.

In 1990 the CTO developed a regional marketing strategy that surpassed its previous initiatives in regional marketing. The strategy may have remained unimplemented were it not for a clarion call at the Caribbean Hotel Industry Conference (CHIC) in June 1991 from Robert Crandall (Chairman and Chief Executive Officer of American Airlines) for a regional approach to marketing Caribbean tourism. This was strongly supported by the Right Honorable Michael Manley (then Prime Minister of Jamaica) at the CARICOM heads of government meeting in St. Kitts and Nevis in July 1991, and was later approved at a special Tourism Summit Meeting of CARICOM heads in Jamaica in February 1992.

The result was the formation of the Caribbean Coalition for Tourism (CCT), comprising the CTO, the CHA, American Airlines, BWIA, American Express, VISA, LIAT, the Sandals hotel chain, the SuperClubs hotel chain, and other major private sector companies involved in Caribbean tourism. The coalition aims to generate a substantial pool of resources for cooperative marketing by drawing on the resources of a wide range of public and private sector players, including nontourism private sector enterprises that are beneficiaries of Caribbean tourism.

The objectives are to create the critical mass required to keep the Caribbean region at the top of the minds of those choosing a holiday destination. This provides a higher platform from which individual Caribbean states can begin their own campaigns (hopefully at less cost) aimed at attracting some of the increased business to their own countries. This cooperative effort produced the world's first regional creative advertising tourism campaign which, while promoting as a single destination an entire region comprising individual countries that normally compete with each other, was able to name 28 countries in a single advertisement.

The 1993 CCT advertising campaign ("The Caribbean—Where to go"), though it fell short of its ideal budget of US$15 million, raised US$8 million and created a major impact in the American market. This campaign can take considerable credit for converting a six-year slide in the Caribbean's share of the American market into a 1993 growth rate of 10 percent, or double the rate of growth of overseas travel by Americans to all other destinations in 1993 (CTO, 1993).

In 1994 a new regional campaign was launched based on the introduction of the *Caribbean Vacation Planner*. This 268-page magazine presented a section on major Caribbean product offers and a country section listing hard basic information on 28 CTO participating countries. It also contained tourism data and an advertising section in which a broad gamut of tourism operators advertised individual products. Surplus funds from this advertising, after meeting publishing and mailing costs, were reinvested in a television and print advertising campaign, largely funded by CTO government contributions.

The campaign urged people calling the 800 number to request the free vacation planner. The CCT distribution service not only collected data on why callers wished to visit the Caribbean, but offered to put them in touch with members of the Agents Coalition for Caribbean Tourism (ACCT) that was specifically formed to train travel agents to sell Caribbean tourism products. The results of the first six weeks of the 1994 campaign were spectacular. Approximately 80,000 persons called and 40 percent requested to be put in touch with an agent in their geographical region. After three months, 160,000 persons had responded. By the end of June 1995, four months ahead of schedule, all 500,000 planners that had been printed had been circulated.

Regional marketing has been a great success to date. In reality, few of the 32 CTO states have a marketing budget that in isolation could make an impact on the marketplace (see Table 8.8). Together with integrated national efforts, the regional approach represents the way forward for the Caribbean and another major step towards sustaining the Caribbean's presence in the marketplace.

Regional Air Transportation

Air transportation[5] is an important instrument of trade, tourism, employment, defense, and economic development. It is the very breath of life in the Caribbean region. Its role in making possible intra-Caribbean travel for social and business purposes is also critical, and its absence would reduce the population of several small states to being virtual prisoners on their islands.

Bilateral air agreements are the instruments by which countries are able to organize the role of their national carriers in furtherance of national interests as well as determine what role foreign carriers should play (Holder, 1994a). No set of countries, economically and geographically placed as are Caribbean countries, can depend solely on foreign carriers that (understandably) must make decisions about services, routes, and schedules according to the best interests of the owners. These decisions will not, and cannot, always coincide with the best interests of the Caribbean states. Moreover, the Caribbean has seen major carriers that served the region disappear almost without notice (e.g., Eastern Airlines and Pan Am).

The argument that a tourism-dependent Caribbean must own carriers of its own becomes even more cogent in the context of world trends in air transportation. The thrust towards deregulation and privatization demands that airlines operate on a strictly commercial basis. The survival instinct for major carriers fosters a philosophy that the competition must be put out of business and that, as far as possible, a monopolistic situation must be created. The most commonly used weapon is the "fare war," which, if perpetuated, can lead to the bankruptcy of some carriers. As the number of carriers is reduced, customer options are also reduced, and a regime of low fares is replaced by high fares that are more characteristic of a monopolistic situation.

A number of national or subregional state-owned carriers in the Caribbean that have been operating on the border of bankruptcy for many years have been kept going by government subsidies. In almost all cases, the carriers had accumulated massive debt that remained in spite of the introduction of some efficiencies to reduce operating costs. Most of the Caribbean's air transportation needs cannot realistically be met by national carriers alone. Therefore, governments have had to combine the burdensome strategy of subsidiz-

TABLE 8.8
Expenditure of National Tourism Organizations, 1993

Country	Administration[a] (US$ Thousands)	Other[b] (US$ Thousands)	Total (US$ Thousands)	Number of Employees	
				Local	Overseas
Anguilla[c]	302	101	403	8	8
Aruba[d]	4,357	9,381	13,738	35	38
Bahamas[d]	19,035	30,981	50,016	259	146
Barbados[e]	4,038	10,628	14,666	68	42
Bermuda[d]	1,865	16,967	28,832	39	37
Bonaire[f]	789	430	1,219	12	8
British Virgin Islands	1,032	1,190	2,222	9	11
Cayman Islands[d]	5,869	7,804	13,673	19	57
Curacao	3,193	5,385	8,578	39	20
Dominica[e]	449	733	1,182	17	2
Grenada	817	881	1,698	58	11
Guyana	NA	NA	700	8	—
Haiti[g]	1,197	225	1,422	171	8
Jamaica[h]	8,256	34,574	42,830	267	52
Montserrat	151	29	180	4	8
Martinique[d]	1,875	4,180	6,055	37	10
Puerto Rico	14,558	210	44,768	380	36
Saba	83	64	147	3	2
St. Eustatius[d]	48	108	156	NA[i]	—
St. Kitts and Nevis[f]	539	427	966	16	6
St. Lucia	981	1,743	2,724	42	10
St. Martin (French)[e]	457	579	1,036	4	—
St. Vincent and the Grenadines[f]	1,060	245	1,305	34	41
Trinidad and Tobago	1,505	138	1,643	56	4
Turks and Caicos Islands[e]	459	241	700	12	—
US Virgin Islands[d]	2,835	9,300	12,135	34	33

[a] Includes the administration costs of local as well as overseas offices.

[b] Covers expenditures on media advertising, marketing and promotion, and press and public relations.

[c] Excludes expenses of local tourism officials.

[d] 1991 data.

[e] 1992 data.

[f] Budgeted figures.

[g] 1989 data.

[h] 1990 data.

[i] NA, not available.

Note: Bermuda and Turks and Caicos Islands (shown in italics) are not CTO members.

ing their carriers, while enticing foreign carriers to service their destinations. To date, these foreign carriers have served the region well.

However, several forces are at work. In an effort to survive, and skilled in the intricacies of yield management and creative pricing, foreign carriers often enact pricing policies that make it nearly impossible for national carriers to compete. Locally owned carriers are then forced to abandon routes or, where they are state-owned, to depend more on government subsidies. It is noticeable that as soon as local carriers leave a route, the fares of the foreign carriers are raised. Government subsidies, however, not only enable national carriers to continue flying, but also make it possible for the local population (the largest users of the national carriers) to travel at reasonable fares.

The 1990s began with most Caribbean governments owning national carriers, burdened by airline debt, and committed to rid themselves of their state-owned carriers. After over 50 years, BWIA (British West Indies Airways), the national carrier of Trinidad and Tobago, had never made a profit and was over US$100 million in debt. At one stage, the losses of Air Jamaica, the national carrier of Jamaica, were estimated at over $US30,000 per day.

The situation of LIAT (Leeward Islands Air Transport), which is owned by nine CARICOM governments, mirrored these, although its losses were smaller. Most of the other regional carriers experienced similar situations. The air transportation problems are not simply those of small Caribbean states. In 1992 Venezuela's major carrier VIASA was taken over by IBERIA of Spain, and in 1992 Aeropostal went bankrupt and quit flying altogether.

In almost all cases, the plan was to privatize, reorganize personnel, and seek an external carrier partner that could supply improved management, marketing, and technology, particularly in the area of reservations. Generally speaking, there was an appreciation of the need to keep control of the privatized carrier in local hands. This led to considerable public debate in Trinidad and Tobago about whether the arrangements being made for the privatization of BWIA in 1994 provided sufficient guarantees of control remaining in Caribbean hands.

In 1992 the 13 English-speaking Caribbean countries which then comprised CARICOM (meeting at the annual Heads of Government Conference in the Bahamas) deliberated the future of their national and subregional carriers. Three proposals were under consideration:

1. Sell LIAT (1974) Ltd. (an interregional carrier largely serving the Eastern Caribbean, Guyana, and Venezuela) to a private sector group known as Caribbean Aviation Enterprises (CAE). All the CARICOM states are shareholders in LIAT except Belize, the Bahamas, and Suriname (the fourteenth member state, which joined CARICOM in 1995).
2. Merge the five CARICOM carriers (Air Jamaica, Bahamasair, BWIA, Guyana Airways, and LIAT) by January 1995.
3. Create a program of functional cooperation among nine carriers: Air Jamaica, ALM Antillean Airlines, Air Aruba, Bahamasair, BWIA International, Cayman Airways, Guyana Airways, LIAT (1974) Ltd., and Suriname Airways. Proposed by the CTO, this concept assumed that other regional carriers could also participate if they wished. This meant sharing services rather than mergers or equity swaps among the carriers.

In July 1992 all three proposals were approved in principle. However, within five months the LIAT proposal was abandoned. By December 1994, cooperation among the regional carriers had been placed on the back burner as each carrier focused on privatization and putting its own house in order.

In February 1995 the government of Trinidad and Tobago completed the privatization of BWIA by turning over 51 percent of the common stock and management of the airline to a private group of American and Caribbean investors headed by an American, Edward Acker, for a price of US$20 million. The government of Trinidad and Tobago retained 33.5 percent, and it allocated the remaining 15.5 percent to airline employees. The Trinidad and Tobago government has provided assurances that clauses exist to protect local interests in BWIA.

Seventy percent of Air Jamaica was sold in November 1994 for US$26.3 million to the Jamaica private sector, of which Stewart's Appliance Traders Ltd. (led by Gordon "Butch" Stewart of Sandals hotel group) owns 35 percent. At the Heads of CARICOM summit held in Guyana in July 1995, a decision was made to privatize LIAT (1974) Ltd. Up to 29 percent of the LIAT shares will be held by BWIA, 10 percent by the government of Antigua and Barbuda, and 10 percent by governments in Barbados, Dominica, Grenada, St. Lucia, and St. Vincent and the Grenadines. The other shares will be taken up by private shareholders.

These same governments own 10 percent of the shares in Carib Express, a new airline headquartered in Barbados. The other shares are owned by British Airways (19.9 percent) and private sector entrepreneurs (70 percent) in the five shareholder countries. Carib Express commenced operations in February 1995 with one 76–seat jet serving Barbados, Dominica, Grenada, St. Lucia, St. Vincent and the Grenadines, and Trinidad and Tobago. A historic multilateral agreement at the July 1995 CARICOM summit to permit open skies policy between the CARICOM states enables Carib Express, BWIA, and LIAT to serve all the Eastern Caribbean destinations as well as Guyana and Suriname.

Air Aruba (67 percent of which is owned by the government) has been making a profit and is considering privatization. In 1995 Bahamasair was undergoing restructuring with a view to privatization.

How do these new or proposed air transportation arrangements serve the Caribbean's purpose with respect to regional carriers? On the plus side:

- The survival of Air Jamaica, BWIA, and LIAT no longer seems in doubt.
- The Eastern Caribbean can be expected to be served by a "new" BWIA, Carib Express, a "new" LIAT, WIN AIR, ALM, the French air carriers, (Air Martinique and Air Guadeloupe), and a range of small private charter airlines.
- Guyana Airways actually makes money. Cayman Airways has downsized and reduced its losses. ALM's losses are still being heavily subsidized although, together with Suriname Airways, it had made more progress with functional cooperation than any of the other carriers up to mid-1995.
- The governments of Trinidad and Tobago, Jamaica, and the CARICOM nations that own LIAT have taken over past debts of their respective carriers but, because of privatization, will be spared further accumulation of debt.
- Individual carriers will benefit from the synergies created through the strategic

alliances formed with foreign carriers. BWIA, for example, has developed code sharing and computer reservations agreements with American Airlines.

- To prepare for privatization, the carriers shed a great deal of excess staff and were made leaner and more efficient.
- Agreement on an open skies policy, and the fact that the five governments referred to earlier will have a director on the board of both the new LIAT and Carib Express, should lead to rationalization of services and improved functional cooperation among the airlines.

Conversely, major concerns remain in the following areas:

- Efforts must be made to ensure that the strategic alliances formed between privatized Caribbean airlines and external airlines that are in competition with each other do not pull the Caribbean airlines apart from each other.
- Governments that have privatized their national carriers may find that, even where control remains in local hands, the new local commercial carriers will be unable to invest in tourism market development or service socially necessary routes that are unprofitable to their shareholders.
- Should any local airline pass into foreign control, the problems cited in the preceding point will be intensified. Some of the funds saved by governments through privatization may have to be used to support otherwise unprofitable routes.
- The creation of distance among the individual Caribbean carriers would frustrate three major desirable long-term objectives:
  —The creation of a better intra-Caribbean air transport system that is vital for intensifying the Caribbean integration process, intra-Caribbean vacation travel, and multidestination vacations.
  —Reducing airline unit costs.
  —Creating a critical mass of Caribbean-owned and Caribbean-controlled air transportation services that could pose serious competition to foreign carriers and, in crisis situations, provide a viable alternative.

FUNCTIONAL COOPERATION   The three objectives cited above are at the heart of the CTO functional cooperation proposal made in a CTO study and presented to CARICOM heads of government in July 1992. The study (Bertrand and Booth, 1993) delineated 30 specific actions that are estimated to earn the group of nine carriers US$31 million dollars in revenue in one year and result in an additional US$34 million in cost containment. The actions include joint interline programs, airport consolidation, joint cargo operations, joint catering, joint fueling and fuel purchasing, shared maintenance, schedule rationing and pooling, centralized charter services, common CRS and distribution, yield management, fleet planning, an aircraft acquisition consortium, and joint training.

Without the implementation of a functional cooperation program among Caribbean carriers, the medium- to long-term air transportation prospect for the Caribbean will see even the present level of control ceded to foreign carriers whose interests must always propel them in the direction of total domination of their regions of operation. A priority policy initiative of Caribbean tourism leaders must, therefore, be to bring Caribbean carriers back into a working relationship in the near future.

Given the dynamic international air transportation scenario in which major carriers go bankrupt or shed routes in their own interest, a strong Pan-Caribbean regional carrier or subregional carriers and/or close functional cooperation among Caribbean carriers remain the only guarantees of maintaining air access to the region and of keeping the fares of foreign carriers competitive. With privatization, governments can no longer mandate these changes. Instead, they must use their powers of persuasion to achieve these desirable ends.

Security and Public Acceptance The fifth factor for sustaining tourism in the Caribbean is security. This is broadly interpreted to include the absence of major threats from crime and illegal drugs, minimizing distress due to natural disasters, and the existence of a receptive social environment. Tourism is an invasive industry which, in small countries, touches the lives of the entire population (Holder, 1994b,c). Tourism planning often fails to recognize the point at which tourism growth leads to social irritation. Doxey (1975) introduced the concept of the "irridex" as a measurement of social irritation resulting from the pressure placed on local populations and local services due to growth in tourist numbers.

An incident of disrespect for the local culture or perceived racial slurs can create considerable social disturbance. Crimes committed against tourists, given wide press coverage, can virtually cripple a tourism season. These factors must be overlaid by the fact that Caribbean tourism, although all-pervasive and in spite of its economic role, is still not totally accepted as an industry or career prospect. It is often seen as an alien activity pursued for the comfort and pleasure of aliens, with the local masses in a position of servitude (Holder, 1979).

The task of changing negative perceptions, especially in a former or present colonial society, is large and daunting. It is critical that the necessary investment be made not only in public education and local public relations, but also to make tourism's benefits and activities more inclusive of the tourism workers and the public at large. Keeping the Caribbean a zone of tranquility and winning the support of Caribbean people for the industry are major tasks requiring a regional effort and collective resources. Negative publicity for any Caribbean country affects all countries in the marketplace, which has come to see the Caribbean as one place. In a real sense, the people who live in the Caribbean Sea are "all in the same boat."

Strengthening Intersectoral Linkages Finally, tourism's economic role must be enhanced by creating and strengthening linkages with other sectors, particularly agriculture and manufacturing, thereby creating jobs outside tourism and expanding tourism's benefits to a wider cross section of the Caribbean community. These linkages must be created not only within individual states, but across state boundaries by enhanced regional trade. A serious effort must be made through such regional cooperation to reduce the bill of some US$4 billion that is spent annually in importing goods and services from outside the region to supply the tourism industry.

Tourism profitability must be seen to directly benefit local populations if their support is to be sustained. The concept of sustainability is reinforced by advocates of ecotourism[6] who promote the development of tourism products that engender respect for environmental resources, produce minimal impact on natural and cultural resources, and both directly involve and materially benefit local communities.[7]

CONCLUSION

This chapter has argued that world economic developments such as deregulation, liberalization, and free trade agreements have tended to marginalize the traditional economic sectors of developing states (especially small ones) that are largely dependent on the export of primary products and small-scale manufactured goods in protected markets. Such states need time to make the transition from their present preferential situations, and some of them may not be able to retain their competitiveness unless a special regime is maintained.

The author is convinced that the scale of airline deregulation, for example, instituted by the US Department of Transportation in 1978, has destabilized American and, therefore, international air transportation. It has led directly to suicidal fare wars among carriers, to the demise of major US carriers and, therefore, to an oligopolistic situation. No end is in sight to the "shake-out," and the disappearance of other major carriers would not be entirely unexpected.

According to François Vellas of the University of Toulouse (France), liberalization of air transport has not yet brought about major changes in the overall distribution of international tourist flows. International tourist arrivals in North America grew 5.5 percent annually from 1983 to 1993 (i.e., at exactly the same rate as the world average). In addition, domestic air traffic in the United States has tended to grow more slowly than world air traffic, and the growth rate forecast for the period from 1990 to 2000 is 4.7 percent as opposed to forecasts of 4.9 percent for world domestic travel and 7.9 percent for international traffic (Vellas, 1995).

Caribbean states with a competitive advantage in tourism find that their dependence on tourism is growing, indicating that their long-term economic future is tied to their ability to sustain the tourism industry. This is often addressed exclusively in terms of environmental and, to a lesser extent, social preservation. This chapter endorses the importance of factors affecting product quality. However, it also argues for recognition of other variables such as profitability, effective marketing, air access at competitive prices, security accompanied by public acceptance, and the development of intersectoral linkages between tourism and other national and regional economic sectors. Moreover, it is suggested that the ability of small Caribbean states to experience the benefits of the above factors can only be achieved in the context of regional cooperation which would give them the critical mass and diverse resources required to compete in the New World Order.

This solution for Caribbean states is not as easy as it sounds. The region is fragmented geographically, a factor that is intensified politically and culturally by the former policies of the major competing colonial powers. Many regional experiments, especially at the political level, have failed. These include the Commonwealth Caribbean Federation that collapsed in 1961 after five years. Proposals made in Tortola, the British Virgin Islands in 1987 for a political union of the Windward Islands are in stalemate. In the Netherlands Antilles in 1994 some national governments, seeking to end an existing federal arrangement, were turned out of power by people who wished to stay in the federation.

In tourism, the experience has been entirely different. A Caribbean Commission, established by the four big colonial powers in Europe in 1942, proposed the establishment of a Caribbean Tourism Association (CTA) in 1946 comprising almost all the countries in the Caribbean and all language groups (Holder, 1993). Its membership included both public and private sector tourism agencies, thereby setting the precedent for the excellent public sector–private sector cooperation that exists today. Its mandate was to promote and market the Caribbean as a single destination. The organization was finally established in 1951 and, through a merger with the Caribbean Tourism Research & Development Centre in 1989, has ultimately become the Caribbean Tourism Organization.

It has taken some 44 years for the organization's marketing program to achieve its full potential, but a great deal of credit must be given because it survived and remained true to its mandate throughout that period of time. This holds out a distinct possibility that the process of regionalization can extend to all the key areas of Caribbean tourism, thereby ensuring both the survival of the industry and the economic future of the Caribbean region.

NOTES

1. See Chapters 4, 5, 7, 17, 18, 22, and 23 for additional discussion relating to sustainable tourism and sustainable tourism development principles and concepts.
2. See Chapters 9, 22, and 23 for additional discussion on carrying capacity and limits of acceptable change.
3. See Chapters 9–11 and 14 for additional examples of tourism's role as a means of economic regeneration or diversification.
4. See Chapters 4 and 7 for further discussion relating to the role of international tour operators in tourism.
5. See Chapter 13 for an overview of tourism–transportation linkages, including air transportation.
6. See Chapters 11, 15, and 20 for additional discussion focusing on ecotourism principles and philosophies.
7. See Chapters 5, 9, 11, 12, and 14–19 for a detailed discussion pertaining to community attitudes and community involvement in the tourism planning and development processes.

REFERENCES

Barrett, G. 1994. *Lomé IV*. Paper presented to delegates from African, Caribbean and Pacific (ACP) states at the midterm meeting of Lomé IV, Barbados, December.

Bertrand, I. and R. Booth. 1993. *Caribbean Regional Airlines Functional Cooperation Study.* Prepared for CTO by El Perial Management Services (Trinidad & Tobago) and Caribbean Management Services (Miami, Florida).

Butler, R.W. 1994. Tourism—an evolutionary perspective. In J.G. Nelson, R. Butler, and G. Wall (eds.), *Tourism and Sustainable Development: Monitoring, Planning, Managing.* Waterloo, Ontario, Canada: University of Waterloo, Department of Geography Publications Series Number 37, pp. 27–43.

Caribbean Tourism Organization. 1994. *1993 Caribbean Tourism Statistical Report, 1993.* St. Michael, Barbados: CTO.

Cruise Line International Association (CLIA). 1994. *Cruise Line International Association Marketing Report.*

Doxey, G. 1975. *A Causation Theory of Visitor–Resident Irritants, Impact of Tourism.* Proceedings of the 6th Annual TTRA Conference, San Diego.

Economist Intelligence Unit (EIU). 1992. *World Cruise Ship Industry Report.*

European Union (EU). 1995. Newsletter of the Delegations of the European Commission in Trinidad & Tobago, Barbados, and the Eastern Caribbean. Special Edition, "The Europe of 15."

Holder, J.S. 1979. Transforming Caribbean tourism. In J.S. Holder (ed.), *Tourism Policies and Impacts*. Bridgetown, Barbados: Caribbean Council of Churches, pp. 3–20.

Holder, J.S. 1988. Pattern and impact of tourism on the environment of the Caribbean, *Tourism Management*, 9(2), 119–127.

Holder, J.S. 1991. Tourism, the world and the Caribbean, *Tourism Management*, 12(4), 291–300.

Holder, J.S. 1992. The need for public/private sector cooperation in tourism, *Tourism Management*, 13(2), 157–162.

Holder, J.S. 1993. The Caribbean Tourism Organization in historical perspective. In D. Gayle and J. Goodrich (eds.), *Tourism Marketing and Management*. London: Routledge, pp. 20–27.

Holder, J.S. 1994a. *Moving Towards Consolidation: Aviation Services in the Region*. Paper presented to the CLAA Miami Conference. December.

Holder, J.S. 1994b. *Quality Tourism—The Key to Caribbean Survival*. Caribbean Tourism Day Message. November.

Holder, J.S. 1994c. *The Tourism Industry: A Global and Regional Perspective in the Context of Sustainable Development*. Keynote address to Tourism Industry Leadership Conference. Grand Bahamas Island, April.

Owen, C. 1992. Building a relationship between government and tourism, *Tourism Management*, 13(4), 358–362.

Pannell Kerr Forster. 1993. *International Hotel Trends, 1993*.

Pannell Kerr Forster. 1995. *Caribbean Hotel Trends*, 1994 edition. A study carried out for CTO, July 1995.

Savignac, A. 1994. *Delivering a Quality Tourism Product*. Paper delivered to the 18th Annual Caribbean Tourism Conference. Ochos Rios, Jamaica, September.

Seale, G. 1994. Cruises most favoured status. *Caribbean Week*, September.

Shafer, E. 1995. *How to Win in Any Negotiation: The Key to Success in the Sustainable Ecotourism Business*. Presented to the 5th CTO Ecotourism Conference. Margarita Island, Venezuela, June.

Simmons, D. 1994. *Impact of Tourism on the Marine Environment*. Study prepared for CTO by Simmons and Associates, May.

Vellas, F. 1995. *Present Status of the Deregulation of Air Transport and its Consequences*. Paper delivered at a WTO Seminar on Tourism and Air Transportation. Martinique, 9–10 February.

World Tourism Organization (WTO). 1990. *Tourism to the Year 2000*.

World Travel and Tourism Environment Review (WTTERC). 1993. The review focuses on the practical aspects of achieving responsible travel and tourism growth in the interest of issues and broad agreements included in the scope of the Rio Earth Summit in June 1992.

World Travel and Tourism Council (WTTC). 1995. *World Travel and Tourism Council Report*.

¶ | PROBLEM SOLVING AND DISCUSSION ACTIVITIES

1. Develop a plan for optimizing cooperation among the Caribbean states by ensuring that the stakeholders, to be identified by you, participate in the policy formulation process and "buy in" to the strategic directions for sustaining Caribbean tourism.

2. Determine what regional approaches to sustaining the tourism industry exist in your region of the world. What created the environment for their initiation (or lack thereof)? Evaluate the initiatives in terms of their potential long-term costs and benefits. Is there potential for more regional cooperation in the future? Justify your response.

3. To what extent are the processes of globalization and strategic alliances between developed states and major corporations affecting the development of small states? What courses of action should be taken by developing states to enhance their sustainable tourism growth?

4. Under what conditions is growth not compatible with sustainable tourism development?

5. Is Caribbean ownership and control of tourism resources necessary for sustainable tourism development in the region?

6. Define "acceptable" tourism and identify the cooperative steps that should be taken to attain this goal. Who must be educated about more "responsible" forms of tourism? Why? What should be the focus of educational programs for various stakeholders?

7. Discuss the advantages and disadvantages of regional cooperation in tourism marketing from the perspective of various stakeholders who should be involved in such activity.

8. What priorities should be assigned to frame conditions for sustainable tourism development? Justify your response.

9. Is Caribbean tourism sustainable outside the context of regional cooperation?

10. The Caribbean hotel industry has one of the highest room rates in the world and yet it is one of the least profitable. What are the implications for tourism sustainability? Suggest possible solutions through cooperative action.

11. Describe the process that should be considered to obtain a higher level of acceptance for tourism among residents of the Caribbean.

9

Setting the Stage to Balance Competing Trade-offs

IDENTIFYING ISSUES AFFECTING TOURISM DEVELOPMENT AND MANAGEMENT ON INIS OÍRR

Michael J. Keane
Micheál S. Ó Cinnéide
Clodagh Cunningham

♪ | KEY LEARNING POINTS

- It is difficult for a small host community to retain control of tourism. Consequently, residents may become victims of the popularity of their community as a tourist destination.

- Strategic planning and management approaches that facilitate widespread and meaningful local participation in all stages of the tourism development process are important mechanisms through which local interests may be protected.

- A dilemma that host communities may face is how to maintain their authentic culture and environment while exploiting these as tourism products. Generating a strong respect for local values and traditions through community animation and education may be necessary to render the local system sufficiently robust to withstand the impacts of tourism.

- It is easy to say that the planning and management of tourism should be about maximizing benefits and minimizing costs. However, it is not possible to simultaneously maximize some effects and minimize others. Trade-offs are required and compromises are necessary. Various development options must be considered prior to committing resources. Options should be assessed for their feasibility and suitability to satisfy the requirements of tourists, those who are commercially involved in tourism, and the local population.

- Interdependence between tourism and local development can be facilitated through visitor evaluation research that assesses the "fit" between tourists' needs and the resources of a location. Such research should do more than just measure tourist reactions. It should also provide planning information for visitor needs.

INTRODUCTION

The emphasis in tourism development is changing from quantity to quality (Fick and Ritchie, 1991). Mass tourism is no longer considered an attractive long-term option. The concern for quality focuses on issues such as maintaining an area's intrinsic appeal, promoting tourism projects at a scale that is suitable and appropriate to an area, and having respect for carrying capacity levels, the way of life, and the cultural traditions of the host community. With the emphasis shifting to quality, the local community must draw more on the potential of the local human resource base if it is to generate the conditions for an ecologically balanced "soft" tourism product within which quality can be sustained.

This chapter focuses on the rapidly expanding tourism industry on the tiny island of Inis Oírr, one of the Aran Islands, situated off the west coast of Ireland. The growing popularity of the island as a tourist destination is generally favored by the resident population of 270 people because it affords them an opportunity to supplement meager incomes derived from subsistence farming and part-time fishing.

On the other hand, the expansion of tourism creates a dilemma in that the community has little control over tourism's development. Ferry operators play a major role in this regard. It also leaves them somewhat divided, with some local product providers preferring the continuation of recent expansionary trends while others search for a better quality and a more sustainable form of tourism. With growing awareness among the island community of the volatile nature of tourism, steps have been initiated to provide greater local control over tourism development on the island. The extent to which the host population will succeed in managing and controlling development is uncertain.

Management approaches to preserving the character of any tourist destination should contain the following key ingredients:

- Securing wide participation by the local community in the management process. A strong human presence is necessary to avoid the likely depletion of the basic resource—the character of the area.
- Nurturing a strong respect among residents for their culture and the character of the area. This calls for a balance in the types of local initiatives undertaken. Such a stance will, in turn, facilitate proper understanding of the area's culture and character among visitors.
- Ensuring the community animation process affirms the local identity and thereby renders the local system sufficiently robust to absorb the impact of external forces.

DEVELOPING AND MANAGING ISLAND TOURISM: CONTEMPORARY PERSPECTIVES AND ISSUES

Small inhabited islands are perceived to be attractive tourist destinations. Their appeal may relate to the feelings of remoteness that one may experience on an island, the peace and quiet there, or the sense of timelessness that islands convey to visitors (Butler, 1990). These special, and sometimes idiosyncratic, features may be threatened by sudden increases in the number of tourists. Such threats must be balanced with a concern for the future of small islands as communities.

For example, most small inhabited islands of the European Union (EU) are undergoing rapid depopulation (EC, 1994). The contraction of traditional economic activities such as farming and fishing has resulted in a severe shortage of employment opportunities, leading inevitably to out-migration and long term population decline. To counteract these adverse trends, many island communities have attempted to diversify their economic bases by promoting alternative forms of economic activity, particularly tourism. Tourism is widely regarded by island communities, as well as by regional and national authorities, as an ideal industry to alleviate the socioeconomic problems that beset these areas.

Many issues relating to island tourism apply to small mainland communities as well. Rural tourism,[1] for example, has emerged as an activity through which rural economies can diversify to compensate for the decline of economic activity on farms (Keane and Quinn, 1990). Rural tourism should not be interpreted as a narrow option that simply complements traditional agriculture. Its potential is far greater than this. Rather, tourism must be considered in very broad terms and in relation to general local development (Greffe, 1994). Tourism development in any location is a complex phenomenon that gives rise to diverse and often contradictory types of effects and differing points of view (Mathieson and Wall, 1982).

It is easy to say that planning and managing tourism should be about maximizing benefits and minimizing costs. However, it is not possible to simultaneously maximize some effects and minimize others. Trade-offs are required and compromises are necessary. Different development options must be considered prior to committing resources. Moreover, all options should be assessed for their feasibility and suitability in terms of satisfying the requirements of the tourist, addressing the interests of those who are commercially involved in tourism, and meeting the requirements and aspirations of the local population. When it is clear that different interests cannot be satisfied simultaneously, trade-offs must be accepted and choices made.

One principle that should be adopted in any local planning process is to view tourism issues as being inextricably linked to broader questions concerning the thrust of overall development. Planning should identify strategies that would render tourism less of a spontaneous process (which is likely to happen in the absence of planning) and more of a coordinated vehicle for development. A second principle important to local management solutions involves encouraging and emphasizing informal solutions to problems whereby the host community identifies ways of managing the various impacts of tourism locally[2] (Travis, 1982). These two principles can be incorporated into a strategic planning approach (Keane et al., 1992; Ó Cinnéide and Keane, 1990).

A strategic planning framework[3] basically involves the preparation of an agreed agenda for local tourism development and management. This includes identifying participants in the planning process, establishing structures for undertaking the process, formulating mission statements and objectives, and agreeing on a timeframe for the completion of the various planning stages. This planning forum should develop a clear vision of the nature of the local economy, the contribution and type of tourism desired, and objectives to be achieved through its existence as well as through the individual and concerted operation of the various bodies it represents. It should also establish a timeframe for accomplishing various objectives. Well-focused research and the analysis of tourism are important inputs.

Wall (1994, p. 238) suggested that it is advisable to develop a theoretical perspective for tourism research that explicitly acknowledges tourism as one among a number of agents of change. He also indicated that it is artificial to abstract tourism from this broader context:

> . . . few communities are static, and vibrant cultures are likely to be in a continual state of flux for a diversity of reasons and not simply because of the onset of tourism. In addition, it is virtually impossible, and perhaps unrealistic, to separate the consequences of tourism from other causes of change which may be occurring in the same place at the same time. However, since it is usually impracticable to study everything at the same time, it is often pragmatic to abstract tourism from the broader context of change to make investigations more manageable. However, the milieu in which these changes occur should not be forgotten and ideally, as has been argued above, should be incorporated into the analysis.

The interdependence between tourism and local development can be seen at a number of levels in any given community through the different involvements of local people in tourism, the views of local people on the future of tourism, the structures (or lack thereof) in place to develop and promote the area and its tourism product, and the problems that must be tackled.

The task of understanding and managing this interdependence can be facilitated by having a sound analytical perspective on the issues involved, as well as through well-designed and well-executed visitor evaluation research that provides information of interest to management practices (Pearce and Moscardo, 1985). Pearce and Moscardo suggest one notion in particular that should be developed in the context of visitor surveys—the "fit" between tourists' needs and the resources of a location. "According to this notion, some tourists are mismatched with the place they visit, in that their motivations for visiting the destinations do not agree with what the visited context can provide" (Pearce and Moscardo, 1985, p. 302). By including such assessment, visitor evaluation research should be able to do more than simply measure tourists' reactions. It can also provide planning information on visitor needs.

One goal of such planning for the host community might be to attract more repeat visitors as opposed to relying on first-time visitors. Visitor evaluation research can help identify how return visitor traffic can be promoted. In this way, return visitors could represent a core clientele who can be relied on for (1) a determined volume of high-value business and (2) as a guarantee of a quality tourism product. This, as the case study that follows shows, is one of the key issues for tourism development on the island of Inis Oírr.

While data from visitor surveys provide information of interest to management practices, what is more critical and fundamental in the long run is the way in which tourism is organized and coordinated at a local level. Local communities, be they small islands or rural communities on the mainland, may be the instigators and focus of tourism activities, but they cannot be sure of being the main beneficiaries. Unless local coordination is integrated into the broader product and marketing structures, it will be difficult for the community to gain control, or break away from what may otherwise be an externally determined development trajectory.

The tourist–transport–leisure chain concept is useful to describe the organization of tourism on small islands. A critical link in this chain is the role played by ferry operators. For example, the key factor in the growth of tourists visiting Inis Oírr has been growth in the capacity of privately owned ferry boats. Given their (i.e., the islanders') position at the end of the "chain," obvious development challenges for islanders and any local tourism management organizations emerge.

Tourism growth is often externally driven and development of tourism may be fragmented. However, by establishing new and agreed structures to coordinate accommodation, standards, bookings, information, and marketing, communities can increase their capacity to make decisions and take greater control in the interests of local people.[4] This is an essential component of local development in practice.

One difficult aspect of this management task is achieving the optimal balance at the local level between what are often highly motivated individual interests and the kind of cooperative and integrated support structures required to promote local development. This is where strategic planning can be of considerable benefit. There are, in a sense, two different and difficult issues involved. One involves the problem of what the optimal management of the tourism sector should be. A typical challenge is created by rapid and highly seasonal growth in tourist numbers. This raises a number of concerns such as the ability of the community to cope with large numbers, the way in which economic benefits are distributed, and the whole future of tourism in the area. The second issue relates to the problem of resolving conflicts over the contribution of different members towards some agreed common management policy. These two aspects of the management problem can be called the *production plan* and the *management plan*, respectively (Seabright, 1993).

Prior to discussing some of the foregoing concepts from the perspective of Inis Oírr, an overview of the inhabited islands of Ireland is presented.

THE INHABITED ISLANDS OF IRELAND

All the inhabited islands of Ireland are situated along the west coast except for Rathlin Island. Situated off the north coast (see Figure 9.1a), Rathlin Island is part of Northern Ireland whereas the other 17 islands belong to the Republic of Ireland. Inis Oírr, with a surface area of only 1440 acres (580 hectares), is the smallest of three islands known collectively as the Aran Islands that are situated at the mouth of Galway Bay (see Figure 9.1b). The total population of all the inhabited islands of Ireland amounted to 3121 in 1991, of which Inis Oírr comprised 270 persons (Census of Population, 1991).

Life on the windswept islands of Ireland has long been characterized by hardship and deprivation. High transportation costs and other general inadequacies associated with transport services (e.g., poor landing facilities, interruptions due to inclement weather conditions) between the mainland and the islands are the primary cause of the long-term population decline that most of these islands have experienced throughout the twentieth century. A vicious circle of decline is precipitated by high transportation costs as they reduce competitiveness and increase the cost of living for islanders (see Figure 9.2).

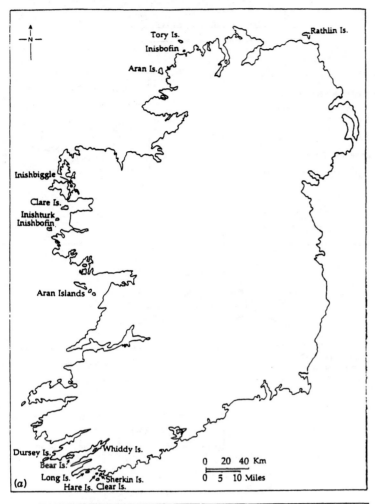

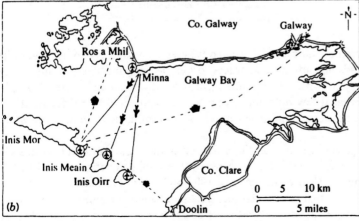

Figure 9.1a
The inhabited islands of Ireland.
Figure 9.1b
Location of Inis Oírr.

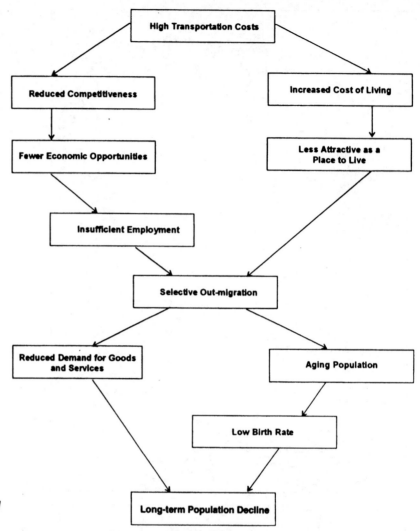

Figure 9.2
*The vicious circle of decline
associated with the inhabited
islands of Ireland.*

These factors restrict the number of opportunities for viable economic enterprises and render the islands less attractive as places to live, leading inevitably to insufficient local employment opportunities and sustained selective out-migration. The residual aging population and associated low birth rate, coupled with reduced demand for goods and services, further restricts economic opportunities and culminates in long-term population decline.

The secular population trends on the inhabited islands of Ireland and on Inis Oírr are depicted in Figures 9.3a and 9.3b, respectively. The total population of 3121 in 1991 represented a decline of 35 percent between 1961 and 1991. Considerable interisland variation is concealed in that overall statistic. The populations of some islands, such as Inishbofin (see Figure 9.1a) off the northwest coast, have declined dramatically, and some islands are now virtually depopulated. Others, such as Inis Oírr, although having

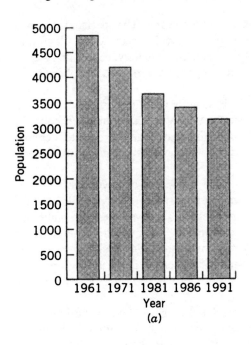

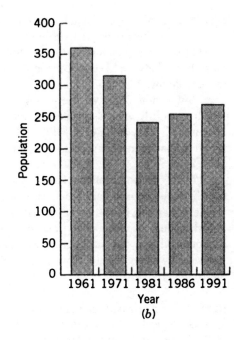

Figure 9.3a
Secular popula-
tion trends on
the inhabited is-
lands of Ireland.
Figure 9.3b
Secular popula-
tion trends on
Inis Oírr.

undergone an aggregate population decline of approximately 50 percent since 1861, and of 25 percent between 1961 and 1991, began to stabilize in the early 1980s and have since experienced modest population increases (see Figure 9.3b).

Even so, most of these island communities are perilously close to extinction. Indeed, several islands along the coast of Ireland, such as the Blasket Islands and the Iniskea Islands, have been abandoned entirely. Clearly, the island communities of Ireland are at a critical juncture and, unless new economic activities can be successfully established in these geographically remote rural areas, their future looks bleak. The extent to which tourism can fulfill this role is addressed in this chapter.

The case study outlines the development of tourism on Inis Oírr and assesses its economic contribution. Tourism development and management strategies that are currently being pursued on the island are also briefly discussed. The information presented was obtained through two pieces of primary research. One involves an analysis conducted in the early 1990s that examined the economic and social impact of tourism on the Aran islands (Keane et al., 1992). The second is an extensive visitor survey conducted on Inis Oírr in the summer of 1994 (Ní Chonghaile et al., 1994). An important secondary source of information was a draft tourism development plan prepared at the end of 1994 (Ó Cinnéide, 1994).

TOURISM ON INIS OÍRR

Tourist No official count of the number of tourists visiting Inis Oírr is available. However, data
Visitation from the transport companies serving the island indicate that approximately 30,000 tourists visit Inis Oírr annually. This figure represents a substantial increase over the past

decade. In 1985, approximately 6000 tourists visited the island. The spectacular growth in tourist numbers is primarily due to major improvements in access to the island provided by the ferry operators starting in 1989. Further additions to ferry services and greater marketing efforts are likely to contribute to an ongoing increase in visitor numbers in the foreseeable future.

Most visitors come via the port of Doolin in County Clare (see Figure 9.1b) from which an hourly service operates during the summer months. Lesser numbers come by ferry from Galway and Ros a' Mhíl, or by air via a nine-seat plane that operates between the Aran Islands and a small airport situated on the mainland at Minna in County Galway (see Figure 9.1b).

Public transportation services to the island are subsidized by government bodies, thereby reducing transportation costs and improving accessibility. However, due to tidal problems, landing on the island's small piers is problematic. In severe weather conditions, the island may be completely isolated from the mainland. Such weather conditions are infrequent during the summer season (peak tourism season). Port facilities have been upgraded by extending the main pier by 60 yards (55 meters). The upgrading was completed in early 1996.

Tourism Resources and Amenities Inis Oírr has many natural and cultural resources that distinguish it is as a tourist destination. Geologically, it is an extension of the unique and strikingly beautiful karst landscape of the Burren in County Clare. Much of it consists of a bare limestone plateau that is dissected by clints and grikes (geomorphological features resulting from weathering and erosion). The natural vegetation is sparse, and trees and shrubs are few. Rare species of orchid and other plants grow in the sheltered limestone crevices. Birds such as seagulls, gannets, crows, wild geese, ducks, mallards, herons, thrushes, blackbirds, and skylarks are abundant. Among the numerous varieties of fish and marine life are lobster, crab, salmon, pollock, ray, sole, mackerel, and seals.

The natural landscape has been shaped by human activity such that small fields surrounded by human-built limestone walls are now a prominent and very distinctive feature of the island. Within the fields, the bare limestone that characterizes the karst landscape is mantled by a thin covering of soil derived mainly from sand and seaweed on the shore. The community still strives to eke out a living in the tradition of their ancestors from these fields and the surrounding seas.

Tourists are also attracted by other aspects of the living culture—especially the Irish language, which is still the vernacular, and traditional music and dance. The island also has many interesting historic and archaeological sites. However, the most important attraction to many visitors is the peace they associate with this small island located on the verge of the Atlantic Ocean.

Tourist amenities include a varied accommodations base, three pubs, three restaurants, a few small shops, a social center, a sports center, and a heritage center. The accommodations base consists of a small hotel (15 bedrooms), a hostel (48 beds), a campsite, approximately 15 island homes (with about 120 beds in total) that offer accommodation and breakfast within the family dwelling, and 27 self-catering traditional houses. Organized tourism activities include cycling, sailboarding, fishing, boat trips, and horse-drawn island tours. Casual walking along the narrow scenic roads and pathways and over the bare limestone plateaus is the most popular tourist activity on the island.

Organization of Tourism Tourism promotion is spearheaded by a local tourism committee that works in conjunction with a multipurpose community cooperative, namely, Comhar Caomhán Teo (CCT). The tourism committee is a subcommittee of the community cooperative. The subcommittee consists of five or six local product providers who are appointed periodically by the CCT. All members of the committee work in a voluntary capacity. Their mandate is to promote tourism on the island in a manner consistent with the host community's best interests. In earlier years their main concern was to generate increased tourism business, but more recently, they have devoted more effort to targeting specific market niches (e.g., cultural tourism) that are deemed to be more in keeping with local values and traditions, and which will also make the optimal contribution to the island economy.

CCT is one of several organizations established in many parts of western Ireland in the 1960s and 1970s to promote the integrated development of lagging localities such as Inis Oírr. They are essentially microdevelopment agencies run by a voluntary committee elected by local communities with a small staff complement, usually no more than two or three persons. They receive an annual subsidy from the state upon which they are heavily dependent. Among the specific activities undertaken by these locally controlled bodies are (1) the organization and marketing of Irish-language summer courses targeted at young school children who wish to improve their command of the Irish language and (2) holiday courses for adults based on the heritage and culture of the island. Both CCT and its tourism subcommittee play a prominent role in improving local tourist amenities and promoting an overall planned approach to tourism development on the island.

Profile of Tourists An extensive visitor survey, involving interviews with 668 tourists throughout the summer of 1994, provides a fairly clear profile of visitors to Inis Oírr. Not surprisingly, the survey revealed that over 60 percent of all visitors to the island were Irish (see Table 9.1). Other nationalities which featured strongly included Germans (10.2 percent), Americans (9.0 percent), French (3.4 percent), and English (3.3 percent). Tourists from most other European countries and from places as far away as Australia also visited Inis Oírr during 1994.

TABLE 9.1
*Nationality of Surveyed Visitors to Inis Oírr,
Summer of 1994*

Nationality	Number	Percent
Irish	416	62.3
German	68	10.2
American	60	9.0
French	23	3.4
English	22	3.3
Other European	26	3.9
Other/No answer	53	7.9
Total	668	100.0

Source: Ní Chonghaile et al. (1994).

TABLE 9.2
Distribution of Surveyed Visitors to Inis Oírr by Occupation and Gender, Summer of 1994

Occupation	Males (%)	Females (%)
Agriculture	1.8	0.0
Producer/Maker/Repairer	15.3	1.8
Clerical worker	4.8	11.7
Commercial/Insurance/Finance	5.7	3.8
Service worker	7.2	10.3
Professional and technical	43.3	37.7
Student	16.0	18.4
Unemployed	0.4	13.3
Retired	5.5	3.1
Total	100.0	100.1

Note: Totals may not equal 100 percent due to rounding.
Source: Ní Chonghaile et al. (1994).

The socioeconomic status of tourists may be gleaned from Table 9.2. Professional and technical employees were by far the largest occupational grouping among the 1994 cohort. In general, the vast majority of visitors belonged to middle and upper socioeconomic groups. This clientele is generally associated with high purchasing power and also with demand for relatively sophisticated tourism products.

The latter point is evidenced in Table 9.3, which summarizes the main expectations

TABLE 9.3
Surveyed Visitors' Expectations of Inis Oírr, Summer of 1994

Expectations	Number	Percent of Total[a]
Peace and quietness	594	88.9
Attractive rural setting	509	76.2
Distinctive local culture	462	69.2
Interaction with local community	286	42.8
Good place for children	226	33.8
Value for money holiday	200	29.9
No particular expectation	20	3.0
Other	40	6.0

[a] Multiple responses. N = 668.
Source: Ní Chonghaile et al. (1994).

of tourists to Inis Oírr. It indicates that the vast majority of visitors sought peace and quietness (88.9 percent), an attractive rural setting (76.2 percent), and a distinctive local culture (69.2 percent). Many were also looking for interaction with the local community (42.8 percent), a safe place for children (33.8 percent), and reasonable value for money (29.9 percent).

Tourists'
Satisfaction
Levels
A major objective of the 1994 visitor survey was to ascertain tourists' degree of satisfaction with the tourism product available on Inis Oírr. It is clear from Table 9.4 that, while tourists were generally pleased with their holiday, they were most satisfied with the physical attributes of the island. Just over 63 percent of tourists who rated peace and quietness highly on their list of expectations were "very pleased," and a further 26.3 percent were "pleased" with the situation that prevailed on the island during their holiday. Similarly, of those expecting an attractive rural setting, 59.1 percent were "very pleased" and 27.9 percent were "pleased."

On the other hand, tourists who were especially looking forward to interaction with the local community were much less content. Only 32.9 percent stated that they were "very pleased," and a further 33.6 percent said that they were "pleased" with the situation as they experienced it. This lower degree of satisfaction was also evident among visitors seeking a distinctive local culture. Approximately 33.0 percent of such visitors expressed themselves as being "very pleased," and 36.1 percent indicated that they were "pleased." Those seeking a good, safe destination for children were most pleased. However, many tourists were not particularly pleased with the value for money received on Inis Oírr.

It appears that, while the physical environment is meeting the expectations of visitors, they are somewhat disappointed with the quality of their encounter with the host community. This is mainly attributable to the large number of visitors relative to the size of the local population, particularly at the height of the tourist season. While the physical carrying capacity[5] of the island is still adequate to cope with present levels of tourism, some visitors no longer feel comfortable due to overcrowding and limited interaction with the

TABLE 9.4
Surveyed Visitors' Degree of Satisfaction with Products on Inis Oírr That Were Rated Highly on Their List of Expectations, Summer of 1994

	Degree of Satisfaction					
Product Sought	Very Pleased (%)	Pleased (%)	Moderate (%)	Poor (%)	Very Poor (%)	Total[a] (%)
Peace and quietness	63.5	26.3	7.2	2.7	0.3	100.0
Distinctive local culture	33.0	36.1	23.0	5.0	2.8	99.9
Attractive rural setting	59.1	27.9	9.4	2.6	1.0	100.0
Good place for children	70.8	21.2	6.6	0.9	0.4	99.9
Value for money holiday	30.0	34.5	24.5	8.0	3.0	100.0
Interaction with local community	32.9	33.6	21.7	8.4	3.5	100.1

[a] Totals may not equal 100 percent due to rounding.
Source: Ní Chonghaile et al. (1994).

local population. In this sense, the social carrying capacity of the island, specifically the degree of crowding that tourists are prepared to accept (O'Reilly, 1986), is being stretched to the limit. This is not surprising considering the small size of the host population and the fact that many residents are preoccupied with tourism, fishing, and farming activities when the tourist influx is at its highest.

Nonetheless, an overwhelming 90 percent of visitors surveyed indicated their intention to return to Inis Oírr for another holiday at some stage in the future. Following O'Reilly's (1986) definition, it can be concluded that the psychological carrying capacity (i.e., the lowest degree of enjoyment that tourists are prepared to accept before they start seeking alternative destinations) has not yet been threatened on Inis Oírr.

Tourist Expenditure and Factors Influencing Tourism's Economic Contribution

The economy of Inis Oírr traditionally has been based on part-time farming and seasonal fishing. Farming on the small rocky holdings is close to subsistence level, with cattle representing the only significant produce offered for sale off-farm. Fishing, mainly for lobster and salmon, is an important supplementary source of income, particularly during the summer months when the weather is more amenable to the use of small craft on the exposed seas surrounding the island.

Tourism is emerging as a new and important economic activity with most households deriving some benefit, particularly through the provision of accommodations for tourists in their homes. Notwithstanding the growth in tourism on the island, the economy of Inis Oírr is still heavily dependent on transfer payments through the social welfare system. One attribute of tourism on Inis Oírr that militates against its contribution to the local economy is the fact that over 80 percent of tourists are day trippers. This means they spend only a short while, ranging from 2 to 12 hours, on the island. By the very nature of their trips, these tourists contribute very little to the island economy by way of expenditure on accommodation, restaurants, pubs, and other services.

The visitor survey conducted during the 1994 tourist season established that approximately 64 percent of day trippers spent less than Ir£10 per capita (about US$14 in 1995 dollars) on Inis Oírr (see Table 9.5). In contrast, 77 percent of tourists who came for an extended holiday (defined for the purposes of the survey as anything in excess of three nights) spent in excess of Ir£50 per capita (about US$70 in 1995 dollars). Indeed, most of these incurred expenses of at least Ir£100 (about US$140 in 1995 dollars). Tourists who came to Inis Oírr for even a short break (defined as a stay of one to three nights) are much more valuable to the island economy than day trippers, as indicated by the fact that just over 64 percent of them spent a minimum of Ir£30 per capita (about US$42 in 1995 dollars) during their visit.

An interesting feature of tourism on Inis Oírr is the relationship between length of stay and whether the tourist is on a return or first-time visit to the island (see Table 9.6). According to the survey findings, just over 33 percent of return visitors come for a long break whereas only 6.8 percent of first-time visitors do so. On the other hand, 49.1 percent of first-time visitors are day trippers in comparison with only 15.1 percent of return visitors. Clearly, repeat visitors have a tendency to remain on the island for a much longer holiday than first-time visitors. Local product suppliers confirm that there is a relatively small group of tourists who return regularly (usually on an annual basis) and who remain for up to one month each time.

TABLE 9.5
Per Capita Expenditure of Surveyed Visitors on Inis Oírr by Nature of Visit, Summer of 1994

	Expenditure						
Nature of Visit	0 Ir£ (%)	1–9 Ir£ (%)	10–29 Ir£ (%)	30–49 Ir£ (%)	50–99 Ir£ (%)	100–299 Ir£ (%)	300+ Ir£ (%)
Day visit	6.9	57.5	29.6	2.6	2.1	1.3	0.0
Short break	0.0	6.1	29.4	28.9	18.8	16.7	0.0
Extended holiday	0.0	0.0	10.7	12.3	34.4	39.3	3.3
Irish college	0.0	0.0	32.4	43.2	0.0	24.3	0.0
Other/No answer	6.5	9.7	12.9	16.1	16.1	25.8	12.9

Note: Totals may not equal 100 percent due to rounding.
Source: Ní Chonghaile et al. (1994).

There is considerable concern among the host population that the large number of day trippers is rendering the island less attractive to the more lucrative and regular long-stay visitors who value the peace and solitude associated with the traditional lifestyles of small island communities. Furthermore, the locals feel powerless about remedying the situation because they have no effective means of controlling the number or type of visitors brought to the island. This is very much in the hands of the ferry companies whose main interest is maximizing total passenger numbers. Given the limited accommodations capacity on the island, the goals of the ferry companies can be achieved only by carrying large numbers of day trippers.

Another unfavorable characteristic of tourism on Inis Oírr is its highly seasonal nature (see Figure 9.4). Tourism is essentially confined to the months of April through October, with approximately 70 percent of all visitors arriving during the midsummer months of July and August. This places the tourism resources and amenities under particular strain for a short and, at times, hectic peak period, leaving them greatly underuti-

TABLE 9.6
Length of Stay of Return Visitors versus First-time Visitors on Inis Oírr, Summer of 1994

		Length of Stay			
Type of Visitor	**Number**	**Day Trip**	**Short Break (One to Three Nights)**	**Long Break (Four or More Nights)**	**Other**
Return visitors	285 (42.7)	43 (15.1)	100 (35.1)	96 (33.7)	46 (16.1)
First-time visitors	383 (57.3)	188 (49.1)	145 (37.8)	26 (6.8)	24 (6.3)
Total	668	231	245	122	70

Source: Ní Chonghaile et al. (1994).

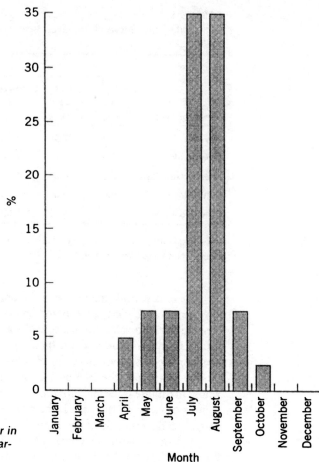

Figure 9.4
Seasonal distribution of visitors to Inis Oírr in recent years (based on data supplied by carriers).

lized, or redundant, for most of the year. Inevitably, this reduces profitability and generally detracts from the overall value of tourism to the island economy.

Despite the preponderance of low-spending day trippers and the highly seasonal nature of tourism on the island, the host community greatly values the contribution that this industry makes to the overall economy. The industry, as currently organized, benefits virtually every household either through the direct provision of tourism products (particularly accommodations) or through casual seasonal employment of household members in various establishments serving the tourists' needs.

Apart from direct benefits, tourism indirectly contributes to maintaining this island community in a variety of ways—for example, helping to sustain an enhanced transportation service, contributing to the viability of shops and other businesses, and improving the quality of life in general by facilitating the creation of a vivacious and pleasant social environment for the enjoyment of both tourists and the host community alike. There is little doubt that the recent growth in tourism on the island is the single most important economic factor leading to the reversal of the long-term downward trend in population around the beginning of the 1980s (see Figure 9.3b). The fact that tourism on the island is community-based, thus benefiting most households, is a critical factor in this regard.

THE NEED FOR A TOURISM DEVELOPMENT STRATEGY

By and large, tourism on Inis Oírr is something that is happening to the island community rather than something that is planned and controlled by them. Until the 1990s there was little or no concern among local residents with either the scale or nature of tourism on the island. Even now, many people on the island, particularly some product providers including restaurateurs and publicans, are more preoccupied with maintaining current growth trends than with securing the current relatively high quality of tourism on the island.

There is growing evidence, however, that several people on the island are becoming increasingly concerned with the direction the industry is taking, particularly with the disproportionate growth in the number of day visitors and the possibility that this trend will destroy both the traditional tourism and the lifestyle that they cherish. This fear is fueled by the very rapid and generally uncontrolled development on another of the Aran Islands, Inis Mór (population 836), which now attracts approximately 150,000 visitors annually.

Greater local awareness of the need for a managed approach has led the local tourism committee, CCT, and Údarás na Gaeltachta (a regional development agency charged with the development of those areas of Ireland in which Irish is still the vernacular) to join forces in preparing a tourism development strategy as part of an overall development plan for the island. They have organized seminars on various aspects of tourism to increase awareness of important issues relating to the industry among the local community. They have also undertaken a comprehensive survey of the local population to ascertain views on current trends and the development strategy that should be pursued. With expert assistance from university researchers, they have undertaken a survey of visitors to the island. Finally, they have commissioned a consultant to prepare a tourism development strategy that is consistent with local aspirations and the optimization of local benefits that may be derived from tourism on a long-term sustainable basis.

Preparatory work on this plan is well underway and already it is clear that, while a broad consensus on the development strategy is emerging, the islanders are in a dilemma with regard to its practical implementation because they have so little control over the number or type of tourists coming to Inis Oírr in the first place. The solution to this problem lies either in arriving at an arrangement with the carriers serving the island or in imposing some statutory control on the extent of their operations.

CONCLUSION

The ability of tourism to contribute to the resolution of the many problems faced by local areas, be they small islands like Inis Oírr or small rural communities on the mainland, depends on how a number of critical issues—how tourism is organized in an area, who can participate, and the structures established to actually develop and exercise some form of quality control over the various tourism products provided—are resolved.

The different planning and development tasks relating to tourism on Inis Oírr are primarily management tasks. What, for example, can be done to offset the considerable market power that carriers (e.g., ferry operators) exert regarding both the number and types of tourists who are attracted to the island? What is needed to sustain quality, and what is the significance of the return and/or longer-stay market segments for quality? How is it possible to achieve the optimum balance between a set of highly motivated individual interests and some mechanism for collective management and control?

It is easy to say that the answers to the different questions should be constructed around balancing various benefits against various costs, or that tourism planning should always be about maximizing benefits and minimizing costs. However, it is not possible to maximize some effects and minimize others at the same time. Thus, trade-offs are nearly always involved. The challenge—and, indeed, the test of how good any strategic approach taken will be—is how well these different trade-offs are handled.

A strategic approach might, for example, manage to convince individuals that their own long-term interests really lie in some form of cooperative behavior, and thereby succeed in reconciling individual action with some informal mechanism of collective management. This kind of achievement is ideal when trade-offs are involved. Finding a suitable balance between competing trade-offs through effective local participation in a strategic planning process is the essence of good practice.

NOTES

1. See Chapter 14 for additional discussion regarding rural tourism.
2. See Chapters 5, 11, 12, and 14–19 for additional discussion and examples of community attitudes and involvement in the tourism planning and development processes.
3. See Chapters 5, 6, 24, 26, and 28 for additional discussion regarding strategic planning, situation analysis, and SWOT analysis.
4. See Chapter 7 for an example of an attempt at gaining local autonomy in Spain. Also, see Chapter 15 for additional discussion of issues relating to balancing power structures.
5. See Chapters 22 and 23 for additional discussion relating to carrying capacity and limits of acceptable change.

REFERENCES

Butler, R.W. 1990. *Tourism Development in Small Islands: Past Influences and Future Directions.* Paper presented at a Conference on Small Island Development, Valetta, Malta.

European Commission (EC). 1994. *Portrait of the Islands.* Luxembourg: Office for Official Publications for the European Community.

Fick, G.R. and J.R.B. Ritchie. 1991. Measuring service quality in the travel and tourism industry, *Journal of Travel Research,* 30, 2–9.

Greffe, X. 1994. Is rural tourism a lever for economic and social development? *Journal of Sustainable Tourism,* 2(1–2), 22–40.

Keane, M.J., P. Brophy, and M. Cuddy. 1992. Strategic management of island tourism: the Aran Islands, *Tourism Management,* 13(4), 406–414.

Keane, M.J. and J. Quinn. 1990. *Rural Development and Rural Tourism.* Galway: Social Sciences Research Centre, University College Galway.

Mathieson, A. and G. Wall. 1982. *Tourism: Economic, Physical and Social Impacts*. London: Longman, Harlow.

Ní Chonghaile, S., C. Cunningham, M. Ó Cinnéide, and M. Keane. 1994. *Suirbhé ar Thurasóirí go hInis Oírr i rith Samhradh, 1994* (Survey of Visitors to Inis Oírr during Summer, 1994). An tIonad um Staidéar san Fhorbairt, Coláiste na hOllscoile, Gaillimh.

Ó Cinnéide, L. 1994. *Plean Turasóireachta do Inis Oírr* (Draft Tourism Plan for Inis Oírr).

Ó Cinnéide, M. and M.J. Keane. 1990. Applying strategic planning to local economic development, *Town Planning Review*, 61(4), 475–486.

O'Reilly, A.M. 1986. Tourism carrying capacity: concept and issues, *Tourism Management*, 7(4), 254–258.

Pearce, P.L. and G. Moscardo. 1985. Visitor evaluation: an appraisal of goals and techniques, *Evaluation Review*, 9(3), 281–306.

Seabright, P. 1993. Managing local commons: theoretical issues in incentive design, *Journal of Economic Perspectives*, 7(4), 113–134.

Travis, A.S. 1982. Managing the environmental and cultural impacts of tourism and leisure development, *Tourism Management*, 3(4), 256–262.

Wall, G. 1994. *Change, Impacts and Opportunities: Turning Victims into Victors*. Proceedings of an Expert Meeting on Sustainability in Tourism and Leisure, Tilburg University, Netherlands, 8–10 December, pp. 279–292.

⸹ | PROBLEM SOLVING AND DISCUSSION ACTIVITIES

1. Review the literature relating to island tourism. Discuss the significance of tourism to island economies and, in particular, the costs and benefits associated with tourism being the economic mainstay of many island communities.

2. What can small island communities do to gain control of tourism development? In particular, what could they do in a situation, such as on Inis Oírr, where the transport carriers dominate the industry and pursue a course of development which maximizes their own (short-term) interests to the detriment of the island community's endeavors to follow a sustainable course of tourism development?

3. Identify examples of tourist destinations where systems of management to control visitor numbers are in place. How effective have these systems been? Why?

4. Prepare a questionnaire that could be used to ascertain local residents' views on current development trends and the development strategy that should be pursued on Inis Oírr or another similar island destination.

5. Three ingredients for preserving the character of a tourist destination were identified in the introduction. Refine or operationalize these criteria so it is possible to actually measure the extent to which these ingredients are present in any particular place. Use the refined criteria to assess the extent to which these conditions are met in a(n) (island) tourist destination of your choice as well as where deficiencies exist. Suggest ways for the resident community to ensure that each of these ingredients is in place.

6. Given the importance of ensuring that there is a "fit" between tourist needs and the resources of an area, what can the tourism committee on Inis Oírr do to heighten satisfaction levels in the future? Identify a number of options that could

be considered (based on visitors' current satisfaction levels), assess the strengths and weaknesses of each, and identify the course that should be followed on Inis Oírr.

7. Identify areas around the world where the threshold level for psychological carrying capacity has been exceeded. Determine the causes for dissatisfaction and prepare a list of factors based on these examples that the tourism committee on Inis Oírr should avoid to ensure that the psychological carrying capacity in this area is not exceeded in the future.

8. Comment on the statement that return or repeat visitors can be perceived as a potential core clientele who can be relied on for a determined volume of high-value business and as a guarantee of a quality tourism product.

9. Identify examples (regardless of climate) where the rapid and highly seasonal growth in tourist numbers has created problems for the host community. What types of problems have emerged? What steps have been taken to rectify the situation in each of the selected destinations? Assess the strengths and weaknesses of the various means of dealing with seasonality and develop a prioritized listing of strategies for dealing with this issue on Inis Oírr.

10. The 1994 visitor survey on Inis Oírr provided evidence that repeat visitors often stay longer in a destination than first-time visitors. Can it be said that information and knowledge about a destination affect the length of stay and ultimately the economic contribution of tourists? What can be done to provide more information to first-time visitors so their stays can be extended?

11. Some believe that day trippers render a destination less attractive to the more lucrative longer-stay visitors. Does this mean that day trippers should not be considered as a valid target market?

12. It was reported that tourism may be something that happens to an area as opposed to something that is planned and controlled by the community. To what extent do you agree with this statement? Identify strengths and weaknesses of the structure of tourism on Inis Oírr (or another community) and recommend a structure to address the shortcomings so that the community may exert more control over its future.

13. Identify examples of "competing trade-offs" that are likely to be relevant on Inis Oírr (or another community) as the tourism development strategy is formulated. Discuss how compromise might be reached so that the end result is beneficial for the future sustainable evolution of the community.

10

Capitalizing on Location and Heritage

TOURISM AND ECONOMIC REGENERATION IN ARGENTIÈRE LA BESSÉE, HIGH FRENCH ALPS

Karl Donert
Duncan Light

ℊ | K E Y   L E A R N I N G   P O I N T S

- Tourism can make an important contribution to economic and industrial regeneration, particularly in areas that have recently experienced industrial decline. However, tourism alone cannot achieve this regeneration.

- In what may seem unlikely circumstances, places can take advantage of their natural environment and historic legacy to provide opportunities for tourism development.

- In an area dominated by mass tourism, places attempting to develop tourism can benefit from offering alternative products aimed at specialist niche markets, rather than attempting to compete within the mass tourism market.

- Local support for and involvement with tourism development projects are highly desirable and should be considered from the earliest stages of the tourism planning process.

INTRODUCTION

During the 1980s many regions of Europe that were previously dependent upon the manufacturing industry experienced severe deindustrialization. These areas faced an urgent need to regenerate their local economies, and so they looked to tourism to make a contribution. There is widespread recognition that tourism can play an important role in economic regeneration through tourist spending in the local area, job creation, and infrastructural improvements.

This chapter focuses on the role of tourism as a response to industrial and economic decline in Argentière la Bessée, a small industrial town in the French Alps that has experienced progressive industrial decline since the 1970s. As part of a strategy to revive the economy, the local authorities have sought to develop various forms of tourism in and around the town. This development has taken place in the context of increasing demand among tourists for experiences that are clearly differentiated from those of "mass" tourism (e.g., ski resorts). Increasing numbers of consumers are seeking specialist, small-scale, and more sustainable forms of tourism and are engaging in new activities in new places, particularly places not previously associated with mass tourism.

The discussion reviews the changing economic fortunes of Argentière and examines the nature of the tourism developments that have taken place in the town, including the introduction of outdoor activities (e.g., water sports and climbing) and heritage tourism, as well as attempts to capitalize on the town's location as a gateway to a nearby national park. A corollary to these tourism developments is a strategy to enhance accommodations provision in the town. This discussion aims to demonstrate that tourism has an important role to play in the regeneration of the town, although tourism alone cannot achieve this regeneration.

TOURISM AND ECONOMIC REGENERATION: CONTEMPORARY PERSPECTIVES AND ISSUES

Europe was the first area of the world to experience industrialization. However, there is evidence that this process has been reversed in the 1980s and 1990s, and many European countries have undergone a process of deindustrialization (Rowthorne, 1986). A number of factors have contributed to this industrial decline (Bull, 1991; Pinder, 1990), including the oil crisis of 1973, the ensuing high inflation and recession during the 1970s, and the increase in global competition, which left many European industries vulnerable to competition from more efficient overseas countries, particularly those of the Pacific Rim.

In many European countries (most notably the United Kingdom), the adoption of monetarist policies [1] by governments led to a decrease in state intervention in the manufacturing industry. Many former nationalized industries were privatized and forced to restructure to become more efficient and competitive. Moreover, this period saw the service sector rise in importance relative to manufacturing. The outcome has been widespread job losses within the manufacturing sector. Between 1980 and 1990, five million manufacturing jobs were lost in Western Europe (Watts, 1990), many of which were concentrated in regions traditionally dependent on manufacturing.

Having experienced the loss of their traditional economic base, many European regions have faced the urgent need to regenerate their local economies and have increasingly looked to various types of tourism to achieve this. [2] There is widespread recognition that tourism can make a contribution to economic regeneration and urban renewal (Swarbrooke, 1993), although the exact extent is a much-debated issue. The economic impacts of tourism have been discussed extensively (Mathieson and Wall, 1982; Pearce, 1981; Ryan, 1991). Tourism is effective in bringing outside revenue into an area in the form of tourist spending. Such spending can have a broad impact through being spread over a range of industries (e.g., transport, accommodations, food) (Fletcher, 1994). Moreover, a large proportion of tourist spending may remain within the local area if tourism is well integrated into the local economy.

In addition, since tourism is a labor-intensive industry, it can support and create considerable employment within an area. Studies in the United Kingdom have found that jobs in tourism can be created at a lesser cost than jobs in the manufacturing industry (Hewison, 1989; Lumley, 1988). Moreover, Archer and Cooper (1994) note that tourism seems to be more effective than other industries in creating jobs in peripheral or less developed parts of a country where opportunities for alternative forms of economic development are limited. Tourism also leads to improvements in infrastructure, to the benefit of both local people and tourists.

For these reasons, tourism is frequently viewed as a source of potential economic salvation in areas that have recently experienced industrial decline (Swarbrooke, 1993). Many towns, cities, and regions formerly dependent upon traditional forms of industry have begun to develop tourist attractions, facilities, and infrastructure. Very often their industrial past is the only resource they have to sell to tourists, and so heritage tourism[3] has boomed (Goodall, 1993; Harris, 1989; Hewison, 1987). This process of using the past to regenerate the present has been termed the "heritage solution" (Hewison, 1987).

Tourism also has its costs or disbenefits (Archer and Cooper, 1994; Mathieson and Wall, 1982). An area may become overdependent upon tourism and, therefore, vulnerable to a decline in the tourist market. Tourism may have an inflationary effect on the price of land so that, as demand generated by the tourism industry increases, local people can no longer afford to live or purchase houses in the local area and are compelled to move away. Jobs in tourism may be unreliable through being part-time and seasonal. Tourism also has broader negative impacts, including pollution, environmental degradation and erosion, and the creation of cultural and moral change among local people as a result of exposure to tourists.[4]

In this chapter Argentière la Bessée is presented as an example of how tourism is being used to regenerate a local economy in France. This small town in the High French Alps was formerly dependent on an aluminum works as the dominant source of employment. But France has experienced deindustrialization in recent years. Between 1975 and 1992 employment in primary and secondary sectors in France fell from 48.7 percent of total employment to 35.3 percent, while employment in the tertiary (service) sector increased from 51.3 percent to 65.7 percent (CREDOC, 1994). Tourism has an important role to play in economic regeneration in France, particularly in rural areas (Boniface and Cooper, 1994) and especially given tourism's ability to create jobs (Tuppen, 1991).

Following the closure of the aluminum works in 1988, the local authorities in Argentière sought to create jobs by developing various forms of specialist tourism. Just as mass tourism was a characteristic of industrial society, so a postindustrial society is increasingly producing "post-mass tourism" (Urry, 1988). While the demand for mass tourism (e.g., ski resorts) remains healthy, many consumers are seeking small-scale, segmented, and specialist tourism experiences. This trend has been variously described as the "new" tourism (Poon, 1989), or post-Fordist tourism (Urry, 1990, 1994). Consumers' tastes are becoming increasingly selective, differentiated, and fussy. Many tourists are becoming bored with familiar experiences and are demanding forms of tourism that offer novelty and difference.

The 1980s also evidenced considerable growth of the professional and managerial classes within Europe. This upwardly mobile group is increasingly likely to regard mass tourism as "vulgar," and to demand something more distinctive, individual, and upscale as a way of affirming and proclaiming their social status. Therefore, there has been considerable growth in types of tourism featuring new activities in new places. In the United

Kingdom, heritage tourism (in a wide variety of forms) has been one of the most obvious examples of this (Urry, 1990).

The 1980s also witnessed greater awareness of environmental problems and the rise of environmentalism and "green" consciousness (Archer and Cooper, 1994). There was increasing recognition that mass tourism was damaging to the environment and frequently motivated by a desire for short-term profits with little consideration for longer-term environmental problems. In this climate new forms of tourism were advocated, including "sustainable" tourism, "responsible" tourism, and "alternative" tourism (e.g., Smith and Eadington, 1992). What these views have in common is a belief that tourism should be developed in a way that minimizes environmental impacts, offers tourist experiences without exceeding the ability of a destination to provide those experiences, and satisfies the needs of tourists without compromising the needs of future generations [5] (Archer and Cooper, 1994).

Argentière is attempting to capitalize on its natural advantages to offer an alternative and more sustainable form of tourism compared to the abundant nearby mass tourism (ski) resorts. Since it will not be able to compete with such resorts for the same consumers, it is attempting to attract an entirely different market segment. The changing fortunes of industry in Argentière la Bessée and the nature of the recent tourism strategy are reviewed in this chapter. This is followed by a discussion of tourism's impacts and consideration of some of the developments that may be undertaken in the future. The discussion draws on a range of secondary sources, including local and regional government organizations, the Centre de Culture Scientifique Technique et Industrielle (CCSTI) in Argentière, and Ecrins National Park visitor surveys (Daude, 1992; Thomatis et al., 1992).

ARGENTIÈRE LA BESSÉE: PAST AND PRESENT

The small industrial town of Argentière la Bessée is located in the Haute Alpes Département (the French equivalent to a county) in the southeast of France (see Figure 10.1). It is highly accessible by road, especially from the south of France. The distance by road from Paris is approximately 435 miles (700 kilometers), while Lyon is approximately 125 miles (200 kilometers) away and Marseilles 185 miles (300 kilometers). Potential motorway access to northern Italy in the future may place this area on a major route through the High Alps. The town is also very accessible by train, with daily direct links to Lyon, Paris, Marseilles, and Grenoble. About 85,000 people each year get on or off the train in Argentière. A train journey from Paris to Argentière takes about 10 hours.

From Roman times to the nineteenth century Argentière had a long history as a mining town. However, in the twentieth century, the town evolved from its initial mining function to one dominated by manufacturing based on the generation of hydroelectric power. The first electricity-generating station was built between 1907 and 1909. In 1907, the Electro-Metallurgy Society of Froges developed an aluminum factory in the Durance Valley at Argentière (see Figure 10.2). Although bauxite is not found locally in large quantities, the new more reliable electricity supply was the key factor influencing the location of the aluminum factory in this area. By 1910 the factory was in operation, using 27,000 kilowatts to produce each ton of metal. In 1930 the factory was bought by the Pechiney Company.

Industrial labor was difficult to find, so immigrants who were prepared to work for

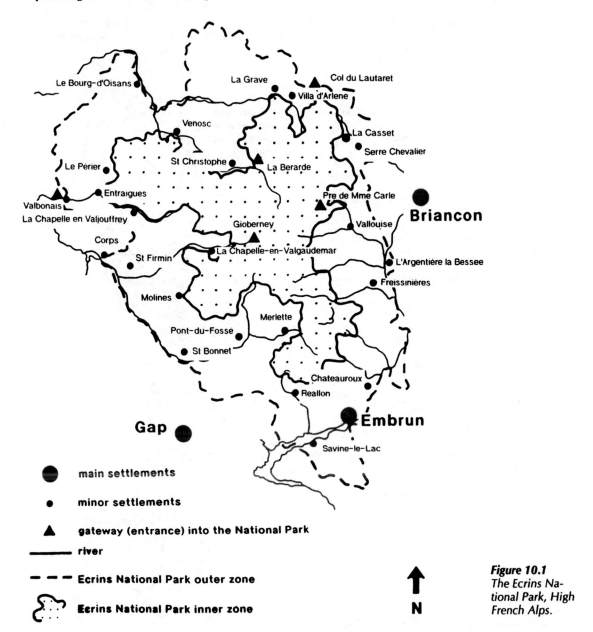

Figure 10.1
The Ecrins Na-
tional Park, High
French Alps.

low pay were imported to this rural mountain area. Argentière la Bessée rapidly became a company town dominated by, and reliant on, the aluminum factory. However, economic decline since the 1970s led to the progressive reduction of the Pechiney works labor force. In 1988 the factory closed, resulting in the loss of 334 jobs. In keeping with the commune's (local council) policy to attract and create new jobs, industrial reconversion has taken place and several new firms have moved into the former industrial site (see Table 10.1). These, together with other developments, brought a total of 260 jobs to Argentière

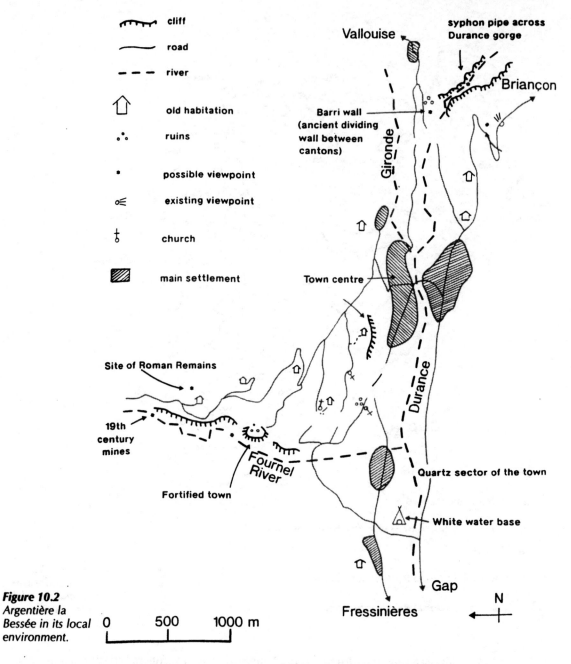

Figure 10.2
Argentière la Bessée in its local environment.

0   500   1000 m

by the end of 1994 (CCSTI, 1994). The unemployment rate in the town, however, increased from 5 percent of the active population in 1982 to 9.6 percent in 1990 (see Table 10.2) and to an estimated 10.6 percent in 1994.

Despite its negative economic impacts, closure of the Pechiney aluminum works had some positive effects on the physical environment. Smoke emissions have ceased, thereby

TABLE 10.1
New Enterprises Created in Argentière la Bessée Since 1988

New Firms Created	Expected Number of Workers	Number Employed in 1994
GMI	12	—
FAP	120	97
SCM	30	—
Transglass	50	14
Sogesiam	22	—
Sandon	34	—
Alit	15	2
Enerbois	20	6
Durance Air Composite	3	—
05 Telematique	10	2
Ferrier	10	5
Total	326	126

Source: CCSTI (1994).

rendering Argentière a more attractive residential area. The improved environment will benefit the town in the coming years. Today Argentière la Bessée acts as a local center providing essential services to those living in the area, while seeking to encourage new industrial employment. Its role as a service center is an important aspect of plans to develop tourist services in the town. Approximately 2500 people live in the town itself, with an additional 1500 people living in the surrounding service area, mainly in the nearby villages of Vallouise and Pelvoux.

TABLE 10.2
Unemployment in Argentière la Bessée, 1990

Age Group	Number Unemployed	Percent of Active Work Force Unemployed
15–21	24	17.5
25–29	18	12.8
30–39	22	9.9
40–59	24	6.0
60+	1	3.6
Total unemployed	89	9.6

Source: CCSTI (personal communication with Ian Cowburn, 1995).

THE TOURISM STRATEGY AND ITS VARIOUS COMPONENTS

Background Based on tourist arrivals, France is the world's most popular international tourist destination (Boniface and Cooper, 1994), receiving 55.7 million tourists in 1991 (Latham, 1994). For much of the postwar period the tourism industry in France has experienced continuous growth which, although slowing, is expected to remain buoyant (Tuppen, 1991). Tourism is a major employer in France, accounting for approximately 1.6 million jobs, or almost 8 percent of the total employed population (Pasgrimaud, 1987; Tuppen, 1991).

The French Alps are one of France's most popular tourist destination areas (Labrune, 1988; Pearce, 1987). This area's altitude and continentality produce excellent conditions for the accumulation of snow (Burton, 1994). Since the 1950s the French Alps have experienced a rapid growth of mass tourism, based primarily on the development of ski resorts at high altitude (Barker, 1982). France and Austria contend for first place in world rankings for winter sports (Barbier, 1991).

Ski-based tourism is very popular among the French. In the winter of 1989–1990, 7.1 percent of the French population went on a skiing holiday (Barbier, 1991), and two-thirds of these holidays took place in the French Alps (Tuppen, 1988). France's ski resorts are visited by approximately 6 million skiers annually (d'Erceville, 1986; Tuppen, 1991) and provide a total of 1.3 million tourist beds (Barbier, 1991). A total of 130,000 holiday beds are provided within the Haute Alpes Département (Comité Départemental du Tourisme, 1995), with the largest resort area being Serre Chevalier-Briançon (see Figure 10.1). This is the third largest ski resort in France, with 35,000 beds and 65 ski lifts (Barbier, 1991). Accommodations in the French Alps include, in order of importance, rented self-catering apartments and houses, campsites, *gites* (rooms in private houses), and hotels.

Not all tourism in the French Alps, however, is based on skiing. The region offers a range of other opportunities, including walking, hiking, climbing, and nature-watching in the national parks. Mountain tourism also includes summer sporting activities (e.g., mountain biking and water sports). Cultural and heritage tourism are also being developed (Daude, 1992). In addition, based on its clean air and sunshine, the region has traditionally been popular for health tourism.[6]

Argentière la Bessée is situated close to Serre Chevalier-Briançon, the administrative and market center for the region. Popular for skiing, heritage, and health tourism, this area, like many other skiing areas, is seeking to extend the season and develop a summer market (Tuppen, 1988). Although Argentière is located in an area of mass tourism, it has traditionally experienced little tourism development or visitation.

The Tourism Development Plan Although skiing and mountain sports dominate Alpine tourism, many towns and villages at lower elevations are seeking to develop their natural advantages for tourism in an effort to diversify the economy. This is particularly the case for settlements, like Argentière, whose industrialization was based on an inexpensive and reliable supply of power or local mineral resources, but which subsequently have experienced great economic decline (Terranche, 1993).

In 1989, Joel Giraud (who was standing for election as mayor of Argentière) proposed a tourism development plan as one component of a package of measures for the town. He was elected with 60 percent support (and reelected in 1995 with 80 percent support) and subsequently set about implementing his plan. Following public consultation,[7] which is a standard part of the French planning system (and to which, in fact, there was little interest among the town's residents), the tourism development plan for Argentière la Bessée was published in 1990 (ACTOUR, 1990).

A major focus of the plan involved an attempt to capitalize on the large number of tourists already visiting the area or passing through. A primary goal was the creation of a distinctive identity for the town. This was to be achieved by providing alternative types of tourism activity, thereby avoiding direct and intense competition from the more established local, traditional Alpine tourist resorts in the surrounding area. The commune decided to develop a range of specific tourism options rather than relying on a single tourism sector. The key components of the tourism development plan, together with their estimated costs, are shown in Table 10.3.

Tourist provision in Argentière is targeted at three market segments: (1) The town has sought to capitalize on its physical location and natural environment to offer various

TABLE 10.3
Major Elements of the Tourism Development Plan for Argentière la Bessée

Tourism Development Project	Estimated Cost (Millions French Francs[a])	Commune's Priority for Implementation [on a Scale of 1 (High) to 5 (Low)]
Renovation of an old industrial building to a multiuse sports hall	5FF (US$1.05 million)	2/3
Extension of hall to provide activity rooms	4FF (US$0.84 million)	3
White water base, including beginner's area, international course, beach area, picnic site and lake, car parks, and tourist information point	3FF (US$0.63 million)	1/2
Tennis center providing five courts next to football stadium	1FF (US$0.21 million)	3/4
Climbing sites providing a range of routes and training sites, picnic areas, and toilets	0.3FF (US$0.63 million)	1/2
Fournel Valley Welcome Center to the national park, woodland trail, cross-country skiing, and heritage trail	0.3FF (US$0.63 million)	1/2
Mining and Industrial Traditions Museum, renovation of old water mill into a convention hall	0.5FF (US$0.105 million)	1/2
Discovery trail in Fournel Valley (nature, water, and flowers) leading to the Mining Museum and the mine	0.25FF (US$0.525 million)	1/2
Children's Residential Health Center	6FF (US$1.26 million)	2/3

[a] Dollar exchange rate as of July 1995: 10FF = US$2.10.
Source: ACTOUR (1990).

forms of activity or adventure tourism (e.g., white water sports and climbing), (2) an attempt has been made to develop and exploit the town's industrial past to cater to heritage tourists, and (3) the town has taken advantage of its position as a gateway to the Ecrins National Park to act as a service center for park visitors.

The key tourism developments focus on summer activities (see Figure 10.3), which is consistent with a general trend in the Alps to broadening the tourist season through diversification away from traditional, winter-based ski tourism (Barker, 1982; Tuppen, 1988). Argentière should benefit directly from tourists visiting the area in the summer months, and also from ski tourists in transit during the winter months.

Activity Tourism WHITE WATER SPORTS Argentière la Bessée is located at the confluence of the Gyr, Onde, Fournel, and Durance rivers. The nature of the water has enabled the development of specialized water sports for both beginners and experts, including white water canoeing, kayaking, and rafting. White water facilities include the provision of a center with instructors and notice boards, a slalom course on the Durance River, a beginner's pool, a picnic area, and a camping and caravan site. The white water base, which became fully operational in 1994, has already been used for international competitions and is now the Olympic training center for the French national team. Activities like these significantly raise the regional, national, and international profile of the town and should lead to further tourism development.

In 1993, over 300,000 people (representing a diverse clientele ranging from school groups to specialist clubs) took advantage of the white water facilities. Because the center offers opportunities for beginners, including the provision of instruction, general tourists to the area have begun to participate in white water sports activities.

CLIMBING Climbing is increasing in popularity in France, with more than 300,000 people practicing the sport (Thomatis et al., 1992). The French are much more "mountain aware" than other Western European nations, and it is common for the French to take both summer and winter holidays in the mountains. Argentière la Bessée is located in a narrow, mountainous valley and is surrounded by cliffs and mountains (some very close to the town center). The rocks are of exceptional climbing quality, offering a wide range of altitudes and levels of difficulty.

Many of the slopes receive high amounts of sunlight and are not covered with snow for long periods, thereby supporting climbing for 10 months a year. Beginner climbing areas that have been established close to the town center are already in use by local people, particularly school groups, and other rock faces have been identified for potential development.

Mining Heritage Tourism Heritage tourism is expanding rapidly throughout Europe (Ashworth and Larkham, 1994; Zeppel and Hall, 1992) and in the Alps. For example, the Mining Museum in Briançon [about 20 miles (30 kilometers) away] annually receives over 15,000 visitors in July and August. The Haute Alpes Département has established a number of heritage trails for the tourist-motorist, including castle heritage trails, vineyard trails, and even a sundial trail.

Many old and previously forgotten French mines have been rediscovered since about 1960. At the same time, underground exploration, especially for the collection of minerals and for archaeological research, has increased in popularity. Old mining sites have

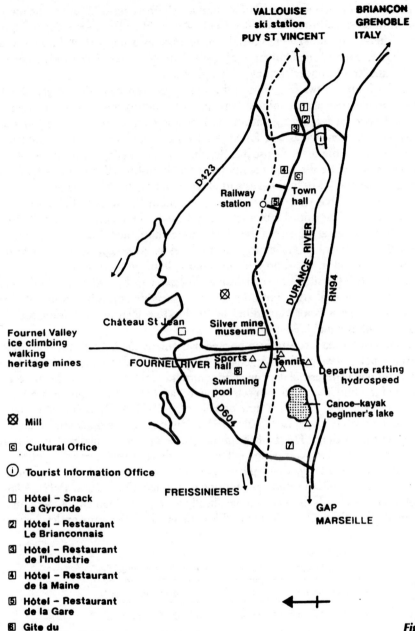

VALLOUISE
ski station
PUY ST VINCENT

BRIANÇON
GRENOBLE
ITALY

D423

Railway
station

Town
hall

DURANCE RIVER

RN94

Mill

Château St Jean

Silver mine
museum

Fournel Valley
ice climbing
walking
heritage mines

FOURNEL RIVER

Sports
hall

Tennis

Departure rafting
hydrospeed

Swimming
pool

Canoe–kayak
beginner's lake

D604

Mill

Cultural Office

Tourist Information Office

Hôtel – Snack
La Gyronde

Hôtel – Restaurant
Le Briançonnais

Hôtel – Restaurant
de l'Industrie

Hôtel – Restaurant
de la Maine

Hôtel – Restaurant
de la Gare

Gite du
Moulin Papillon

Camping
Caravaneige

FREISSINIERES

GAP
MARSEILLE

Figure 10.3
Tourism developments in Ar-
gentière la Bessée.

been the object of a French national plan for multidisciplinary research under the direction of the Minister of Culture and CNRS (Centre National de Recherche Scientifique) since 1982. After 1986, mines were officially recognized as being part of the industrial heritage of France. Protection of former mining sites, which can now be accorded historic monument status, can be undertaken by local authorities.

With relics from the twelfth, fourteenth, and nineteenth centuries, Argentière la Bessée has a privileged place in mining heritage. The mining and industrial works at Argentière la Bessée have left a significant mark on the countryside. Mining galleries, mine workings, treatment works and foundries, spoil tips, and areas of toxic industrial waste are all found in the area. Consequently, the Fournel Valley mine site has been classified and protected by the local commune as an "industrial edifice" or historic antique, though it has not yet been listed as part of regional or national heritage.

The Fournel River has eroded several areas, and many buildings in the mining village are deteriorating. The ruined buildings and collapsed galleries on the mine site have remained in this state since the end of the nineteenth century, and thus they are in need of considerable investment to enable tourism to develop. Although poor access to the mine site is a constraint in the short term for mining heritage tourism in Argentière la Bessée, it does protect the site from vandalism and/or pilferage by visitors and collectors. Mining occurred at several sites, but only one site is readily accessible to tourists. An inventory of the mines is being carried out by the local geological and mining society, which is a long but essential task.

In common with other areas in Europe, and particularly the United Kingdom, heritage tourism is being developed in Argentière as part of a wider strategy of economic development following industrial decline. The commune wants to conserve the mine and restore some of the buildings, with projects being initiated to evaluate their potential for future use. Consequently, a heritage development plan (ACTOUR, 1990) with a range of funding sources was prepared (see Table 10.4) to initiate the development of a heritage site in the Fournel Valley. The heritage mining development is planned to be self-sustaining, with an initial support period followed by a dynamic self-supporting phase.

The purpose of the heritage development plan is to maintain the character of the site in a manner to justify its classification as a historic monument (ACTOUR, 1990). A large number of proposals have been prepared specifically for the development of the heritage of the mine site (see Table 10.5). Much of this component of the tourism development

TABLE 10.4

Funding Sources for Enhancement of the Heritage Site

Funding Source	Funding Provided[a]	
European funding (INTERREG)	514,000FF	(US$107,940)
Region and Haute Alpes Département	50,000FF	(US$10,500)
Commune	113,000FF	(US$23,730)
Others	100,000FF	(US$21,000)

[a] Dollar exchange rate as of July 1995 10FF = US$2.10.
Source: ACTOUR (1990).

TABLE 10.5
Heritage Site Development Proposals in the Fournel Valley

Theme	Feature, Challenges, and Opportunities	Outcome
Publicity	Road signs, need permission for main road but not the current policy; unlikely to obtain permission to attract tourists this way on the N94	Expect to be able to put advertisements at the entrance and exit of the commune identifying sites that can be visited
Parking	Presently on a communal road; need to improve parking facilities and access roads; roads are very narrow, with a precipice and few protecting barriers	Plans to improve access road to the mine are yet to be approved
Footpaths	Site extends over a large area; most interesting sites are concentrated in the gorge	Aim to provide three access paths: one by the river, another through the forest, and one on the existing steep track (i.e., produce two new tracks)
Documentation	Tourism development requires increased publicity	Plan to produce brochures for tourists, including a free plan of the site and a site booklet for sale
Viewpoints	Need to inform and educate tourists	Panoramic viewpoints to be built on three sites giving a variety of views of the geographic context of mining and the geology, flora, and fauna in the valley; benches to be provided; path to be enlarged and cleared
Improvements in the valley above the site	Some areas of the site are still unstable and there is also some risk of flooding and erosion; need to further protect river banks	Plan has yet to be developed
Main entrance to the mine	There are concerns about the safe access to and security of the mine; work has been carried out and the entrance was reopened in 1994	Further clearance in the mine is needed to allow tourist circulation underground, enabling increased numbers
Restoration of buildings	All in ruin, these include the old shop which could become a welcome center and starting point for guided visits	Former mine director's house to be restored in the long term as it may slip into the gorge; creation of a picnic site on ruined area
Mining artifacts	Need to protect wood structures; they are being scientifically studied to evaluate best method	Wood to be protected; hydraulic wheel and some other major structures to be rebuilt

Source: Derived from ACTOUR (1990) and CCSTI (personal communication with Ian Cowburn, 1995).

plan has yet to be implemented. Maintenance and improvements are to be integrated into the character of the existing site.

Some initial clearance work has been undertaken and interpretive boards about the heritage of the Fournel Valley have been erected in the center of town. Sufficient heritage materials had been collected to open a museum in the town in 1992. There were also

TABLE 10.6
Tourist Visits to the Fournel Mine Site, 1992–1994

Year	Total Number of Tourists	Number of Tourists Visiting in July and August (Percent of Total)	Income from Tourists (French Francs[a])
1992	1000	800 (80%)	11,000FF (US$2,310)
1993	1300	1000 (77%)	34,000FF (US$7,140)
1994	2159	1800 (83%)	74,000FF (US$15,540)

[a] Dollar exchange rate as of July 1995: 10FF = US$2.10.

Source: CCSTI (personal communication with Ian Cowburn, 1995).

many requests for guided tours that had originally been organized by old miners around the mine site. In response to the evident, if initially small, demand for heritage tourism, the main mine site at Argentière la Bessée has been nominally open to the paying public since 1992.

Visits to the mine and ruins are organized and coordinated from the town hall by the Municipal Cultural Service (CCSTI). The number of official visits to the site has steadily increased (see Table 10.6), with the main heritage tourist season being the summer months.

A visit to Argentière offers tourists a "small-scale" experience, the antithesis of the "mass" tourism experience of the ski resorts. Most visitors are French, but there have been some of Belgian, German, Dutch, and British origin. There have been very few Italian visitors despite the site's proximity to the Italian frontier. The clientele is varied, although, in common with the Haute Alpes region as a whole, family groups dominate (ACTOUR, 1990). Specialist organizations also visit the site (e.g., geological and histori-cal societies). Other visitors include school groups (lodgings have been constructed for this group), tourists visiting Ecrins National Park, and heritage tourists. The latter tend to be well educated and from the middle classes (Light and Prentice, 1994; Prentice, 1993; Richards, 1994). This high-spending group represents an ideal market for a place like Argentière that is seeking to use tourism to contribute to economic renewal.

Although local people visit the site, they have generally shown little interest in being involved in tourism developments in the town, either as entrepreneurs or as participants in local projects. This has been a source of disappointment among local authorities, especially since local interest and synergy for the project are essential to its long-term success. Consequently, the commune is undertaking a campaign to sensitize people to the local heritage and its tourism potential.

Community awareness activities have taken the form of publicizing the commune's activities and organizing local events and meetings, as well as making an effort to intro-duce children to the new facilities and involve them in their promotion. Local children have participated in a number of competitions, such as designing a logo for the heritage area. These activities are beginning to have some effect as more local people are recogniz-ing the tourism potential of the town and are accepting the role of tourism in the future of the area.

To complement the mine developments, the commune formalized previous *ad hoc* facilities and activities and developed the Museum of Mining and Industrial Traditions in the Chateau St. Jean. The museum, which houses an archaeological display and features multimedia interpretation of the area's cultural heritage, opened in 1995 and is expected to be a major addition to the town's tourist provision.

PLANNING ISSUES ASSOCIATED WITH HERITAGE TOURISM   Historic monuments and sites in France like the Fournel mine and village can be protected under the Law of December 31, 1913. Three steps must be followed to obtain such protection: (1) site identification, (2) site protection and survey, and (3) site evaluation to establish the grounds for protection. The Fournel mine site was protected in 1993 under the local land use plan (Plan d'Occupation des Sol, or POS) because of the quality of the site, the exceptional natural environment, and the interesting countryside in the Fournel Valley (historically, ecologically, and esthetically). This temporarily guaranteed the preservation of the site, forbidding new construction, but otherwise it was neither protected nor classified as a regional or national historic site.

Full protection of the mine and village is being sought by the commune to conserve the buildings for history, art, and public interest as well as to classify the area as a historic site on the surface and underground. This would confirm the site's status as a public utility, with the state encouraging the restoration and opening of the site to the public. Moreover, state subsidies covering up to 50 percent of the costs of restoring classified buildings could be accessed (Cowburn, 1994).

The mine and its buildings are on the edge of the steep valley of the Fournel River at an altitude between 3840 feet (1170 meters) and 3900 feet (1190 meters) and at 655 feet (200 meters) below the narrowing of the Fournel Gorge. Positioned in a deep gorge with very steep rocks, the west side of the valley has an avalanche cone, creating potential problems for further development if the forest is removed. Although the river has frequently flooded the valley and damaged the mining village several times, it has now been stabilized upstream, thereby reducing the likelihood of this happening again.

The Fournel mines are located on both communal and private lands, rendering ownership of the site a key issue for future tourism development. In particular, the entrance lane to the village (18 on Figure 10.4), the large workshop (27 on Figure 10.4), the central buildings enclosing the forge and shop (26 on Figure 10.4), and the eighteenth century washhouse (16 on Figure 10.4) are all located on private land.

The commune has been negotiating with the owner to purchase the land. However, while the owner prefers to rent the land on a 10-year lease, the commune wants a minimum 30-year lease to make it a viable option (Perez, 1993). In 1993, archaeologists were allowed access to the site for one year and the commune explored the option of compulsory purchase which would only be possible if the site is classified as a historic monument.

The Ecrins National Park Argentière la Bessée lies at the gateway to the Ecrins National Park, a high mountain wilderness with peaks over 13,120 feet (4000 meters) high. Between June and September of 1991, 595,359 people visited the Ecrins National Park (Thomatis et al., 1992). The Vallouise Valley offers well-developed activities for tourists in both winter and summer, as well as a total of 16,000 tourist beds in hotels, rented accommodations, campsites, and holiday centers (Thomatis et al., 1992). There is, however, little commercial development (i.e., shops and services) in the valley.

It is estimated that over 200,000 tourists travel along the Vallouise Valley to the

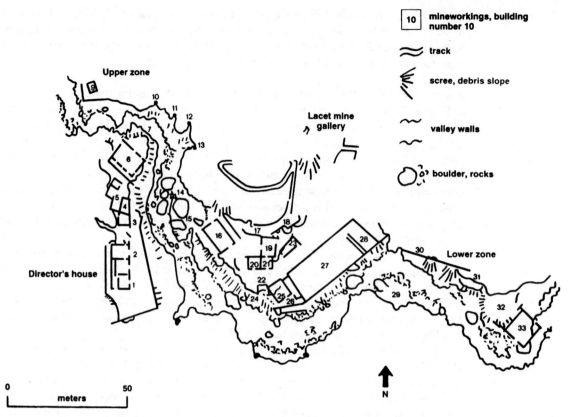

Figure 10.4
The mine site near Argentière la Bessée.

entrance of the national park at the Pré de Madam Carle each year (Thomatis et al., 1992). Approximately 35 percent of these are repeat visitors, and many of them are perceived by the local commune as being receptive to the natural and cultural heritage of the area. Argentière la Bessée could conceivably benefit from its location at the bottom of the Vallouise Valley to become the key service center for visitors to this part of the Ecrins.

Many of the tourism developments in the town could attract visitors on their way to the national park. For example, a former industrial building has been renovated and converted to a sports hall (see Figure 10.3) for use by both tourists and local residents. In recent years a new shopping area in the town center has been developed and several shops have started to sell tourist-oriented goods. The visual environment of parts of the town center has been improved, including the area around the bandstand which has been "pedestrianized" and now forms the central focus of the town.

Further improvements have been proposed for the middle of Argentière, including the planting of shrubs, trees, and lawns, the creation of a car park, and the development of other "pedestrianized" areas and pedestrian crossings. These developments are estimated to cost 3 million French francs (US$630,000) (Perez, 1993). The overall goal is to render the center of Argentière a more attractive place for tourists to stop and shop.

TABLE 10.7
Accommodations Used by "White Water Tourists" in the Haute Alpes,[a] 1993–1994

Type of Accommodations Used	Percent[b]
Gites	61
Camping	52
Hotel	20
Rented furnished flat	23
Holiday center	23
Home of family or friends	23

[a] Similar data for heritage tourists and visitors to the Ecrins National Park are not available.

[b] The total percent value is over 100 percent because many visitors use more than one type of accommodations.

Source: CCSTI (1993).

Accommodations Part of the tourism development strategy is concerned with improving the accommodations supply of Argentière. The commune recognizes the need for compatibility between the type and nature of tourists and the facilities they require. For example, a survey carried out in the Haute Alpes in 1993–1994 indicated that most people using white water facilities stayed either in *gites* (large houses with furnished rooms) or at campsites (see Table 10.7). In contrast, heritage tourists tend to be passing through the region and, therefore, do not require accommodation, while skiers tend to use rented accommodations. Most visitors look for comfort and quality whatever the style of lodgings.

As part of the tourism development plan, the commune has encouraged improvements to existing accommodations, along with an extension and diversification of the range of accommodations (see Table 10.8). By the end of 1994 the Welcome Center (which has accommodations for 40–50 people) was nearing completion. The roof of the college, which will provide dormitories for school and university groups, was replaced and the interior improved. The Papillon Mill has been developed for family accommodations. One of the hotels has improved its facilities and has been reclassified as a three-star property.

Other tourist accommodations in Argentière la Bessée in 1994 included a *carava-neige* site (caravan accommodation in winter and summer) for 60 people, a campsite, three *gites*, and five hotels with a total of 46 rooms. Nonetheless, for a town seeking to promote tourism, the current level of hotel provision is rather low (see Figure 10.3).

EVALUATION AND CONCLUSION

Faced with a situation of industrial decline, the commune of Argentière la Bessée has been successful in its efforts to redevelop and regenerate the economy. The town has been able to attract new industry and is gaining an increasing role as a service center for

TABLE 10.8
Proposed Accommodations Development in Argentière la Bessée

Type of Tourist Accommodations Development	Predicted Cost (Millions of French Francs[a])	Commune's Priority for Implementation [on a Scale of 1 (High) to 5 (Low)]
Welcome Center to be created in a renovated Pechiney Building. The center is to have accommodations for 40 to 50 people.	2.9FF (US$609,000)	2/3
The College to provide lodging in dormitories with a surface area of 500 square meters. Target school and university groups for skiing and other sports.	0.6FF (US$126,000)	2/3
The Papillon (Butterfly) Mill, a large building with character, is to be restored with 40 beds (to be rented or sold).	No cost to commune	1
Improvement of hotel provision, better standard of provision.	No cost to commune	1/2

[a] Dollar exchange rate as of July 1995: 10FF = US$2.10.
Source: ACTOUR (1990).

the surrounding area. New amenities have been provided in the town, and the quality of the townscape has been improved. The residential sector of the town is also growing. Overall, the commune has succeeded in enhancing the profile of Argentière la Bessée locally, regionally, and nationally.

Tourism has been an integral part of the economic redevelopment of Argentière la Bessée. The commune has successfully developed a tourism plan with both short- and long-term objectives. Funding, which was acquired from various sources (see Table 10.4), has been used effectively. Tourism developments have sensibly focused on utilizing the natural environment and historical legacy of the area to provide specialist, small-scale tourist services that are not in competition with the mass ski tourism of the surrounding area. The development of a range of tourism products avoids the risks associated with a highly undiversified economy. Short-term, higher-priority projects appear to have been successfully implemented in most cases (e.g., the creation of the white water base, the renovation of an industrial building for a sports hall, and the Mining and Industrial Traditions Museum).

By July 1995, 80 percent of the initial tourism development plan had been implemented, with the redevelopment of the Fournel Valley mine site being the main outstanding achievement. Quantitative data to assess the effectiveness of the tourism strategy are difficult to attain. However, visitor numbers to the former mine site (see Table 10.6) have increased steadily during the period from 1992 to 1994, suggesting that there *is* demand for heritage tourism in Argentière la Bessée. The income derived from the mine, most of which will remain in the local area, has also increased steadily.

Tourist use of the Fournel mine site is in its early stages, and visitor numbers and income generated are on a modest scale compared to developments elsewhere in the region. Nonetheless, potential for further growth seems evident. Once the Fournel mine is fully operational, the commune envisages groups of tourists visiting the mine circuit every 15 minutes. If well organized, the site could expect a maximum of about 30,000 visitors each year.

The final evaluation of the success of the tourism development strategy for Argentière la Bessée may rest with a change in the town's image. Argentière la Bessée was a declining industrial town, but the regeneration plans have turned it into a modern industrial area with tourism as an important corollary. The commune wishes to raise the profile of the town in the Haute Alpes region. One goal to this end is for Argentière la Bessée to be included in the Haute Alpes Département plan for tourism.

Previously derelict sites in the town have been redeveloped, and new uses have been found for them (e.g., the Sports Hall). Accommodations provision in the town has been enhanced, thus providing a foundation for further tourism developments and strategies to attract more visitors to the town. The protection, conservation, and scientific analysis of the Fournel Valley mine site have been achieved and, at the same time, the site has acted as a catalyst for further heritage tourism developments in Argentière, including a museum and interpretive center for the area's mining past.

The financial ability of the commune to encourage such developments must be considered, along with an appreciation of their priorities. The town has obligations other than simply developing its tourism, especially with respect to improving existing infrastructure and the generation of local services. Argentière's tourism strategy is dependent on the support of both local people and the town's elected mayor. The involvement of local people is crucial if plans to develop tourism in the town are to be effective.

Although initially this support seems to have been lacking, there is now evidence that the town's inhabitants are recognizing the role of tourism in bringing money and jobs into the town. Given support by the voters, the town might yet emerge from its recent industrial devastation towards a brighter future. However, the successful implementation of the entire tourism development plan also relies on the political support of the town's elected mayor. A change of mayor could lead to a change in emphasis in that a new mayor might be less sympathetic to the role of tourism in the economic redevelopment of the town.

Although there is much potential for future tourism development in Argentière la Bessée, a consistent and coordinated policy will be necessary. There is a need to ensure that future tourism developments are truly sustainable (i.e., they should bring maximum benefits to the area with the least impact on the environment). There may be a need to undertake impact studies (social, ecological, and economic) of tourism on Argentière and also to consider establishing carrying capacities[8] for tourism within the town and immediate surroundings. Such procedures have not been part of tourism planning to date.

Future developments of the Fournel mine will need to be carried out not only for the tourist, but also with consideration of the technical and scientific community. An understanding of mining heritage and the fragility of its environment is essential to provide the most acceptable framework for heritage tourism to develop successfully. Other possible tourism developments have been sparked by the heritage tourism of the Fournel Valley near the mining settlement. The Office National des Forets (Forestry Commission) has recognized the potential of providing a nature trail there, and work is being undertaken to achieve this.

Argentière la Bessée provides a good illustration of trends in modern tourism, including the role of tourism in job creation, the focus on small-scale and specialist tourism products, and an emphasis on sustainability. Evaluation of this strategy is still in its early stages, but the town offers much potential for more detailed formal evaluation of the impacts, costs, and benefits of tourism in remote and mountainous regions.

ACKNOWLEDGMENTS

We would like to thank Ian Cowburn (CCSTI) and Geoff Taylor (Liverpool Hope University College) for their assistance in providing information for this chapter. We would also like to thank our cartographer, Elaine Shannon, for the production of the figures presented in this chapter.

NOTES

1. Monetarist policies are those whereby economic stability and growth are determined primarily by the maintenance of a steady rate of growth in the supply of money.
2. See Chapters 8, 9, 11, and 14 for additional examples of areas where tourism has been adopted as a means of economic regeneration or diversification.
3. See Chapters 11, 24, and 25 for additional discussion and examples pertaining to heritage tourism.
4. See Chapters 12 and 14 for additional discussion relating to some of the costs and benefits of tourism.
5. See Chapters 4, 5, 8, 11, 15, 17, 18, 20, 22, and 23 for additional discussion regarding these alternative forms of tourism, including overviews of sustainable tourism development and sustainable tourism principles and philosophies.
6. See Chapter 28 for an overview of the evolution of spa and health tourism (primarily in Spain).
7. See Chapters 5, 9, 11, 12, and 14–19 for additional discussion of community attitudes and involvement in tourism planning and development processes.
8. See Chapters 9, 22, and 23 for additional discussion regarding carrying capacity and limits of acceptable change.

REFERENCES

ACTOUR. 1990. *Plan Pluri-Annuel de Development Touristique*. Toulon: ACTOUR.

Archer, B. and C. Cooper. 1994. The positive and negative impacts of tourism. In W. Theobald (ed.), *Global Tourism: The Next Decade*. Oxford: Butterworth Heinemann, pp. 73–91.

Ashworth, G.J. and P.J. Larkham. 1994. *Building a New Heritage: Tourism, Culture and Identity in the New Europe*. London: Routledge.

Barbier, B. 1991. Problèmes des stations Françaises de sports d'hiver, *Bulletin Société de Geographie de Marseilles*, 91(20), 18–33.

Barker M.L. 1982. Traditional landscape and mass tourism in the Alps, *Geographical Review*, 72, 395–415.

Boniface, B.G. and C. Cooper. 1994. *The Geography of Travel and Tourism*, 2nd ed. Oxford: Butterworth Heinemann.

Bull, P.A. 1991. The changing geography of manufacturing industry. In R.J. Johnston and V. Gardiner (eds.), *The Changing Geography of the United Kingdom*, 2nd ed. London: Routledge, pp. 198–232.

Burton, R.C.J. 1994. Geographical patterns of tourism in Europe. In C.P. Cooper and A. Lockwood (eds.), *Progress in Tourism, Recreation and Hospitality Management*, Vol. 5. Chichester: John Wiley & Sons, pp. 3–25.

Centre de Culture Scientifique Technique et Industrielle (CCSTI). 1994. *Aluminum Pechiney and Argentière la Bessée: Géographie Urbaine*. Argentière la Bessée: CCSTI.

Comité Départemental du Tourisme. 1995. *Hautes-Alpes: Guide des Hebergements*. Gap: Comité Départemental du Tourisme.

Cowburn, I. 1994. L'aménagement du territoire en zone frontalière avec le patrimoine comme outil de développement, *Quaderno*, 14, 25–27.

CREDOC. 1994. *L'Etat de la France, 94–95*. Paris: La Découverte.

Daude, G. 1992. Culture, nature et tourisme: à travers l'example du Parc National du Ecrins, *Revue de Geographie de Lyon*, 67(1), 31–48.

d'Erceville, I. 1986. Premiéres neiges au salon, *Le Monde*, 18 October.

Fletcher, J.E. 1994. Economic impact. In S.F. Witt and L. Moutinho (eds.), *Tourism Marketing and Management Handbook*, 2nd ed. London: Prentice-Hall, pp. 475–479.

Goodall, B. 1993. Industrial heritage and tourism, *Built Environment*, 19(2), 93–104.

Harris, F. 1989. From the industrial revolution to the heritage industry, *Geographical Magazine*, 61(5), 38–42.

Hewison, R. 1987. *The Heritage Industry: Britain in a Climate of Decline*. London: Methuen.

Hewison, R. 1989. Heritage: an interpretation. In D. Uzzell (ed.), *Heritage Interpretation*, Vol. 1. London: Belhaven Press, pp. 15–23.

Labrune, G. 1988. *La Geographie de la France*. Paris: Nathan.

Latham, J. 1994. International tourism statistics 1991. In C.P. Cooper and A. Lockwood (eds.), *Progress in Tourism, Recreation and Hospitality Management*, Vol. 5. Chichester: John Wiley & Sons, pp. 327–333.

Light, D. and R. Prentice. 1994. Who consumes the heritage product?: implications for European heritage tourism. In G. Ashworth and P. Larkham (eds.), *Building a New Heritage: Tourism, Culture and Identity in the New Europe*. London: Routledge, pp. 90–116.

Lumley, R. 1988. Introduction. In R. Lumley (ed.), *The Museum Time Machine*. London: Routledge, pp. 1–23.

Mathieson, A. and G. Wall. 1982. *Tourism: Economic, Physical and Social Impacts*. New York: Longmans.

Pasgrimaud, A. 1987. Le tourism: une activité en pointe, *Ecoflash*, (INSEE), 15.

Pearce, D. 1981. *Tourist Development*. New York: Longmans.

Pearce, D. 1987. *Tourism Today: A Geographical Analysis*. New York: Longmans.

Perez S. 1993. *Aménagements pour la Mise en Valeur du Site des Mines d'Argent du Fournel*. Unpublished Masters paper. Argentière la Bessée: CCSTI.

Pinder, D. 1990. Challenge and change in Western Europe: an overview. In D. Pinder (ed.), *Western Europe: Challenge and Change*, London: Belhaven Press, pp. 1–16.

Poon, A. 1989. Competitive strategies for a "new" tourism. In C. Cooper (ed.), *Progress in Recreation and Hospitality Management*, Vol. 1. London: Belhaven Press, pp. 91–102.

Prentice, R. 1993. *Tourism and Heritage Attractions*. London: Routledge.

Richards, G. 1994. Developments in European cultural tourism. In A.V. Seaton, C.L. Jenkins, R.C. Wood, P.U.C. Dieke, M.M. Bennett, L.R. MacLellan, and R. Smith (eds.), *Tourism: The State of the Art*. London: John Wiley & Sons, pp. 366–376.

Rowthorne, B. 1986. De-industrialisation in Britain. In R. Martin (ed.), *The Geography of De-industrialisation*. London: Macmillan, pp. 1–30.

Ryan, C. 1991. *Recreational Tourism: A Social Science Perspective*. London: Routledge.

Smith, V.L and W.R. Eadington. 1992. *Tourism Alternatives: Potentials and Problems in the Development of Tourism*. Chichester: John Wiley & Sons.

Swarbrooke, J. 1993. Attractions touristiques, grands évènements et régénération urbaine dans le Nord de l'Angleterre, *Hommes et Terres du Nord*, 2, 91–99.

Terranche, P. 1993. Ugine Ville-Usine, *Alpes Magazine*, 24, 72–81.

Thomatis, J., F. Victor, and B. Patin. 1992. *La Fréquentation touristique du Parc National des Ecrins*. Gap: PNE.

Tuppen, J.N. 1988. Tourism in France: recent trends in winter sports, *Geography*, 73, 359–363.

Tuppen, J. 1991. France: the changing character of a key industry. In A.M. Williams and G. Shaw (eds.), *Tourism and Economic Development: Western European Experiences*, 2nd ed. London: Belhaven Press, pp. 191–206.

Urry, J. 1988. Cultural change and contemporary holiday-making, *Theory, Culture and Society*, 5, 34–55.

Urry, J. 1990. *The Tourist Gaze*. London: Sage.

Urry, J. 1992. The tourist gaze and the "environment," *Theory, Culture and Society*, 9, 1–26.

Urry, J. 1994. Cultural change and contemporary tourism, *Leisure Studies*, 13, 233–238.

Watts, H.D. 1990. Manufacturing trends, corporate restructuring and spatial change. In D. Pinder (ed.), *Western Europe: Challenge and Change*, London: Belhaven Press, pp. 56–71.

Zeppel, H. and C.M. Hall. 1992. Arts and heritage tourism. In B. Weiler and C.M. Hall, *Special Interest Tourism*, London: Belhaven Press, pp. 47–68.

� | PROBLEM SOLVING AND DISCUSSION ACTIVITIES

1. What risks might be associated with the use of natural and cultural heritage resources for touristic purposes? How can the development of a tourism plan and policies ameliorate some of these risks?

2. What measures have been taken and what other steps might be taken to ensure that tourism development in Argentière can be undertaken on a truly sustainable basis?

3. Explain why economic impact assessments should be considered within an overall program of evaluation of the success of tourism in Argentière. What data would be required to assess both the economic costs and benefits of tourism in the area? Outline a process for collecting such data.

4. Devise a program to ensure maximum community involvement and support for tourism development in Argentière. Identify the objectives of the program and make recommendations for how these objectives might be achieved.

5. Comment on the fact that tourism developments in Argentière owe their origins to the efforts of one person (the local mayor) and might not be continued by his successors. Identify the mechanisms and organizations that might be put in place to ensure that the development of tourism continues into the future, regardless of local politics.

6. Given the potential developments in Argentière la Bessée (Table 10.5), rank the

various activities in order of priority for development over the next five years. Justify the priorities in terms of both costs and benefits.

7. Assume that nine million French francs are available for tourism developments, of which five million are available immediately and the rest will be available in three years. Using data from Table 10.3, identify which developments should be initiated and in what order to produce the maximum overall benefit for the town. What further information should be collected to undertake this analysis, and how could such information be obtained?

8. Hold a debate on the role of tourism in places like Argentière. One side should be in favor of tourism as a contributor to economic redevelopment in such places, and the other side should favor alternative means of economic regeneration. Groups on both sides should assume the roles of various stakeholders within the community. Present cases in the form of a public inquiry to a jury who will decide on what future direction tourism developments should take. The jury should state their views both before and after the debate to determine how the debate itself has affected or changed their attitudes.

9. Devise an interpretive and development strategy for the mining village (Figure 10.4) in Argentière or for a heritage attraction in your area. Identify which interpretive media and other visitor services should be included. Make specific reference to the ways in which the site could be interpreted and made accessible for visitors with various special needs (e.g., mobility impairment, deaf, blind, elderly). Suggest the main features to be included in a self-guided tour and devise a proposed route around the attraction. The trail should be as accessible as possible, should avoid crossing its own path, and should avoid any potentially dangerous sites, but should also be as interesting as possible for the visitor.

11

Striving for Sustainability and Financial Self-Sufficiency

NELSON'S DOCKYARD NATIONAL PARK, ANTIGUA

David Russell
Ann Marie Martin
Wrenford Ferrance

❡|KEY LEARNING POINTS

- The challenge of creating a self-financing national park that draws on tourist markets for revenue generation, protects resources, and proactively fosters opportunities for local economic development is immense. Although institutional structures may be regarded as sound, sustainability can still be a question.

- Institutional capacity building, effective and practical management systems, revenue and cost monitoring, upgrading of skills, and team building are all required to strengthen a park's organization and the delivery of its mandate.

- Park staff must reach out to stakeholders and strengthen their linkages, forge and sustain a common vision on future development, establish effective communication mechanisms to resolve issues, and generally build partnerships to ensure ongoing sustainability.

- Revenue generation can suffer if marketing plans are not implemented. Parks should engage in cooperative marketing with others in the tourism industry and seek their support in resolving issues (e.g., market access).

- If parks are not able to generate sufficient revenues to implement their own capital investment programs, they should implement a financing plan that seeks to access additional capital project funding from various agencies, foundations, and the private sector interested in joint ventures. This must be undertaken in collaboration with macrolevel economic development programs.

- The challenge of simply managing and operating a park may be greater than originally imagined. Therefore, management may be unable to implement a comprehensive program of economic development. Parks should forge partnerships with the appropriate economic development agencies and organizations to encourage greater local participation and to work cooperatively in delivering programs.

INTRODUCTION

Tourism product diversification has recently become a major preoccupation of many destinations, reflecting shifts in market trends toward a much greater interest in a destination's natural, cultural, and heritage attributes. This trend is particularly relevant in the Caribbean region, where a "sun, sea, and sand" product has been the dominant force for decades. However, given the economic circumstances of these small nations, natural resource protection and heritage restoration have been limited at best.

Nonetheless, such market trends offer an excellent opportunity to link resource protection with tourist market interests to finance national parks and historic sites as well as create local economic opportunities. This potential is being explored in the Caribbean country of Antigua, where the country's first park, Nelson's Dockyard National Park, was created in 1984 as a "self-financing" agency.

The park was conceived with two objectives: (1) protecting important natural and historic resources and (2) creating an economic engine for new business opportunities for Antiguans in the tourism industry. This chapter describes the Antiguan experience in establishing a sound, self-financing agency, developing approaches for the provision of economic development opportunities, and balancing park development and interpretation with the need to finance the management and operation of these resources. It has resulted in a number of useful models that can be applied elsewhere, including the following:

- Designing institutional structures and legislative authorities related to park development control.
- Establishing private sector concessions.
- Creating a viable economic climate for private sector activity.
- Developing partnerships with the tourism industry.

The foregoing are overviewed within this chapter, which concludes with a summary of suggestions for achieving success in developing national parks that will enhance the value-added economic contribution of tourism to a country's economy.

TOURISM AND NATIONAL PARKS AS POSITIVE INTEGRATING FORCES: CONTEMPORARY PERSPECTIVES AND ISSUES

Tourism: The Economic Phenomenon During the past few decades, the travel and tourism industry has emerged as a key generator of income and employment worldwide.[1] In the Caribbean region, the influence of the tourism industry is even more striking.[2] Specifically, for 1994 the travel and tourism industry was expected to account for 24.5 percent of the gross domestic product (GDP) generated by the Caribbean economies and 18.7 percent of employment in the Caribbean, or about one in every six jobs (WTTC, 1993). As a proportion of total investment, the Caribbean is expected to be the largest regional investor in tourism-related services, pouring 17.4 percent of its capital into the tourism industry in 1994 (CTO, 1992).

Tourism: An Emerging New Look

For the last several decades, tourism has been about vacation experiences—things to do and places to see. Only more recently has it been about learning about the destinations that one visits. Tourism practitioners have been preoccupied with competitive forces, accessing and appealing to markets, and developing product. In developing countries, this has led to reliance on offshore investment with limited opportunities for the local private sector to participate in tourism.

This traditional thinking is increasingly coming under scrutiny as these countries try to develop stronger private sectors and more fully integrate tourism within their economies. The focus on economic integration also encompasses more local involvement in tourism product development,[3] more attention to environmental sustainability,[4] and more consideration for the role of the countries' resources (ranging from natural areas to cultural and entertainment industries) in the tourism industry. In short, economic integration focuses on enhancing the quality of life and economic opportunities in a destination—not just related to tourism activities but to a wide range of sectors.

Tourism development can be structured as a positive integrating force for a country's growth and change, or it can follow old-style formulae leading to traditional tourism activities and all its attendant social and cultural problems. These problems, which include increases in crime, menial employment opportunities, and a sense of disenfranchisement, are typical of the Caribbean region where investment capital in tourism comes mainly from offshore.

There are positive market trends that offer considerable optimism for structuring a more sustainable and integrated tourism industry for the Caribbean region. Destination diversity is increasingly regarded as one of the key attributes for a successful tourism industry. This quest for diversity on the part of consumers is underscored by recent consumer research in the United States. A syndicated survey focusing on beach vacationers found that the top two factors affecting vacation decisions were not the beach vacation itself but rather excitement and diversity together with experiencing the destination's culture.[5]

The recent growth of ecotourism,[6] in all its facets, has been astounding the industry. Although once construed as a small specialty market offering active vacations focused primarily on adventure products, it is now defined generally as involving natural, cultural (including heritage), and adventure products. Demand for ecotourism is being satisfied not only by specialist companies but also by tour operators and destinations catering to a much broader range of consumers.

Although market data are scarce, some estimates show astounding growth, with ecotourism representing 12–15 percent of the overall leisure travel market. According to the US Travel Data Center, 43 million Americans will take an ecotourism trip in the mid- to late 1990s. More recent research in 1994 found optimism among 176 wholesalers offering ecotourism products (defined as nature, culture, and adventure experiences in a rural setting) from North America, Europe, and Asia. It also found significant interest among consumers. All respondents in a 1994 consumer telephone survey in seven North American metropolitan areas expressed interest in a nature, culture, or adventure experience (HLA Consultants and ARA Consulting Group, 1995).

Although Caribbean tourism is dominated by a "sun, sea, and sand" product, the importance of diversification into natural, cultural, and heritage products to remain competitive and respond to market trends has become one of the major challenges facing the

Caribbean region in the next decade.[7] With a tourism plant that is largely targeted to "sun and beach" vacations, the region stands to lose customers in the face of trends toward a preference for vacation packages that offer interpretive activities and opportunities to "learn" about one's destination.

These market trends, together with the need to finance national park development and operations, offer superb opportunities for destinations. In Canada, the national park system is actively pursuing stronger linkages to the tourism industry based on a mandate of revenue generation in the face of shrinking fiscal capacity. The same principles apply in the Caribbean, even without a history of national parks.

TOURISM AND NATIONAL PARKS IN ANTIGUA

Unlike North America and other developed countries, the Caribbean region does not have a legacy of ecological and resource protection through national park mechanisms.[8] Part of the problem historically has been the absence of fiscal capacity for park development. However, market trends present a significant opportunity to develop and operate national parks through tourism revenues, positioning parks as tourism products and generating revenue through complementary private sector development within parks, admission fees, tours, and other experiences.

Such an approach also recognizes the difficulty of "entry" into the tourism industry by the local private sector. Small businesses offering such products as tours and retail shops can take advantage of tourists attracted to the park and need not have major capital resources to establish within a park. This is unlike the resort market, the Caribbean's mainstay, where major capital resources are required for entry. Thus, a national park system, by virtue of its control of the resource base, can pursue local economic integration on a proactive basis through development agreements and concessions.

It is in this context that Antigua has pursued a development strategy since the mid-1980s that attempts to enrich the visitor experience with opportunities to visit national park attractions. Under the provisions of the *National Parks Act*, Antigua's National Parks Authority (NPA) was created in 1984 as a "self-financing" crown agency to operate and manage national parks in Antigua and Barbuda. This diversification approach was designed to achieve two complementary objectives for the country: (1) protection of the nation's natural, cultural, and historic resources and (2) creation of an attractions base that distinguishes Antigua as offering not only a sun and beach product, but also rich natural and cultural experiences.

More importantly, for the purposes of this chapter, is the opportunity to enhance the economic value-added contribution of the tourism industry to the country.[9] Antigua is typical in having an accommodations plant that is largely foreign-owned and for which purchases of the inputs to the hotel industry (other than labor) are made from offshore. The large investment required to successfully develop the hotel product generally preclude Antiguans from participation in all but the smallest of hotel facilities. Thus, a strategy of diversifying the tourism product may also provide opportunities for Antiguans to participate in economic benefits—not only from employment opportunities, but also from ownership of tourism businesses with significantly lower capital entry requirements.

To demonstrate the challenges and the potential of this approach, this chapter draws upon the experience of the authors who have been intimately involved in the develop-ment of the park from 1983 to today. It also documents the progress that Antigua has made in creating and managing Nelson's Dockyard National Park, the country's first national park. Designed from the outset as a "self-financing" park, the challenge has been to find new models for designing national park systems, accommodating complementary development within the park, protecting the park's resource base, and generating local economic opportunities (Antigua and Barbuda, National Parks Authority, 1985a). Blessed with extensive natural coastal resources, a thriving yachting destination, a Georgian naval dockyard, and historic buildings abandoned by the British army in the seventeenth and eighteenth centuries, the park offers interesting and unique natural and heritage[10] experi-ences.

With a population of about 65,000, Antigua is largely dependent on the tourism industry for its economic base. A country of about 110 square miles (285 square kilome-ters), Antigua is strategically located in the Caribbean (see Figure 11.1), with interna-tional air access to both the North American and European markets. The country's tour-ism product is almost exclusively devoted to resort tourism offering "sun, sea, and sand" experiences.

Antigua attracted 249,000 air arrivals and an additional 238,000 cruise ship passen-gers in 1993. Yachting occupies a small but important facet of the tourism industry based on historic Nelson's Dockyard and its position as a hurricane-free harbor. It is the site of the annual "Antigua's Sailing Week," that attracts participants from around the world.

Figure 11.1
Location of Antigua and Barbuda.

The country does not have a strong legacy of natural and heritage resource protection and, prior to the creation of Nelson's Dockyard National Park, did not have a national park system.

NELSON'S DOCKYARD NATIONAL PARK

Background English Harbour has served the world yachting community as a favorite hurricane-safe port of call in the Caribbean since the 1950s. Part of the attraction is the rich heritage of the English Harbour area, once host to the British Navy, which maintained a working dockyard providing a base of operations, supply, and maintenance for the British fleet in the Caribbean region. An extensive network of army forts and supporting facilities was developed in the eighteenth and nineteenth centuries to protect British interests in Antigua and the dockyard itself.

Many of the dockyard buildings still stand today and have been adapted for reuse to serve the modern yachting community. A program of restoration and adaptive reuse was informally initiated in the 1950s by the yachting community and continued to 1983 under the aegis of the Friends of English Harbour, a "not-for-profit" volunteer organization comprising expatriates and local community representatives. The government of the day was content to permit the Friends to manage Nelson's Dockyard, given that it was generally consistent with the country's aspirations for maintaining a healthy yachting industry.

Development Issues In the early 1980s, Antigua's yachting sector attracted about 1500 yachts per year from North America and Europe. It was regarded as the premiere yachting destination for charter yachts, complementing the bareboat yachting industry of the US and British Virgin Islands. At that time, two converging factors compelled the government to focus on the future of the English Harbour area. First, the need for development of a stronger infrastructure and service base to serve the yachting community exceeded the financial resources of the Friends, largely due to the general increase in yachting business and the introduction of competitive facilities in other areas of the Caribbean. Second, local Antiguans expressed increasing frustration with the control exercised by the expatriate community in developing and managing Nelson's Dockyard.

These factors, which brought several issues into sharp relief, required some action by government. The issues included the following:

- *The absence of a legal authority for managing Nelson's Dockyard.* The Friends were a volunteer organization, able to maintain their authority only because their objectives also served the objectives of government. When actions were proposed by the dockyard supervisor (under the authority of the Friends of English Harbour) that were inconsistent with government objectives or that created political problems, the issue of legal authority emerged as a major concern.
- *The lack of planning guidelines.* There were no planning guidelines against which to consider the increasing number of development applications being made by both hoteliers and the yacht service industry.
- *Anti-yacht administration.* In the early 1980s, the dockyard supervisor and his administration faced significant financial shortfalls based on the services they were

expected to deliver. Given that yacht mooring and berthing charges were the only stable source of revenue, the administration increased yacht fees to the point where many observers suggested that yachts were being driven away. This pricing change, which was made in spite of arguments by the local yachting community, reflected a lack of understanding of market forces.

- A *disastrous investment climate.* In the absence of due process and a dockyard administration that did not favor private sector investments, considerable frustration was expressed by the investment community (largely expatriate) about the future of the area.
- A *focus on "subsidy" projects.* The dockyard administration had a reasonably successful record of obtaining capital funds from aid agencies. However, the difficulty was that these projects were non-revenue-generating and served to increase the strain on operating requirements.
- *Peppercorn leases.*[11] Provided to expatriate investors by the government in the 1950s and 1960s, peppercorn leases were regarded as unfair by many Antiguans.
- *Unreliable power sources.* The absence of a reliable source of power that could accommodate increased development created challenges.

It was in this environment that the government of Antigua submitted a request for funding for about 26 small projects in the English Harbour area to the Canadian International Development Agency (CIDA). The request was for grant funding under the provision of CIDA's Caribbean Aid Program. The intent was to provide necessary infrastructure and related projects to enhance the tourism potential of the area.

Development Opportunities Not surprisingly, CIDA's response to the funding request was conditional on the government agreeing to establish a legal framework for development activity, resolve the development debates between the communities and expatriate private sector, and pursue resource protection with linkages to the tourism industry. In 1983 a CIDA team concluded that the area, with its rich natural, cultural, and heritage features, could serve as a world class tourist attraction if properly developed. They also observed that there was a real need to develop a comprehensive plan for the area to ensure protection of the resources for the benefit of all Antiguans.

The vehicle recommended by the CIDA consultants, which was subsequently adopted by government, was the creation of a national park with proper legal authority. A long-term view was taken with the recommendations for national park boundaries to include a significant undeveloped area to the west of English Harbour and a more developed area along the coastline east of English Harbour.

The recommended size of the park amounted to about 10 percent of the country's land mass. The recommendation included provision for communities to exist within the national park. As such, the park structure is not typical of its North American counterparts. Three communities with a total population of about 6000 are located within the park boundaries. In addition, several yacht service industries, three hotels, and a number of restaurants and foodservice establishments mainly catering to the yachting industry are also found within the park. Many are located on crown lands[12] or occupy crown-owned historic buildings.

The conclusions of the CIDA team were predicated in part on extensive consultation with stakeholder groups (i.e., communities, yacht visitors, the yachting industry, dock-yard staff, and government agencies). The theme of consultation reflected in the CIDA team approach was carried forward throughout the creation and ongoing operation of the national park. Indeed, the public meetings held on the proposed park plan were the first public meetings pertaining to land use in the country.

The objectives ultimately established for the park encompassed protection of important natural and historic features, the creation of a world class tourist destination area, the maintenance of a sound environment for economic development, and improvements in the quality of life for the park's residents. The park's rich resource base was regarded as offering the potential for a variety of tourist attractions that would appeal to many market segments, including the following:

- The "traditional" tourist seeking a beach-related vacation with some opportunities for touring.
- Tourists interested in historic and/or archaeological artifacts and restoration activities.
- Tourists interested in exploring a natural wilderness area.
- Environmental/research/university organizations interested in the opportunity to participate in historic and archaeological research in a natural park setting.
- Tourists interested in and attracted by a world class yachting harbor.

Establishing the Park The concept for Nelson's Dockyard National Park was predicated on four overriding principles that have served to guide activities since the park was established in 1984:

- *Self-sustaining park operation.* This was critical given that funding was not then available from central government nor could it be expected in the future. Therefore, attention was focused on the revenue sources for the park.
- A *planning framework.* To guide the activities of park management and private sector investment within the park, a legally adopted plan was required that incorporated the development control provisions of Antigua for all lands within the country. The planning framework also served to establish the natural, cultural, and heritage features that should be protected for future generations of Antiguans.
- An *orientation to economic development.* Sometimes called "Antiguanization," one of the objectives was to increase the opportunity for local participation, including not only job opportunities but also entrepreneurial potential.
- *Maintenance of a positive investment climate.* To realize economic benefits for Antigua, park management had to strike a balance between the need for conservation and protection on the one hand and the need to encourage appropriate investment by the private sector on the other. Park management provided the necessary infrastructure and support services and also cooperated in marketing efforts, while the private sector responded with investment.

In essence, the vision was one of protection of the resource base and the creation of a quality experience for visitors through interpretation of the park's resources. Thus, the park served not only as a public good, but also as an engine for increasing the value-added contribution of tourism to Antigua's economy. The process that was followed in establishing the park is summarized in Figure 11.2.

Legislative To ensure consistency with the principles established for the park and to provide a lasting
Framework legal framework for a park system in Antigua, a *National Parks Act* was required. The act
provided for the establishment of a National Parks Authority (NPA), which is essentially
a crown agency separate from central government and whose members are appointed
by the minister responsible for the *National Parks Act*. Several powers were mandated to this authority, including those listed at the top of page 205.

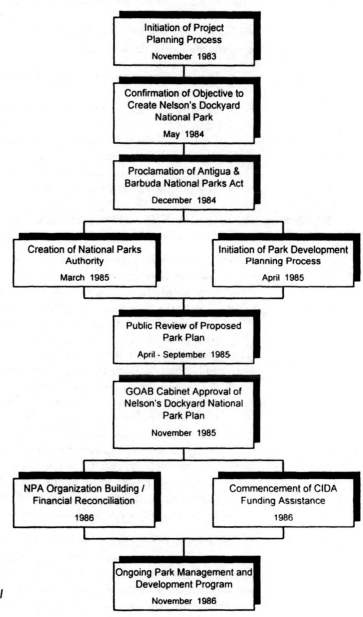

Figure 11.2
Establishing Nelson's Dockyard National
Park: the process.

- Responsibility for the management of all crown lands within the park, including retention of the revenues from these crown lands for the purposes of park development and operations.
- Authority to approve development applications within the park, provided that approval had been received by the country's Development Control Authority (DCA). The test for consistency with the park development objectives was a legally adopted park development plan. In other words, development within the park could not proceed without approval of the NPA as well as the DCA.
- Authority to establish regulations for the maintenance of the park and levy concessions and fees for park services.
- A requirement for a public review of park plans and an annual report on the activities of the National Park Authority.

The NPA comprises ex-officio membership by the country's Town and Country planner and the parks commissioner as well as appointed members, with at least one from the tourism industry and one from the local community in Nelson's Dockyard National Park. In all, there are seven members.

The act provides for the NPA to manage all parks within Antigua and Barbuda. Although the country has not created additional national parks, a candidate list of four sites has been assembled and is currently under consideration. The *National Parks Act* provides the tools for the NPA to manage and operate national parks on a self-financing basis. Without this feature, the most important component of which is the transfer of crown lands within park areas to the NPA, efforts at developing national parks to serve the objectives set for them would be severely constrained.

Institutional Design An appointed body, the NPA was established to function as a "board of directors" for national park management in the country. The act also provided for the appointment of a parks commissioner by the minister on the recommendation of the NPA. The function of the parks commissioner is to provide administrative, management, and planning support for the NPA. Upon its appointment, the NPA assumed responsibility for the Nelson's Dockyard organization that was created under the regime of the Friends of English Harbour. This included responsibility for all staff and outstanding legal and financial obligations.

The first task of the NPA was to prepare park development and management plans with technical assistance from CIDA. Such plans were adopted by Antigua's cabinet in 1985. A key feature of the planning process was extensive public review. The CIDA team and the new park administration recognized the importance of building a partnership among the park's communities, yachting private sector, businesses, and Nelson's Dockyard National Park staff. Several public meetings were held, announced beforehand through advertisements in local newspapers and "loud speaker" announcements in local communities. Flyers were distributed to all residents and businesses, encouraging them to attend and discuss the draft park plans. Since the initial planning process, the park has established a Community Advisory Committee comprising representatives from all stakeholder groups with whom it meets semiannually to discuss park development and operations issues.

The plans were specific to Nelson's Dockyard National Park, the only park area so designated under the new act, and included both a development plan setting guidelines for future development and a management plan to guide the activities of the NPA. The plans were to be reviewed annually as part of the NPA's annual report to the minister.

Following adoption of the plans, the NPA turned its attention to reconciling the financial situation it inherited. The NPA found itself in severe financial straits. The revenue base, largely drawn from yachting activities, was about EC$420,000. Expenses exceeded revenues, and operating shortfalls were met by increasing lines of credit. Outstanding demand loans and draws on lines of credit amounted to an additional EC$500,000. The financial strategy of the NPA followed its policy for the source and application of funds (see Table 11.1).

Funding from the government of Antigua was restricted to efforts by the NPA to encourage local enterprise development. All funding sources for operating and managing the park were to come from park revenues and/or lending institutions, with the assistance of aid agencies and donors for major non-revenue-producing capital projects (e.g., sewer service, road upgrades). The power of the NPA to retain revenues from crown land leases or rentals was particularly important. The NPA was able to renegotiate peppercorn leases on crown lands and facilities, thereby increasing its revenue base significantly in the first two to three years of operation.

The NPA inherited an organization that was ill-suited to national park management requirements. The most pressing concern was a collection of retail ventures operated by the former Dockyard administration. Although providing a revenue source, these initiatives turned out to be a net drain on the financial situation due largely to mismanagement. For example, money was spent on capital equipment for ventures such as a bakery, T-shirt operation, and wood-carving facility that exceeded the revenue potential for each. In addition, there was no bookkeeping on a profit center basis or financial control of

TABLE 11.1
Source and Application of Funds: National Parks Authority, 1985

	Application of Funds					
Source of Funds	**Operating Costs**	**Small-Scale Capital Works**	**Revenue-Generating Infrastructure**	**Major Capital Works**	**Special Capital Projects**	**Local Enterprise Development Assistance**
Government of Antigua	—	—	—	—	—	X
Park Revenue						
Leases or rents	X	X	—	—	—	X
Concessions	X	X	—	X	—	X
Service charges	X	X	X	—	—	—
Lending institutions	X	—	X	—	X	—
Aid agencies	—	—	—	X	X	X
Private donors	—	—	—	—	X	—

Source: Antigua and Barbuda National Parks Authority (1985b).

revenues generated. The NPA privatized these operations, placing them on a rental/concession basis. These businesses were turned over to Antiguan owners and marked a first step on the part of the NPA to encourage enterprise development within the park.

CREATING AN OPERATIONAL PARK

The creation of a sound legal framework and adoption of a park plan provided the incentive for CIDA to commit to a bilateral project oriented to three activities: (1) institution building through technical assistance, (2) development of a capital program for infrastructure and park interpretation/attractions, and (3) encouraging enterprise development.

The capital program was premised on the principle that park infrastructure and interpretation would be provided through CIDA funding. This "seed" funding was intended to provide the basis for the park to enhance its revenue base (through increased tourist visitation) and ultimately establish its own capital project budget. The activities of the NPA, in partnership with CIDA's bilateral project team, are summarized below.

Institution Building To enhance the operation of a national park that was also intended to serve as a tourist destination, several training programs for park staff were initiated, including (1) on-site training in restoration techniques and procedures using one of the park's powder magazines and (2) training in parks interpretation and park operations. In addition, a counterpart parks specialist was to be provided for a period of about three years to work with the park's commissioner and staff to establish appropriate procedures and policies.

The success of the training programs was hampered to some extent by changes in key staff positions. In particular, the first parks commissioner, interpretation director, and maintenance supervisor all left to seek other employment opportunities. Nevertheless, the training activity did provide a sound foundation on which to fine-tune park management and establish working procedures that continue to this day. In particular, the restoration training program provided the basis for an ongoing restoration and stabilization effort on other historic sites within the park.

Development Program The philosophy of the development program—advancing the protection of park resources and creating a world class tourist attraction—was aimed at (1) ensuring that NPA revenues were sufficient to incorporate a capital budget for ongoing park development, (2) "bringing the market" to the park's businesses and creating opportunities for entrepreneurial endeavors by Antiguans, and (3) providing a sound investment climate.

From 1985 to 1988, emphasis was placed on the provision of basic infrastructure that would either enable increased (though appropriate) development within the park (e.g., the construction of a new power line to service the park) or reduce potential hazards from faulty services (e.g., reelectrification to place services underground, thereby achieving a safer and more esthetic service).

Infrastructure and park interpretation/attraction requirements were significant (see Figure 11.3). Therefore, in the second phase (1988–1992) the challenge was to design a balanced development program. Evaluation criteria applied to alternative development scenarios included the need to (1) ensure continued self-financing for the park, (2) resolve basic infrastructure constraints, and (3) create a quality experience to attract more visitors.

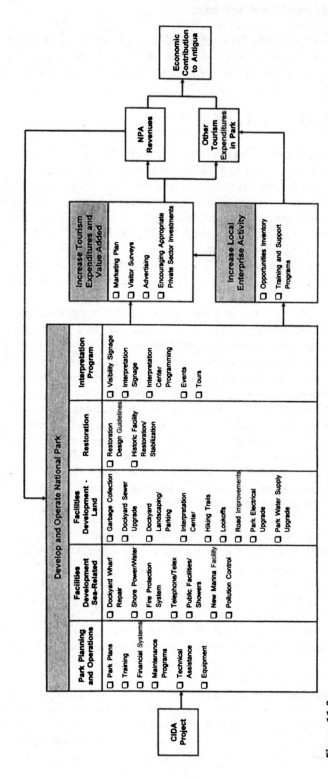

Figure 11.3
Overall development/management plan: Nelson's Dockyard National Park.

The benefits of alternative short-term park development strategies were assessed in terms of impact on park revenues, ability to attract new visitors and build Antiguan commitment to the park, and impact on enterprise development objectives (i.e., "Antiguanization").

Short-term infrastructure and development projects focused on those necessary to address issues of environmental degradation, development capacity, and quality of the environment. Priority projects, given the resources available, included a new sewer treatment plant, improvements in the water supply system, and garbage collection and firefighting services.

Analysis of existing markets in 1988 revealed that Nelson's Dockyard was strong in the yachting and cruise ship markets but very weak in attracting stayover visitors. In appreciation of the role of interpretive activities in enhancing the visitor experience, extensive signage and a major interpretive center were included as important elements of the development program. Complementing this was the creation of attraction "sites" equipped with interpretive signage and, in some cases, parking and public toilet facilities at key locations in the park.

The most important component of the development program from the NPA's perspective was the interpretation center which was completed in 1992. Situated adjacent to a major restoration site, it incorporates a world class multimedia exhibit depicting the history of Antigua and the park and an interior "sound and light" show which is a unique attraction in the region. The interpretation center provides an anchor for attracting visitors to explore the park.

Enterprise Development The first efforts at locally based enterprise development proceeded with the privatization of several small business activities that were run under the former Dockyard administration. The NPA now rents space to these businesses, all of which are still in operation.

The NPA also rationalized space use within the dockyard itself and offered a number of spaces for rent to the private sector. These were offered in the form of public tender calls with a priority on Antiguan-owned businesses. As a result, the park now accommodates about 27 businesses in rental space, 22 of which are Antiguan-owned.

A comprehensive enterprise development program is awaiting implementation. In 1993 the NPA decided that the focus in the next two to three years should be on increasing the attractiveness and quality of experience, thereby enhancing the market capture rate. The resulting environment will also be more amenable to an enterprise development program. New business development opportunities for Antiguans include guided tours, marine service businesses (e.g., engine repair), food and beverage concessions, and retail enterprises.

A complete inventory of needs and opportunities was undertaken to provide a foundation for the design of an enterprise development program.

ACHIEVEMENTS TO DATE

The park has made considerable progress in achieving its original objectives for establishing linkages to the tourism industry, self-financing, protection of the resource base, tourism product diversification, and contribution to Antigua's economy.

Tourism Industry Linkages and Market Penetration Excellent progress was made in the late 1980s and early 1990s in attracting visitors to the park. Nonetheless, as the visitation and capture rates shown in Figure 11.4 illustrate, attraction of stayover visitors to the park remains an ongoing challenge. In 1988 the park attracted about 8 percent of the air arrivals destined for hotels outside the park. While this has increased to 19 percent, there is still room for improvement given that the average length of stay for air arrivals is about seven days. Cruise ship visitation has not increased substantially, although the park does attract a significant proportion of cruise ship passenger arrivals (17 percent). Yacht arrivals constitute the greatest success story, with increases from about 2000 yachts per year in the mid-1980s to about 4000 yacht arrivals per year by 1993.

Market penetration is critical to maintaining self-financing status. The interpretation center took longer than anticipated to become functional, partially because of a lack of marketing and prolonged negotiations with ground operators. However, a more important constraint which still remains today is the organization of the taxi system in Antigua. Tour operators are not able to make "pick ups" at multiple hotels to provide tours of the park and the dockyard. The taxi system is structured so that hotel "pick ups" can only be made by taxis assigned exclusively to individual hotels. This situation must change if greater numbers of stayover arrivals experiencing the park are to be facilitated.

Self-Financing Status When the NPA assumed control of Nelson's Dockyard in 1985, its financial situation (from a self-financing perspective) was extremely difficult. The total debt amounted to

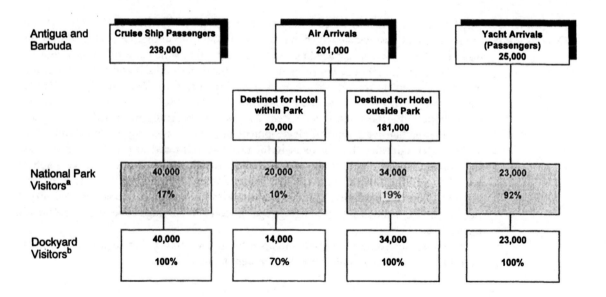

[a] *Capture rate as percent of Antigua and Barbuda total by market segment.*
[b] *Capture rate as percent of National Park visitors total by market segment.*

Figure 11.4
Nelson's Dockyard National Park: visitor volume and market capture rate in key tourism markets, 1993.

about EC$500,000, and it was operating on a deficit basis through lines of credit at several banks.

The revenue base of the NPA has been diversified in accordance with original park objectives to include (1) revenue from the yachting community, (2) crown land leases and building rentals, and (3) park admission fees and tour revenues. The 1990 revenues of the NPA were EC$1.8 million, distributed among the revenue sources shown in Table 11.2. In addition to renegotiating peppercorn leases, two decisions were made that helped to strengthen the revenue picture: (1) a reduction of yacht fees which resulted in substantial increases in yacht arrivals and (2) establishing tours conducted by NPA staff in the dockyard area and selling these to the cruise ship industry. The NPA negotiated agreements with major cruise ship ground operators to establish a package tour that included payments to the NPA covering tour guide costs and park admission fees. This was highly successful and, in its first year, the program accommodated 35,000 cruise ship visitors.

NPA revenues for 1994 were about EC$3.0 million, representing an average increase of about 14 percent per year since 1990. Until 1991–1992, the NPA was able to operate with surpluses in revenues and retired the EC$500,000 debt in that fiscal year. In the succeeding two years, however, the NPA incurred substantial losses because (1) marketing was not implemented effectively and anticipated visitor revenues were not realized, (2) there was a significant increase in staff that was not justified by the revenue base, and (3) capital and maintenance requirements of the NPA were higher than anticipated.

Recognizing these problems, the NPA introduced a restructuring program in early 1995 that included a significant staff reduction and greater attention to expenditure control. In addition, the NPA experienced what other businesses in Antigua experienced, namely, increasing electricity and insurance rates on capital assets. The challenge to remain self-financing will continue and can be met with a more focused and aggressive marketing campaign, overcoming the constraints related to the stayover market penetration issue, and greater control of expenditures.

There are capital investment issues that cannot be accommodated within the existing revenue base. For example, the historic dockyard wharf wall is collapsing and requires rebuilding. Estimates for this work are in excess of US$1 million. Efforts are now being made to launch a donations campaign to raise revenues for this capital item. While it is

TABLE 11.2
Revenue Sources: National Parks Authority, 1983–1994

Source of Revenue	1983 (EC$)	1990 (EC$)	1994 (EC$)
Yachts	300,000	500,000	950,000
Visitors (Gate and tour fees)	40,000	435,000	706,000
Leases or rents	—	410,000	646,000
Enterprises (NPA gift shop)	80,000	277,000	477,000
Other revenues	—	185,000	308,000
Total	$420,000	$1,807,000	$3,087,000

clear that the park can maintain a self-financing operation, outside revenue sources are still required for major capital items and will continue to be required into the future, given the size of the physical plant.

Protection of Park Resources Protection of park resources is a significant challenge, involving activities ranging from the formulation of strong development control procedures to implementation of a capital program for the restoration of historic structures. The development control process within the park is, under the provisions of the act, the ultimate responsibility of the NPA. Even with concurrence of the nation's Development Control Authority, an application cannot proceed without NPA approval. The park plan provides guidance for NPA decisions and, while there have been instances of political interference, the NPA has generally exercised its responsibility in accordance with the park plan.

It is expected that more public support will be engendered for a strong development control process. In the meantime, a major challenge relates to a shortage of residential land for Antiguans, thereby creating a situation where squatting[13] has become a normal practice. Thus far, the NPA has had the broad support of the nation for its development control policies. The organization has shown that it can exercise this responsibility even in the face of development pressure (e.g., with a court injunction that forced an illegal gambling use from the park in 1993).

Progress on the restoration and stabilization of historic structures has been relatively slow. The sheer magnitude of the task (about US$15 million for a full restoration/stabilization program) and the lack of technical expertise have been the major stumbling blocks. Therefore, the NPA has adopted a program which has as its priorities the training of staff for restoration/stabilization, provision of equipment to support this effort, and development of a priority list for a long-term restoration program.

To date, park management has not been able to fund the research and analysis required to address environmental issues and establish appropriate regulations to protect the park's natural environment. This, however, is emerging as a major priority as park residents and the nation generally become more sensitized to environmental issues. Interpretation of the park's resources at sites throughout the park and through the interpretive center exhibits will increase the profile of this issue and encourage greater efforts in this regard. Some of the major priorities include (1) addressing the problem of pollution in English and Falmouth harbors, (2) developing policies to ensure environmentally sensitive private sector developments, and (3) preparing specific strategies for important natural areas within the park (e.g., Indian Creek and the Rendezvous Bay turtle breeding grounds).

Tourism Product Diversification Nelson's Dockyard is emerging as Antigua's most important tourist attraction other than the sun and beach experience on which the industry is currently based. Major advances have been made in the yachting market, and cruise ship passenger visitation has been introduced to the park. However, the park continues to appeal to only a small segment of the stayover market. In the long term, the NPA believes that this market represents a major growth area because it is a captive market with an average length of stay of about seven days in Antigua. It is partly in recognition of this market potential and the difficulties in attracting stayover visitors that an interpretation center of such scope and quality was developed.

However, it is not sufficient to simply attract visitors to an interpretation center or to a 15-minute tour of dockyard historic buildings. A product that encourages longer stays by visitors in the park, thereby enhancing the prospects for more expenditures at park businesses, must be created. The NPA intends to implement several strategies aimed at increasing the time spent by visitors in the park:

- Designing tour packages, including evening package tours, in association with Antiguan ground operators that incorporate exploration of the park resources and a stop at one of the park's food and beverage establishments.
- Developing an annual event to increase the profile of the park in the marketplace.
- Offering tours by vehicle in addition to walking tours.
- Developing a cultural program for the high season.

The NPA had intended to initiate action on these items prior to 1995 but was unable to do so given fiscal challenges and the staff complement. Recognizing the problems with the marketing effort, a much greater focus on marketing and product diversification in cooperation with the private sector and the Ministry of Tourism will be pursued in the next one to two years.

Contribution The incremental impact of Nelson's Dockyard National Park on Antigua's economy has
to the not been measured in any definitive way. However, several indicators suggest that the
Economy impact has been positive and significant. Based on a 1988 study (Phase II Feasibility Study for CIDA bilateral project), it was estimated that 1988 tourist expenditures in the national park area amounted to EC$97 million, an increase of EC$65 million from 1983 (see Table 11.3).

The majority of tourist expenditures are generated by the local hotel industry within the park. Indeed, the increase in hotel-related expenditures between 1983 and 1988 was generated largely by the introduction of the St. James Club, a high-end hotel/condominium development. Adjusting for expenditures exclusive of accommodation, it is estimated that annual non-hotel-related tourist expenditures in 1988 were EC$39 million compared to EC$22 million in 1983. This represents a 77 percent increase (or 12.1 percent per year).

In the absence of detailed empirical data, a rough estimate based on proportional increases in visitation to the park (see Table 11.4) indicates that non-hotel-related tourist expenditures increased to an estimated order of magnitude ranging from EC$63 million to EC$75 million in 1993.

Value-added estimates for these expenditure levels amount to 37.5 percent of expenditures as a minimum based on a 1983 study (the only definitive impact analysis of Antigua's tourism economy conducted in the last decade) by the CRTC (now known as the Caribbean Tourism Organization). A further indicator of positive economic impacts is the creation/privatization of about 22 Antiguan-owned businesses in the park area. Most were established shortly after the park was created and are still in business today.

TABLE 11.3
*Tourism Expenditures and Economic Contribution,
1983 and 1988 Estimates*

	1983[a] (EC$)	1988[b] (EC$)	Average Annual Growth (%)
Tourist expenditures (EC$ millions)			
Hotel-related	10	58	42.1
Non-hotel-related	22	39	12.1
	32	97	24.8
Value-added (at 37.5%, EC$ million)[c,d]			
Non-hotel-related	8	15	13.4
Total	12	36	24.6
New Antiguan businesses (number of establishments): 22			

[a] The 1983 tourist expenditure estimates are from DPA Group Inc. Phase I, English Harbour Development, Antigua, 1984.

[b] The 1988 tourist expenditure estimates are from DPA Group Inc. Phase II, Feasibility Study, Nelson's Dockyard National Park, 1989.

[c] The 1988 estimates are judged to be conservative given the introduction of new Antiguan service businesses in the park. Figures, however, are not available for a more up-to-date value-added estimate than that of 1983 (see footnote b).

[d] Value-added estimate from CTRC, *Sailing Week Economic Analysis*, 1983.

FUTURE PROSPECTS

The completion of the capital development program in 1993 (the CIDA Phase II project)—in particular, the completion of the interpretation center—provides a solid foundation from which to enhance the park's capture rates from current tourist markets. The most notable increase is expected to be in the attraction of stayover visitors (air arrivals) to the park. Discussions with ground tour operators have confirmed that tour packages from hotels to the park are a viable proposition, especially with the introduction of the interpretation center. Reviews of the interpretation center based on discussions with cruise line directors and a review of the "comments" sign-in book at the center have been excellent.

However, a significant increase in market capture rate will not take place without a much improved marketing approach, linkages to the tourism industry, and resolution of Antigua's taxi industry structure as it relates to ground tour activity throughout the country.

It is also recognized that ongoing capital investment and major maintenance requirements of the park cannot be funded, at least in the foreseeable future, from operating revenues. Therefore, more intensive efforts at fundraising and attracting assistance will be necessary.

TABLE 11.4
Park Visitation, 1988 and 1993

Market Segment	1988	1993	Increase (%)	Average Annual Growth (%)
Cruise ship passengers	31,500	40,000	27	4.8
Air arrivals	31,400	54,000	72	11.4
Yacht arrivals (passengers)	13,400	23,000	72	11.4
Total	76,300	117,000	53	8.9

CONCLUSION

The experience of Nelson's Dockyard National Park has demonstrated that national parks can play an important role in the Caribbean tourism industry based on the potential they offer for tourism product diversification. The model followed in Antigua, however, is not one that has typically been used in developing national parks in other parts of the world (e.g., North America). Antigua's national park includes a variety of tourism businesses, communities, and other activities in addition to the normal incentives for national park designation.

From the outset, the approach incorporated two complementary objectives: (1) creation of a national park to protect important natural, cultural, and heritage resources of the nation and (2) improving the contribution of tourism to Antigua's economy through the development of a world class tourist attraction. This, too, represents a departure from typical western models for national parks where the motivating factor is resource protection.

While not all objectives have been achieved, considerable progress has been made and a strong foundation for the future has been established. This progress has been due in large part to the following mechanisms and strategies that were put in place to govern national park development in Antigua:

- *An independent institutional mechanism.* The separation of the NPA from line functions of Antigua's central government has been an important factor. Through its crown agency structure, the NPA has been able to focus efforts fully on its park development and management mission.
- A *sound financial structure.* The transfer of crown lands to the administration of the NPA and the ability to retain crown land revenues have been instrumental in providing a sound revenue base. The imposition of a self-financing model recognized that funds were not available from central government and focused the NPA's attention more sharply on the tourism aspect of the business mission.
- A *national park plan.* The vision inherent in the plan provided the basis for establishing the policy framework under which the NPA operates and has been advantageous in attracting donor contributions for the park's programs.

- *Recognition of the role of the private sector.* The private sector has been a partner in efforts to develop and operate the park. A balance between the mandate to protect and conserve resources and encourage tourism development is critical to the ongoing viability of both the NPA and private sector organizations conducting business within the park.
- A *strong institution.* Qualified staff, financial systems, the introduction of capital budgeting, and coordinating development programs with the financial and technical capacity of park staff have been major priorities. However, these efforts have been hampered by many changes in senior park management and by the lack of strong coordination with central government agencies (e.g., linkages to marketing and funding sources for both capital investment and technical assistance). Also important is the learning curve associated with running a self-financing national park. For example, a major restructuring was required in 1995 to reduce NPA staff in line with the revenue base and to apply more stringent expenditure controls.
- *Strategic development approaches.* Because of its self-financing policy, the NPA must embrace a strategic approach in considering the development that it will undertake. The overall program must balance the need for revenue-producing activities (e.g., the interpretation center) against the need to protect the resource base (e.g., historic resource stabilization). The NPA will soon be implementing its own capital program. Recognition of this long-term requirement is important when considering development projects.
- *Marketing and marketing partnerships.* The long-term revenue base is dependent on successful implementation of marketing programs, both on its own and in partnership with industry and government agencies. Marketing is currently one of the major weaknesses of the NPA.

Although there are many possible models that could be followed in establishing national parks, the model that has been applied in creating Nelson's Dockyard National Park offers considerable promise for continued success in the future. Indeed, it is expected that the NPA will emerge as one of the nation's most important institutions with respect to protecting significant resources and providing tourism product diversification opportunities for Antiguans. The experience of Nelson's Dockyard National Park leads one to conclude that adaptation of the national park approach to fulfill traditional resource protection objectives and capture economic benefits is a powerful and realistic paradigm to consider in the Caribbean context.

ACKNOWLEDGMENTS

The authors wish to acknowledge the assistance of the Canadian International Development Agency, the Antigua and Barbuda Ministry of Tourism, and the businesses and communities within Nelson's Dockyard National Park for providing background information for this chapter.

NOTES

1. See Chapter 1 for an overview of international tourism trends.
2. See Chapter 8 for an overview of tourism trends in the Caribbean region.
3. See Chapters 5, 9, 11, 12, and 14–19 for various perspectives on local involvement in tourism planning and development processes.

4. See Chapters 4, 5, 7, 8, 17, 18, 22, and 23 for detailed discussion relating to sustainable tourism and sustainable tourism development principles and philosophies.
5. Personal correspondence with State of Hawaii tourism officials. Hawaii subscribed to a 1994 US Consumer Survey of the motivations of beach vacationers.
6. See Chapters 15 and 20 for an overview of ecotourism principles.
7. Based on personal discussions with ministers of tourism for the Cayman Islands, St. Lucia, Antigua, and Trindad and Tobago, 1994–1995.
8. See Chapters 22 and 23 for more discussion of protected areas and national park systems.
9. See Chapters 8, 9, 10, and 14 for additional discussion pertaining to tourism's role in economic regeneration or diversification strategies.
10. See Chapters 10, 24, and 25 for additional examples of heritage tourism experiences.
11. *Peppercorn lease* is a term used to describe leases given by governments that are significantly below market rates (e.g., EC$1200 per year for a 15–unit hotel).
12. A crown agency in the Antiguan context involves the creation of an independent authority for national park development and management with provision for the authority to raise revenues through crown land rentals, bank financing, levying of fees, and agreements on concessions. It is created under the provisions of an Act of Parliament and, in the case of the NPA, is responsible under the provisions of that legislation to the Ministry of Tourism and Economic Development.
13. *Squatting* is a term for occupation of crown land without permission for the purposes of maintaining a residence or business. Within Nelson's Dockyard National Park, squatting for residential purposes is common. Less common but also occurring is squatting by local entrepreneurs operating unauthorized businesses. The National Parks Authority has been unable to satisfactorily resolve the squatting situation to date.

REFERENCES

Antigua and Barbuda National Parks Authority. 1985a. *Park Development Plan*.
Antigua and Barbuda National Parks Authority. 1985b. *Park Management Plan*.
Caribbean Tourism Organization (CTO). 1992. *Caribbean Tourism Statisical Report*.
HLA Consultants and ARA Consulting Group. 1995. *B.C. and Alberta Ecotourism Market Demand*. Provinces of British Columbia and Alberta, Government of Canada.
World Travel and Tourism Council (WTTC). 1993. *Travel and Tourism, A New Economic Perspective*.

♵ | PROBLEM SOLVING AND DISCUSSION ACTIVITIES

1. The NPA must strengthen its partnership activities in tourism, capital project financing, and resource protection. Suggest how this may be accomplished, bearing in mind the NPA's limited staff resources.
2. One of the issues affecting revenue generation within the park is the lack of an effective marketing program. Part of the problem is the absence of strong linkages to the tourism industry and the Ministry of Tourism. What institutional framework should be established to position Nelson's Dockyard National Park squarely in the tourism industry and as a partner with other tourism interests in the country?
3. Although the NPA intended to be proactive in providing economic opportunities for Antiguans, this was not achieved. What role should the park play

in economic development given its mandate to manage and operate on a self-financing basis?

4. Although the NPA has made considerable progress in public communications and consultation, financial and operational priorities continue to get in the way. An effective communications and consultation program will foster stronger partnerships and linkages. Suggest ways to strengthen the NPA's performance in this regard.

5. Identify environmental considerations that should be brought to the forefront as Nelson's Dockyard National Park continues to evolve. What research activities should be considered to determine and assess potential environmental impacts within the park?

6. What are keys to success for "Antiguanization"? Why?

7. What are some examples of development controls relevant to national park development and management that could be considered within the context of Nelson's Dockyard National Park? What form of education and/or public consultation program should be considered to gain support for the implementation of such initiatives? Who should be invited to participate in such a program and why? Identify constraints to implementing a program of development controls that should be acknowledged at the outset.

8. What are potential risks or costs (from a sustainable tourism perspective) associated with the product diversification strategies identified in this chapter? What implications do these have for the development and implementation of growth management strategies within the park?

9. What can be done to resolve the issues relating to the taxi system in Antigua, especially the ability of the taxi system to make Nelson's Dockyard more accessible to hotel guests?

10. What strategies should be considered to increase the park's capture rate of stayover visitors?

12

Impacts of the Grand Traverse Resort, Michigan, USA

ARE PERCEPTIONS CONSISTENT WITH "REALITY"?

Daniel J. Stynes
Susan I. Stewart

❡ | K E Y   L E A R N I N G   P O I N T S

- Tourism development can have social, economic, fiscal, and environmental impacts on local communities. A comprehensive assessment of tourism's impacts must therefore draw from a variety of sources of information to identify both positive and negative consequences in each of these categories.

- In evaluating the impacts of any project or policy, it is important to measure the effects "with versus without" the given action, not just "before and after." The impacts of the action being evaluated must be isolated from other potential causes of change. Achieving this, especially in the context of a community, may be a challenging task.

- More accurate and complete assessments of impacts can be made by "triangulation." This involves using multiple sources of both qualitative and quantitative evidence and utilizing methods that rely on assumptions or interpretations of the evidence.

- Tourism affects different subgroups in the community in different ways. Some groups benefit from tourism, while others may bear more of the costs. Different individuals and groups in a community weigh the benefits and costs of tourism in distinct ways leading to different perceptions of tourism and its impacts.

- Both actual and perceived impacts are important. Perceptions can differ from reality because of a lack of information or differing interpretations of a situation. Local community perceptions and attitudes about tourism and its impacts can be measured using survey research.

INTRODUCTION

An example of formal case study research design is presented in this chapter to address the question of what impacts a major resort may have on a community. The answer will vary depending on the type of resort, the number and types of visitors it attracts, the characteristics and history of the community where it is located, and how various planning, development, marketing, and community relations issues are handled. Rather than trying to explain how resort impacts vary by studying many resorts in different communities, the case study approach seeks an in-depth understanding of impacts based on the comprehensive study of a single case.

The Grand Traverse Resort (GTR)—a US$17 million dollar resort which was developed in several phases during the 1980s just outside the northern Michigan (USA) community of Traverse City—is the focus of discussion in this chapter. Like many resorts developed during the 1970s and 1980s in North America, the GTR combines hotel accommodations with recreational (health club, golf courses, alpine ski trails, swimming, and tennis) and convention facilities. Both community perceptions and objective measures of change are examined to provide a comprehensive picture of the resort's impacts on the local community. Conducted in 1990, the research assesses the local impacts of the resort approximately 10 years after it opened. While the original study was conducted to help evaluate a similar resort being proposed in another northern Michigan community, it is presented here as an example of case study research and tourism impact assessment.

ASSESSING IMPACTS OF TOURISM RESORTS: CONTEMPORARY PERSPECTIVES AND ISSUES

Before presenting the case study, background about resort developments,[1] impact assessment, impact assessment methods,[2] and case study research is presented.

Resorts Resorts are a special type of property within the hotel industry. They tend to be located in high-amenity areas (beaches, mountains, hot springs) where they provide not only lodging, but also entertainment and recreation (Gee, 1988; Inskeep and Kallenberger, 1992). Ski resorts, beach resorts, hunting and fishes lodges, casinos, and health spas are popular types of resorts throughout the world.

Impact Impact assessment is an integral part of the planning and development of any tourism
Assessment facility, including resorts (Gee, 1988). Like tourism developments more generally, resorts have a variety of social, economic, and environmental impacts,[3] both positive and negative, and short and long range. Because acceptance by, and the cooperation of, the host community[4] is essential to the success of a resort (Gee, 1988), resident opinions and local impacts must be carefully considered and addressed in the development and management of resorts. Resorts depend on the host community for supporting infrastructure and, generally, to enhance the experience of their guests. Furthermore, local residents are often an important or supplemental market for the resort's facilities (e.g., banquet halls, meet-

ing rooms, recreational facilities), programs (e.g., fitness and recreation classes, golf and ski lessons), and services (e.g., restaurants, bars, and shops) (Stynes and Stewart, 1993).

Impact assessment, or the process of evaluating the effects of some action, may be conducted prior to the action (*ex ante*), may be ongoing (monitoring), or may be carried out after the fact (*ex post*). *Ex ante* assessments of impacts are often part of feasibility or planning studies. Formal impact assessments may be required by government authorities prior to the approval of a plan. Indeed, much of the literature and methodology for conducting impact assessments in the United States arose primarily from the need to implement provisions of the *National Environmental Policy Act* (NEPA) (Leistritz and Murdock, 1981). Passed by the US Congress in 1969, NEPA requires an assessment of social, environmental, and economic impacts of major federal actions affecting the environment. The NEPA requirements have been extended in various forms at the state and local level to cover other public and private sector developments, including resorts.

Ex ante impact assessments are used to identify, measure, and evaluate the positive and negative effects of a proposal before it is implemented. Hence, they can be used to avoid or mitigate anticipated negative consequences or enhance positive ones.

Impact Assessment Methods A variety of specialized and general impact assessment methods have been developed (Leistritz and Murdock, 1981; Mathieson and Wall, 1982). Formal quantitative models (e.g., input–output models) are available for assessing economic impacts and have been applied extensively to tourism developments (e.g., Johnson and Sullivan, 1993; Wearing and Parsonson, 1991). The most frequently cited benefits of tourism developments are the jobs, income, and foreign exchange that they can bring to an area (Frechtling, 1994a). Tourism developments can also involve significant costs (e.g., infrastructure, roads, police, fire protection, parks, and other social services) (Frechtling, 1994b, c). Fiscal impact assessment methods are used to assess these impacts (Burchell and Listokin, 1978; Teisl and Reiling, 1992).

Social impacts are more difficult to quantify, and they are often evaluated using social indicators or "quality-of-life" measures (Burdge, 1994; Finsterbusch et al., 1990; Freudenberg, 1986; Taylor et al., 1990). Studies of the social impacts of tourism often focus on congestion and crowding, crime, social disruption, and cultural impacts (Crandall, 1994; Teo, 1994). Social benefits of tourism such as contributions to cross-cultural or interregional understanding, community pride, or the benefits to the tourists themselves (e.g., education, stress reduction, fitness) are less likely to be covered (Prentice et al., 1994).

A variety of methods are also available to evaluate environmental impacts (Hart et al., 1984; Westman, 1985). These range from checklists for identifying potential environmental impacts to various models for tracing environmental effects (Williams, 1994). Environmental impacts that may result from resort development include erosion and stream sedimentation during construction, water pollution from fertilizers and pesticide use in landscaping and particularly on golf courses, air pollution from increased traffic, and visual impacts of resort structures in natural settings. In many cases, environmental concerns are not generated by the resort itself but by the general contribution of a resort to growth and development in an area. Environmental and social impacts are sometimes assessed by measuring resident perceptions of the impacts (e.g., Liu and Var, 1986).

Any assessment of impacts rests upon a solid understanding of the systems being studied, be they social, economic, or environmental. Impact assessments therefore rest on a combination of expert opinion and formal models. Models are generally developed by measuring and monitoring the response of systems to various actions. Models developed in monitoring or *ex post* evaluation studies are subsequently applied in *ex ante* situations to predict the likely impacts in similar situations. Since almost all tourism developments involve some unique circumstances and factors not captured in existing impact models, judgment and expert opinion also play important roles in applying and interpreting formal models.

Evaluations of proposed actions based on their impacts should always estimate the effects "with versus without" the proposed action, not simply "before and after." This means that when measuring the effects of an action, one must separate the effects of the specific action from changes resulting from other factors. For example, if visits to an area increase by 20 percent after a major promotional campaign, can all of this increase be attributed to the campaign? Not necessarily—visits may have increased because of more favorable weather, lower prices, changes in competing markets, or increases in populations, for example.

The changes attributable to an action may be isolated from those attributable to other causes using experimental or quasi-experimental designs (Mohr, 1988). Because these designs are difficult to implement in nonlaboratory settings, somewhat less rigorous control procedures are often used in field research. The four most common approaches use historical trends, existing theory, logical arguments, or statistical controls.

These approaches could be used to estimate the impacts of a resort on traffic in an area, for example. If historical data on traffic volumes outside the resort were available, the trend prior to the resort could be extended to capture the "without" scenario and then subtracted from the observed changes "with" the resort. This approach assumes that recent historical trends would likely have continued in the absence of the resort development. A theory-based estimate might predict how many trips would be generated by the resort and which routes these trips would use. A simple, logical approach might assume that a typical guest would take four one-way trips during their stay: one when arriving, one when departing, and at least one excursion (out and back) during their stay. Using this approach, one would multiply the expected number of guest parties by four to estimate the number of one-way trips.

The statistical control approach identifies one or more highway segments similar to the one(s) near the resort (the "controls") and measures changes in traffic volumes before and after the resort development on each segment. The effect of the resort is the difference between the change in traffic on the segment(s) near the resort and the change on the control segments. The change in traffic near the resort is a "before-after" measure. Control segments are assumed to capture the effects on traffic of all other factors that may have changed over the given period (e.g., population growth, changes in travel propensity or vehicle ownership). Subtracting the change on the control segments isolates the effect of the resort from other factors.

Case Study Research As a research strategy, case studies seek a comprehensive understanding of complex phenomena by examining a single instance of the phenomenon within its real life context (Yin, 1989). Case studies generally employ multiple sources of evidence, both quantitative and qualitative, and can accommodate multiple interpretations of this evidence. Using several distinct methods or sources of information to establish a particular finding is called "triangulation." Since each method and source of information involves different kinds of errors, confidence in a result can be increased by showing that distinct methods and sources point to the same conclusions. Most impact assessments are inherently case studies because they address questions of how and why changes occurred within a particular context (Stynes, 1991). Impact assessments rely on many sources of information and must take into account the different perceptions and interpretations of various interests.

GRAND TRAVERSE RESORT: LOCATIONAL CONTEXT AND BACKGROUND

The following discussion provides some background about the study area and the Grand Traverse Resort itself, delineates the scope of the case study, and summarizes the methods used.

The Traverse City Area Traverse City is a community of 16,000 people, accounting for roughly one-quarter of the population of Grand Traverse County (US Census, 1990). Located in northwestern Michigan on the shores of Lake Michigan, Traverse City is the largest city in the surrounding 10-county region (see Figure 12.1). Grand Traverse County's population grew by 40 percent between 1970 and 1980, largely from in-migration, and slowed to a 16 percent increase between 1980 and 1988. The tourism industry has been an important component of the local economy since the early 1960s. The four primary tourism sectors (lodging, eating and drinking, amusements, and auto services) account for about 18 percent of all jobs in the county. These are concentrated in the Traverse City area.

Traverse City's numerous amusements and small- to medium-sized motels have traditionally catered to short-stay tourists. The area attracts visitors from metropolitan areas in southern Michigan approximately 200 miles (320 kilometers) away as well as from the surrounding states of Ohio, Illinois, and Indiana. The Traverse City area offers four seasons of attractions, including its beaches and annual Cherry Festival during the summer, fall colors in the autumn, and several nearby ski areas in the winter.

The Grand Traverse Resort The opening of the Grand Traverse Resort (GTR) represented a major increase in scale and quality compared to existing facilities, thereby elevating the area's national reputation and its ability to attract major conferences. The resort is located about 6 miles (10 kilometers) northeast of Traverse City in Acme Township, Michigan (see Figure 12.1). Situated in a high-amenity rural area, the primary attraction is the natural setting of Grand Traverse Bay on Lake Michigan.

The 920-acre (370 hectare) property opened in 1980 as a 240-room Hilton franchise, and it expanded during the next 10 years to include 350 privately owned condominiums, 430 hotel rooms and suites, a major convention facility, several restaurants and lounges, 36 holes of golf, 22 specialty shops, and various indoor and outdoor recreation facilities, including a health and racquet club and a 12-mile (20-kilometer) Nordic ski facility. Major expansions included an 18-hole championship golf course designed by Jack Nicklaus, a conference center, and 174 condominiums in 1984, and a 15-story hotel

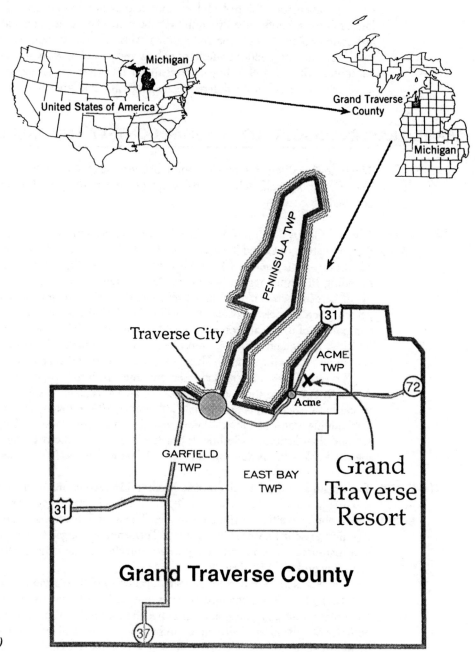

tower in 1986. There are 45 home sites along the golf courses, as well as plans for future condominium and golf course expansion. The resort claims to have hosted about 250,000 overnight guests in 1988. Due to ongoing financial problems the resort declared bankruptcy in 1993. However, the resort was reorganized under new management, and today it continues to operate much as it did when the study was conducted.

The resort fostered several controversies in Traverse City, including issues related to loan financing, environmental impacts, hiring practices, property tax assessments, and general growth and development. While the relationship between the resort and the local community has generally been good, there has been opposition to the resort from some environmental and antigrowth groups in the community. Resort management has on several occasions altered development and management plans in response to community concerns. For example, the high-rise hotel was a compromise to preserve more open space than the original plan that had proposed low-rise cluster development.

Scope and The demographic and social, economic, and fiscal impacts of the GTR on the local
Study Methods community are evaluated in this chapter. The definition of "local community" varies somewhat depending upon the type of impact being assessed and corresponding data availability. For example, fiscal impacts are most evident in Acme Township (where the resort is located), social impacts are assessed primarily for the Traverse City area (including Traverse City and three surrounding townships), and economic impacts cover all of Grand Traverse County (see Figure 12.1) since most economic data are reported at the county level.

Impacts associated with the construction of the resort have not been included. Construction impacts can be substantial but, for the most part, they are temporary (e.g., the economic stimulus of construction activity, temporary disruptions of traffic, erosion and stream sedimentation from grading and road building, social impacts of temporary construction workers and their families). The operation of the resort, on the other hand, has continuing and long-term impacts and is therefore the focus of this chapter.

Using the best available information, impacts have been estimated on an annual basis, usually represented by the year 1988 or 1989, or as the percentage change in activity between 1980 and 1988 attributable to the GTR. Like all impact assessments, those for the GTR rest on numerous assumptions, especially with respect to estimating its contribution to changes in the area during the 10-year period.

The case study measures actual changes that took place in the Traverse City area during the period from 1980 to 1989 and estimates the contribution of the GTR to these changes. Actual and perceived impacts were documented through extensive analysis of historical data, interviews with community leaders, and a community attitude survey.

Residents' perceptions of impacts measured in the community attitude survey and qualitative information from interviews with community leaders are used to interpret and/or validate the quantitative measures of change. Special efforts were made to assess impacts "with versus without" the resort, rather than simply measuring changes in the area over a 10-year period "before and after" the resort development. This involved the use of control counties or townships, tracing impacts directly from resort activities, and qualitative assessments.

The study involves an *ex post* assessment using case study research, impact assessment, and general research methods. While planners and developers are primarily interested in the impacts of future actions, the basis for making such assessments requires having a clear understanding of what has happened in the past under similar circumstances. *Ex post* analyses provide the basis for making predictions of impacts in an *ex ante* analysis. In fact, this is how this case study was originally used.

Four distinct data collection approaches were employed:

- Historical data covering the period from 1960 through 1989 were gathered from a variety of federal, state, and local secondary data sources. Data included population estimates, school enrollments, traffic counts, crime statistics, and data on housing, retail sales, income, employment, and local government costs and revenues. The GTR also provided confidential information on payroll, expenses, sales, taxes, and selected market information.
- Loosely structured in-depth personal interviews averaging about 45 minutes each were conducted with 13 community leaders to obtain subjective assessments of the resort's impacts. Leaders included representatives of the tourism industry, including one from the GTR, local planning and zoning officials, environmental groups, the county sheriff's office, and other key individuals in the community.
- A telephone survey of a random sample of 174 local residents (adults) measured perceptions of changes in the community during the past five years as well as the resort's contribution to these changes. Telephone interviews were conducted in April and early May of 1990 using a Computer-Assisted Telephone Interviewing (CATI) system.
- Coverage of resort-related issues in the local newspaper (*Traverse City Record Eagle*) between 1975 and 1990 was also reviewed for further background information and to help interpret the results.

ASSESSMENT OF IMPACTS

The following section draws upon secondary sources to summarize the impacts of the resort within three broad categories: (1) demographic and social, (2) economic, and (3) fiscal. Impacts corresponding to the three major sets of impact variables are summarized in Tables 12.1 to 12.3. Before–after assessments are made by comparing selected social, economic, and fiscal indicators for 1980 and 1988. The first year represents the "before" situation, while 1988 provides a good representation of the changes in the area 5–10 years after the development. The study was conducted in 1990. Hence, 1988 was usually the most recent year for which data were available at that time. Trend data were examined for many variables to better identify the path of change in the area, but are not reported within this chapter.

The resort's contribution to changes in the area during this period is assessed using a combination of expert opinion, informed judgment, logical connections, formal models, and statistical controls. No attempt to fully document methods for evaluating the contribution of the resort to each impact variable is made. Instead, a summary of the general approach for each type of impact is provided. Examples are then presented to illustrate the methods. Stynes and Stewart (1991) report methods in greater detail.

Demographic Demographic and social changes were documented using secondary sources (e.g., US
and Social Census of population and housing, local sources for school enrollments, crime, and sea-
Impacts sonal populations). The contribution of the resort to changes in these variables was assessed largely based on expert opinion and logical grounds, supported occasionally by
comparisons with similar areas.

The most significant demographic and social impacts were (1) the GTR's contribution to transient and seasonal populations in the area and (2) the corresponding increases
in traffic and congestion. The resort did not significantly impact the size of the resident
population or school enrollments, although it did have some impact on housing, crime,
and local air service (see Table 12.1).

RESIDENT POPULATION By 1988, the resort had not directly contributed much to growth
in the number of permanent residents in the area. While there was some population
growth and in-migration in the 1980s, these were substantially below the rates for the
previous decade and not significantly different from similar areas of northern Michigan.
Housing provided by the resort was almost entirely for seasonal or transient visitors, and
the number of in-migrants attracted to work year round at the resort was small. The resort
is expected to contribute more to population growth in the future by stimulating other
growth and development, as well as improving the reputation of the area as an attractive
place to live, retire, or locate a business.

SEASONAL AND TRANSIENT POPULATIONS The GTR, through its overnight accommodations, directly contributes about 5 percent of total visitors to the county in July, representing about 20 percent of visitors in hotel/motel accommodations. When all rooms at the
resort are full, it can contribute over 2000 overnight visitors to the area on a given day.
The resort also attracts visitors who stay elsewhere in the area but who attend events at
the resort or use its facilities. The proportion of visitors attributable to the resort increases
from about 5 percent for the county as a whole to probably more than 75 percent in
Acme Township. The resort accounts for between 10 percent and 20 percent of overnight
visitors to Traverse City.

SCHOOL ENROLLMENTS Public school enrollments increased by only 7 percent between
1980 and 1988. The resort added less than one dozen new students to the school system,
according to GTR staff. However, although the GTR added few new students, it had a
significant positive impact on schools in the area through paying between US$350,000
and US$500,000 in school taxes each year.

HOUSING The GTR added 350 condominium units to area housing and had plans for
further expansion of condominiums and single-family housing. The resort's housing
raised quality standards, prices, and rents in the area. Based on housing permit data,
there appeared to be little housing development induced by the resort. Housing price and
rent increases caused some problems in affordability of housing for lower-income residents, including the resort's seasonal employees and housekeeping staff.

CRIME Uniform crime reports for the area showed an increase in crime rates of 78 percent in Acme Township between the 1982–1984 period and the 1986–1988 period. This

TABLE 12.1

Summary of the Social Impacts of the Grand Traverse Resort in 1980 Compared to Those in 1988

Variable	1980	1988	Percent Change	Resort Contribution
Resident Population				
Grand Traverse (GT) County	54,899	63,900	16	Little to date. Future potential in attracting retirees,
Traverse City (TC)	15,516	16,261	5	other businesses, and labor.
Acme Township (AT)	2,909	3,863	33	
Seasonal Population, GT County				
Overnight rooms	1,600	2,776	74	GTR has added 750 rooms, including condos, since 1979. About half of growth in rooms since 1980.
July overnight visitors per day in GT County	25,000	43,000	72	2000 resort guests per day at capacity. About 5% of GT County summer visitors, 10–20% of TC visitors.
July average daily overnight visitors as percent of residents and visitors (%)	46	67	48	About 20% of visitors in hotels/motels in GT County.
School Enrollments				
Population age 5–19 (GT)	13,959	15,005	7	Little impact.
TC public school enrollment	9,398	10,067	7	
Housing				
Units, GT County	23,613			Resort added 350 condo units, plans for 45 single-family homes. Recent data unavailable and permit data unreliable.
Units, TC	6,068			
Units, AT	1,198			
Crime				
Reported crimes, AT	247[a]	440[b]	78	GTR contribution of about 10%. Crimes up 22% in TC, 81% in nearby Peninsula Township.
Traffic (ADT = average daily traffic count)				
US 31 N of M 72 (ADT)	5,500	11,800	115	GTR generates 3500 average daily vehicle trips representing about 30% of traffic on US 31 N and 10–15% on M72 and on US31 S. of M72.
US 31 S of M 72 (ADT)	16,200	20,900	29	
M 72 E of US 31 (ADT)	7,700	8,700	13	
Air Traffic				
Cherry Capital Airport				GTR a factor in airport service.
Passengers (thousands)	139	161	16	GTR contributed about 25% of the passenger growth since 1983. If 2 of guests arrive by air, GTR generates 5000 trips = 36% of passengers.
Recreation				Added indoor and outdoor recreation opportunities. Taxes from resort helped purchase park land.
Other				GTR has stirred controversy and debate in community. Have versus have not, local versus outsider conflicts. Changing image of area, types of tourists attracted.

[a] Data are for 1982–1984.

[b] Data are for 1986–1988.

is similar to the rate of growth experienced in nearby Peninsula Township. According to local law enforcement officials and an analysis of the types of crimes reported, it is estimated that the resort contributed about 10 percent of this increase, particularly to traffic and DUI (driving under the influence of alcohol) violations.

AIR TRAFFIC   Traffic at Cherry Capital Airport grew by 16 percent between 1980 and 1988. The vast majority of GTR visitors arrived by car, but the small percentage of convention attendees and weekend vacationers who arrived by air constituted about 3 percent of all passengers at the airport. Therefore, the GTR accounted for about one-fourth of the growth in air traffic from 1980 to 1988, and it continues to be a factor in decisions relating to expanding or maintaining services at the local airport.

HIGHWAY TRAFFIC   The GTR accounted for about 30 percent of the traffic on the major US highway (US Route 31) that passes the resort entrance. Resort traffic represented about half of the growth on this segment of the highway between 1980 and 1988 (based on state highway department traffic counts). The resort's impact is diluted to between 10 percent and 15 percent of vehicles on highway segments leading into Traverse City. In 1988, the GTR was estimated to have generated about 3500 average daily vehicle trips to or from the resort. Traffic to and from the resort was less peaked than other traffic, but the peaks coincided with general peak traffic from 3 P.M. to 5 P.M., particularly on Fridays. These patterns contributed to traffic congestion around the resort.

Economic Impacts   The GTR contributes substantially to sales, income, and jobs in the area. It has also contributed to increases in property values, prices, and the cost of living (see Table 12.2). Economic impacts were assessed using formal regional economic models. The direct contribution of the resort was estimated from employment and operating expense data provided by the resort. Visitor spending in the community was estimated by multiplying the number of guest-nights by a per-night estimate of guest spending outside the resort. Secondary economic effects were estimated using multipliers and an input–ouput model for the county. The GTR's impact on property values was assessed via comparisons with similar townships. Tax revenue effects of the property value changes are covered under fiscal impacts.

EMPLOYMENT   The GTR employed about 850 people on an annual basis in 1988 (between 60 percent and 70 percent full time), with employment reaching a peak of over 1100 during the summer. Using regional economic multipliers and employment to sales ratios for Michigan (US Department of Commerce, BEA, 1992), it is estimated that the resort *indirectly* contributed to another 950 jobs through resort spending, spending by resort visitors elsewhere in the county, and the induced effects of wage and salary income of GTR employees. Therefore, the total employment effects of the GTR were around 1800 jobs in 1988. Jobs directly supported by the resort's activity were concentrated in hotel, restaurant, recreation, entertainment, and other retail sectors, although the GTR's activities contributed to sales and earnings in a wide range of local businesses through its indirect and induced effects.

TABLE 12.2

Summary of the Economic Impacts of the Grand Traverse Resort in 1980 Compared to Those in 1988

Variable	1980	1988	Percent Change	Resort Contribution
Employment: Grand Traverse County				
Total jobs	31,451	40,175	28	Total GTR job contribution is about 1800
Service jobs	7,833	10,842	38	jobs. Roughly 80% of these stem from
Percent services	25	27	7	GTR operations, another 20% from
				GTR guest spending elsewhere in the
				community.
Total private sector jobs		28,285		Estimate 850 direct jobs at the GTR, 200
Tourism-related sectors	2,896	4,972	72	direct jobs from spending of GTR
Hotel and motel (SIC 701)		1,522		guests in the community, and 750 jobs
Eat and drink (SIC 581)		2,788		from indirect and induced effects.
Miscellaneous amusements (SIC 799)		169		
Gas service (SIC 554)		467		GTR represents half of jobs in SIC 701
				and 16% of jobs in key tourism-related
				sectors. 1800 jobs associated with GTR
				activity is about 16% of new jobs in
				the county since 1980.
Income, Grand Traverse County				
Per capita personal income ($US)	9,140	14,740	61	Payroll of US$9.6 million, including bene-
Total personal income ($US millions)	504,272	899,115	78	fits. Another US$2.1 million in wages
Service income ($US millions)	97,493	198,372	103	and salaries from an estimated US$10
Percent service (%)	19	22	14	million spending by GTR guests in the
				community. Total contribution of
				US$20 million to earnings with indi-
				rect and induced effects.
Sales and Use Taxes ($US thousands)				
Hotel use tax	519[a]	1,147	121	GTR accounted for 38% of growth in ho-
Hotel sales tax	282[a]	493	75	tel use taxes over the 1983–1988
				period.
GTR Guest Spending ($US millions)				
At resort		21		Based on 250,000 guest-nights and
In community		10		125,000 room-nights. At least half of
Total		31		this spending would not have occurred
				in TC area in the absence of the GTR.
Other				Prices, cost of living, distribution effects.
				Seasonality, stability of economy.

[a] These data are from 1983.

INCOME GTR payroll in 1988 was reported to be US$9.6 million. Subtracting 26 percent for benefits leaves US$7.1 million in wages and salaries. Including earnings generated by some US$10 million of spending by GTR visitors elsewhere in the county, and indirect and induced effects, it is estimated that total earnings in the county resulting from the resort in 1988 were US$20 million. This represents 10 percent of all earnings in the service sectors in the county and about 2.2 percent of all earnings in the county.

SALES AND SALES TAXES Approximately 250,000 overnight guests at the resort in 1988 spent an estimated US$20 million at the resort and another US$10 million outside the resort in the county. This spending represents direct income to the GTR and other local businesses. The resort's direct effects on sales can be seen in the Grand Traverse County hotel sales and use tax data. Sales taxes collected by hotels and motels in the county grew by 75 percent between 1983 and 1988, and hotel use taxes (covers only costs of the room) increased by 121 percent. The resort accounted for about 38 percent of the growth in hotel use taxes in the county between 1983 and 1988. Sales and use taxes do not directly benefit the local area because these accrue to the state and are redistributed to local communities on the basis of population.

GRAND TRAVERSE CONVENTION AND VISITOR'S BUREAU The resort estimated that its 1988 contribution to the Convention and Visitor's Bureau (CVB) was US$235,000. In 1989, it is estimated that the resort contributed almost US$300,000 in room assessment tax. The GTR contributions represent about 30 percent of the CVB assessment revenue and half of the revenue from within Grand Traverse County. The resort's CVB contributions along with its own US$1.7 million marketing and sales program in 1988 helped promote the Traverse City area.

PROPERTY VALUES The GTR represented 13 percent of all real and personal property in Acme Township in 1988. Total (real plus personal) state equalized property values (SEV) in Acme Township nearly tripled between 1979 and 1988, increasing from US$29.3 million in 1979 to US$80.0 million in 1988 (see Table 12.3). The increased value of the resort accounted for 14 percent of this change, indirect effects of the resort accounted for another 43 percent, and general inflationary trends accounted for 43 percent.

Fiscal Impacts Fiscal impacts represent changes in the costs and revenues for government units and/or changes in the level of public services that are made necessary by some action, in this case resort development. Fiscal impacts of the resort were felt most directly in Acme Township. Fiscal impacts on Grand Traverse County and Traverse City were small because these government units had limited jurisdiction over the resort and much larger existing operations relative to Acme Township.

The resort has had major impacts on township revenues and costs, although isolating the resort's precise contribution is extremely difficult. A combination of logical connections and statistical controls was used to assess fiscal impacts. For example, some costs such as extending and expanding sewer lines can be logically linked to the resort, while the general growth in the operating costs of the township office are only partly attributable to the resort. Embedded in the added township operating costs are expanded and improved services, some of which may or may not have been added if the GTR had not been developed.

Estimates for a "with versus without" scenario were obtained by comparing the growth in township operating costs and revenues in Acme Township with two similar townships, one nearby (Peninsula Township) and another 60 miles (95 kilometers) away (Resort Township in Emmett County). These "control" townships were chosen because they had fiscal structures similar to that of Acme Township in 1979 and corresponding growth trends during the 1970s. The control townships were assumed to have captured

TABLE 12.3

Summary of the Fiscal Impacts of the Grand Traverse Resort in 1979 Compared to Those in 1988

Variable	1979	1988	Percent Change	Resort Contribution
Acme Township Property Values[a]				
Total SEV (US$ millions)	29.30	80.00	173	GTR = 13% of property value in 1988. GTR directly accounted for 14% of change in SEV, indirectly, another 43%.
Total SEV per acre	1.88	5.15	174	
Acme Township Revenues (US$ thousands)				
Property tax	27.50	89.40	225	GTR 1988 taxes = US$444,400. US$19,700 to Acme Township = 22% of township property taxes. Little impact on revenue sharing. GTR contributed to fire truck purchase in 1980.
State revenue sharing	72.50	133.80	85	
Other revenues	24.60	37.60	53	
General fund revenue	124.60	260.80	109	
Township millage rate	1.93	1.97	2	
Acme Township Expenditures ($US thousands)				
General government	43.0	96.9	125	Acme Township expenditures have nearly tripled since 1979. Two-thirds of the increase is associated with the GTR including costs of expanded and improved services. Added revenues cover 35% of added costs.
Protective services	9.2	39.9[b]	333	
Health, culture, recreation	0.5	30.0[c]	5900	
Planning and employee benefits	9.3	76.5	722	
Total general fund expenses	62.0	243.3	292	
Other Fiscal Benefits and Costs				In 1988 GTR paid US$356,000 in school taxes and US$68,700 in county taxes. Some costs on county and city government. Sewer line from Acme was brought to capacity; GTR has purchased 43% of sewerage benefits to date, although at 44% of rate to be charged new users to cover the needed expansion.

[a] The 1988 property values presented here reflect GTR reassessment from market to income basis, which resulted in a US$7.6 million decrease in assessed value. SEV = state equalized value.
[b] Ten percent of US$83,117 fire expense in 1988 included.
[c] Ten percent of US$292,867 park land purchase in 1988 included.

both the general inflationary growth in township operations as well as the pattern of historical growth in the Traverse City area and northern Michigan. Most "with versus without" analyses assume that historical growth patterns would have continued in the absence of a new development, although this need not always be the case.

REVENUES While general fund revenues in Acme Township grew by 109 percent between 1979 and 1988, and property tax revenues increased by 225 percent, revenue sharing and other sources grew more slowly. The GTR paid US$444,400 in property taxes in 1988. Approximately US$356,000 went to schools, US$68,700 to Grand Traverse County, and US$19,700 to Acme Township. The latter represented 22 percent of all township tax revenue in 1988. Although GTR taxes represented a smaller share of school and county revenues, the resort added virtually no school expenses and made only modest demands on county services (see Table 12.3).

COSTS Acme Township's general fund expenditures grew from US$62,000 in 1979 to US$243,300 in 1988, almost a threefold increase. Only 10 percent of the costs of large one-time allocations for park land (US$292,867) and fire equipment (US$83,117) in 1988 are included in this figure because these are not typical or recurring costs. The park land was purchased with funds accumulated over several years from the GTR's tax payments, and the fire engine was also financed through arrangements with the resort. Township expenses grew by 292 percent between 1979 and 1988. Based on the experience of the two control townships, it is estimated that costs would have grown by about 100 percent without the resort. This growth in township operating costs includes both new and expanded services.

NET FISCAL IMPACTS The most substantial net fiscal benefits from the resort accrued to the school system because it experienced limited enrollment impacts from the resort while receiving the bulk of the incremental tax revenues. Grand Traverse County also benefited, although to a lesser extent. The picture was less clear in Acme Township because it was difficult to isolate which township operating costs could be directly or indirectly attributed to the resort. Including both direct and indirect effects, it was estimated that the increase in township property taxes due to the GTR covered about 35 percent of the increase in township costs since 1979.

COMMUNITY ATTITUDES ABOUT THE RESORT'S IMPACTS

Community perceptions of the GTR's impacts were assessed through a household telephone survey, interviews with 13 community leaders, and a review of articles appearing in the local newspaper between 1975 and 1989. The survey of a random sample of 174 local adult residents provided a representative sample of attitudes in the community. This size sample yields sampling errors of between 5 and 8 percent for the attitude measures (95 percent confidence level).

The survey covered Traverse City and the three surrounding townships, including Acme. The purpose of the telephone survey was to measure community attitudes about changes in the area and the resort's contribution to these changes. Quantitative data from the telephone survey were supplemented with more qualitative information from interviews with community leaders and a review of news coverage. These sources helped in interpreting the findings of both the secondary data analysis and community survey and assisted in the identification of issues that may have contributed to the formation of attitudes about the resort.

Attitudes About Growth and Development To avoid potential bias, questions about changes in the community and general attitudes about growth and development were asked prior to questions about the resort and its impacts. The respondents were divided in their attitudes about the rate of population growth, the amount of tourism development, and the number of "outsiders" in the Traverse City area. About half of the local residents believed that growth in the population and development in the area were proceeding too fast, and the other half indicated that they were about right or even too slow. The community was more positive regarding tourism development, with 60 percent suggesting that it was about right or could be increased, and 40 percent stating that there was too much tourism development.

Change in the Community Those rating the Traverse City area as a much or somewhat better place to live in 1990 compared with five years previously outnumbered those who reported that it was a much or somewhat worse place to live by two to one. Four community attributes were perceived to be better (national reputation, recreation, shopping, and cultural opportunities), four worse (traffic, local taxes, cost of living, and crime), and four about the same (air and water quality, scenic beauty, housing, and jobs) compared to five years previously (see Figure 12.2).

Perceptions of the Impacts of the Grand Traverse Resort The majority of local residents, particularly Acme residents, believed that the GTR had major impacts on the community. There was general agreement on the positive impacts, primarily centering around the resort's contribution to the local tourism industry and, in turn, to the local economy and employment opportunities. Recreation, shopping, and cultural opportunities for local residents were also perceived to have been improved by the GTR. Contributions to tourism included the increase in numbers of tourists, changes in the kinds of tourists attracted, expanded convention capability, increased quality standards, and heightened promotion of the area.

There was, however, less agreement on the negative impacts of the resort. In response to a direct question, over one-quarter of the respondents would not, or could not, identify a negative impact. The responses of those who did identify a negative impact cut across a variety of social, economic, environmental, and special issues. Effects of the resort on

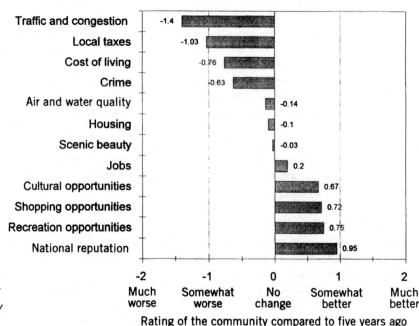

Figure 12.2
Community perceptions of change in the Traverse City area.

wages and salaries, traffic and congestion, community relations, land use, esthetics, and general growth and development were the most frequently cited negative impacts.

The GTR's overall impact was seen to be positive by most residents. The resort was credited with enhancing each of the community attributes that were seen as improving during the five years prior to the survey: national reputation, recreation, shopping, and cultural opportunities (see Figure 12.3). Although job opportunities were seen as improving only slightly, residents believed that the resort contributed quite positively in this regard. The increase in jobs from the resort offset some losses in other sectors of the local economy (e.g., the closing of a state hospital in Traverse City).

Of the four community attributes perceived to be getting worse, the resort was seen as contributing negatively to three: traffic, local taxes, and the cost of living. Residents had different views on the local tax effects, (almost one in five believed that the resort's effect was positive). People perceived the GTR to have had little effect on crime. Perceptions of the resort's effects on scenic beauty and housing were mixed, with some recognizing positive effects and others reporting negative effects.

Familiarity with and Use of the Grand Traverse Resort Virtually everyone was familiar with the GTR. About half of the sample had read, seen, or heard something in the media about the resort on a weekly basis, with over one-third claiming to have paid "a lot of attention" to the information. All but 5 percent had been to the resort within the last year (1989). Residents averaged 12 visits in 1989. Over 70 percent of local visitors in 1989 had visited the resort at least once for shopping, eating in restaurants, or attending an indoor event. About 30 percent had used the resort's health club, between 10 and 20 percent had used tennis, cross-country ski, or golf facilities, and 7 percent had stayed overnight.

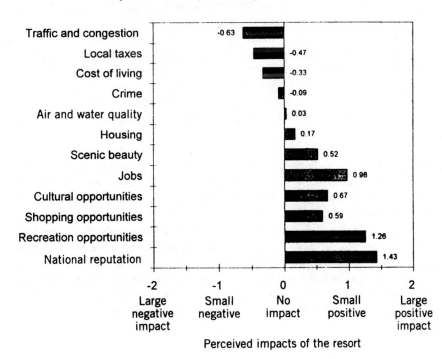

Figure 12.3 Community perceptions of the impacts of the Grand Traverse Resort.

Differences Among Population Subgroups Because tourism affects different people in different ways, it is important to evaluate impacts on subgroups of people as well as on the community as a whole. Perceptions of change in the area and the GTR's impacts varied most significantly among subgroups defined by location of residence, tenure in the community, use of the resort, and general attitudes about growth and development. Differences among groups defined by demographic variables (i.e., age, gender, and education) or ties to tourism (i.e., friends or family working in the tourism industry) were not as significant.

Acme Township residents reported larger impacts and generally rated the GTR's contribution more favorably (with the exception of effects on traffic and crime) than did the residents of the area living outside Acme Township. People born in the Traverse City area or moving there prior to 1971 perceived more negative changes in the community than more recent migrants to the area, particularly compared to people moving to the area from southern Michigan metropolitan areas. For example, newer residents from southern Michigan were less likely to perceive a deterioration in crime, the cost of living, or traffic and congestion. People not born in the area but moving there prior to 1971 perceived the GTR's effects most negatively, and more recent migrants from southern Michigan evaluated the resort most positively.

Frequent visitors to the resort tended to evaluate positive impacts more positively compared to infrequent visitors. Resort facilities and grounds are readily available to local residents. A health club in the resort serves both guests of the resort and local area residents who may purchase memberships. The resort sponsors a variety of events for the local community. The policy of encouraging local use of the resort appears to have contributed positively to attitudes about the resort in the local area (Stewart and Stynes, 1991). Frequent visitors in particular credited the resort for improvements in Traverse City's national reputation and for greater recreation opportunities.

General attitudes about growth and tourism were related to perceptions of the resort's impacts, with "progrowth" groups generally evaluating the resort more favorably. Evaluation of the resort's impacts were particularly more negative for people opposed to both population growth and tourism development. This "antigrowth" segment rated the resort's impacts on the growth of the area, scenic beauty, recreation opportunities, property values, traffic, the cost of living, and local taxes significantly less positively than other segments.

Community Leaders' Perceptions The 13 community leaders indicated that few impacts of the resort were entirely unanticipated. They believed that positive impacts had generally been underestimated and that negative impacts were overestimated. Among the negative impacts of the resort were several issues relating to the resort's financial dealings (e.g., loans, taxes), traffic and congestion, and changes in land use. Positive impacts centered on the quality of the resort and its influence on other development in the area. Growth in the area was frequently mentioned as an impact, sometimes in a positive context and sometimes in a negative one. Given the opportunity to start the development process over again, most leaders indicated that they would favor low-rise cluster development as opposed to the 15-story glass tower. Overall, the leaders believed that the GTR's impact on the community had been mostly quite positive.

CONCLUSION

This chapter has presented an *ex post* assessment of the social, economic, fiscal, and environmental impacts of the Grand Traverse Resort on the surrounding community. An improved understanding of how resort developments affect communities can be achieved by documenting changes in an area over time and isolating the contribution of a specific development to these changes. This understanding can then be used to enhance positive impacts, mitigate negative ones, and more generally, predict the likely impacts of resort developments in other places.

Tourism developments can have a variety of impacts on an area, some positive and some negative. The magnitude and nature of these impacts depend on the nature of the community, the scale and character of development, and perhaps most importantly, how well growth and change are managed. Different stakeholder groups within a community will perceive and evaluate the impacts somewhat differently. Those receiving the benefits will tend to support further tourism developments, while groups incurring more costs and inconvenience than benefits may oppose them.

Actual and perceived impacts have been examined. Whether one relies on the perceptions of local residents or the analysis of secondary data, the resort clearly has had significant impacts on the area. To some it has meant further development and accompanying congestion, while to others the resort has helped promote the area, provide jobs, expand markets, and elevate the quality of tourism facilities.

Assessing the specific short-term impacts of the resort requires consistent measurement of key impact variables over time. Impact assessments also rely heavily upon assumptions or models of change to isolate the resort's contribution from many other possible causes of change in the community. The impact assessment should not just compare the situation "before and after" the resort, but should compare the results "with versus without" the resort. Perhaps the most difficult question in an impact assessment is what would have happened if the resort had not been built. The community certainly would not have stood still, which is what a before–after analysis implicitly assumes.

Impact assessments become somewhat clearer if there are two or more viable alternatives to compare. In this case, for example, the existing development could have been contrasted with a smaller-scale resort in the same location or with a proposal to preserve farm land in Acme Township. A smaller-scale resort would probably have had similar but reduced impacts, while a decision to restrict growth more generally in Acme Township would likely have shifted the growth and development to another nearby township.

Given the complexity of assessing impacts and the varying perspectives of different stakeholder groups, it is wise to employ multiple sources of evidence, examine impacts from several viewpoints, and include both quantitative and qualitative dimensions. In the GTR case, the community attitude survey both supported and extended what was learned from the quantitative analysis of secondary data. The survey also captured important differences in how various stakeholder groups perceive and evaluate the resort and its impacts. Conversely, the quantitative analyses helped in interpreting the survey results and provided the "hard" numbers that decision makers frequently want or need.

ACKNOWLEDGMENTS

The research upon which this case is based was supported by funds from U.S. Inc. (a not-for-profit organization based in Petoskey, Michigan) and the Michigan State University Agricultural Experiment Station.

NOTES

1. For further background about resorts see Gee's (1988) comprehensive text on resort management.
2. Chapters in Ritchie and Goeldner's (1994) tourism research handbook cover research and impact assessment methods as applied in tourism.
3. See Chapters 10 and 14 for additional discussion of the costs and benefits of tourism.
4. See Chapters 5, 9, 11, and 14–19 for additional information pertaining to community attitudes and involvement in the tourism planning and development processes.

REFERENCES

Burchell, R.W. and D. Listokin. 1978. *The Fiscal Impact Handbook*. New Brunswick, NJ: Center for Urban Policy Research.

Burdge, R. 1994. A *Community Guide to Social Impact Assessment*. Middleton, WI: Social Ecology Press.

Crandall, L. 1994. The social impact of tourism on developing regions and its measurement. In J.R.B. Ritchie and C.R. Goeldner (eds.), *Travel, Tourism and Hospitality Research: A Handbook for Managers and Researchers*. New York: John Wiley & Sons, pp. 413–424.

Finsterbusch, K., J. Ingersol, and L. Llewellyn (eds.). 1990. *Methods for Social Analysis in Developing Countries*. Boulder, CO: Westview Press.

Frechtling, D.C. 1994a. Assessing the impacts of travel and tourism: introduction to travel economic impact estimation. In J.R.B. Ritchie and C.R. Goeldner (eds.), *Travel, Tourism and Hospitality Research: A Handbook for Managers and Researchers*. New York: John Wiley & Sons, pp. 359–366.

Frechtling, D.C. 1994b. Assessing the impacts of travel and tourism: measuring economic benefits. In J.R.B. Ritchie and C.R. Goeldner (eds.), *Travel, Tourism and Hospitality Research: A Handbook for Managers and Researchers*, New York: John Wiley & Sons, pp. 367–392.

Frechtling, D.C. 1994c. Assessing the impacts of travel and tourism: measuring economic costs. In J.R.B. Ritchie and C.R. Goeldner (eds.), *Travel, Tourism and Hospitality Research: A Handbook for Managers and Researchers*, New York: John Wiley & Sons, pp. 393–402.

Freudenberg, W.R. 1986. Social impact assessment, *Annual Review of Sociology*, 12, 451–478.

Gee, C.Y. 1988. *Resort Development and Management*, 2nd ed. East Lansing, MI: Educational Institute of the American Hotel and Motel Association.

Hart, S.L., G.A. Enk, and W.F. Hornick. 1984. *Improving Impact Assessment: Increasing the Relevance and Utilization of Scientific Information*. Boulder, CO: Westview Press.

Inskeep, E. and M. Kallenberger. 1992. *An Integrated Approach to Resort Development*. Madrid: World Tourism Organization.

Johnson, D.G. and J. Sullivan. 1993. Economic impacts of Civil War battlefield preservation: an *ex ante* evaluation, *Journal of Travel Research*, 32(1), 21–29.

Leistritz, F.L. and S.M. Murdock. 1981. *The Socioeconomic Impact of Resource Development: Methods for Assessment*. Boulder, CO: Westview Press.

Liu, J.C. and T. Var. 1986. Resident attitudes toward tourism impacts in Hawaii, *Annals of Tourism Research*, 13, 193–214.

Mathieson, A. and G. Wall. 1982. *Tourism Economic, Physical and Social Impacts*. London: Longman, Harlow.

Mohr, L.B. 1988. *Impact Analysis for Program Evaluation*. Newbury Park, CA: Sage.

Northwest Michigan Council of Governments. 1989. *1988 Population and Economic Characteristics*. Traverse City, Michigan.

Prentice, R.C., S.F. Witt, and E.G. Wydenbach. 1994. The endearment behaviour of tourists through their interaction with the host community, *Tourism Management*, 15(2), 117–125.

Ritchie, J.R.B. and C.R. Goeldner (eds.). 1994. *Travel, Tourism and Hospitality Research: A Handbook for Managers and Researchers*, 2nd ed. New York: John Wiley & Sons.

Stewart, S.I. and D.J. Stynes. 1991. *Impacts of Three Fires Pointe on the Petoskey Area: Implications of the Grand Traverse Resort Case Study*. East Lansing: Michigan State University, Department of Park and Recreation Resources.

Stynes, D.J. 1991. Case study approaches to assessing tourism impacts. *TTRA CenStates News*, 8(2), 9. East Lansing, MI: Travel, Tourism, and Recreation Resource Center.

Stynes, D.J. and S.I. Stewart. 1991. *The Impacts of the Grand Traverse Resort on the Local Community: A Case Study*. East Lansing: Michigan State University, Department of Park, Recreation, and Tourism Resources.

Stynes, D.J. and S.I. Stewart. 1993. Tourism development and local recreation: some findings from a case study, *Journal of Park and Recreation Administration*, 11(4), 30–44.

Taylor, C., C. Nicholas, H. Bryan, and C.C. Goodrich. 1990. *Social Assessment: Theory, Process and Techniques*. Center for Resource Management: Lincoln University, New Zealand.

Teisl, M.F. and S.D. Reiling. 1992. The impact of tourism on local government public service expenditures. In S. Reiling (ed.), *Measuring Tourism Impacts at the Community Level*. Orono, Maine: Maine Agricultural Experiment Station, Miscellaneous Report #374.

Teo, P. 1994. Assessing socio-cultural impacts: the case of Singapore, *Tourism Management*, 15(2), 126–136.

US Department of Commerce, Bureau of Economic Analysis. 1992. *Regional Multipliers: A User Handbook for the Regional Input–Output Modeling System (RIMS II)*, 2nd ed. Washington, D.C.: U.S. Government Printing Office.

Wearing, S. and R. Parsonson. 1991. Rainforest tourism, *Tourism Management*, 12(3), 236–244.

Westman, W. 1985. *Ecology, Impact Assessment and Environmental Planning*. New York: John Wiley & Sons.

Williams, P.W. 1994. Frameworks for assessing tourism's environmental impacts. In J.R.B. Ritchie and C.R. Goeldner (eds.), *Travel, Tourism and Hospitality Research: A Handbook for Managers and Researchers*. New York: John Wiley & Sons, pp. 425–436.

Yin, R.K. 1989. *Case Study Research: Design and Methods*. Newbury Park, CA: Sage.

¶ | PROBLEM SOLVING AND DISCUSSION ACTIVITIES

1. Find an article in a newspaper, magazine, or journal discussing the expected or actual impacts of a tourism facility or event. Which of the types of impacts presented for the GTR are mentioned and which are not? Are both positive and negative impacts discussed? Does the article assess impacts "with versus without"

the facility or event, or just "before and after"? How were the impacts measured, estimated, or predicted?

2. Identify an existing or proposed resort development in an area familiar to you.
    a. Which of the kinds of data examined in the GTR case study are available from federal, state, provincial, or local government or from private sources? Evaluate the availability, reliability, and relevance of each kind of data for conducting an impact assessment. What types of data are not available or are of questionable reliability?
    b. Select one of the specific types of impacts examined in the GTR case study and prepare both a quantitative and qualitative assessment of the impacts in your area.
    c. Design a telephone survey to assess attitudes of the local community about this resort and its impacts. Include a sampling plan and questionnaire.

3. Review the literature on methods for assessing one of the following types of impacts: envirnomental, economic, social, or fiscal. Prepare a summary and identify which methods you would use for the resort development examined in Activity 2.

4. Hold a "public hearing" on a proposed resort development that would be twice the size of the GTR (or a large factory outlet mall, a family theme park, a gambling casino). Form groups, with each group representing the perspective of a special interest or group of stakeholders. Develop and support the positions that each group might take on the proposal. Possible stakeholder groups include the developers, local or state (provincial) environmental officials, community business leaders, permanent residents, seasonal residents, other industry sectors, and local government officials.

5. Using hindsight, what aspects of the Grand Traverse Resort development and its implementation would you modify to either enhance the positive impacts or reduce negative ones?

6. Assume that the Grand Traverse Resort disappeared in 1997 (went bankrupt, burned down, or reverted to agricultural or vacant lands). How much of the changes in the community that were attributable to the resort would likely be lost? Would the community return to baseline (1980) levels of all variables, and under what assumptions? Are the impacts of removing tourism developments simply the opposite of adding them?

7. Identify a community or region that was formerly a high-quality tourist destination but no longer is. How is it different today than during its prime or prior to that?

8. Develop quantitative estimates of the changes that you would have expected between 1980 and 1988 if the GTR had been developed at either half or double the existing scale. How would Tables 12.1 to 12.3 be different? Justify your answers.

9. Assume the position of the public relations director at the GTR. Use the results of the community attitude survey to develop a community relations program for the resort. What areas should be addressed to further enhance public perceptions of the resort? How would you go about capitalizing on strengths and mitigating weaknesses associated with community attitudes to the resort?

13

Tourism and Transportation in Ontario, Canada

A VITAL LINK

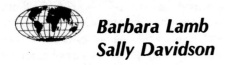

Barbara Lamb
Sally Davidson

¶|K E Y   L E A R N I N G   P O I N T S

- Tourists require convenient and affordable access to destinations. Some destinations, which have recognized the strategic relationship between tourism and transportation, are now increasing their market share over those that have not recognized and actively strengthened tourism–transportation linkages.

- From a government policy perspective, transportation can play a key role in the rejuvenation of a declining tourism industry, particularly where gaps in the development and/or maintenance of transportation infrastructure act as impediments to tourism growth.

- Not only does tourism benefit from transportation, but the transportation industry is also a major beneficiary of tourism. National, provincial/state, regional, municipal, and private sector transportation and tourism agencies and sectors would benefit from recognizing and exploring mutual interests, communicating more effectively, and cooperating more closely.

- Criteria to identify areas where tourism's interests are worthy of support by transportation ministries and industry need to be developed, particularly in times of daunting government deficits and fiscal austerity. One of the most important of these criteria, but often the least understood and most underestimated, is the economic contribution that tourism can make to local, regional, and national economies. Recognition of these often extensive economic benefits may help transportation ministries lobby more effectively for the upgrading and maintenance of transportation facilities.

- Because transportation infrastructure (e.g., highways, public transit systems, airports) tends to be expensive, long-lasting, fixed in location, and not readily converted to other uses, it has tended to rely heavily on public sector intervention. Thus, the extent to which the key role of transportation is, or is not, recognized by a ministry/department of transport can make a very important difference in the long-term competitiveness of a destination's tourism industry.

INTRODUCTION

Government tourism agencies should concern themselves with tourism matters only, and government transportation agencies should confine themselves to transportation concerns—or should they? While government organizational structures in many jurisdictions around the world still follow this traditional sectoral approach, the need for closer cooperation between and among sectors is becoming increasingly compelling. The fact that a decision made by one agency can have significant impacts on others makes consideration of intersectoral linkages in policy formulation and decision-making processes a necessity.

Linkages between the transportation and tourism sectors are not merely of academic interest, but are of fundamental importance to the success of a region or country's tourism industry. While significant to many industries, transportation is vital to the tourism industry, which depends on convenient, affordable, and easy access of tourists to destinations. There are many examples throughout the world that demonstrate how transportation has been the single most important factor in attracting tourists to a country. Caribbean countries owe their relatively successful tourism industries to the advent of the jet age. The Eurorail Pass, the Train-à-Grande Vitesse (TGV) and other bullet trains, the Chunnel, and Mediterranean and Caribbean cruise lines have enabled and promoted tourism by providing markets with access to a variety of tourist destinations.

At some point in the early 1990s, tourism became the largest value-added industry in the world.[1] However, while tourism continued to thrive worldwide, warning signs that Canada and Ontario's tourism industries were failing to keep pace began to appear. Questions regarding transportation's capacity to support the tourism industry became particularly relevant in Ontario. A study was commissioned by Ontario's transportation ministry to explore, and better understand, the nature of the province's transportation system linkages with tourism. The study set out to answer the following questions, among others:

- To what extent is Ontario's transportation system linked with the tourism industry?
- How strategically important are these tourism–transportation linkages?
- To what extent, if any, does Ontario's transportation ministry recognize and integrate tourism-related interests and considerations into its decision-making process?
- What is/should be the relationship between the province's transportation ministry and the ministry responsible for tourism?
- What policies and/or processes can be put into place in the ministry of transportation to ensure that tourism interests are fully considered?

Tourism and transportation linkages in Ontario were found to be numerous, complex, and of great strategic importance to the future of the tourism industry. By exploring these linkages, it became clear that there were policies and processes that, if adopted by the transportation ministry, would be supportive of the tourism ministry and the province's tourism industry. Moreover, it was found that the tourism ministry often had a relatively *ad hoc* relationship with the transportation ministry and had little or no involvement in some critical transportation-related decisions that held implications for the tourism industry. One of the most important lessons arising from the study is that a focus by government agencies on intersectoral linkages can illuminate issues and opportunities for action that would simply not be seen using a unisectoral approach to decision making.

INTEGRATED APPROACHES TO TOURISM AND TRANSPORTATION PLANNING: CONTEMPORARY PERSPECTIVES AND ISSUES

The Role of A comprehensive survey of 24 countries undertaken by the Organisation for Economic
Intersectoral Cooperation and Development (OECD) in 1992 revealed wide variation among countries
Linkages in with respect to government intervention in tourism. While, in some cases, governments
Tourism were increasing their allocation of resources to tourism, others were reducing their sup-
Planning port and involvement (OECD, 1992, pp. 15–19). In most cases, the dominant purpose
of government involvement in tourism was seen by the national tourism agencies (NTAs)
to be marketing and promotion. Overall, the survey indicated a trend towards privatization of responsibility for tourism because of constrained budgets. This trend, the OECD
(1992, p. 21) concluded, should be of considerable concern:

> The general climate today is towards privatisation, but there are inherent risks in the privatisa-
> tion of national tourism promotion and marketing. Governments are responsible for national
> transportation policy and economic policy aimed at maximising tourism's contribution to the
> nation's economy. It is also government's responsibility to deal with issues related to the work-
> force, training matters, consumer affairs and public awareness campaigns. . . . The provision
> of specific public infrastructure and facilities for the tourism industry, as well as local planning
> and zoning arrangements, land use, environmental protection matters and national parks, are
> other examples. . . . If national tourism promotion and marketing were left entirely to the
> private sector, this could result in the unbalanced development of infrastructure and market
> expansion, with the risk of congestion and increased pressure on environmental resources.

What determines decisions of government? The fundamental and guiding beacon of government action is policy. Policy is typically developed to address a problem or an opportunity. It articulates a goal or a decision; it specifies a direction that must be fol-lowed, or alternatively, one that must not be followed. In the OECD example above, some governments developed a policy that said "We are leaving tourism promotion and marketing to the private sector to save scarce public sector financial resources." It is evi-dent from the OECD comments that the choice of a policy and its implementation can have significant and, at times, unforeseen and undesirable consequences that may actu-ally defeat the purpose of the original policy.

Thus, the process of policy formulation—the process by which governments deter-mine future courses of action—is very important. If the process is flawed and policy is implemented, problems that could have been avoided through an effective policy formu-lation process are likely to arise. Key components of an effective policy formulation pro-cess include the following:

- *Defining the policy issue as clearly and specifically as possible.* What are we really trying to achieve by creating a new policy? Is our vision specific enough? Without answers to such questions, there may be misinterpretations by those engaged in formulating policy, and a flawed policy will emerge.

- *Involving all stakeholders who are part of the policy problem and who are likely to be part of the solution.*[2] Their input is vital. A decision to privatize tourism promotion, the OECD surmised, could be costly because other government stakeholders involved in the provision of infrastructure affecting tourism or environmental protection may be rendered less effective.

- *Incorporating meaningful stakeholder consultation early in the process.* Failure to do so is likely to cause strife, resistance to new direction, flawed policy formulation, and a lack of support from those affected during implementation. Stakeholders can provide invaluable assistance in defining and shaping policy. Avoidance of consultation risks serious consequences if stakeholders believe that a policy has been forced on them and/or if major unforeseen consequences of a policy occur that stakeholder input might have averted.

- *Basing policy on complete and current data and analyses from all relevant sectors.* Incomplete information can lead to decisions that are flawed.

These components of effective policy formulation underscore the critical importance of an integrated approach to tourism planning and policy development. As the OECD example shows, tourism goals cannot be achieved without consideration of the implications of tourism's close linkages with many other sectors. For example, the failure to consider tourism–environment linkages is nowhere more evident than in the Caribbean, where the very resources on which tourism depends (the beaches and natural attractions of some countries) have been compromised by degradation from many sources, including the tourism industry itself.[3] The importance of considering linkages between tax laws and minimum wage rates and tourism is also evident because these can, and do, affect a destination's competitiveness.

A Vital Link: Transportation and Tourism Transportation is one of three fundamental components of tourism. The other two are the tourism product (or supply) and the tourism market (or demand). Without transportation, most forms of tourism could not exist. Indeed, so closely linked are the two sectors that tourism is often termed "the travel industry." In some cases, the transportation experience *is* the tourism experience (e.g., cruises, scenic and heritage rail trips, and motorcoach, automobile, and bicycle tours).

The transportation industry can be a major beneficiary of tourism. In 1990, leisure travel in Canada accounted for almost 75 percent of all intercity trips, making tourism the largest user of intercity passenger transportation services in the country and underscoring the interdependence of the two sectors (ISTC-Tourism, 1992, p. 1). Moreover, 45 percent of total revenue generated by Canada's tourism industry in 1990 was in the transportation sector, compared to 21 percent in food and beverage, 16 percent in accommodation, and 7 percent in recreation/entertainment (ISTC-Tourism, 1992, p. 3). Transportation was estimated to account for 40 percent of tourists' expenditures in Ontario in 1991 (Ontario Ministry of Transportation, 1993, p. 4). The touring aspect of Ontario's tourism product has also been a mainstay of the provincial tourism industry.

Unlike the freight industry which brings its products to the market, the reverse is the case with tourism. This has strategic implications. Since the purchaser of the tourism product (the tourist) must experience the trip to access the product, the quality of the transportation experience becomes an important aspect of the tourism experience and, therefore, a key criterion that enters into destination choice. Poor service, scheduling problems, and/or long delays associated with a transportation service, for example, can seriously affect a traveler's perceptions and levels of enjoyment with respect to a trip. Tourists require safe, comfortable, affordable, and efficient intermodal[4] transportation networks that enable precious vacation periods to be enjoyed to their maximum potential.

Figure 13.1 portrays some of the many interfaces that exist between transportation and tourism. The diagram illustrates the varied and multifaceted transportation universe that tourism industries and government tourism agencies should consider in their policies, programs, and actions. Only through recognition and exploration of such linkages can new and important dimensions of the competitiveness of a tourism industry be comprehended.

The integration of tourism–transportation linkage considerations into government policy development is also crucial to the success of a tourism industry. Indeed, as the OECD (1992, 19) concluded:

There is little doubt . . . as to the relevance of government intervention in the tourism industry—in the context of market failures,[5] or minimising impediments to growth, such as unnec-

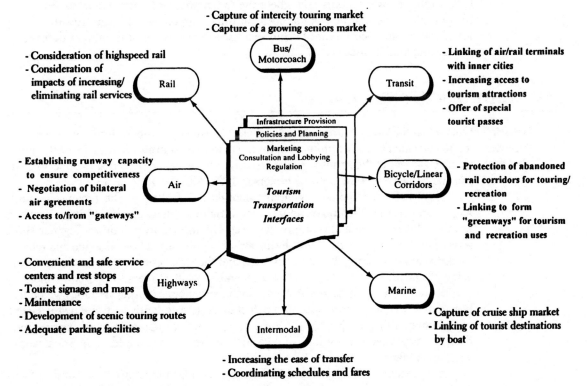

Figure 13.1
Examples of tourism–transportation linkages.

essary regulations and taxes, inefficiencies in the provision of transport services, or distortions in existing tax or regulatory systems which discriminate against the industry.

France provides an excellent example of successful tourism development in the 1990s spurred by policies that led to improvements to transportation. Recognizing that the country had been losing its share of the global market, in 1987 the French government made a concerted effort to arrest the downward trend, establishing a promotional organization (*Maison de la France*) and enacting several other initiatives. The results have been extremely favorable, with the country having consolidated its position as the world's second-ranking tourism earner behind the United States by the early 1990s.

One example of the French government's approach involved establishing a series of joint activities between its tourism and transportation ministries focusing on such matters as tourism-related road signs and the classification of motorcoaches for tourism purposes. Its investments in the TGV and the tunnel connection to Great Britain are also indicative of the country's recognition of the key role of an effective intermodal transportation system to tourism. As reported by the OECD (1992), the primary reason that France is a leading tourist destination is transportation.

There are precedents for transportation ministries and departments to become proactively engaged in measures to support tourism, particularly where governments judge the economic importance of tourism to be sufficient to merit development of strategies to cater to the industry's needs and where the importance of transportation to tourism is recognized. Those that do not consider tourism–transportation linkages run the risk of losing significant opportunities to gain increased market share or to prevent declines in the existing tourism industry.

CASE STUDY ORIGIN AND GOALS

Ontario's Tourism Industry Ontario has the largest tourism industry of any Canadian province or territory, accounting for 36 percent of Canada's (domestic plus international) tourism revenues in 1991. As the primary gateway to the country, Ontario received 66 percent of American visitors to Canada and 53 percent of the overseas visitors in 1992 (MCTR, 1994, p. 13).

Tourism is an important economic contributor, ranking as the province's fourth largest export earner after motor vehicles, industrial/machinery manufacturing, and wood products. Like the rest of the country, however, Ontario's tourism industry began to show signs of decline in the early 1990s, losing visitation in terms of both absolute and relative market share. Increasing global competition and the emergence of new destinations, the aging of Ontario's tourism product, a demographic shift of the all-important American market away from border states, and a decline in automobile touring vacations which had been a mainstay of Ontario's tourism product for American tourists are among the factors contributing to this decline. At the same time, American domestic travel became relatively less expensive as a result of air deregulation, which encouraged more Americans to vacation at home.

In its analysis of Canada's (and Ontario's) declining competitiveness, Tourism Canada[6] cited poor air links with American cities, an aging highway infrastructure, airport congestion, a decline in intercity rail services, and the failure to capitalize on the high growth in the cruise ship industry. These issues underscore the integral role of transportation in the competitiveness of Ontario's tourism industry.

In 1993, the Ontario ministry responsible for tourism[7] undertook its own major stakeholder consultation process to determine priorities for improving performance in Ontario's tourism industry. As some of the following priorities for action suggest, the key role of transportation was highlighted:

- Improvements and upgrading were recommended for Pearson International Airport in Toronto, which is the arrival point for 43 percent of all air arrivals to Canada.
- Ottawa, Niagara Falls, Toronto, Windsor, and Sault Ste. Marie were recognized as "gateways" for American travelers and, as such, should be developed to draw tourists and to become "stepping off" points for regional tours.
- Improvements to Ontario's highway, air, and waterway facilities were recognized as being necessary.

The case study presented in this chapter arose from a project initiated by Ontario's transportation ministry, a powerful provincial government agency with a broad mandate and high profile. The ministry is responsible for many areas including infrastructure development, signage, maintenance, transportation policy development, and lobbying at the national level with respect to air access issues, passenger rail, and other federal government-controlled areas.

In recognition of the importance of tourism to Ontario's economy, a study was undertaken to determine whether the many divisions of the ministry (responsible for issues related to air, rail, provincial highways, bus, transit, marine, and intermodal transportation) included tourism interests in their diverse decision-making processes. Specifically, the objectives were to generate an improved understanding of the nature of tourism–transportation linkages, identify issues of specific relevance to Ontario, and review the extent to which the ministry was directly or indirectly engaged in policies, programming, or operations that affected tourism. The ultimate goal was to assess whether the transportation ministry could be more directly and proactively engaged in supporting tourism and, if so, how and where.

A steering committee that included representatives from the ministry responsible for tourism was formed. The project itself involved several tasks, including extensive review of federal and provincial government documents from several ministries (e.g., planning, transportation, tourism, northern development), a literature review, an analysis of the experience of other (non-Ontario) destinations, consultation with public and private sector tourism and transportation representatives, group discussions with stakeholders, and preparation of reports. Key transportation–tourism linkages of interest to Ontario are discussed below.

TOURISM–TRANSPORTATION LINKAGES IN ONTARIO

Air Access and Transportation   The strong linkages between air transportation and tourism[8] are perhaps the most immediately obvious, particularly in the context of long-haul travel where tourists have little or no alternative to airlines for reaching a destination. For overseas tourists to access Ontario, affordable, efficient, and safe air transportation is essential. This is also the case for any tourist wishing to access remote northern parts of the province.

Given that air travel from Europe to other continents is forecast to increase by 10 or 11 percent each year through the 1990s (Wheatcroft, 1989, p. 213), and because tourists arriving by air are the source of a disproportionately large share of Ontario's tourism receipts, the capacity and quality of the province's airports, frequency and diversity of air connections, and ground and intermodal transportation services become extremely important. In a recent report prepared for Tourism Canada, it was noted that " . . . airport congestion has now become the leading [tourism] industry constraint" (Sypher: Mueller, 1993, p. 8).

Generally, a tourism industry's primary needs with respect to air transportation include the following: (1) good geographic coverage, particularly from primary markets, (2) adequate frequency of service, (3) competitive air fares to and from primary markets, and (4) efficient, attractive, informative, and "user friendly" airport infrastructure, from customs, ticketing, and baggage handling through to leaving the airport.

In a Canadian context, bilateral air agreements between Canada and other countries (to which Ontario must comply) have likely played a considerable role in determining coverage, service frequency, and cost competitiveness. These agreements define permitted routes, maximum number of airlines per route, airline capacity, and the method of pricing (ISTC-Tourism, 1993, p. 9–10). Growth in the number of Japanese tourists visiting Canada, for example, has been attributed in large part to the air services agreement between the governments of Canada and Japan in 1988 that allowed services between Toronto/Tokyo, Vancouver/Nagoya, and Edmonton/Tokyo and that led to significant increases in the capacity of both Canadian and Japanese airlines. Similarly, the leveling off of American tourists to Canada is seen as a function, to some extent, of an outdated bilateral agreement that has not afforded American and Canadian airlines the flexibility to respond to changes in the market.

In Ontario, Pearson International Airport in Toronto, which is by far the province's most significant airport, accounts for an estimated 43 percent of all international arrivals to Canada and handles an estimated 22 million passengers per year (Ontario Ministry of Culture, Tourism and Recreation, 1994, p. 36). Its economic contribution to Ontario has been estimated at $4 billion (CAD) in business income, $42 billion (CAD) in personal income, and $630 million (CAD) in taxes, as well as 50,000 direct and indirect jobs (*Toronto Star*, 1994, p. B2).

In 1992, approximately two million visitors (same day and overnight visitors from overseas and the United States) entered Ontario through Pearson International Airport, making it a key component of the province's tourism-related infrastructure. Visitors to Canada who arrive by air spend, on average, three times more than those arriving by automobile (excluding the cost of transportation). Moreover, overseas visitors to Ontario and to Canada as a whole, on a per capita basis, are a much greater source of revenue than are tourists from the United States. Because of the economic importance of the overseas market, the tourism ministry in 1994 established targets that, if achieved, would see overseas visitors more than double from 1.7 million to 3.5 million by the year 2000. In terms of revenue generated by overseas visitors, the ministry targeted an increase from 7 percent to 12 percent of total receipts by 2000.

Referring to the future potential of air travel, the World Tourism Organization (WTO, 1993a, p. 24) observed the following:

> Despite the growing fears concerning airspace congestion, air transport is projected to increase its overall share of world travel during the next decade. The Boeing forecast of a 5.9 percent average annual increase in global passenger air travel is higher than the "high" forecast for international tourism growth to 2000 [i.e., 5% per year]. Among the contributory factors to this variation are the trends towards longer haul travel, and away from road transport in modal choice.

Some specific issues of relevance to Ontario are as follows:

- *"Open Skies" initiative.* This involves a renegotiation of Canada's bilateral agreement with the United States. The initiative should have a very positive effect on tourism, allowing for the opening up of air routes based on market-driven considerations (i.e., unrestricted entry by carriers to any transborder route, no restrictions on the numbers of carriers permitted to fly between any city-pair).
- *Liberalization of air service agreements with other countries.* Air service agreements with many other countries, which are generally based on a "balance of benefits" principle (whereby each country's carriers are to receive equal benefit from the arrangement), have impeded a market-driven approach to air service and constrained benefits associated with more open air services.
- *Runway capacity.* A recent report on air transportation policies (Sypher: Mueller, 1993, p. vii) emphasizes the necessity for increased runway capacity if Pearson International Airport is to be able to accommodate the increased air services that liberalized air service agreements would afford.
- *Possibility of Pearson International becoming an intercontinental hub.* In the event that liberalized air service agreements with the United States and other markets are operationalized (particularly without a "phase-in"), Pearson International Airport may realize a new status as a large-scale intercontinental hub. The economic benefits associated with achieving such a level of traffic would be significant.
- *Negotiation of air service agreements outside of bilateral arrangements.* Precedents exist for the negotiation by Ontario of air service agreements outside of the bilateral framework under certain conditions. Because of the federal government's jurisdiction over international air access and because national carriers (that have fought for the phase-in of Open Skies and the protection of their status) have a strong voice at the federal level, achievement of these air services will require strong lobbying from Ontario interests.

In recognition of the importance of air transportation to tourism, Ontario's transportation ministry commissioned a study (completed but not released to the public) to provide them with an informed basis on which to lobby at the federal level. However, despite the importance of air transportation to the province's tourism industry, the tourism ministry apparently sought to have little or no involvement in this initiative.

Passenger Rail Rail transport in Ontario plays a smaller role in tourism than other modes such as air and road. Rail lines are being abandoned throughout the province and, indeed, across the country where extreme distances between centers have made the mode a relatively expensive and time-consuming choice for most travelers. The ongoing discontinuation of rail services is lamentable for many, given Canada's historic connections to train travel. It is possible that the widespread loss of key linear corridors may be widely regretted in the future if circumstances shift to rekindle interest in passenger rail, if high-speed rail becomes a technologically and financially more appealing alternative, and/or if other modes become less attractive and/or expensive.

In contrast, continental Europe continues to improve and expand its rail transport network. Indeed, it has been predicted that rail may some day surpass air as the preferred mode for travel between many centers (*Globe and Mail*, 1994). Passenger rail transportation, along with the automobile, is a favored mode of travel among tourists in Europe. Rail networks are extensive, frequency of service is high, high-speed trips are possible, and the alternative, air transportation, is very expensive.

In Canada, VIA Rail, which is under federal government jurisdiction, has been responsible for passenger rail and has been severely cut back as a result of substantial deficits. As noted earlier, some routes have been discontinued and, with some exceptions in heavily traveled corridors, the frequency of service has diminished. Although Ontario's passenger rail services have also decreased, some intercity travel continues to occur, particularly among cities and towns in the more highly populated southern part of the province. Ontario also offers some scenic rail tours (e.g., the Agawa Canyon route and Polar Bear Express).

In the late 1980s, a study was undertaken to establish the feasibility of a Windsor–Quebec City high-speed rail corridor (VIA Rail Canada Inc., 1989). In 1992, another study was commissioned by the federal government in partnership with the governments of Quebec and Ontario to reexamine the viability of such a corridor, with Ontario's transportation ministry being one of the overseers of the study. Tourism was to be considered in this study (unreleased as of this writing). From a tourism perspective, such a corridor would likely stimulate growth in visitors and receipts. The American border market would have easy access (at Windsor and Kingston) to this system, which would provide an attractive and time-effective vacation opportunity for visitors to see many areas of southern Ontario and Quebec. It would also likely be of interest to the European market, which is more accustomed to train travel.

Good intermodal links with air (at Pearson), the motorcoach industry, and a potential cruise ship industry on the Great Lakes would likely also induce tourism growth. However, there is some speculation that the travel costs, if passed on to the consumer, would be comparable to air travel costs. If the true costs were not passed on to the user, subsidies would be required to keep fares attractive and affordable.

While Ontario's transportation ministry had input to the study and was involved as an overseer, the tourism ministry was not. Thus, it appears that the onus for substantive response to any tourism-related findings would be left to the transportation ministry, which had no in-house tourism expertise.

Roads, Ontario has over 15,500 miles (close to 25,000 kilometers) of provincial highways, in-
Highways, and cluding major highways of four or more lanes that are important economic corridors for
Motorcoach tourists, freight, and commuters as well as many two-lane highways that are more rural in nature, some of which are of scenic interest. Ontario's highway network has a signifi-

cant linkage to the tourism industry. "Rubber tire" traffic accounted for 75 percent of arrivals to Ontario in 1991. Most of this traffic is generated from the United States, which accounts for 80 percent of out-of-province visitors. However, total American visitors to Ontario declined by over 10 percent between 1987 and 1991 due primarily to demographic changes in the United States, increasing global competition for the American market, a decline in the popularity of touring vacations, and higher gas prices.

Although auto touring began to decline in popularity in the mid-1980s, it has remained an important component of the provinces's tourism industry. So important is automobile access that Ontario's tourism ministry identified the need to significantly upgrade the tourism infrastructure in Ontario's automobile gateway cities from the United States (e.g., Niagara Falls, Windsor, Sault Ste. Marie, and Sarnia) to improve ease of access, sense of arrival, and access to information as well as to stimulate longer stays by visitors (Ontario Ministry of Culture, Tourism and Recreation 1994, p. 48).

Motorcoach (bus) tours are becoming increasingly popular, particularly among the growing seniors market. Based on its licensing agreements with the Ontario Ministry of Transport (MTO), the motorcoach industry has agreed to provide service to commuters/ nontourists on less profitable routes as long as they are permitted to provide service on other, more profitable tourism-related routes and charters. To this degree, tourism supports or subsidizes nontourism transportation services. As passenger rail operations continue to be phased out, road travel and the significance of the quality of the infrastructure may increase in importance from a motorcoach touring standpoint.

A recent survey of motorcoach travelers across North America (National Tour Association, 1992) found that (1) there is an increasing preference for a shorter trip, where participants fly to a destination and take a motorcoach tour, (2) tour travelers tend to be the growing seniors market, with a median age of between 66 and 70 years of age, and (3) convenience, comfort, and ease of access to motorcoaches are very important.

Because motorcoach tours encourage overnight stays and, therefore, increased expenditures and because the market is a growing one, the linkages between the motorcoach industry and good roads, supportive infrastructure, and well-developed scenic touring routes and lookouts are evident.

Ontario's transportation ministry also oversees important highway support infrastructure to motorists, including signage, service centers, tourism information centers, maps, and computerized freeway traffic management systems that are intended to increase safety, convenience, and ease and speed of access for travelers. Signage that provides information on attractions, scenic routes, and support facilities (i.e., restaurants, service centers, information centers, and rest stops) is closely regulated by the province. Scenic touring routes have been identified by the tourism ministry (e.g., Loyalist Parkway, Lake Huron Circle Tour), but they are poorly identified on provincial highway maps.

Some of the main issues affecting Ontario's roads and tourism include the following:

- *Quality of infrastructure.* Highways across Ontario are experiencing deterioration. Auto and bus tourism ideally requires good infrastructure including, for example, multilane high-speed routes, well-designed and efficient "gateways" at entrance points, good signage, and support facilities. Continued deterioration of Ontario's highways could have a deterrent effect on scenic touring.

- *Road congestion.* Increasing congestion on some routes, notably around Lake Ontario, is an impediment to tourism as well as to other industries because it could deter visitors from exploring popular attractions and scenic routes.
- *Signage.* Improvement to Ontario's tourism signage has been identified as an overriding goal of Ontario's tourism ministry. The tourism ministry, along with a large private sector constituency including resorts, restaurants, and attractions, identified signage as one of the highest priorities for action and emphasized the need to cater to the interests of different types of travelers, among whom are the "spur of the moment" versus the "planned" traveler. In addition, they cited the increasing prevalence of circuit tourists who travel with no destination target and who, given the open nature of the trip, would benefit from highway signage that directs them to motels, attractions, and scenic touring routes. To the extent that signage can inform travelers of sites of interest, the tourism industry would be enhanced.

The dialogue around signage represented one of the few instances where close consultation between the two ministries was found to occur and where the tourism ministry was able to articulate the interests of its stakeholders to its transportation counterpart, whose overriding concern was safety.

Access and Mobility Issues As "baby boomers" age, the seniors tourism market will increase markedly and issues related to accessibility/mobility for seniors will increasingly come to the fore. The implications for transportation–tourism linkages are numerous and diverse. Signage, for example, should be developed with an aging population in mind (i.e., size, visibility). Bus touring and cruising vacations will continue to increase in popularity, and provisions for this will have to be more intensively considered during transportation planning processes. Tourism facilities will also need to be made accessible to accommodate tourists with various types of physical challenges (e.g., wheelchair ramps, railings).

Despite the importance of these issues to the future of Ontario's tourism industry, there appears to have been a lack of communication between the tourism and transportation ministries regarding future accessibility policies.

Intermodal Factors In its tourism strategy, the ministry responsible for tourism identified a strong intermodal transportation network as one of the highest priorities from a tourism perspective (Ontario Ministry of Culture, Tourism and Recreation, 1994, p. 79). Ease of intermodal connections, integrated fares and schedules, affordability, and convenience are cornerstones of a competitive tourism industry because they encourage increased length of stay and the distribution of economic benefits from primary "gateways" (e.g., Toronto and Niagara Falls) to other parts of the province.

Some specific intermodal improvements that could benefit tourism in Ontario in a direct way include (1) improved access between Pearson International Airport and central Toronto, (2) strengthened Niagara Falls–Toronto ferry/rail/other links, and (3) development of linear land and water corridors integrating various forms of transportation—such as cycling, hiking, and boating—to explore scenic parts of Ontario.

Greater recognition of the economic benefits of tourism could strengthen MTO's case for improved intermodal systems. Moreover, increased appreciation of tourism on the part of MTO could also influence priorities for the type and location of transportation system upgrading. There is considerable support from the tourism industry for improved intermodal systems. In this area, therefore, unlike with other subsectors, there is a congruence of interests among tourism and municipal and provincial organizations.

IMPLICATIONS OF TOURISM–TRANSPORTATION LINKAGES AND CONCLUSION

Clearly, there is a need for ongoing communication and cooperation between the tourism and transportation ministries at all levels of their operations (i.e., policy formulation, infrastructure development, public consultation, marketing). In some instances the linkages appear to be so pervasive that the transportation ministry should consider acquiring its own tourism expert to assist in evaluating the implications for tourism of its decisions and as a point of contact for formal, ongoing liaison with the tourism ministry.

The following points provide a summary of the key findings of the study:

- Tourism is a significant but underrecognized contributor to Ontario's economy. However, the province is showing signs of losing its competitiveness. If current trends persist and international competition continues to increase, tourism's economic contributions will continue to be in jeopardy.
- Transportation is a fundamental determinant of the competitiveness of a tourism industry. Therefore, the quality of transportation infrastructure influences tourism's strength.
- Ontario's transportation ministry is, *de facto*, involved in many decisions that directly affect the quality of Ontario's tourism industry, although it has no formalized structure or policy framework to address tourism issues in a coordinated way. Therefore, opportunities may be lost as a result of a lack of consistent recognition of tourism-related interests.
- Ontario's tourism ministry has identified transportation improvements as a high priority in its tourism strategy.
- Liaison between transportation and tourism in Ontario has largely been carried out on an *ad hoc* (issue-by-issue) basis in the absence of more formalized procedure.
- Both the tourism and transportation ministries could benefit from a more formalized process for interministerial cooperation. For example, rigorous identification and/or quantification of the tourism benefits associated with proposed transportation investments may galvanize political support for the allocation of appropriate levels of funding to support proposed transportation programs.

Given the foregoing, several actions were suggested to the transportation ministry for their consideration. Among them were (1) development of an institutional capacity to address the wide range of tourism-related issues and decisions, (2) accommodation of tourism within transportation policies, (3) integration of tourism impacts into cost–benefit models, (4) continuing promotion of a seamless provincewide transportation system that will serve tourist as well as provincial resident needs and expectations, and (5) development of formal vehicles to establish ongoing cooperation between the ministries responsible for tourism and transportation.

In a broad sense, the results of the study support the contention that *direct* consideration of tourism–transportation linkages is required for a vital tourism industry. Where tourism–transportation linkages are not appropriately explored or well understood, significant opportunities may be lost. In contrast, those jurisdictions that *do* recognize the potential importance of such linkages give themselves the opportunity to gain a competitive advantage over tourist destinations that continue to view tourism and transportation as two separate entities.

No longer is it realistic to view the two sectors as entirely discrete entities, with separate jurisdictional agencies/ministries pursuing their own goals along parallel paths. The importance of each sector to the other must be clearly recognized and addressed, and cooperative mechanisms, policies, and activities must be initiated to promote and strengthen the linkages for the benefit of all stakeholders.

NOTES

This chapter represents the views and ideas of the authors and does not necessarily reflect the views and policies of the Ontario government ministries referred to.
1. See Chapter 1 for an overview of international tourism trends.
2. See Chapters 5, 9, 11, 12, and 14–19 for additional disscussion of community attitudes and involvement in the tourism planning and development processes.
3. See Chapter 8 for more detailed discussion relating to the sustainability of Caribbean tourism.
4. *Intermodal* refers to a trip requiring the use of more than one transportation mode. For example, when one arrives at an unfamiliar airport, the ease, cost, and time-efficiency of transfer to a rail, automobile, marine (cruise), and/or bus mode can make a considerable difference to the tourism experience.
5. See Chapter 22 for additional discussion relating to market failure.
6. Tourism Canada is now referred to as the Canadian Tourism Commission.
7. As of mid-1995, Ontario's tourism ministry was housed within the Ministry of Economic Development, Trade and Tourism.
8. See Chapter 8 for a discussion of tourism–air transportation linkages in the Caribbean region.

REFERENCES

Globe and Mail. 1994. Working on the railway. January 18, Toronto.

ISTC-Tourism. 1992. *Tourism and Transportation: The Vital Link*. Submission to the Royal Commission on National Passenger Transportation, April.

ISTC-Tourism. 1993. *Tourism Benefits to Canada from a More Liberalized Air Services Agreement Between Canada and the United States*.

National Tour Association (NTA). 1992. *Tourism Traveller Index: The Benchmark Study*. USA.

Ontario Ministry of Culture, Tourism and Recreation (MCTR). 1994. *Ontario's Tourism Industry: Opportunity, Progress, Innovation*. Toronto/Canada.

Ontario Ministry of Transportation. 1993. *Strategic Directions*. Draft, March. Toronto/Canada.

Organisation for Economic Cooperation and Development. 1992 and 1993. *Tourism Policy and International Tourism in OECD Countries*. Paris.

Sypher: Mueller. 1993. *Air Transportation Policies: Priorities for the Economy of Ontario*.

Toronto Star. 1994. Airport maintenance can't wait, February 6, B2.

Via Rail Canada Inc. 1989. *Review of Passenger Rail Transportation in Canada*. July.

Wheatcroft, Stephen. 1989. Current trends in aviation, *Tourism Management*, September, 213–217.

World Tourism Organization. 1993a. *Aviation and Tourism Policies: Balancing the Benefits—A Summary*.

Further Reading

Foster, C. (n.d.). Transport infrastructure as the key to successful tourism development, working for pleasure, *Tourism and Leisure Tomorrow*.

Ontario Ministry of Culture, Tourism and Recreation. 1993a. *The Ontario Tourism Strategy: Report on Marketing and Product Development—Making a Difference*. October.

Ontario Ministry of Culture, Tourism and Recreation. 1993b. *The Seamless Tourism Network*. Submission of the Tourism Infrastructure Working Group, October.

Ontario Ministry of Transportation. 1992. *Ontario Submission to the Royal Commission on National Passenger Transportation*.

Royal Commission on National Passenger Transportation. 1991. *Getting There: The Interim Report of the Royal Commission on National Passenger Transportation*. April.

World Bank. 1988. *Transport Policy and Planning: An Integrated Analytical Approach*. Economic Development Institute of the World Bank.

World Tourism Organization. 1991. *Tourism to the Year 2000: Qualitative Aspects Affecting Global Growth*.

World Tourism Organization. 1993b. *Tourism Trends Worldwide and in East Asia and the Pacific: 1980–1992*.

World Tourism Organization. 1993c. *Tourism Trends Worldwide and in Europe: 1980–1992*.

ℊ | PROBLEM SOLVING AND DISCUSSION ACTIVITIES

1. Using Figure 13.1 as a guide, determine the interfaces between the transportation and tourism sectors that are most important to your region, province, state, or country. Identify the critical issues that tourism authorities and decision makers should consider when attempting to optimize the competitiveness of tourism. Provide a rationale for your choices.

2. Does your government's main transportation agency recognize the importance of tourism in its policy documents? What evidence exists to support your conclusions? Does it have an acknowledged mandate to be involved in tourism? If so, describe and assess it. If not, discuss why tourism should, or should not, be included in the transportation agency's mandates.

3. If you were the director of your province or state transportation department, in what ways could you integrate tourism considerations into the agency's decision-making processes? Which of the following would you advocate, and why: (a) specific policy actions, (b) training, (c) addition of new tourism personnel, (d) linkages with the tourism ministry (what types), and/or (e) creation of multidisciplinary committees with public and private sector tourism–transportation representation?

4. What do you consider to be the five most important tourism–transportation linkages that need to be strengthened in your region, province/state, or country? Some of the following may be important to your answer: (a) air connections with

nearby states or provinces, (b) air connections with long-haul/overseas centers, (c) improved intermodal transportation systems, (d) expanded/new train systems, (e) expanded transit systems, (f) a better harbor, (g) development of a better understanding of the economic benefits of tourism within the transportation department, (h) highway maintenance, (i) consideration of tourism's costs and benefits in government options regarding transportation infrastructure investments, (j) development of a tourism manual for use by the transportation ministry's personnel, or (k) other items not listed. What criteria did you use to make such a determination? Justify your response.

5. Describe an experience you have had as a tourist where transportation played a favorable role and satisfied your needs as a vacationing traveler. Identify the specific elements that contributed to your satisfaction and explain why. Now, describe an experience you have had as a tourist where transportation had a negative impact on your holiday, including identification of the specific factors that detracted from your vacation experience. What recommendations could you make to address some of the deficiencies? Prepare a list of at least five success factors that would contribute to a more satisfying tourism experience given the interdependence between transportation and tourism.

14

Rural Tourism Development

ARE COMMUNITIES IN SOUTHWEST RURAL PENNSYLVANIA READY TO PARTICIPATE?

Lisa Bourke
A.E. Luloff

ℐ|KEY LEARNING POINTS

- Local input into the planning of tourism development can help identify potential problems, successes, and failures. Therefore, assessing local perceptions and expectations of tourism can greatly facilitate decisions relating to the development and promotion of tourism.

- Local participation, investments, and input greatly enhance the chance for success of tourism projects because they reflect the local community's commitment to the industry.

- Residents of different rural communities may vary in their responses to tourism development. As a result, just because one community favors tourism development does not mean that another community, similar in history and social structure, will accept the same tourism development proposal.

- Tourism can generate both benefits and costs. Moreover, rural community residents may perceive the social and economic impacts from tourism as being both negative and positive. Therefore, residents of the host community should plan for both the costs and benefits when anticipating rural tourism development.

- Despite strong federal and/or state (provincial) support, tourism may be perceived by local residents as playing *only a role* in local economies, not as being *the solution* to reversing economic decline. Consequently, not all residents expect tourism to be the panacea to economic ills. For rural tourism development to be successful, a readiness of the host community is required—readiness in local attitudes, resources, and commitment.

INTRODUCTION

Traditionally, natural resource extractive industries (i.e., agriculture, forestry, fishing, and mining) have played a dominant role in the local economies of rural areas in the

United States. With a decline in these industries and technological advances that have resulted in further reductions to the work force, many rural economies began to actively promote themselves as settings for the location of manufacturing plants (Krannich and Luloff, 1991). However, due to recent global economic changes, including the centralization of manufacturing facilities in low-cost areas, many American manufacturing companies have abandoned rural areas for foreign locations (particularly Mexico and Pacific Rim nations).

Consequently, rural areas have once again been forced to restructure their economies. Many have turned to the service sector generally, and tourism more specifically, as a strategy for advancing economic development. To date, the economic, social, and cultural consequences of this shift remain unclear (Bourke and Luloff, 1995; Krannich and Luloff, 1991).

This chapter reports on a case study of rural tourism conducted in a five-county area of nonmetropolitan Appalachian Pennsylvania during 1992 and 1993. An analysis of the impact of tourism on rurality, the economy, and the local social fabric provides insight into the potential success of further tourism development and promotion. Particular attention is placed on local response to, and initiation of, tourism projects that reflect the attitudes of local residents as well as their readiness to participate.

RURAL TOURISM AND PARTICIPATION READINESS: CONTEMPORARY PERSPECTIVES AND ISSUES

The study of tourism has received increased attention since the 1980s, particularly as it relates to tourism's role in adjusting to macroeconomic transformations.[1] Little is known about the implications of such changes for rural and small communities. Following earlier work (Luloff and Swanson, 1990; Luloff et al., 1984; Wilkinson, 1991), rural areas are defined as less densely populated places that are marked by their distance from large population centers and traditional reliance on primary industries for existence (extractive activities include agriculture, fisheries, mining, and forestry).

Rural Tourism: Implications for the Host Community Studies of rural tourism development have highlighted four main conclusions about tourism's impacts on communities. Tourism (1) threatens the local rural ambience, (2) has economic benefits, (3) creates social problems, and (4) has been more successful when initiated locally (Bourke and Luloff, 1995; Cohen, 1984).

This chapter extends the literature by suggesting that incorporating a measure of tourism *participation readiness*, or understanding levels of response and anticipation by the host community, is a necessary first step in the successful development and promotion of tourism, particularly in small rural communities (Luloff, 1990; Luloff et al., 1994; Wilkinson, 1991). Participation readiness refers to the local community's endorsement of tourism development (economically, socially, and culturally), acceptance of nonlocal tourists, and willingness to invest in the promotion and development of specific tourism projects.[2]

THREATS TO THE LOCAL RURAL AMBIENCE   Some have argued that rural tourism is inherently contradictory because mature tourism development involves a process of urbanization (Cohen, 1984). Noronha (in Cohen, 1984) alleged that when tourism is fully developed, it becomes institutionalized, resulting in the host community's loss of control over the industry and its share of the benefits. Hence, if tourism results in urbanization, it can threaten the local rural ambience when it is promoted. Where rurality is cherished, loss of rural ambience is a high cost of tourism development.

LOCAL ECONOMIC BENEFITS   Tourism studies have emphasized the beneficial economic impacts associated with tourism development, including the provision of local employment (Cohen, 1984) and its ability to revitalize local economies (Dahms, 1991; Fleming, 1988; Hester, 1990; Jensen and Blevins, 1992; Stokowski, 1992). Such studies have been cited (by academics, politicians, and developers) as justification for encouraging tourism development.

Despite this, it would appear that rural areas in the United States have not always been as effective as their urban counterparts in capturing tourist dollars. Recent studies have established that nonmetropolitan regions in Illinois received fewer benefits from travel and tourism than did metropolitan areas (Bowling, 1992). Furthermore, despite having the largest rural population in the nation, rural areas of Pennsylvania have not shared equitably in tourism's impacts. In 1988, for example, travel was a thriving industry, generating over US$13 billion (including both direct and indirect travel expenditures) in Pennsylvania (US Travel Data Center, 1994). However, only about 23 percent of this (around US$3 billion) was spent in predominantly rural counties (Center for Rural Pennsylvania, 1991).

While tourism has played an important role in helping many economies adjust to losses both in extractive industries and in manufacturing, these changes have frequently been associated with "lower-quality" jobs. Employment in service industries generally, and for rural areas in particular, has usually translated to lower wages and a reduced likelihood of medical benefits (Kassab and Luloff, 1993; Kassab et al., 1995), particularly when employment is largely seasonal or involves part-time work.

SOCIAL COSTS   A review of the extant literature suggests that tourism development is not without costs, particularly with reference to the creation of social problems. Moreover, that these problems tend to be neither anticipated nor directly observed makes them all the more pernicious. For example, in some cases the development of a tourism industry has changed friendship patterns as well as types of relationships among residents of the host community (Hester, 1990; Stokowski, 1992). According to Greenwood (in Cohen, 1984), tourism tends to expand the economic domain into aspects of social life by commercializing social phenomena.

In many rural and small communities, traditional "hangouts" (including diners, bars, and Dairy Queens) are often the scene of local gossip and discussion of issues central to the locality. With the advent of tourism activity, these "sacred" places (Hester, 1990; Luloff et al., 1994) may no longer fill these roles because they increasingly cater to the needs of the rapidly growing tourist population, particularly before other establishments are developed to meet their expanding needs. It is also common for local promoters of tourism activity to make use of overstated and highly optimistic predictions about the opportunities for social mobility and advancement that may accompany tourism (Cohen, 1984).

Even when efforts are made to respect local culture, lifestyles, and sacred places, problems such as traffic congestion may emerge. These factors may discourage locals from venturing into town and socializing with other residents (Hester, 1990).

LOCAL INITIATION OF TOURISM ACTIVITY   Projects that were planned locally have been more successful than those directed from outside (Dahms, 1991; Fleming, 1988; Gitelson et al., 1992; Hester, 1990; Jensen and Blevins, 1992). Consequently, local initiation has been recognized as being necessary for successful tourism development (Bourke and Luloff, 1995; Luloff et al., 1994; Walsh and Burr, 1993).

Most local initiatives begin with a group of local residents who are concerned about their community (Luloff, 1990; Wilkinson, 1991). This group is more likely to consider local interests, culture, and noneconomic impacts than are nonlocal developers (Fleming, 1988; Wells et al., 1991). Dahms (1991) believes that local entrepreneurial spirit is key to developing attractions that not only draw tourists but are beneficial for the host community.

PARTICIPATION READINESS   When tourism development efforts are initiated locally, a heightened sensitivity to the protection and preservation of local ambience occurs and efforts to optimize economic and social benefits are made, thereby increasing the probability of local support (Bourke and Luloff, 1995). The degree of support reflects the level of participation readiness, or the willingness of a local population—both leaders and general public—to favor growth of the tourism industry commensurate with the potential of the local infrastructure to support development.

The roots of participation readiness are traceable to the level of activeness (Luloff and Wilkinson, 1990; Tilly, 1973) expressed by members of the community. According to *community field theory*, interactional characteristics such as involvement by local residents, patterns of local interactions, and bonds shared by community members play essential roles in the levels of activeness (i.e., the degree to which citizens play decisive roles in directing purposive change) in a community. That is, interactional characteristics greatly assist in explaining the patterns of mobilization (i.e., how people come together to address issues of shared concern) used to achieve development goals (Kaufman, 1959; Wilkinson, 1990, 1991).

Community field theory maintains that the community is a structure of relationships that emerges from the place-oriented (i.e., characteristics of the the community) social interactions of a group of people who meet their common daily needs together and express common interests in the locality (Wilkinson, 1991). This interaction helps build bridges among members of the community, and it fosters solidarity and mutual identity among people who may share little else in common (Humphrey and Wilkinson, 1993; Zekeri et al., 1994).

From an *interactional theory* perspective, the essence of a community is discovered in an examination of the activities of local organizations, groups, and activists who work to address the needs of their local society while maintaining its social identity (Wilkinson, 1970, 1991). Priority is given to the role of local actors whose interactions focus on local issues. When relating this perspective to tourism, attention must be given to the level of participation readiness of rural communities. The host community needs to have more than a welcoming attitude toward visitors. Tourism development requires both financial investments and adequate staffing for the organization and promotion of specific projects. Community sentiment supporting tourism activities must be coupled with a willingness by residents to participate and promote them.

RURAL TOURISM DEVELOPMENT IN PENNSYLVANIA

Pennsylvania's proximity to the eastern seaboard, the presence of two large metropolitan areas (Philadelphia and Pittsburgh) as well as several smaller metropolitan centers, and the location of other large cities across state lines (Baltimore, Maryland; Washington, D.C.; and New York, New York) often result in the characterization of Pennsylvania as a predominantly urban state. However, Pennsylvania is quite rural. The state boasts the largest rural population in the country (3.7 million people or 31 percent of the total state population) as well as thousands of small and rural towns where agriculture, forestry, mining, and manufacturing dominate the local economies. Approximately 84 percent of Pennsylvania's ridge and valley topography is farm land [8 million acres (3.2 million hectares), or 28 percent of the total land base] or forest land [16 million acres (6.5 million hectares), or 56 percent of the total].

The geographic and demographic distribution of the population has historically reflected the state's natural resource endowments. This has tended to create regional dependency on a single extractive industry (generally mining, forestry, or agriculture). However, such dependency on natural resource-based industries has declined due to a stronger commitment to preserving these resources as well as technological advancements that have decreased employment in traditional primary industries and lowered demand for such products (Krannich and Luloff, 1991). As a result, alternatives were sought to stop the hemorrhaging associated with economic decline in these rural areas. Following signals from agencies of the federal government, in the 1980s the Commonwealth of Pennsylvania moved rapidly to promote rural tourism as a replacement industry (Gitelson et al., 1992).

To justify such economic restructuring, state officials pointed to significant rural tourism attractions throughout the state, including the Amish regions, numerous state forests, the Poconos, the Lake Erie shore communities, ski resorts, and historic towns. The success of these areas provided evidence for the idea that tourism could secure a thriving local economy in rural areas throughout Pennsylvania (Gitelson et al., 1992).

However, not all rural and small communities have the potential to capitalize on the attractiveness of their natural resources. Having attractions is certainly a prerequisite, but other factors, such as local acceptance and financial support, are also important for the creation of a successful tourism industry (Bourke and Luloff, 1995). Recently, Bourke and Luloff (1995) concluded that rural areas often lack local financial resources and have to struggle to compete for limited state and federal funding for tourism development. Consequently, in an effort to maximize the likelihood of successfully capturing such support, rural areas may focus more on satisfying grant requirements (the criteria for which may contradict the initial goals of the tourism project) than on assessing local community needs or assets.

Following an interactional theory of community, this chapter proposes that when capital and human resources are available and a local mindset that welcomes and wants tourism is present, a foundation can be established for the successful advancement of the tourism industry. Tourism efforts in communities of five nonmetropolitan counties in southwestern Pennsylvania that vary in their stages of tourism development[3] are discussed. Greene County is located in the most southwestern corner of the state and borders West Virginia to the west and south. The other four (Somerset, Bedford, Fulton, and Franklin) are contiguous and form part of the state's border with Maryland (see Figure 14.1). Between Greene and Somerset is Fayette County, which was excluded from this study because it is a metropolitan area.

RURAL TOURISM IN SOUTHWESTERN PENNSYLVANIA

Methods In the springs of 1992 and 1993, interviews were conducted with local officials and tourism representatives in the five counties as part of a larger study on regional and local approaches to rural tourism as a means of economic development. Two protocols were established prior to conducting any fieldwork. The first set of respondents, known as "key informants," consisted of 86 local officials and representatives of the tourism industry within the five counties. Using a standardized set of open-ended questions, the key informants were asked general questions about the local community, economy, tourism facilities and services, tourism projects and proposals, and the future of the tourism industry. Interviewers added other questions as necessary to clarify points (e.g., Why do you think that? or Can you be more specific?)

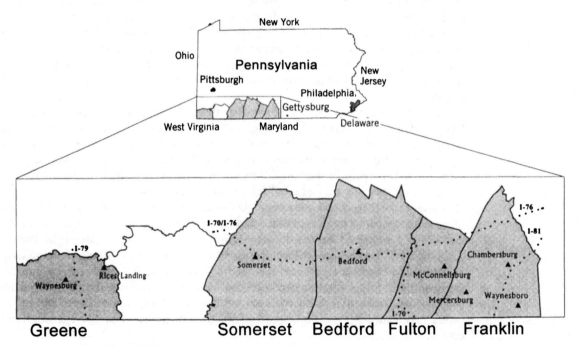

Figure 14.1
Location of the five counties within Pennsylvania.

The key informants were also asked to identify specific persons who were actively involved in a specific tourism activity or project. These individuals, known as "action informants," provided important and detailed insights into their particular involvement, as well as the actions of others, in the various stages of the tourism development activities. This set of interviews was less structured. Forty-eight individuals were identified in this process.

A total of 134 interviews were conducted: 26 in Greene County, 21 in Somerset County, 42 in Bedford County, 19 in Fulton County, and 26 in Franklin County (see Table 14.1). All but nine of the interviews were conducted face-to-face. The remaining nine were telephone interviews with respondents who were unavailable when the fieldwork was conducted.

Socioeconomic Characteristics of the Five Counties The study area has a tradition of being dependent on natural resources, with long histories of mining, forestry, farming, and manufacturing activities (Krannich and Luloff, 1991). The economy of Greene County has long been tied to the vagaries of mining, which may account for its stronger resemblance to other Appalachian coal regions, like those in West Virginia and Kentucky, than to the other counties in the study area. The remaining counties have comparatively smaller mining operations, but farming and forestry activities are more prevalent.

Manufacturing enterprises play a more important role in the four contiguous counties than in Greene. Although strongest in Franklin, where just over one-third of all employment was tied to manufacturing in 1990, employment in this industry declined between 1980 and 1990 (see Table 14.2). Manufacturing employed approximately one-fifth of the labor force in Somerset.

There are a variety of service industries throughout the study area. Despite declines during the 1980s, more than four of every five workers in Bedford, and two of every three in Fulton, were employed in the service industry in 1990. Somerset and Franklin both experienced growth in service jobs, and in Greene the number of employees more than doubled between 1980 and 1990 to a total of 97 percent of the work force (see Table 14.2).

Tourism is strongest in Somerset County, where approximately 2740 people were employed in tourism-related jobs in 1992. This county also evidenced the highest levels of travel expenditures and local tax receipts from travel within the study area. Bedford appears to have had the largest and most stable proportion of its work force employed in tourism between 1980 and 1990. Historic attractions and recreational resources form the basis of tourism in Somerset and Bedford.

Franklin, the least rural of the five counties, also possesses a relatively strong tourism industry that is fueled by its proximity to Gettysburg and the core metropolitan centers of Philadelphia (Pennsylvania), Washington, D.C., and Baltimore (Maryland). Employment in tourism as a percentage of the total work force declined slightly in this county between 1980 and 1990.

Although the two most rural counties, Fulton and Greene, experienced (respectively) the second and third highest proportions of the labor force employed within tourism, these two areas generated relatively lower levels of travel expenditures, tax receipts, and lodging receipts. This reflects the fact that few lodging properties exist in these counties where tourism activity tends to be based on hunting, fishing, camping, and interstate highway travelers stopping for services.

TABLE 14.1
Individuals Interviewed by County

Position	Number of Organizations Consulted[a]					
	Greene	Somerset	Bedford	Fulton	Franklin	Total[a]
County planner	1	1	2	1	1	6
County official	2	1	3	1	1	8
TPA director	1	1	1	1	1	5
Extension agent	1	1	1	1	1	5
United Way representative	1	—	—	1	—	2
Bank manager	1	1	1	1	1	5
Representative from economic developmental groups	2	1	1	1	1	6
Leaders of tourism opposition groups	NA[b]	NA	2	NA	NA	2
Newspaper editor/reporter	1	1	2	NA	1	5
Chamber of Commerce	1	1	1	1	3	7
Local goverment officials	2	2	2	2	4	12
Local historian	2	1	3	1	2	9
Representative from arts and crafts groups	1	1	1	1	1	5
Motel manager	3	2	3	1	1	10
Business manager	—	2	1	1	—	4
Gift store owner	2	1	1	1	1	6
Directors of tourist sites	2	3	1	2	1	9
Directors of tourist information services	NA	NA	1	NA	2	3
Initiators of tourism projects	5	4	8	3	5	25
Representatives from tourism projects	2	2	4	1	2	11
Number of individuals interviewed[a]	26	21	42	19	26	134

[a] Because of the rural nature of these counties, many individuals have more than one role and their interview may be counted more than once.
[b] NA, not applicable.

Between 1980 and 1990, the more eastern counties, Franklin and Fulton, experienced substantial population growth, and the population of Bedford grew at a faster rate than the state (see Table 14.3). Somerset and Greene, on the other hand, both experienced population decline which was related in part to economic decline, especially in the mining industry.

Per capita income in the study area was consistently below the state average throughout the 1980s. Franklin, which had the highest per capita income in both 1980 and 1990,

TABLE 14.2
Tourism-related and Socioeconomic Characteristics of the Five Counties and the State of Pennsylvania

Characteristic	Greene	Somerset	Bedford	Fulton	Franklin	Pennsylvania
1992 direct travel expenditures[a] (US$ millions)	6	134	46	2	55	9,642
1992 local tax receipts from travel (US$ thousands)	90	1,920	990	140	680	134,290
Number of lodging establishments	6	14	24	4	14	—
1987 lodging receipts (US$ millions)	1.2	5.8	10.6	0.3	7.7	1,649
1992 employment from tourism[b]	70	2,740	800	10	930	160,510
Percent employed in manufacturing						
1980	1.5	24.0	5.1	4.7	49.0	33.1
1990	*[c]	21.7	10.9	7.7	35.3	21.3
Percent employed in all services						
1980	46.2	53.5	92.2	85.2	46.6	60.2
1990	97.2	65.8	84.3	66.5	58.8	72.0
Percent employed in retail/tourism[d]						
1980	5.3	12.8	26.5	15.8	9.7	9.9
1990	13.6	9.2	25.3	18.2	8.5	11.7

[a] In 1992, direct and indirect travel expenditures in Pennsylvania were US$17.3 billion. Stateside the industry has grown between 1988 and 1992. Direct and indirect travel expenditures by county are not available (US Travel Data Center, 1994).

[b] Tourism employment as defined by the US Travel Data Center.

[c] There is a disclosure problem for this county in manufacturing, the asterisk reflects a small number of manufacturing businesses or few people employed in manufacturing.

[d] Categorization of retail/tourism is based on SIC codes 58, 59, and 70.

was the only county that exhibited a poverty rate below the state average. Poverty rates were considerably higher in Greene, Bedford, and Somerset. During the 1980s, some poverty alleviation occurred in Bedford and Fulton. However, poverty rates worsened in Franklin and Somerset, and in Greene the rate was almost double the state average by 1990. Only Franklin had unemployment rates below the state averages in both 1980 and 1990. Nevertheless, unemployment declined during the 1980s in all counties but Greene.

Taken as a whole, these indicators suggest that the economy of the study area lagged behind the state. Franklin consistently had the strongest economy, Bedford and Fulton experienced moderate improvements, Somerset was stable, and Greene suffered economic decline during the 1980s resulting in more than one in five individuals in that county being in poverty.

Tourism Development in the Five Counties Tourism is at different stages of development in each of the five counties. An aggregate count of existing tourist attractions and proposed developments suggests that Somerset, Bedford, and Franklin have had higher levels of tourism-related experiences than either Fulton or Greene (see Table 14.4).

Annual festivals and events exist throughout the study area, ranging from two festivals

TABLE 14.3

General Characteristics of the Five Counties and the State of Pennsylvania

Characteristic	Greene	Somerset	Bedford	Fulton	Franklin	Pennsylvania
Size (square miles)	576	1,075	1,015	438	772	44,820
Population (1990)	39,550	78,218	47,919	13,837	121,082	11,881,643
Population change 1980–1990 (%)	(2.3)	(3.7)	2.4	7.7	6.6	0.1
Population of largest town	4,270	8,732	4,949	2,167	16,647	—
Income per capita (US$)						
1980	$5,995	$6,011	$5,430	$5,402	$6,675	$7,077
1990	$10,005	$10,442	$9,954	$10,267	$13,060	$14,068
Percent of individuals in poverty						
1980	14.0	11.7	14.7	14.4	7.4	10.5
1990	21.4	14.3	13.6	12.2	8.3	11.1
Percent of work force unemployed						
1980	9.8	10.2	12.6	7.8	4.6	7.4
1990	12.2	7.4	8.0	5.9	3.9	6.0

and events in Bedford to eight in Somerset. Types vary from festivals with a seasonal or harvest theme, to county fairs, historic celebrations, and antique or flea market events. The majority of these festivals and events are organized by local groups, although some are organized by county agencies or officials. None is organized from outside the county. Each festival or event is unique in terms of its activities and atmosphere, but all provide an opportunity for local residents to participate and raise money. The festivals and events range in size from the newer ones that attract less than 1000 people to those that draw crowds of 30,000 or more, including people from metropolitan areas.

Historic attractions, including large museums and archives, historic buildings, old courthouses, historic districts, and walking tours, were commonly mentioned as tourist attractions by respondents in Somerset, Franklin, and especially Bedford. Development of historic sites was usually initiated by a small number of local people who sought state, federal, or private funding for restoration and development. While respondents who were involved in such developments (planning and delivery) tended to be very excited about them, others were more critical. Some leaders suggested that developing numerous historic sites was key to making history attractive. Others were less concerned about the number of sites and more interested in the operation of "live" museums which they believed would be more popular to a general audience.

Bedford and Somerset both received considerable federal support from America's Industrial Heritage Project (AIHP) to develop historic attractions such as establishing an agricultural museum in Somerset and a transportation museum in Bedford, renovating four old buildings into smaller museums in Bedford, and developing the Lincoln Highway (State Route 30) as a historic drive. At the time of data collection, only feasibility studies had been conducted on these AIHP projects.

Although outdoor recreation was reported as a popular activity in each county, such activity tended to be seasonal, and most facilities were not owned by local residents. Consequently, estimates of economic benefits from such activities varied.

TABLE 14.4
Tourism Activities in Each County, 1992–1993

Tourism Actions[a]	Greene	Somerset	Bedford	Fulton	Franklin
Festivals and events					
Festivals	4	4	1	3	4
County fairs	1	1	0	0	1
Historic celebrations	0	1	1	0	0
Markets	0	2	0	0	0
Subtotal	5	8	2	3	5
Historic attractions					
Museums	1	3	4	0	2
Historic artifacts	0	2	6	0	2
Historic districts	0	1	2	0	3
Subtotal	1	6	12	0	7
Outdoor recreation activities					
Hunting/fishing	Yes[b]	Yes	Yes	Yes	Yes
Camping/hiking	Yes	Yes	Yes	Yes	—
Ski areas	0	2	1	0	1
State parks	1	4	3	1	4
Boating	0	2	1	0	0
Scenic drives	0	0	1	0	0
Rails-to-trails	0	1	0	0	0
Subtotal	3	11	8	3	6
Shops					
Historic	1	1	1	0	1
Outlet malls	0	1	0	0	0
Subtotal	1	2	1	0	1
Hotel/convention centers/resorts	0	1	1	0	1
Tourist promotion centers	1	1	1	1	2
Total	11	29	25	7	22

[a] Actions refer to tourist attractions as well as tourism developments, projects, and efforts. Categories of these actions are not mutually exclusive.

[b] A "yes" refers to the fact that there are numerous tourist-related hunting/fishing and/or camping/hiking activities. For simplicity, the presence of a "yes" has been treated as "1" to reach the totals for the outdoor recreation activities rows.

Shops were identified as another form of attraction for tourists. All counties but Fulton and Greene attracted tourists shopping for antiques. Greene has historic shops associated with its riverfront development (including renovated buildings and mills as part of a marina, boutiques, craft shops, and restaurants) in Rices Landing. Somerset has an outlet mall that is popular, but respondents suggested that shoppers spent little money outside the mall.

Resorts are another attraction. One privately owned ski area in Somerset is also a year-round convention center and resort, while the country club in Franklin attracts both golfers and conventions. These resorts were reported as promoting themselves independently. Bedford has secured funds to renovate an old four-star hotel. While this project has been controversial because of cost (Bourke, 1995), the county has undertaken this development and is seeking private investment. All shops and resorts were privately owned, except for the state-owned Blue Knob Ski Area. Some respondents claimed that, as a result of nonlocal ownership, the leakage of economic benefits was common.

Each county has tourist promotion centers, except Greene, where a state Welcome Center is in the planning stages. Franklin has a large information center located on an interstate highway, which was built entirely through donations, is staffed by 270 volunteers and records 55,000 visitor-days annually (mostly tourists enroute to Gettysburg). Somerset and Bedford have small tourist information centers located in the county seat.

The Tourism Promotion Agency (TPA—a state-sponsored office charged with promoting local tourism) was cited as another important service in tourism development and promotion within the study area. However, the perceived effectiveness of TPA activities varied across the counties. This reflected, in part, diversity in size and staffing. For example, while both Greene and Somerset shared TPAs with other counties, Somerset had a staff person from the TPA located in the county. Bedford had one full-time TPA director, Fulton had one part-time director, and Franklin had a full-time director, a part-time staff member, and volunteers. Not surprisingly, respondents from Fulton and Greene were dissatisfied with the current funding of tourism promotion.

Overall, these data suggest that in 1992–1993, tourism in Greene and Fulton was based largely on festivals and outdoor recreation, which are seasonal activities. Fulton had no proposals for new tourism development, while Greene had proposals only for the riverfront development and the Welcome Center. The former was in its early stages with only a few grants of US$500 each, while the latter is a state promotion center not specific to Greene.

Somerset had numerous festivals, some historic attractions, and a variety of outdoor recreation opportunities. Of Somerset's 29 activities, only four were "in progress." In Bedford, on the other hand, nine of the 25 projects reported were in the developmental stage. Tourism was being championed in Bedford, largely reflecting the availability of federal money. Franklin, with 22 activities, had only one new tourism development in progress. It has several festivals, outdoor recreation activities, and small historic attractions.

IMPACTS OF RURAL TOURISM

Examination of secondary data on numbers of attractions, services, travel expenditures, and/or employment in retail/tourism-related activities provides only part of the picture. To adequately assess tourism's impacts and potential, perceptions of local residents and leaders in the context of the five factors outlined previously must also be considered.

Rural Threats to the rural atmosphere was a decided concern of many respondents who not
Ambience only were anxious about losing the rural nature of their county, but were also concerned about nonlocals dominating their "sacred places" (see Hester, 1990). Many were concerned that economic growth of any kind (including tourism development) would detract from the rurality of the region. Such concerns were expressed most often by respondents from Greene and Fulton, the most rural of the counties, and less often by those in Franklin, the least rural of the five counties.

Some respondents in Somerset, Bedford, and Fulton believed that the rurality of their area was itself an attraction for campers, hikers, and outdoor recreationists as well as for metropolitan residents seeking a "weekend getaway" to a small town or rural bed and breakfast. The preservation and protection of the rural setting was seen by many residents as vital to both tourism and quality-of-life issues. On the other hand, the lack of fine dining and other services was seen as a potential deterrent.

Economic Benefits Issues relating to the economic benefits resulting from tourism were more frequently discussed by respondents in Bedford, Somerset, and Franklin (i.e., those counties where tourism was comparatively well established). While many respondents, particularly in Somerset and Bedford, believed that tourism contributed to the local economy, most did not want tourism to become the sole foundation for their local economic base. Because of tourism's seasonal nature and vulnerability to fluctuations in the national economy, these respondents were skeptical of it becoming the major local industry. Indeed, few saw tourism as a panacea to rural economic decline.

Instead, many viewed tourism as providing low-wage jobs without benefits. Some were concerned that the tourism industry's profits leaked from the host community. Still others, especially those from the poorer counties, viewed tourism development as investing money in outsiders rather than in the local community. In addition, concerns about the initial costs of developing tourism (constructing and promoting attractions) were expressed.

Not surprisingly, those directly involved in the tourism industry and/or economic development were more likely to anticipate economic benefits from tourism development. In addition, tourism development was most endorsed in areas where the existing industry was perceived as being successful (Somerset and Bedford) and least supported where economic growth and development were most needed (Greene).

Social Impacts While changes to the rurality of an area or to the local economy tended to be the initial focus of discussion during the interviews, potential social impacts resulting from tourism development were also identified by the respondents. Traffic congestion, the lack of parking, and an increased diversity of people were among the negative impacts identified. A few residents reported avoiding traditional social places when "the tourists" were in town.

On the other hand, increased community pride, more services, improvement of downtown areas, identity of place ("It would put us on the map!"), and more diversity of people were noted by others as being positive social repercussions arising from tourism. Respondents often expressed great pride in the festivals and believed that they served as promoters of community (Wilkinson, 1991).

Local Participation Participation by local residents was believed to have been a key to the success of rural tourism projects in these nonmetropolitan counties. Festivals drew the largest crowds, were the most profitable, had the least negative social impacts, and involved the greatest number of community citizens (all measures of success as defined by the citizens and leaders of these counties). They tended to be community-based (not countywide) and organized through the collective efforts of a coordinated group of local residents and organizations.

The least successful tourism efforts were those associated with external funding. This was particularly the case when the project satisfied *funding criteria* rather than the *development needs* of the local community. In these cases, the projects commonly stalled when the initial grant expired. Furthermore, despite official efforts at promoting these externally based activities, local commitment and investment have been scarce. For example, despite strong local official support for a plan to develop the old hotel at taxpayer expense, residents in Bedford expressed overwhelming opposition, which contributed to the withdrawal of the proposal.

While the privately owned resorts were profitable, they were not always supported or promoted by the local community. Some respondents viewed them as detached from the local community because they promoted themselves independently and generally did not refer tourists to other local services.

In summary, those activities that involved locals in the design and implementation of tourism events or in planning a series of attractions, and that required local funds or matches-in-kind were found to be more successful, both in terms of long-term community participation in projects and in capturing a market.

Participation Readiness

Participation readiness was an important factor that influenced many other perceptions about tourism development, including readiness in mindset, resources, and commitment of the local population. Participation readiness extends beyond the number of existing attractions (Franklin had more existing tourist attractions than Bedford in 1992–1993) to include local citizens' attitudes about, and involvement in, the development and/or expansion of a successful tourism industry.

Bedford and Somerset were more ready for tourism than the other counties. Local leaders in Bedford and Somerset actively pursued grants for tourism development and believed that existing services and tourism sites provided a strong base for expansion. They anticipated economic benefits and believed that the necessary financial resources could be attained. Furthermore, they suggested that development and improved marketing of existing attractions (historic buildings, services, ski resorts, recreation, and local rural atmosphere) would result in a stronger tourism industry.

In addition, residents from these two counties were more likely to view tourism as being important to the local economy and part of the community's way of life. Despite such local support, all developments were not without conflict. Residents of Bedford and Somerset tended to be aware of specific tourism projects, and while they might have been hostile towards some, they were generally supportive of the industry as a whole.

Readiness in Greene County, which is facing serious economic problems, was quite different. Respondents believed problems of poverty and the lack of economic opportunities were more pressing local issues to be addressed. Directing fiscal and human capital efforts into developing tourist attractions was not a high priority. They wanted traditional industrial expansion, usually in the form of manufacturing jobs, which they believed would alleviate unemployment, poverty, and welfare dependence more quickly than advances in tourism.

Fulton County lacked local resources to develop tourism. In addition, there was strong local opposition to growth. When viewed together, these factors help explain why this region did not aggressively seek tourism development. Both Greene and Fulton lacked the staff to regularly apply for grants and pursue outside funds for tourism. In addition, both lacked local funds to develop tourist sites themselves or even satisfy the requirements of matching fund grants. Key informants from Franklin suggested that they did not want to develop a tourism industry because their strong manufacturing economy provided good jobs and good wages.

DISCUSSION AND CONCLUSION

This case study highlights some important issues about rural tourism. While the previous literature has found that tourism development tends to be economically beneficial, not all respondents in this study agreed. Respondent attitudes varied from those who expressed the belief that tourism development would overcome economic decline and stagnation, to those who held a skeptical view and focused on its low paying seasonal jobs and the initial costs of development. The majority of responses was based on perceptions rather than actual impacts, but as pointed out by Thomas (1928), what is perceived to be real is real in its consequences. Perceptions influence local involvement and participation readiness. Researchers should not assume that economic impacts are all positive. Healthy skepticism may result in more efficient expenditure of money on tourism development.

This study does confirm previous notions of fears or concerns relating to such negative social impacts as traffic congestion, decline in the rural atmosphere, and a loss of local "sacred places." However, social benefits were also identified. In particular, the various festivals were believed to have promoted interaction, community participation, community pride, and a sense of community (see Wilkinson, 1991).

Successful tourism projects were generally found to have strong local involvement and were often locally initiated. Some forms of tourism development were found to increase the level of urbanization more than others. Certainly, rurality is important to many residents' quality of life. More research is required to address the actual impact of tourism on rurality.

The major implication of this study is that participation readiness is an essential element affecting the potential success of public efforts at tourism development. Energies should be concentrated in areas where local residents are committed to tourism and ready to become involved. Where residents lack participation readiness, developing successful tourism projects is likely to be more difficult. This conforms with community development studies which have found that developments which involve the community, receive local investment, and extend beyond economic factors are more enduring and tend to have more positive impacts. Developing a tourism industry in connection with the atmosphere of the local community and the needs of the local people, as well as respecting their place of residence and quality of life, is likely to ensure both a better community and a more compatible tourism industry. This is consistent with the interactional perspective of community.

An assessment of the perceptions of local residents, tourism resources and services, the local economy, and the history of the project are primary considerations for measuring the potential success of any tourism venture. Relying on secondary indicators such as numbers of visitor-days, gross sales or receipts, and occupancy rates does not provide adequate evidence for such an assessment. For example, while the visitor center in Franklin was well used, the staff reported that most tourists wanted directions to Gettysburg. Most local leaders in this county did not perceive tourism to be important or worthy of further investment. Incorporating community theories into the study of tourism and assessing local response can provide more accurate indicators of the potential impacts of rural tourism.

It can be concluded that rural economies are not simple structures and that no single industry will alleviate economic decline. Tourism cannot be viewed by state officials or local leaders as the panacea for a struggling economy. Tourism, like most industries, can contribute to an economy, assist in diversifying that economy, and promote a sense of community. But, at the same time, tourism has costs. Careful planning, local involvement, and accounting for signs of participation readiness could assist in more successful tourism development in rural areas.

ACKNOWLEDGMENTS

The authors greatly appreciate the assistance of Claudio Frumento with the preparation of the map, and the collection of some of the secondary data. Furthermore, we acknowledge Gaynell Meij, Nana Nti, Steve Jacob, and Steve Burr for their assistance in collecting primary data.

NOTES

1. See Chapters 8–11 for additional examples of tourism's role as a means of economic regeneration or diversification.
2. See Chapters 5, 9, 11, 12, and 15–19 for a detailed discussion pertaining to community attitudes and involvement in the tourism planning and development processes.
3. See Chapters 2, 3, 5, 7, and 28 for further discussion relating to life cycle models and the tourist area cycle of evolution.

REFERENCES

Bourke, L. 1995. Development for whom? A case study of Bedford, Pennsylvania, *Small Town*, 25(5), 14–21.

Bourke, L. and A.E. Luloff. 1995. Leaders perspectives on rural tourism: case studies in Pennsylvania, *Journal of the Community Development Society*, 26(2), 224–239.

Bowling, M. 1992. Illinois rural tourism, *Small Town*, 22(4),19–26.

Center for Rural Pennsylvania. 1991. *Rural Tourism: New Opportunities for Rural Pennsylvania* (April Newsletter). Harrisburg, PA: Center for Rural Pennsylvania.

Cohen, E. 1984. The sociology of tourism: approaches, issues, and findings, *Annual Review of Sociology*, 10, 373–392.

Dahms, F. 1991. Economic revitalization in St. Jacobs, Ontario: ingredients for transforming a dying village into a thriving small town, *Small Town*, 21(6), 12–18.

Fleming, C. 1988. A tale of two towns: using tourism to revitalize Iowa's small communities, *Small Town*, 19(2), 22–24.

Gitelson, R., A. Graefe, A.E. Luloff, and K. Martin. 1992. *An Assessment of Alternative Policy Initiatives to Foster Rural Tourism as a Viable Economic Development Tool in Pennsylvania*. Report prepared for the Center for Rural Pennsylvania. State College, PA: The Center for Travel and Tourism Research.

Hester, R.T. Jr. 1990. The sacred structure in small towns: a return to Manteo, North Carolina, *Small Town*, 20(4), 5–21.

Humphrey, C.R. and K.P. Wilkinson. 1993. Growth promotion activities in rural areas: do they make a difference? *Rural Sociology*, 58(2), 175–189.

Jensen, K. and A. Blevins. 1992. Lead, South Dakota: the remaking of a company mining town, *Small Town*, 22(6), 4–11.

Kassab, C. and A.E. Luloff. 1993. The new buffalo hunt: chasing the service sector, *Journal of the Community Development Society*, 24(2), 175–195.

Kassab, C., A.E. Luloff, and F. Schmidt. 1995. The changing impact of industry, household structure, and residence on household well-being, *Rural Sociology*, 60(1), 67–90.

Kaufman, H.F. 1959. Toward an interactional conception of community, *Social Forces*, 38(1), 8–17.

Krannich, R.S. and A.E. Luloff. 1991. Problems of resource dependency in U.S. rural communities. In A.W. Gilg (ed.), *Rural Policy and Planning*, Vol. 1. New York: Belhaven Press, pp. 5–18.

Luloff, A.E. 1990. Communities and social change: how do small communities act? In A.E. Luloff and L.E. Swanson (eds.), *American Rural Communities*. Boulder, CO: Westview Press, pp. 214–227.

Luloff, A.E. and L.E. Swanson (eds.). 1990. *American Rural Communities*. Boulder, CO: Westview.

Luloff, A.E. and K.P. Wilkinson. 1990. Community action and the national rural development agenda, *Sociological Practice*, 8, 48–57.

Luloff, A.E., J.C. Bridger, A. Graefe, M. Saylor, K. Martin, and R. Gitelson. 1994. Assessing rural tourism efforts in the United States, *Annals of Tourism Research*, 21, 46–64.

Luloff, A.E., B. Yager, and D. Francis. 1984. *Case Studies of New Hampshire Communities* (NE-129 Project Report). Durham, NH: New Hampshire Agricultural Experiment Station.

Stokowski, P.A. 1992. The Colorado gambling boom: an experiment in rural community development, *Small Town*, 22(6), 12–19.

Thomas, W.I. 1928. *The Child in America*. New York: Knopf.

Tilly, C. 1973. Do communities act? *Sociological Inquiry*, 43(3–4), 209–240.

US Travel Data Center. 1994. *The Economic Impact of Travel on Pennsylvania Counties 1991 & 1992*. Washington, D.C.: US Travel Data Center.

Walsh, J.A. and S.W. Burr. 1993. The role of rural tourism in community development—a caveat. In *Proceedings of the Northeastern Recreation Research Meetings*, April; General Technical Report NE-185. Radnor, PA: U.S. Department of Agriculture, Forest Service, Northeastern Forest Experiment Station, pp. 160–163.

Wells, B., L. Sternweis, and T. Borich. 1991. Intercommunity cooperation: how Iowa towns band together for community development, *Small Town*, 21(6), 25–27.

Wilkinson, K.P. 1970. The community as a social field, *Social Forces*, 48(3), 311–322.

Wilkinson, K.P. 1990. Crime and community. In A.E. Luloff and L.E. Swanson (eds.), *American Rural Communities*. Boulder, CO: Westview Press, pp. 151–168.

Wilkinson, K.P. 1991. *The Community in Rural America*. Westport, CT: Greenwood Press.

Zekeri, A.A., K.P. Wilkinson, and C.R. Humphrey. 1994. Past activeness, solidarity, and local development efforts, *Rural Sociology*, 59(2), 216–235.

ⓢ | PROBLEM SOLVING AND DISCUSSION ACTIVITIES

1. Tourism development may threaten rurality as well as generate social costs. What are the characteristics of rural communities that make them vulnerable to such threats and costs? Select a rural community that is pursuing tourism to some degree and use the technique of "windshield reconnaissance" (i.e., an initial step in a research or planning project whereby the researcher or planner drives through the study community to make initial observations) to formulate an opinion about this area's potential vulnerability to the loss of ambience and other social costs associated with tourism development. Try to observe interactions among community residents to determine whether this is a community wherein people are likely to come together to address issues of shared concern.

2. Collect secondary data for a tourism-dependent town. Identify statistics that describe the area. Also, look for history books and other references. Use this information to address the following questions: How would you describe this area (geographically, politically, demographically, economically)? How important is tourism to the local economy? How far is the area from metropolitan areas? Why would this be important? Where do tourists come from, what type of people come, when and why do they come? How many come? Is tourism growing/declining? Is tourism a major industry? Prepare a brief that summarizes and interprets the relevance of this information for tourism in this community. Assume that this brief is to be presented to the local chamber of commerce, which would like to see more tourism development in this town.

3. Design a procedure for identifying key informants in a community. Why would you choose certain individuals and not others? Prepare a list of key and action informants and/or the organizations they represent that would be relevant to a specific community of interest to you.

4. It has been suggested that rural areas in some parts of the United States have not always been as effective as their urban counterparts in capturing tourist dollars. Why might this be the case? To what extent is this true for rural areas in other parts of the world? What steps can rural communities take to strengthen their position? What costs might the community incur if it focuses only on economic goals?

5. To what extent are social costs and threats to the ambience of an area relevant in larger urban centers? Why? Substantiate your response using "real-life" examples drawn from secondary source materials and/or personal observations.

6. Critique the concept of participation readiness. Be sure to include what you consider to be the strengths and weaknesses of the concept. Indicate whether it is a useful concept for rural tourism development. Justify your opinion.

7. Assume the role of a regional tourism planner for a rural area with which you are familiar.
   a. What type of tourism development would you encourage? Why?
   b. How would this form of tourism development impact the region's rurality and what would you do about this?
   c. How would this form of tourism impact the economy of the host community?

  d. What are potential social impacts of the type of tourism development you are suggesting, and how would you overcome them/capitalize on them?

  e. How would you encourage local participation?

  f. How would you assess participation readiness in the region? How could you increase participation readiness for this form of tourism development in the region?

  g. What other factors would you consider to ensure successful development in the region?

15

An Approach to Community-Based Tourism Planning in the Baffin Region, Canada's Far North

A RETROSPECTIVE

 *Liz Addison*

ℊ | K E Y   L E A R N I N G   P O I N T S

- Sensitive community-based tourism planning requires that residents be involved throughout the planning process in a two-way exchange of information and views.
- Vehicles to provide residents with ongoing control over tourism development (including physical development, programs and services, and marketing) should be established as part of a community-based tourism plan.
- Recommended tourism developments and programs should complement traditional lifestyles, while providing employment and business opportunities.
- Despite sensitive planning, community participation and implementation of plans may be constrained by factors relating to the lack of formal education, business experience, and support from lending institutions, insufficient awareness and understanding of tourism opportunities, and the activities of government agencies in protecting their own investments and those of established private sector businesses. Such constraints should be acknowledged early in the planning process, and means to mitigate them should be developed.

INTRODUCTION

The Baffin Region is a fascinating and starkly beautiful part of Canada's far north. Tourism development is a relatively new phenomenon in this part of the world. In the early 1980s, when the *Baffin Regional Tourism Planning Project* (BRTPP) was initiated, tourism development in this region was largely the work of entrepreneurs from the "south." The low participation rate by aboriginal northerners had resulted in some antagonism between native residents and tourism operators as well as resource conflicts at a time when resources were already being strained by a rapidly expanding native population and when employment opportunities for native northerners were in short supply. The BRTPP was commissioned by the Territorial Government's (GNWT) Department of Economic Development and Tourism (ED&T) to alleviate some of these problems by stimulating the interest and participation of native residents in the tourism industry.

This chapter describes an approach to community-based tourism planning in a remote area that was to (1) promote culturally and environmentally appropriate tourism development and marketing, (2) involve local residents in the tourism planning process, and (3) provide economic and social benefits to local residents.

Ten years following completion of the BRTPP, a study of the impact of community-based tourism planning in one of the region's most visited communities—Pangnirtung—was conducted. It was concluded that, despite well-intentioned planning and educational efforts, "this type of development [had] not given the community control over tourism. Rather, it [had] been a means for greater community involvement in economic development" (Reimer and Dialla, 1992).

The BRTPP was one of the first major Canadian planning initiatives in what has become widely known as "ecotourism." Ecotourism opportunities that claim to be sensitive to local cultures and natural systems have become increasingly attractive to tourist markets and tourism marketers alike. This chapter also reviews recent literature on the merits and limitations of ecotourism as a context within which the BRTPP can be assessed.

ECOTOURISM AND TOURISM DEVELOPMENT IN SMALL COMMUNITIES: CONTEMPORARY PERSPECTIVES AND ISSUES

One of the fastest-growing tourism sectors and the subject of a great number of recent publications and conferences, ecotourism[1] is a manifestation of growing environmental and social awareness in the developed world, including awareness of the negative impacts caused by mass tourism. This phenomenon, which has been given many names (e.g., alternative, appropriate, sustainable,[2] progressive, soft, sensitive, green, nature, postindustrial, responsive, responsible,[3] and other usually approbative terms) has been characterized as follows:

- "Travel to enjoy the world's amazing diversity of natural life and human culture without causing damage to either" (Cater and Lowman, 1994, Foreward).
- "Responsible travel that conserves the environment and sustains the well-being of local people" (Orams, 1995, p. 5—quoting the United States Ecotourism Society's definition of ecotourism).
- "An enlightening nature travel experience that contributes to conservation of the ecosystem, while respecting the integrity of host communities" (Wight, 1993, p. 3—as defined by the Canadian Environmental Advisory Council Workshop on Ecotourism, 1992).
- "Independent, drifter travel by relatively small numbers of people to remote destinations, principally in the developing world" (Jones, 1992, p. 102).
- "Development . . . focusing simultaneously on the integration of major elements, closely charted development, conservation, cultural compatibility, and local in-

put" (Farrell and Runyan, 1991, p. 35—summarizing the conclusions from the World Commission on Environment and Development, also known as the Brundtland Report, 1987).

- A "supposedly more caring, aware form of tourism" (Wheeller, 1991, p. 92).
- "An alternative to the least desired or most undesired type of tourism, or essentially what is known as mass tourism . . . an alternative to the Costa Bravas, the Daytona Strips, Atlantic Citys and Blackpools of the world . . . alternative to large numbers, tasteless and ubiquitous development, environmental and social alienation and homogenization" (Butler, 1990, p. 40).
- "Fairer contacts and greater mutual understanding and respect between business and leisure travellers and their hosts . . . travel responsive to non-Westernized cultures and environments, reciprocity in travel, [helping to] conserve the diversity of the world's human communities and natural habitats" (Millman, 1989, p. 277).

The common thread is the principle that tourism should not compromise the integrity of the resources upon which it is based and, ideally, both the tourist and the host community should benefit from tourism activity. Widespread endorsement of this principle is manifested even in contemporary media culture. The "Prime Directive," in the ever-popular television series *Star Trek* and its successors, ensures that travelers in the farthest reaches of the galaxy do not interfere with the natural order of things or with the evolution of "alien" cultures (Müller, 1994).

Recent literature on the subject is generally divided between those who see ecotourism as a positive trend (Choy, 1991; Millman, 1989) and those who see it either as no better (and possibly worse) than what it purports to replace—that is, mass tourism (Butler, 1990; Munt, 1994; Wheeller, 1991, 1992)—or as cynical marketing "hype" (Wight, 1993). Many who view ecotourism as generally positive are aware that it is far from a panacea for community economic development (Cater, 1993; Hughes, 1995; Jones, 1992).

However, no one is likely to quibble with the irreproachable aims of *The Columbia Charter* (Vancouver, B.C., 1988) to encourage tourism that (1) promotes mutual understanding, trust, and goodwill, (2) reduces economic inequities, (3) develops in an integrated manner, with the full participation of local host communities, (4) improves the quality of life, (5) protects and preserves the environment, both built and natural, and other local resources, and (6) contributes to the world conservation strategy of sustainable development.

The differences in attitudes towards ecotourism seem to stem from variations in the degree to which one believes that these goals are achievable and the extent to which one believes that the various tourism industry stakeholders sincerely subscribe to these goals.

The concept of, and attitudes towards, ecotourism are perhaps best understood if one looks at it as a continuum of paradigms bounded by polar extremes (Orams, 1995). Quoting Miller and Kaae (1993, pp. 30, 35–41), Orams (1995) presents ecotourism as a conceptual continuum where, at one pole, all tourism can be viewed as ecotourism and, at the other, no tourism can be viewed as ecotourism. At one extreme, humans are viewed as living organisms whose behavior is natural and who are, therefore, incapable of behaving "un-ecotouristically." Thus, all tourism is ecotourism. At the other extreme, all tourism is seen to have negative impacts on the natural world. Ecotourism is, in this view, impossible because any tourism will have some form of negative effect.

Most perceptions of ecotourism lie somewhere between these extremes, classified according to expectations of human responsibility. High-level expectations, which few ecotourism operations satisfy, insist on actively positive contributions to the environment, including changes to public attitudes and behavior. Low-level expectations of human responsibility accept more passive approaches that seek simply to appreciate the natural environment and minimize damage to it. Wight (1994) presents a series of principles that can be used to determine where along this continuum any specific tourism activity lies:

- It should not degrade the resource and should be developed in an environmentally sound manner.
- It should provide long-term benefits (conservation, scientific, social, cultural, or economic) to the resource, the local community, and the industry.
- It should provide first-hand, participatory, and enlightening experiences for the tourist.
- It should involve education among all parties: local communities, government, nongovernmental organizations, industry, and tourists (before, during, and after the trip).
- It should encourage all-party recognition of the intrinsic values of the resource.
- It should involve acceptance of the resource on its own terms and recognition of its limits, which involves supply-oriented management.
- It should promote understanding and involve partnerships between many players which could include government, nongovernmental organizations, industry, scientists, and local residents (both before and during the trip).
- It should promote ethical responsibilities and behavior towards the natural and cultural environment by all players.

The impacts of ecotourism on the Baffin Region's small aboriginal communities are comparable in many ways to the impacts of tourism on other small-scale societies around the world. Issues relevant to these situations are discussed by Mansperger (1995), who compares tourism's impacts on communities on Yap Island in Micronesia with impacts among the Masai in Kenya and the Yagua of the Peruvian and Columbian Amazon. Mansperger notes the many positive impacts that tourism can have on indigenous populations, including (1) economic growth and development (e.g., jobs and business opportunities), (2) increased government expenditure on tourism infrastructure that may also benefit residents (e.g., improvements to roads, water supply and sewage treatment, electrical servicing), (3) cross-cultural education/communication, and (4) preservation of local traditions.

He also identifies potential costs, some of which are particularly relevant to the Baffin Region situation, including (1) disruptions to normal economic or subsistence activities, (2) adoption of tourists' consumer behavior and expectations, (3) interference with social reciprocity and kinship obligations and increased social differentiation and inequality as a result of the amount of money flowing into an area, (4) social factionalism caused by disagreements over whether tourism should be allowed to occur at all, and (5) allocation of limited public sector capital resources to tourism infrastructure over the needs of the resident community.

"It is one of the great inequities of tourism that people in small-scale societies often incur these costs without receiving many of the benefits. By owning the local hotels, restaurants, . . . and most of the other tourism infrastructure, foreign tour businesses are able to control tourism processes and capture most of the revenues" (Mansperger, 1995, p. 92).[4] Quoting Dogan (1989), Mansperger notes that "often the net effect of tourism among an unindustrialized, small-scale population is to weaken the people's cultural system and autonomy and place them in a higher state of dependency on the outside world" (Mansperger, 1995, p. 92).

Mansperger's conclusions on how to minimize damaging impacts of tourism on small-scale communities are also relevant to the Baffin situation:

- The scale of tourism must be kept low to moderate. The fewer the tourists, the lesser the impact.
- Tourists should be educated on matters of local etiquette and how to avoid intrusions and other disruptive situations.
- There should be local involvement in the decision-making process concerning touristic developments.
- There should be host control or ownership of touristic infrastructure.
- Indigenous land utilization systems should be preserved.

Within the context of these different ways of looking at ecotourism, and especially ecotourism in small-scale communities, the Baffin Region case study raises a number of questions concerning tourism in remote, sensitive communities. Prior to discussing the process associated with development of the BRTPP, an overview of the Baffin Region is presented.

THE BAFFIN REGION: LOCATIONAL CONTEXT AND BACKGROUND

Location   The Baffin Region is the easternmost of six travel zones within Canada's Northwest Territories (see Figure 15.1). This sparsely populated expanse encompasses Baffin and Ellesmere Island, the Melville Peninsula on the mainland to the west, and numerous smaller islands stretching from James Bay in the south to the North Pole. Most of its largely Inuit population of about 10,000 live in one of 14 small communities that dot the coastline. A small percentage live in outpost camps.

Settlement   Prior to the twentieth century, there were no permanent settlements in the Baffin Region. Its nomadic or seminomadic inhabitants followed the migratory animals that were their chief source of food and material for clothing, shelter, and fuel. The dispersion of the Inuit population maximized the harvesting potential of limited biological resources. It was also the policy of early fur traders to maintain a dispersed Inuit population to exploit wildlife resources over as large an area as possible.

Settlements were established when the Inuit saw the opportunity to obtain commercial goods by working for, or trading with, fixed enterprises or stations (e.g., Hudson's Bay Posts, DEW Line Stations) or when they wished to remain close to a fixed service (e.g., missions, hospitals, schools). As more people moved to permanent settlements,

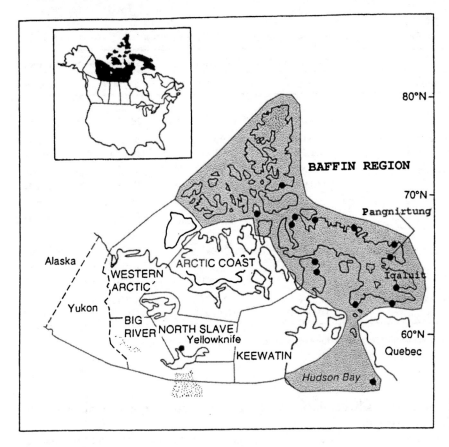

Figure 15.1
Northwest Territories
travel zones. (Adapted
from Anderson, 1991,
p. 210.)

● **Communities**

more government services have been provided so the need for most Inuit to remain in a settlement has been intensified.

The major migration of Inuit from the land to permanent communities did not take place until the 1960s. Most Inuit elders were born and raised on the land in vastly different circumstances than they find themselves in today. The great majority of the region's population now live in permanent settlements with basic services such as power, air transportation, water supply, education, medical services, and some form of sanitary service.

The Tourism Industry in the Early 1980s In the early 1980s, the Baffin Region's tourism industry was at a very early stage of development relative to other parts of Canada and the less remote parts of the Northwest Territories. As indicated in Table 15.1, the Baffin Region's tourism industry in 1979 consisted of only 27 businesses catering to a total of about 1280 summer pleasure visitors.

Although tourism resources were plentiful and interest in the region had increased dramatically in the late 1970s, services and infrastructure were inadequate and the resident population, who had very limited awareness of the opportunities presented by tour-

TABLE 15.1
Travel Data for Northwest Territories Travel Zones, 1979 and 1988

Tourism Zone	Number of Travel Businesses		Summer Pleasure Visitors	
	1979	1988	1979	1988
Big River	45 (23.2%)	64 (17.2%)	6,320 (28.1%)	8,250 (25.0%)
Northern Slave (Northern Frontier)	51 (26.3%)	90 (24.2%)	8,300 (36.9%)	11,350 (34.4%)
Western Arctic	40 (20.6%)	59 (15.9%)	6,080 (27.0%)	8,250 (25.0%)
Arctic Coast	10 (5.2%)	23 (6.2%)	200 (0.9%)	690 (2.1%)
Keewatin	21 (10.8%)	55 (14.8%)	320 (1.4%)	1,720 (5.2%)
Baffin	27 (13.9%)	81 (21.8%)	1,280 (5.7%)	2,740 (8.3%)
All Northwest Territories	194 (100.0%)	372 (100.1%)[a]	22,500 (100.0%)	33,000 (100.0%)

[a] Totals may not equal 100 percent due to rounding.
Source: Adapted from Anderson (1991).

ism, had neither the skills nor the financial resources to capitalize on even those opportunities that they recognized.

Tourism development had, for the most part, been the work of entrepreneurs who were not native to the area. The low participation rate by native northerners had resulted in some antagonism between local residents and tourism operators as well as resource conflicts at a time when resources were already being strained by the rapidly expanding native population and when employment opportunities for native northerners were in short supply. Moreover, development had been haphazard. Resources had not been adequately assessed, and development coordination had been almost nonexistent.

The Baffin Region combines adventure, history, scenery, and wildlife experiences with unique cultural opportunities. Its relatively small number of pleasure visitors pursue a wide range of activities. There is no "typical" visit, and a trip to the region may range from a fishing camp holiday to a snowmobile safari, from a flightseeing trip to the North Pole to a one-night sightseeing tour from Toronto or Montreal to Iqaluit (formerly Frobisher Bay) (see Figure 15.1). Auyuittuq National Park, which draws on the order of 400–500 visitors per year, is the region's most significant attraction.

Most tourist activity takes place during the summer, when the days are long and relatively warm and when the seas are relatively ice-free. Spring, before the ice breaks up, is a less popular tourist season with considerable potential for growth. Little tourist activity takes place once the ice freezes in the fall due to extreme cold and long hours of darkness.

Although the region's natural and cultural resource base is of a high caliber with inherent potential to attract a diversity of markets, the tourism industry has suffered from an underdeveloped tourism infrastructure which severely constrains the number and type of tourists that can be attracted and accommodated. When the BRTPP began in 1981, many communities had only the most basic visitor accommodations, often consisting of a small transient center with dormitories, nonflush toilets (whose plastic "honey bags" had to be removed and left outside for pick up), and self-catering foodservices (i.e., a kitchen with a sink that drained into the street). Only the larger communities had restaurants, and even these were of dubious quality in terms of both food and service. Outside the regional center of Iqaluit, "full-service" hotels generally provided dormitory accommodation with dining rooms that had fixed menus and fixed schedules (i.e., guests ate whatever was offered whenever it was served).

When the study began, the only direct regularly scheduled passenger flights into the Baffin Region from southern Canada were provided by Nordair, which flew seven times a week to Iqaluit. There were also indirect connections via Yellowknife, as well as flights from the northern communities of Timmins (Ontario) and Lynn Lake (Manitoba). Internally, regular passenger services provided connections among the region's 14 communities. Also, a few charter services operated out of some Baffin communities.

THE BAFFIN REGIONAL TOURISM PLANNING PROJECT

Community-Based Tourism Planning Objectives The *Baffin Regional Tourism Planning Project* (BRTPP) was commissioned in 1981 by the Territorial Government's (GNWT) Department of Economic Development and Tourism (ED&T) to provide a blueprint for tourism development and marketing, as well as to serve as an educational tool to promote the full participation of native residents. Table 15.2 identifies the specific objectives of the planning project.

ED&T administrators believed that a community-based approach to tourism, with an emphasis on "learn/observe/experience" rather than resource-consumptive activities, was the most appropriate strategy for the Baffin Region. Tourism activity and development centered in the region's small communities would minimize infrastructural and service requirements while maximizing economic and social benefits for local residents. Administrators also recognized that the tourism industry could only develop in these communities with the full cooperation and participation of their primarily native populations.[5] It was, after all, on their behalf that the industry was being developed as an alternative to the traditional subsistence economy that was no longer able to support the burgeoning population with its expectations for a higher standard of living.

The community-based approach, which called for community advice, participation, and support in all proposed tourism plans and projects, represented both an economic and political shift in GNWT policy and practice. An ED&T policy statement produced in 1983 (after completion of the BRTPP) clearly articulates the GNWT's intent with regard to community-based tourism (Reimer and Dialla, 1992, p. 10, quoting ED&T, 1983, p. 14):

The intention of community-based tourism is to allow communities to use the tourism industry as a means to self-determination, especially economically. This Government's role in com-

TABLE 15.2

Baffin Regional Tourism Planning Project Objectives

To develop a planning process that will permit and encourage the involvement of community residents in data gathering and analysis, strategy formulation, and plan preparation.

To increase awareness of residents of the possible benefits to be derived from tourism and the type of demands that tourists may place upon the community.

To identify and examine the tourism and recreational resources of the Baffin Region in general, and each of its communities in detail, and to describe the general and specific opportunities and constraints to the development and growth of the tourism industry in the Baffin Region.

To identify and describe the market potential of the identified tourism and recreation resources.

Within the context of market potential, to isolate and describe specific, realistic tourism development/investment opportunities within each community and throughout the Baffin Region.

To outline the general economic feasibility of various types of development.

To develop/recommend specific policies, guidelines, programs, and public/private sector actions required to realize the development/investment opportunities.

To prepare a five-year general tourism development strategy for the Baffin Region that integrates and provides a context for the implementation of the individual community tourism development plans.

To provide a synthesis of supporting and background information to support ongoing planning activities.

Source: Marshall Macklin Monaghan Ltd. (1981a, p. 2).

munity-based tourism is that of a consultant in the planning stages, and that of a provider of direct financial support in the developmental stage.

The community-based approach meant that the most important, and probably the most challenging, aspect of the study was the development of a public participation program that would make clear to local residents the benefits and potential hazards of the tourism industry, thereby enabling them to reach an educated decision as to whether they wanted tourism development, and under what conditions. The public participation program not only determined the aspirations and concerns of local residents, but also tapped their vast knowledge of the land and its resources.

GNWT Tourism Policy—"Good" Versus "Bad" Tourism When the BRTPP began, there was no comprehensive official policy for the development of tourism in the Northwest Territories. However, ED&T had made an effort to define a tourism policy that would be understandable to native people whose cooperation they hoped to elicit. According to this policy, tourism development was divided into that which was "good" and that which was "bad." The GNWT's definitions of "good" and "bad" will be familiar to anyone who has read recent literature on ecotourism and tourism impacts.

"Good" tourism was defined as that which (1) was beneficial to northerners, (2) resulted in northern purchases and profit, (3) resulted in wildlife preservation, (4) preserved traditional values and lifestyles, (5) resulted in northern employment and management, (6) resulted in secondary infrastructure benefits, (7) informed visitors and promoted understanding, (8) did not overwhelm communities, (9) resulted in local control and ownership, and (10) advocated external investments directed towards these ends.

"Bad" tourism, on the other hand, was seen to be characterized by (1) overcapitalization, (2) fast profits, (3) "snotty" tourists, and (4) erroneous tourist expectations and perceptions.

Although priorities for "good" tourism had not been established, the most important aspect was that tourism should create jobs complementary to traditional lifestyles. ED&T also believed that tourism in the eastern Arctic should emphasize small, low capital, seasonal businesses requiring limited infrastructure. The GNWT's work with native people had established that the priorities of northern residents emphasized local control, local benefits, and local management.

BRTPP
Fieldwork

FIELDWORK OBJECTIVES   Much of the study was directed toward three objectives:

- To help the Baffin Region communities understand what tourism is, as well as what benefits and other impacts might result from tourism development.
- To determine if community residents were interested in developing tourism and, if they were, what kind of tourism and under what conditions.
- To evaluate tourism potential by examining the resources in and around each community.

In keeping with these objectives, visits to each of the communities that ranged from one to two weeks each comprised a major part of the study.

FIELDWORK PREPARATION   To prepare for this extensive fieldwork, the planning team undertook a number of tasks:

- They conducted extensive secondary source research to ensure a basic understanding of the region in general and the individual communities in particular. This research culminated in the preparation of a *Preliminary Background Information Report* (Marshall Macklin Monaghan, 1981a) that distilled an enormous range of literature (much of which had been produced by the federal or territorial governments) on topics that included, for example, tourism and recreation resources and activities, natural resources, climate, community profiles and demographic characteristics, native issues, historic and archaeological resources, and relevant policies and legislation.
- They prepared a taped slide presentation (with soundtrack) to be shown to residents to explain the concept of tourism, including why tourists might be interested in visiting their community, what tourists needed and expected, and how the community might benefit from the tourism industry.
- They prepared a newsletter that explained the study and tourism in general.
- They made arrangements to ensure that residents were aware of the study before the planners arrived (including notices, with photographs of the planners, placed at key community gathering places such as the local co-op store, and announcements on community radio stations).
- They developed inventory sheets to ensure that information obtained by each of the planners was comprehensive and consistent in both form and content.

FIELDWORK ACTIVITIES   Based on the methodology developed during a pilot project in the Baffin Island hamlet of Pangnirtung (Marshall Macklin Monaghan, 1981b), tourism planners carried out a rigorous schedule of fieldwork within the remaining 12 communities.[6] During these community visits, the planners spoke with as many local residents as possible and evaluated each community's potential for tourism development.

In each community, the planner worked with an Area Economic Development Officer (AEDO) from ED&T who was regularly assigned to and familiar with that community. The role of the AEDOs was critical because they knew, and were known by, the local residents whose support and participation would be essential to community-based tourism development. Assisted by the AEDO and, where necessary, by a local interpreter, the planner undertook a series of activities to ensure that residents were aware of the study and its objectives and to encourage their participation in the study and in tourism in general, including the following:

- He or she arranged for radio announcement(s) advising of the arrival of a tourism planner and the AEDO.[7]
- He or she distributed the previously prepared newsletters to each household. In some of the smaller communities, these were delivered personally to provide opportunities for any initial questions or comments.[8]
- He or she organized one or two phone-in shows on the local radio station to provide listeners with an opportunity to ask questions of the planner and the AEDO, as well as to make comments about tourism and/or the study.
- He or she invited residents to a drop-in session at a convenient location to speak with the planner and the AEDO.
- He or she held group meetings with, for example, local council,[9] community elders, the hunters and trappers association, the land claims committee, the education society, the recreation committee, arts and crafts groups, the historical society, and senior school classes.
- He or she met with individuals who had, or might have had, some connection with the local tourism industry (e.g., elected officials, government representatives, hamlet managers, co-op managers, community leaders, outfitters, hotel owners, transportation operators, educators, church representatives, people with knowledge of local resources).

Community Attitudes As the study progressed, a number of prevalent attitudes and concerns within the communities became apparent:

- Most communities[10] were generally in favor of tourism if growth was slow and if residents were able to maintain a high degree of control over numbers of visitors, timing of visits, and the activities of visitors.
- Residents wanted more information about the local benefits of tourism.
- Many experiences with tourists had been negative, and concerns were expressed about the intrusive impact of uncontrolled tourism on existing lifestyles.
- Many residents believed that tourists should not be allowed to access traditional hunting and fishing areas.
- Most communities wanted to control the tourism business and be involved in specific tourism developments.
- Residents wanted tourists to have an Inu[11] as a guide.
- Residents believed that tourists should know more about the likes and dislikes of the Inuit before coming to the region and should not ask too many questions.

Reporting The recommended regional tourism development strategy (1982a, b) proposed the following:

> . . . To stimulate the development of predominantly non-consumptive community-centered tourism in an integrated network of tourism destination areas and destination communities that are linked together by air transportation or boat tours. Development of tourism facilities, attractions and programs will take place along specific themes that will attempt to reflect the natural, cultural and historic resources and lifestyles of the region.
>
> These will aim to attract specific specialty markets to provide structured, programmed opportunities that can be packaged for small group visitation. The bulk of the tourism development will be initiated by the public sector and managed and operated by the private sector. The individual community's decision regarding tourism development will ultimately decide the type and extent of tourism development that will take place in that community.

Table 15.3 summarizes the intent of the strategy.

To promote locally initiated tourism development, reports for each community were written in relatively simple language that could be read by people with basic English reading skills or that could be readily translated into Inuktitu.[12] Each report contained a summary of findings, conclusions, and recommendations from the study, including an inventory of resources, a description of the community field trip activities, and a series of sheets describing tourism development opportunities and recommendations. The local government office of each community was also provided with copies of other study documents, including the following:

- *Background Information Report*. General information about the Baffin Region, including roles and responsibilities of government agencies and major Inuit organizations, land use and ownership characteristics, economic activity, climate, tourism resources and activities, and tourist markets.

TABLE 15.3
Intent of the Baffin Region Tourism Strategy

To develop a hierarchy of tourist destination areas, attractions and facilities that will define the role each community will play in the strategy.

To develop specific tourism attractions in or near each community based on the potential of cultural, natural, or historic resources.

To develop attractions, facilities, events, and programs that stress resource nonconsumptive, "learn, observe, and experience" forms of tourist activities.

To structure the primary tourism activities with each element of the experience coordinated to ensure that the tourist receives a quality experience.

To attract carefully selected and targeted markets, primarily from the group/package tour market.

To encourage extended stays by tourists in the region during all seasons.

To minimize the impact of the tourism industry on traditional lifestyles.

To provide the Inuit with the required skills to operate the tourism developments.

To minimize competition on a regional basis between select destination areas.

Source: Marshall Macklin Monaghan Ltd. (1982a).

- *Planning Process Report.* Methods used to complete the study.
- *Regional Tourism Development Strategy.* Recommendations for tourism development programs for the region as a whole.
- *Technical Appendix.* Additional research and findings.

REVIEW OF COMMUNITY-BASED TOURISM PLANNING IN THE BAFFIN REGION—TEN YEARS AFTER

Ten years after the completion of the BRTPP, a report was prepared to examine the results of the community-based tourism planning initiative. The hamlet of Pangnirtung,[13] the subject of the 1980–1981 pilot project, was selected for analysis. While each Baffin community's tourism industry has developed somewhat differently, the Pangnirtung experience provides an indication of the political, economic, educational, and cultural consequences of community-based tourism development in the eastern Arctic region.

Sponsored by Pangnirtung Hamlet Council and ED&T, the research project was carried out cooperatively by two investigators (one from McMaster University and the other from Pangnirtung) who conducted about 100 interviews, studied files, and coordinated household surveys. The report (Reimer and Dialla, 1992) summarized the conclusions of nine months of research as follows:

> Overall, this type of development has not given the community control over tourism. Rather, it has been a means for greater community involvement in economic development. In the final analysis, government agencies have held financial, and hence political control over the tourism development in Pangnirtung. Tourism's economic benefits have been significant and appropriate. In particular, local people have been able to supplement their family income by informal, direct sales to tourists. However, training and management skills have not kept pace with capital development. This has presented problems in terms of keeping command over the industry at the local level.

This 1992 report ends with a number of more detailed conclusions that can be summarized as follows:

- The goals of community control[14] over tourism had not yet been fulfilled. Tourism development remained largely driven and controlled by ED&T.
- A local Tourism Committee had taken on an advisory role rather than the decision-making and initiating role that had been intended. It had also tended to involve itself primarily in capital projects, neglecting other more general tourism issues such as awareness, training, management, and industry growth. Hence, when the capital projects (largely government-driven) were complete, the Tourism Committee had ceased to function. It was unprepared to take control of the operational phase of development.
- Factors thought to be limiting community participation in the tourism industry included the lack of formal education, business experience and support from lending institutions, insufficient awareness and understanding of tourism industry opportunities, and the activities of government agencies in protecting their own investments and those of established private sector businesses.

- Insufficient training opportunities and an overall underinvestment in human resource development were repeatedly identified as reasons for limited community participation in the tourism industry. It was also stated that training had not kept pace with the growing demands for quality service in the tourism industry. Moreover, women felt excluded from training opportunities.
- Although the general attitude towards tourists was good, community awareness of tourism had decreased over the years. This was particularly true of Pangnirtung's youth, who did not recognize tourism as a potential career choice and were developing negative attitudes towards tourists.
- Some local residents believed that the historic picture presented to tourists of their culture and history (one which emphasized the whaling period and early postcontact history) presented a rather narrow, one-sided view of Inuit culture and history. It was also widely felt that community elders were not sufficiently involved in cultural interpretation.

On a more positive note, the 1992 report concluded that community-based tourism was, for the most part, an appropriate form of economic development. Although relatively few formal "wage economy" jobs had been created by the tourism industry (six person-years in 1991), tourist visitation provided an opportunity for local individuals to supplement their family incomes (through occasional outfitting, the sale of art and crafts) while pursuing a more traditional land-based economy. Although the community had not taken control, community-based tourism was seen to be an appropriate step towards greater political self-determination.

CONCLUSION

The BRTPP and its preceding pilot project in Pangnirtung illustrate many of the principles and practices now being promoted under the banner of "ecotourism." Being among the early efforts to plan for environmentally and socially sensitive tourism, these projects can now be evaluated for their effectiveness in creating a form of tourism that is truly beneficial to the native population.

This chapter actually raises more questions than it answers. The government department and its planning consultants followed all the rules of sensitive community-based planning and ecotourism in that (1) native residents were involved throughout the planning process in a two-way exchange of information and views, (2) residents were provided with vehicles for ongoing control over tourism development, and (3) recommended tourism developments and programs were complementary to traditional lifestyles, while providing employment and business opportunities. The original tourism planning work was carried out with great care, sensitivity, and concern for the interests of the native residents of Baffin Region communities.

Nevertheless, as revealed in the 1992 report, the results have been mixed and the objectives of this extensive work have not been entirely fulfilled. Although some development has taken place and some economic benefits have been generated, the Baffin Region's communities have not obtained the level of control over tourism they would have wished. It remains for future planners to determine whether alternative approaches to tourism development and administration might more fully satisfy the stated objectives of the BRTPP. Among the questions that remain unanswered are:

- What might have been done differently to overcome the obstacles that continue to limit the benefits accruing to native residents from the tourism industry? What might still be done?
- What are realistic objectives for tourism in remote, relatively undeveloped communities?
- Must all goals be satisfied before one concludes that tourism has been a positive influence? At what point, if any, does one conclude that tourism has been a negative influence?

ACKNOWLEDGMENTS

Many thanks to Garry Singer and Rick Hamburg of GNWT Department of Economic Development and Tourism for their kind permission to use this study and for providing me with the invaluable updated material.

NOTES

1. See Chapters 11 and 20 for additional discussion relating to ecotourism principles and philosophies.
2. See Chapters 4, 5, 7, 8, 17, 18, 22, and 23 for more detailed discussion of sustainable tourism and sustainable tourism development principles and concepts.
3. See Chapter 1 for an overview of responsible tourism philosophies.
4. See Chapters 4 and 7 for additional discussion of the roles and implications of foreign tour operators.
5. See Chapters 5, 9, 11, 12, 14, and 16–19 for further discussion and examples of community attitudes and involvement in tourism planning and development processes.
6. Three tourism planners were each assigned four communities. Pangnirtung had already been surveyed as part of the Pangnirtung Pilot Project (Marshall Macklin Monaghan, 1981b). Nanisivik, a mostly non-Inuit mining company community, was not involved in the public participation process, but was surveyed as a potential tourism resource. The author of this chapter conducted fieldwork in Broughton Island, (Marshall Macklin Monaghan, 1982c), Clyde River, Arctic Bay, and Pond Inlet.
7. Radio was an important communication medium for the planners because every community had a locally run Inuktitut-language radio station that was regularly listened to by a large percentage of residents.
8. All but one of the communities had fewer than 1000 residents. Most had populations under 500.
9. Community organization is an important aspect of the social structure in contemporary Inuit society. In the communities of the Baffin Region, various community groups or special-purpose committees act in an advisory capacity to provide expertise to public agencies making decisions related to the provision of social and economic services, land use, and the preservation and/or harvesting of renewable resources. In most of the communities in the region, the most important committees were the hunters and trappers association, land claims committee, education advisory committee, housing association, and alcohol committee.
10. In the early 1980s, four of the Baffin Region communities were "designated settlements", eight were "hamlets", and one (Frobisher Bay, now Iqaluit) had attained "town" status.
11. Singular form of Inuit.

12. The Inuit language.
13. Next to the regional center of Iqaluit, Pangnirtung has the region's largest population (about 900 in 1980) and most highly developed tourism industry.
14. See Chapters 7 and 9 for additional discussion of changing and balancing the power structures within the tourism industry.

REFERENCES

Anderson, M.J. 1991. Problems with tourism development in Canada's eastern Arctic, *Tourism Management*, September, 209–220.

Butler, R.W. 1990. Alternative tourism: pious hope or Trojan horse? *Journal of Travel Research*, Winter, 40–45.

Cater, E. 1993. Ecotourism in the third world—problems for sustainable tourism development, *Tourism Management*, April, 85–90.

Cater, E. and G. Lowman. 1994. *Ecotourism: A Sustainable Option?* New York: John Wiley & Sons.

Choy, D. J.L. 1991. Tourism planning: the case for market failure, *Tourism Management*, December, 313–330.

Farrell, B.H. and D. Runyon. 1991. Ecology and toursim, *Annals of Tourism Research*, 18, 26–40.

Hughes, G. 1995. The cultural construction of sustainable tourism, *Tourism Management*, 16(1), 49–59.

Jones, A. 1992. Is there a real "alternative" tourism? *Tourism Management*, March, 102–103.

Mansperger, M.C. 1995. Tourism and cultural change in small-scale societies, *Human Organization*, 54(1), 87–94.

Marshall Macklin Monaghan Ltd. 1981a. *Preliminary Background Information Report, Baffin Regional Tourism Planning Project.* Report prepared for the Department of Economic Development and Tourism, Government of the Northwest Territories.

Marshall Macklin Monaghan Ltd. 1981b. *Pangnirtung Community Tourism Study.* Report prepared for the Department of Economic Development and Tourism, Government of the Northwest Territories.

Marshall Macklin Monaghan Ltd. 1982a. *Executive Summary Report, Baffin Regional Tourism Planning Project.* Report prepared for the Department of Economic Development and Tourism, Government of the Northwest Territories.

Marshall Macklin Monaghan Ltd. 1982b. *Regional Strategy Report, Baffin Regional Tourism Planning Project.* Report prepared for the Department of Economic Development and Tourism, Government of the Northwest Territories.

Marshall Macklin Monaghan Ltd. 1982c. *Community Tourism Development Plan—Broughton Island, Baffin Regional Tourism Planning Project.* Report prepared for the Department of Economic Development and Tourism, Government of the Northwest Territories.

Miller, M.L. and B.C. Kaae. 1993. Coastal and marine ecotourism: a formula for sustainable development? *Trends*, 30, 35–41.

Millman, R. 1989. Pleasure seeking v the "greening" of world tourism, *Tourism Management*, December, 275–278.

Müller, P. 1994. *The American Dream Continued? The Crisis of the American Dream in the 1960s and Its Reflection in a Contemporary TV Series. Unpublished essay.* Denmark: University of Oldenburg.

Munt, I. 1994. Eco-tourism or ego-tourism? *Race & Class*, 36, 1.

Orams, M.B. 1995. Towards a more desirable form of ecotourism, *Tourism Management*, 16(1), 3–8.

Reimer, G. and A. Dialla. 1992. *Community Based Tourism Development in Pangnirtung, North-west Territories: Looking Back and Looking Ahead.* Report prepared for the Department of Economic Development and Tourism, Government of the Northwest Territories and the Hamlet of Pangnirtung.

Wheeler, B. 1991. Tourism's troubled times: responsible tourism is not the answer, *Tourism Management*, June, 91–96.

Wheeler, B. 1992. Is progressive tourism appropriate? *Tourism Management*, March, 104–105.

Wight, P. 1993. Ecotourism: ethics or eco-sell? *Journal of Travel Research*, Winter, 3–9.

Wight, P. 1994. Environmentally responsible marketing of tourism. In E. Cater and G. Lowman (eds.), *Ecotourism: A Sustainable Option?* New York: John Wiley & Sons.

℘ | PROBLEM SOLVING AND DISCUSSION ACTIVITIES

1. Overall, has the tourism industry in the Baffin Region been a positive or a negative force? Who has benefited most, and who has benefited least?

2. What level of responsibility for economic development should the tourism industry assume in the Baffin Region? Must tourism be a positive influence or simply avoid being a negative one?

3. Can tourism be developed in a region as ecologically and culturally sensitive as Canada's far north in a way that eliminates *all* negative environmental and social impacts? Is this a reasonable expectation?

4. At what point, if any, can one conclude that the economic benefits of tourism in the Baffin Region (existing and potential) outweigh its negative impacts?

5. Have the measures that have been taken to enhance the positive and minimize the negative aspects of tourism in the region been effective? What might have been done differently?

6. Comment on the public participation process of the BRTPP. Would you have done anything differently? Have the passage of time and the evolution of concepts and principles relating to sustainable and responsible tourism planning changed the way in which such a study would be conducted today?

7. If the local community is unprepared to initiate and control tourism development, should the government push its own agenda in the name of economic development? When is a community ready to take control of its own tourism industry? What actions can be initiated within the Baffin Region to help the local people to have more control?

8. What measures might be taken to train local residents in a relatively undeveloped region to take control of their own tourism industry?

9. Select an undeveloped remote destination and prepare an audiovisual presentation (i.e. videotape, slide show, multimedia computer program, etc.) to explain and promote tourism to the local residents, especially the youth.

10. Develop appropriate tour packages and marketing campaigns for a northern destination or other remote tourism destination.

16

Everything Must Be Connected to Everything Else

AN ECOSYSTEM APPROACH TO TOURISM DEVELOPMENT IN NORTHUMBERLAND COUNTY, ONTARIO, CANADA

 *Marion Joppe*

🎱 | KEY LEARNING POINTS

- There is an expectation that leadership will naturally be provided in the case of community-driven tourism. However, this should not be taken for granted. The establishment of interim leadership to provide balance, vision, and direction at the beginning of the process is essential.

- A workable method for achieving and maintaining political support must be identified early in the process. This is critical to facilitating both implementation and funding efforts. Councils need to be approached to obtain formal "buy in" and staff resources.

- A clear statement of principles at the beginning is critical to establishing norms of working and a framework for objectively setting priorities. Such guiding principles or values may also reduce the risk associated with the formation of cliques that can fracture the focus of community groups.

- A community development process must strive to involve a broad number of stakeholders and to ensure a high level of awareness among residents in general. This can prove to be very challenging, particularly with respect to process-oriented tasks.

- The composition of subcommittees should be based not solely on volunteerism, but also on the focus or theme of the community development process. The roles and responsibilities for all committees and subcommittees should be explicitly outlined. Committee members must be informed of the time commitment associated with a community-driven process. Volunteer and staff "burnout" is a reality, and it is a constant struggle to bring in new players.

INTRODUCTION

The rise in community consciousness in North America and Europe since the 1980s is due in part to a growing awareness of local heritage,[1] both natural and cultural, and its progressive loss. Local residents have become far more vocal in their desire to be involved in planning the economic future of their communities,[2] especially insofar as it impacts their quality of life and the natural environment. "With the trend toward decentralized decision-making and community action, plus tourism's dependence on destination area resources and goodwill, it is important to gauge the chances of successfully merging industry and community aspirations" (Murphy, 1988, p. 97).

Although much has been written about community development and community-driven planning, as well as about the principles that underpin them and the benefits to be derived, relatively little work has been conducted on the actual steps, trials, and tribulations of developing a successful and integrated community-driven tourism strategy.

This chapter documents a multijurisdictional community process (four municipalities in the western part of Northumberland County, Ontario) from its inception to the completion of the long-term strategy. Although influenced by factors such as the political will and financial resources of the community, the strength of its tourism industry, the civic-mindedness of community and business leaders, and past successes or failures with public participation, some of the lessons learned may help other communities to initiate a similar process and avoid at least some of the pitfalls that are otherwise likely to be encountered along the way.

COMMUNITY DEVELOPMENT AND COMMUNITY-DRIVEN PLANNING: CONTEMPORARY PERSPECTIVES AND ISSUES

A definition of community is important to understanding community development. Community is self-defining, based on a sense of shared purpose and common goals. It may be geographical or a community of interest. For example, communities built on heritage and cultural values may cluster together beyond municipal boundaries based on an assessment of the benefits of working together.

An ecosystem approach to community development requires that economic, social, and environmental structures and interests of communities work together to plan and implement development strategies. This process should be inclusive, involving all elements of a community. As Haywood (1988, p. 105) stated:

> The rationale is as follows—the positive and negative aspects of tourism (economic, social, and ecological) have their most profound impact in and on host communities. Whenever tourism activity is concentrated in time and space, builds rapidly, dominates a local economy, disrupts community life, endangers the environment, and ignores community input, the seeds of discontent are sown.

Many communities have tourism strategies and/or tourism master plans that were commissioned by municipal staff and developed by a consulting firm. Public involvement is relatively limited, usually involving interviews with a series of key "influencers." Findings are presented at a public forum. However, consultants generally make few changes as a result of this public meeting. It is generally left to councils (i.e., the elected officials at the local government level) and staff to implement the strategy. As a result, many strategies are not implemented in the manner intended, leading to much frustration among residents.

This kind of tokenism has far too often been referred to as a public process or even community-based decision making, when it is actually only a conscious (or unconscious) effort to ensure that the process will lead to conclusions decided upon by the particular level of government or agency that initiated the process. As Hall (1994, p. 169) noted, "communities rarely have the opportunity to say no." Fostering cooperation among jurisdictions and different sectors of the economy to reduce gridlock, share resources, and coordinate planning activities requires a very different approach than this so-called "consultation."

Community development based on an ecosystem approach differs in that it ensures that all interested parties truly have the opportunity to shape the outcome by determining the process. This is often a tedious, long, and drawn-out process involving many meetings, hearings, focus groups, and charettes. Moreover, many institutional and systems-related obstacles can impede the process (Haywood, 1988). Consequently, it is often difficult to predict where the process will lead.

People's reactions to tourism development may be in conflict. In times of greater environmental awareness, people tend not to be disposed to large developments of any kind, even though they prefer a manufacturing business that will create 500 jobs over the opportunities that smaller tourism enterprises may bring. Although many municipalities want to see tourism develop, they generally do not want to change the character of the community, nor do they want tourists to become noticeable because of their number. Developing a tourism industry under these circumstances is no small task. Nonetheless, an ecosystem approach to planning that is interdisciplinary, balanced, and comprehensive can enhance a community's ability to address some of these challenges.

The Ecosystem Approach to Planning Odum (1970, p. 262) defines an ecosystem as "any area of nature that includes living organisms and non-living substances interacting to produce an exchange of materials between the living and non-living parts." It has also been stated (Waterfront Regeneration Trust, 1995, p. 18) that:

> The ecosystem approach recognizes that humans are part of the ecosystems, and that everything—economic, social and environmental—is connected to everything else. To work towards healthy and sustainable ecosystems, the ways that activities are planned and decisions are made must change. Instead of working with separate disciplines, linkages and integration must be given higher priority.

The ecosystem approach to planning attempts to address the overlapping spheres of the environment, economy, and community, and coordinate the actions of existing agencies rather than impose solutions from above. This approach presupposes extensive public consultation and participation. This chapter draws on the author's involvement in such a process on behalf of the Waterfront Regeneration Trust. The chapter provides a brief discussion of why the municipalities in question launched a community-driven tourism strategy and places the initiative in its larger context. This is followed by a description of the communities, their assets, and their potential for tourism development. The process itself is outlined next, with a separate section on the lessons learned. Lastly, some of the longer-term implications for the region are highlighted in the conclusion.

THE WATERFRONT REGENERATION TRUST: BACKGROUND AND LOCATIONAL CONTEXT

In the mid-1980s, the Canadian government, which owned the lands adjacent to Toronto's inner harbor, gave permission to a number of developers to construct high-rise apartment, office, and hotel complexes. The result was that the city of Toronto was, to a certain extent, cut off from its central waterfront. The public outcry was such that a freeze on development was enforced by the province of Ontario, the Royal Commission on the Future of the Toronto Waterfront under Commissioner David Crombie was established by the federal government in 1988, and public hearings were held on the issue. It quickly became apparent that people were greatly concerned over access to the waterfront in general, as well as the state of pollution in Lake Ontario.

Commissioner Crombie was able to convince the federal and provincial governments that to address these broader public concerns, the commission's mandate needed to be expanded to cover the entire Greater Toronto Bioregion from the Niagara Escarpment in the west to the Trent River in the east, and from Lake Ontario in the south to the Oak Ridges Moraine in the north. The final report, released in 1992 (entitled *Regeneration, Toronto's Waterfront and the Sustainable City*), advocated an ecosystem approach that was interdisciplinary and multijurisdictional to determine solutions for the longer term.

When the Waterfront Regeneration Trust (hereafter referred to as the "Trust") was established by the province of Ontario in 1992, it was given the specific objective to implement the recommendations put forward by the Royal Commission on the Future of the Toronto Waterfront. In particular, the Trust was mandated to develop a plan for shoreline regeneration, including a greenway and a waterfront trail extending from Burlington Bay to the Trent River in Trenton using the ecosystem approach to planning. Built into the concept was the notion that current development must satisfy present needs without compromising the ability of future generations to meet their own needs.

The lands and waters that show a direct ecological, cultural, or economic connection to the waterfront from Burlington Bay to the Trent River have come to be known as the Lake Ontario Greenway. The Greenway

extends into the lake, generally to the ten metre depth within which most of the nearshore coastal processes and fishery activities occur. Inland the Greenway generally extends to the first significant rise in elevation, which often corresponds to the former Lake Iroquois shoreline. Where significant natural areas extend up major river valleys, they are usually included. . . . The Waterfront Trail forms the backbone of the Greenway, in a setting that includes protected natural areas, cultural heritage, appropriate waterfront development, and compatible commercial ventures [Waterfront Regeneration Trust, 1995, pp. 20–21].

The development of the Lake Ontario Greenway and the Waterfront Trail provides some unique opportunities for tourism development. In assessing these opportunities, a number of nodes [3] were identified. One of the primary nodes comprised the towns of Port Hope and Cobourg, along with the townships of Hamilton and Hope in the western part of Northumberland County (see Figure 16.1).

There has a been long-standing and deep-felt political rivalry among these communities which, for the most part, was linked to growth and the rationalization of services. Cobourg has been growing more quickly than its surrounding neighbors and would like to expand its municipal boundaries into Hamilton Township. There has also been discussion of merging the two towns of Cobourg and Port Hope to rationalize municipal services.

The Waterfront Trail was met with opposition in certain parts of the Lake Ontario Greenway, particularly in areas where much of the shoreline is in the hands of private landowners and is used for residential and agricultural purposes. This is the case in Hope Township where the council refused to endorse the proposed trail alignment. Thus, when the Trust first suggested that there was merit in looking at the four municipalities as one destination area for the purposes of promoting tourism, there was a certain amount of suspicion regarding possible ulterior motives.

The Communities The communities of Port Hope, Cobourg, Hamilton Township, and Hope Township form the southwestern portion of Northumberland County, about 60 miles (95 kilometers) east of Toronto and 30 miles (50 kilometers) west of Trenton. Highway 401 serves as the main transportation artery. The historically significant towns of Port Hope and Cobourg are also on Highway #2 and on the main Canadian National/Canadian Pacific (CN/CP) rail line between Toronto and Montreal. Lake Ontario forms the southern boundary.

PORT HOPE A beautiful Victorian town of 12,500 inhabitants at the mouth of the Ganaraska River, Port Hope has traditionally been a service center for the surrounding agricultural community. Industrial activity has historically been located around the port, although newer industries have located in the industrial parks close to Highway 401. One of its largest industries is uranium refinement, which has left much of the harbor and other lands polluted with low-level radioactive waste. This long-standing issue has impeded the town's development efforts and affected its reputation as a destination among boaters and other visitors.

Dating back to 1797, Port Hope is one of the oldest towns in Ontario. Its main street is considered to be the best-preserved nineteenth-century streetscape in Ontario. Its past as a thriving mill town and lake port is reflected in many of its stately homes, and the town boasts one of the most extensive aggregations of heritage domestic architecture in Ontario. The restoration of the Capitol Theatre, an old-ambience movie theater, and its conversion for use by the performing arts, will strengthen the area's image for quality cultural programming.

The Ganaraska River has given rise to a variety of events throughout the year (e.g., fishing derbies, a celebration of the periodic flooding of the town). Its trail also provides an excellent north–south linkage with the Waterfront Trail, the Oak Ridges Moraine, and the trail system of the Ganaraska Forest.

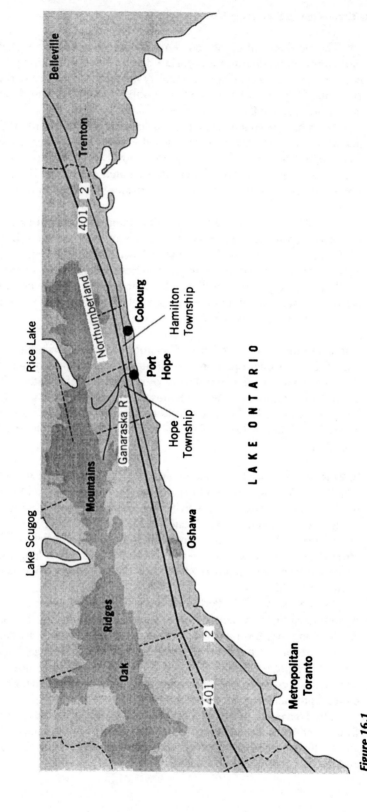

Figure 16.1
Location of the four communities and Northumberland County.

COBOURG Located about 5 miles (8 kilometers) east of Port Hope, Cobourg is the largest town in Northumberland County (14,700 inhabitants) and is the home to the county seat. It has a solid industrial base, especially in plastics. During the nineteenth century, the town grew to a mill center and port of some importance, while in mid-century it also became a fashionable resort for Americans who built numerous summer mansions along the shore. Well into the twentieth century, Cobourg's harbor was busy with freight shipping and served as a port for passenger, car, and rail ferries crossing Lake Ontario to and from the United States.

Today Cobourg is well known for its waterfront (marina and beach promenade) development. It has numerous heritage buildings, although it cannot compare with Port Hope's architectural heritage. Cobourg's many and varied events (e.g., the three-day Canada Day festival) attract significant crowds from May to October, which have established the town as a destination for Torontonians, particularly boaters.

There are only a limited number of accommodation establishments in Cobourg, most of which are in need of upgrading and modernization. Its downtown requires revitalization, both from a business and an architectural perspective. The grandeur of the stone classical revival Victoria Hall, which serves as the town hall, theater, and art gallery, dominates the main street.

HAMILTON AND HOPE TOWNSHIPS Hamilton Township (9200 inhabitants) stretches from Lake Ontario to Rice Lake and boasts a thriving resort community. Along the Lake Ontario shore, between the two towns of Port Hope and Cobourg, there are extensive wetlands and some mixed farming activity.

Hope Township (3500 inhabitants) covers roughly the same area as Hamilton Township. Largely rural in character, its Lake Ontario shoreline is dominated by the Ontario Hydro Wesleyville generating station. Very close to this facility is the village of Wesleyville which contains several historically significant buildings.

The townships offer natural heritage components which are fundamental to the attraction held by visitors to the area. The Oak Ridges Moraine and the close to 10,000-acre (over 4000-hectare) Ganaraska Forest are contained within these townships.

THE PROCESS OF DEVELOPING A COMMUNITY-DRIVEN TOURISM STRATEGY

The Trust's research determined that the Port Hope/Cobourg area had the potential to become a primary destination area within the Lake Ontario Greenway. After several weeks of discussion, the communities decided to embark upon an ecosystem-based process for developing a tourism strategy. This process was divided into four distinct phases:

- The *preparatory phase*, which lasted six months (from January 1994 to September 1994) and concluded with the four councils adopting a plan for the development of a strategy.
- *Phase I*, which lasted four months (from June 1994 to September 1994) and concluded with a framework for a long-term strategy being adopted by the four councils.

- *Phase II*, which lasted six months (from October 1994 to March 1995) and concluded with the presentation of a long-term strategy to the four councils.
- *Phase III*, the actual implementation of the long-term strategy (not discussed in this chapter because it had just been launched at the time of writing in April 1995).

Preparatory A community workshop was organized by the Trust in January 1994 to familiarize the
Phase communities with the concept of "greenway nodes," or primary destination areas in the
Lake Ontario Greenway, and to discuss why the Trust thought that these communities
had the potential to become one of the nodes. A workshop format was chosen to keep
discussion informal and provide participants with the opportunity to decide not to pursue tourism.

Participants were invited from each of the four municipalities and represented a diverse cross section of local politicians, senior community staff, cultural and natural heritage as well as environmental groups, the performing arts and other artistic communities, local businesses, business associations, and the tourism coordinators from the local and regional levels. Provincial representatives from the Ministries of Culture, Tourism and Recreation,[4] Municipal Affairs, and Economic Development and Trade attended as well.

The Trust had researched and summarized all existing official and secondary plans, in addition to previous strategies dealing with growth and settlement, tourism development, waterfront development, and parks and recreation. The commonalities in issues (which were striking) were presented to the workshop participants. All four municipalites expressed concern over the preservation of the natural and cultural heritage. Park land dedication was identified as a condition of (re)development, and expansion of the pedestrian and bicycle path system was considered to be an essential part of any green space and other (re)developments. There was a general commitment to improving accessibility and environmental restoration, as well as agreement that the waterfront should be a focus for public uses (including tourism and recreation, and residential development).

Information on the area's strengths and weaknesses, collected from the various strategies, was also presented and formed a basis for discussion among workshop participants. Through this exercise, it became apparent to everyone that collectively the four communities had a significant number of complementary assets, but individually their strengths were not sufficient to justify investments to attract increased overnight visitors.

When the discussion turned to which markets should be considered, the Trust presented information on tourism and recreation trends, focusing especially on two of the largest demand growth trends in southern Ontario: cultural tourism and soft adventure/ outdoor tourism. The assets of the four communities and their proximity to Metro Toronto suggested that a concerted effort could lead to excellent positioning within these niches.

The workshop participants reached the following conclusions: (1) A longer-term strategy was necessary to chart the course for common actions, (2) at least one initiative had to be undertaken in the short term to demonstrate that something concrete could come out of the process, since participants believed that they had been through many similar exercises without realizing any benefits, and (3) the group wanted to be kept informed of progress.

Workshop participants decided on the development of a cycling guide as a realistic short-term initiative. A small working group [which became the Greenway Node Coordinating Committee (GNCC)] was established to scope out action steps and structures, gain political and public support and commitment, and identify and assess outstanding issues. The Trust agreed to continue acting as a facilitator.

The GNCC decided that the first step should be the endorsement of the overall process to be taken by the four councils, since support from municipal staff was essential. There was also concern that the group would not be backed by councils when it came time to financially support various initiatives. Given the long-standing rivalries among councils, it was believed that a "neutral" body had to invite all four to a joint meeting to present the concept of the "greenway node" and ask for their endorsement of the approach put forward by the stakeholders at the workshop. The Commissioner of the Trust was asked to play that role.

In April 1994, the four councils met and formally endorsed the formation of the GNCC. Its members were requested to pursue a number of short-term initiatives as well as prepare a longer-term work plan with funding implications. It was agreed that the committee would report back to the councils at the end of September 1994. The four heads of council and the commissioner would act as a Political Liaison Committee during that period to ensure that the directions taken would receive council support.

Phase I Launched in June 1994, the first phase of the formal process involved establishing a number of subcommittees to deal with short-term initiatives, explore new projects, and prepare a framework outlining the process by which a strategic plan for the Greenway Node could be developed. The number of groups formed and the ambitious meeting schedule required dedicated resources to facilitate the process, assist in the preparation and follow-up of meetings, and help guide the efforts of the community volunteers and staff. The Trust retained a consulting firm to provide these services to the GNCC.

As agreed during the workshop, the first subcommittee was established to develop and produce an on-road cycling guide. Led by staff of the Port Hope Recreation Department, the Cycling Committee brought together a diverse number of players, including the Ganaraska Region Conservation Authority, the chambers of commerce, Energreen Teem, the Cobourg Cycle Club, the District Health Unit, and the Trust. The Political Liaison Committee was approached to guarantee that the municipalities would be responsible for any funding shortfalls not covered through a provincial grant, advertising, or other financial support.

Establishing a name, and hence common market recognition, for the four waterfront communities was also deemed a priority. The "Name That Node" Committee organized a media conference to launch this initiative, reviewed submissions received from the community, and selected the name to be presented to the GNCC and the four councils for endorsement. The Political Liaison Committee agreed to the process and the funds required, and it invited the community at large to "name our node." After testing to determine its acceptance by local residents and potential visitors, the name *Heritage Shores*, with the byline "Port Hope Cobourg Rice Lake," was adopted for joint promotional purposes.

It was deemed important to discuss the work to date with the broader community prior to presenting its short-term accomplishments and the strategic planning steps to the four councils. Therefore, the GNCC held another workshop with community stakeholders, inviting all those who had been involved in the January workshop as well as others who had indicated an interest or were involved in one of the numerous sub-committees.

During the September 1994 meeting, the GNCC presented the councils with (1) a report on its activities since its inception in June 1994, (2) a draft of the cycling guide, (3) the name selected for the Greenway Node, (4) an announcement that there would be a public forum on trails to bring all interested groups together to examine the status of ongoing and proposed trail projects as well as explore common issues for trail groups in the area, and (5) the process and timeframe proposed to build on the involvement of stakeholders and volunteers and ensure that their commitment and enthusiasm would remain high for the development of a long-term strategic plan.

Phase II   Three of the four councils endorsed the recommendations of the GNCC's report in principle, and they subsequently agreed to provide the funding necessary for ongoing facilitation during Phase II. Hope Township chose not to contribute financially, claiming a smaller tax base and population than the other communities. However, it requested observer status during the ongoing work of the GNCC. The other community members believed that it was important to have input from Hope Township on the expectation that its political leadership would recognize the benefit of participating more fully in the initiative at a future date. A number of Hope Township residents continued their work with subcommittees and the GNCC. Their insights were much appreciated by the group.

This six-month phase resulted in the completion of several of the short-term initiatives started during Phase I, as well as the formulation of the long-term strategy. Although the early subcommittees were established according to a commonly recognized need or opportunity, the GNCC believed that it was necessary to identify general principles that had to underlie all projects:

- In the Greenway Node, a healthier and more sustainable waterfront environment that should be clean, green, connected, open, accessible, usable, diverse, affordable, and attractive would be endorsed. These are the nine principles of the Royal Commission on the Future of the Toronto Waterfront that underlie the Trust's work.
- The various committees involved with the Greenway Node would work in cooperation with all local agencies involved in tourism to provide a collaborative planning approach and a streamlined, effective, and efficient delivery of tourism development and promotion.
- In advancing the Greenway Node the community would be involved in the development of the strategic plan and all aspects of its implementation, monitoring, and evaluation.

Public input into the long-term strategic directions was sought in several ways. The results of the September 1994 stakeholder workshop, including objectives to be accomplished, guided the subcommittee throughout this phase. A questionnaire distributed to over 250 individuals from various associations, community groups, and businesses solicited additional input and advice from the stakeholders, particularly with respect to their views on the effectiveness of marketing activities by different organizations within the region, their own marketing budgets and where these were invested, and their willingness to assist with the implementation of future initiatives. This questionnaire also provided recipients with an update on activities and, thus, kept them involved in the strategic planning process. A third stakeholder workshop dealing with strategic actions and implementation was held in January 1995.

Ongoing political support was sought through information sessions held with each council during December 1994. These sessions also informed new councillors (municipal elections were held in November) of the initiative as a whole and the various projects being advanced by the GNCC. The outcome of the January 1995 workshop was presented to the Political Liaison Committee in February 1995, while a full presentation on the strategic plan, its priorities, and actions plans was made to the councils at the end of March 1995.

Implementation of the long-term strategy began in April 1995, with the expectation that it would be reviewed annually to sustain the process by setting yearly objectives in a voluntary collaborative way, and every three years for general direction. A model for evaluating results and a monitoring process will be part of the strategy implementation to ensure accountability and the justification of investments.

LESSONS LEARNED

Community development processes will always be evolutionary and, to a large degree, dependent on the dedication, support, and personalities of key individuals as well as the visionary ability of elected officials and other leading citizens. Community development based on the ecosystem approach implies a high degree of public participation. As Arnstein (1969, cited in Hall, 1994, p. 169) argued, public participation implies that the local community will have a degree of control over planning and decision-making processes. The residents must be the focal point of community tourism development since they will ultimately bear the largest share of the costs associated with tourism development and must, therefore, also be placed in a position of determining how they will share in the benefits.

The following lessons can provide guidance to any community wishing to undertake an ecosystem approach to community planning, particularly if the focus of development is tourism.

Leadership *The community must assume leadership roles in the tourism strategy development process.* There is an expectation that leadership will emerge naturally from elected officials, community staff, or those who have the most to gain from the process (in this case, the tourism industry and its representatives). This should not be taken for granted. Those who would appear to be "natural" leaders often shun the responsibility, afraid of being too close to the issues or of being seen as possibly too self-serving. They may also be unable to make the necessary time commitment.

Establishment of "interim leadership" at the outset is essential. When forming a community committee, a strong, well-organized objective leader should be solicited to ensure that the committee "gets off to the right start." Establishing the tone, operating guidelines, budget, and work plan at the beginning will assist in achieving clarity of vision and direction for all. The leader must also have the time to provide adequate communication to all members, and the ability to work through conflict resolution as differences of opinion and approach will most certainly arise. The leader must provide balance, vision, and direction to ensure that the initiative is not derailed.

Committee Membership

The focus of the community process must determine membership. Thought should be given prior to committee formation as to which agencies and individuals should serve on committees. Membership should be based not only on volunteerism, but also on the focus or theme of the community development process. In the case of the Greenway Node, the focus is tourism development that builds on the cultural and natural heritage of the local area, making the conservation authority a critical player. Membership size is another important consideration. While more members provide for greater workload distribution, larger memberships may result in greater inefficiency and more difficult communication. A balance must be struck and supported by all committee members.

General Principles and Evaluation of Projects

A clear series of principle statements is required to establish norms of working and a framework for setting priorities. Criteria for determining which projects conformed to the objectives of the GNCC were based on the three principles outlined in Phase II, and they ensured that inappropriate projects would be recognized as such in an objective way. The criteria dealt with (1) opportunity for financial benefit to the community, (2) opportunity for enhancement to the local quality of life, (3) partnership and collaboration potential, and (4) the ecosystem and environmental impact.

Establishing guiding principles and values to determine how problems will be solved at the outset can avoid discussions outside of official meetings and the formation of cliques that fracture the focus of the community group.

Roles and Responsibilities of Committee Members

A broad development goal allows an interdisciplinary and multisectoral group to focus on shared opportunities. The concept of critical mass and a focus on shared attractions was necessary to redirect traditional tourism planning and advertising that was based on existing administrative structures rather than the identification of market-driven products. The process was initiated with more enthusiasm than with a clear delineation of roles and responsibilities. This lack of delineation was a good way to encourage GNCC members to draw upon resources from their respective areas of responsibility to satisfy broader community needs. Thus, Port Hope was able to assume leadership in developing the cycling guide for all four communities.

As the GNCC matured, expanded, and dealt with a greater variety of issues, it was necessary to clarify the roles and responsibilities of community members, provincial representatives, and consultants. Moreover, similarities, differences, and economies of scale among the Greenway Node process and other initiatives being undertaken at the same time (e.g., Port Hope tourism plan) also needed to be determined and clarified.

Precise terms of reference should be written for all committees and subcommittees. They should state unequivocally that community members representing an organization are expected to report to that organization on a monthly basis regarding the process and activities, as well as keep the committee(s) informed as to the positions and decisions taken by their respective organizations.

A focus on, and balance between, short- and long-term objectives must be maintained, and priorities must be established. It is very easy to compromise the long-term vision and planning as a result of volunteer "burnout."

Political Support *A workable method for achieving and maintaining political support must be identified early in the process.* Although political support was sought throughout, some councillors still questioned the process and directions. Reporting to councillors on a regular basis was also seen as necessary, yet problematic. Councillors appointed to the GNCC and/or subcommittees did not necessarily keep their colleagues informed. Where a citizen had been asked to act as a liaison with the elected officials, the reporting relationship was even more problematic.

Each council should be asked to designate its representative *by resolution*, to be unequivocal regarding that person's status and authority, and to outline the reporting requirements of their designate. Minutes of meetings should be sent to each of the chief administrative officers. This is believed to be the only way to ensure that the minutes are distributed to councillors as part of their regular information package. The same applies to all correspondence with councillors and heads of councils, since this ensures logging within council records.

Time Commitment and Financial Support *Community development processes are very lengthy and time-consuming, and they require funding for facilitation and research.* How much time community members must invest in a community-driven process cannot be overstated. Involving the public is a very time-consuming endeavor, but it pays off in the long run through broad-based community commitment and support. Relying to a large extent on a volunteer effort also brings greater flux in committee membership. Members should clearly understand the time commitment involved when agreeing to serve. To determine time commitments, a meeting schedule should be established at the outset. If time commitments become too onerous, many people—in particular, private sector representatives—will not serve on the committee or attend regularly enough to be effective. To ensure that the committee is as effective, efficient, and nonbureaucratic as possible, some ground rules should be decided upon regarding such issues as voting (versus consensus decision making) and membership.

Every effort should be made to keep records of volunteer time to ensure that a gift-in-kind dollar value can be accounted for. This is particularly important because it allows politicians to understand more clearly the importance that community members attach to the process. Because of the significant amount of time invested (the GNCC estimated Phase I required over 1000 hours, not counting staff time or the presence of provincial representatives), it is critical that facilitation services be available to support the activities. This can be in the form of professionals being brought in or staff being dedicated by one municipality/agency. Total reliance on volunteer efforts will invariably slow the process and could lead to its failure. The time required to organize meetings, agendas, preparatory material, minutes, and reach out to other members of the public, for example, should not be added to the already significant time constraints faced by most participants.

The resources the Trust brought to bear, particularly in the early part of the process, allowed for a much faster than normal community development process. The Waterfront Trail and Greenway initiatives convinced many local politicians that their area was part of a much larger vision. This made it somewhat easier to convince councils to provide the necessary funding to the GNCC so that facilitation and support services could be contracted.

Public *A community development process must strive to involve a broad number of stakeholders*
Involvement *and to ensure a high level of awareness among residents.* Although the first stakeholder
meeting (January 1994) had undoubtedly been successful and provided support for the
process, keeping the public involved and active proved challenging throughout. Many
people did not hesitate to contribute to a short-term, action-oriented subcommittee; fewer
were prepared to help guide the more strategic, process-oriented work. Surveys, focus
groups, and stakeholder meetings can overcome this lack of participation somewhat by at
least ensuring that input is sought from a wide variety of individuals and groups.

Business and economic development organizations, which should have been leading
the process since their membership would be the first to benefit, are often too stretched
for resources to assume a leadership role. As with the requests made to councils to officially appoint a representative to the committee, the boards of these organizations need
to be approached for formal "buy in" and allocation of staff resources. This is particularly
important since existing organizations will be expected to incorporate shared opportunities into their own objectives. The process should not lead to the creation of yet another
organizational layer, but rather to refocusing existing resources to accomplish more efficient tourism development.

Volunteer and staff burnout is a reality in many communities today, and it is a
constant struggle to reach out and bring in new players. An intense, time-consuming
process such as the one undertaken by the four waterfront communities exacerbates that
problem. While people might be prepared to become involved for a couple of months, it
is very difficult to build a community process on a constantly changing volunteer base.

Media *The media must be brought onside early and a plan developed to ensure the process is*
Relations *regularly in the public eye.* At key intervals, the activities of the GNCC attracted media
attention, particularly when the four councils came together for presentations. Also, the
process for naming the area relied on the media to spread the message as widely as possible. In its reporting and editorials, the local newspaper tended to be rather skeptical of
the process and several of the initiatives. Rather than focusing on the positive aspects of
the partnerships that were being built, the newspaper emphasized historic differences
between the communities and the challenges of overcoming these. Community members
of the GNCC found this persistent negativism on the part of local journalists demoraliz-
ing, and they believed it was undermining broader public support for their work. The
problem was intensified to some degree by the municipal election campaign.

Effective public relations is essential to the success of any community-driven initiative. Consideration should be given to bringing a local communications expert onto the
committee at the start. A key task of this individual would be to develop a communications plan for all phases of the work. In addition, the chairperson must be prepared to
interact with the media and solicit media support at the outset and throughout the
process.

BENEFITS OF A COMMUNITY DEVELOPMENT PROCESS

Although the challenges are many, community-driven initiatives will ultimately ensure
support for the direction adopted by the community at large. Locally initiated activities

that seek to develop the economy of a community and improve the quality of life for the benefit of its residents will result in locally sustainable employment opportunities and the promotion of the community's financial health.

The benefits resulting from a community development process have been abundantly documented [e.g., Mondragon, Spain which is probably the most famous case of community development (MacLeod, 1995); Baltimore's Inner Harbour and Cleveland in the United States (King, 1995); Victoria and Kamloops, British Columbia (Murphy, 1988); and tourism in the Northwest Territories (Government of the Northwest Territories, 1983)]. Key benefits of such a process include (1) greater opportunity for residents to participate in the development of their community, (2) a flexible approach to identifying and supporting community priorities, (3) facilitation of partnerships within communities, (4) increased cooperation among communities to meet shared development objectives, (5) nurturing local leadership and an enhancement of people's skills, information, and linkages to promote their community, and (6) nurturing local entrepreneurship and small-scale economic activity.

CONCLUSION

A community development process is difficult to sustain unless elected officials and community members work very closely together. At times, politicians will feel threatened by such a process. Only a close working relationship throughout will ensure that they remain supportive of the directions the community determines for itself. If the process involves several jurisdictions, as in the Greenway Node, the problem will likely be heightened by rivalries and mistrust. Hence, a "champion" must be found (i.e., a person or organization acceptable to politicians and residents alike). In the case of the Greenway Node, this role was filled by the Honourable David Crombie, Commissioner of the Waterfront Regeneration Trust.

Aside from this "champion," the strategic plan and its implementation must be associated with a dedicated group of local individuals, not a consulting firm. It is too easy for the community and its elected officials to disengage themselves if they believe that they have paid for advice they can accept or reject.

Community development takes time. The process cannot be hurried and there are no shortcuts. Residents and politicians rarely want to hear that it will take at least one to two years to develop a long-term strategy. They want immediate results. However, an action orientation without a framework will lead to wasted time and financial resources. Many private sector representatives, not used to process, will become frustrated with what they see as a bureaucratic approach. Yet, rushing into projects without ensuring that the community at large understands the underlying rationale will result in residents feeling disenfranchised. The projects will suffer as people will become disinterested at best, hostile to them at worst.

ACKNOWLEDGMENTS

The *Heritage Shores* project benefited from the diligence and dedication of David Crombie and Suzanne Barrett (Commissioner and Director of Environmental Studies, respectively, of the Waterfront Regeneration Trust) and Gail Wood (Ganaraska Region Conservation Authority and Chair of the GNCC). Many other people supported my work with the Trust and the four municipalities throughout, most notably Lori Waldbrook (the Ministry of Culture, Tourism and Recreation), Frank Godfrey of Cobourg, Starr Olsen and Dugald McDonald (Mowbray, Frankum & Associates), and Gord Phillips (the Economic Planning Group of Canada). Thanks also to Mike Morel for his assistance in preparing the map for this chapter.

NOTES

1. See Chapters 10, 11, 24, and 25 for additional discussion and examples of heritage tourism.
2. See Chapters 5, 9, 11, 12, 14, and 16–19 for a detailed discussion pertaining to community attitudes and involvement in the tourism planning and development processes.
3. Nodes are areas presenting a cluster of facilities, attractions, services, and natural and cultural resources that have the potential to attract visitors from outside the local community.
4. As of mid-1995, Ontario's tourism ministry was housed within the Ministry of Economic Development, Trade, and Tourism.

REFERENCES

Government of the Northwest Territories (GNWT), Department of Economic Development and Tourism. 1983. *Summary Report—Community-Based Tourism: A Strategy for the Northwest Territories Tourism Industry.* Yellowknife: GNWT.

Hall, C.M. 1994. *Tourism and Politics: Policy, Power and Place.* Chichester: John Wiley & Sons.

Haywood, K.M. 1988. Responsible and responsive tourism planning in the community, *Tourism Management*, 9(2), 105–118.

King, P. 1995. Cleveland's rebirth, *Leisureways*, April, 43–46.

MacLeod, G. 1995. *Ideas with Legs: From Mondragon to American.* Tompkins Institute.

Murphy, P.E. 1988. Community-driven tourism planning, *Tourism Management*, 9(2), 96–104.

Odum, E.P. 1970. The strategy of ecosystem development, *Science*, 164, 262–270.

Royal Commission on the Future of the Toronto Waterfront. 1992. *Regeneration, Toronto's Waterfront and the Sustainable City: Final Report.* Minister of Supply and Services Canada.

Waterfront Regeneration Trust. 1995. *Lake Ontario Greenway Strategy.* Toronto.

Further Reading

Benwell, M. 1980. Public participation in planning—a research report, *Long Range Planning*, 13, August, 71–79.

Doering, R. 1994. Sustainable communities: progress, problems and potential, *Sustainable Round Table Review*, Spring.

Economic Planning Group of Canada. 1986. *A Community Strategy Manual.* Ottawa/Victoria: Department of Regional Industrial Expansion, Ministry of Tourism, Recreation and Culture.

Interministry Committee. 1993. *Building Capacity for Community Economic Development: Interministry Committee.* Government of Ontario.

Joppe, M. 1995. A tourism, recreation and economic strategy for the Lake Ontario Greenway. *Toolkit.* Toronto: Waterfront Regeneration Trust.

Joppe, M. 1995. Consultation versus community development: the Lake Ontario greenway strategy—a Canadian experience. *Proceedings*, 26th Annual Tourism and Travel Research Association Conference, Acapulco.

Kasperson, R.E. 1978. Citizen participation in environmental policy-making: the U.S.A. experience. In B. Sadler (ed.), *Involvement and Environment: Proceedings of the Canadian Confer-

ence on Public Participation, Vol. 1, Edmonton: Environment Council of Alberta, pp. 128–138.

Mill, R.C. 1995. Key Success Factors in Community Tourism. *Proceedings*, 26th Annual Tourism and Travel Research Association Conference, Acapulco.

Ministry of Tourism, Recreation and Culture. (n.d.). *Community Tourism Action Program*. Province of British Columbia.

Murphy, P.E. 1985. *Tourism: A Community Approach*. New York: Methuen.

Ritchie, J.R.B. 1988. Consensus policy formulation in tourism: measuring resident views via survey research, *Tourism Management*, 9(3), 199–212.

Roseland, M. 1994. Bottom-up initiative, top-down leadership, *Sustainable Round Table Review*, Spring.

Task Force on Economic Viability and Community Economic Development. 1988. *Discussion Paper on Economic Viability and the Ministry of Municipal Affairs' Role in Community Economic Development*. Government of Ontario.

ℊ | PROBLEM SOLVING AND DISCUSSION ACTIVITIES

1. Discuss the key differences between traditional consultation of "key stakeholders" and community development based on an ecosystem approach. Who is likely to be excluded, and why, under the more traditional approach?

2. Who should lead the actual implementation of the long-term strategy in the case study discussed in this chapter? Consider that there are four municipalities, a regional municipality, and many other organizations such as the chambers of commerce, the Ganaraska Region Conservation Authority, and cultural, environmental, and heritage groups that all have a role to play. Consider also that funding and staffing from public sector sources is highly unlikely due to government cutbacks in spending at all levels.

3. Politicians increasingly want proof that promotional efforts and investments in tourism are paying off for the community. Therefore, monitoring the impacts (both positive and negative) is becoming more important. This usually means that appropriate data have to be collected, analyzed, and presented. What kind of data should be collected and how? Bear in mind that the data should not be merely anecdotal and should be collected as efficiently as possible.

4. Why might tourism operators be relatively unenthusiastic about the process-oriented development of a long-term tourism strategy? Do you think that this attitude would be representative of operators in locations other than Southern Ontario? What should be done to have tourism operators contribute more of their time and insights throughout the process?

5. Discuss some of the relationships among the economic, social, and natural environments that should be considered when adopting an ecosystem approach to community tourism planning. Consider the interests of various stakeholder groups and the potential conflicts that might arise during public consultation activities. How might these "differences" be resolved and compromises reached?

17

Instilling Community Confidence and Commitment in Tourism

COMMUNITY PLANNING AND PUBLIC PARTICIPATION IN GOVERNMENT CAMP, OREGON, USA

Samuel V. Lankford
Jill Knowles-Lankford
David C. Povey

₰ | KEY LEARNING POINTS

- Issues associated with competition for resources among stakeholders, seasonal fluctuations in population, land ownership, and infrastructure development and maintenance create interesting challenges within outdoor recreation and resort communities wishing to pursue tourism.

- The extent to which a community decides to offer services desired by visitors and manage the community accordingly is a critical question that leads ultimately to the need for comprehensive community planning which relies heavily on public involvement.

- Public participation in the community planning process must be tailored to the specific community. If a community is not prepared to handle the volume of visitors desiring services, the quality of life for permanent residents may deteriorate and the visitor experience may be adversely affected.

- Public participation can be instrumental in achieving sustainable tourism development if it involves decision making that is locally determined and cooperatively implemented, planning and management that nurture local values, and marketing that solicits local input.

- The degree of community participation is related to the public's attitude toward change and public sector planning efforts. Critical to achieving high levels of participation is the creation of an environment where stakeholders believe that they have a stake in the course of events and that their participation can affect the course of events.

INTRODUCTION

Public participation in the community planning process is essential for quality sustainable tourism development and the dual values of community solidarity and economic growth. A sustainable tourism industry is characterized by a comprehensive planning approach that considers the economic, social, and ecological implications of tourism and recreation development. Decisions should be made locally and should be cooperatively implemented. The involvement of those affected by tourism plans should build support for the plans and should strengthen trust and confidence among planners, the general public, and tourism operators. This should lead to a better understanding of tourism development impacts and ways to deal with them effectively.

A cooperative public participation process that identifies issues, concerns, and discrepancies in preferences and attitudes toward tourism and recreation development is critical. To be responsive to both local residents and visitors, it is necessary to gain an understanding of the nature of tourism and the outdoor recreation resources within the areas targeted for development and promotion. Specifically, it is important that tourism and economic development efforts be approached with an understanding of existing local and regional values and culture, yet be grounded in planning theory so there is a sound, reasoned, and tested basis for planned actions of public policy development, promotion, and both the public services and infrastructure required.

This chapter summarizes the community planning process, significant findings, and recommendations of three years (1987–1990) of planning and design work concerning Government Camp on Mount Hood in Oregon, USA. The research agenda included a review of existing conditions and plans in the study area, a market analysis, development of transportation strategies, and delineation of recommended development options for the community. Survey research, nominal group techniques, public information meetings, visual presentations where feedback was solicited, and a community design workshop were used to involve a diverse cast of community members and interests. These efforts allowed many perspectives to be integrated, and they provided different ways of envisioning the future of this small mountain community.

Specifically, this chapter provides (1) an overview of a comprehensive economic development planning effort that addressed tourism and recreation opportunities as the key strategy, (2) an understanding of the various techniques available to involve residents, business, government officials, and visitors in the planning process, and (3) an awareness of the issues and concerns of various stakeholders when planning for community change.

COMMUNITY PLANNING, PUBLIC PARTICIPATION, AND SUSTAINABLE TOURISM DEVELOPMENT: CONTEMPORARY PERSPECTIVES AND ISSUES

Travel for the purposes of recreation and tourism has increased dramatically since the 1980s. With this, some specific community management problems emerge. Communities may not be prepared[1] or sufficiently developed to handle the volume of visitors desiring services. Consequently, the quality of life for the permanent resident deteriorates and the visitor experience is adversely affected.

Outdoor recreation and resort communities have to balance the interests of the business community with the interests of the permanent resident. Moreover, many issues arise due to the considerable population fluctuations winter recreation communities experience. For example, housing costs are high during the peak visitor season, which makes it difficult to attract employees willing to pay those higher costs (Gill and Williams, 1994; Kouba, 1985). This impacts the quality and level of services provided to the visitor and resident. To service the peaks, unique staffing patterns for government and business must be developed.

Infrastructure development and maintenance must reflect peak use patterns. The level of maintenance (e.g., snow removal, transportation, and the provision of warming shelters) can greatly affect the success of local tourism developments (McIntosh and Goeldner, 1990) and recreation-based businesses. Another common issue is that land is predominantly held by nonresidents. This ownership pattern affects the level, style, and volume of development in the community, sometimes against the desires and values of the host population.

Tourists and outdoor recreation enthusiasts inevitably require a series of goods and services including accommodations, restaurants, entertainment options, professional services such as banking, and retail stores. These services basically encompass private and commercial enterprises, public and quasi-public services, and recreation facilities and services. The challenge is how to best serve the needs and desires of a diverse outdoor recreation and tourist clientele as well as those of the residents (Lankford and Knowles-Lankford, 1992).

Balancing various needs and desires is crucial in any community development activity, and it is amplified in tourist resort and outdoor recreation communities. The extent to which the community decides to offer the services desired by visitors and manage the community accordingly is a critical question that leads ultimately to the need for comprehensive community planning,[2] which relies heavily on public involvement.[3]

Why should tourism planning and development organizations be concerned about public involvement in the decision-making process? Public participation developed within the municipal and regional planning arenas because citizens believed that they were not being adequately represented by local elected officials and government employees. Consequently, attempts have been made to redefine the roles and level of responsibility of all those involved in community development as well as tourism development.

At a basic level, citizens help define the public interest through involvement in public participation programs. At a more complex level, public participation is required to identify and define what is sacred and valued by local people. The underlying hypothesis is that the degree of participation is related to the public's attitude and behavior toward change and government planning efforts (Loukissas, 1983).

Public participation is instrumental in achieving sustainable tourism development[4] in that it helps to develop plans and programs that may be more responsive to local needs, values, and norms and, therefore, have a better chance of acceptance. Draper and Kariel (1990) suggested that sustainable tourism development requires (1) decision-making processes that are locally determined and cooperatively implemented, (2) planning and management that nurture local cultures, and (3) promotion and marketing activities that are conducted with input from local people.

Public participation should play an important role in any development scenario

(Gunn, 1988; Lankford, 1994; Loukissas, 1983; Murphy, 1985). A study of planners and landscape architects in Northern California, Oregon, and Washington revealed that public participation methods and programs are extremely important to the success of their current practices and that future public participation programs should be expanded to include a diverse group of stakeholders (Knowles-Lankford, 1992; Knowles-Lankford and Lankford, 1994). Additionally, Brindley (1991) identified several goals of sustainable development, including the need to consult with the public, plan small-scale projects, let the people benefiting from the project make the decisions, and provide education and training to the public and employees.

Unfortunately, apathy, mistrust of public authorities, and the inability of the host population to project their needs and articulate their interests have kept much of the general public from participating in planning (Loukissas, 1983). Political, environmental, religious, cultural, ethnic, and other groups in an area can make or break a tourism development (Gunn, 1988, p. 75). Consequently, public participation to guide proposed projects in ways that are sensitive to local values, recognize and address constraints identified by citizens, and satisfy critical functional and management issues determined through public consultation must be actively encouraged.

Planners must be fully versed in what tourism planning is about, and what changes are generated locally by tourism development. Much of this understanding can be gained through public participation programs. Such programs can enhance the legitimacy of the planning process and improve the quality and acceptability of decisions made during the planning process.

Public involvement can be viewed as one mechanism within an overall process of democratic consensus building. Resulting from public input should be decisions about resource allocation and public service priorities that are designed to address the needs and interests of those who are affected and concerned. Participation should ultimately move a process in the direction of consensus by providing opportunities for dialogue with interested citizens. This dialogue enables planners to design recommendations that are responsive to the public's concerns.

A study of tourism impacts on residents in the Pacific Northwest region of the United States revealed that involvement in local planning and decision-making processes significantly influenced the level of support and attitude toward tourism and tourists (Lankford, 1991a, b, 1994; Lankford and Howard, 1994). Residents have been found to be less supportive of tourism development than decision makers, government officials, and business owners. However, when involved with various community activities (self-assessed community involvement), residents appeared to hold more favorable attitudes toward community change and development (Allen and Gibson, 1987; Ayers and Potter, 1989; Goudy, 1977; Napier and Wright, 1974; Rosentraub and Thompson, 1981).

Lankford (1994) revealed that residents appeared to be suspicious of the ability of decision makers to listen to and acknowledge their concerns regarding tourism development. Interestingly, elected/appointed officials believed that they did listen to the community. Planners and administrators also suggested, although to a lesser degree, that community concerns were heard at the decision-making level. Business owners, on the other hand, seemed to be slightly more cautious about whether their tourism development interests were heard by decision makers. It also appeared that residents were inclined to believe that they had less access to decision-making processes than did business owners, government employees, and elected/appointed officials.

Local decision makers, planners, and administrators should heed the finding that residents may believe that they do not have access to the planning/public review process and that their concerns are not being considered. An open planning process that facilitates participation by *everyone* in the community can enhance decisions made at the local level. More open discourse among stakeholders early in the tourism development process is required if local residents are to believe that their input has made a difference in the nature of the tourism development strategy adopted by local decision makers.

Open discussion also facilitates gaining community confidence and will allow tourism promoters to initiate appropriate corrective action as necessary (Lankford, 1994). Critical to achieving high levels of participation is the creation of an environment where stakeholders (1) recognize that they have a stake in the course of events and (2) believe that their participation can affect the course of events in a desired direction.

Government officials and/or tourism planners must convince and demonstrate to the public that their input and involvement in local affairs is vital to the community and worthy of their efforts. Some methods of involving the community, business owners, government officials, and visitors in tourism planning and development processes include (1) representative surveys of random samples of visitors and residents that use attitudinal scaling and target satisfaction with services and concerns for the future, (2) design workshops and visual presentations, (3) educational programs focusing on the significance of the tourism industry, (4) advisory groups, committees, and commissions who study issues and concerns, (5) volunteers to help design, implement, and evaluate services, (6) empowerment of business owners through "self-help" programs, (7) nominal group techniques[5] to identify opportunities and issues, (8) public hearings on research findings, planning processes, and proposals, and (9) balloting by visitors and residents on various proposals or aspects of proposals.

The remainder of this chapter describes a planning effort that included the use of many of the foregoing techniques. This case study examines the development of an economic improvement plan for the Village of Government Camp on Mount Hood, Oregon that was based entirely upon local and regional input and dialogue.

GOVERNMENT CAMP: LOCATIONAL CONTEXT AND BACKGROUND

Government Camp is a mountain village situated at an elevation of 4000 feet (1220 meters). Sitting on the slopes of Mount Hood, Oregon (see Figure 17.1), Government Camp is located in one of the most popular, attractive, and easily accessible tourist and recreation destinations in the northwest United States. Accessed by the Mount Hood Scenic Loop, which passes through the Columbia River Gorge National Scenic Area (one of the sailboarding centers of the world), Mount Hood is located within one hour's drive of Portland, the largest metropolitan area in Oregon. Mount Hood is the only mountain in the United States that offers skiing throughout the year. This ski area, Timberline, is within a 10 minute drive of Government Camp and is associated with Timberline Lodge, a national historic landmark.

Government Camp is currently the only urban area in Oregon and Washington from

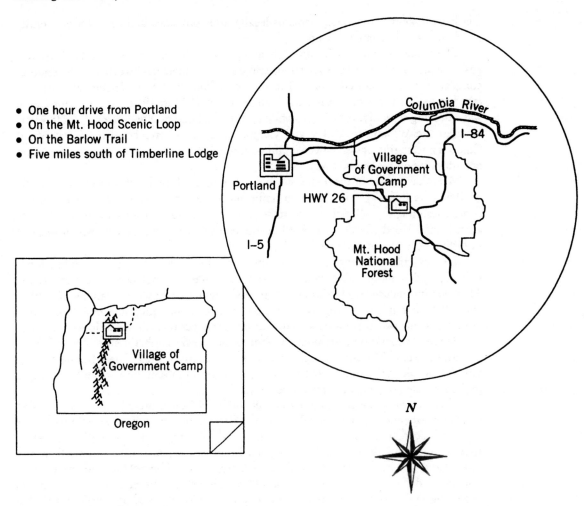

- One hour drive from Portland
- On the Mt. Hood Scenic Loop
- On the Barlow Trail
- Five miles south of Timberline Lodge

Figure 17.1
Location of Government Camp, Oregon, USA.

which ski facilities can be directly accessed from lodging facilities. The village is located on the business loop just off Highway 26, the third most traveled highway in Oregon. An estimated 1.7 million vehicles pass Government Camp on Highway 26 each year. The Mount Hood National Forest which surrounds the village is a 320-acre (130-hectare) "island" of privately owned land that registered nearly 7 million visits annually during the period from 1986 to 1993.

As with many tourism communities, Government Camp experiences considerable population fluctuations. The estimated permanent population is 135 people, or 18 percent of the total village population of 735 persons (includes both permanent and seasonal residents). The residents have a strong sense of independence, which probably has influenced their desire to remain without local government control and influence. Located in

Clackamas County, the village remains legally unincorporated and relies on the county for planning and revenue support.

The name *Government Camp* refers to a point on the Barlow Pioneer Trail where a government regiment in 1849 abandoned 46 wagons in inclement weather in an effort to complete the mountain crossing and reach the Willamette Valley. Historically, the village has been a recreation visitor destination. From 1927 to 1960, Government Camp was a thriving center for Alpine recreation as well as a frequent stopping place for travelers between the Willamette Valley and Central Oregon. Today, however, Government Camp is a scattering of disconnected buildings offering a narrow spectrum of services and opportunities on the old highway.

What happened? In the 1940s, several fires destroyed the hotels in the community. In 1957, the highway was altered so traffic no longer passed through the commercial center, resulting in a 40 percent decrease in sales of goods and services. In 1967, a ski area, Mount Hood Meadows, opened on the east side of the mountain, which resulted in further decreases in commercial sales.

The majority of businesses in Government Camp provide services—including food, lodging, and outdoor equipment sales and rental—to the outdoor recreation visitor. There are five foodservice businesses, a grocery, a winery, two service stations, two other gas outlets, one inn providing six rooms, and four outdoor equipment rentals and sales outlets. Twenty percent of total demand for these services is attributed to local residents.

Alpine ski operations, including Multorpor Ski Bowl, Timberline (see Figure 17.2), and Mount Hood Meadows, are the major employers in the area. These businesses employ 730 people in the winter (92 percent of private sector jobs in the area) and 215 people in the summer (78 percent of private sector jobs).

There are some encouraging signs for the future of Government Camp. Tourism and recreation expenditures now rank third among Oregon industries. The ski facilities on the mountain account for 20 percent of Oregon and Washington ski visits (Povey, 1986). Indeed, in the 1980s, Mount Hood attracted more winter recreation visitors than any other mountain in the Pacific Northwest (Povey, 1986). The potential for year-round visitation exists given that Mount Hood offers alpine skiing throughout the year and is becoming an important summer ski training area. Mount Hood attracted about 5000 skiers in 1987 who participated in an organized race training camp.

Government Camp is ideally located to provide recreation and tourist support services that complement seasonal activities and attractions on Mount Hood. How this can be achieved is the focus of this chapter. The tourism industry in the village possesses great potential for social and economic benefits, each of which can be addressed through the tourism planning and development process.

In 1987, the Clackamas County Community Development Division funded a proposal prepared by the University of Oregon's Community Planning Workshop to assist the Government Camp Recreation Association (the equivalent of a chamber of commerce) in involving local citizens in efforts to improve the appearance of the village and stimulate the local economy. Matching funds for the *Government Camp Economic Improvement Plan* were provided by the Government Camp Recreation Association. A multidisciplinary planning and design team was established comprising faculty and students from the departments of Urban and Regional Planning, Landscape Architecture, Architecture, and Leisure Studies and Services. The planning and design work involved collecting and

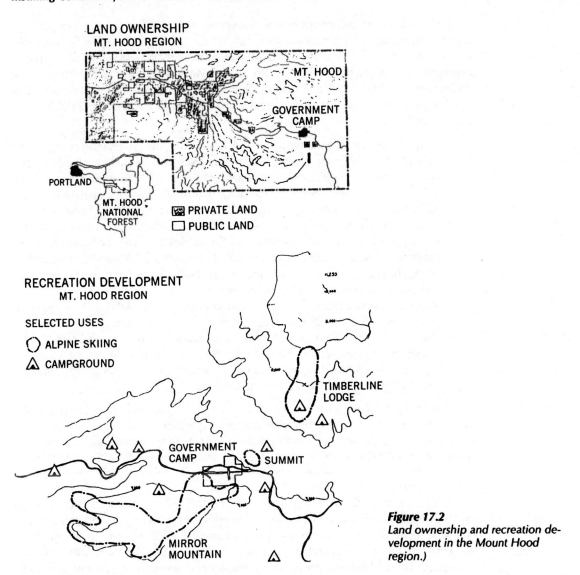

LAND OWNERSHIP
MT. HOOD REGION

MT. HOOD

GOVERNMENT
CAMP

PORTLAND

MT. HOOD
NATIONAL
FOREST

▨ PRIVATE LAND
☐ PUBLIC LAND

RECREATION DEVELOPMENT
MT. HOOD REGION

SELECTED USES

◯ ALPINE SKIING
△ CAMPGROUND

TIMBERLINE
LODGE

GOVERNMENT
CAMP   SUMMIT

MIRROR
MOUNTAIN

Figure 17.2
Land ownership and recreation de-
velopment in the Mount Hood
region.)

analyzing demographic and market data as well as developing guidelines for a series of
projects designed to revitalize the village.

OVERVIEW OF THE PLANNING PROCESS

The planning process used for the *Government Camp Economic Improvement Plan* recognized that those amenities important to the quality of life and social well-being of the
resident population should be protected to avoid degradation. The local planning process
also aimed to obviate some of the problems identified by the community and visitors.

The economic improvement plan for Government Camp had three sets of goals: (1) determining strategies for improving the economic conditions, (2) assessing the feasibility of developing selected destination resort facilities and services, and (3) presenting recommendations for making the village more attractive and economically viable for permanent residents, seasonal residents, and visitors. To achieve these goals, a work plan was established comprising four phases, each of which concluded with a report(s) and public input and presentations:

- *Phase I*. Review of existing plans and studies to gain an understanding of the current situation in the village. The report presented an analysis of information collected from surveys, public meetings, interviews, and secondary data sources and addressed issues relating to land use, physical and natural characteristics, recreation resources, visibility, signage, and the sociodemographics of residents.
- *Phase II*. Analysis of current and potential demand affecting local development as well as identification and description of the market area and the feasibility of expanding the market. Specifically, seasonal recreation activities, the adequacy of overnight accommodations, existing and potential future commercial activities, and visitor characteristics and profiles were assessed.
- *Phase III*. Development of transportation strategies for circulation, access, parking, pedestrian traffic, visibility, and signage for the main highway.
- *Phase IV*. Identification, analysis, and presentation of recommendations on the development potential and feasibility for resort/recreation facilities, conceptual design proposals for existing and future development, community design concepts, and strategies for future development and financing.

Resident perceptions of what should be offered the tourist formed the underlying basis of the economic improvement planning effort. This involved the assessment of natural resources suitable for tourism, the potential and existing market base, business and economic considerations, service provision, and evaluation of social and cultural issues. Several public input/information techniques were used to solicit comments and gain insight into local problems, issues, and opportunities.

Initially, to focus the planning, design, and research efforts, members of the Government Camp Recreation Association identified issues, constraints, and opportunities for change through the use of a nominal group technique. Another nominal group session was conducted with visitors and business owners. Additionally, personal interviews were conducted with all business owners and public service providers to gain insight into the local economic situation. This information was utilized in the development and implementation of a comprehensive survey research process. As issues were identified, the need for additional research was often identified. Table 17.1 summarizes the types of surveys conducted during the planning effort.

Two additional questionnaires were administered to business owners and representatives of public service/governmental agencies (police, fire, water, electric, and telephone). Telephone interviews were conducted with village officials, citizens, county officials, elected officials, and federal agencies.

Public meetings were held to present the research findings, discuss alternative approaches for developing the tourist market, and review planning and design proposals. Three public meetings were held in the village for residents. Two other public meetings

TABLE 17.1
Survey Research Studies and Methods

Survey and Purpose	Population Targeted	Sample Size	Return Rate	Method Used
Household survey: Census of housing; identify desired changes and services; determine issues that residents want addressed	Residents (permanent and seasonal)	275	85 (30.9%)	Mail
Visitor survey: Identify desired changes and services required to increase visitation; delineate visitor profiles and trip characteristics	Visitors (ski area season passholders and lodging guest lists)	493	278 (56.4%)	Mail and intercept
Ski camp survey: Identify desired changes and services required to increase visitation	Youth groups utilizing ski instruction (12–18 years of age)	400	106 (26.5%)	Intercept
Business survey: Identify issues and opportunities, including facility and space requirements, traffic counts, parking, preferred adjacent businesses, and customer requirements	Business owners	11	11 (100.0%)	Structured interview
Public services survey: Identify characteristics and issues of all public services in the village	Managers	6	6 (100.0%)	Structured interview
Business development survey: Identify customer, facility, and location requirements of potential businesses for the village	Potential business types	23	15 (65.2%)	Telephone
Destination resort survey: Identify management and marketing issues in Alpine communities of a similar size, including business recruitment, financing of snow removal, decreasing traffic congestion, parking alterations, signage, and promotion	Mayors and city administrators in selected Alpine communities in the Pacific Northwest and Colorado	30	17 (56.7%)	Mail
Convention/Conference trends survey: Identify competing Oregon convention and visitor hotels and resorts as well as characteristics of the market	Hotels and resorts in the Pacific Northwest	15	8 (53.3%)	Mail and telephone

Source: Government Camp Improvement Project: Summary Report (1990).

that encouraged all Mount Hood residents (four different communities) to attend were held in Government Camp. Finally, three presentations to the County Board of Commissioners and professional planning staff were made by the planning and design team. In total, seven reports and six design alternatives were completed for public review and comment.

To gain additional input, a three-day design workshop with professional planners, designers, artists, community residents, business owners, United States Forest Service

(USFS) personnel, and visitors was held in the village. This workshop provided a way to assess, via a balloting process, the key stakeholders' reactions to the various design alternatives. Extensive efforts were also made to encourage radio, newspaper, and television coverage of all efforts, meetings, and findings during the three-year planning effort. Figure 17.3 presents an article from the Portland newspaper, *The Oregonian*.

SUMMARY OF FINDINGS AND PLAN RECOMMENDATIONS

Challenging policy and community development questions arose when trying to satisfy the needs and address the issues of visitors and residents. Initial findings from the nominal group sessions and surveys indicated that there were concerns regarding the range of services to be developed and how that development would impact the esthetic qualities and ambience of the village. As the planning process progressed, different opinions surfaced regarding the types of services desired and how they should be developed. The multidisciplinary composition of the planning and design team helped to address two sets of interrelated concerns: (1) desired services and facilities and (2) improving the image of the village.

Desired Services and Facilities
Desired services and facilities were categorized into (1) commercial service and facility improvements, (2) recreation service and facility improvements, and (3) public and quasi-public service and facility improvements. Commercial services gaining the most support were visitor-oriented. Compared to the visitor population, permanent and seasonal residents indicated little support for developments such as a large retail drug/variety store, believing that this type of development would detract from the esthetics of the town. All groups (visitors and permanent and seasonal residents) supported installation of a bank teller machine, development of a restaurant (24-hour operation), and additional lodging facilities.

Support for public and quasi-public service development and provisions that would improve the quality of life/experience for all groups was widespread (see Table 17.2). The need to provide services such as parking, public restrooms, police and fire services, snow removal service, and affordable employee housing was identified by all three groups. This information helped Clackamas County develop strategies to focus resources in this unincorporated, urban area. It was determined that incorporation would not enable the village to provide the range and extent of services required due to the size of the tax base.

Support for various recreation facilities and service development options was mixed. Interestingly, visitors did not support the development of tennis courts, while permanent and seasonal residents did. It is possible that visitors viewed Government Camp as a place to enjoy resource-oriented outdoor recreation activities, whereas tennis can be enjoyed elsewhere in different seasons. Visitors and permanent residents desired a central park/play area, while seasonal residents did not. Potential explanations could relate to seasonal residents' fears of tax increases to pay for this type of development and/or concerns that a park would detract from the rugged atmosphere of the area. On the other hand, permanent residents may have been indicating a need for social gathering places that could be used by residents and visitors alike.

All groups supported an increase in the number of cross-country ski trails and the

The Oregonian

Founded Dec. 4, 1850. Established as a daily Feb. 4, 1861. The Sunday Oregonian established Dec. 4, 1881. Published daily and Sunday by the Oregonian Publishing Co., 1320 S.W. Broadway, Portland, Oregon 97201

FRED A. STICKEL, President and Publisher

WILLIAM A. HILLIARD, Editor

ROBERT M. LANDAUER, Editorial Page Editor
BRIAN E. BOUNOUS, Advertising Dir.
DONALD J. STERLING JR., Asst. to the Publisher

PETER THOMPSON, Managing Editor
PATRICK L. MARLTON, Circulation Dir.

MONDAY, DECEMBER 4, 1989

Right time, right plan

The proposal for the revitalization of Government Camp is an outstanding example of citizens and state and local governments working together to improve a community.

It promises to make Government Camp what it should be but never has managed to become: a choice alpine resort and commercial center for Oregon's most popular mountain playground, Mount Hood.

For decades Government Camp has struggled with the question of how an unincorporated village that today has only about 150 full-time residents can serve the thousands of visitors who flock to the mountain on winter weekends. Not all of them stop there, but most of them at least pass by.

Even Government Camp's name is against it. It commemorates a U.S. Army detachment that bogged down in heavy snow at the site in 1849. But research has found that many tourists, who might otherwise stop whiz past because they think the place must be a Forest Service installation or even a military base.

Business people and cabin owners of Government Camp have organized to do something about its stagnation. They have developed a proposal with the help of the University of Oregon's Department of Planning and Clackamas County's Planning and Economic Development Division.

Their aim is to remake Government Camp into an alpine town with harmonizing buildings featuring stone and heavy timbers, in the Cascadian style that Timberline Lodge represents.

Public money would be invested in improvements such as street paving, parking, sidewalks, trash cleanup, street lighting, a playground park — and entrance signs. Also in the plan but probably further in the future are a skating rink, nature center and studies for a new tramway between Government Camp and Timberline.

Private investors already have said that if the village can be revitalized, they are prepared to build motels, shops and other accommodations to take advantage of it.

The public improvements would be paid for by tax-increment financing. That is, for the next 15 years the property tax revenue from any increases in assessed values in the revitalization area would be used to pay for the public improvements. The plan would be fail-safe in that if the hoped-for new private investments did not produce the revenue, the public projects would not be undertaken.

One challenge that still would face the people of Government Camp would be to figure out how to maintain the new public facilities. They probably either would have to incorporate Government Camp as a city or form a service district to perform such chores as plowing snow from the side streets and mowing the grass in the park.

The Clackamas County Board of Commissioners must adopt an ordinance in order to create the tax-increment financing district. It has scheduled the last of several public hearings for Dec. 14. Then the commission should approve the ordinance and start Government Camp on its way.

Figure 17.3
Publicity concerning Government Camp's tourism proposals. (Courtesy of The Oregonian *Publishing Company.)*

341

TABLE 17.2
Public and Quasi-Public Improvements

Public/Quasi-Public Services	Community-Pedestrian Development
Fire/Health safety	Path system
Snow removal	Drainage/Water
Small business development loans	Sidewalks
Building renovation loans	Curbs/Gutters
Employee housing	Trash receptacles
Entrance improvements	Street lighting

Source: Government Camp Economic Improvement Project: Summary Report (1990).

development of an indoor swimming pool. Bike trails, picnic areas, soccer and softball fields, and movie rentals were not desired by any of the groups to any significant degree. Quite possibly, these services and facilities were not desired because they were viewed as being inconsistent with a winter recreation area.

Improving the Village Image Through the use of surveys, public meetings, and nominal group techniques, permanent and seasonal residents were asked to indicate aspects of the community they wanted to preserve and aspects that needed changing (see Table 17.3). The resulting list of positive aspects of Government Camp included skiing, hiking, and the beauty, quiet, and peacefulness of the village. The appearance of the village and the lack of services were commonly mentioned as the "least desirable" aspects of the village.

Potential solutions for changing the least desirable aspects had to be carefully considered by the planning and design team because they could have an impact on the outstanding aspects of the village. For example, the lack of parking was perceived to be a significant problem. Paving some of the roads within the village and thereby reducing reliance on the main highway was one solution to address the parking problem. On the other hand, doing so would detract from the rustic atmosphere of the village that had been created by virtue of the fact that the majority of roads within the village are unpaved.

Recommendations to improve the image of the village included (1) creating a village that encouraged exploration on foot, (2) promoting the village as part of the Mount Hood region, (3) promoting the village as a whole as opposed to focusing on individual businesses, (4) informing developers and designers of regional conditions and opportunities by creating a design support group, and (5) providing a public gathering place in the village center on the main highway or "Main Street."

Because Government Camp no longer sits on the major highway, improvements to access and visibility were required. It was recommended that signage at the main entrances to the village be placed on the highway and that existing signage be replaced with signs crafted from wood, metal, or formed glass.

The village also needed to adjust its "street manner" to accommodate visitors for an extended stay rather than merely attracting them for a quick stop. It was suggested that this could be accomplished by adding walkways to existing buildings and requiring new

TABLE 17.3

Outstanding and Least Desirable Aspects of the Village According to Residents (in Rank Order)

Outstanding Aspects to Preserve/Enhance	Least Desirable Aspects Needing Change
1. Rustic atmosphere	1. Appearance of village
2. Quiet/Peacefulness	2. Garbage and litter
3. Village character/Architecture	3. No recreation programs
4. Fresh air/Mountain scenery	4. No parking
5. Historic Barlow Trail Marker (Pioneer Trail)	5. Lack of commercial facilities
6. Proximity to Portland, Oregon	6. Snow removal
7. Unincorporated village	7. Noise
8. Winter sports	8. Traffic/Speeding
9. Hiking	9. Visitors from ski camp
10. Wildflowers	10. Lack of lodging
11. Huckleberry picking	11. Unemployment
12. Mushroom gathering	12. Attitudes toward visitors
13. Wood cutting	13. No police services

Source: Government Camp Economic Improvement Project: Summary Report (1990).

buildings on "Main Street" to provide covered walks, sitting walls, trash cans, and lighting.

A combination of three strategies for parking was adopted, including (1) establishing parking around the perimeter of the village center and a parking permit program that might include charging parking fees, (2) requiring a permit and/or promoting the use of transit systems, and (3) staggering demand with a reduced and variable rate for ski tickets during periods when demand for parking was low.

To address the issue of snow removal, a problem that is common to many winter recreation communities, contracting of snow removal, grading specific roads to facilitate snow plow operation, and modifying snow removal to reduce damage to the vegetation adjacent to the west entry of the village were recommended.

IMPLEMENTATION

A phased approach to developing and funding projects was recommended. Three phases were identified for implementation over a 10-year period. Phase I comprised developments and improvements that were required immediately and would support subsequent developments. These included improvements to commercial facilities and services such as lodging (specification of lot location, size, type, and recommended price per night), retail (outline of type of establishment, goods to be offered, and location), and visitor services (focusing on ski·storage and child care). Most of Phase I involved investment by the private sector. Table 17.2 presents some of the Phase I public and quasi-public improvements that were supported by village residents.

Phase II included a recommendation to develop a regional convention facility on one of two large parcels of land located in the community. Commercial services recommended included laundry facilities, a general store, and convenience foods and specialty clothing stores. Public and quasi-public initiatives included a number of recommendations for main street pedestrian developments (e.g., planter beds, drinking fountains, and sitting walls). It was also recommended that a budget be developed for advertising and promoting the community. This expenditure was recommended assuming that Phase I improvements would have been implemented and that the basic services and image of the village would have been improved. Main street pedestrian developments and promotion efforts have been implemented. However, the convention center is on hold due to unfavorable economic conditions.

Phase III development focused on the provision of more extensive recreation amenity development and public improvement (e.g., picnic areas, trails for cross-country skiing, biking, and hiking, a park in the village core, tennis courts, and a ski/mountain museum). Based on the study of comparable regional convention and resort centers, along with consensus building via community meetings and workshops, these improvements were believed to be necessary to support future resort developments. Public and quasi-public amenities included the provision of restrooms, a visitor center, additional employee housing, and additional funds for marketing. Phase III has yet to be implemented because Phases I and II have not been implemented in full.

A funding program that identified potential sources of funds available from the federal, state, and county governments as well as private foundations was developed. Estimated costs, funding potential, and sources were identified for each project within each phase. Tax increment financing (TIF) was recommended as a tool to enable the village to earmark tax revenue generated from property improvements within the area for use for additional planned development. This method is particularly appropriate to unincorporated villages like Government Camp because income generated via taxes will be reinvested in the village based upon the recommendations identified in the phasing plan just described.

CONCLUDING OBSERVATIONS ON CITIZEN PARTICIPATION AND PLANNING FOR TOURISM

Using a variety of means to solicit input from stakeholder groups to identify issues and concerns is crucial in initiating the planning process. The information helps define the objectives of community planning and development efforts. Specifically, planners should help citizens, business owners, and the decision-making authorities to be visionary with regard to the desired results of the planning effort.

Research findings and recommendations must be presented in a user-friendly manner so the community can clearly understand the implications. The use of pictures, graphics, slides, and guest speakers from successful tourism communities may be helpful. Additionally, the use of public balloting which allows residents and visitors to vote for aspects of each proposed strategy or alternative plan and design is key to involving the public. Each alternative usually has unique and desirable qualities. Balloting and graphic techniques proved useful in developing consensus in Government Camp.

Planners should listen to residents. If residents believe that they are being listened to, they will tend to support change within their community and region. If nothing else, the concerns of residents can be integrated into the planning processes. For example, residents of Government Camp were very concerned that tourism development would detract from the "rustic" nature of their community and bring an onslaught of fast-food chains with their bright plastic neon signs.

The planning process should not be solely reliant on public hearings, which tend to be intimidating. Instead, the process should utilize a variety of means (e.g., small group processes, surveys, brainstorming, balloting) to solicit comment and input from residents and the business community.

Planners should be prepared to provide training and educational sessions for citizens. Bringing in outside speakers and experts who can verify conclusions and findings may prove useful. Providing reading materials and film documentaries (available at many university libraries) may also be of assistance.

Finally, an atmosphere that encourages citizens to speak freely must be developed. Community members' concerns must never be belittled. If community members perceive that the planners and decision makers are not sincere, problems may arise later in the adoption phase of the plan(s). Total congruency of opinion may not be possible, but a fair, effective, and accessible planning process that includes participation and representation of the public is possible and necessary.

What does all this mean? How should managers, planners, and tourism promoters use this information? Listed below are several points to consider for planning and managing the development of a tourism community:

- *Local planning and control.* Local control[6] of the development process is important to clarify local values. Integrating local residents into the planning process ensures support for the local tourism and recreation industry.
- *Community direction and values.* Addressing community and visitor values is essential for improving the quality of life and visitor experience. The residents, permanent and seasonal, can help to decide on a general direction for changing the "sense" of their community. Their input is motivated by a need for economic stimulation and preservation of a sense of place. Through the planning process, values related to the quality of life can be identified. Consequently, all improvements should be evaluated and measured against these expressed values and concerns.
- *Market research.* Continual evaluation of visitor characteristics will provide the opportunity to determine the potential clientele for existing and future services.
- *Service needs and desires.* Residents and visitors in tourism and recreation-based communities sometimes appear to have conflicting needs. Seasonal residents want the community to remain a rustic place of refuge. Permanent residents desire and need the jobs that may be generated through economic stimulation and sound visitor management programs. Finally, visitors need and desire improved and well-maintained visitor facilities within a rugged and rustic atmosphere. Plans must

address these differences and ensure a service mix compatible with the similarities and differences identified.

- *Quality services.* Since the tourism-based community's economic livelihood depends on its visitor services (lodging, restaurants, equipment rentals), it is critical to provide quality services and to facilitate the utilization of those services. The physical design of the community should address these issues by providing a setting that will enhance the visitor experience.

- *Taxes and assessments.* Local officials must demonstrate that government expenditures benefit residents by bringing the visitor to town, which, in turn, helps the local economy.

- *Community impact research.* Continual monitoring and evaluation of permanent and seasonal resident needs, concerns, and issues will enable the community to manage tourism and recreation in a way that limits or reduces negative influences on the local quality of life.

Economic improvement using tourism and recreation development is a complex and time-consuming process requiring considerable coordination among all concerned individuals and groups. The planning, analysis, organization, and prioritizing of economic development strategies is only the beginning of the process. The challenge involves how to proceed in promoting positive growth while continually attempting to improve the village image for the purpose of attracting visitors. Fortunately, the residents of Government Camp seem to be prepared to meet the challenge. Their willingness is shown by their intense interest and participation in the planning effort. With a concerted effort, the residents and business owners should realize their goal of improving the economic health of this small, unincorporated village in an Alpine region of the Pacific Northwest Cascade mountains.

ACKNOWLEDGMENTS

We would like to thank the Government Camp Recreation Association, RLK Company, Timberline Lodge, Mount Hood Meadows, Clackamas County Department of Human Services, Division of Community Development, and the US Forest Service, Mount Hood District Office for their support and involvement in the project. Just a few of the Government Camp community members who provided the impetus and key support include Duane Bridges, Mary Anne Hill, Bud England, and Richard Kohnstamm. The comprehensive nature of this project was achieved based on their concern for the future of their community. Thanks also to Jie Chen and the University of Oregon Department of Planning, Public Policy, and Management for their assistance in preparing the maps presented in this chapter.

NOTES

1. See Chapter 14 for a comprehensive overview of issues relating to participation readiness.
2. See Chapters 3–6, 9, and 28 for overviews of tourism planning processes and philosophies.
3. See Chapters 5, 9, 11, 12, 14–16, 18, and 19 for additional discussion of community attitudes and involvement in tourism planning and development processes.
4. See Chapters 4, 5, 7, 8, 17, 18, 22, and 23 for additional discussion relating to sustainable tourism and sustainable tourism development.
5. The nominal group technique (NGT) can be used as a tool for consensus building (Ritchie, 1994, pp. 493–501). It is normally implemented in six stages: (1) presentation of an initial

statement of the topic area, (2) individual reflection and recording of personal responses, (3) round table discussion of responses, (4) consolidation and review of the complete set of ideas, (5) prioritizing of responses on an individual basis, and (6) compilation of results based on aggregate rankings. Three strengths of the NGT are that it provides structured output that can be analyzed at an individual level, it can result in high respondent involvement and commitment, and it is possible to study both intra- and intergroup differences (Ritchie, 1994, pp. 498–499). The major disadvantages relate to sampling and high levels of nonresponse bias (i.e., participants may choose not to attend the session) (Ritchie, 1994, p. 499).

6. See Chapters 7, 9, and 15 for additional discussion concerning power structures and control of the local tourism industry.

REFERENCES

Allen, L.R. and R. Gibson. 1987. Perceptions of community life and services: a comparison between leaders and community residents, *Journal of the Community Development Society*, 18(1), 89–103.

Ayers, J.S. and H.R. Potter. 1989. Attitudes toward community change: a comparison between rural leaders and residents, *Journal of the Community Development Society*, 20(1), 1–18.

Brindley, B. 1991. What is "sustainable"? Ceres: *FAO Review*, 35–38.

Draper, D. and H.G. Kariel. 1990. Metatourism: dealing critically with the future of tourism environments, *Journal of Cultural Geography*, 11(1), 139–150.

Gill, A. and P.W. Williams. 1994. Managing growth in mountain tourism communities, *Tourism Management*, 15, 212–220.

Goudy, W.J. 1977. Evaluations of local attributes and community satisfaction in small towns, *Rural Sociology*, 42(3), 371–382.

Government Camp Economic Improvement Project: Summary Report. 1990. Community Planning Workshop, University of Oregon.

Gunn, C.A. 1988. *Tourism Planning*, 2nd ed. New York: Taylor and Francis.

Knowles-Lankford, J. 1992. *Sustainable Practices: A Study of the Change Professions.* Unpublished Master's thesis. University of Oregon, Eugene: Department of Landscape Architecture.

Knowles-Lankford, J. and S. Lankford. 1994. *Sustainable Practices: Implications for Tourism and Recreation Development.* Abstracts from the 1994 National Recreation and Park Association Leisure Research Symposium. Minneapolis, MN: NRPA.

Kouba, D.M. 1985. Managing resort communities, *MIS Report* (ICMA), 17(7), 1–15.

Lankford, S. 1991a. *An Analysis of Resident Preferences, Attitudes and Opinions Toward Tourism and Rural Regional Development in the Columbia River Gorge.* Unpublished PhD Dissertation. Eugene: University of Oregon.

Lankford, S. 1991b. *Attitudes Toward Tourism in the Columbia River Gorge.* University of Oregon, Eugene: Community Planning Workshop.

Lankford, S. 1994. Attitudes and perceptions toward tourism and rural regional development, *Journal of Travel Research*, 32(3), 35–43.

Lankford, S. and D. Howard. 1994. Developing a tourism impact attitude scale, *Annals of Tourism Research*, 21(1), 121–139.

Lankford, S. and J. Knowles-Lankford. 1992. Managing your community for winter recreation activities: considerations for promoters and managers, *Winter Cities*, 10(1), 25–27.

Loukissas, P.J. 1983. Public participation in community tourism planning: a gaming simulation approach, *Journal of Travel Research*, 22(1), 18–23.

McIntosh, R.W. and C.R. Goeldner. 1990. *Tourism: Principles, Practices, Philosophies*, 6th ed. New York: John Wiley & Sons.

Murphy, P.E. 1985. *Tourism: A Community Approach*. New York: Methuen.

Napier, T.L. and C.J. Wright. 1974. Impact of rural development: case study of forced relocation, *Journal of the Community Development Society*, 5(2), 107–115.

Povey, D. 1986. *Oregon Ski Economics Study, 1986–1987*. University of Oregon, Eugene, Oregon: Community Planning Workshop.

Ritchie, J.R.B. 1994. The nominal group technique—applications in tourism research. In J.R.B. Ritchie and G.R. Goeldner (eds.), *Travel, Tourism, and Hospitality Research—A Handbook for Managers and Researchers*, 2nd ed. New York: John Wiley & Sons, pp. 493–501.

Rosentraub, M. and L. Thompson. 1981. The use of surveys of satisfaction for evaluations, *Policy Studies Journal*, 9(7), 990–1000.

ɠ | PROBLEM SOLVING AND DISCUSSION ACTIVITIES

1. The Black Point National Scenic Area (BPNSA) Administration requests proposals for a study to (1) address preliminary planning and research initiatives for tourism and recreation development and (2) assist in the development of long-range plans and strategies aimed at developing the local economy of Makapu'u. Makapu'u is situated in the Pacific region. Its natural harbors and marine life have attracted fisherman and explorers for centuries. The area has extensive geologic formations, ancient fishing caves, and many trails. Fishing, tourism and agriculture are primary sources of income. There is a population of 9000 people. The BPNSA Administration has determined that the area resources can be diversified to spur local growth and developed to alleviate crowded conditions on other islands.

   An extensive development plan is being considered to include short-term residential uses, limited business and commercial uses, and additional recreational uses such as fishing areas, golfing, car racing, motorcycle and dune buggy areas, and hiking areas. Short-term accommodations with resort capabilities and long-term accommodations to include timeshare units will also be developed.

   The following stakeholders must be integrated into the proposed process: Coastal Zone Management Commission, BPNSA Administration, County Planning and Economic Development Office, tourism operators, business owners, tourists, residents, and developers. The BPNSA desires to examine a number of scenarios and planning processes. Proposals must provide an overview of the process that will be used to determine the following:

   a. Recreational amenities and services for tourists and residents.

   b. A promotional plan (to whom, how, where).

   c. The level, type, and extent of tourist facilities.

   d. The impacts (economic, social, ecological) of tourism.

   Work in groups to respond to the Request for Proposals. A work plan, process, timeline, and research agenda should be prepared. Of particular importance are your recommendations for incorporating public consultation within the planning process.

2. Prepare an overview of the process (i.e., a script) for using the nominal group technique to solicit input from local residents on the nature of development they would like to see on Makapu'u. What approach should be taken to ensure a high level of participation at this session?

3. Interview two persons from among the following: a developer, a local conservation group representative, and/or a government official (planner etc.) to discuss what constitutes a good planning process and a solid public participation program. Compare the perspectives resulting from the interviews.

4. Attend a public meeting or hearing in your community. Prepare a critique of the effectiveness of this form of public consultation based on your experience at that meeting/hearing. Was public input actually "heard"? Did it appear that attendance at the meeting/hearing was worth the effort of the public? What suggestions would you make to improve the effectiveness of such a forum?

18

It Is "Never-Never Land" When Interest Groups Prevail

DISNEY'S AMERICA PROJECT, PRINCE WILLIAM COUNTY, VIRGINIA, USA

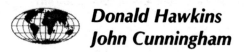

Donald Hawkins
John Cunningham

✎ | KEY LEARNING POINTS

- Even the most prestigious, high-profile, multinational company must recognize the critical role of public consultation if they are to succeed in today's environment.

- Public participation should be incorporated in the planning of new developments to mitigate problems before they become serious issues that impede development. Developers who include local residents and other interest groups in the planning process and address their concerns have a greater chance of success than those who do not.

- Local residents should be encouraged to participate in the planning process for new developments because they have a stake in the future direction of their communities.

- Local residents should be provided with objective and comprehensive information about the nature of development and its effect on the human and cultural environments prior to and throughout the development process. Although this may be time-consuming and costly, such communication affords opportunities to identify and mitigate potential sources of conflict between communities of interest and the developer before they become major issues that could thwart the development process.

INTRODUCTION

This chapter discusses issues relating to Disney's America theme park that was proposed for development in the Prince William County area outside the town of Haymarket,

Virginia, USA. The Walt Disney Company's approach to developing Disney's America theme park provides an example of a megaproject that failed to follow one of the key principles of sustainable tourism development—the need to involve all stakeholders in all aspects of planning and decision making in projects affecting their community. It serves as a testimonial to what can happen if local citizens are excluded from the planning process, regardless of the scope and potential economic benefits of development.

A series of milestones is presented that covers the period from the project's announcement in November 1993 to its cancellation in September 1994. During this time, the Walt Disney Company experienced a number of victories, including vocal support from local, regional, and state politicians and business leaders and a US$163.2 million incentive package from the state of Virginia. On the other hand, the Walt Disney Company also encountered fierce opposition from residents concerned with the environmental and cultural degradation they believed would accompany the project. The opposition's organization and intensity created serious stumbling blocks for the Disney Company and ultimately contributed to the project's demise.

Information presented in this chapter was compiled from secondary source materials, primarily information released to the general public by the Washington media, the Disney Company, and the Greater Washington Board of Trade between November 1993 and September 1994.

SUSTAINABLE TOURISM DEVELOPMENT AND PUBLIC CONSULTATION: CONTEMPORARY PERSPECTIVES AND ISSUES

The concepts of sustainable tourism development and conservation are increasingly being linked to public participation and decentralized decision making. They have evolved as a result of an educated society's increased emphasis on preserving cultural and natural resources, particularly when development occurs near their place of residence.

Sustainable Tourism Development Sustainable tourism development[1] relates to the interdependency among tourism industry developers, community authorities, and environmentalists who work in tandem to ensure an improved quality of life for area residents and to maintain area resources for future generations (see Figure 18.1) (McIntyre, 1993). This approach emphasizes that planning for sustainable tourism development should be cross-sectional and integrated, involving government agencies, private corporations, citizens groups, and individuals affected by development.

Critical to sustainable tourism development is the involvement of local residents in the planning and implementation of new developments. Local residents must be provided with objective and comprehensive information, research, and communication about the nature of development and its effects on the human and cultural environments (McIntyre, 1993). This information should be made available to local residents prior to, and throughout, the development process.

Public Participation Local participation during the early stages of the planning process is critical to tourism development. Lankford[2] (1994, p. 35) indicates that, to mitigate negative sociocultural impacts, "goals and strategies of tourism development must reflect or incorporate local

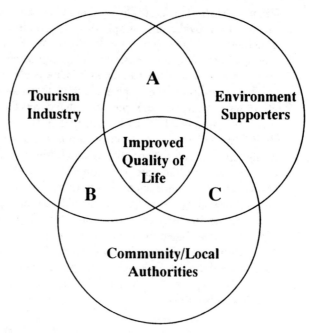

Figure 18.1
Relationships for
sustainability.
(From McIntyre,
1993, p. 35.
Courtesy of
WTO.)

The tourism industry seeks a healthy business environment with:
* financial security
* a trained and responsible work force
* attractions of sufficient quality to ensure a steady flow of visitors—who stay longer and visit more often

Those interested in natural environment and cultural/heritage issues seek:
* protection of the environment through prevention, improvement, correction of damage, and restoration
* to motivate people to be more aware—and therefore "care for" rather than "use up" resources

Community members seek a healthy place in which to live with:
* food, adequate and clean water, health care, rewarding work for equitable pay, education and recreation
* respect for cultural traditions
* opportunities to make decisions about the future

Some concerns that each pair may hold in common include:
* issues of access, such as when, where, and how tourists visit and move from place to place
* host and guest issues, such as cultural impact or common use of infrastructure
* land use issues, such as hunting/wildlife habitat, agriculture/recreation, preservation/development, etc.

residents' views to ensure consensus on development policies and programs." Lankford makes reference to Pearce, who states that "if resident perceptions and preferences do not support tourism development policies and programs, then programs are likely to fail or be ineffective in their implementation" (Pearce, 1980 as cited in Lankford, 1994, p. 35).

Studies summarized by Bhatnager and Williams (1992) for the World Bank document numerous cases where local participation increased the effectiveness and sustainability of development projects. A 1985 study of 25 development projects achieving long-term sustainability concluded that 12 were the result of a high degree of local participation (Bhatnager and Williams, 1992).

Local participation may range from unstructured methods such as public meetings to specialized techniques, including the nominal group technique[3] and scenario writing. In cases of conflict and confrontation, negotiated rule making, arbitration, and mediation techniques may be employed (Colwell, 1993). Although local participation can be time-consuming and costly to developers, these public feedback tools can identify tourism development issues that are important to various interest groups in the community. Identifying potential conflict areas so they can be mitigated before they become major issues is essential to the development process.

DISNEY'S AMERICA PROJECT: BACKGROUND AND LOCATIONAL CONTEXT

Disney Company Profile Nearly 30 years after the death of the company's founder, the Walt Disney Company has become firmly imbedded in American culture as an entertainment empire. In 1984, Michael Eisner became chief executive officer (CEO) of the Walt Disney Company. During the period to 1990, under the leadership of Eisner, the company's earnings quadrupled, making Disney one of the highest growth stocks on Wall Street. Disney stock increased almost eightfold during that period.

Eisner focused on the business of making movies with such megahits as *Pretty Woman, Who Framed Roger Rabbit?, Beauty and the Beast*, and *The Lion King* (Moreau, 1992). By 1992, films represented the second largest source (42 percent) of company revenue. Disney's share of the American movie market was 29 percent. Disney's July 31, 1995 US$19 billion takeover agreement with Capital Cities/ABC (America's second-largest merger ever—including Capital Cities/ABC's television and radio stations, publishing, and multimedia groups) provides the company with the opportunity to have its films and products viewed, heard, and read by a large segment of the American public. Under Eisner's leadership, Disney also ventured into other areas. By 1992, Disney operated 144 Disney retail stores, the Disney Channel was in operation, a book division was started, Disney hotels had opened, and two new health-conscious fast-food restaurants had been opened.

In addition to being the most profitable aspect of Disney business, theme parks were the most significant source of revenue for Disney in 1992. The two theme parks located in California and Florida accounted for 46 percent of company revenue and 53 percent of company profits in 1992 (Moreau, 1992). Visitation within the US$6 billion theme park industry was expected to increase by 5–7 percent during 1994 (Cohen, 1993). Despite losses of more than US$900 million at Euro Disney during its first fiscal year (1992–1993), the predicted increase in popularity and potential for high profit margins may have set the stage for Disney's continued focus on developing new theme parks such as the proposed Disney's America project.

Disney's America Project Announcement The Walt Disney Company announced its plans to develop a new theme park in Prince William County, Virginia near Haymarket, approximately 35 miles (55 kilometers) west of Washington, D.C. (see Figure 18.2) in November 1993. The theme park was to be located at the junction of Interstate 66 and US Route 15. The proposal for the US$625 million 3000-acre (1215-hectare) development included an American heritage theme

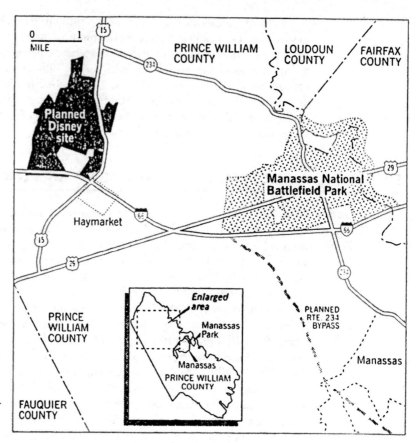

Figure 18.2
Disney's America project: proposed site. (Courtesy of The Washington Post.)

park, 2500 homes, 1300 hotel rooms, recreation facilities, and up to two million square feet (185,800 square meters) of commercial space (Hsu, 1994a). The theme park was scheduled to commence operations by 1998 and be completed by 2007.

The project was plagued by controversy from the outset due to a development proposal that was perceived to be vague and which, therefore, caused concern among area environmental, conservation, and historical preservation interest groups. This chapter presents a narrative focusing on the Disney's America project from the time of its announcement by Disney officials in mid-November 1993 to its termination on September 28, 1994. Milestones apparent during the project's initial stages are highlighted.

The underlying theme is that the traditional approaches associated with successful major developments in the past cannot be taken for granted today, even when a world class developer like Disney is involved. Furthermore, Disney's past successes, such as those in Orlando and Anaheim, cannot necessarily be replicated in today's environment. Indeed, Disney has recently suffered setbacks with several project initiatives in the United States, not to mention the initial challenges with the Euro Disney effort in Paris, France (see Table 18.1).

TABLE 18.1

"Never-Never Land": Canceled Disney Projects

Name	Location	Project	Estimated Cost	Date Launched	Date Project Canceled
MGM Studio Backlot	Burbank, California	Retail and entertainment complex	US$611 million	Early 1987	May 1988
Disney Sea	Long Beach, California	Waterfront theme park	US$2–US$3 billion	August 1990	March 1992
Westcot	Anaheim, California	Theme park based on Epcot	US$3 billion	1990	On hold, Summer 1994
Disney's America	Haymarket, Virginia	History-oriented theme park	US$625 million	November 1993	September 1994

Source: The Washington Post (October 3, 1994). (Courtesy of *The Washington Post*).

DISNEY'S AMERICA PROJECT: THE ROLES, PERCEPTIONS, INTERESTS, AND ACTIONS OF DISNEY AND OTHER STAKEHOLDERS

The following milestones (not necessarily presented in chronological order) document efforts by Disney, its supporters, and the opposition to influence the actions of Disney's America during the 10-month period from November 1993 to September 1994.

Milestone 1: Overwhelming Support from Local Businesses Between November 1993 and April 1994, Disney officials met with approximately 10,000 people representing about 200 community and business organizations to gather support for the project. Disney officials also launched a community outreach blitz and "joined high-profile business groups, dispatched local staff members to myriad business luncheons, dinners and other meetings, and generally played a role of solitious new kid in town" (Powers, 1994).

Local business leaders perceived Disney's America to be a windfall for Prince William County and the surrounding area in that it would stimulate additional tourism revenue. According to the Virginia Department of Economic Development, Division of Tourism, annual tourism revenue generated by Prince William County increased by only 6.7 percent between 1988 and 1993 (from US$150 million to US$160 million), whereas tourism revenue generated by the state of Virginia increased by 19.7 percent (from US$7.6 billion to US$9.1 billion) during that time.

Local business leaders also believed that the project would generate increased tourism-related employment. According to the Virginia Department of Economic Development, Division of Tourism, state tourism employment decreased marginally (less than 1 percent) between 1988 and 1993, while tourism employment in Prince William County declined by 26.4 percent during this period.

Many Prince William County business leaders and residents believed that Disney's America offered an opportunity of a lifetime to "progress." Anticipated were new jobs, new investment, and increased sales for the area. This new business activity would translate into tax revenue that could finance a much needed expansion in the area's infrastructure. Specifically, it was believed that, given the Disney company's sound development history, the proposed theme park offered opportunities for the following:

- An improved lifestyle for many residents and business owners.
- 2700 permanent jobs when the park opened in 1998 and up to 19,000 when the project was completed in 2007. Increased employment for the area would help reduce (1) the number of people who commuted from Haymarket to Washington D.C. to work and (2) the leakage of young employable workers who otherwise leave the area in search of jobs.
- New business investment.
- Improved infrastructure and community facilities and services including water supply, waste disposal, roads, health care, and security.
- Increased markets for local products.
- Improved recreational and cultural facilities and activities for both residents and tourists.
- An increase in the number of new and repeat visitors.
- An increase in the area's average length of stay.
- Annual tax revenue of US$28.9 million by 2010, which represented the capital required for infrastructure improvements and expansion.

Milestone 2: Commitment Obtained for a State Incentive Package The proposed Disney's America project became a magnet for support from Virginia politicians based on the scope of development and the high-profile image of the Walt Disney Company. Disney officials negotiated a state incentive package totaling US$163.2 million for road improvements, tourism promotion, equipment relocation, and worker training.

The Governor's Road package, which comprised the largest segment of the incentive package for Disney, totaled US$82 million (see Figure 18.3). Proposed road improvements included the widening of US Route 15 from two to four lanes, an interchange to access the site from Interstate 66, and the addition of two new roads inside the park. In return, Disney agreed to pay debt service on US$49 million in road bonds which would be used to finance road improvements around the site.

Although most state politicians supported the project, there was division with respect to the perceived "generosity" of the package. In February 1994, further negotiation in the Virginia General Assembly resulted in an attempt by the state to (1) impose a US$1.00 per person tax on admission tickets to the theme park to ensure recovery of some state money and (2) reduce the amount of the package initially proposed (Baker, 1994a).

Disney officials reacted swiftly, stating that if the US$1.00 tax were imposed or the incentive package reduced, they would not locate in Virginia (Hsu and Harris, 1994). The newly elected state governor, who favored the project, applied pressure to several lawmakers by holding back as many as 10 judicial appointments (Baker and Harris, 1994). Ultimately, the threat of Disney's pullout, combined with creative politicking, resulted

Fact: I-66 Improvements Occur a Generation Early

Funding for I-66 Congestion Relief <u>Without</u> Governor's Road Package

$82 Million in Funding for Long-Planned I-66 Improvements <u>With</u> Governor's Road Package

$82

$0

•No New Taxes

•State Income from park will be 4X Annual Cost of Road Bonds

$49

Figure 18.3
F.A.I.R. facts: Governor's Road package. (The F.A.I.R. Issues Campaign. Courtesy of the Greater Washington Board of Trade.)

in the Virginia General Assembly passing the US$163.2 million package without the US$1.00 admissions tax on March 11, 1994 (Baker and Harris, 1994).

Milestone 3: Problems Surface The social and environmental costs associated with Disney's America project were perceived by many to be too high. Some believed that the increase in traffic and suburban sprawl resulting from peripheral developments would contribute to the exploitation and degradation of an area considered to be the most historically significant in the United States. The project would be situated less than one-half hour's drive from 18 Civil War battlefields and 64 historic sites—an area tagged the "Cradle of American Democracy." As Protect Historic America co-chair C. Vann Woodward said in the *Washington Post* (McPherson, 1994):

> This part of Northern Virginia has soaked up more of the blood, sweat, and tears of American history than any other area of the country. It has bred more founding fathers, inspired more soaring hopes and ideals and witnessed more triumphs and failures, victories and lost causes than any other place in the country.

Many residents were also concerned that the dramatic increase in traffic predicted to accompany Disney's America would affect the Manassas Battlefield, a priceless national heritage site located 4 miles (6.5 kilometers) east of the proposed theme park, which was already under pressure from Washington D.C.'s suburban sprawl.

Although many Prince William County residents favored Disney's America, some feared that they would lose control in determining the future direction of the area once such development occurred. In addition, some residents expressed concern that the development would pose a threat to the quality of life for existing residents in this rural area and result in the following:

- A permanent change in the esthetic appeal of the region. Prince William County is a rapidly growing residential community. Residential growth between 1985 and 1993 placed the county second among 10 geographic regions in Northern Virginia. Prince William County ranked fourth in nonresidential/commercial development during that same time period. Some residents were concerned about the negative impacts of a large-scale development.
- Increased prices for land and new construction. Land speculation had already increased property values. Demand for construction would increase as well.
- The creation of generally low-paying, seasonal employment. The peak tourist season in the county occurs during the months of April through October. Up to 19,000 people would have been directly employed by Disney during the peak months. However, there was uncertainty concerning the numbers who would be employed during the winter season.
- Increases to the population and, thus, increased crime.
- Increased environmental damage from increased transient traffic and the emergence of new businesses.
- Degraded and depleted water resources. Some residents were concerned that the proposed theme park would overwhelm the county's water treatment capabilities.
- Increased traffic, resulting in congestion and diminished air quality.

Moreover, some residents voiced concern that, if the Disney Company did not meet its financial obligations, the burden would rest with the taxpayer. Three related concerns included the following: (1) Area tax rates would be affected similar to what happened in Orlando, Florida and Anaheim, California, where government subsidies and incentives provided for the Disney Company were recovered by increased taxation; (2) if the Disney Company could not make its payments to the state for its share of the road improvements, the state would be forced to make these payments, with the burden ultimately falling on the taxpayer; and (3) the possibility that Disney officials and county planners had overestimated theme park benefits while understating the costs of the project to the community in terms of schooling, fire, and policing expenses.

In essence, some residents were concerned that the project posed a significant threat to their quality of life. For many, the "price of progress" was considered to be too high.

Milestone 4: The Opposition Consolidates and Strengthens Its Position Interest groups in and around Prince William County, as well as nationally, shared many of the concerns expressed by local residents. More than 20 local and national interest groups joined forces to oppose the theme park. The opposition was spearheaded by a broad coalition of existing and newly formed environmental, historic preservation, and citizens organizations as well as a powerful component of wealthy citizens, Washington political and media advisors, and consumer advocates. As stated in the *Washington Post* in June 1994 (Fehr and Shear, 1994):

> Since the company unveiled its plans last fall, the fight over Disney's America has built gradually from a neighborhood squabble to a high stakes struggle involving environmentalists, historians, federal agencies and now congress.

One major source of opposition was the National Trust for Historic Preservation, consisting of approximately 250,000 members. The National Trust represented a number of other interest groups concerned with the theme park and the resulting urban sprawl. Some of the activity on the part of the opposition included the following:

- On February 2, 1994, The Environmental Defense Fund, the Natural Resources Defense Council, and the Sierra Club (three of the nation's largest environmental groups) announced that they were going to oppose the project amid concerns relating to transportation, zoning, and infrastructure (Baker, 1994a).
- Piedmont Environmental Council's (PEC) membership doubled its donations to US$1.2 million. PEC's lobbying costs increased from US$4,200 per year to more than US$105,000 in 1994, while the Disney Company spent US$444,000 to lobby the assembly during that same period (Tousignant, 1994).
- Protect Historic America located chairpersons in several states to reach a mailing list of approximately 30,000 history advocates (Hsu, 1994c).
- A group of 20 prominent historians and writers united to oppose the Disney's America project, and served as an advisory committee to Protect Historic America (Hsu, 1994b).

The organization, commitment, and clout of the opponents was underestimated by Disney officials, including the top Disney official, Michael Eisner. During a scheduled Capitol Hill luncheon in June he expressed his surprise at the intensity and financial resources of the opposition.

Milestone 5: Disney Offers Concessions High visibility on the part of the opposition contributed to increased public pressure against the project. By September 1994, the Disney Company responded by pledging a substantial concessions package to persuade the opposition to accept the new theme park development. Among the concessions were pledges to (Untitled Disney's America release Sept. 1, 1994):

- Make annual donations to historic preservation groups.
- Provide financial contributions for improvements to the Manassas National Battlefield Park located approximately 4 miles (6.5 kilometers) from the proposed theme park site.
- Donate an area visitors center.
- Commit to adopting recycling practices, the consumption of nonpolluting fuels in the Disney operating fleet and ride attractions, and using alternatives to pesticides.
- Provide concessions on land use for new schools, parks, a library, and a police station for Prince William County amounting to approximately 90 acres (36.5 hectares) on the site of the proposed theme park.
- Place a cap on the amount of new traffic utilizing the roadways to visit Disney's America. This limit was to be enforced by Prince William County if the annualized average reached 77,000 vehicles per day.

These concessions did not dissuade interest groups from continuing to publicly oppose the development. Ongoing negative publicity in the *Washington Post* as well as in local and regional newspapers prompted Disney officials and supporters of the development to mount a public relations campaign to counteract the momentum of the opposition groups. As a result, Facts About Intra-Regional Issues (F.A.I.R) was formed.

Fact: Disney Will Not Be Visible from Any Point on the Battlefield

Figure 18.4
F.A.I.R. facts: Disney's America project location relative to Manassas Battlefield. (The F.A.I.R. Issues Campaign. Courtesy of the Greater Washington Board of Trade.)

Disney's America

Four miles from battlefield on a map

(same as National Airport to RFK)

7 miles from battlefield by car

Manassas Battlefield

Milestone 6: On September 1, 1994, the leaders of the Greater Washington Board of Trade announced
F.A.I.R. the formation of F.A.I.R., an advocacy group comprising regional business leaders who
Formed to favored Disney's America. F.A.I.R. was established to counterbalance what was per-
Counterbalance ceived as misinformation being spread by the opposition groups (Fehr, 1994a). F.A.I.R.
Opposition released information to alleviate public concerns regarding the development. For exam-
ple, two releases were aimed at mitigating concerns relating to the impact of the Disney
project on the Manassas Battlefield (see Figures 18.4 and 18.5), particularly concerns that

Fact: Location

■**Disney's America is as far from the Manassas Battlefield by auto as:**

    – Tyson's Corner to Oakton, VA

    – The Beltway to Laurel, MD

    – W. Wilson Bridge to Andrews Air Force Base

    – The Capitol to I-66/Glebe Road Exit

    – Montrose Road on 270 to Gaithersburg, MD

Figure 18.5
More F.A.I.R. facts: Disney's America project location relative to Manassas Battlefield. (The F.A.I.R. Issues Campaign. Courtesy of the Greater Washington Board of Trade.)

■**It is not on, adjacent, or contiguous at any point to the battlefield.**

Fact: Highly Skilled Workers

■About half 2,700 Disney jobs will be in:

- ■Management
- ■Engineering
- ■Accounting
- ■Design
- ■Human Relations
- ■Maintenance

Figure 18.6
*F.A.I.R. facts: Employ-
ment opportunities
arising from Disney's
America project. (The
F.A.I.R. Issues Cam-
paign. Courtesy of the
Greater Washington
Board of Trade.)*

the theme park would be visible from the Manassas Battlefield and diminish the esthetic appeal of the battlefield site.

Two other releases attempted to minimize concerns that the jobs provided by the project would be low paying and low skilled (see Figures 18.6 and 18.7).

Milestone 7: Disney's Final Attempt to Counter the Opposition Disney officials also prepared documentation to support their argument for development and counteract the concerns voiced by the interest groups. On September 1, 1994, a 14-page document outlining the benefits of the project was released in which Disney elaborated several issues, including their commitment to (1) complement the area's historic theme, (2) establish community partnerships, (3) create economic opportunities, and (4) act as an agent for responsible growth and environmental protection. It is believed, however, that the efforts by Disney and F.A.I.R. were "too little and too late."

Milestone 8: Disney's Future Plans On September 28, 1994, less than 11 months after the announcement of the proposed Disney's America, Michael Eisner publicly announced the termination of the project (Downey Grimsley, 1994). It was later revealed that Disney officials believed that the company image was being hurt by the constant attacks from environmentalists, historians, and community leaders who were opposed to the project.

Disney officials believed that each new zoning application would be met with delays resulting from legal maneuvers initiated by opposition groups. Therefore, it would take a great deal of management's time to overcome obstacles at every stage of the development (Farhi and Spayd, 1994). Disney officials also indicated that there were contingency plans to locate elsewhere in Virginia. However, as of August 1, 1995, there was no indication of an alternative site. The Disney Company may very well consider other options and leave the State of Virginia behind.

Fact: Fully one-half Disney Orlando Workers Earn Over $12/Hour

Figure 18.7
More F.A.I.R. facts: Employment opportunities arising from Disney's America project. (The F.A.I.R. Issues Campaign. Courtesy of the Greater Washington Board of Trade.)

• **Disney Orlando minimum wage is over 30% above Federal minimum wage.**

• **Disney will pay Washington area competitive, above-minimum wage starting salaries.**

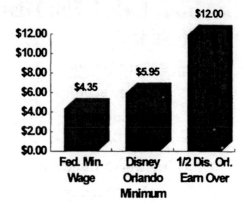

Milestone 9: Prince William County Development Back to Ground Zero Upon hearing the news of the Disney pullout, many community business owners and residents as well as local, regional, and state politicians were in a state of shock. Supporters of the development were left feeling confused and betrayed (Hsu and Tousignant, 1994). Those who opposed the development felt satisfied and victorious. Whatever the personal feelings of the individuals, Prince William County and the state of Virginia lost a significant number of jobs and tax revenue that would have accompanied the theme park. Moreover, it is unlikely that major infrastructure development projects that were predicted to be accelerated by the Disney theme park will occur within the next 10 years.

Nonetheless, development is inevitable because much of Disney's land is zoned for growth. The major challenge for Prince William County will be to (1) overcome its image of being hostile to new development (Hamilton and Webb Pressler, 1994), which resulted from the strong "not in my backyard" opposition and (2) move forward with community supported initiatives.

CONCLUSION

Disney's America project provides a contemporary example of what can happen if public concerns are not properly mediated and are allowed to grow into serious issues that impede development. Disney officials chose to solicit support from politicians and local business leaders who, in the past, may have had the power to impose development in an area with little organized resistance. In Prince William County, however, Disney officials were approached by more than 20 organized citizens groups who believed that the Disney project posed a threat to the area's cultural and natural resources.

Disney officials may have been able to counter opposition to the project had they held more open discussions, provided the opportunity for more public input, and involved area residents in the planning of Disney's America, thereby giving them a stake in planning the future of their area. Instead, Disney's "backroom" tactics left many residents feeling uneasy with the potential long-term ramifications of the project. It was feared that the development of Disney's America would result in the same perpetual expansion as other Disney theme parks in Anaheim, California and Orlando, Florida. Disney's America was perceived by many to be an incoming megadevelopment that would exploit the area's cultural heritage and irreparably damage an area already being encroached by the suburban sprawl emanating from Washington, D.C.

Disney's approach proved to be a significant mistake in its public relations strategy. According to the *Washington Post* (1994):

> Disney relied upon the mystique of its name, its impressive record of corporate success over several decades, its financial clout and the naiveté of local and state politicians, hungry for an economic development plum of any kind at any cost . . . allow[ing] arrogance to get in the way of common sense and basic principles of community and public relations. It was only after opposition surfaced that Disney unleashed a public relations blitz to win citizens' support for the project. Disney attempted to muscle its way into Haymarket, demanding subsidies and concessions from state and local officials.

Only when opposition strengthened did Disney offer its own concessions. In the past, economic opportunities and incentives may have been sufficient to bind together a community leadership coalition to support Disney development. However, today, economic opportunities do not necessarily outweigh the perceived negative social, cultural, and environmental impacts of development.

NOTES

1. See Chapters 4, 5, 7, 8, 17, 22, and 23 for additional discussion regarding the concepts of sustainable tourism and sustainable tourism development.
2. See Chapter 17 for more discussion of Lankford's 1994 study and an overview of community attitudes and involvement in the tourism planning and development processes. Additional discussion of community participation can be found in Chapters 5, 9, 11, 12, 14–17, and 19.
3. See the notes in Chapter 17 for a description of the nominal group technique.

REFERENCES

Baker, P. 1994a. Panel slaps Disney with ticket tax, *The Washington Post*, February 11, D1.

Baker, P. and J.F. Harris. 1994. Allen–Disney plan wins key support, *The Washington Post*, March 12, A1.

Bhatnager, B. and A.C. Williams. 1992. *Participatory Development and the World Bank: Potential Directions for Change*. Washington, D.C.: The World Bank.

Cohen, W. 1993. Fun boom, *US News and World Report*, 115(20), 22.

Colwell, S.D. 1993. *Negotiated Rulemaking: A Process for Facilitating Public Participation in Tourism Planning*. Unpublished Master of Arts Thesis presented to The George Washington University, December.

Downey Grimsley, K. 1994. Disney packs its bags, *The Washington Post*, October 3, Supplement, 1.

Farhl, P. and L. Spayd. 1994. Eisner ended Disney plan, *The Washington Post*, September 30, A1.

Fehr, S.C. 1994a. Board of Trade advocacy group formed to support Disney park, *The Washington Post*, September 1, A18.

Fehr, S.C. and M. Shear. 1994. For Disney, fight takes a new twist, *The Washington Post*, June 17, A1.

Hamilton, M.M. and M. Webb Pressler. 1994. Executives fear Disney move will give area hostile image, The *Washington Post*, September 30, B1.

Hsu, S.S. 1994a. Disney plans sent back for more, *The Washington Post*, January 14, D5.

Hsu, S.S. 1994b. Historians, writers organize against Disney theme park, *The Washington Post*, May 11, B7.

Hsu, S.S. 1994c. Legacy of land casts long shadow in Disney debate, *The Washington Post*, May 15, B1.

Hsu, S.S. and J.F. Harris. 1994. For Disney, it's all or goodbye, *The Washington Post*, March 4, D1.

Hsu, S.S. and M. Tousignant. 1994. No joy in Haymarket, *The Washington Post*, September 30, A1.

Lankford, S. 1994. Attitudes and perceptions toward tourism and rural regional development, *Journal of Travel Research*, Winter, 35–43.

McIntyre, G. 1993. *Sustainable Tourism Development: Guide for Local Planners*. Madrid, Spain: World Tourism Organization.

McPherson, J.M. 1994. Hauntingly like it was, *The Washington Post*, August 24, A19.

Moreau, D. 1992. Blue chips: a real life fairy tale for Disney investors, *Kiplinger's Personal Finance Magazine*, 49(4), 30.

Pearce, P.L. 1980. A favorability–satisfaction model of tourists' evaluations, *Journal of Travel Research*, (18(4), 13–17.

Powers, W. 1994. The Mickey Mouse Club, *The Washington Post*, April 25, Supplement, 1.

Tousignant, M. 1994. Disney foes display motivation, means, *The Washington Post*, August 21, B1.

Washington Post (The). 1994. In making plans for theme park, Disney let arrogance be its guide, October 3, Supplement, 1.

Further Reading

Baker, P. 1994b. Those persuasive guys in the Mickey Mouse ties, *The Washington Post*, February 7, D1.

Baker, P. 1994c. In VA, two stumbling blocks on Disney subsidy removed, *The Washington Post*, March 2, A14.

Fehr, S.C. 1994b. Disney traffic plan disputed, *The Washington Post*, July 14, B8.

Hsu, S.S. 1994d. Traffic studies of Disney proposal collide, *The Washington Post*, January 12, C6.

Hsu, S.S. 1994e. Prince William planners seek common ground with Disney, *The Washington Post*, January 18, D1.

Hsu, S.S. 1994f. Disney braces for environmentalists, *The Washington Post*, March 28, B3.

Hsu, S.S. 1994g. Different spins put on Disney's traffic study, *The Washington Post*, May 24, C1.

Hsu, S.S. 1994h. Disney revenue estimate triples, *The Washington Post*, May 27, C4.

Hsu, S.S. 1994i. For Disney, a long, hot summer, *The Washington Post*, June 5, B1.

Hsu, S.S. 1994j. Disney dollars, jobs tempt county, *The Washington Post*, July 3, A1.

Melton, R.H. 1994. Demise of another major project helps define a region's character, *The Washington Post*, September 3, D1.

Shear, M.D. 1994. 2 sides in Disney debate argue a sewer point, *The Washington Post*, June 14, A18.

¶ | PROBLEM SOLVING AND DISCUSSION ACTIVITIES

1. Discuss the potential negative and/or positive ecological, cultural, and economic impacts of the Disney's America project in Prince William County. What types of research would be required to evaluate these impacts?

2. Who were the stakeholders in the Disney's America project and how might they be affected by the Disney pullout? What could Disney officials have done to mitigate opposition and obtain a "buy in" for their project? What role could negotiation techniques like arbitration or mediation have played?

3. Research and compare other Disney projects to identify whether similar problems could be associated with their development strategy.

4. Identify an attraction similar in size to the Disney's America project and determine what patterns and problems arise due to their scope. What are the opportunities for communities located within close proximity of such attractions?

5. Discuss the relationship between entertainment and authenticity when dealing with a "built" historical interpretive center adjacent to an actual historical site. Are they complementary or competitive facilities?

6. Identify the process or mechanisms that should be put in place in Prince William County to (a) minimize the risks that a situation similar to what was experienced with Disney arises again and (b) optimize the chances that community supported initiatives are brought forward and implemented in the future.

7. Identify other examples of situations where community interest groups have lobbied successfully against tourism development or the staging of an event. What explanation can be offered for why the various stakeholder groups were unable to reach a compromise?

8. Can the lessons learned from the experiences of Disney and Prince William County be applied at a more macro level, say for a state or province, region, or entire country? Justify your response.

19

Hallmark Events and Urban Reimaging Strategies

COERCION, COMMUNITY, AND THE SYDNEY 2000 OLYMPICS

 C. Michael Hall

𝄢 | K E Y   L E A R N I N G   P O I N T S

- Hallmark events are an integral component of urban reimaging strategies that are geared towards attracting investment, generating income for government and business, creating employment opportunities, and improving the image of a city or region.

- The impacts of a hallmark event should be considered not just for the period in which the event is held, but also for the period leading up to, and beyond, hosting the event. Indeed, the legacies of an event on a city are significant, yet under-researched.

- Because they exist as attractions for only a short period of time, hallmark events can generate a feeling of "crisis" in an effort to meet deadlines. Therefore, the planning of large-scale events often circumvents traditional planning procedures because the event is "fast-tracked" through the system.

- Given the sense of "crisis" that supporters of hallmark events often generate, the events are sometimes developed in an environment in which public debate is stifled and opponents are labeled "unpatriotic." Therefore, the planning process and the media often remain closed to expressions of opposition to hosting events.

INTRODUCTION

Hallmark events such as the Olympic Games and world fairs are major factors in tourism development, urban revitalization, and urban reimaging strategies. However, despite their economic, social, and political significance, it is only since the 1980s that substantial attention has been paid to their impacts and legacies. This chapter presents the Sydney 2000 Summer Olympics as an example of hosting and planning hallmark events within the context of urban reimaging strategies.

The case study highlights how political and business interests can stifle public participation processes. Government often focuses more on the perceived economic and employment benefits of the event and its contribution to broader urban redevelopment policy and place promotion than on traditional welfare roles. Indeed, it is somewhat ironic that one of the most significant factors in the conduct of megaevents—the political dimension—is probably the least studied.

HALLMARK EVENTS AND URBAN REIMAGING STRATEGIES: CONTEMPORARY PERSPECTIVES AND ISSUES

Definition and Role of Hallmark Events
The standard definition of hallmark events[1] is provided by Ritchie (1984, p. 2), who defined them as follows:

> Major one-time or recurring events of limited duration, developed primarily to enhance the awareness, appeal and profitability of a tourist destination in the short and/or long term. Such events rely for their success on uniqueness, status, or timely significance to create interest and attract attention.

Hallmark events, otherwise referred to as *mega* or *special events,* may include major fairs, festivals, expositions, cultural events, and sporting events (Hall, 1992). Nations, regions, and cities have used hallmark events to provide a favorable image in the international tourism and business marketplace (Ashworth and Goodall, 1988). Hallmark events are also significant because they often leave behind legacies, such as infrastructure and public debt, that may have a far greater impact on the host community than the event itself. The Olympic Games and world fairs have been associated with large-scale public expenditure, construction of facilities and infrastructure, and redevelopment and revitalization of urban areas that may have substantial impacts on local communities (Hall, 1992, 1994).

According to Law (1993, p. 107), such events act

> . . . as a catalyst for change by persuading people to work together around a common objective and as a fast track for obtaining extra finance and getting building projects off the drawing board. This is not without its problems, since some would argue that it gives priority to development issues over those of welfare. The physical aspect of this strategy is that it has been linked with inner city regeneration and in particular with that of the city centre.

Although urban areas have long attracted tourists, it is only recently that cities and regions have consciously sought to develop, position and brand, and promote themselves to increase the influx of tourists. Tourism has been perceived as a key mechanism to regenerate urban areas through the creation of an attractive urban environment. This process appears almost universal in western society. As Urry (1990, p. 119) observed, "in recent years almost every town and city in Britain has been producing mixed development waterfront schemes in which tourist appeal is one element."

In many cities, the nature of the urban core is changing. Although the commercial functions of central business districts are still important, "the entire urban core is presently looked upon as a recreational environment and as a tourism resource" (Jansen-Verbeke, 1989, p. 233). The ramifications are far-reaching. As Bramham et al. (1989, p. 9) observed, "it is no longer unusual to see the city as a tourist product [to be sold and promoted], although on the level of local policy this may still be more an expression of certain political ideas than a coherent policy with practical consequences."

The emergence of a more economically oriented urban policy aimed at the revitalization of the city has led to "projects, developed in public–private partnerships, [that] are meant not for the integration of disadvantaged groups within society, but for servicing the pleasures of the well-to-do" (Mommaas and van der Poel, 1989, p. 263). Indeed, the positioning of the city to attract the middle-class market and the associated focus on the economic benefits of tourism have "reinforced the idea of the city as a kind of commodity to be marketed" (Mommaas and van der Poel, 1989, p. 264).

Hallmark Events, Re-development, Imaging, and Place Promotion Urban imaging processes are characterized by some or all of the following: (1) development of a critical mass of visitor attractions and facilities, including new buildings and/or prestige centers; (2) hallmark events; (3) development of urban tourism strategies and policies which are often associated with new or renewed organization and development of city marketing; (4) public–private sector partnerships; and (5) development of leisure and cultural services and projects to support the marketing and tourism effort (Hall, 1994).

The principal aims of urban imaging strategies are to attract tourist expenditure, generate employment, foster positive images for potential investors [often by "reimaging" previous negative perceptions—for example, the attempted transformation of Sheffield, England from an "industrial" to a "modern" city through the hosting of the World Student Games (Roche, 1992, 1994)], and provide an urban environment that will attract and retain the interest of professionals and white collar workers.

Hosting hallmark events is often deliberately exploited in an attempt to "rejuvenate" urban areas through the construction and development of new infrastructure, including improved transport links, sewage, and housing. This has been used to revitalize inner city locations that are regarded by government, municipalities, and business interests as requiring renewal. World fairs and the Olympic Games, in particular, have been used to provide a boost to urban development projects.

Indeed, the majority of bids for the 1996 and 2000 Summer Olympics involved substantial investment in new capital and infrastructure (e.g., transport facilities) quite separate from that of sports facilities (Hall, 1992). For example, Toronto's (Canada) bid for the 1996 Olympics was an important element in federal, provincial, and city moves to revitalize Toronto's waterfront. Similarly, Melbourne's (Australia) bid for the 1996 Olympics was key to a massive dockland redevelopment project. Sydney's (Australia) bid was a major component of, and justification for, a massive redevelopment of the city's waterfront. Noting Manchester's (England) bid for the 2000 Summer Olympics, Hughes (1993, p. 157, 159) observed that "the Olympics may be of particular significance in relation to the 'inner city' problems that beset many urban areas of Europe and N[orth] America."

The revitalization of downtown areas through the creation of new tourism and leisure spaces is regarded by some as being indicative of a crisis of the local state in which the importance of welfare functions is lessened (Henry and Bramham, 1986). In a broader context, the use of tourism to reimage the city may also be seen as a response by urban elites to the globalization of capital and the changing nature of the role of the state in society (Hall, 1994). As Harvey (1989) noted, imaging a city through the organization of spectacular urban space by, for example, hosting a hallmark event is a mechanism for attracting capital and people (of the "right" sort) in a period of intense interurban competition and urban entrepreneurialism.

An improved image seems to be one of the most significant legacies of the Calgary 1988 Winter Olympic Games (Martin, 1988, p. 31, in Mount and Leroux, 1994, p. 15):

> In the end, declares Art Smith [co-chair of the Calgary Economic Development Authority], the prime Olympic legacy may be the casting aside of Calgary's age-old reputation as an outpost. People will know us as not just a western frontier town, but as a metropolitan, sophisticated city. . . .

This chapter examines the role of hallmark events in urban revitalization projects and urban reimaging strategies in Australia, focusing on the Sydney 2000 Olympics. The discussion focuses on the relationship between image and reality in the planning and policy context that surrounds events and urban redevelopment. A combination of primary and secondary source investigations, including those in which the author was involved, provided the information highlighted in this chapter.

SYDNEY 2000 OLYMPICS: LOCATIONAL CONTEXT AND BACKGROUND

Located on the eastern seaboard of Australia, Sydney (see Figure 26.1) is the capital of the state of New South Wales. A sprawling multicultural city of over 3.5 million people, Sydney is the largest city in Australia. It is a major industrial and service center, and the principal aviation gateway for Australia. Because of its size and the potential employment opportunities it offers, Sydney is the primary setting for domestic and international migration in Australia. However, concerns have been expressed that Sydney may need to restrict its population growth because of environmental costs and the cost of developing new infrastructure.

Given its gateway status, Sydney is the major urban tourist destination in Australia. New South Wales, like the rest of Australia, has been experiencing strong inbound tourism growth since the 1980s. However, Queensland's rapid growth in domestic and international tourism in recent years influenced the New South Wales government to search for strategies that could improve the state's positioning in the tourism market.

Cities are becoming increasingly competitive in their attempts to attract investment and industry and to create employment opportunities in the global economy. Bidding to host events and developing financial packages to attract industry are two widely applied competitive strategies. To position itself as a "world class city," Sydney is being promoted as a major financial and business center not only in Australia, but also in Southeast Asia and the Pacific Rim. To this end, Sydney and the New South Wales government have embarked on urban redevelopment and reimaging strategies, including the development of waterfront revitalization projects, festival marketplaces, casinos, convention and exhibition centers, heritage precincts, museums, and art galleries. Megaevents that can be used as promotional tools, a means of attracting investment, and a justification for circumventing established planning procedures (Hall, 1992) are part of this overall redevelopment strategy.

Competition among Australian cities for events and projects is intense. For example, the site of the Australian Formula One Grand Prix is shifting from Adelaide to Melbourne, based on the Victorian government's willingness to pay substantially more for the Grand Prix rights than the South Australian government. This negotiation was initially unknown to the South Australian government, which had held the rights for the previous 10 years.

Sydney's successful bid for the 2000 Olympics was the culmination of years of intense competition both domestically and internationally. The Sydney bid was the third successive bid by an Australian city to host the Summer Olympics (Brisbane bid for the 1992 Olympics and Melbourne for those in 1996). Australian cities have two layers of competition in any Games bid. First, the Australian Olympic Committee selects a city. Second, the Australian "winner" then competes with other cities worldwide to host the Games with the International Olympic Committee (IOC). In the case of the 1996 Olympics, Sydney and Melbourne waged an intense contest for the rights to be the Australian bidder. The traditional rivalry between the two cities became so fierce that Sydney supporters were accused of deliberately sabotaging the Melbourne Olympic bid.

The exact origins of the Sydney bid are hard to ascertain. Suffice it to note that, as soon as the Melbourne bid proved unsuccessful, the New South Wales government began to move towards making their own push to host the Games. Sydney was in competition with Beijing, Berlin, Istanbul, and Manchester and had to win the votes of the 91 members of the IOC. The Games bid was, therefore, a public relations exercise *par excellence*. Some may also describe this as "vote buying."

According to Booth and Tatz (1993–1994, p. 7), "the lobbying process has degenerated into a shameful and shameless gravitational spiral towards the lowest ethical base." Indeed, criticism of the Games came to be regarded by some as "un-Australian." As the New South Wales minister responsible for the Games bid at the time, Mr. Bruce Baird asserted that "anyone who threatens Sydney's Olympic bid had better watch out" (PM Australian Broadcasting Commission Radio, 16 July, 1993, in Booth and Tatz, 1993–1994, p. 10).

When the winning bid, by one vote over Beijing, was announced on September 23, 1993, the reaction in Sydney was one of euphoria. Sydney was "on the map" as the eyes of the international media focused on the celebrations. However, since that time, fears have been expressed about the costs of the Games and the need to have the facilities ready by the year 2000. The Olympics are now being analyzed and debated in a manner that was not possible during the bidding period. Questions are being asked not only about the bidding process itself, but also about the impacts and planning of the event.

THE SYDNEY OLYMPICS AND THE ENVIRONMENT

The environment has become a critical component of the imaging process for the Olympic Movement and Olympic cities. Following the lead of Lillehammer (Norway), Sydney focused on the environment as a key element in its bidding strategy. The Sydney Olympics 2000 Bid Limited (SOB) (1993a, p. 2) argued that Sydney would stage a great Olympics in 2000 because it is

> . . . pioneering environmentalism for the Olympics. Throughout Sydney's Olympic plan, from venue and residential construction to event management, the highest environmental principles are applied. Sydney's Olympic Village design, prepared in collaboration with Greenpeace, foreshadows the sustainable city of the 21st century.

According to SOB (1993b, p. 2), the environmental guidelines developed for the bid, which address five major global environmental concerns (global warming, ozone depletion, biodiversity, pollution, and resource depletion), "would make Sydney's Olympic Plan a prime example of ecologically sustainable development in the 21st century" and "integrate the latest technologies with tried and tested measures into a co-ordinated environmental protection plan for a summer Olympic Games." Specific examples of environmental guidelines developed with support from Greenpeace (Greenpeace Australia, 1993) include the following:

- The use of solar power, water recycling, and public transport in the athletes' village. Buildings that do not require air conditioning and refrigerators that contain no ozone-destroying gases will be designed.
- Recyclable building materials, energy-efficient systems, and water recycling will be used in new sporting facilities.
- Electronic mail to reduce the need for paper, multiuse tickets (for events, transport, food), and minimal food packaging will be critical aspects of event management.
- Companies tendering for a contract will have to satisfy the environmental guidelines stipulated by the Organising Committee for the Sydney Olympic Games (Sydney Olympics 2000 Bid Limited, 1993b, p. 3).

The "greening" of the Sydney Olympic bid will also enable Australia to market its environmental technology to other countries bidding for the Games in the future. Indeed, an International Olympic Committee/United Nations Environment Programme Working Party on the environmental standards for future Olympic Games has been established (Foreshaw, 1994). However, debate is growing over whether the "green Games" is just a marketing and imaging ploy rather than a substantial contribution to issues facing sustainable tourism development[2] in Australia. In fact, the Games have been perceived by some to be ". . . the best marketing exercise ever undertaken in Australia" (Greiner, 1994, p. 13).

THE POLITICAL IMPACTS OF HALLMARK EVENTS: COERCION, COMMUNITY, AND IMAGE

The postindustrial urban environment associated with contemporary hallmark events often has a major impact on the socioeconomic groups occupying the inner city or deindustrialized areas designated for renewal. The creation of a desirable "middle-class environment" invariably leads to increased rates and rents and is often accompanied by a corresponding breakdown in community structure as families and individuals are forced to relocate.

Moreover, the people who are often most impacted by hallmark events are typically those who are least able to form community groups and protect their interests (Hall, 1992). For example, the Asian Coalition for Housing Rights (1989, p. 92) noted that South Korea's preparations for the 1988 Olympic Games led to the "rehabilitation" and "beautification" of numerous areas in Seoul whereby "many communities were evicted from sites, simply because they were next to the path along which the Olympic torch was to be carried and the public authorities did not want these communities to be visible to the reporters and television cameras." It appears that the political and economic benefits to the local elites and the state often outweigh the costs to segments of the host community, usually the poor and those with minimal political power.

Hallmark events are typically dependent on a large outlay of public monies to host and bid for such events. For example, SOB, with support from the corporate sector, the Australian federal government, the New South Wales state government, and other state and territory governments, spent over A$20 million in their bid. As Bonnemaison (1990, p. 25) commented, ". . . a city wanting to upgrade its infrastructure or its political image will use a large-scale event as a tool to generate funds from higher levels of government and corporations."

Despite substantial costs and benefits, the net contribution of hallmark events to local communities and their social, economic, and environmental impacts are rarely studied. Indeed, there are pressures operating against such evaluation (Crompton and McKay, 1994). As Hiller (1989, p. 127) noted in the case of the 1988 Calgary Winter Olympics, "The overarching compelling rationale of preparation for the Olympics in general tended to minimise opposition and controversy thereby supporting capital cost expenditures." Why does this happen?

Coercion A mixture of coercion and co-option centered around maintenance of real estate values and employment and investment generation, as well as a belief that growth is inherently good, has led to the creation of growth coalitions in many urban centers. Coercion arises either through interplace competition for capital investment and employment (accede to the capitalist's demands or go out of business; create a "good business climate" or lose jobs) or, more simply, through the direct political repression and oppression of dissident voices (e.g., cutting off media access) (Harvey, 1993, p. 9).

The former New South Wales state premier, Nick Greiner (1994, p. 13), argued that "The secret of the success was undoubtedly the creation of a community of interest, not only in Sydney, but across the nation, unprecedented in our peacetime history." The reference to a "community of interest"[3] is itself interesting. The implication is that community interest was far-reaching when, in fact, "community of interest" generally indicates a rather narrow community in the form of elite interests that direct and influence proposals.

In this case, the Sydney media played a critical role in creating a favorable climate for the bid (McGeoch and Korporal, 1994). As Greiner (1994, p. 13) stated:

Early in 1991, I invited senior media representatives to the premier's office, told them frankly that a bid could not succeed if the media played their normal "knocking role" and that I was not prepared to commit the taxpayers' money unless I had their support. Both News Ltd. and Fairfax subsequently went out of their way to ensure the bid received fair, perhaps even favourable, treatment. The electronic media also joined in the sense of community purpose.

Community Greiner's statement begs the question, "Which community?" Certainly, the lack of social impact assessment prior to the Games bid (Office of Social Policy, 1993) indicates the failure of growth coalitions to recognize that there may well be negative impacts on some sections of the community. As mentioned earlier, those who are most impacted (i.e., those living in rental accommodation and hostels or in the vicinity of Games-related infrastructure projects) are also the ones who are least able, politically and otherwise, to affect policy and planning processes (Polesy and Watson, 1994).

One of the most surprising elements of the Sydney bid was the lack of debate surrounding the costs and benefits of hosting the Olympics. Darcy and Veal (1994, pp. 7–8) observed the following:

> During the period up to the announcement of the successful bid there were few local critics of Sydney's bid, leading to some questioning of the independence of the media, especially given that leading media executives were members of the bid committee . . . Whether or not it was a result of a media/government conspiracy or a genuine desire on all sides not to jeopardise the bid by providing competing cities with critical ammunition, criticism of the idea of holding the Games in Sydney was muted. No pressure groups emerged to oppose the bid as happened, for example, in Berlin.

The lack of debate surrounding the Olympics will have substantial implications for the long-term economic and social development of both Sydney and New South Wales. During the bidding, the New South Wales government maintained that the cost of staging the Olympic Games was A$1.7 billion. Yet, almost immediately after Sydney won the bid, the government conceded that the total cost, including essential infrastructure primarily at the main Games site at Homebush Bay, was A$3.23 billion (*Sydney Morning Herald*, 1993). During the latter stages of the Games bid, then Premier John Fahey claimed that the redevelopment of the sports facilities at Homebush Bay was independent of the decision on the hosting of the Games. However, according to Booth and Tatz (1993–1994, p. 10):

> This is wilfully misleading: Sydney's victory condensed and converted a 20-year *discretionary* project into a seven-year *essential* project. Redevelopment of Homebush Bay will not provide an economic return (although it may be a worthwhile environmental project) and it will compete with other capital works associated with health, education, housing, roads and so forth. Taxpayers deserved the courtesy of being informed . . . In the end, there was no organised criticism of Sydney's bid . . . deceived about the full costs of the Games, SOBC's seductive promise of a Games-led economic recovery engendered hope.

The New South Wales government has also been taken to task over its handling of the deal for the construction of the Airport Link rail project. Disregarding its own 1990 guidelines recommending competitive bidding by private sector firms for public sector infrastructure projects, the project was awarded without tender.

Professor Bob Walker of the University of New South Wales has suggested that "the government, in its haste to finalise the 2000 Olympics-related deal, has been outsmarted, at a heavy cost to the taxpayer" (*Sydney Morning Herald*, 1994, p. 14). The terms of the deal mean that the private sector consortium is insulated from inflation risk and stands to earn a prospective real rate of return in the range of 21–25 percent over a 30-year period. On the other hand, despite contributing most of the finance and bearing most of the operating risk, the government would earn a return of only 2 percent per annum.

As Walker states, "it seems absurd that annual budget allocations for cash expenditures require parliamentary scrutiny and approval, while major contracts involving the alienation of revenue streams and financial commitments stretching over 30 years can be handled in secret by executive government" (*Sydney Morning Herald*, 1994, p. 14).

Stifling opposition may be more overt than the restriction of public debate seen in the creation of a "community of interest" comprised of politicians, the media, and real estate developers. For example, there was substantial community protest (including a rally by more than 10,000 people) against the 1996 Formula One Grand Prix to be staged in Melbourne, Victoria. However, the Victorian government's Grand Prix Bill extinguishes "substantive" rights of appeal and grants indemnity to the Grand Prix from court action by residents or businesses who believe that they are entitled to compensation. This led the vice-president of the Victorian Council of Liberties to tell a hearing of the Scrutiny of Acts and Regulations Committee that elements of the Grand Prix Bill were "abhorrent" (Henry, 1994, p. 4).

Values and Interests in Urban Redevelopment: Imaging Strategies

Urban redevelopment associated with hallmark events may conceal the history of struggle over place and space. Inner city space, therefore, becomes a space of conspicuous consumption, celebrating commodities rather than civic values (Debord, 1973; Harvey, 1990). The new inner city space of leisure consumption reflects not only particular values but also particular interests. The "new" civic values reflect those of the local elites that influence urban redevelopment and planning processes. As Mommaas and van der Poel (1989, p. 267) observed, "local policy has increasingly sought to stimulate the mixture of economic enterprise, culture and leisure, attempting in this manner to attract the new economic élite to the city." However, in focusing on one set of economic and social interests, other community interests, particularly those of traditional inner city residents, are increasingly neglected

> . . . because urban policy has adopted and legitimated the profiles and potentials of the lifestyle of this new economic élite, thereby also legitimating the economic dimensions involved (the acceptance of making leisure, culture, and welfare strategies and criteria), the interests of those not having the opportunity to emulate the new economic élite in its pleasures fail to be considered [Mommaas and van der Poel, 1989, p. 267].

The creation of a "bourgeois playground" (Mommaas and van der Poel, 1989, p. 263) in the name of economic progress may create considerable tension in the urban policy-making environment. For example, the integration of tourism functions in the inner city may compete with more traditional functions such as housing. This occurred in Melbourne, where the track for the Formula One Grand Prix is being constructed in a park in the inner city.

The redevelopment of the inner city to improve its attractiveness to visitors can lead to the transformation of the community-based organization of local spaces and populations into an individual or family-based organization. Castells (1983) characterized this phenomenon as the "disconnection of people from spatial forms." In the case of Sydney, the Olympic Games and other associated projects (such as a casino development) are accelerating rates of gentrification and changing the social and community characteristics of the inner city (Hall and Hamon, 1995). The implications of the transformation of the core of many cities, including Sydney, for lower socioeconomic groups are amplified by the reallocation of local state resources from social welfare to imaging functions. As the inner city is being promoted and developed as a leisure resource, public spending on social programs has been decreasing (Mommaas and van der Poel, 1989).

CONCLUSION

The role of hallmark events in urban imaging strategies cannot be separated from the political and fiscal crisis of the local state in western society. Hallmark events are a mechanism by which places can be "commodified" as part of an attempt to attract investments, white collar employment, and tourists. They can also be used to engineer consensus among residents by creating an image that the city is "on the right track."

The crisis of the local state reflects a more general crisis of legitimacy in which certain interests, particularly the powerless and disadvantaged in the inner cities, have become disenchanted with existing political arrangements that have failed to deliver much needed social, economic, and infrastructural improvements. In addition, it appears that city centers, the focal point of the new urban tourism, are gaining resources at the expense of the suburbs (Bramham et al., 1989, p. 4):

> . . . the question arises as to whether or not there should be some form of public life or culture, accessible to all local citizens of the city; and if so, how this can be stimulated by local policies. This last question is particularly relevant in local politics. Is the city a product to be sold on the tourism market and/or as a location in which to invest money? Or is a city a place to live, where people can express themselves, even if it is in terms of resistance to, rather than rejoicing in, the dominant culture?

A second crisis is what may be termed a "fiscal crisis" in which:

> The central state is attempting to revitalize private industry by reducing expenditure on social consumption, and therefore reducing grant aid to local government which is responsible for many such services, while local government, deprived of such income and with a declining tax base (as the local economy suffers), is faced with increasing demands both for welfare services and for local economic development [Henry and Bramham, 1986, p. 190].

The two crises are intimately related. The reallocation of scarce financial resources exacerbates the frustration and marginalization of certain disadvantaged groups in society. Although many civic governments claim that the development of visitor attractions will encourage employment and investment, many of the jobs do not go to those most directly affected by such developments because they often do not possess the requisite skills.

Moreover, the new jobs are frequently low paying and part time or temporary in nature (Booth and Tatz, 1993/1994; Hall and Jenkins, 1995).

A hallmark event may improve the image of a destination (Ritchie and Smith, 1991). However, whether this can be turned into a sustained increase in visitor numbers and investment is highly debatable (Mount and Leroux, 1994). As Hughes (1993, p. 162) argued, tourism

> . . . can only be a component of an overall strategy for urban regeneration rather than a major force in its own right. Tourism associated with the Olympics, given its short-term nature, provides even less direct opportunity for urban regeneration. The hopes of regeneration lie largely in the belief that inward investment in other industries and increased long-term tourist flows will result. The prospect is based on improvements to the environment and infrastructure and a generally enhanced image or awareness of an area. The case for this has, however, not yet been demonstrated.

Indeed, hosting a hallmark event, such as the Olympics, may even disturb "the 'normal' development of tourism and other activity" because these events may constitute "a distraction from the pursuit of a more fundamental development strategy that will ensure long-term sustainable growth" (Hughes, 1993, 162). Appropriately scaled and planned events can revitalize, redevelop, and reimage communities and destinations (Hall, p. 1992). However, large-scale hallmark events, and the Sydney Olympics in particular, generally serve a narrow range of interests. These events reflect imaging and marketing concerns as opposed to the search for sustainable forms of tourism development and improvements to the welfare of impacted urban populations.

ACKNOWLEDGMENTS

The author would like to acknowledge the research assistance of Sandra Haywood, Nicolle Lavelle, and Vanessa O'Sullivan in the preparation of this paper. A previous version of this paper was presented at the Urban Tourism Conference, University of Victoria, British Columbia in November 1994.

NOTES

1. See Chapter 27 for additional discussion relating to event tourism.
2. See Chapter 4, 5, 7, 8, 17, 18, 22, and 23 for additional discussion of sustainable tourism and sustainable tourism development concepts.
3. See Chapter 16 for additional discussion of "community of interest."

REFERENCES

Ashworth, G. and B. Goodall. 1988. Tourist images: marketing considerations. In B. Goodall and G. Ashworth (eds.), *Marketing in the Tourism Industry: The Promotion of Destination Regions*. London: Routledge, pp. 213–238.

Asian Coalition for Housing Rights. 1989. Evictions in Seoul, South Korea, *Environment and Urbanization*, 1, 89–94.

Bonnemaison, S. 1990. City policies and cyclical event. In *Celebrations: Urban Spaces Transformed, Design Quarterly*, Vol. 147, Cambridge, MA: Massachusets Institute of Technology for the Walker Art Center, pp. 24–32.

Booth, D. and C. Tatz. 1993–1994. Sydney 2000: the games people play, *Current Affairs Bulletin*, 70(7), 4–11.

Bramham, P., I. Henry, H. Mommaas, and H. van der Poel. 1989. Introduction. In P. Bramham, I. Henry, H. Mommaas and H. van der Poel (eds.), *Leisure and Urban Processes: Critical Studies of Leisure Policy in Western European Cities*. London and New York: Routledge, pp. 1–13.

Castells, M. 1983. Crisis, planning, and the quality of life: managing the new historical relationships between space and society, *Environment and Planning D, Society and Space*, 1, 3–21.

Crompton, J.L. and S.L. McKay. 1994. Measuring the economic impact of festivals and events: some myths, misapplications and ethical dilemmas, *Festival Management and Event Tourism*, 2(1), 33–43.

Darcy, S. and A.J. Veal. 1994. The Sydney 2000 Olympic Games: the story so far, *Leisure Options: Australian Journal of Leisure and Recreation*, 4(1), 5–14.

Debord, G. 1973. *Society of the Spectacle*. Detroit: Black and Red.

Foreshaw, J. 1994. Olympic green good as gold for environment firms, *The Weekend Australian*, 24–25 September, 13.

Greenpeace Australia. 1993. *Press Release: Greenpeace Calls on International Olympic Committee to Adopt Environmental Criteria for Games*. Greenpeace Australia, Balmain, 23 March.

Greiner, N. 1994. Inside running on Olympic bid, *The Australian*, 19 September, 13.

Hall, C.M. 1992. *Hallmark Tourist Events: Impacts, Management and Planning*. London: Belhaven Press.

Hall, C.M. 1994. *Tourism and Politics: Policy, Power and Place*. London: John Wiley & Sons.

Hall, C.M. and C. Hamon. 1995. *Casinos and Urban Redevelopment in Australia*. University of Canberra, Canberra: Centre for Tourism and Leisure Policy Research.

Hall, C.M. and J.M. Jenkins. 1995. *Tourism and Public Policy*. London: Routledge.

Harvey, D. 1989. *The Condition of Postmodernity: An Enquiry into the Origins of Cultural Change*. Oxford: Basil Blackwell.

Harvey, D. 1990. Between space and time: reflections on the geographical imagination, *Annals of the Association of American Geographers*, 80(3), 418–434.

Harvey, D. 1993. From space to place and back again: reflections on the condition of postmodernity. In J. Bird, B. Curtis, T. Putnam, G. Robertson and L. Tickner (eds.), *Mapping the Futures: Local Cultures, Global Change*. London: Routledge, pp. 3–29.

Henry, I. and P. Bramham. 1986. Leisure, the local state and social order, *Leisure Studies*, 5, 189–209.

Henry, S. 1994. Grand Prix Bill branded 'abhorrent', *Australian*, 28 September, 4.

Hiller, H. 1989. Impact and image: the convergence of urban factors in preparing for the 1988 Calgary Winter Olympics. In G.J. Syme, B.J. Shaw, D.M. Fenton, and W.S. Mueller (eds.), *The Planning and Evaluation of Hallmark Events*. Avebury, Aldershot, pp. 119–131.

Hughes, H.L. 1993. Olympic tourism and urban regeneration, *Festival Management and Event Tourism*, 1(4), 157–159.

Jansen-Verbeke, M. 1989. Inner cities and urban tourism in the Netherlands: new challenges for local authorities. In P. Bramham, I. Henry, H. Mommaas, and H. van der Poel (eds.), *Leisure and Urban Processes: Critical Studies of Leisure Policy in Western European Cities*. London and New York: Routledge, pp. 233–253.

Law, C.M. 1993. *Urban Tourism: Attracting Visitors to Large Cities*. London: Mansell.

Martin, D. 1988. Olympian effort pays off, *Calgary Herald Business Outlook 88*.

McGeoch, R. and G. Korporal. 1994. *The Bid: How Australia Won the 2000 Games*. Sydney: William Heinemann.

Mommaas, H. and H. van der Poel. 1989. Changes in economy, politics and lifestyles: an essay on the restructuring of urban leisure. In P. Bramham, I. Henry, H. Mommaas and H. van der Poel (eds.), *Leisure and Urban Processes: Critical Studies of Leisure Policy in Western European Cities*. London and New York: Routledge, pp. 254–276.

Mount, J. and C. Leroux. 1994. Assessing the effects of a mega-event: a retrospective study of the impact of the Olympic Games on the Calgary business sector, *Festival Management and Event Tourism*, 2(1), 15–23.

Office of Social Policy. 1993. *Sydney Olympics 2000: Approaches and Issues for Management of Social Impacts*. New South Wales Government, Sydney: Social Policy Directorate.

Polesy, N. and P. Watson. 1994. *Sydney 2000 Olympics: Economic and Social Impacts on Housing*. Unpublished paper. University of Canberra, Canberra: Centre for Tourism and Leisure Policy Research.

Ritchie, J.R.B. 1984. Assessing the impact of hallmark events: conceptual and research issues, *Journal of Travel Research*, 23(1), 2–11.

Ritchie, J.R.B. and B.H. Smith. 1991. The impact of a mega-event on host region awareness: a longitudinal study, *Journal of Travel Research*, 30(1), 3–10.

Roche, M. 1992. Mega-events and micro-modernization: on the sociology of the new urban tourism, *British Journal of Sociology*, 43(4), 563–600.

Roche, M. 1994. Mega-events and urban policy, *Annals of Tourism Research*, 21(1), 1–19.

Sydney Morning Herald. 1993. $1.3 billion blowout proves it's big Games, 14 October.

Sydney Morning Herald. 1994. Editorial: Taken for a ride to the airport, 22 September, 14.

Sydney Olympics 2000 Bid Limited. 1993a. *News Release: Why Sydney Would Stage a Great Olympics in 2000*. Sydney Olympics 2000 Bid Limited, Sydney.

Sydney Olympics 2000 Bid Limited. 1993b. *News Release: Sydney's Plans for an environmental Olympics in 2000*. Sydney Olympics 2000 Bid Limited, Sydney.

Urry, J. 1990. *The Tourist Gaze: Leisure and Travel in Contemporary Societies*. London: Sage Publications.

¶ | PROBLEM SOLVING AND DISCUSSION ACTIVITIES

1. How can the public provide greater input into the planning and policy formulation processes associated with hallmark events? Develop a model that would encourage more community involvement in setting the goals and objectives for events.
2. Does hosting hallmark events create a crisis for planning because deadlines for the event are inflexible? To what extent does this lead to "fast-track" planning? What might be some of the consequences of "fast-track" planning?
3. When should evaluations of the impacts of hallmark events be conducted? Consider the costs and benefits of such evaluations and how the results of pre- and post-event evaluation may be incorporated into the planning process.
4. Can politics and planning be separated? In particular, consider the roles of values, interests, and power in policy making and event planning.
5. Hallmark events provide opportunities to examine the image of a destination.

Conduct a content analysis of the media coverage of an event to identify how much, and the nature of, information conveyed about the destination.

6. Select a large event or tourism-related project. Identify the amount of public participation that exists in the planning and policy processes surrounding the event. Discuss how the level of participation relates to ideas of democracy in tourism planning.

7. What alternatives (i.e., other than staging hallmark events) might an urban center consider to achieve its reimaging goals? What are the advantages and disadvantages of such alternatives compared to the staging of hallmark events? Comment on whether and why there tends to be a leaning toward hallmark events.

20

Seeing the Forest Through the Trees

USING GEOGRAPHICAL INFORMATION SYSTEMS TO IDENTIFY POTENTIAL ECOTOURISM SITES IN NORTHERN ONTARIO, CANADA

Stephen W. Boyd
Richard W. Butler

✊|KEY LEARNING POINTS

- Geographical information systems (GIS) technology comprises computer programs that can be used to process and answer questions about spatial data. In essence, GIS is a form of interactive mapping that facilitates the preparation of an inventory of an area's attributes that can be used in the decision-making process.

- GIS allows researchers and decision makers to collect, synthesize, and manipulate large data sets with relative ease, thereby enhancing decisions associated with the use and allocation of resources.

- Even with GIS, there is a need for field examination and local consultation before decisions are made.

- The type of tourism pursued in an area should be consistent with the area's attributes and should enhance the well-being of local populations.

INTRODUCTION

Beginning in the 1970s, the field of resource and environmental management has been revolutionized by the collection of large amounts of data using techniques such as remote sensing and geographical information systems (GIS). These data offer potential for the skillful and effective management of resources and, to some degree, the management of people using those resources.

The field of remote sensing, developed in the 1960s, has been concerned with data acquisition that has little application to tourism and recreation. In part, this is because the data were not at a scale or resolution suitable for site management and planning (Coppock and Rhind, 1991). The development of GIS in the 1960s made available new tools and techniques for utilizing vast pools of data in ways that enable planners and managers to make better decisions about the use and allocation of resources (Aronoff, 1991; Maguire et al., 1991; Star and Estes, 1990).

The application of GIS to tourism and recreation is still in its infancy. However, GIS offers considerable promise to decision makers and planners in allocating resources between what are often conflicting demands (Townshend, 1991). One of the main advantages of GIS over many other techniques and technologies of data manipulation lies in its ability to handle spatial attributes. This allows uses such as tourism to be analyzed more effectively, particularly where tourism is proposed for peripheral or sensitive areas and where the spatial pattern of use is a significant consideration (Berry, 1991).

This chapter focuses on the identification of areas suitable for ecotourism in a specific spatial context—Northern Ontario (see Figure 20.1). Ecotourism is drawn to and dependent upon natural areas, often those that may contain rare or endangered species or habitats, are remote or peripheral, and about which little may be known or recorded. The

Figure 20.1
Ontario and the study area.

emphasis is not on the appropriateness of ecotourism in Northern Ontario, nor is it on technical aspects of GIS technology. Rather, the chapter addresses GIS's suitability for identifying ecotourism areas in the region. The fact that the application has been developed in a specific spatial context does not necessarily invalidate its application in other areas. However, its suitability in other settings is not guaranteed.

The study was conducted under contract with the Canadian Forest Service and the Ontario Ministry of Natural Resources as part of the Northern Ontario Development Agreement (NODA)[1] during a three-year period from 1993 to 1995. It is one of a number of studies within this agreement that focused on ecotourism.

The chapter begins with a brief history of the development of GIS, including comments on its role in resource inventory and analysis. This is followed by an overview of ecotourism and its linkage to other types of tourism and environmental management concepts. Next, the suitability of Northern Ontario for ecotourism based on the mix of physical and human attributes present in the region is discussed, followed by the delineation of elements and criteria of ecotourism suitable for Northern Ontario. The various stages in the methodology are then set out. This is followed by the application of GIS to the study area and, finally, some conclusions and implications.

GIS, RESOURCE INVENTORIES, AND ANALYSIS: CONTEMPORARY PERSPECTIVES AND ISSUES

The creation of software for spatial data analysis has made possible the collation and manipulation of massive amounts of data covering large areas, and the analysis of the complex interrelations between different elements sharing the same space (Aronoff, 1991). Commonly referred to as GIS, geographical information systems can be defined as "systems composed of software used to collect, store, and manipulate spatially referenced data" (Pazner, 1989, p. 7). In short, GIS technology comprises computer programs that can be used to process and answer questions about spatial data. It is, in other words, a form of interactive mapping. According to Star and Estes (1990), a GIS must contain the following five essential elements: (1) data acquisition, (2) preprocessing (manipulating data to enter into the GIS), (3) data management both in terms of creating the data base itself and gaining access to it, (4) manipulation and analysis involving linkages to external systems to assist with the fifth element, and (5) product generation or output from the GIS (i.e., maps, statistics, and tables).

GIS evolved as a response to increased interest in managing the environment and concern with balancing competing uses of environmental resources (Aronoff, 1991). Response to these factors resulted in an explosion in information, fueled by advances in technology and computer development. Consequently, systems that had the ability to analyze, store, manipulate, retrieve, and present data in forms that were useful to the end user were developed.

The first automated GIS appeared in the 1960s and was linked to the Suitability/Capability Analysis (SCA) found in the work of McHarg (1969). Within Canada, the first GIS, known as the Canada Geographic Information Systems (CGIS), was designed in 1964 for the *Agriculture Rehabilitation Development Act* (ARDA) to analyze *Canada*

Land Inventory (CLI) data.[2] By 1980, the US Department of Fish and Wildlife Service noted that 54 GISs had been developed, of which fewer than 10 were commercial. The 1980s to the present may be characterized as a period where growth in the *application* of GIS was predominant. Few new systems appeared, the emphasis being placed on the refinement of existing systems.

Only recently have researchers within resources management adopted GIS as a tool for analyzing and presenting data. For instance, Sussmann and Rashad (1994) examined the level of awareness that managers had of GIS in the area of tourism marketing, noting problems of cost for capital layout, training, and personnel. Devine and Kuo (1991) used GIS to delimit effective service areas for recreational programs with respect to expanding the quality dimension of urban recreation planning. GIS has also been useful in the identification and delineation of buffer areas for biodiversity conservation in Nepal (Nepal and Weber, 1994), the planning of linear facilities in Southern Ontario, and impact assessment (Smith, 1993).

Although Northern Ontario has been extensively mapped and surveyed by ground-level surveys, GIS and remotely sensed data from satellite imagery have allowed for vastly improved surveying and analysis of many components of this landscape, especially for relatively unexplored areas (Siderelis, 1991). The Ontario Forest Research Institute, located in Sault Ste. Marie (see Figure 20.1), has collated much data, especially with respect to forest resources and their exploitation. Data collected on physical (i.e., vegetation coverage, water, relief, wildlife capability) and human attributes (i.e., settlements, location of resource-based industry, road networks) in Northern Ontario can be used to evaluate the potential of areas for various activities.

GIS is used to produce a series of maps for the area under consideration. The maps can be thought of as layers of data that can be overlain in any specified or random order (see Figure 20.2). The data are portrayed as numeric scores for each pixel (unit area), the size of which depends on the resolution of the data collected. The number of pixels making up each map or layer of the GIS depends on the degree of detail or resolution of the data collected—the greater the resolution, the greater the number of pixels. As each map or layer is overlain, accumulated scores develop which can then be represented in total form on the final map. In the study reported in this chapter, the final output was a set of maps depicting what are termed "ecotourism units."

ECOTOURISM: CONTEMPORARY PERSPECTIVES AND ISSUES

Ecotourism[3] has emerged as one of the fastest-growing forms of tourism, influenced primarily by public demand for more environmentally and socially responsible tourism. In response, the industry has attempted to portray itself as being committed to maintaining the resource base upon which it depends. As a result, ecotourism has spread throughout many parts of the world (Boo, 1990; Eagles et al., 1993). While it has generally been regarded as fostering environmentally responsible principles, in many areas it has resulted in significant negative impacts upon the human and physical environments (Boo, 1990; Dearden and Harron, 1992; Kenchington, 1989). These impacts are often similar to those found in areas that have experienced conventional tourism. The areas to which ecotourism has been introduced have been quite often devoid of the effects of

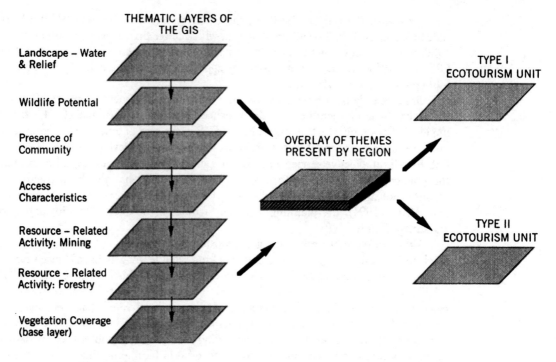

Figure 20.2
Overlay procedure used to identify potential ecotourism sites. (From Boyd and Butler, 1994.)

tourism and, in some cases, extremely sensitive and vulnerable environments. This makes its negative effects all the more serious and regrettable.

Areas ranging from Antarctica (Marsh, 1992) to the tropical rain forests of Central America and Southeast Asia have experienced the development of various forms of ecotourism (Dearden, 1989; Fennell and Eagles, 1990). Growth in interest has also resulted in opportunities for ecotourism being sought in less exotic temperate landscapes of the developed world. This latter trend has emerged in recognition of the potential that ecotourism may offer the economies of marginal areas, and also because of the realization that there may be a declining number of new exotic and rare landscapes available that can be marketed as ecotourism destinations (International Resources Group, 1992; Ziffer, 1989).

Given that ecotourism continues to grow, both in terms of volume of participants and the number of areas viewed as suitable ecotourism destinations, it is imperative that only those areas which have a resource base to sustain this form of activity should be developed. Therefore, it is necessary to ensure that the requirements of ecotourism development are matched with the resource base characteristics, as well as the preferences of local residents.

Definition and Linkages Ecotourism is fraught with problems of definition. There is no generally accepted definition, and many terms have been used to describe the same phenomenon. Examples include terms like nature travel (Laarman and Durst, 1987), nature-oriented tourism (Durst and Ingram, 1988), and special interest tourism (Inskeep, 1987; Weiler and Hall, 1992). Others have identified over 35 terms that may be linked to ecotourism, such as sustainable tourism and alternative tourism (Scace et al., 1992). The danger inherent in allowing definitions of ecotourism such scope is that the term can fall prey to indiscriminate use as a catchall phrase for almost anything that links tourism with nature (Farrell and Runyan, 1991).

One of the most commonly cited definitions is that by Hector Ceballos-Lascurain (citied in Boo, 1990), who first coined the term "ecotourism" in Mexico in 1980. He defined ecotourism as

> . . . traveling to relatively undisturbed or uncontaminated natural areas with the specific objective of studying, admiring, and enjoying the scenery and its wild plants and animals, as well as any existing cultural manifestations (both past and present) found in these areas.

This definition suggests a form of tourism that is little different in effect from what has traditionally been regarded as "wilderness recreation" in North America. It says nothing about avoiding resource degradation, having positive impacts on the flora or fauna, optimizing economic impacts or benefits, and/or enhancing the visitors' experience or levels of satisfaction. These ideological and value-laden attributes have been added to subsequent definitions of ecotourism and have often served to obscure rather than clarify the meaning of ecotourism. Abuse of the term, often for marketing purposes, has diluted attempts towards conciseness in defining the term.

The authors view ecotourism as a dynamic concept, prone to change given the various settings in which it occurs (e.g., coastal regions, forested landscapes, national parks and protected areas, wildlife reserves, private land) and the range of experiences sought by those traveling to such varied landscapes. A flexible approach is required where it is understood that no one definition is suitable for all settings, and that certain elements will have greater value than others depending on the environment in which ecotourism is being promoted.

Ecotourism has been linked to many other types of tourism and ideas related to environmental management (Scace et al., 1992). Similarities exist between ecotourism and adventure travel, with the latter often being viewed as a form of ecotourism that involves a higher degree of risk and, possibly, environmental impact. Ecotourism can also be viewed as fitting within a sustainable development[4] framework, addressing principles (e.g., equity, carrying capacity,[5] conservation), planning[6] (e.g., proactive, integrative, and long term), and management (e.g., integrative, assigned responsibility) (Boyd and Butler, 1993).

Being able to define ecotourism is important to facilitate the identification of elements that are suitable in specific settings. No single definition appears suitable given the variety of specific activities involved and the great range of settings in which they take place. Certain elements have greater importance in some settings than others. It is not realistic to expect that ecotourism would be acceptable and promoted in an area if it were clearly in conflict with well-established existing land uses and sources of employment.

Ecotourism within the context of Northern Ontario is defined as (Boyd and Butler, 1993, 13)

> . . . a responsible nature travel experience that contributes to the conservation of the ecosystem while respecting the integrity of host communities and, where possible, ensuring that activities are complementary, or at least compatible, with existing resource-based uses present at the ecosystem level.

This definition also includes value-laden terms (e.g., "responsible" and "compatible"). However, such is the confusion over the meaning of the term that it would be unrealistic to use it without providing a working definition.

NORTHERN ONTARIO AS A SETTING FOR ECOTOURISM

In this section, the specific attributes and image of Northern Ontario as they pertain to ecotourism are noted. This is followed by the identification of inconsistencies that may exist between the perceptions of Northern Ontario held by the tourist and its suitability as a setting for ecotourism based on the area's characteristics.

Ecotourists are generally perceived to be well educated, affluent, and mature. They also appear to be sympathetic to "green" principles, essentially those of sustainable development that emphasize (1) small scale rather than large scale, (2) traditional or indigenous rather than modern resource development (i.e., industrial-based), (3) nonconsumptive rather than consumptive use of wildlife except by indigenous peoples, and (4) protection rather than exploitation of resources and landscapes. The ecotourism population is also primarily urban in origin and is attracted to areas that epitomize the opposite of the home environment.

Northern Ontario initially appears to have many of the attributes required for ecotourism. It is largely free from urban settlements and has vast expanses of "untouched" landscape, a rich vegetation cover, considerable wildlife, and an indigenous population which, in some locations, still lives off the land. There has also been recreational and tourist use of the area for a considerable time, and thus some basic facilities and infrastructure exist. Finally, the area's provincial parks and one national park support the presence of tourists and help safeguard some of the natural features.[7]

Nonetheless, ecotourism in Northern Ontario will have to be somewhat different from that found, for example, in Latin America, Africa, or Asia. While Northern Ontario does have the attributes noted, many of these factors create difficulties for the development of ecotourism. For example, urban settlements in Northern Ontario hold few attractions for the potential ecotourist. Moreover, many communities rely on a single industry based on resource extraction that generates few scenic values.

The resource development activities of Northern Ontario, basically forestry (and pulp/paper production), mining, and trapping/hunting, are not viewed as attractive, or even as acceptable, by some ecotourists who regard such activity as being unsympathetic to the natural environment. Furthermore, although the portrayal of the historic importance and development of fur trapping should be of interest, this activity does not rank high with ecotourists, even when practiced by indigenous peoples. As well, clear-cutting of forests is not generally viewed with sympathy by ecotourists.

Recreational opportunities, mostly in the form of wilderness and back-country recreation, presently exist in Northern Ontario and lend themselves well to ecotourism. Indeed, some would argue that much of the current recreation activity is ecotourism. Major exceptions, despite their significant contribution to tourism revenue in the region, are consumptive activities such as sport hunting and sport fishing. Hunting and fishing by indigenous peoples are viewed by some ecotourists as acceptable, but only within certain limits.

In many ecotourism destinations, the indigenous population is promoted as a major attraction. They may be used as guides, provide accommodations in traditional villages and houses, and produce and sell native artifacts. Above all, and regardless of the inaccuracy, bias, and insensitivity, they are "sold" as exotic, primitive, different, and desirable. In general, such a portrayal of Northern Ontario native peoples would be unacceptable and would, possibly, conflict with the legal system. Moreover, most Indian reserves and settlements in Northern Ontario probably do not have the same exotic appeal of a Thai hill tribe village, for example. In fact, in many cases they may not be much different from other small northern urban communities.

Forest coverage, wildlife potential, variations in relief and the presence of water throughout the region, and the scale (size) of the Northern Ontario landscape render the area a prime candidate for ecotourism. However, the area is prone to problems of access and seasonality. Access within the region is restricted to several main highways, with the majority of the road network comprising minor classed roads and those used by the logging industry. In addition, the distance between features and attractions in this area may be vast, certainly compared to some tropical ecotourism destinations. The flora and fauna of Northern Ontario are not comparable in variety, guaranteed visibility, or accessibility to many other ecotourism areas such as the rain forests or cloud forests of the tropics.

These points have been noted not to disparage the appeal of Northern Ontario to ecotourism, but to clarify some of the issues. Ecotourism in this area will, by necessity, be different in many respects from that found in more traditional areas. The attributes of Northern Ontario must be carefully matched to the attributes and demands of ecotourism and must respect the needs and preferences of the local population if ecotourism development is to be appropriate and acceptable, let alone successful.

The remainder of this chapter focuses on the development and application of GIS for the purpose of identifying specific regions in Northern Ontario that are suitable for ecotourism.

INVENTORYING POTENTIAL ECOTOURISM SITES IN NORTHERN ONTARIO

The seven procedural steps involved in this study are outlined in Figure 20.3 and discussed below, beginning with Stage 2. Stage 1 was discussed previously in this chapter. This comprehensive process recognizes that to "make the right decision requires that the relevant data be presented in the framework of an appropriate model" (Aronoff, 1991, p. 31).

STAGE 1:	**REVIEW OF LITERATURE AND CONCEPTUALIZATION OF THE PROBLEM**

Outcome:
* No consensus over definition of ecotourism
* Ecotourism has a long and diverse history
* Ecotourism has recognized linkages with other types of tourism (alternative) and ideas related to environmental management (sustainable tourism development)

STAGE 2: **DETERMINATION OF CRITERIA TO BE USED**
Outcome:
* Identification of key attributes of ecotourism applied to Northern Ontario
* Northern Ontario landscape best characterized by the criteria of: naturalness, wildlife, cultural heritage, landscape & community (see Table 20.1)

STAGE 3: **DETERMINATION OF THE CONCEPT OF NATURALNESS**
Outcome:
* Degrees of naturalness exist in the form of a continuum (see Figure 20.4)

STAGE 4: **DETERMINATION OF ECOTOURISM UNITS**
Outcome:
Step 1
* Identification of features of ecotourism criteria (see Table 20.2) that can be recorded using GIS
Step 2:
* Determining an area's naturalness
* Recognition of attributes of naturalness
* Incorporation of ideas used in other studies
* Assigning value ranges for all aspects naturalness from which an overall score of naturalness for areas can be determined (see Table 20.3)
Step 3:
* Hierarchical arrangement of naturalness attributes (see Figure 20.2)
* Utilizing a system of veto to determine the type of naturalness a region is given based on the overall cumulative score it achieved

STAGE 5: **TESTING THE PROCEDURE IN A PILOT AREA**

STAGE 6: **APPLICATION OF GIS METHOD TO STUDY AREA AND THE IDENTIFICATION OF POTENTIAL ECOTOURISM AREA**
(see Figures 20.5 and 20.6)

Figure 20.3
Procedural steps in the methodology.

STAGE 7: **INCORPORATION OF THE RESULTS OF GIS INTO THE DECISION-MAKING AND PLANNING PROCESS IN THE AREA INVOLVED**
(see Figure 20.7)

Stage 2: Elements and Criteria of Ecotourism Suitable for Northern Ontario To identify elements and criteria for the purpose of determining areas in Northern Ontario that might be suitable for ecotourism activity, a compromise between a conceptually "pure" ecotourism (i.e., absence of conflicting activities or resource use) and an acceptable and realistic form of development (i.e., ecotourism as one of many activities vying for limited resources) is required. Based on a review of the literature and the physical and human composition of Northern Ontario, a number of key attributes were identified (Boyd and Butler, 1993). For ecotourism to be environmentally and socially responsible, it should be (1) focused on elements of the natural environment, (2) managed in such a way as to have minimal environmental and social impacts, (3) nonconsumptive, (4) capable of providing desired economic benefits to local residents, (5) compatible with other resource uses in the area, and (6) appropriate in scale for the setting. These attributes are not the only characteristics of ecotourism, nor are they universally applicable.

Evaluation of the compatibility of ecotourism with other resource uses must acknowledge economic and political realities. There is a long history of both extractive resource use and local recreational consumptive use of natural resources in the region, and it would be naive to expect a fledgling ecotourism industry to take precedence over existing forms of resource use, especially where these are sanctioned by the public sector and supported by the local population. Similar conclusions have been drawn in other locations (International Resources Group, 1992).

Stage 3: Determining the Concept of Naturalness When defining indicators of ecotourism suitability for Northern Ontario, one major concern is the "naturalness" or "pristineness" of the area under consideration. It can be argued that in Northern Ontario, only a few "pristine" or untouched environments exist. The region has been heavily forested and resource extraction is widespread, with the pervading influence of pollutants, emissions, and possible people-induced climatic change on even those areas that have not been exposed to extractive activities. There is, therefore, a range of degrees of "naturalness." This is shown in the form of a continuum in Figure 20.4, in which the relative influences of the natural and human processes operating on the landscape determine where a particular site would fall within the spectrum.

Five landscape types are illustrated, with Type 1 being the most "pristine" and the one most preferred for ecotourism. This does not imply that ecotourism could not occur elsewhere, but reflects ecotourists' preference for the most natural and untouched landscapes (Boo, 1990; Valentine, 1992; Whelan, 1991). The descriptions provided should be viewed as examples of possible landscape characteristics only, and not as characteristics that must be present for an area to be given a certain designation of "naturalness." What is important is demonstrating how the landscape becomes less natural as one moves through the spectrum.

The presence of forest and aquatic environments is important with respect to the area's naturalness. Both are also important for tourism uses, albeit in different ways, depending on the type of activity. For instance, in the case of land-based activities, ecotourists moving through the forest will be confronted with numerous detailed forest characteristics. Aquatic areas may provide important backdrops mostly in the form of scenery, but subtle changes in quality may be of little significance. Water-based activities, on the other hand, reverse this situation, with the forest merely providing the scenic backdrop for a water-based ecotourism experience.

Although naturalness is considered a key criterion for identifying ecotourism sites, wildlife, cultural heritage, landscape, and community are also significant and appropriate indicators. Table 20.1 lists characteristics and measures of these criteria, where variation is expressed as absolutes or in the form of a continuum.

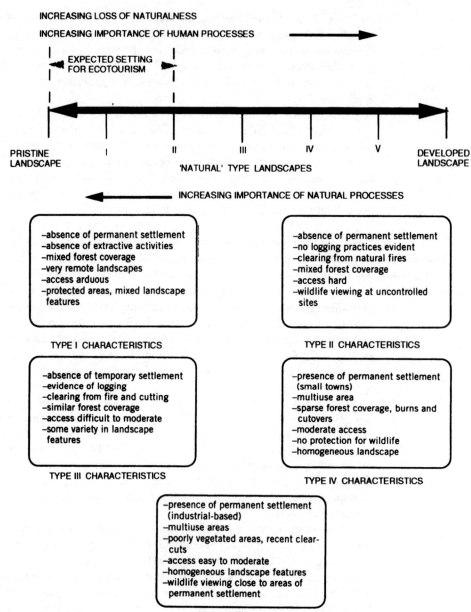

INCREASING LOSS OF NATURALNESS

INCREASING IMPORTANCE OF HUMAN PROCESSES

EXPECTED SETTING
FOR ECOTOURISM

PRISTINE   I   II   III   IV   V   DEVELOPED
LANDSCAPE   LANDSCAPE

'NATURAL' TYPE LANDSCAPES

INCREASING IMPORTANCE OF NATURAL PROCESSES

–absence of permanent settlement
–absence of extractive activities
–mixed forest coverage
–very remote landscapes
–access arduous
–protected areas, mixed landscape
 features

TYPE I CHARACTERISTICS

–absence of permanent settlement
–no logging practices evident
–clearing from natural fires
–mixed forest coverage
–access hard
–wildlife viewing at uncontrolled
 sites

TYPE II CHARACTERISTICS

–absence of temporary settlement
–evidence of logging
–clearing from fire and cutting
–similar forest coverage
–access difficult to moderate
–some variety in landscape
 features

TYPE III CHARACTERISTICS

–presence of permanent settlement
 (small towns)
–multiuse area
–sparse forest coverage, burns and
 cutovers
–moderate access
–no protection for wildlife
–homogeneous landscape

TYPE IV CHARACTERISTICS

–presence of permanent settlement
 (industrial-based)
–multiuse areas
–poorly vegetated areas, recent clear-
 cuts
–access easy to moderate
–homogeneous landscape features
–wildlife viewing close to areas of
 permanent settlement

TYPE V CHARACTERISTICS

Figure 20.4
The naturalness
continuum.
(From Boyd and
Butler, 1994, pp.
11, 29–30.)

Stage 4: Three steps are associated with identifying specific ecotourism units (Boyd and Butler,
Determination 1994). First, those features of each criterion that can be recorded using GIS must be
of Ecotourism identified (see Table 20.2). Elements within a region can be recorded by the GIS as
Units points (e.g., mills, mines), polygons (e.g., areas of clear-cut forest), or lines (e.g., rivers,
logging roads). Distance components are accommodated through placing buffers of a

TABLE 20.1
Characteristics and Measures of Ecotourism Criteria

Characteristics	Measures	
Naturalness		
Permanent settlement in area	Absent	Present
Absence of cutting	>10% red/white pine	>80% deciduous
Undrained wetland	Absence of dams	Dam
Unmodified rivers (Type 1)	Absence of dams	Dam
Unmodified rivers (Type 2)	Absence of bridges	Bridges
Absence of intrusive sound	10 km to near sound	1 km
Wildlife		
Suitable habitat	ARDA 1 capability	ARDA 7 capability
Migration route	On primary routeway	Not on routeway
Wintering site	Yes	No evidence
Feeding site	Yes	No evidence
Nature reserve	Nature reserve provincial park	Nature reserve zone within provincial park
Cultural Heritage		
Designated historic sites	Yes	None
Historic parks	Historical provincial park	Historical zone within provincial park
Historical routes	Present	Absent
Indian reserve	Traditional desired	Modern not desired
Landscape		
Significant feature	High relative relief >100 meters	No relief
Viewpoints	Present	Absent
Community		
Not within site, but close enough to provide base, services, and local population for economic benefit	5 km	Over 20 km
Close enough for primary access to site(s)	Access features	No access

Source: Boyd and Butler (1993, pp. 45–46).

certain distance around features (e.g., where noise may be a deterrent, a buffer of say 6 miles or 10 kilometers is placed around current extractive activities).

The second step focuses on determining an area's naturalness. This is expressed in terms of the following seven attributes: (1) presence or absence of permanent settlement, (2) biophysical (vegetation) characteristics, (3) extent of resource-related activity present, (4) type of access, (5) presence of wildlife, (6) nature of recreational activity, and (7) landscape characteristics. An assumption is made that the degree of naturalness is an

TABLE 20.2
Spatial and Temporal Characteristics of Ecotourism Criteria

Negative Aspects		Positive Aspects	
Feature	**Frequency**	**Feature**	**Frequency**
Spatial (Area)			
Clear-cut	Any	Old forest	Relative, all
Mining (spoil tips)	Any	Water bodies	Relative
Urban development	Any	Streams	Relative
Mining affected areas	Any	Historic routes	Relative, all
Nodal (Points)			
Mines	All	Localized habitat	Relative
Mills	All	Viewpoint	Relative
Airports	All	Historic site	Relative, all
Dams	All		
Temporal (Fluctuating short and long term)			
Logging	Any	Migratory sites	Relative
Hunting	Any	Wintering sites	Relative
Trapping	Any		
Linear (Access)			
Roads	All, few	Roads	Relative, few
Rail	All	Old logging roads	Relative
Used logging roads	All, relative	Rivers	Relative, all

Source: Boyd and Butler (1994, p. 20).

important factor in determining which areas are best suited to different types of ecotourists and ecotourism experiences.

These seven attributes of naturalness were used in the actual procedure to identify ecotourism units described later. The items listed under the heading of naturalness in Table 20.1 should only be viewed as possible examples of aspects of "naturalness," and should not be tied specifically to those mentioned above. In deciding what criterion to use (Table 20.1), the emphasis should be on choosing appropriate criteria and not on determining the specific features of the landscape that could be labeled under each one.

The methodology proposed in this fourth stage is similar to that used in Australia for the production of a national wilderness inventory and wilderness evaluation (Lesslie and Taylor, 1985; Lesslie et al., 1988, 1993). A value range is assigned to the various aspects of each attribute, from which an overall score can be determined. Table 20.3 provides an itemized list of possible scores for each attribute (six primary and one secondary, namely, landscape), a description of the various elements of each attribute, and a

TABLE 20.3
Scores, Attributes, and Value Ranges Used to Establish an Area's "Naturalness"

Score	Attributes	Value Range

Primary Characteristics

Presence of Community

Score	Community Type	Population Size
5	Absence of permanent settlement	0
3	Unincorporated communities	1–1000
2	Small towns	1001–10000
1	Urban settlements (industrial-based)	>10,000

Resource-Related Activity (Forestry)

Score	Resource Type	Percent of Area
5	No presence of forestry activities	100%
3	Forestry practices I (cutover area)	<20% cutover 30–40 years
2	Forestry practices II	>20% cutover 20–30 years
1	Forestry practices III	>20% cutover 10–20 years

Resource-Related Activity (Mining)

Score	Resource Type	Percent of Area
5	No presence of mining	100%
3	Mining practices I	Abandoned mines present
1	Mining practices II	Operational mines present

Vegetation Coverage

Score	Vegetation Type	Percent of Area
5	Mixed forest (Type 1)	>50% coniferous, >10% white and red pine
4	Mixed forest (Type 2)	>50% deciduous/coniferous, <10% white or red pine
3	Dense coniferous forest	>80% jack pine, black spruce
2	Sparse coniferous forest burns and cutover	>80% deciduous, >10 years old
1	Poorly vegetated areas, clear-cuts, burns	Shrub cover, <10 years old

Access Characteristics

Score	Type	Value Range
5	Access area I	Areas outside any buffers around all roads
3	Access area II	Areas within 2-km buffer around logging roads
2	Access area III	Areas within 5-km buffer around loose surface roads
1	Access area IV	Areas within 10-km buffer around paved roads

Wildlife Setting

Score	Value Range	Type
5	Wildlife setting I	ARDA class areas 1–2
3	Wildlife setting II	ARDA class areas 3–5
1	Wildlife setting III	ARDA class areas 6–7

TABLE 20.3
(Continued)

Score	Attributes	Value Range
	Secondary Characteristics	

Landscape (Relief)

Score	Characteristic	Measure
5	High relative relief	>25 meters
3	Medium relative relief	10–25 meters
1	Little relative relief	Less than 10 meters

Landscape (Water)

Score	Characteristic	Percent of Area
5	Presence of water	5–20%
3	Presence of water	10–50%
1	Presence of water	0–5% or >50%

Source: Boyd and Butler (1994).

measure to determine the score. While all attributes have a range from "5" to "1," not all have the same subdivisions within the range.

The third and final step in this stage requires the overlay of the attributes. The sequence of the overlays is not particularly critical because the overall score an area receives will be the same regardless of the order chosen. The order used in this study is similar to that shown in Figure 20.2, in which the scores for vegetation cover were calculated first and to which were added resource-related activities, access characteristics, community presence, wildlife potential, and landscape characteristics.

An area's type and degree of naturalness is determined by the cumulative score it receives for all of the attributes/biophysical characteristics present for respective areas. The following scores were used for the levels of naturalness: Type I, 31–35; Type II, 21–30; Type III, 15–20; Type IV, 8–14; and Type V, 1–7. A veto system is employed in classifying areas. A Type I area is not possible if a score of "3" is recorded for two or more attributes present within the area. Type II landscapes require that no more than two attributes have a score less than "3," with at least one attribute scoring a "5." A Type III landscape is not possible if a score lower than "2" is recorded for three or more attributes. A Type IV is not possible if an area scores a "1" for more than three attributes.

Areas that received a Type I or II classification and that include components of cultural heritage (determined after GIS is completed) are considered as the best options for ecotourism. The next best areas are those classed as a Type III landscape that also evidence cultural features. It is important that the areas are of a minimum size sufficient for ecotourism use. An area of 120–200 square miles (300–500 square kilometers) is considered to be suitable, in that it allows several days' travel to occur with a diversity of flora and fauna present. In regions where few areas of this size are identified, smaller areas may be considered suitable for ecotourism experiences that are offered as day excursions, or with the added attraction of an overnight stay.

Stage 5:
Testing the
Procedure in a
Pilot Area
During this stage, the procedure as noted in Stages 2 to 4 was applied to the test area (shown in Figure 20.1). This revealed some minor problems that required modification of how the buffers around features were scored to ensure that the road network and communities were not included in any of the ecotourism units. It should be noted that not all attributes were used in the pilot because the test area did not contain the full range of attributes listed in Table 20.3 (e.g., no mining activity was present and incomplete information was available on wildlife potential).

Also, the thematic layers as shown in Figure 20.2 were not arranged in a hierarchy for purposes of ranking the criteria as initially proposed. Instead, scores were added on a pixel-by-pixel basis for each of the layers because the final score an area received remained the same regardless of the order in which they were placed in the hierarchy.

Stage 6:
Application of
GIS
The study area comprised some 31,250 square miles (80,000 square kilometers), covering the area from near Sault Ste. Marie in the southwest to North Bay in the southeast, and from the northern edge of Lake Superior Provincial Park in the northwest to beyond Kirkland Lake in the northeast (see Figure 20.1). Its boundaries were the 48th parallel to the north, Lake Superior to the west, the Ontario–Quebec border to the east, and a line from slightly south of Sault Ste. Marie to North Bay in the south. Using Figure 20.2 as the frame of reference, a general description of the characteristics of each thematic layer can be discussed. More detailed discussion of the results of the mapping of the GIS is available in Boyd et al. (1994).

Vegetation types were varied and fragmented (Table 20.3 provides an overview of vegetation types). Only the western portion of the region had extensive areas of sparse coniferous forest, with a belt of poorly vegetated areas on the southern edge. Vegetation types regarded as most suitable for ecotourism (mixed forest) were found mostly in the central and northern parts of the region. Areas of mixed forest (Type 2) (see Table 20.3) were found to be highly fragmented, having no significantly sized contiguous areas. The greatest concentrations were in the southeast. Mixed forest (Type 1) vegetation was found to occur in more sizable segments throughout the central and northern parts, indicating areas of high potential for ecotourism.

With regard to the first aspect of resource-related activity (forestry), a few older cuts (more than 30 years) exist in the south and southeast, with more recent ones covering the northern half of the area. The overall pattern of cutovers revealed that considerable areas in the south and west had not been affected. However, this region is mostly covered by forms of vegetation that are less attractive for ecotourism. Although many of the cutovers are small, the fact that they exist in close proximity to each other (especially in the north and central parts of the region) meant that they affected significant portions of the overall study area.

Landscape attributes were depicted by layers recording the presence of water and the absolute relief. Water bodies were present throughout the entire area, with significant concentrations found in the central regions and towards the eastern edge of the area. An overall north-south pattern of drainage exists for the entire region, as revealed by the orientation of many of the lakes and rivers shown in GIS output.

A variation in absolute relief of almost 1650 feet (500 meters) was found to occur over the entire study area. The general pattern displayed one of two significant features:

the east and south were relatively low, with elevations rising to the north and west, except in the vicinity of the lakeshore.

The potential for wildlife was inferred from the ARDA land capability map coverage for ungulates and waterfowl. The combined results of these two classes comprised a fourth layer in the GIS. Areas with the lowest potential for wildlife were found to lie in the southern part, with a concentration in the central portion of the study area. The GIS output revealed that very few areas attained a high score representative of ARDA Classes 1 and 2, the largest of which were located in the extreme northwest. The implication is that the diversity in capability for wildlife that does exist within the study area is present at a very small scale only, if at all.

The last "natural" element considered was the presence of protected areas (provincial parks). "Recreation" and "natural environment" parks were found throughout the study area, with one "waterway" and one "wilderness" park present. With the exception of the Missisagi River "waterway" park and the Lady Evelyn-Smoothwater "wilderness" park, these parks were generally small and, therefore, were not viewed as particularly relevant to ecotourism, unless used as campsites.

The remaining layers of the GIS comprised human elements present within the region in the form of community type and access characteristics. Buffers of varying size were placed around these elements (see Table 20.3 for buffer sizes) to identify areas that should remain outside of all "ecotourism units" identified. The output of the GIS layer for presence of communities revealed that three types exist over the study area: unincorporated communities, small towns, and cities. Major urban centers, such as Sault Ste. Marie, Elliot Lake, Sudbury, and North Bay, are all located on the southern edge of the study area in the generally lower-scoring regions.

The majority of the smaller towns are also located in the south, except those around Kirkland Lake in the extreme northeast. A belt of small unincorporated communities reflected, to a large degree, an access network that ran west to east across the northern part of the study area. Overall, the vast majority of the study area was found to be unaffected by communities and urban development.

However, when access characteristics and the buffers placed around them (see Table 20.3 for details of buffer size) are considered, substantial human intrusion into the study area is revealed. The GIS output for the road network shows an absence of paved roads, with the exception of three major north–south routes, including the Trans Canada Highway in the extreme west. Loose surface roads, however, were found to be extremely dense in three regions: the northeast around Kirkland Lake, the southeast around Sudbury and North Bay, and the southwest around Sault Ste. Marie. For the most part, this is representative of the spread of settlement. Logging roads followed the pattern of cutovers and were widespread and clustered, reflecting the pattern of timber development and exploitation. When buffers were applied to the access network, very little of the study area was found to remain outside of any of the buffers. A discontinuous belt of several moderately sized areas did emerge, however, in the central portion of the study area, with smaller blocks scattered over the remainder of the region.

The final element (and GIS layer) of the human impact on the landscape was mining. Because this activity is generally unattractive to ecotourists, it was buffered to avoid being included in any potential "ecotourism unit." In particular, two areas of major mining activity were noted: One was in the northeast to the west of Kirkland Lake, and the other was in the south centered on Sudbury and running west to Elliot Lake.

These "thematic" layers, representing the physical and human elements present in the study area, were overlain to determine the total score an area could receive. Total scores were derived by accumulating the scores for each of the attributes in turn. The result was a complicated picture of the potential of the area for ecotourism. The predominant impression gained was the absence of significant areas in the south, northeast, and southwest sections of the region, but the relative abundance of potentially high-quality ecotourism sites in the central and northern–central portions of the region.

The total score an area could receive was 35 points (a score of five for six of the seven attributes and a score of five for "landscape" features combined). To produce some order out of the mass of detail, it was necessary to reassemble the data to eliminate areas close to major access routes, add in the landscape component, and identify contiguous areas with a minimum size of 120 square miles (300 square kilometers). It was then possible to identify Type I and Type II ecotourism units.

Four Type I ecotourism units (see Figure 20.5), scoring between 31 and 35 points, were identified as having the most potential for ecotourism development on the basis of the criteria used. Not surprisingly, none of these units was in the south or west of the study area. One was found in the central part of the region, one in the north–central, and two in the eastern part, south of Elk Lake. Moreover, none of the areas was entirely homogenous; that is, there were small areas within the overall units that were not of an equally high value, as shown by the empty pixels. Also, not surprisingly, their shapes were generally far from symmetrical, reflecting (1) natural elements such as water bodies and topographic features and (2) the absence of intrusive human impacts.

The less rigorous criteria involved in delimiting Type II ecotourism units (see Figure 20.6) is reflected in the map of these units. A considerable proportion of the study area fell in Type II ecotourism units (12 areas that scored between 21 and 30 points) although, again, the southern part of the region received little coverage. The majority of the units

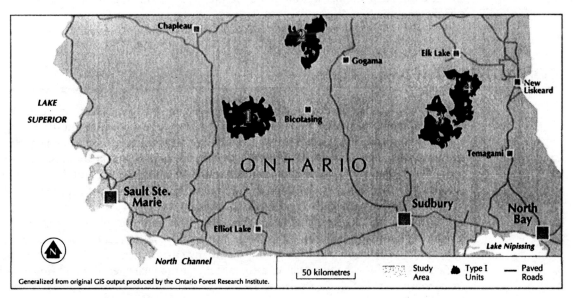

Figure 20.5
Ecotourism Type I units.

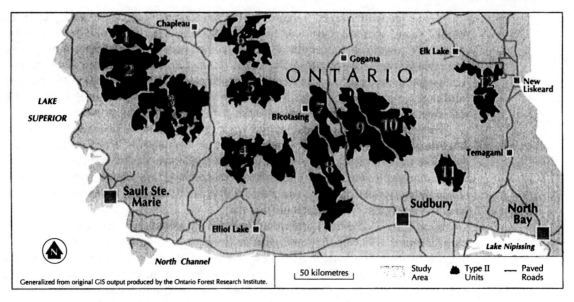

Figure 20.6
Ecotourism Type II units.

were located in the central belt, although there were several units in the west of the area.

The average size of units was considerably larger than the size of the Type I ecotourism units, although a number of units (#7, #8, #9, and #10) had obviously been dissected by elements of the access network. The units in the northwest were found to be more contiguous and uniform than was the case for the Type I units. Overall, access characteristics and wildlife were found to be the most important criteria in shaping the ecotourism units.

CONCLUSION AND IMPLICATIONS

This chapter has described a method to identify ecotourism sites within Northern Ontario. The nature of the methodology is such that it can be applied in similar settings elsewhere if suitable data exist. The value of GIS can best be appreciated when large data sets are available for analysis, because the costs of acquiring such data are normally very high. The availability of specific data can determine which elements or attributes can be examined and which have to be ignored. Such considerations clearly influence the validity of the results of such studies and applications (Dale, 1991).

Matching the characteristics of an area with those attributes most appropriate for ecotourism has major implications for tourism operators and recreation planners. By its very nature, ecotourism will have an impact on any environment. Limiting ecotourism (which has within it the potential to assume some of the characteristics and impacts of "mass tourism" although on a small scale) to areas that can best withstand such use will, to some extent, reduce negative impacts compared to more "fragile" areas.

GIS provides information in a form from which decisions can be made. In the con-

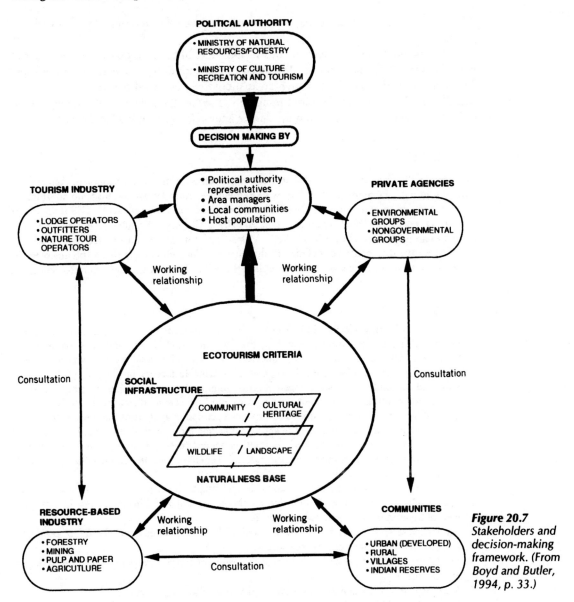

POLITICAL AUTHORITY
- MINISTRY OF NATURAL RESOURCES/FORESTRY
- MINISTRY OF CULTURE RECREATION AND TOURISM

DECISION MAKING BY

- Political authority representatives
- Area managers
- Local communities
- Host population

TOURISM INDUSTRY
- LODGE OPERATORS
- OUTFITTERS
- NATURE TOUR OPERATORS

PRIVATE AGENCIES
- ENVIRONMENTAL GROUPS
- NONGOVERNMENTAL GROUPS

Working relationship

Working relationship

Consultation

Consultation

ECOTOURISM CRITERIA

SOCIAL INFRASTRUCTURE

COMMUNITY / CULTURAL HERITAGE

WILDLIFE / LANDSCAPE

NATURALNESS BASE

RESOURCE-BASED INDUSTRY
- FORESTRY
- MINING
- PULP AND PAPER
- AGRICUTLURE

Working relationship

Working relationship

Consultation

COMMUNITIES
- URBAN (DEVELOPED)
- RURAL
- VILLAGES
- INDIAN RESERVES

*Figure 20.7
Stakeholders and decision-making framework. (From Boyd and Butler, 1994, p. 33.)*

text of Northern Ontario, the GIS application and the data produced can represent a saving of many hours of fieldwork. As well, it allows for continuous updating and provides visual images of areas that could not otherwise have been obtained (Aronoff, 1991).

Development of areas identified as having high potential for ecotourism requires cooperation and consultation among agencies, communities, and industry to make decisions that not only are based on the interests of the various stakeholders, but also consider the characteristics of the area itself. Various interest groups in a region interact with each other and use information in different ways. Some of these relationships are shown in Figure 20.7. The data obtained from the application of GIS are shown in the center of this figure because, in principle, the information will be available to all interested parties.

The methodology described in this chapter identifies areas that show the greatest potential and which may then be developed through fostering cooperative partnerships. The actual decision on whether such areas should be developed has to be made in the overall context of existing plans and resource use within the general area, the economic viability of such development, and the desires and preferences of the local residents.[8]

ACKNOWLEDGMENTS

Funding for this project was provided through the Northern Ontario Development Agreement, Northern Forestry Program. The authors wish to thank Dr. Ajith Perera and his team at OFRI for their cooperation in compiling the data base producing the various layers in the GIS from which analysis was possible. Thanks are also extended to Patricia Chalk, cartographic section in the Geography Department at the University of Western Ontario, for modifying the colored maps produced by OFRI so that they could be included in this chapter. The authors also thank the independent reviewers for their critical commentary, as well as the editors for their excellent editorial skills.

NOTES

1. The Canada-Ontario Northern Ontario Development Agreement (NODA) is a four-year, $95 million (CAD) initiative funded equally by the Government of Canada and the Government of Ontario. It has four objectives: (1) to undertake programs of applied research and technology transfer that provide information in support of sustainable forestry in Ontario; (2) to provide improved capability to forest managers through improved decision-support systems, advanced silvicultural training, development of alternative forest management techniques, collection and publication of forestry information, and expanded economic analysis of the forest sector; (3) to support the economic development of aboriginal people through on-reserve forest management programs, access to off-reserve resources and enhanced forestry training; and (4) to promote broader understanding of the forest, the values it generates, and the contributions of Canada and Ontario to its sustainable use.
2. See Chapter 21 for a comprehensive discussion relating to the Canada Land Inventory (CLI).
3. See Chapter 15 for additional discussion relating to ecotourism. Chapter 11 provides an overview of trends relating to nature-based tourism.
4. See Chapters 4, 5, 7, 8, 16, 17, 18, 22, and 23 for further discussion relating to sustainable tourism and sustainable tourism development.
5. See Chapters 9, 22, and 23 for additional discussion of carrying capacity and limits of acceptable change.
6. See Chapters 3–6, 9, and 28 for overviews of tourism planning processes.
7. See Chapters 22 and 23 for additional discussion pertaining to protected areas and national parks.
8. See Chapters 5, 9, 11, 12, and 14–19 for additional discussion regarding community attitudes and involvement in tourism planning and development processes.

REFERENCES

Aronoff, S. 1991. *Geographic Information Systems: A Management Perspective*. Ottawa, Ontario, Canada: WDL Publications.
Berry, J.K. 1991. GIS in island resource planning: a case study in map analysis. In D.J. Maguire,

M.F. Goodchild, and D.W. Rhind (eds.), *Geographical Information Systems: Principles and Applications*, Vol. 2. Harlow, UK: Longman Scientific and Technical, pp. 285–295.

Boo, E. 1990. *Ecotourism: The Potentials and Pitfalls*, Vols. 1 and 2. Washington, D.C.: World Wildlife Fund.

Boyd, S.W. and R.W. Butler. 1993. *Review of the Development of Ecotourism with Respect to Identifying Criteria for Ecotourism for Northern Ontario*. Report for Department of Natural Resources/Forestry, Ministry of Natural Resources. Sault Ste. Marie, Ontario, Canada.

Boyd, S.W. and R.W. Butler. 1994. *Geographical Information Systems: A Tool for Establishing Parameters for Ecotourism Criteria*. Report for Department of Natural Resources/Forestry, Ministry of Natural Resources. Sault Ste. Marie, Ontario, Canada.

Boyd, S.W., R.W. Butler, R.E. Bae, A. Perera, and W. Haider. 1994. *GIS Mapping of Potential Areas for Ecotourism in Northern Ontario*. Report for Department of Natural Resources/Forestry, Ministry of Natural Resources. Sault Ste. Marie, Ontario, Canada.

Coppock, J.T. and D.W. Rhind. 1991. History of GIS. In D.J. Maguire, M.F. Goodchild and D.W. Rhind (eds.), *Geographical Information Systems: Principles and Applications*, Vol. 1. Harlow, UK: Longman Scientific and Technical, pp. 21–43.

Dale, P.F. 1991. Land information systems. In D.J. Maguire, M.F. Goodchild, and D.W. Rhind (eds.), *Geographical Information Systems: Principles and Applications*, Vol. 2. Harlow, UK: Longman Scientific and Technical, pp. 85–99.

Dearden, P. 1989. Tourism in developing societies: some observations on trekking in the highlands of North Thailand, *World Leisure and Recreation*, 31(4), 40–47.

Dearden, P. and S. Harron. 1992. Tourism and the hilltribes of Thailand. In B. Weiler and C.M. Hall (eds.), *Special Interest Tourism*, London: Belhaven Press, pp. 96–104.

Devine, H.A. and J. Kuo. 1991. Geographic information systems applications to urban recreation research and management. In C. Sylvester and L. Caldwell (eds.), *Abstracts of the Proceedings of the 1991 NRPA Leisure Research Symposium*, Baltimore, Maryland, 17–20 October, p. 83.

Durst, P.B. and C.D. Ingram. 1988. Nature-oriented tourism promotion by developing countries, *Tourism Management*, 9(1), 39–43.

Eagles, P.F.J., S.D. Buse, and G.T. Hvengaard. 1993. *Ecotourism: An Annotated Bibliography for Planners and Managers*. North Bennington, VT: The Ecotourism Society.

Farrell, B.H. and D. Runyan. 1991. Ecology and tourism, *Annals of Tourism Research*, 18(1), 26–40.

Fennell, D.A. and P.F.J. Eagles. 1990. Ecotourism in Costa Rica: a conceptual framework, *Journal of Park and Recreation Administration*, 8(1), 23–34.

Inskeep, E. 1987. Environmental planning for tourism, *Annals of Tourism Research*, 14(1), 118–135.

International Resources Group. 1992. *Ecotourism: A Viable Alternative for Sustainable Management of Natural Resources in Africa*. Washington, D.C.: Agency for International Development Bureau for Africa.

Kenchington, R.A. 1989. Tourism in the Galapagos Islands: the dilemma of conservation, *Environmental Conservation*, 16(3), 227–232.

Laarman, J.G. and P.B. Durst. 1987. Nature travel in the tropics, *Journal of Forestry*, 85(5), 43–46.

Lesslie, R.G. and S.G. Taylor. 1985. The wilderness continuum concept and its implications for Australian wilderness preservation policy, *Biological Conservation*, 32, 309–333.

Lesslie, R.G., B.G. Mackey, and K.M. Preece. 1988. A computer-based method of wilderness evaluation, *Environmental Conservation*, 15(3), 225–232.

Lesslie, R.G., S.G. Taylor, and M. Maslen. 1993. *National Wilderness Inventory: Handbook of Principles, Procedures and Usage.* University of Adelaide, Department of Geography.

Maguire, D.J., M.F. Goodchild, and D.W. Rhind (eds.). 1991. *Geographical Information Systems: Principles and Applications,* Vols. 1 and 2. Harlow, UK: Longman Scientific and Technical.

Marsh, J. 1992. *Tourism in Antarctica and Its Implications for Conservation.* Fourth Congress on National Parks and Protected Areas, Caracas, Venezuela.

McHarg I.L. 1969. *Design With Nature.* New York: Doubleday Natural History Press.

Nepal, S.K. and K.E. Weber. 1994. A buffer zone for biodiversity conservation: viability of the concept in Nepal's Royal Chitwan National Park, *Environmental Conservation,* 21(4), 333–341.

Pazner, M. 1989. *Map II Map Processor: A Geographical Information System for the Macintosh.* New York: John Wiley & Sons.

Scace, R.C., E. Grifone, and R. Usher (SENTAR Consultants Ltd.). 1992. *Ecotourism in Canada.* Report for the Canadian Environmental Advisory Council, Ottawa, Ontario, Canada.

Siderelis, K.C. 1991. Land resource information systems. In D. Maguire, M.F. Goodchild, and D.W. Rhind (eds.), *Geographical Information Systems: Principles and Applications,* Vol. 2. Harlow, UK: Longman Scientific and Technical, pp. 261–273.

Smith, L.G. 1993. *Impact Assessment and Sustainable Resource Management.* New York: John Wiley & Sons.

Star, J. and J. Estes. 1990. *Geographic Information Systems: An Introduction.* Englewood Cliffs, NJ: Prentice-Hall.

Sussmann, S. and T. Rashad. 1994. Geographic information systems in tourism marketing. In C. Cooper and A. Lockwood (eds.), *Progress in Tourism, Recreation and Hospitality Management,* Vol. 6, London: Belhaven Press, pp. 250–258.

Townshend, J.R.G. 1991. Environmental data bases and GIS. In D.J. Maguire, M.F. Goodchild, and D.W. Rhind (eds.), *Geographical Information Systems: Principles and Applications,* Vol. 2. Harlow, UK: Longman Scientific and Technical, pp. 201–216.

Valentine, P.S. 1992. Review: nature-based tourism. In B. Weiler and C.M. Hall (eds.), *Special Interest Tourism,* 105–127. London: Belhaven Press.

Weiler, B. and C.M. Hall (eds.). 1992. *Special Interest Tourism.* London: Belhaven Press.

Whelan, T. (ed.). 1991. *Nature Tourism: Managing for the Environment.* Washington, D.C.: Island Press.

Ziffer, K.A. 1989. *Ecotourism: The Uneasy Alliance.* Washington, D.C.: Conservation International.

¶ | PROBLEM SOLVING AND DISCUSSION ACTIVITIES

1. Identify the various interests of the stakeholders presented in Figure 20.7 with respect to the development of ecotourism. What potential conflicts might exist? How can these conflicts be resolved?
2. Select a specific type of tourism (e.g., cultural, event) and generate criteria for its development in a specific area similiar to what was undertaken in this chapter.
3. Select an area, determine its key elements, produce maps of these key elements, and manually overlay them using transparencies. What does the final picture of

the combined elements reveal? Did overlaying maps reveal any issues or attractions that might not otherwise have been clear?

4. How does one integrate different uses of an area and how should these be prioritized?

5. What role should the private sector play versus the public sector in selecting areas to promote certain types of tourism?

6. Techniques such as GIS represent exciting new developments that have seen little use within tourism and recreation research. How far should/can computers go in influencing decision making for tourism development?

21

Keeping Track of What Really Counts

TOURISM RESOURCE INVENTORY SYSTEMS
IN BRITISH COLUMBIA, CANADA

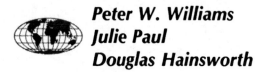

Peter W. Williams
Julie Paul
Douglas Hainsworth

§ | K E Y   L E A R N I N G   P O I N T S

- The effectiveness of tourism resource inventories depends on the extent to which they record and represent the quality of resources that are important to the visitor's experience.

- To adequately represent the relative value of locations for tourism, tourism resource inventory systems must include a combination of biophysical and human features.

- Quality, diversity, capacity, accessibility, availability, and quantity are critical measures of a resource's potential usefulness for tourism purposes.

- Incorporating stakeholder input into the identification and measurement of tourism resource attributes is an essential part of the development and implementation process associated with any credible tourism resource inventory system.

- Using geographical information system technologies (GIS) to record and analyze tourism resource inventory information is an efficient and effective method of assisting stakeholders to assess the implications of varying land use decisions for tourism development.

INTRODUCTION

For many destinations, the splendor of the natural and/or cultural environment drives tourism. For example, scenic attractions such as Canada's Niagara Falls and Rocky Mountains have drawn literally hundreds of thousands of visitors for decades. However, in other locations, the critical resources have not been clearly defined.

Numerous examples of industrially polluted beaches adjacent to resort areas, over-harvested commercial fishing zones in proximity to sport fishing lodges, and clear-cut forest mountain slopes adjacent to cruising and automobile scenic travel corridors all point to failures in recognizing the importance of protecting the natural and cultural resource base for tourism. In many cases, this loss of natural resource quality has not been deliberate. Quite often the necessary data may not exist or are not available in a fashion suited to the needs of tourism and other land use decision makers.

Tourism inventory systems are recording procedures that provide critical information for many resource allocation and land use planning decisions. Their usefulness depends on a variety of factors, including (1) how rigorously and credibly they reflect the relative importance tourists and tourism operators place on an area's natural, cultural, and heritage attributes and (2) how effectively they support resource planning and management decision making (Pigram, 1983). This chapter provides both theoretical and applied perspectives on the structure and application of tourism inventory systems in resource planning initiatives, focusing primarily on British Columbia's tourism resource inventory system.

TOURISM INVENTORY SYSTEMS: CONTEMPORARY PERSPECTIVES AND ISSUES

Tourism inventories are generally designed with specific purposes in mind. The resources selected (e.g., climate, wildlife, heritage), the attributes of these features (e.g., temperature, waterfowl, aboriginal settlements), and the relative ratings given to these attributes (e.g., high, medium, and low use capability) provide insights into the intentions of the inventory.

Some inventories record the extent and type of facility development present in a region. For example, tourism directories often record the range (e.g., bed and breakfast, motel, motor hotel, hotel, campground) and capacity (e.g., number of rooms, bed units, operating season) of fixed-roof accommodations available for tourists in a region. As such, they are relatively straightforward and useful inventories that describe the capability of the built environment. These and other *capability inventories* assess the maximum potential of a land unit or region for specific tourism uses.

Inventories may also record those natural and cultural features of a geographic area that are suited to tourism use. For example, inventories of climate, water depth, and beach conditions help determine the suitability of a region for various forms of water-oriented tourism development. These *suitability* inventories not only assess the potential of a specified land unit for tourist use, but also identify features that may represent constraints on development. For example, particularly strong water currents in a beach area may reduce its suitability for swimming activity.

Tourism Inventory Approaches Approaches to developing capability and suitability inventories can be categorized in two ways: (1) recording properties of the resource base without reference to any single planning or management objective (e.g., generic descriptions of existing wildlife populations and fixed accommodation supply are recorded irrespective of the intent of the exercise) and (2) itemizing only select elements of the resource base associated with specific forms of tourism.

The approach selected depends on the objectives and financial circumstances. The more holistic process identified in the first point above is most applicable when the inventory can be used in a variety of ongoing and evolving land use decision-making situations. In British Columbia (B.C.), there are several ongoing provincial and regional resource and land use planning programs in process. These programs require tourism inventory information that can be retrieved on a repetitive and flexible basis in a variety of configurations. In such cases, the costs of developing the inventory system can be borne over a series of applications.

The second more focused inventory procedure is best suited to addressing nonrepetitive planning and resource allocation decisions. These planning processes are typically linked to the development of site plans in areas designated for specific forms of tourism use (e.g., golf courses, ski trails, marine parks). In such situations, this approach reduces the time and cost required to develop the resource information needed for planning. However, the information generated is limited in its application to broader land use planning processes.

The overall effectiveness of a particular inventory approach will, in large part, be measured by the extent to which it is able to record and represent the quality of those resources that are central to the tourist's experience. The importance of such factors as accessibility, facility development, scenic quality, and natural resource diversity often differ significantly among tourists. Both the commonalities and differences in the relative importance of these attributes should be recognized in the development and use of resource inventory systems (Brown et al., 1978).

Inventory Elements   A combination of biophysical and human features gives locations their relative value from a tourism perspective. Each of these features plays a role in establishing an area's capability, suitability, and overall uniqueness for tourism.

BIOPHYSICAL PARAMETERS   Some inventory systems focus on the classification of resource features according to their physiographic, climatic, and biological characteristics. In combination, these landscape features determine the overall appeal of the setting for many tourism experiences. For instance, the patterns of rivers and streams, as well as the distribution of ground water and soils, often dictate those locations that tourists can access, as well as where the development of facilities may be feasible (Cressman and Hoffman, 1968; Taylor and Thomson, 1966). Climate, which is often an attraction in itself, plays an important role in establishing the intensity and seasonality of tourist demand (Besancenot et al., 1978; Crowe, 1975). Biological features such as vegetation and wildlife that are often sensitive to overuse by travelers frequently give regions their unique "sense of place" (Gunn, 1988; Swanson and Miles, 1988).

HUMAN PARAMETERS   Many human factors influence the attractiveness of the resource base for tourism. As a result, inventories often catalog the built features of destinations. These features include such elements as transportation, landscape esthetics, and land tenure (Gunn and McMillen, 1979).

Because transportation and access play key roles in the time-constrained travel behaviors of tourists,[1] many inventory systems record the physical and market accessibility attributes of destination resources. Physical access is usually recorded with reference to the type, quantity, and capacity of the existing transportation infrastructure. Market accessibility is normally measured based on resource proximity (i.e., time, financial, or physical distance) to tourist-generating regions (Smith, 1987).

Growing demand for tourism experiences in high-quality natural environments has created a need to recognize landscape esthetics as tourism resources. As a consequence, some resource inventory methods incorporate landscape attributes such as heritage sites, topographic relief, and scenic viewscapes into their systems (Schroeder, 1983).

Ownership of the resource base is an important concern for tourism planning and management, especially in jurisdictions where resource tenure is central to the long-term stability and economic viability of tourism operations. For example, ski and golf resorts require lengthy land tenures to provide enough time to generate an acceptable return on their extensive front-end capital investments. Ownership is also critical in situations where changes in neighboring tenure may influence the basic character of existing tourism operations. Commercial back-country tourism operations such as fishing resorts are especially vulnerable to changes in the quality of the resource base caused by nearby commercial enterprises such as mining and logging businesses.

Variations in land tenure and ownership can play an important role not only in determining the location of tourism facilities, but also in shaping the form and type of developments that occur (Pearce, 1979). In B.C., where the vast majority of the natural resource base is vested in the crown, tenure and stewardship of the land is a particularly important policy issue (ARA Consulting Group, 1993). For most parts of the province, the government dictates who uses the land base, for what tourism purposes, for how long, and at what cost.

Measuring Inventory Attributes Whether based on natural landscape features (e.g., hiking and cross-country skiing trails) or developed facilities (e.g., theme parks and marinas), the challenge facing most inventory systems is to identify the most important attributes of these resources. Quantity, diversity, capacity, availability, accessibility, and quality indicators are often used to describe the condition of these attributes (Laventhol and Horwath, 1982).

Once the characteristics of each resource attribute have been identified, they must be weighted in terms of their relative importance to tourists and tourism operators. Past approaches to weighting have involved incorporating the views of tourists through visitor surveys (Ferrario, 1979), the "expert" assessments of industry operators and other tourism specialists (Ritchie and Zins, 1978), and the subjective perspectives of tourism planners (Gunn, 1988). The technique chosen depends on (1) the richness of the information base available concerning resource preferences and (2) the time and economic constraints of the inventory process. Regardless of the approach, the inherent subjectivity in the process must be recognized. Resource inventories become increasingly subjective as more resource attributes are added to the process.

BRITISH COLUMBIA'S TOURISM RESOURCE INVENTORY SYSTEM

Rationale and Locational Context Located on Canada's Pacific coast, British Columbia (B.C.) has an overall land and fresh water area of approximately 235 million acres (95 million hectares). It is Canada's third largest province and comprises 9.5 percent of the country's total area. It is also one of the country's most popular tourist destinations. The province has both pristine wilderness areas (e.g., Vancouver Island's Pacific Rim National Park) and cosmopolitan urban centers (e.g., Vancouver and Victoria) that depend on scenic natural settings for a significant part of their tourist appeal. The qualities of the natural environment have evolved from simply being the setting for tourist activities to representing a fundamental part of the infrastructure required for a range of visitor products. Tourist activities that depend directly on a high-quality natural environment for their appeal range from heli-skiing to scenic driving, river rafting to fishing, ocean cruising to mountain trekking, and wilderness camping to golfing.

A diversity of ecosystems, wildlife species, and natural landscapes, in addition to clean air and water, contribute indirectly to the appeal of many of the province's regions for a broader range of economic and social activities (e.g., small meetings and conventions, festivals, and special events). In combination, these high-quality natural and cultural resources have helped to establish B.C. as an internationally competitive tourist destination (Industry, Science and Technology Canada–Tourism Canada, 1991).

Tourism is an important employment and revenue producer for B.C. It has been estimated that tourism generates well over 24 million overnight visitors, $5.5 billion dollars (CAD) in tourist spending, and 182,000 jobs during the peak season within the province (B.C. Ministry of Tourism, 1992). In the highly resource-dependent adventure tourism sector alone, more than 1700 jobs are directly attributable to the availability of the province's natural resource base (Tourism Canada, 1995).

To remain competitive in the global marketplace, the government can no longer rely on traditional marketing and finance techniques to manage the development and delivery of its nature-based tourism experiences. While these tools have played a significant role in building an awareness of B.C.'s natural assets and creating an impressive range of product lines, they have also increased pressures on the natural environment. As never before, the province's tourism stakeholders are being confronted with issues of resource scarcity, inter- and intraindustry resource use competition, and land tenure issues (Commission on Resources and the Environment, 1994).

This is not just the case in B.C., but is a circumstance that is being experienced worldwide (Williams, 1992). Indeed, there is growing support for the careful scrutiny of all land use development programs that place demands on the capacity of the natural resource base. Governments and industry in many areas are responding to the new ethic of sustainability by seeking better ways of managing the use of natural resources for all sectors of the economy, including tourism (National Park Service, 1993).

The issue of sustainable resource use is being confronted on several fronts in B.C. Most issues relating to the use of tourism resources have traditionally been addressed only incidentally through other acts and legislative mandates related to the use of resources such as forests, land, and fish (Williams, 1991). Since 1991, tourism industry associations and government agencies have participated in several integrated land use decision-making processes (e.g., Commission on Resources and the Environment, 1994).

Such involvement represents both an opportunity and a challenge for stakeholders. It is an opportunity because tourism interest groups are now in a better position to present their perspectives on issues pertaining to the use of land and resources. However, it is a challenge because, unlike other natural resource users such as forestry and mining, tourism stakeholders have not had the types of information required to effectively assert their perspectives on specific land use planning issues. In part, this is why a systematic inventory of natural and cultural resources important to tourists and the tourism industry in B.C. has been developed.

Evolution Tourism-related natural resource inventory systems in British Columbia are rooted in the *Canada Land Inventory* (CLI) (Cressman and Hoffman, 1968). Launched in 1963, the CLI was developed to measure the quality, quantity, and distribution of Canada's land resources. Recreation resource potential was assessed on the basis of the quantity of use that might be generated and sustained within specific geographic areas or "land units." The ability to attract and accommodate recreation use guided the development of this system. The "attraction power" of an area was based on the presence or absence of 26 different landscape features (e.g., beaches, forest cover, rivers) required for participation in a wide range of outdoor recreation pursuits popular at that time.

The ability of each land unit to accommodate recreation was inferred through the amount of site maintenance required to sustain maximum recreational use. This assessment was based on the ability of a site's soil characteristics to sustain various kinds of on-site recreation facilities (e.g., camping sites, outhouses). The overall capability of the land unit was then determined according to the average of the site's ability to attract and accommodate recreational activities.

The CLI was developed in a management context that sought to facilitate expansion of the rapidly growing outdoor recreation sector. It did not comprehensively address the potential negative impacts of recreation on the land resource base. Incorporation of attributes important to the experiential dimensions of recreation (e.g., scenic quality, crowding, adjacent population centers) was also limited. The system focused on classifying the recreation resources of an area based on the match between specific recreation activities and their physical requirements.

Recognizing the inherent shortcomings in the CLI, the province developed the *Outdoor Recreation Classification of British Columbia* (ORCBC) in 1977 (ORCBC, 1982). The evaluation focus shifted from the CLI emphasis on quantity to the quality of recreational opportunities. Quality in this context referred to a resource feature's ability to attract and hold user interest. ORCBC's three-tiered classification system (comprising feature groups, subgroups, and modifiers) provided a more in-depth description of the probable characteristics of the recreation opportunities to be provided in each land unit inventoried.

ORCBC was developed in a period characterized by protracted growth in outdoor recreation demand and emerging environmental awareness. The resource management concerns of government were beginning to shift from maximizing resource exploitation to growth management. This was reflected in the priority placed on providing high-quality recreation opportunities as opposed to maximizing the quantity of experiences. In addition, this inventory system recognized the growing complexities of the linkages between recreation and the biophysical environment. Where soil characteristics had been the primary measure of site capability in the past, ORCBC used nine biophysical features (e.g., wildlife, vegetation, climate) to rate site capability.

Due to the growing economic significance of tourism, in 1990 the focus began to shift towards the development of an inventory system that identified the specific resource requirements of this sector of the economy (Ethos, 1990). It built on the strengths and experiences gained from the recreation inventory approaches, as well as on the growing opportunities and efficiencies associated with the use of geographical information system (GIS) technologies.[2]

In earlier inventory approaches, too much emphasis was placed on identifying land unit features for specific pursuits (e.g., camping and hiking). Not only were these data often too narrow in focus, but they frequently became outdated as new recreation pursuits developed (e.g., snowboarding and mountain biking) and older activities modified their resource requirements due to technological advancements in the equipment used (e.g., sea kayaking and cross-country skiing). In contrast, B.C.'s tourism resource inventory system recorded more generic features (e.g., slope, gradient, vegetation cover, wildlife diversity) that could be interpreted for a broader range of evolving recreation activities. As well, the new system avoided the use of previous inefficient and manually driven mapping and interpretation procedures by incorporating the powerful data integrating and analytical capabilities associated with GIS technologies.

The B.C. Unlike many previous approaches, the B.C. tourism resource inventory system was initi-
Tourism ated as a tool for assisting in the development and maintenance of a sustainable tourism
Resource industry.[3] In this context, it focused more on identifying resources that required manage-
Inventory ment and protection for existing and future tourism activities than it did on flagging new
System tourism development opportunities (Gale, 1991). It was designed not only to supply pub-
lic and private sector tourism stakeholders with information required to present credible
positions on tourism issues, but also to provide tourism input to broader resource planning and management activities.

While other sectors of the B.C. economy, especially forestry, had at their disposal credible inventories reflecting the value of the resource base from their perspective, this had not been the case for the tourism industry. As a consequence, in many cases the perspectives of tourism interest groups had not been adequately advanced or protected in land use decisions across the province. For instance, it was not unusual to have forestry clear-cutting operations approved without due consideration for the implications on the quality of streams and wildlife essential to the sustainability of neighboring adventure tourism businesses. The B.C. tourism resource inventory system was designed to help address this concern and, therefore, merits recognition as a management tool suited for use in a variety of tourism resource planning contexts.

The *Coastal Tourism Resource Inventory* (CTRI) represents the first generation of this system (ARA Consulting Group, 1992). It has been used to guide the creation of a provincewide inventory system that is almost completely in place. It is used in this chapter to illustrate the structure and potential uses of inventory tools. The CTRI takes advantage of the efficiencies, display, and analytic capabilities of GIS technologies (Gunn, 1994), thereby allowing tourism stakeholders to respond to a variety of resource-related concerns. GIS capabilities enable industry and government representatives to quickly and efficiently produce maps and other tabular displays of important tourism resource features that permit direct comparisons with those advanced by other resource users.

The B.C. The B.C. tourism resource inventory framework records three different types of data.
Tourism This information is contained within electronic data files and maps that describe existing
Resource tourism resources, uses, and capabilities (Paul, 1993).
Inventory
Framework TOURISM RESOURCE MAPS Resource maps identify the most important natural (e.g., vegetation, waterways), historic (e.g., heritage buildings), and cultural (e.g., native sites) tourism attributes found in specific regions of the province. Identification of critical re-
source attributes to be inventoried is based on information obtained from focus group

sessions with tourism operators in a specific region as well as available market research on the preferred resource attributes of tourists. These attribute data have been collected primarily from credible resource inventories generated by other government planning agencies.

In the case of the CTRI, more than 50 different tourism resource map layers were created. For example, three of these maps are related to (1) shoreline configuration (e.g., attributes important to kayakers and overnight power boat cruisers such as pocket beaches, islets, and protected bays), (2) coastal native heritage areas (e.g., characteristics such as site type, visibility, access, availability of interpretive information, level of development), and (3) scenic resources (e.g., landscape unit features such as slope gradient, vegetation coverage, and degree of human alteration from activities like logging, mining and other industrial endeavors). Figure 21.1 provides further insight into the range of attributes used to develop heritage and scenic tourism values within the inventory system.

TOURISM USE MAPS Tourism use maps provide an appreciation of what resources are currently being used by tourists, tourism businesses, and recreationists. Typical information inventoried includes the supply of existing tourism facilities, their capacity, months and seasons of operation, and types of services and facilities provided. In the case of the CTRI, this includes a detailed listing of the locations of all lodges and related businesses directly servicing coastal tourists.

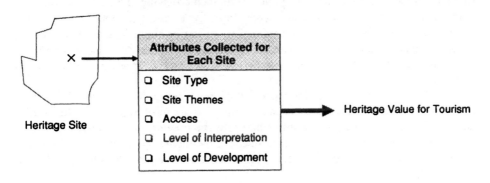

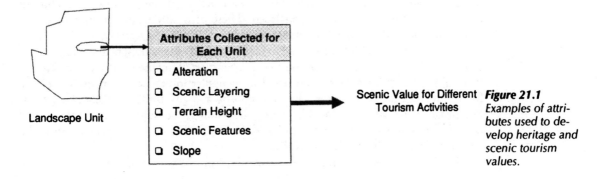

Figure 21.1 Examples of attributes used to develop heritage and scenic tourism values.

More than 20 tourism resource use maps were developed, including maps related to specific resource uses such as sport fishing and coastal cruising. For example, information recorded in the cruising inventory map contains a variety of coastal resource attributes normally featured in cruise tour experiences (e.g., aquatic wildlife, small fishing communities, and local waterfalls). This includes cruise operator use patterns as well as the resources upon which the tours depend.

TOURISM CAPABILITY MAPS   The resource attributes identified in the "resource" and "use" components of the system are used to generate the third and most dynamic part of the tourism resource inventory framework, namely, tourism capability maps. Through careful selection of those resource attributes to be included in the analysis of the preceding inventory files, customized tourism capability map displays can be generated (see Figure 21.2).

With the use of GIS, stakeholder groups can readily model the effects of different combinations of resource use on specific sections of the B.C. coastline. This capability, which makes the system particularly attractive, is important for ensuring that the ramifications of specific uses of an area's resource base are understood by all parties to the decision.

For example, if small cruise ship businesses were to be introduced to a specific section of the province's coastline, capability maps could be used to identify sections of shoreline forest cover that should be protected for scenic viewing. This information could help resource planners make decisions concerning the extent, type, and location of tree cutting that would be most appropriate under varying levels of logging or cruise ship activity. Figure 21.2 provides a schematic representation of how the data provided from B.C.'s tourism resource inventory system might be used to guide resource decision making.

In a typical capability mapping process, the input received from stakeholders initially defines resource features and associated attributes that are most important to the tourism activity. The process identifies features that must be present for the activity to happen (e.g., fish for sport fishing). A map assessment of the highest concentrations of the most favorable attributes helps to establish the broad set of potential locations for specific tourism pursuits.

Stakeholders then identify attributes that would enhance the overall quality of the specific activity (e.g., calm waters, scenic settings, wildlife viewing, heritage/cultural sites). Mapping of these "quality-enhancing" attributes, along with the original activity resource features, provides an indication of each potential site's relative capability for the specific tourism activity being analyzed. These capability maps can be revisited by stakeholders to further refine the resource assessment criteria if necessary.

In the case of B.C.'s CTRI, nine tourism capability maps designed to meet the resource needs of the major tourism businesses occurring along the coastline were created (see Table 21.1). These were constructed in computer format based on input received from numerous focus group sessions with industry and government stakeholder groups. For instance, for small cruise ships along the southern coastline, scenic areas, small coastal communities, concentrations of wildlife, day fishing areas, and staging areas with air access were identified as being critical.

For sport fishing, the critical resources were concentrations of Chinook and Coho

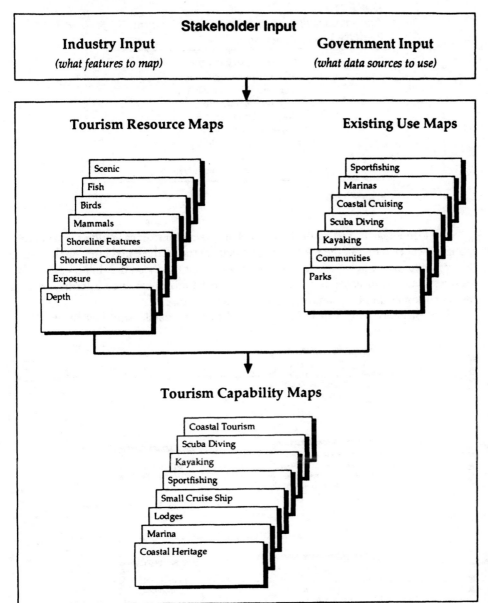

Stakeholder Input

Industry Input
(what features to map)

Government Input
(what data sources to use)

Tourism Resource Maps

- Scenic
- Fish
- Birds
- Mammals
- Shoreline Features
- Shoreline Configuration
- Exposure
- Depth

Existing Use Maps

- Sportfishing
- Marinas
- Coastal Cruising
- Scuba Diving
- Kayaking
- Communities
- Parks

Tourism Capability Maps

- Coastal Tourism
- Scuba Diving
- Kayaking
- Sportfishing
- Small Cruise Ship
- Lodges
- Marina
- Coastal Heritage

Figure 21.2
*B.C. tourism re-
source inventory
framework.*

salmon, remote areas away from day fishing activities, and scenic settings. In combination, the locations of the highest concentrations of these attributes help define those sections of the coastline in need of the greatest protection from other potentially conflicting
activity. Figure 21.3 provides an example of how the capability of an area for sport fishing
would be established based on the key resource attributes.

TABLE 21.1
Tourism Capability Maps for the Coastal Tourism Resource Inventory System

Coastal cruising day trip
Coastal cruising multiday trip
Small cruise ship multiday trip
Kayaking day trip
Kayaking multiday trip
Sport fishing day trip
Sport fishing lodge multiday trip
Marinas
Coastal heritage/culture multiday trip

Source: Williams (1992).

GIS technology facilitated the creation of an overall tourism capability map incorporating critical elements of the preceding nine map layers. In these and other applications, this computer-based inventory and modeling system has expanded the abilities of tourism resource planners to generate accurate and current tourism resource information in a format customized to the management issues under review.

The capability maps can indicate areas of high, moderate, and low capability for

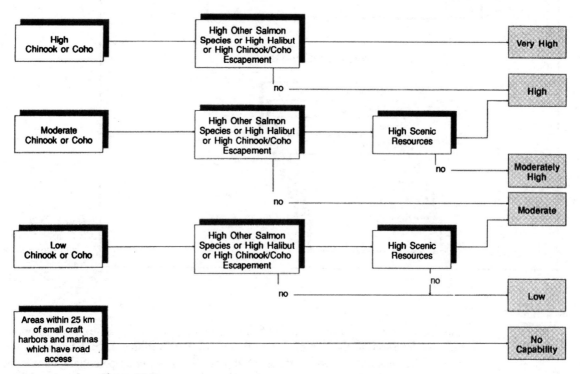

Figure 21.3
Capability for sport fishing day model.

specific tourism activities. This provides a good starting point for developing and protecting new and existing tourism products. Knowing what natural and cultural resources are most critical for specific forms of tourism activity, where the best of these resources exist, how they are currently being used, and what are the potential constraints to their future development can provide an excellent starting point for establishing the long-term sustainability of most coastal tourism products.

The inventory system also has potential for use in a variety of tourism planning contexts that typically involve nontourism resource user groups. It is a tool with great potential for use in negotiating with other resource users such as forestry and mining stakeholders on matters related to integrated resource planning and conflict resolution. An interesting example involves its application to resource planning in Clayoquot Sound.

THE CLAYOQUOT SOUND CASE

Clayoquot Sound is an 864,850-acre (350,000-hectare) resource-rich region situated on the west coast of Vancouver Island (see Figure 21.4). Since the mid-1980s, the region has been the subject of considerable controversy over the use and management of its spectacular natural and cultural resources. Loggers, sport and commercial fishers, environmentalists, First Nations groups, and community organizations have all expressed compelling and frequently emotional feelings concerning the allocation of resources within the region. On some occasions, this led to outright confrontation between stakeholder groups.

In 1992, the government of British Columbia assigned the Ministries of Small Business, Tourism and Culture, and Forests joint responsibility[4] for the development of a *Landscape Management Plan* for the newly designated scenic corridors along all transportation routes (marine and land) within the Clayoquot Sound area. This was the first time in the province's history that a provincial tourism agency had been given responsibility to manage natural resources important to tourism. With its CTRI in place, the tourism agency entered into negotiations with other public and private sector partners (e.g., local tourism operators, environmental groups, logging companies, local community political representatives) to develop the area's *Landscape Management Plan* (Government of B.C., 1995).

The *Clayoquot Sound Land Use Decision* had designated approximately 15 percent of the area's land base as being within scenic corridor zones (see Figure 21.4). The intent of the new *Landscape Management Plan* was to ensure that "key scenic values important to tourism and recreation would not be compromised" (Government of B.C., 1993). The plan was to guide all use and development within these scenic corridors. Given the varied perspectives, ranging from preservation to managed use, held by stakeholders concerning the thrust of the *Landscape Management Plan*, a process incorporating both public and private sector input into development of the plan (see Figure 21.5) was established.

Early in the planning process, sector-specific stakeholder groups (e.g., tourism, forestry, aqua-culture, mining, recreation, conservation) prepared use maps identifying areas within Clayoquot Sound that were most important to them for their current and future activities. The tourism representatives were able to map their current use areas. The CTRI system was then used to help identify areas of existing and future tourism use.

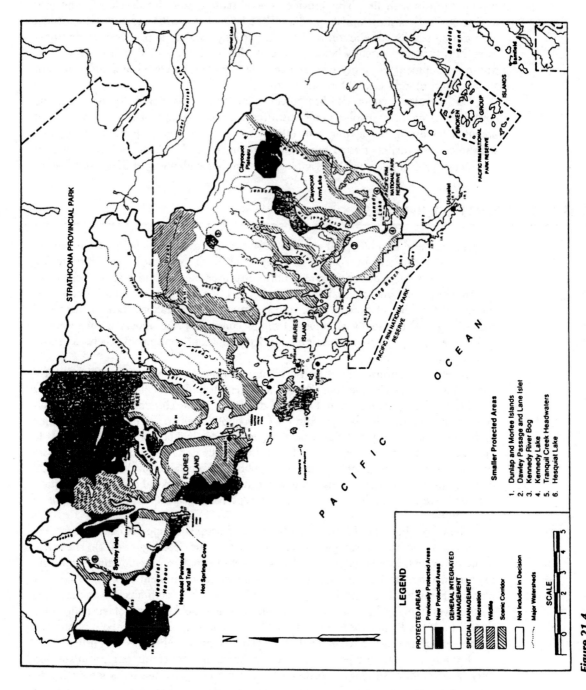

Figure 21.4
Clayoquot Sound Land Use Decision, 1993. (Base map provided by the Ministry of Forests.)

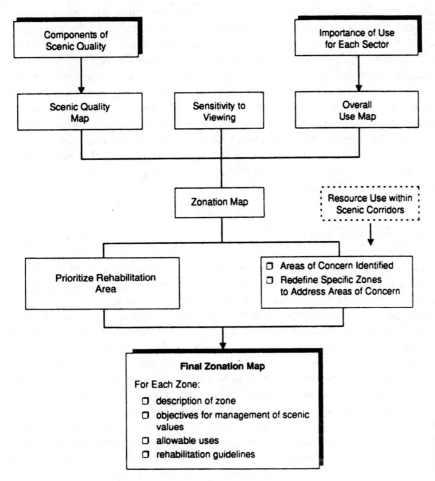

Figure 21.5
Process for integrating scenic values into the Landscape Management Plan.

Areas designated as having particularly high capability were then field-checked to verify their ratings. These maps then became powerful visual tools for use in developing the *Landscape Management Plan.*

Furthermore, information generated by the provincewide tourism resource inventory system clearly identified the Clayoquot Sound area as possessing a particularly rich base of scenic resources. The potential loss of these scenic values through other resource uses that might inadvertently modify the landscape led to a more detailed inventory of the area's scenic resource characteristics.

This more detailed inventory, which built on the foundations of the CTRI, not only described more attributes within each landscape unit (e.g., 16 versus five attributes/ landscape units), but also recorded them at a much refined scale (e.g., 1:20,000 versus 1:250,000). More extensive fieldwork was undertaken to collect and ground-truth information needed for decision making.

Through this process, more detailed scenic quality maps were created. Input received from the sector stakeholders was then used to integrate the information gained from these two mapping procedures (i.e., to establish "importance of use" maps for each landscape unit). GIS procedures were used to integrate the information obtained from the scenic quality and "importance of use" maps. As a result, stakeholders were in a better position to rationally divide Clayoquot Sound's scenic corridors into specific segments, as well as identify the ideal types and levels of resource-use management appropriate to each zone.

The participatory nature of this planning process, the detailed information contained within the inventory created, and the interactive nature of CTRI's GIS capabilities made it much easier for tourism stakeholders to present informed and visually powerful positions concerning the implications of different land use actions on the area's scenic corridors. Without this credible and formal inventory information, it is likely that many scenic attributes central to the sustainability of the tourism industry (e.g., watershed forest cover, shoreline vegetation) in this region might have been lost.

OTHER POTENTIAL APPLICATIONS

While still in its early stages of implementation, B.C.'s tourism resource inventory system offers considerable potential for use in a wide variety of land use and resource management situations. There are three reasons why this inventory is important.

Initially, the system can help to answer the question, "How much is available and where is it?" It allows planners and resource managers to determine the capability of the natural resource base for the creation of new tourism products and services. Computer accessible digital information, maps, and tourism product-specific reports inform decision makers about general locations most suited to tourism. Such information is critical not only to resource allocation issues, but also to broader integrated planning processes (e.g., local resource use management planning processes) that occur on a regular basis.

Secondly, the B.C. Tourism Resource Inventory System can help planners decide which of a variety of land use management options influencing tourism and other adjacent resource uses is most suitable in an area. When tourism activities are perceived to be in conflict with other resource sector pursuits, the tourism resource inventory system can be used to eliminate potential conflict and/or establish zones of complementary usage. By using a common set of criteria established by the resource stakeholders involved in the conflict, the inventory acts as a tool for systematically narrowing the range of choices.

For example, the inventory can provide decision makers with explicit spatial information concerning access points, water bodies, and wildlife habitats critical to wilderness camping that may be affected by varying strategies and timing of forest harvesting in Clayoquot Sound. Through the efficiencies of GIS, comparisons of the implications associated with a variety of clear- or selective-cutting practices can occur relatively easily.

At a third level, this inventory system can be used to address difficult policy and planning questions such as how long-term trends in land use may affect tourism capability. In Clayoquot Sound, the inventory facilitates controversial but important decisions about the use of the area's resources. For example, it can help answer questions such as the following: Are some important tourism resources (e.g., wetlands, wildlife, water quality) at risk because of poor management practices? Are trends in resource use associated with other economic sectors (e.g., forestry, fisheries) affecting tourism's capability in the area?

These and other environmental impact assessment questions can be addressed when tourism-specific inventory information is integrated with other social (e.g., community locations and services), environmental (e.g., endangered species habitats), and economic data (e.g., employment patterns, work force capabilities). The complexity of these kinds of problems usually renders analysis using GIS procedures necessary.

CONCLUSION

Tourism resource inventory systems can enhance decisions about the use of natural resources. Moreover, they can influence the perceptions and understanding of land use decision makers concerning tourism's reliance on a healthy natural environment. As planning for a more sustainable tourism industry becomes more sophisticated, the information generated by systematic tourism resource inventory systems will become even more crucial to land use policy decisions. B.C.'s tourism resource inventory system is but one example of the type of tool the next generation of land use planners and managers will use to protect the growing scarcity of high-quality natural environments for tourism.

NOTES

1. See Chapter 13 for additional discussion relating to tourism and transportation linkages.
2. See Chapter 20 for detailed discussion pertaining to GIS technology.
3. See Chapters 4, 5, 7, 8, 17, 18, 22, and 23 for additional discussion relating to sustainable tourism and sustainable tourism development concepts and principles.
4. See Chapter 13 for additional discussion of the importance of intersectoral approaches to tourism planning and policy formulation.

REFERENCES

ARA Consulting Group. 1992. Coastal Tourism Resource Inventory. Victoria, B.C.: B.C. Ministry of Tourism, Inventory and Resource Planning Branch.

ARA Consulting Group. 1993. *Tourism Industry's Resource Management Needs*. Victoria, B.C.: B.C. Ministry Of Tourism, Inventory and Resource Planning Branch.

B.C. Ministry of Tourism. 1992. Prepared by Canadian Facts. *Tourism's Value to British Columbia*. Victoria: Government of British Columbia.

Besancenot, J.P., J. Mounier, and F. de Lavenne. 1978. Les conditions climatiques du tourisme littoral: une methode de recherche comprehensive, *Norois*, 99, 357–382.

Brown, P.J., B.L. Driver, and C. McDonnell. 1978. The opportunity spectrum concept and behavioural information by outdoor recreation resource supply inventories: background and application. In *Integrated Inventories of Renewable Natural Resources: Proceedings of the Workshop*. Fort Collins, Colorado: Rocky Mountain Forest and Range Experiment Station, US Forest Station.

Commission on Resources and the Environment. 1994. *Provincial Land Use Strategy: A Sustainability Act For British Columbia*. Victoria: Government of British Columbia.

Cressman, D.R. and D.W. Hoffman. 1968. Classifying land for recreation, *Journal of Soil and Water Conservation*, 23(3), 91–93.

Crowe, R.B. 1975. Recreation, tourism and climate—a Canadian perspective, *Weather*, 30(8), 248–254.

Ethos. 1990. *Tourism Resource Sustainable Development Planning: The Whistler Case Study*. Victoria: B.C. Ministry of Tourism and Culture.

Ferrario, F.F. 1979. The evaluation of tourism resources: an applied methodology, *Journal of Travel Research*, 17(3), 18–22 and 17(4), 24–30.

Gale, S. 1991. *Challenges in Tourism Resource Management: The British Columbia Experience.* Unpublished paper presented at the 1991 World Congress on Adventure Travel and Eco-Tourism, Whistler B.C., August.

Government of British Columbia. 1993. *Clayoquot Sound Land Use Decision.* Victoria, B.C.: Government of British Columbia.

Government of British Columbia. 1995. *Clayoquot Sound Scenic Corridors Landscape Management Plan.* Victoria, B.C.: Ministry of Small Business, Tourism and Culture, and Ministry of Forests.

Gunn, C.A. 1988. *Tourism Planning,* 2nd ed. New York: Taylor and Francis.

Gunn, C.A. 1994. Emergence of effective tourism planning and development. In A.V. Seaton, C.L. Jenkins, R.C. Wood, P.U.C. Dieke, M.M. Bennett, L.R. MacLellan, and R. Smith (eds.), *Tourism The State of the Art.* Toronto: John Wiley & Sons, pp. 10–19.

Gunn, C.A. and J.B. McMillen. 1979. *Tourism Development: Assessment of Potential in Texas,* Technical Report MP-1416. College Station, Texas: The Texas Agricultural Experiment Station.

Industry, Science and Technology Canada–Tourism Canada. 1991. *Federal Tourism Strategy for Western Canada.* Ottawa: Industry Science and Technology Canada.

Laventhol & Horwath. 1981. *Peterborough-Haliburton Tourism Development Strategy.* Toronto, Ontario: Ontario Ministry of Industry and Tourism.

National Park Service. 1993. *Guiding Principles of Sustainable Design.* Denver, CO: United States Department of the Interior.

Outdoor Recreation Classification of British Columbia. 1982. *Outdoor Recreation Classification of British Columbia.* APD Technical Paper 8. Victoria, B.C.: B.C. Ministry of Environment, Assessment and Planning Division.

Paul, J. 1993. Tourism resource planning—British Columbia's approach. In M.J. Staite and R.A.G. Wong (eds.), *Regional Marketing Partnerships and Adventure Tourism, TTRA Canada and New England Chapters Joint Conference Proceedings,* Portland, Maine, pp. 62–68.

Pearce, D.G. 1979. Land tenure and tourist development: a review. *Proceedings of the 10th Geography Conference,* Auckland, New Zealand Geography Society, pp. 148–150.

Pigram, J. 1983. *Outdoor Recreation and Resource Management.* New York: St. Martin's Press.

Ritchie, J.R. and M. Zins. 1978. Culture as a determinant of the attractiveness of a tourism region, *Annals of Tourism Research,* 5(2), 252–267.

Schroeder, H.W. 1983. Measuring visual features of recreational landscapes. In S.R. Lieber and D.R. Fesenmaier (eds.), *Recreational Planning and Management.* Pennsylvania: Venture.

Smith, S.L.J. 1987. Regional analysis of tourism resources, *Annals of Tourism Research,* 14(2), 254–273.

Swanson, S. and S.L. Miles. 1988. Classifying range and riparian areas: the Nevada Task Force approach, *Journal of Soil and Water Conservation,* 43(3), 259–263.

Taylor, G.D. and C.W. Thomson. 1966. Proposed methodology for an inventory and classification of land for recreational use, *Forestry Chronicle,* June, 153–159.

Tourism Canada. 1995. *Adventure Travel In Canada: An Overview.* Ottawa, Ontario: Government of Canada.

Williams, P.W. 1991. Tourism resource management issues in the coastal zone. In P.E. Murphy (ed.), *Tourism Research: Meeting the Needs of Industry, Conference Proceedings—TTRA Canada.* Victoria, B.C.: University of Victoria.

Williams, P. W. 1992. Tourism and the environment: no place to hide, *World Leisure and Recreation*, 34(2), Summer, 13–17.

₅ | PROBLEM SOLVING AND DISCUSSION ACTIVITIES

1. You have been assigned responsibility for managing tourism for the regional government in your area. The mandate of your agency includes ensuring the region's natural and cultural resources are protected and used responsibly. Your agency does not have a clear idea of either the range or extent of existing tourism resources in the region. Hence, your first task is to develop a comprehensive tourism resource inventory system for the area. Be sure to:
   a. Identify resources of primary concern to your agency.
   b. Indicate features or attributes of these resources that are most important to record.
   c. Describe how you will quantify/measure these attributes.
   d. Indicate how various kinds of tourism development might influence the quality of these resources.
   e. Suggest how various other kinds of economic activity in the area might influence the quality of these resources.
   f. Describe how the inventory might be used by your agency in future planning processes.

2. The government has decided to develop an integrated land use strategy for your region to promote the sustainable use of the natural resources by tourism and other economic sectors. You have been asked to represent the interests of your tourism industry partners in negotiations concerning the future use of the area's natural resources.
   a. Indicate how characteristics of the natural resource base should be described from a tourism perspective.
   b. Suggest how your perspective concerning the natural resource base may differ from those of forestry and manufacturing interests.
   c. Indicate how these other sectors can be convinced that tourism interests in the resources must be protected.
   d. Describe how a strategy could be developed to provide opportunities for, as well as enhance, sustainable coexistence between all resource industry sectors in the region.

3. Difficulties typically arise when resource inventories fail to account for the experiential benefits associated with tourism activities. Articulating these experiential qualities represents a major challenge and weakness in most tourism inventory systems. Nevertheless, methods of identifying and recording these attributes must be developed. To overcome this methodological challenge:
   a. Identify what is experiential about tourism.
   b. Indicate how experiential elements can be quantified.
   c. Describe how these elements will vary between outdoor recreation and culturally-based tourism activities.
   d. Indicate how these elements can be recorded in an effective inventory system.

22

Sustainable Tourism Development or a Case of Loving a Special Place to Death?

SCUBA DIVING IN THE JULIAN ROCKS AQUATIC RESERVE, EASTERN AUSTRALIA

Derrin Davis
Vicki J. Harriott

𝖌 | KEY LEARNING POINTS

- Conflict between recreational uses and conservation needs may arise when a nature-based tourism industry relies on access to protected areas.

- As a tourist activity, recreational scuba diving may be potentially hazardous to underwater tourism resources. Moreover, beyond certain use levels, human contact with natural resources detracts from the quality of the recreational experience.

- Marine protected areas (MPAs) are of considerable economic significance to the dive tourism industry, and therefore it is in the industry's interest to ensure that MPAs are used in a sustainable manner.

- Techniques that assist in the evaluation and management of human use of protected areas include the analysis of biological and social carrying capacities and the determination of limits of acceptable change, both of which are difficult to implement in a practical way.

- Economic valuation of protected areas is important because it indicates the real value of those areas, thereby providing information that may be used when deciding what funding should be allocated to an area and determining the level of charges that might be applied to their use. Economic valuation challenges the idea that these special natural areas provide services that have no value and should be provided at zero price.

- The use of geographical information systems (GIS) adds valuable management information relating to those sites most in need of protection.

- Management responses to intense diver pressure must enhance the sustainability of protected areas by limiting the level of use where necessary and ensuring that environmental damage is minimized.

INTRODUCTION

The dive tourism industry, which is rapidly growing in popularity worldwide, is heavily reliant on access to marine protected areas (MPAs) that are established principally to protect special biological and environmental values. However, overuse and subsequent environmental degradation are possible because of open access to marine resources in MPAs and because of the associated market failure that normally occurs. Market failure may occur when the full costs of the use of natural resources are not met by users. In MPAs, resources are normally available at a low or zero price, and it is usually difficult to exclude individuals and groups from such areas. Consequently, MPAs may be subject to excessive use, overcrowding, and biological degradation.

Such challenges are discussed in this chapter in the context of the Julian Rocks Aquatic Reserve in Eastern Australia, a site that has one of the highest rates of diver usage in Australia. The potential for conflict between users, the social and biological carrying capacities, limits of acceptable change, and the potential for environmental degradation are examined. In addition, economic valuation methods and the use of geographical information systems (GIS) are explored. Finally, management options to enhance the sustainability of dive tourism in the Julian Rocks Aquatic Reserve are discussed.

MARINE PROTECTED AREAS AND DIVE TOURISM: CONTEMPORARY PERSPECTIVES AND ISSUES

The Role and Significance of Marine Protected Areas The case for establishing marine parks and reserves rests on three main factors (Ivanovici, 1984). First, marine parks and reserves are seen as a logical development of the terrestrial park movement. The concept has sprung from an awareness of "the beauty and scientific interest of the world of nature beneath the sea, coupled with the increasing evidence of the vulnerability of this world to damage and alteration by man" (Ivanovici, 1984, p. 427). Second, the high level of interest and increased participation in water-based recreation adds to the relevance of MPAs. Third, MPAs are important for extractive activities (e.g., commercial fishing) and scientific research given the biological diversity in marine waters, particularly in near-shore locations and coral reef areas in tropical and subtropical zones.

The International Union for the Conservation of Nature and Natural Resources (IUCN) (now the World Conservation Union) identified eight categories of marine park and protected areas, ranging from strict nature reserves to multiple-use management areas[1] (IUCN, 1986). This has been extended to 10 categories[2] in Australia, where MPAs cover a total area of 97.8 million acres (39.6 million hectares) (Hooy and Shaughnessy, 1992).

MPAs serve a host of functions, including conservation (i.e., "wise," managed use for both recreational and commercial purposes) and preservation (i.e., minimal or zero disturbance by humans), as well as scientific, recreational, and educational purposes. Questions arise, however, as to the conflicts that may occur among these purposes, particularly between conservation and recreation. This may be translated into concern for whether MPAs can be managed in a sustainable[3] fashion when a range of uses is being pursued.

Carrying Application of the carrying capacity concept[4] to recreation areas became popular in the
Capacity early 1970s due to the overuse and overcrowding of recreation resources [Urban Research
and Development Corporation (URDC), 1980]. The concept is relevant to recreational
scuba diving, given the potential for biological damage and loss of amenity[5] at heavily
used sites.

Carrying capacity has traditionally referred to the number of people and animals
that could use a resource without causing "unacceptable impacts" [Resource Assessment
Commission (RAC), 1993]. It focused on determining the maximum population density
that could be supported in a given area without causing environmental degradation. The
principal contemporary use of this concept refers to the management of outdoor recreation. However, many variations of the concept have been used to define different kinds
of impacts (i.e., social, cultural, perceptual, physical, and ecological) and interactions
among these impacts (RAC, 1993).

Although it is well-accepted and conceptually appealing, Clark (1990) commented
that, regardless of the logic of the approach or of how good individual models are, the
carrying capacity concept has largely been ignored by environmental agencies. Despite
some use for the purposes of controlling visitor loads in national parks, as well as in
controlling range herds, Clark complained that it is difficult to find a good example of a
government that limits coastal/marine tourism according to environmental carrying capacity. If the purpose of carrying capacity is to promote the long-term sustainability of a
resource, then it is important to establish why management agencies have been reluctant
to implement strategies based on the concept.

Part of the explanation relates to the difficulties in measuring carrying capacity in
coastal ecosystems. The uncertainties associated with understanding ecological relationships and predicting change in these ecosystems mean that defining a carrying capacity
relies on the "common sense logic of the managers involved." Therefore, the amount of
change in an area that is both likely and acceptable "is usually a judgement call" (Clark,
1991, p. 15). The concept also implies a degree of precision and objectivity that is difficult
to achieve in resource management (RAC, 1993). Hence, carrying capacity estimates
should be treated as ranges rather than as absolute limits or thresholds.

RAC (1993, p. 8) also noted that a "problem with the carrying capacity concept lies
in its demand for a technical solution to a subjective question." This arises because there
are a number of criteria (biological, social, legal, cultural, economic, and esthetic) for
deciding on the overuse of a resource. Moreover, particularly in recreational settings, the
social carrying capacity may be quite different from the ecological carrying capacity.

Difficulties associated with applying the carrying capacity concept have led RAC
(1993) to conclude that the main strength of the concept is that it helps managers think in
a structured way about resource problems, user activities and experiences, and ecological
constraints. It may also be valuable in community education and in raising awareness
about the environmental consequences of human activities.

Notwithstanding the uncertainties associated with determining the carrying capacity
of some resources, Clark (1990, 1991), along with Salm (1986) and others, has called for
its application to tourism activities in coastal areas. Clark (1991) provided guidelines for
determining the carrying capacity of coastal ecosystems, noting that the appropriate level
of use varies with the site location and changes in the resource through time. Key parameters in defining carrying capacity, according to Clark, include the (1) type of recreational

activity, (2) season, (3) time of day, (4) present health of the resource, (5) existing support facilities, and (6) the satisfaction being realized by users.

These parameters indicate that research and monitoring have important roles in establishing carrying capacities. Baseline data are needed and monitoring is required to identify changes in the condition of the resource in question. Very often, however, management agencies do not have these baseline data, nor do they have the human and financial resources required to undertake long-term monitoring programs.

Salm (1986) identified determinants of the carrying capacity of coral reefs for underwater tourism, noting that important factors include (1) the size and shape of the reef, (2) the composition of coral communities, (3) the types of underwater activities (e.g., consumptive activities such as spearfishing versus nonconsumptive pursuits like fish watching), and (4) the level of experience of snorkelers and divers. Salm concluded that the challenge is to manage reefs and people in a way that allows maximum use without diminishing the quality of the underwater experience.

Limits of Acceptable Change The carrying capacity concept is based on the question of "how much use is too much." Shortcomings of this concept have led to the formulation of alternative approaches to resource management. A well-known alternative is the "limits of acceptable change" (LAC) framework developed by Stankey et al. (1985) in which it is acknowledged that change is inevitable, but the question of "how much change is acceptable" must be asked. LAC involves identifying desired social and resource conditions and, subsequently, orienting management towards the maintenance or restoration of those conditions (Stankey and McCool, 1989).

LAC is used as an aid in the management of impacts rather than as an aid to the management of use itself. That it is focused on the environmental and social conditions desired in an area is a strength. LAC requires careful definition of explicit objectives for the establishment of appropriate management techniques, as well as for monitoring and evaluating the management regime.

It is generally agreed that the LAC framework, which was set out as a nine-step process (see Figure 22.1) by Stankey et al. (1985), leads to more effective resource management than do estimates of carrying capacity. This is because the definition of social and ecological thresholds, along with performance standards, are easier to quantify and monitor than are efforts to establish one capacity figure for a recreational resource (RAC, 1993). Prosser (1986, p. 9) also argued that LAC provides a practical framework for applying the carrying capacity concept because, "When conditions are within acceptable standards, it is sufficient to know that the capacity of an area is greater than the current levels of use."

Despite its claimed advantages, LAC is not without its shortcomings. Gaining agreement from stakeholders on acceptable ecological and social conditions may be extremely difficult. Suitable ecological and social indicators that define the desired conditions and which can be measured and monitored must also be selected. Furthermore, as with carrying capacity, there is a need for baseline data and also a need for the resources to be monitored over the long term.

Methods capable of measuring environmental change with appropriate statistical resolution have been the basis of considerable recent research and discussion (Fairweather, 1991; Oliver and Schneider, 1993). However, the measurement of anthropogenic change

Step 1:	Identify the specific features and values of the area
Step 2:	Define and describe 'opportunity classes' These classes represent subunits of the management area with each subunit providing different conditions, thereby reflecting the area's diversity. The different conditions are measured through indicators (see Step 3) which should be quantifiable, and which show the resource and social conditions for which management is striving.
Step 3:	Select indicators of resource and social conditions
Step 4:	Inventory existing resource and social conditions Data are collected, recorded and mapped, and serve as the basis for the definition (see Step 5) of standards for each indicator in each opportunity class.
Step 5:	Specify standards for the resource and social indicators for each opportunity class
Step 6:	Identify alternative opportunity class allocations reflecting area issues and concerns, and existing resource and social conditions
Step 7:	Identify management actions for each alternative This step requires an analysis of the various costs and benefits of each alternative, in terms of environmental impacts, impacts on visitors, and administrative costs.
Step 8:	Evaluate and select a preferred alternative The costs and benefits of each alternative are evaluated and a final alternative is selected.
Step 9:	Implement actions and monitor feedback

Figure 22.1
The nine-step limits of acceptable change framework. (Adapted from Resource Assessment Commission, 1993.)

(i.e., change caused by human activities) using monitoring techniques is complicated where large natural changes occur as a consequence of events such as major storms, since natural change can mask human impacts over time. Given the long timeframes in which ecological processes occur and the possibility that biological degradation may be subtle and cumulative until some threshold is reached, the application of LAC is not totally free of uncertainty.

Economic Valuations of Marine Protected Areas   Pearce et al. (1989) argued that the valuation of the services provided by natural resources is central to the concept of sustainable use of those resources. This is because the services are usually provided free or at minimal cost due to open access. Open access resources are those that are owned by no one in particular[6] and/or from which it is difficult to exclude users (Pearce and Turner, 1990). Where open access exists, individual users appear to have no incentive to conserve the site (i.e., they do not take user costs into account). Moreover, there is always a risk that even when an individual user takes care, the area will be damaged by others. This supports the adage that the property of all becomes the responsibility of none (Davis and Tisdell, 1995).

Open access to resources such as dive sites may also create market failure[7] because the price for using the good is zero. This is a condition of environmental goods in general, and it means that their "true" value has been underestimated or even ignored (Turner et al., 1994). According to Turner et al., the fact that such goods have remained unpriced has resulted in overuse. This, in turn, leads to negative impacts such as damaged corals, impaired ecological functions, and reduced amenity values. The cost of these impacts is not recovered from those who have benefited from use of the site and who may have caused the damage.

Management agencies might respond to apparent market failure by introducing new or tougher regulations such as restricting diver numbers or by requiring that divers do not touch corals or other features of the underwater environment. Alternatively, they may attempt to introduce user fees, with the revenue being used to support monitoring and management activities. This approach requires a greater understanding of the economic value of MPAs. A mix of regulation and user fees might also be used.

Open access also involves questions of exclusion, rivalry, and congestion at recreational sites. For example, the benefits of the "wilderness experience" associated with recreational diving are likely to be affected by the extent of congestion at a site or competitiveness in the use of the resource. This concept is often discussed in terms of rivalry and the ability to exclude some users from a site.

Rivalry is absent when one person's consumption does not affect the total amount available to anyone else. That is, the total amount of a good available can be enjoyed without diminishing the supply of that good (Davis and Tisdell, 1995). Scuba diving sites might be expected to meet a criterion of "nonrivalry." However, Dixon and Sherman (1990) made the point that some goods, particularly recreational goods, are in fact congestible. That is, rivalry is absent up to a certain level of use, but beyond that level, rivalry will set in. Hundloe (1979, p. 36) suggested that, by "Disregarding ecological impacts (which, presumably, could be controlled by regulating visitor numbers), there is a very real loss of satisfaction to some visitors if they are but some of a multitude that have visited the area."

Hundloe's suggestion about regulating visitor numbers raises the possibility of exclusion: Is it feasible to exclude anyone from consuming the good? A "nonexcludable" good is one where the cost of excluding consumers is greater than the benefit received from such exclusion (Dixon and Sherman, 1990). A degree of nonexcludability does exist with respect to scuba diving in MPAs. It is very difficult, except in areas where all public use is disallowed (as in the scientific research and preservation zones in Australia's Great Barrier Reef Marine Park), to exclude private divers and recreational anglers. However, sensitivity to the problems of rivalry and exclusion contributes to managers' understanding of the issues to be resolved in managing MPAs, while efforts to value natural resources provide additional important management information.

Economic valuation of environmental goods involves placing monetary values on previously unpriced or underpriced natural resources and the benefits they provide. Currently, divers at Julian Rocks are asked (i.e., it is noncompulsory) to pay a nominal fee (A\$1 or US\$0.72) per dive as a contribution towards the management of the reserve. However, information about the real economic value of Julian Rocks will allow the managers (i.e., New South Wales Fisheries[8]) to make more informed decisions about management of the resource and about the funding that should be available to support that management.

While the market price of natural resources is not determined by supply and demand (because of open access), it is possible to use the relationships that exist between the environment and marketed goods to derive an economic value for such resources (Bennett, 1991). Underlying such techniques is society's willingness to pay for the benefits received from natural resources. It has generally been found that the actual price charged represents a significant underestimate of the value that society actually places upon the resources.

Techniques used for economic valuation include hedonic pricing,[9] contingent valuation,[10] and the travel cost method (TCM).[11] These methods, which are the subject of extensive literature, have been summarized by DeLacy (1990) and Bennett (1991).

Recreational Scuba diving is one of the fastest-growing recreational activities in the world (Dignam,
Scuba Diving 1990; Tabata, 1992). The largest market is in the United States, where more than 2.3
million people participated in this activity in 1993 (National Sporting Goods Association,
1994). In February 1994 the Professional Association of Dive Instructors (PADI), which
began operations in 1967 and is now the world's largest dive training organization, issued
its five millionth certification. In 1993 alone, PADI issued 565,000 certifications worldwide. Indeed, in the 10 years from 1984 to 1993, PADI experienced an average annual
growth in certifications of 13 percent.

Japan has become an important source of divers in the Pacific Basin, with tours to
Chuuk (formerly Truk), Palau, the Philippines, and Australia's Great Barrier Reef being
popular. American divers travel widely, mainly to Florida, the Bahamas, and other Caribbean destinations. Hawaii, Australia, and Micronesia are also popular destinations for
American divers (Tabata, 1992).

The dive travel association of Australia estimated that more than 100,000 certifications are issued each year in Australia, around two million individual dives are made,
and the total value of the recreational diving business exceeds A\$360 million (US\$259.2
million) annually (Dive Australia, 1994). Dive Queensland estimates that the number of
dive retail and training businesses in Queensland (from where the Great Barrier Reef is
accessed; see Figure 22.2) tripled in the 10 years to 1995 (Greenwood, personal communication).

The level of reliance on MPAs for recreational scuba diving worldwide is unknown.
In Australia, however, it is estimated that more than 50 percent of dives occur in MPAs
(Wilks, 1993). This is not surprising given that areas with special values (i.e., attractive
and interesting underwater flora, fauna, and geologic formations) are more likely to be
given protected area status. These special values also attract divers. Hence, it may be
asked whether the granting of protected area status makes these areas more well known
and, therefore, more heavily used for recreational pursuits (i.e., the "loving an area to
death" syndrome).

Continued growth in recreational scuba diving may conflict with the ecological values that form the basis of MPA status. In addition, growth may lead to accelerated environmental degradation in marine areas and/or reduce the amenity values in those areas
(Davis and Tisdell, 1995). The concentration of divers in certain locations may also degrade the "wilderness experience" that is often associated with scuba diving.

A three-year study of coral reef damage on recreationally used reefs in Florida led to
the conclusion that human impacts were small compared to the damage caused by natural wave action and storms (Tilmant and Schmal, 1981). Nonetheless, Tilmant and
Schmal also stated that higher rates of use by humans would lead to a greater incidence
of coral damage. Others have also found that biological damage caused by diving was
relatively unimportant (Hawkins and Roberts, 1992, 1993a). However, in a later study,
Hawkins and Roberts (1993b) indicated that the present level of usage of Egyptian reef
sites (i.e., 30,000 to 50,000 dives per year) was approaching the maximum sustainable
carrying capacity of the reefs and that the projected tenfold increase in divers at these sites
would result in serious environmental damage.

Dixon et al. (1993) reported that diver impacts at certain locations in Bonaire Marine
Park (BMP) in the Caribbean were beyond an acceptable level. They estimated the carrying capacity of BMP at 190,000 to 200,000 individual dives per year, with an upper

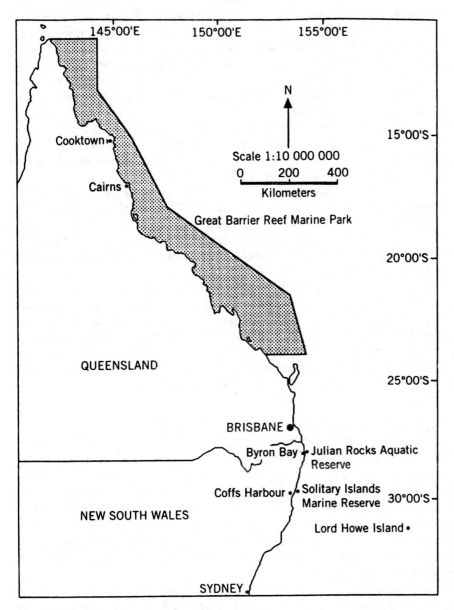

145°00'E   150°00'E   155°00'E

N

Scale 1:10 000 000

0   200   400

Kilometers

15°00'S

Cooktown

Cairns

Great Barrier Reef Marine Park

20°00'S

QUEENSLAND

25°00'S

BRISBANE

Byron Bay — Julian Rocks Aquatic
Reserve

Coffs Harbour — Solitary Islands
Marine Reserve   30°00'S

NEW SOUTH WALES

Lord Howe Island

SYDNEY

Figure 22.2
Northwest coast of Australia: Julian Rocks and the Great Barrier Reef Marine Park.

limit of 5000 at each dive site. They also warned that, beyond some threshold level of use, biological impacts might be severe and irreversible and that significant loss of amenity may arise from diver damage and overcrowding. Dixon (1993) also concluded that localized overuse within an MPA is commonly observed before large-scale degradation begins, possibly serving as an "early warning system."

In Florida, Ward (1990) concluded that the level of diving activity at the five most popular sites in John Pennecamp National Park (150,000 dives per year) probably exceeded the park's carrying capacity. However, in a study of the interactions between divers and corals in the Florida Keys, Talge (1993) suggested that briefly touching and finning near corals at normal levels of diver activity did not cause detectable damage to coral colonies. Of greater concern is the fact that divers break corals, particularly the more fragile branching species (Hawkins and Roberts, 1993a). These breakages, which are mostly accidental, occur when divers strike corals with their fins, gauges, hands, or other parts of their body such as their knees.

The various estimates of carrying capacity reported above relate to the number of divers who access a site during a 12-month period. However, in many locations, including Julian Rocks, there is some seasonality of use which, while acknowledged, has not been considered when formulating carrying capacity estimates.

The skill of divers is also important in that inexperienced divers are generally less able to control their buoyancy, tend to be overweighted (lead weights are used by divers to help them descend and stay underwater), and have poorer control over their finning and other behavior. The question of diver ability and training was considered by Dixon et al. (1993), who concluded that the number of divers could potentially be doubled in Bonaire Marine Park with further training.

A case study of recreational scuba diving in Julian Rocks Aquatic Reserve is used in this chapter to illustrate many of the issues relating to the management of nature-based tourism in MPAs. The reserve is described, as is its use for recreational diving. Issues relating to the biology, management, and economics of MPAs are outlined, and possible management strategies to alleviate user pressures are identified. The information was assembled through a series of research projects undertaken between 1992 and 1994, with particular assistance from dive tourism operators in Byron Bay.

JULIAN ROCKS AQUATIC RESERVE: LOCATIONAL CONTEXT

The Julian Rocks Aquatic Reserve is located just over 1 mile (approximately 2 kilometers) off the coast, northeast of the township of Byron Bay, which is the most easterly point of the Australian mainland and a popular holiday destination in the northern part of New South Wales (NSW) (see Figure 22.2). While accurate data on the number of visitors to Byron Bay are not available, information from surveys indicates that the main reason for visiting Byron Bay is to holiday (76 percent of visitors), and the main attraction is the surfing beaches (Ludwig Rieder and Associates, 1988; Taylor, 1994). Scuba diving is also a significant activity in the area.

Approximately 85 percent of visitors come from outside the region in which Byron Bay is located (Ludwig Reider and Associates, 1988). Backpackers comprise the fastest-growing segment, accounting for 156,000 visitor-nights in 1993 (Taylor, 1994). There are relatively few international visitors in the Byron Bay area apart from the backpacker market, of which an estimated one-third come from overseas (Taylor, 1994). Backpacker facilities are well developed, as are other types of accommodations such as motels, camping and caravan parks, and holiday apartments.

The rocky outcrop known as Julian Rocks (see Figure 22.3) has nature reserve status, and the surrounding waters [within a 550–yard (500–meter) radius] have been an aquatic reserve since March 1982. In both cases, "reserve status" means that the primary aim of

Figure 22.3
Aerial view of Julian Rocks with Cape Byron in the background. (Courtesy of Max Egan.)

management is to protect, manage, and conserve the environment and the existing uses of the sites and to ensure that their ecological diversity and significance are maintained (Copeland and Phillips, 1993). Apart from line fishing, collecting from the reserves is not allowed. The aquatic reserve covers approximately 198 acres (80 hectares) of ocean and is managed by NSW Fisheries.

Wright (1990) described Julian Rocks as one of the best diving locations on the Australian east coast. Julian Rocks is in a tropical–temperate overlap zone, typified by the mixing of warm equatorial waters from the north with cooler southern waters. Consequently, it contains an abundant marine community consisting of both tropical and warm temperate species. Despite being approximately 375 miles (600 kilometers) south of the southern extremities of the Great Barrier Reef (GBR), Julian Rocks features around 33 species of coral (about 10 percent of the number recorded for the entire GBR), with coral covering up to 12.2 percent of the area of some sites (Harriott, unpublished data).

Julian Rocks also contains a range of habitats, including rock reefs, steep rocky ledges, caves, tunnels and boulder floors, and sand gutters and channels that support a diverse marine flora and fauna community. The reserve is an important breeding, feeding, and sheltering area for migratory and territorial fish species. Julian Rocks is also known for the presence of marine turtles and, at certain times of the year, the congregation of gray nurse sharks.

SCUBA DIVING AT JULIAN ROCKS AQUATIC RESERVE

Diving Intensity Resulting from its diverse attractions, proximity to Byron Bay, and relatively easy access, the Julian Rocks Aquatic Reserve is a popular and intensively used scuba diving site. As mentioned earlier, Byron Bay is a popular holiday destination on the Australian east coast, and many people who dive at Julian Rocks do so as an "add-on" to their beach holiday. Concomitantly, there is some seasonality in diving, with the peak diving seasons being the summer holiday period (November to January) and the Easter holiday break. Diver numbers in December are more than double those experienced in the cooler mid-winter months of June and July.

In 1992, records of the three commercial dive enterprises then operating in Byron Bay were analyzed, and the number and location of all dives were noted. More than 20,000 dives were recorded, 86 percent of which occurred at the "Nursery" and the "Cod Hole" (see Figure 22.4). Together, these dive sites account for an area of approximately 86,000 square feet (8000 square meters) (Roberts and Harriott, 1995). In a survey of dive tourism in the Great Barrier Reef, Thomas (1992) identified only two sites that had slightly greater usage levels than Julian Rocks, but both of these sites were more extensive in area. The greatest threat to the sustainability of the aquatic reserve at Byron Bay is the level of use of popular dive sites (Copeland and Phillips, 1993).

While exact figures are not available, it appears that the number of divers using

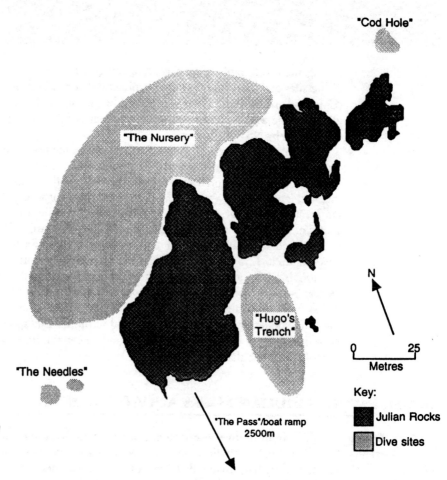

Figure 22.4
Location of the main dive sites in Julian Rocks Aquatic Reserve.

Julian Rocks has increased steadily. In 1985, there were only two dive operators who normally operated three or four vessels. By 1994, there were four operators running up to 10 dive boats. Based on the growth in the Australian and world recreational diving industries, it seems likely that use of Julian Rocks will also continue to grow. However, this growth may not be as spectacular as that likely to occur in the Great Barrier Reef Marine Park, which is visited by a rapidly growing number of international tourists, because Byron Bay and Julian Rocks are not as accessible to overseas tourists.

The vessels used for diving at Julian Rocks can carry up to 12 divers each (although there are often fewer divers than this on board). During 1992, the vessels made 3795 launches at "The Pass" (the local boat launching ramp), suggesting that there is capacity for more than 40,000 dives per year. Therefore, it would appear that dive operators could accommodate still greater numbers of divers if and when demand increases, although at peak times, such as the Christmas summer holiday period, excess capacity is rarely evidenced.

While the predominant use of the reserve is generated by divers utilizing the services of the Byron Bay commercial operators, other commercial operators (e.g., from Brisbane) use Julian Rocks, although on an infrequent basis. Private divers with their own vessels also use the resource as do recreational anglers (mostly using small boats and generally in small groups of only two to three anglers per vessel).

Environmental Impacts of Boats and Divers at Julian Rocks Aquatic Reserve

Does the intensity of use of Julian Rocks cause environmental degradation and conflict with its conservation and/or amenity values? This is a critical question because degradation of the site may lead to a simultaneous reduction in its economic value. Reports from long-term divers at the site have indicated a perceived decline in the condition of the marine environment since the 1980s (Copeland and Phillips, 1993). Damage attributed to boat anchors from both fishing vessels and dive boats is thought to be the principal cause of the environmental degradation.

Concerns about overuse at particular dive sites were the catalyst for a study of diver behavior and potential diver impacts at Julian Rocks in 1993 (Roberts and Harriott, 1995). A random sample of recreational divers was followed throughout their dives, and the frequency and duration of contacts made by divers with substratum (the bottom type: sand, rock, or rubble) and benthic organisms (nonliving animals and plants such as coral, sponges, and algae) were recorded, as was the type of contact (i.e., whether the contact was by fin, hand, knee, or gauges). Observed damage was rated as either major (broken) or minor (marked, abraded, release of mucus by corals).

Thirty divers contacted substratum or benthic organisms an average of 35 times (range: 2–121) during a 30-minute dive. Fins were involved in more than 50 percent of the contacts. The majority of contacts resulted in very little observable damage, with only 7.2 percent causing a noticeable level of impact. The majority of damaging contacts were made with hard corals, while lesser damage was inflicted on sponges and turf algae.

More experienced divers (those who had made more than 100 dives) made significantly fewer uncontrolled contacts than did inexperienced divers. It was noted that less experienced divers tended to swim at a "fins-down" angle to the bottom, probably because of overweighting, thereby increasing their tendency to strike the substrate with their fins. Furthermore, the buoyancy control of inexperienced divers was less well developed.

Other Because of the popularity of Byron Bay as a holiday location and diving site, conflicts
Conflicts among recreational users of beaches have arisen. Given a lack of protected beaches or
estuaries in the region, the only vehicle access for boat launching is via a popular swimming beach known as "The Pass." There have been disputes among recreational and
commercial boat operators and holiday makers concerning the safety of swimmers and
surfers in the path of motor boats in surf conditions (see Figure 22.5).

Conflicts also arise between divers and recreational anglers. Divers have complained
about damage caused by anchors, fishers occupying mooring buoys for long periods, the
destruction of corals from snagged lines, the catch of nontarget species (e.g., inedible
fish, stingrays), and the incidence of gray nurse sharks and turtles (both protected species)
with hooks in their mouths.

Figure 22.5
*Surfers and dive boats compete for space at
"The Pass." (Courtesy of Max Egan.)*

ECONOMIC ANALYSIS OF DIVING ACTIVITY AT JULIAN ROCKS

The travel cost method (TCM) has been widely applied to the valuation of recreational sites. The central concept is that the cost of traveling to a recreational site will influence the number and frequency of visits to that site. With the support of the Byron Bay dive operators, TCM surveys for Julian Rocks were administered between September 1993 and January 1994. A total of 272 divers responded to questions on their expenditures while traveling to, visiting, and diving at Byron Bay. The total annual expenditure of divers for accommodations, meals, fuel, fares, gifts, diving, and "other costs" was estimated at around A$2.8 million (US$2.016 million) per year (based on 20,878 dives per year, the actual number of individual dives made through the three commercial operators providing charters in 1992).

Based on data collected during the survey and using 1992 diver numbers, the "consumer surplus" (i.e., the economic benefit received by divers over and above the cost of using the Julian Rocks Aquatic Reserve; see Edwards, 1987) was estimated at A$728,000 (US$524,000). This figure is only about 25 percent of the A$2.8 million (US$2.016 million) spent by divers, because much of that expenditure was allocated to other holiday activities. That is, the estimated consumer surplus is related only to the portion of expenditure allocated to diving.[12]

It would appear that Julian Rocks is of significant economic value to scuba divers (in addition to its ecological and other values). Yet, due to budgetary restrictions, NSW Fisheries is unable to allocate funds specifically for its management. This is a situation that has prevailed since the reserve was declared in 1982. As observed by Dixon (1993), marine park management costs are small compared to the gross economic benefits associated with the use of those parks.

The TCM underestimates the total economic value of Julian Rocks because the estimate is derived only from users of Byron Bay's commercial dive operations (which, however, generate by far the majority of total divers using the site). It does not include the values realized by other users, nor does it account for a range of nonuse values that contribute to the "total economic value" of the reserve. Nonetheless, the estimated consumer surplus indicates the substantial economic value of Julian Rocks and provides management with useful information on which to make resource allocation and management decisions.

MANAGEMENT RESPONSES

The intensity of use and the resulting potential for impacts suggest that management actions are required if the ecological and economic values of the reserve are to be placed on a sustainable footing. Some of these (e.g., the installation of mooring buoys) are included in the management plan prepared by NSW Fisheries (Copeland and Phillips, 1993), while others (e.g., determining the carrying capacity and the limits of acceptable change) are recommended longer-term initiatives for enhancing the sustainable management of the reserve.

Determining Carrying Capacity Defining the carrying capacity of Julian Rocks has been hampered by a paucity of baseline data on the ecology of the area (e.g., the recovery and regrowth rates of different coral species) as well as a lack of information on diver attitudes towards congestion at popular dive sites (which is needed to determine the important social components of carrying capacity). In the only study yet available on determining underwater carrying capacity, Dixon et al. (1993) suggested an upper limit of 5000 dives annually at each site in Bonaire Marine Park (BMP)— a figure that represents only about half of that recorded at the "Cod Hole" and "Nursery" at Julian Rocks. Such comparisons, unfortunately, are not helpful because of the different features found at different locations. For example, BMP has a much higher level of cover of more fragile coral species than does Julian Rocks.

Establishment of an ongoing program for monitoring changes in the level of coral cover and in the species composition of corals, sponges, fish, and other organisms would be a first step towards determining the carrying capacity of Julian Rocks. Information on user attitudes to congestion and apparent degradation within the reserve is also required.

Defining Limits of Acceptable Change Assessing the limits of acceptable change (LAC) in Julian Rocks Aquatic Reserve is equally complicated, especially given the lack of baseline data. The nine-step procedure for determining LAC (see Figure 22.1) indicates that knowledge of existing conditions is required before indicators of acceptable resource and social conditions can be developed. Moreover, the lack of coordinated information on the attitudes of users about what changes are acceptable further constrains the assessment of LAC.

Given anecdotal evidence of past degradation in the reserve, it is likely, for example, that divers would conclude that no change is acceptable. Apparent or potential degradation was a primary reason for declaring Julian Rocks an MPA, implying that the management agency, NSW Fisheries, would also perceive further change as being unacceptable. Moreover, user perceptions of acceptable levels of change with respect to social values such as crowding may be just as significant as environmental change [i.e., even if current management practices lead to an improved environment, social (experiential) factors might impose an upper limit on user numbers].

Encouragement of Sensitive Diver Practices While diver impacts resulting from overweighting and lack of buoyancy control are generally unintentional, more sensitive diver practices will enhance the potential for sustainable use of the reserve and will also raise carrying capacity and biological impact thresholds. Improved and ongoing diver training is believed to be important in this regard.

International interest in the development of ecologically sensitive diving practices is growing. For example, PADI has implemented "Project AWARE" to enhance environmental preservation in marine areas, and the National Association of Underwater Instructors (NAUI) has produced a series of three training videos on environmentally responsible diving and has also updated other training materials (Jackson, personal communication). Other agencies such as Scuba Schools International (SSI) and the National Association of Scuba Diving Schools (NASDS) are also promoting careful use of the marine environment. Furthermore, dive publications, mainly magazines, regularly include articles dealing with environmental matters and promote environmentally sensitive use of the marine world.

Although such messages are frequently aimed at instructors and more experienced divers, they need to be incorporated into basic diver training as well, with a focus on awareness of the fragility of the environment and development of suitable buoyancy control skills. Further diver training and environmental briefings before dives are two important actions being promoted.

Concerns about the degradation of dive sites may also necessitate increased regulation of diver certification and diver activities. The entry level certification (known as the "C-Card") is a lifetime certification which does not require divers to upgrade their skills even if they have not dived for a long period of time. MPA managers may be well served by calling for greater regulation of this aspect of the dive industry. Many dive operators have policies limiting inexperienced divers to "hard" sites (i.e., sandy areas where potential damage is minimized) in much the same way that inexperienced divers are not permitted beyond restricted depths. Such policy, if more widely adopted, should reduce impacts at sensitive sites.

In Australian waters, as distinct from locations such as Florida (Talge, 1993), there are few regulations on touching or breaking marine organisms such as corals. If environmental degradation is an issue, the question of a "look but do not touch" policy backed by regulation should be reviewed.

Provision and Use of Boat Moorings Mooring buoys are the single most important factor in reducing reef damage from diving (Hawkins and Roberts, 1993b). A program of mooring installations within Julian Rocks since 1985 acknowledges that the state of the marine environment is critical for attracting and retaining the dive market. Although use of the moorings is voluntary and anchoring is still permitted, this program has reduced the incidence of boat anchors. Nonetheless, Copeland and Phillips (1993) recommended that additional moorings be installed, especially at sites used by anglers. If sufficient moorings were installed, anchoring could ultimately be prohibited.

There are ongoing problems in many Australian marine management agencies concerning the financial burden of legal liability if there is damage to people or property resulting from public use of moorings installed by government agencies (Great Barrier Reef Marine Park Authority, personal communication). These problems have been addressed in the United States (e.g., in the Florida Keys) primarily by taking due care in the installation and maintenance of moorings and through public notification concerning the appropriate use of those moorings (van Breda and Gjerde, 1992).

Tactics to Reduce Conflict and Crowding Efforts by the local council to deal with problems concerning the safety of swimmers and surfers have included issuing boat launching permits for a fee, paying staff to regulate boat and swimmer activities during periods of high demand, and regulating the number of users during peak summer periods by installing a control gate and restricting boating access to regular local users who pay a small fee. Other alternatives, such as artificially enlarging a nearby estuary and constructing a jetty in the township, have also been canvassed, but much ill-feeling has been generated over this issue. In general, management responses have been "stop-gap" in nature, and no viable long-term solution has yet been found.

NSW Fisheries and Byron Council recognize that crowding is a potential problem within the reserve and at the boat ramp. Dive operators have volunteered to stagger diving times to reduce crowding, particularly at the boat ramp where public safety is a major issue. The council uses licence fees to fund a staff position to direct boat operations during times of peak activity.

User Fees to Fund Management and Research and to Control Use

At present, divers pay a voluntary A$1 (US$0.72) fee to dive operators, and the money is returned to NSW Fisheries as a contribution to management and research. Such a system has also been implemented in Australia's Great Barrier Reef Marine Park. Although the fee is only A$1, the scheme has met considerable opposition from tourist operators.

The small fee at Julian Rocks is not a deterrent to users. However, if a reduction in visitor numbers is required in the future, the imposition of a larger user fee could conceivably act as a disincentive to some. The fees introduced at Julian Rocks and the Great Barrier Reef Marine Park were not designed to overcome market failure. Rather, they are merely a means of contributing to management and research activities.

Regulation of Activities Under the Fisheries Act

The only activity expressly prohibited in Julian Rocks is the removal of marine life (except fin fish by hook and line). In other MPAs, stricter restrictions exist (e.g., zoned areas where line fishing or diving are not permitted). In reserves located in other parts of the world, there are prohibitions on touching the substratum while diving, which are enforced at great cost. Such legislation remains an option in the study area if increasing numbers of divers begin to produce unacceptable levels of damage.

Provision of an Artificial Reef and Alternative Sites to Spread Diver Pressure

Another possibility involves directing more diving activity to areas within Byron Bay that currently exhibit relatively low levels of use. However, alternative sites are limited in number and quality, and their use is more dependent on the weather than is the use of popular sites in the reserve. Hence, the potential for establishing an artificial reef within Byron Bay was examined in 1993. Kerr (1992) reported that 72 artificial reefs have been constructed in Australian waters using materials such as tires, obsolete ships, old cars and trams, concrete modules and culverts, and bridge rubble.

Interviews with Byron Bay dive operators revealed a high level of interest in establishing an artificial reef. They suggested a site to the northwest of Julian Rocks with a depth of approximately 65 feet (20 meters) and a sandy bottom. This site features easy navigation, some protection by Julian Rocks from southeasterly swell, weak oceanic currents, and likely rapid colonization of the reef from Julian Rocks and other nearby rocky reefs. The preferred structure for initiating reef growth was an old vessel. Although this is an attractive mechanism for reducing the pressure on the Julian Rocks Aquatic Reserve, several environmental issues would have to be addressed before this proposal is implemented, including (1) legal requirements under the Environmental Protection (Sea Dumping) Act 1981 and (2) regulations governing the management and funding of an artificial reef.

Establishing an Environmental Monitoring Program

The monitoring of marine environments to measure potential impacts of human activities has received a great deal of attention in recent years (Fairweather, 1991). A substantial suite of methodological and analytical tools has been developed [eg., water quality (Brodie and Furnas, 1993), photographic techniques (Gittings et al., 1993), line transects (Liddle and Ohlhorst, 1993; Wilkinson et al., 1993)].

A program to monitor environmental changes is required to detect potential improvements in the condition of the marine communities as a result of management actions such as the installation of moorings, or to measure potential environmental degradation, and to determine whether the carrying capacity has been approached or exceeded. Underwater video transects (to record benthic community structure) have been completed at 11 sites (4 x 30-m transects per site) in the reserve and at three sites in Byron Bay (Harriott et al., 1996). Percentage cover of the major categories of biota has been recorded. This data set will permit analysis of changes in cover of these categories. Resurveys at intervals of approximately two years have been recommended.

Establishment of a GIS Data Base to Measure Usage, Impacts, and Environmental Change A GIS[13] data base focusing on the Byron Bay and Julian Rocks region has been established. Information on the location and structure of the islands, marine community structures, location of moorings, and bottom features in certain areas of the reserve has been stored in the data base. This system provides a powerful tool to measure the effects of changing usage patterns and will assist future management decisions, particularly those relating to the establishment of an artificial reef, the location of additional mooring buoys, and the need to preclude diving from certain areas to allow marine community structures (corals, etc.) to recover.

CONCLUSION

Most marine protected areas (MPAs) in Australia are managed as multiple-use resources and have a range of ecological, economic, and recreational values. Recreational scuba diving in MPAs is increasing and intensive diving activities at certain sites, such as the Julian Rocks Aquatic Reserve, may conflict with ecological values, reduce amenity values, and result in the nonsustainability of such sites.

An examination of the use of Julian Rocks for recreational scuba diving suggests that it is of significant economic value to the diving fraternity. The environmental impacts of individual divers appear to be minor, although the cumulative impacts of diver contacts with the substrate and benthos found in the reserve may be substantial. Consequently, an environmental monitoring program that can detect future changes in marine communities due to the cumulative effects of diving has been initiated and will provide management with information relating to user pressures. This program could be used as the basis for an assessment of the carrying capacity of Julian Rocks. Such an assessment would need to incorporate attitudinal data on matters such as congestion at the main dive sites, acceptable changes to the environment, and ideas for resolving existing user conflicts.

Certain management responses, such as the installation of boat moorings and staggered dive times, have been implemented. However, there may still be a need to reduce the number of divers using the most popular sites in the reserve. One possible strategy is to establish an artificial reef in Byron Bay. This strategy is currently constrained by financing and uncertainty regarding the source of responsibility for permission to construct such a facility.

NOTES

1. See Chapter 23 for additional discussion relating to the IUCN.
2. The Australian categories of marine parks and protected areas include aquatic reserves, conservation areas, fish habitat reserves, fish sanctuaries, historic shipwreck protected zones, marine

and coastal parks, marine parks, marine reserves, national nature reserves, and wetland reserves.

3. See Chapters 4, 5, 7, 8, 17, 18, 22, and 23 for additional discussion relating to sustainable tourism and sustainable tourism development concepts and philosophies.

4. See Chapters 9 and 23 for additional discussion of the carrying capacity concept and limits of acceptable change.

5. "Loss of amenity" may occur in heavily used sites. For example, the appeal of attractive corals may be lost because they are damaged by excessive use. If a dive site is converted from a pristine area to one that is showing considerable damage, then that site will be less attractive to divers, and the value and benefits they derive from it will be similarly reduced.

6. Marine protected areas are in public sector ownership, but access to them is still generally "open." For example, there is no private ownership of scuba diving sites, and therefore individual users may see no long-term benefits to themselves in being careful when using such sites.

7. The concept of market failure is central to much of the work undertaken in the field of environmental economics. Policies on "user pays" for environmental goods (such as water, clean air, recreational sites), taxes on the use of natural resources, and transferable permits and quotas for using natural resources, all of which come under the heading of "economic instruments," are designed specifically to overcome the market failure that results from the use of free (or very cheap) environmental goods. An excellent discussion of market failure can be found in Chapters 5 and 6 of Turner et al. (1994).

8. New South Wales Fisheries is a state government agency that has responsibility for establishing and implementing policy on the management and use of marine resources, including MPAs, recreational fisheries, and commercial fisheries. The agency undertakes public consultation when developing management plans for MPAs, but has ultimate control over those areas.

9. The *hedonic price technique* employs statistical techniques and approaches such as regression analysis to isolate environmental values that contribute to observed differences in product prices. This approach is not generally used in valuing recreational areas.

10. *Contingent valuation* is a method of placing a figure on the benefits that people derive from consuming a good by directly questioning a sample of consumers to determine (a) their maximum willingness to pay for the good or (b) their minimum compensation to go without it.

11. *The travel cost method* relies on time and travel cost information to derive a demand curve for a recreational site. This curve is then used to estimate the value of the site to all users. This method is used widely to value the recreational benefits of public parks and other natural areas.

12. Travel cost estimates such as those provided here do not provide any guidance on economic flow-ons to other parts of the local economy. Such estimates are used simply to indicate the value to users (i.e., divers in this case) of the natural resource. Obviously, however, the availability of a quality dive experience does generate considerable local economic activity, much of which would disappear if the experience was not available.

13. See Chapter 20 for a more comprehensive overview of GIS.

REFERENCES

Bennett, J. 1991. Valuing the environment, *Evaluation Journal of Australia*, 3(1), 3–11.

Brodie J. and M. Furnas. 1993. Long term monitoring programs for eutrophication and the design of a monitoring program for the Great Barrier Reef. *Proceedings of 7th International Coral Reef Symposium*, Guam, 1992, 77–84.

Clark, J.R. 1990. *Carrying Capacity: The Limits to Tourism*. Paper presented at the Congress on Marine Tourism, East–West Conference Center, University of Hawaii, 23–29 May.

Clark, J.R. (ed.). 1991. *Carrying Capacity: A Status Report on Marine and Coastal Parks and*

Reserves. Report prepared by the participants of the Third International Seminar on Coastal and Marine Parks and Protected Areas, Miami, Florida and Costa Rica, 11 May–5 June.

Copeland, C. and S. Phillips. 1993. *Julian Rocks Aquatic Reserve: Draft Plan of Management 1993–1995*. Wollongbar: NSW Fisheries.

Davis, D.C. and C.A. Tisdell. 1995. Recreational scuba diving and carrying capacity in marine protected areas, *Ocean and Coastal Management*, 26(1), 19–40.

DeLacy, T. 1990. Economic valuation of nature conservation and outdoor recreation resources, *Australian Parks and Recreation*, 26(3), 16–28.

Dignam, D. 1990. Scuba gaining among mainstream travelers, *Tour and Travel News*, 26 March.

Dive Australia. 1994. Media Release No. 57/94, Diving Industry and Travel Association of Australia, Lindfield, NSW, Australia.

Dixon, J.A. 1993. Economic benefits of marine protected areas, *Oceanus*, 36(3), Fall, 35–40.

Dixon, J.A. and P.B. Sherman. 1990. *Economics of Protected Areas: A New Look at Benefits and Costs*. London: Earthscan Publications.

Dixon, J.A., L.F. Scura, and T. van't Hof. 1993. Meeting ecological and economic goals: marine parks in the Caribbean, *Ambio*, 22 (2–3), 117–125.

Edwards, S.F. 1987. *An Introduction to Coastal Zone Economics: Concepts, Methods and Case Studies*. New York: Taylor and Francis.

Fairweather, P.G. 1991. Statistical power and design requirements for environmental monitoring, *Australian Journal of Marine and Freshwater Research*, 42, 555–567.

Gittings, S.R., K.J.P. Deslarzes, D.K. Hagman, and G.S. Boland. 1993. Reef coral populations and growth on the Flower Garden Banks, Northwest Gulf of Mexico, *Proceedings of the 7th International Coral Reef Symposium*, 90–96. Guam, 1992.

Harriott, V.J., P.L. Harrison, and S.A. Banks. 1996. The coral communities of Lord Howe Island, *Australian Journal of Marine and Freshwater Research*.

Hawkins, J.P. and C.M. Roberts. 1992. Effects of recreational scuba diving on fore-reef slope communities of coral reefs, *Biological Conservation*, 62, 171–178.

Hawkins, J.P. and C.M. Roberts. 1993a. Effects of recreational scuba diving on coral reefs: trampling on reef-flat communities, *Journal of Applied Ecology*, 30, 25–30.

Hawkins, J.P. and C.M. Roberts. 1993b. Can Egypt's coral reefs support ambitious plans for diving tourism? *Proceedings of the 7th International Coral Reef Symposium*, Guam, 1992, pp. 1007–1013.

Hooy, T. and G. Shaughnessy (eds.). 1992. *Terrestrial and Marine Protected Areas in Australia (1991)*. Canberra: Australian National Parks and Wildlife Service, Australian Government Publishing Service.

Hundloe, T. J. 1979. Parks in the marine environment. In J. Messer and G. Mosley (eds.), *The Value of National Parks to the Community: Values and Ways of Improving the Contribution of Australian National Parks to the Community*. Melbourne: Australian Conservation Foundation Inc.

International Union for the Conservation of Nature and Natural Resources (IUCN). 1986. *Review of the Protected Areas System in Oceania*. Gland, Switzerland: IUCN, Commission on National Parks and Protected Areas.

Ivanovici, A.M. (ed.). 1984. *Inventory of Declared Marine and Estuarine Protected Areas*, Vols. I and II, Special Publication 12. Canberra: Australian National Parks and Wildlife Service.

Kerr, S. 1992. *Artificial Reefs in Australia: Their Construction, Location and Function*. Canberra: Bureau of Rural Resources, Working Paper No. WP/8/92.

Liddle, W.D. and S.L. Ohlhorst. 1993. Ten years of disturbance and change on a Jamaican fringing reef, *Proceedings of the 7th International Coral Reef Symposium*, Guam, 1992, pp. 144–150.

Ludwig Rieder and Associates. 1988. *Byron Shire Tourism Plan*. Byron Bay, NSW, Australia: Byron Shire Council.

National Sporting Goods Association. 1994. *Sports Participation in 1993: Series II*. Mt. Prospect, IL: NSGA.

Oliver, J. and R. Schneider. 1993. Monitoring the impact of tourist developments in the Great Barrier Reef Marine Park: some case studies [Abstract], *Proceedings of the 7th International Coral Reef Symposium*, Guam, 1992, p. 167.

Pearce, D.W., A. Markandya, and E. Barbier. 1989. *Blueprint for a Green Economy*. London: Earthscan Publications.

Pearce, D.W. and R.K. Turner. 1990. *Economics of Natural Resources and the Environment*. London: Harvester Wheatsheaf.

Prosser, G. 1986. The limits of acceptable change: an introduction to a framework for national area planning, *Australian Parks and Recreation*, 22(2), 5–10.

Resource Assessment Commission (RAC). 1993. *The Carrying Capacity Concept and Its Application to the Management of Coastal Zone Resources*, Information Paper No. 8. Canberra: Coastal Zone Inquiry, Australian Government Publishing Service.

Roberts, L. and V. Harriott. 1995. Recreational scuba diving and its potential for environmental impact in a marine reserve. In O. Bellwood, J.H. Choat, and N.K. Satena (eds.), *Recent Advances in Marine Science and Technology*. Townsville, Australia: James Cook University.

Salm, R.V. 1986. Coral reefs and tourist carrying capacity: the Indian Ocean experience, *UNEP Industry and Environment*, Jan-March, 11–14.

Stankey, G.H. and S.F. McCool. 1989. Carrying capacity in recreational settings: evolution, appraisal, and application, *Leisure Sciences*, 6(4), 453–473.

Stankey, G.H., D.N. Cole, R.C. Lucas, M.M. Peterson, and S.S. Frissell. 1985. *The Limits of Acceptable Change (LAC) System for Wilderness Planning*, General Technical Report INT-176. Washington, D.C.: Forest Service, United States Department of Agriculture.

Tabata, R.S. 1992. Scuba diving holidays. In B. Weiler and C.M. Hall (eds.), *Special Interest Tourism*. London: Belhaven Press.

Talge, H. 1993. Impact of recreational divers on scleractinian corals at Looe Key, Florida, *Proceedings of the 7th International Coral Reef Symposium*, Guam, 1992, pp. 1077–1082.

Taylor, D. 1994. *An Analysis of the Backpacker Segment of the Travel Market in Byron Bay*. Lismore, NSW, Australia: Centre for Tourism, Southern Cross University.

Thomas, C. 1992. *Dive Tourism in the Great Barrier Reef Region*. Study report for the Great Barrier Reef Marine Park Authority, Townsville, Queensland.

Tilmant, J.T. and G.P. Schmal. 1981. A comparative analysis of coral damage on recreationally used reefs within Biscayne National Park, Florida, *Proceedings of the 4th International Coral Reef Symposium*, Manila, pp. 187–192.

Turner, R.K., D. Pearce, and I. Bateman. 1994. *Environmental Economics: An Elementary Introduction*. London: Harvester Wheatsheaf.

Urban Research and Development Corporation (URDC). 1980. *Recreation Carrying Capacity Handbook: Methods and Management*. Prepared for the US Army Corps of Engineers, Washington, D.C.

van Breda, A. and K. Gjerde. 1992. *The Use of Mooring Buoys as a Management Tool.* Washington D.C.: Center for Marine Conservation.

Ward, F. 1990. Florida's coral reefs are imperilled, *National Geographic*, July, 115–132.

Wilkinson, C.R., L.M. Chou, E. Gomez, I. Mohammed, S. Soekarno, and S. Sudara. 1993. A regional approach to monitoring coral reefs: studies in Southeast Asia by the ASEAN-Australia Living Coastal Resources project, *Proceedings of the 7th International Coral Reef Symposium*, Guam, 1992, pp. 138–143.

Wilks, J. 1993. Calculating diver numbers: critical information for scuba safety and marketing programs, *SPUMS Journal*, 23(1), 11–14.

Wright, J. 1990. *Diving Southern Queensland: A Guide to 40 of the Top Dive Sites From Heron Island to Byron Bay.* Brisbane, Queensland: Division of Information, Department of Lands.

¶ | PROBLEM SOLVING AND DISCUSSION ACTIVITIES

1. Is it practical to estimate carrying capacity for marine locations such as the Julian Rocks Aquatic Reserve, or are alternative approaches such as LAC more feasible?

2. What factors are of the most significance when estimating the carrying capacity of a marine protected area? Recommend an approach to collecting the baseline data that are required to determine the carrying capacity and limits of acceptable change in Julian Rocks Aquatic Reserve.

3. Design a research project for gathering information on social aspects of the use of Julian Rocks by divers, including a questionnaire to determine the attitudes of divers towards congestion at the site.

4. In North Queensland, many dive tourists are Japanese. Japanese and Australians probably differ from each other in the way that crowding is perceived in relation to leisure activities. How can these differences be taken into account when evaluating the social carrying capacity of dive sites?

5. At present, because of weather and safety considerations, the majority of divers at Julian Rocks are confined to a relatively small area, thus creating intense use of that area and relatively low use of the remainder of the reserve. This may restrict diver impacts to a small proportion of the reserve. Is it better to maintain a policy where damage is potentially limited to a relatively small area, or should there be efforts to spread the divers and, hence, potential impacts more widely? Justify your answer.

6. How important is it to place economic values on environmental resources such as Julian Rocks? Review methods of economic valuation for recreational resources, and identify the various components of "total economic value."

7. It is suggested that a small proportion of divers are responsible for a large proportion of the damage caused by divers. Who is responsible for modifying the behavior of destructive divers so that they become more environmentally friendly? If they display no desire to amend their diving practices and reduce their contacts with the biota, should they be permitted to continue diving in the reserve? Should the commercial operator risk unpopularity and loss of revenue by not taking the divers to that site again, or should there be legislation against

contact with the fauna and enforcement by the management agency, such as exists in several American marine reserves?

8. If a monitoring program demonstrates that a major natural event (such as a storm) is more destructive than several years of diver activity, is it acceptable to dismiss diver impacts as insignificant?

9. Julian Rocks is potentially a disturbed environment because of the level of activity, particularly boat anchoring, over the past 10–20 years. If a monitoring program indicated an increase in coral cover in the next five years, as well as an increase in diver numbers, can it be concluded that more divers are good for the environment?

10. Prepare a position paper (a brief) for presentation at an international dive conference to encourage a cooperative approach to addressing the potential negative implications of diving in marine protected areas.

23

Divergence and Conflict, or Convergence and Harmony?

NATURE CONSERVATION AND TOURISM POTENTIAL IN HOHE TAUERN NATIONAL PARK, AUSTRIA

 Christoph Stadel

✊|K E Y   L E A R N I N G   P O I N T S

- Sustainability implies courses of action that do not jeopardize the long-term stability of ecological systems or the survival of key features of the cultural landscape. Achieving sustainability in national park regions that are part of the living space of local populations should be based on a management approach that integrates ecological, economic, social, and cultural parameters and that balances the needs and objectives of both residents and visitors alike.

- Partnerships between park authorities and local communities are critical to addressing the diverse and often conflicting goals and interests of stakeholder groups. Through partnership, public education, and public consultation, the principles of ecorealism may be realized by harmonizing ecological and economic imperatives.

- The implementation of national park objectives can be facilitated through a number of strategies geared towards education and guidance of tourists, voluntary limitation of activities, and a respect for nature. The channeling of visitor flows into specific areas and careful management of sites of tourist concentration are critical.

- Carefully planned and implemented zoning regulations may prevent conflicts between conservation and the pursuit of economic viabiity.

INTRODUCTION

By international definition, national parks are generally natural areas whose ecosystems have not been substantially modified by human activity. These areas have been set aside to protect and conserve features of the landscape. This chapter focuses on the Hohe Tauern National Park in Austria, a high mountain area that combines a diversified Alpine landscape and ecosystem with long-standing social, cultural, and economic traditions of the resident population. The area has considerable appeal for tourism based on its impressive natural resource base.

This national park (covering approximately 700 square miles or 1800 square kilometers), which was created between 1983 and 1991 by the three Austrian länder (provinces) of Carinthia, Salzburg, and Tyrol, comprises 29 mountain communities. This chapter discusses the evolution of the park, including conflicts that have marked its history. These conflicts have arisen from the often diverse objectives and forms of utilization of various stakeholders, the resolution of which has required a number of delicate compromises.

In an attempt to accommodate these different objectives, the national park region has implemented a zoning scheme that differentiates between the high Alpine core zone consisting of largely unspoiled nature, an outer zone that includes a landscape modified by the human impact of mountain agriculture, and an adjacent zone in the major valleys with villages and towns that largely depend on tourism.

This chapter emphasizes the importance of adopting a partnership approach to minimize conflict. Such an approach between Hohe Tauern National Park authorities and the communities has resulted in widespread acceptance of the park concept by the local population. Through partnership, the objectives of conserving the ecology of the region can be harmonized with those of sustaining the economic base for the local population. The term "ecorealism" has been used by national park officials in conjunction with this principle.

SUSTAINABILITY, CARRYING CAPACITIES, AND NATIONAL PARKS: CONTEMPORARY PERSPECTIVES AND ISSUES

The Concept of Sustainability In concept and practice, the notion of sustainability[1] is particularly applicable to the highly sensitive environments of mountain regions, as well as to the well-being of the communities located there. *Environmental sustainability* implies courses of action that do not jeopardize either the long-term stability of ecological systems or the survival of key features of the cultural landscape. For local populations, sustainable development focuses on promoting the well-being of people through the provision of healthy and supportive economic and social conditions. By practicing sustainable development, people seek to chart a future that is both environmentally sustainable and economically viable (Stadel and Everitt, 1995, p. 6).

Sustainable tourism involves managing resources "in such a way that we can fulfill economic, social, and aesthetic needs while maintaining cultural integrity, essential ecological processes, biological diversity and life support systems" (Tourism Canada, 1990 in Murphy, 1994, p. 279). Sustainability in national park regions that support local populations is a complex issue which should be based on a management approach that integrates ecological, economic, social, and cultural parameters and that balances the needs and objectives of both residents and visitors alike.

The Concept The concept of sustainability is closely related to the notion of *carrying capacity*[2] which
of Carrying implies the existence of (or the goal of establishing) determinable limits to development,
Capacity population pressure, and infrastructures in a particular area. As a management tool for
tourism, carrying capacity (Williams and Gill, 1994, p. 174)

> . . . appeals to a recognized need to limit and control tourism which may threaten the sus-
> tained use of limited resources. Simultaneously, it runs at odds with other desires for maximis-
> ing opportunities for growth and the benefits associated with increased visitor use.

Varying perspectives on carrying capacities may be distinguished when the concept
is applied to the interrelationship between the environment, tourism, and local communities. Moreover, different stakeholders frequently express divergent views on carrying
capacity management. In environmental terms, the concept refers to "the maximum
number of people who can use a site without an unacceptable decline in the quality of
the experience gained by visitors" (Mathieson and Wall, 1982, p. 21). From a community
perspective, on the other hand, "carrying capacity concerns a destination area's capability
to absorb tourism before negative effects are felt by the community" (Williams and Gill,
1994, p. 177).

In environmentally outstanding and/or sensitive areas, attempts are being made to
develop and promote sustainable forms of tourism, or at least to impose restrictions where
mass tourism is potentially harmful to the physical and cultural environments. In such
areas, management objectives often adhere to the following guidelines (Pigram, 1990 in
Williams and Gill, 1994, pp. 178–179): (1) development that reflects an architectural
character and style that is sensitive to an area's heritage and environment; (2) preservation,
protection, and enhancement of the quality of local resources; (3) development of visitor
services that enhance local heritage and environmental resources; and (4) growth that
improves the quality of life of the local community.

Objectives Internationally, national parks are predominantly natural areas whose ecosystems have
and Roles of not been substantially modified by human activity and which have been set aside to
National Parks protect and conserve the features of a relatively unspoiled landscape. Nonetheless, since
the establishment of Yellowstone National Park (USA) in 1872, an important objective
of national parks worldwide has been to provide for the recreation and enjoyment of
people who live in urban industrial settings and find themselves largely removed from
nature. To this end, national parks not only represent valuable natural environments
(ecotopes) that have to be protected, but also highly appreciated recreational landscapes
for stressed people (psychotopes).

In most parts of the world, national parks increasingly appeal to visitors who (1) are
attracted to these regions based on their scenic beauty, (2) are seeking unspoiled natural
areas where they can pursue alternative forms of tourism (e.g., nature observation, wilderness experience), and/or (3) desire to take advantage of the wide range of services and
infrasructures provided. In this way, national parks have become powerful magnets for an
ever-increasing number of tourists.

However, some observers have questioned whether the physical carrying capacities
of these parks are being exceeded, and they have even suggested that the growing popular-

ity of parks for leisure and tourism activities could lead to a lowering of their recreational quality, the demise of their attractiveness, and a reduction in the role they play in regional development (Schürrer, 1994, p. 13). In short, there is a risk that parks could be "loved to death."[3.]

In regions such as the European Alps where local natural resources had been exploited by resident populations prior to the establishment of parks, national parks have another objective—that is, to provide a sustainable social and economic base for the local population. This is especially critical since, with a decrease in the viability of many traditional forms of economic activity (e.g., agriculture), many communities have begun to consider tourism as a means to strengthen and/or diversify their economies.[4] Various factors have contributed to this interest in tourism development, including the relatively low economic return from traditional forms of employment compared to other economic activities, a preference for white collar jobs, and perhaps most important, the fact that tourism has offered new and attractive economic alternatives to regions where such choices did not exist previously.

Given that one of the principal mandates of national parks is to conserve nature and limit human impacts, resident populations tend to be skeptical (at least in the initial phases) of being included in a national park region, or even of living close to such an area where there might be a curtailment of some economic activities. In this context there may be a fundamental contradiction between national parks and the pursuit of tourism. Hence, park planning and management require a delicate balancing of the different aspirations of stakeholders, the functions of a region, and the nature of land use and other activities. Achieving this balance is the responsibility of a variety of individuals, communities, organizations, and political authorities (e.g., landowners, farmers, tourists, villages, lobby groups, and provincial/state and federal institutions).

NATIONAL PARKS IN THE EUROPEAN ALPS

The Alpine region, including most areas where national parks exist today, has been settled for many centuries. Therefore, with the exception of some high Alpine zones, areas that remain in a completely natural state are rare. Consequently, there has been considerable debate about the feasibility or desirability of a strict adherence to the principles of nature preservation within the regional context of the European Alps as stipulated by the International Union for the Conservation of Nature (IUCN).[5]

National parks fall into Category II of the IUCN management categories for protected areas (see Table 23.1). For some, the complete renunciation of all forms of human resource utilization within national parks appears unrealistic and is politically untenable. Hence, it has been suggested that national park policies in the European Alps should attempt to conserve the region's cultural landscape, not in the form of an "open-air museum" but by providing the social and economic prerequisites for a sustainable living space for the local population.

This means that, while an attempt should be made to conserve traditional features of the material culture and some social traditions of the region, national parks should not eliminate modernizing influences that make living and working conditions easier and more comfortable. Above all, resident populations should not have to make economic

TABLE 23.1
IUCN Management Categories for Protected Areas

Category I: Strict Nature Reserve/Wilderness Area
Protected area managed mainly for science or wilderness protection.

Category II: National Park
Protected area managed mainly for ecosystem protection and recreation.

Definition
Natural area of land and/or sea designated to (1) protect the ecological integrity of one or more ecosystems for present and future generations, (2) exclude exploitation or occupation inimical to the purposes of the designation of the area, and (3) provide a foundation for spiritual, scientific, educational, recreational, and visitor opportunities, all of which must be environmentally and culturally compatible.

Objectives of Management
- To protect natural and scenic areas of national and international significance for spiritual, scientific, recreational, or tourist purposes.
- To perpetuate, in as natural a state as possible, representative examples of physiographic region, biotic communities, genetic resources, and species to provide ecological stability and diversity.
- To manage visitor use for inspirational, educational, cultural, and recreational purposes at a level that will maintain the area in a natural, or near natural, state.
- To eliminate, and thereafter, prevent exploitation or occupation inimical to the purposes of the designation.
- To maintain respect for the ecological, geomorphologic, sacred, or esthetic attributes that warranted designation.
- To take into account the need of indigenous people, including subsistence resource use, insofar as these will not adversely affect the other objectives of management.

Guidance for Selection
- The area should contain a representative sample of major natural regions, features, or scenery, where plant and animal species, habitats, and geomorphologic sites are of special spiritual, scientific, educational, recreational, and tourist significance.
- The area should be large enough to contain one or more entire ecosystems not materially altered by current human occupation or exploitation.

Organizational Responsibility
Ownership and management should normally be the highest competent authority of the nation having jurisdiction over it. However, they may also be vested in another level of government, council of indigenous people, foundation, or other legally established body that has dedicated the area to long-term conservation.

Category III: Natural Monument
Protected area managed mainly for conservation of specific natural features.

Category IV: Habitat/Species Management Area
Protected area managed mainly for conservation through management intervention.

Category V: Protected Landscape/Seascape
Protected area managed mainly for landscape/seascape conservation and recreation.

Category VI: Managed Resource Protected Area
Protected area managed for the sustainable use of the natural ecosystem.

Source: Poore (1992).

sacrifices by living in national parks or adjacent regions. Rather, they should be able to provide themselves and future generations with attractive and secure economic and social conditions.

Given this often precarious situation, national parks in the European Alps have been established not only in areas where landscapes or ecosystems merit conservation, but also in regions where (1) the potential for conflict between national park objectives and those of other stakeholders was relatively low, (2) there was interest and support for the national park concept by "key players," communities, organizations, and political parties, and/or (3) there was a promise and commitment by authorities to provide people living in the region with adequate compensation for curtailed activities or land taken out of production.

The regions designated as national parks in the European Alps were generally not pristine wilderness spaces. Rather, over a long period of time, some areas were utilized quite intensively by individuals and political authorities and were characterized by complex land ownership or land lease patterns. This explains why most national parks in Europe were established only during the second half of the twentieth century, are relatively small in their extension, and often had to consider the aspirations of the resident population and private or public sector organizations eager to exploit the natural resources of the region.

Twelve national parks have been established, or are in the process of being developed, in the European Alps (see Table 23.2). They cover about 3000 square miles (7800 square kilometers), or 4.3 percent of the Alpine region, and are located in Austria, France, Germany, Italy, Slovenia, and Switzerland (see Figure 23.1). Seven are recognized as national parks by the IUCN in the protected area Category II (Broggi and Tödter, 1994, p. 168).

The Swiss National Park in the Engadine (41,728 acres, 16,887 hectares), founded in 1914, was the first Alpine national park. Although economic activities such as agriculture, forestry, hunting, and other forms of utilization are prohibited, no such prohibition exists with respect to tourism. To compensate for the restrictions, long-term lease arrangements for the land of the communities located within the national park have been negotiated.

The issue of land tenure is different in the Italian Gran Paradiso Park (178,722 acres, 72,328 hectares), the second national park established in the Alps. Its territory comprises a former royal hunting region that was subsequently transferred to the state of Italy. The third national park, the Italian Stelvio (332,646 acres, 134,620 hectares), was unilaterally developed in 1936 by the Fascist government despite resistance by the local population who subsequently lost traditional hunting privileges. The remaining parks in the Alpine region were founded between 1963 (La Vanoise in France) and 1992 (Val Grande in Italy).

In the European Alps, a variety of options exist for the use of land and water resources and for the nature of conservation or development. These options range from preservation to curtailing certain activities and land uses to allowing largely unrestricted forms of development. However, questions remain about how to reconcile the interests of different segments of the local population and various "external" interest groups with regard to nature conservation, agriculture, forestry, mining, hydroelectric development, transportation, and tourism.

TABLE 23.2
National Parks in the Alps, 1995

National Park	Area (Hectares)	Forest (Hectares)	Year Founded	IUCN Rating	Area Zoned (Hectares)	Buffer Zone (Hectares)
France						
Le Mercantour	68,500	20,637	1979	II	0	145,500
Les Ecrins	91,800	4,400	1973	II	0	178,600
La Vanoise	52,839	950	1963	II	0	145,000
Italy						
Gran Paradiso	72,328	6,000	1922	II	0 Five-part zoning proposed	34,000
Stelvio	134,620	42,000	1935	V	0	nd[a]
Val Grande[b]	11,700	nd	1992	nd	In planning 7,500 protected 1,000 core 3,200 general	nd
Dolomiti Bellares[b]	31,000	nd	1990	nd	nd	nd
Switzerland						
Swiss Endadin	16,887	5,000	1914	II	0	nd
Germany						
Berchtesgaden	20,800	8,100	1978	V	2,640 protected forest 5,450 forest calm zone 700 protected high pastures	25,000
Austria						
Hohe Tauern	178,600	17,160	1983/1992	II	114,600 core 59,800 outer 4,200 special	nd
Nockberge	18,410	5,966	1986	V	7,730 core 10,680 outer	nd
Kalkhochalpen[c]	18,000	nd	nd	nd	nd	nd
Kalkapen[c]	75,400	nd	nd	nd	nd	nd
Slovenia Triglav	84,815	55,000	1981	II	54,220 core 30,585 fringe 20,000 protected forest 35,000 utilized forest	nd

[a] nd, no data.
[b] Under development.
[c] Proposed.

Sources: Broggi (1993); Broggi and Tödter (1994).

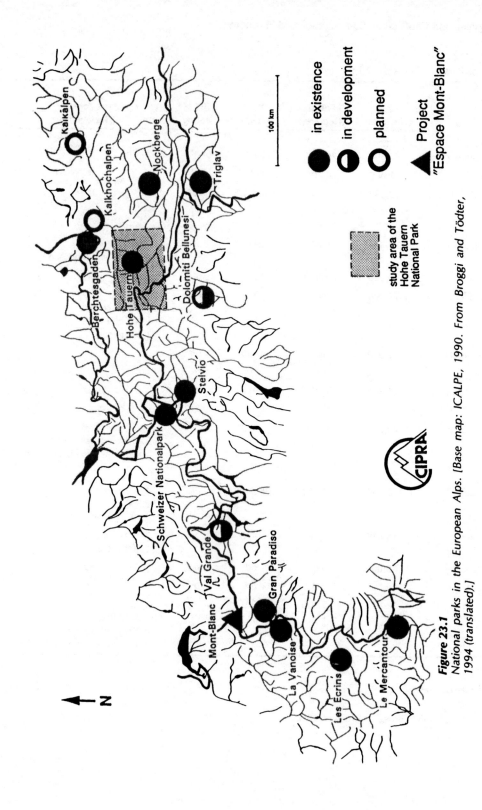

Figure 23.1
National parks in the European Alps. [Base map: ICALPE, 1990. From Broggi and Tödter, 1994 (translated).]

in existence

in development

planned

Project
"Espace Mont-Blanc"

study area of the
Hohe Tauern
National Park

100 km

Kalkalpen

Kalkhochalpen

Nockberge

Triglav

Berchtesgaden

Hohe Tauern

Dolomiti Bellunesi

Stelvio

Schweizer Nationalpark

Gran Paradiso

Val Grande

Mont-Blanc

La Vanoise

Les Ecrins

Le Mercantour

CIPRA

N

To reach a compromise and accommodate the diverse objectives and interests of stakeholders, national parks have been subdivided into different zones depending on the significance of their natural environment attributes or the importance of specific areas as cultural landscapes and viable living spaces. In many instances, the designation of such zones has been reached through public consultation processes involving the local population, political authorities, and external interest groups.[6]

There is considerable variation among parks in how these zones are designated and regulated. However, they usually include (1) a zone geared to large-scale tourism activity for which few restrictions apply and an optimal level of services is provided for visitors, (2) a zone of tranquility and preservation where traditional settlement and economic activities as well as modest and "gentle" forms of tourism are permitted, and (3) a "wilderness" or ecological protection zone to which access is restricted and where economic activity is often prohibited. In addition to the zoning of park regions proper, special zones adjacent to park boundaries may be designated. The establishment of such zones can provide a framework for avoiding some of the problems associated with largely uncontrolled and unregulated developments outside park boundaries.

To achieve a higher level of awareness of environmental concerns in the communities inside or adjacent to the parks, as well as among visitors, there is widespread agreement among park planners that the public has to be sensitized to ecological issues. This may be achieved in part through public education programs. A cooperative approach to park management, which involves the local population and various other stakeholders and interest groups at every stage of park planning and management is critical to achieving policies and strategies that foster sustainability.

Partnerships are a preferred option compared to rigid restrictions on visitor numbers and activities that are unilaterally imposed. With partnerships, carrying capacity issues will no longer appear as technical jargon and management tools that are poorly understood and simply accepted by the resident population and tourists. Instead, these issues will be understood and supported by the public as strategies that are necessary to sustain the environmental qualities and appeal of the region.

One strategy for regulating carrying capacities in specific areas of national parks involves allowing, or even encouraging, the concentration of people at specific points of major touristic appeal (e.g., waterfalls, scenic viewpoints) or along specially designed paths. However, such a strategy prohibits, or at least discourages, people from venturing into other areas, especially those that are ecologically sensitive. This "channeling" of visitor flows can be accomplished through:

- Legal measures and active surveillance of permitted and prohibited activities and resource uses.
- Incentives and disincentives. For example, offering attractive services in spatially confined areas (e,g., comfortable paved trails with interpretive signs, souvenir shops, restaurants, picnic areas) and/or greatly curtailing amenities or even removing facilities from large areas of the park (e.g., not maintaining a well-marked trail system; not allowing camping or picnicking; discouraging car access; not permitting the construction of restaurants and accommodation facilities) (Kremser, 1994a, pp. 45–46; Rupitsch, 1994, pp. 47–49).

In addition to these spatially oriented strategies of park management, Czerny (1994, pp. 52–54) proposed a mechanism that focuses on the time management of tourist and visitor flows, the objective being to limit excessive temporal peaks. He also suggests that greater attention must be given to philosophical and organizational frameworks in national park planning. He not only mentions the need for a reevaluation of existing park objectives and guidelines, but also proposes a new approach to public relations and marketing issues, with the goal of promoting national parks as attractive natural environments and as regions ideally suited for gentle forms of tourism (see Figure 23.2).

The establishment of national parks in regions where there is overlapping political jurisdiction has proved to be particularly challenging. In such cases, coherent natural regions (e.g., watersheds), ecosystems (e.g., regions of specific vegetation and/or types or fauna), or cultural landscapes (e.g., similar vernacular landscapes) may be divided through the superimposition of political boundaries. On the other hand, in a climate of increasing political and/or economic integration in central and western Europe, a more intensive transboundary cooperation appears desirable. The ultimate goal would be the establishment of "international parks." The Federation of Nature and National Parks of Europe supports these efforts. Such support is expressed in its slogan "Conservation without Frontiers." The prime objective of the federation is "to foster and promote national park ideals by seeking to strengthen and enhance the European network of protected areas" (Clark, 1993, p. 9).

One example of transfrontier cooperation is the management agreement between Mercantour National Park (France) and Argentera Regional Park (Italy). Cooperation in a less formalized fashion exists between other parks across international boundaries (e.g., the Swiss National Park and the Italian Stelvio National Park; the Slovenian Triglav National Park and the Italian Alpi Giulie Nature Park). Moreover, the recently established transboundary Neusiedler See (Ferto Tava) National Park located in eastern Austria and western Hungary could be a milestone in the creation of European international parks.

Figure 23.2
Sustainable tourism in a high Alpine environment. (Courtesy of Nationalparkverwaltung Salzburg.)

HOHE TAUERN NATIONAL PARK: AN EXAMPLE OF TRIPARTITE COOPERATION AMONG AUSTRIAN *LÄNDER*

In October 1971, the Austrian provinces of Carinthia, Salzburg, and Tyrol signed an agreement in the Carinthian resort of Heiligenblut with the objective of establishing the Hohe Tauern National Park "for the benefit of the population, for the use of science, and for the promotion of the economy for the future" (Katschthaler, 1994, p. 10). Because the issues of nature protection and national parks fall under the jurisdiction of the *länder*, the legislative framework and implementation of the national park were carried out by the *länder*. Carinthia passed the national park legislation in 1981 and designated a region on the south side of the Hohe Tauern massif as a national park (see Figure 23.3). Salzburg and Tyrol followed in 1983 and 1992, respectively (see Table 23.3).

The considerable time lag between the so-called *Heiligenblut Agreement* of 1971 and the establishment of the different sections of the national park between 1983 and 1992 reflects the rather thorny road taken toward the realization of the first Austrian national park. Foremost were the varying interests of the hydroelectric lobby (which sought to fully exploit the considerable water resources of this mountain region), tourism (with its specific interest in developing the potential of ski tourism), and property owners and communities (who feared a curtailment of economic opportunities). These divergent interests slowed implementation.

The resistance was gradually overcome by (1) creating awareness among the commu-

TABLE 23.3
Hohe Tauern National Park: Chronology of Development

Year	Square Miles (Square Kilometers)	Region
Carinthia		
1981	72 (186)	Glockner and Schober Mountains
1986	72 (186)	Ankogel Mountain
Total	144 (372) 50% of the originally planned area	
Salzburg		
1983	257 (667)	Reichenspitz, Venediger, Granatspitz, Glockner Mountain, Goldberg Mountain
1991	53 (157)	Ankogel Mountain
Total	310 (804) 70% of the originally planned area	
Tyrol		
1992	235 (610)	Lasörling, Rieserferner, Venediger, Granatspitz, Glockner Mountain, Schober Mountain
Total	689/1786 86% of the originally planned area	

Source: Stotter (1994).

TABLE 23.4
Hohe Tauern National Park Zones

Länder	Core Zone, Square Miles (Square Kilometers)	Outer Zone, Square Miles (Square Kilometers)	Special Protection Zone, Square Miles (Square Kilometers)	Total[a] Square Miles (Square Kilometers)
Carinthia	103 (264) 71%	28 (72) 19%	14 (37) 10%	145 (372) 100%
Salzburg	208 (533) 66%	104 (266) 33%	2 (5) 1%	315 (804) 100%
Tyrol	135 (350) 57%	103 (260) 43%	0 (0) 0%	238 (610) 100%
Total[a]	448 (1,147) 64%	235 (598) 34%	16 (42) 2%	698 (1,786) 100%

[a] The sum of the zones and the sum of the länder may differ slightly from the totals shown in the last row and the last column due to errors in rounding during conversion.
Source: Salzburger Institut für Raumordnung und Wohnen (1993).

nities through creating awareness that the establishment of a national park did not necessarily mean economic sacrifices, (2) growing skepticism towards further expansion of ski tourism infrastructure, especially for glacier skiing, (3) widespread resistance against further proliferation of dams and reservoirs, and (4) a change in the political climate within the *länder*.

Between 1981 and 1992, the Hohe Tauern National Park increased in size from 72 square miles (186 square kilometers) to nearly 690 square miles (1786 square kilometers), making it by far the largest national park in the Alps. Of this total area, 315 square miles (804 square kilometers) are located in Salzburg, 238 square miles (610 square kilometers) in Tyrol, and 145 square miles (372 square kilometers) in Carinthia (see Table 23.4). In total, 29 communities have at least some of their municipal land located within the Hohe Tauern National Park (13 in Salzburg, 10 in Tyrol, and 6 in Carinthia).

In 1991, the combined population of these communities amounted to 56,541, with 55.2 percent (31,224 persons) in Salzburg, 30.6 percent (17,289 persons) in Tyrol, and 14.2 percent (8028 persons) in Carinthia (see Table 23.5). The functional orientation of these communities varies considerably, ranging from villages where agriculture is still an important economic activity (e.g., Winklern in Carinthia) to famous spas and resorts (e.g., Bad Gastein in Salzburg or Heiligenblut in Carinthia). Generally, agriculture is declining in importance, and most communities now rely on tourism.

Location and Geographical Identity of Hohe Tauern National Park The Hohe Tauern National Park, which is located in the heart of Alpine Austria, overlaps the boundaries of the provinces of Carinthia, Salzburg, and Tyrol. The Hohe Tauern, one of the major mountain massifs of the Eastern Alps, forms a watershed of principal river systems. To the north, the Salzach Valley is the major settlement area and the principal west–east transportation axis of the region. To the south, in Carinthia, the drainage system feeds into the Möll and Drau rivers.

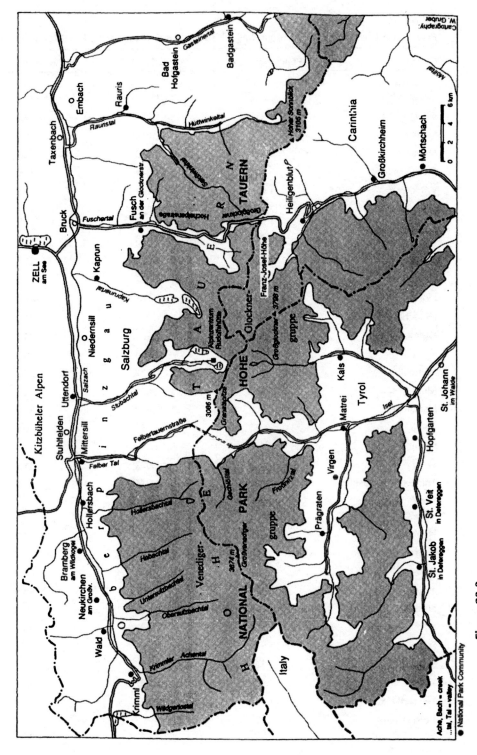

Figure 23.3
Hohe Tauern National Park, Austria.

457

TABLE 23.5
Population Change in the Communities of Hohe Tauern National Park, 1951–1991

Community	Population 1951	Population 1991	% Change 1951–1991
Carinthia			
Grosskirchheim	1,326	1,604	21.0
Heiligenblut	1,211	1,259	4.0
Mallnitz	1,126	1,014	(9.9)
Malta	1,463	2,080	42.2
Mörtschach	858	944	10.0
Winklern	1,020	1,127	10.5
Six communities	7,004	8,028	14.6
Salzburg			
Bad Gastein	5,048	5,662	12.2
Bramberg	2,418	3,658	51.3
Fusch	774	771	(0.4)
Hollersbach	803	1,164	45.0
Hüttschlag	690	906	31.3
Kaprun	2,138	2,901	35.7
Krimml	657	858	30.6
Mittersill	3,155	5,427	72.0
Muhr	718	673	(6.3)
Neukirchen	1,800	2,479	37.8
Rauris	2,261	2,957	30.8
Uttendorf	2,415	2,746	13.7
Wald	775	1,022	31.9
Thirteen communities	23,652	31,224	32.0
Tyrol			
Dölsach	1,482	2,079	40.3
Hopfgarten	816	912	11.8
Iselsberg-Stronach	395	505	27.8
Kals	1,082	1,312	21.3
Matrei	3,104	4,621	48.9
Nussdorf-Debant	842	2,825	235.5
Prägraten	906	1,237	36.5
St. Jakob	914	1,027	12.4
St. Veit	764	784	2.6
Virgen	1,275	1,987	55.8
Ten communities	11,580	17,289	49.3
Vorfeldregion			
Bad Hofgastein	4,000	6,085	52.1

TABLE 23.5
(Continued)

Community	Population 1951	Population 1991	% Change 1951–1991
Bruck	3,258	3,926	20.5
Dorfgastein	1,143	1,481	29.6
Grossarl	2,326	3,276	40.8
Lend	2,253	1,633	(27.5)
Niedernsill	1,365	2,085	52.7
Piesendorf	1,946	2,997	54.0
Stuhlfelden	990 ·	1,388	40.2
Taxenbach	2,579	2,966	15.0
Nine communities	19,860	25,837	30.1

Sources: Barnick (1991); Fally (1994).

Hohe Tauern National Park (see Figure 23.3) is particularly well known for its high mountain scenery, with the Grossglockner (12,470 feet; 3800 meters) located in Carinthia forming the highest peak in Austria (see Figure 23.4). The Hohe Tauern also represents one of the largest glaciated areas of the Eastern Alps, with the Pasterze forming the largest valley glacier in the country. Its diversity of natural features renders Hohe Tauern as a representative yet unique mountain region within Austria.

The park displays significant altitudinal differentiation. The range in altitude from less than 3000 feet (900 meters) in the major valleys to over 13,000 feet (4000 meters) at the highest peaks has resulted in pronounced altitudinal belts of natural environments

Figure 23.4
Grossglockner Peak, Austria. (Courtesy of Nationalparkverwaltung Salzburg.)

(e.g., climate and vegetation zones) and human landscapes (e.g., zones of agricultural activity, settlement regions) (Stocker, 1993, p. 63). Although the marked relief gives rise to pronounced gradational processes (e.g., landslides, flash floods, avalanches), it has some advantages. For instance, the area is well endowed with hydroelectric resources, impressive scenery, and steep slopes attractive to experienced skiers.

The glaciers and other aspects of glacial and fluvioglacial morphology are another significant feature. Glaciated areas still cover some 67 square miles (173 square kilometers), or about 10 percent of the total area of the Hohe Tauern National Park. During the summer, the Pasterze glacier has become one of the most noted mountain tourist attractions of Austria, a development that was greatly enhanced by the construction of the Grossglockner Road which allows motorists to drive to the immediate vicinity of the glacier. This has led to the development of mass tourism facilities, such as large restaurants, extensive parking spaces [including a parkade at an elevation of some 8200 feet or 2500 meters (see Figure 23.5)], and even an "elevator" that transports tourists from the viewing platform to the edge of the glacier. Such developments explain why the Grossglockner Road area has been excluded from the territory of the national park.

The Hohe Tauern is a region with a long history of human settlement and resource utilization dating back to the Neolithic period (about 3000–1800 B.C.). Over a long period of time, the abundance of mineral resources (primarily copper and gold) and the transportation function of the mountain passes linking Central Europe to Mediterranean Europe were economically important for the region's inhabitants. This gave the region a reputation and strategic importance that extended well beyond the Hohe Tauern. Initially, the preferred settlement areas were the relatively dry and warm lower south-facing slopes of the valleys where extensive forest-clearing took place. In addition, farmers used the grassland areas above the forest line for summer pastures.

Since the sixteenth century, the Hohe Tauern, similar to most other Alpine areas, has experienced a decline in its major economic activities, along with the associated

Figure 23.5
Franz-Josephs-Hohe, Grossglockner High Mountain Road, Austria. (Courtesy of C. Stadel.)

decay of many features of the cultural landscape. There was a significant abandonment of farms, mostly because of deteriorating climatic conditions. Most of the mines were closed because of the exhaustion of the ore bodies, new competition from overseas mines, and advancing glaciers. In addition, new trans-Alpine roads bypassed the Tauern region.

Beginning in the mid-nineteenth century, but more evident during the twentieth century, the economy of the Hohe Tauern region recovered. The region began increasingly to rely on tourism. New employment opportunities created by tourism helped to counteract the general trend of out-migration from the agriculturally oriented mountain areas to urban centers.

The growth of mass tourism during the second half of the twentieth century, and its ubiquitous penetration into virtually every community and mountain valley, and even to glacier and summit regions, began to threaten the ecological stability of the Alpine environment, as well as the autochthonous heritage and culture of the population. Hence, the need to protect the beauty and integrity of the unique mountain landscapes and their ecology was recognized by a growing number of individuals, groups, and political authorities. One result was the eventual founding of Hohe Tauern National Park.

Challenges Associated with the Establishment of Hohe Tauern National Park

The establishment of Hohe Tauern National Park was complicated and difficult to achieve. The designated region included not only the territory of the three *länder* with their respective legislative controls, but also included a large number of communities and a multitude of property owners, each of whom had divergent interests that needed to be addressed.

The contrast with many other national parks is reflected in its land use patterns. A large proportion of the land is still used for agricultural purposes, albeit mainly in the form of extensively used high mountain pastures and meadows for haymaking (see Figure 23.6). If the area adjacent to the park (*vorfeldzone*) is included, a four-part subdivision

Figure 23.6
Traditional agricultural mountain landscape, Hohe Tauern National Park, Austria. (Courtesy of Nationalparkverwaltung Salzburg.)

of distinct landscapes and land uses can be distinguished: (1) the intensively utilized, multifunctional, and permanently occupied settlement zone of the valley floors and lower slopes that are characterized by rather high population densities; (2) the forest belt at intermediate elevations; (3) the zone of high mountain pastures (*almen*); and (4) the largely unspoiled rock/debris and glacier zone.

Within the permanently settled areas of the major valley regions (e.g., the Salzach Valley in Salzburg), population densities may exceed 500 people per square mile (200 people per square kilometer) in many parts. If the seasonal influx of tourists is included, densities of close to 3900 people per square mile (1500 people per square kilometer) may be reached. Outstanding examples of such seasonal peak densities are the Gastein Valley, the region around Zell am See in Salzburg, and the upper Möll Valley around Heiligenblut (see Figure 23.7).

Figure 23.7
Möll river valley and community of Heili-genblut, Carinthia, Austria. (Courtesy of C. Stadel.)

These regions have also witnessed the largest growth in residential population and dramatic increases in the number of buildings, mainly in the form of secondary residences for the leisure population (Salzburger Institut für Raumordnung und Wohnen 1993, p. 38). Not only do population and building densities exert substantial pressure on the valley floors, they also create significant ramifications within the adjacent national park region.

There is widespread agreement that the Alpine region should fulfill the functions associated with ecological protection, economic development, and recreation and tourism. Nonetheless, it is also obvious that a balance among these three overlapping roles is difficult to achieve. The economic and recreation functions represent serious threats to the ecology and culture (Kaspar, 1992, p. 69). Moreover, it is also recognized that tourism can only be maintained if the important potential of nature and culture can be sustained. This is possible only if the Alps continue to be the living space of an active and economically secure population.

Given that the Hohe Tauern has been settled and its resources exploited for many centuries, the objective of a national park in this region could not have been solely environmental protection or the "renaturalization" of the landscape. Instead, the challenge was to establish a careful balance between the goals of preservation, providing the basis for a sustainable livelihood for residents, and rendering this unique heritage region accessible to tourists and scientists.

Despite these generally accepted objectives, a number of externally promoted, and probably environmentally harmful, development projects have generated considerable controversy. The most debated issues in this region revolved around future energy demands and the further promotion of tourism, especially in the form of mass skiing on glaciers. Glacier skiing, facilitated by cable cars and ski lifts, is enjoying considerable popularity. On the other hand, skiable glaciers for mass tourism are not abundant. Therefore, some communities in the Hohe Tauern region considered the development of glaciers for skiing as a potential bonanza. However, development of glacier skiing may impair the natural environment of the glaciers through the installation of services and infrastructure (e.g., restaurants, cable car structures). Moreover, this sort of development also entails building ancillary structures and facilities in adjacent regions. Most notable is the building or improvement of access roads, large parking areas, and the grooming of ski runs.

Even without glacier skiing, the impact of tourism has been considerable. Tourism appears in different forms and spatial frameworks, which generate distinct forms of impact. For example, summer mass tourism converges on the spectacular Krimml Waterfalls in the province of Salzburg and on the Grossglockner High Alpine Road. At the Krimml Waterfalls, some 700,000 visitors are recorded annually on average during the period from May to October. On peak days in July and August, between 8000 and 10,000 people may visit the Falls (see Figure 23.8).

On the Grossglockner Road, 325,000 trips were registered in 1992, about 40 percent of which were bus trips, with a total of well over one million visitors (Salzburger Institut für Raumordnung und Wohnen, 1993, pp. 101–102). The Kaprun dammed lakes and the power plant, as well as the so-called "Glacier Express" to the summer skiing area of the Kitzsteinhorn (both located in the province of Salzburg), are other major tourist attractions. These peak flows of tourists result in high traffic densities on the major access

Figure 23.8
Mass tourism at the Krimml Waterfalls, Salz-
burg, Austria. (Courtesy of C. Stadel.)

highways and roads. They also generate negative environmental consequences (e.g., air pollution, garbage disposal).

Moreover, in addition to the well-documented problems associated with the mass Alpine ski industry, other touristic and/or sports activities have also become the focus of debate in terms of their potential incompatibility with the goals of a national park.

Recreational aviation, for example, causes some concern. Legally, motorized flights in the Hohe Tauern National Park below an altitude of about 16,400 feet (5000 meters) above sea level are only allowed with a special permit. This permit is generally restricted to necessary transport flights (e.g., to Alpine pastures or mountain huts), rescue operations, or documentation and scientific purposes. The Austrian Civil Aviation Authority, as a federal institution, has an unrestricted right to use the airspace at its discretion. However, although difficult to prove or to pursue through legal channels, numerous infractions have been reported. Furthermore, flight operators argue that the *Austrian Civil Aviation Law* does not contain a clause about a minimum flying height (Nowotny, 1994, p. 60).

Modern sports, such as mountain biking, rafting, hang gliding, or paragliding, are also potential sources of conflict. Such activities have been criticized by hikers, hunters, and mountain farmers as being nuisance factors and/or harmful to the environment (Nowotny, 1994, p. 63).

Hunting represents another issue. Regulations for hunting wild animals are covered in principle by the hunting laws of the *länder*, not by the *National Park Law*. However, in 1993, Salzburg amended its hunting laws to place a stronger emphasis on ecological considerations, especially in terms of providing more effective protection for endangered animals in specific regions. Nevertheless, the existing hunting laws, in the opinion of many ecologists, have not been satisfactorily harmonized with the objectives of a national park. Similarly, it has been argued that sport fishing in the national park should be further restricted or even prohibited (Nowotny, 1994, pp. 67–68).

Because of its rich variety of minerals and crystals, the region has attracted the interest of collectors for a long time. Mountain farmers have earned incomes from collecting and selling minerals. However, increasing numbers of tourists have been collecting minerals. Under the *National Park Law*, the commercial mining of stones is prohibited. In the core zone of the park, only small pieces that have not been extracted from the bedrock can be taken (Nowotny, 1994, pp. 60–61). In light of these potential problems, it would appear that regulations governing the protection of plant life are now of only minor importance.

National Park Laws and Zoning Regulations In the national park laws of the three *länder*, an attempt was made to uphold the principles and objectives of nature conservation while at the same time respecting the existing land ownership pattern, cultural identity, and economic interests of the resident population. However, the fact that large areas of the national park are owned by the Federal Department of Forestry complicates the issue. For instance, forestry and hunting rights on federal land contradict the goals of a national park, but these activities have been traditionally carried out on the lands of the Federal Department of Forestry.

The *Salzburg National Park Law* of 1983 is based on the following general objectives: (1) The region should be preserved in its beauty and originality, (2) the indigenous animals and plants and their habitats should be protected and preserved, and (3) the national park should facilitate the provision of impressive experiences to a wide range of people.

The legislation emphasized the adoption of a partnership among the communities, property owners, and the resident population. This concept of ecorealism attempts to respect the traditions, needs, and aspirations of the local population, while at the same time adhering to ecologically sound objectives and measures. To a large extent, this has contributed to the establishment of a climate of mutual trust and the acceptance and support of the park by the vast majority of the population (Katschthaler, 1994, pp. 10–11).

In Tyrol, the *National Park Law* was passed in 1991 and was implemented on January 1, 1992. In conjunction with the establishment of the national park, a regional development program for the communities of the national park was initiated. The major objectives were to support peripheral areas where factors relating to isolation and economic deprivation required special measures for the improvement of work conditions and the quality of life. The *National Park Law* and the regional development program attempt to arrive at a reasonable compromise between the objective of protecting and utilizing resources within the "living space, the economic realm, and the tourism region of Eastern Tyrol" (Barnick, 1991, p. 7).

In Carinthia, the *National Park Law* was passed in 1983, with later amendments in 1986 and 1992. It was guided by the following premises (Kärntner Bergwacht, 1994, p. 1). The area should (1) comprise impressive, diverse, and/or historically significant landscapes that are representative of Austria, (2) not be profoundly impaired by human activity and, to a large extent, should maintain its original character, (3) contain ecosystems of a particular landscape identity and of specific scientific interest, and (4) not be small (its minimum extension, however, was not precisely defined).

To more easily accommodate the different functions of the national park region and reduce the conflicts of interest, the stakeholders agreed that Hohe Tauern National Park should be subdivided into three distinct zones (see Table 23.4) as described below.

THE CORE ZONE (KERNZONE) The main function of this zone of approximately 448 square miles (1147 square kilometers) is nature conservation and minimizing human impacts. It includes the highest and most remote areas outside the zone of permanent settlement and contiguous land use. Areas designated as core zones are totally, or largely, preserved in their original state and the natural landscape is protected for scientific or cultural reasons.

THE OUTER ZONE (AUSSENZONE) The principal objective in this zone of 235 square miles (598 square kilometers) is the maintenance of cultural landscapes (primarily those that have been shaped by mountain farmers over many centuries), the preservation of native plants and animals, and the promotion of environmentally compatible forms of tourism. This zone comprises high mountain pastures and forests. Prohibited, or at least subject to special approval procedures, are activities or measures that have the potential to persistently or profoundly impair the landscape identity or beauty and/or its recreational and ecological balance.

SPECIAL PROTECTED AREAS (SONDERSCHUTZGEBIETE) These areas, which cover only 16 square miles (42 square kilometers), include sections that are of outstanding beauty, have special scientific interest, and/or are particularly valuable from an ecological perspective. In these areas, interference with the natural or ecological balance and the impairment of the landscape are prohibited, or are at least subject to special approval.

In addition, a number of communities that are not within the actual boundaries of the national park, but are adjacent to and functionally closely linked to the park, have been designated as being part of a so-called adjacent zone (*vorfeldzone*).

HOW MUCH TOURISM IS SUSTAINABLE IN A NATIONAL PARK? EXPERIENCES AND LESSONS FROM AUSTRIA

There is widespread agreement that tourism in national parks should be geared towards "gentle tourism," "intelligent tourism," "ecotourism,"[7] "socially responsible tourism," or "sustainable tourism." This type of tourism should not threaten the ecological integrity of the area. Moreover, it should respect the social traditions of local populations while also securing the economic future of the region.

The following objectives for tourism in national parks were highlighted in a book published by the Austrian Society of Ecology (Christian and Hubinek, 1994, p. 8): (1) adaptation of tourism to the principles of nature protection, (2) quality tourism instead of mass tourism, (3) emphasis on nature experiences and education instead of artificial events alien to the culture of the region, and (4) economic support for the local population under conditions of optimal utilization of the available resource base, rather than profit maximization.

The implementation of these objectives can be facilitated through strategies geared towards the education and guidance of tourists, voluntary limitation of activities, and a respect for nature. The channeling of visitor flows into specific areas and careful management of sites of tourist concentration are critical.

Carefully planned and implemented zoning regulations in national parks are likely to minimize potential conflicts. Thus, in the case of Hohe Tauern, there is a decline in visitation as one moves away from the major attractions of the Krimml Waterfalls, the Grossglockner Mountain Road, or the Pasterze glacier. Experiences from many national parks have also shown that a large number of restrictions or bans are annoying to tourists and may even be counterproductive.

Planning measures and implementation strategies relating to the environment and tourist activities in a national park do not exist in an idealized, interest-free space. In referring to Hohe Tauern National Park, Rupitsch (1994, pp. 47–49) underlines the century-old traditions of the resident population and the specific legal framework of existing land titles and permitted uses, as well as the importance of the history of alpinism with its old established network of trails and mountain huts. He proposes an improvement to the quality of existing Alpine infrastructures instead of the further proliferation of additional huts, trails, and other amenities. He further emphasizes the need to address the unsolved problem of motorized visitor access. This suggests a need to reduce private vehicle traffic in favor of more environmentally compatible public transportation systems (e.g., shuttle buses). The latter could be achieved by limiting private vehicle access, restricting parking areas in the national park to public transportation, and establishing additional parking spaces for private cars outside national parks.

CONCLUSION AND OUTLOOK

In spite of its shortcomings and remaining problems, the creation of Hohe Tauern National Park has evidenced a number of positive consequences. Of utmost importance has been the conservation of one of the most outstanding regions of the Eastern Alps and legal protection from potential large-scale development and ecological destruction. It has also provided three benefits. First, scientific disciplines are provided with a unique opportunity to conduct research in a largely unspoiled natural and cultural environment. Second, the general public has access to the recreational potential of the region based on a "gentle" form of tourism. They also have the opportunity to learn about the natural and cultural heritage of the region through a range of educational services. Finally, the local population has been provided with opportunities for employment and income, thereby improving the chances for a sustainable living space and economic future.

On the other hand, the two major functions of the national park—nature protection and human utilization—have frequently been sources of divergence and conflict rather than convergence and harmony. The creation of the national park has only been accepted by the population and the politicians on the basis of compromises that, at times, went beyond the spirit and function of a genuine national park. Nonetheless, one should not forget that national park communities have benefited economically from government incentives, particularly in the outer zone where environmental protection has a relatively weak legal acceptance. Environmentalists have argued that, to obtain international recognition as a national park by the IUCN, a stricter legal adherence to the principles of nature protection, even in the park's outer zone, has to be spelled out unequivocally (Nowotny, 1994, p. 71).

Conversely, officials of the Hohe Tauern National Park have proposed new conservation and management criteria that, in their opinion, more adequately take into account the reality of European countries. They believe that, through zoning, an appropriate meshing and interaction of wilderness areas with adjacent seminatural cultural landscapes should be achieved. This will require the involvement of all levels of government, as well as compensation to owners of private land where appropriate.

Within the spatial and cultural context of Europe, the total protection of all national park areas from any form of human impact is impossible, but the legal and real guarantees for the maintenance or fostering of certain ecological standards are indispensable. These efforts have the best chance for success if they are linked to an effective program of environmental education and public awareness. Thus, the objectives of Hohe Tauern National Park should (1) ensure a high level of acceptance of the park among the population, (2) strengthen proven successes, and (3) continuously strive to reach goals that have not yet been attained (Kremser, 1994b, p. 155). Support for these efforts has to come from individual landowners, the communities, the *länder*, and the federal government.

Sustainable forms of tourism in the Alps are necessary alternatives to the exploitation of the resources by mass tourism. There is substantial evidence to support the contention that these developments have led to an impairment of the natural environments and traditional landscapes and, as a consequence, have also reduced the recreational value and tourist appeal of some Alpine regions.

National parks and their adjacent regions can become pioneers in adopting a new form of tourism that is based not only on relatively unspoiled, diversified, and attractive natural environments, but also on the integrity and appeal of cultural heritage. National parks should prohibit highly consumptive forms of resource utilization "that rest principally on the inclination toward power and domination," and focus more on forms that stimulate a "reflective and contemplative recreation" (Sax, 1980, p. 105). In conclusion, it can be stated that (Sax, 1980, 111–112)

. . . parks are places where recreation reflects the aspirations of a free and independent people. They are places where no one else prepares entertainment for the visitor, predetermines his responses, or tells him what to do. In a national park the visitor is on his own, setting an agenda for himself, discovering what is interesting, going at his own pace. . . . parks are places that have not been tamed, contemporary symbols to men and women who are themselves ready to resist being tamed into passivity. . . . In the national parks the visitor learns that satisfaction is not correlated to the rate at which he expends resources, but that just the opposite is true. . . . parks promote intensive experience, rather than intensive use. . . . The quantity of resources the visitor needs to consume shrinks as he discovers the secret of intensiveness of experience, and his capacity for intensive satisfaction depends on what is in his own head.

NOTES

1. See Chapters 4, 5, 7, 8, 17, 18, and 22 for more discussion relating to the principles of sustainable tourism and sustainable tourism development.
2. See Chapters 9 and 22 for additional discussion relating to the concept of carrying capacity and limits of acceptable change.
3. See Chapter 22 for additional discussion relating to the notion of "loving resources to death."
4. See Chapters 8–11 and 14 for comprehensive discussion relating to tourism's role as an economic regenerator.
5. The IUCN is now referred to as the World Conservation Union.
6. See Chapters 5, 9, 11, 12, and 14–19 for additional discussion relating to community attitudes and community-based planning and development principles and practices.
7. See Chapters 15 and 20 for additonal discussions pertaining to ecotourism.

REFERENCES

Barnick, H. 1991. *Entwicklungsprogramm Nationalpark Hohe Tauern*. Innsbruck: Amt der Tiroler Landesregierung.

Broggi, M.F. 1993. *Aufbruchstimmung für Weitere Nationalpark in den Alpen?* CIPRA (Commission de Protection de la Région Alpine).

Broggi, M.F. and U. Tödter. 1994. Nationalparks in den Alpen gestern–heute–morgen. In R. Floimair (ed.), *Umdenken. Zehn Jahre Nationalpark Hohe Tauern in Salzburg—eine Bestandsaufnahme, Salzburger Diskussionen*. Schriftenreihe des Landespressebüros, pp. 168–176.

Christian, R. and M. Hubinek. 1994. Vorwort. In R. Christian (ed.), *Nationalpark und Tourismus—ein Widerspruch?*, Vol. 8. Wien: Österreichische Gesellschaft für Ökologie.

Clark, A. 1993. Conservation without frontiers: the guiding principle of the Federation of Nature and National Parks of Europe. In Bundesministerium für Umwelt, Jugend und Familie (eds.), *Nationalparks in Österreich*. Vienna, pp. 9–11.

Czerny, W. 1994. Planung–werbung–attraktionen: konzepte für eine nationalparkregion. In R. Christian (ed.), *Nationalpark und Tourismus—ein Widerspruch?* Vol. 8 Wien: Österreichische Gesellschaft für Ökologie, pp. 52–54.

Fally, W. 1994. Die region "nationalpark und vorfeld." In R. Floimair (eds.), *Umdenken Zehn Nationalpark. Hohe Tauern in Salzburg—eine Bestandsaufnahme, Salzburger Diskussionen*. Schriftenreihe des Landespresseburäs, pp. 107–120.

Kärntner Bergwacht. 1994. *Kärntner Nationalparkrecht*. Klagenfurt.

Kaspar, C. 1992. Umweltrelevante aspekte der tourismusentwicklung im Alpenraum. In Hannes Flühler et al. (eds.), *Die Alpen—Naturpark oder Opfer des künftigen Europas?* Basel: Birkhäuser, pp. 69–75.

Katschthaler, H. 1994. Zehn jahre einsatz für die natur. In R. Floimair (ed.), *Umdenkan. Zehn Jahre Nationalpark Hŏhe Tauern in Salzburg—eine Bestandsaufnahme, Salzburger Diskussionen.* Schriftenreihe des Landespressebüros, pp. 9–17.

Kremser, H. 1994a. Besucherlenkung im Nationalpark Hohe Tauern-Salzburg. In R. Christian (ed.), *Nationalpark und Tourismus—ein Widerspruch?* Wien: Österreichische Gesellschaft für Ökologie, pp. 45–46.

Kremser, H. 1994b. Zehn jahre unbedingt—für den Nationalpark Hohe Tauern. In R. Floimair (ed.), *Umdenken. Zehn Jahre Nationalpark Hohe Tauern in Salzburg—eine Bestandsaufnahme, Salzburger Diskussionen.* Schriftenreihe des Landespressebüros, pp. 150–167.

Mathieson, A. and G. Wall. 1982. *Tourism: Economic, Physical and Social Impacts.* London: Longman.

Murphy, P.E. 1994. Tourism and sustainable development. In W.F. Theobald (ed.), *Global Tourism: The Next Decade.* Oxford: Butterworth–Heinemann, pp. 274–290.

Nowotny, G. 1994. *Naturschutz.* In R. Floimair (ed.), *Umdenken. Zehn Jahre Nationalpark Hohe Tauern in Salzburg—eine Bestandsaufnahme, Salzburger Diskussionen.* Schriftenreihe des Landespressebüros, pp. 52–71.

Poore, D. (ed.). 1992. *Guidelines for Mountain Protected Areas.* Gland: International Union for the Conservation of Nature (IUCN).

Rupitsch, P. 1994. Besucherlenkung im Nationalpark Hohe Tauern-Kärnten. In R. Christian (ed.), *Nationalpark und Tourismus—ein Widerspruch?* Wien: Österreichische Gesellschaft für Ökologie, pp. 47–49.

Salzburger Institut für Raumordnung und Wohnen (SIR). 1993. *Entwicklung- und Förderungskonzept für die Nationalpark Hohe Tauern Vorfeldregion im Bundesland Salzburg. Teil I. Bestandsaufnahme und Analyse.* Salzburg: SIR.

Sax, Joseph L. 1980. *Mountains Without Handrails: Reflections on National Parks.* Ann Arbor, MI: The University of Michigan Press.

Schürrer, W. 1994. Wie attraktiv sind Nationalparks für die Tourismuswirtschaft? In R. Christian (ed.). *Nationalpark und Tourismus—ein Widerspruch?* Wien: Österreichische Gesellschaft für Ökologie, pp. 13–16.

Stadel, C. and J.C. Everitt. 1995. *Sustainable Micropolitan Communities in the Canadian Prairies.* Paper presented at the Fourth International Symposium of the Institute for Canadian Studies, Augsburg.

Stocker, E. 1993. Geomorphologische fragestellungenim bereich des Nationalparks Hohe Tauern, *Salzburger Geographische Materialien,* 19, 63–65.

Stotter, H. 1994. Ökologie kontra Ökonomie—der sieg der vernunft. In R. Floimair (ed.). *Umdenken. Zehn Jahre Nationalpark Hohe Tauern—eine Bestandsaufnahme, Salzburger Diskussionen,* 19, Schriftenreihe des Landespressebüros, pp. 26–37.

Williams, P.W. and A. Gill. 1994. Tourism carrying capacity management issues. In W.F. Theobald (ed.), *Global Tourism: The Next Decade.* Oxford: Butterworth–Heinemann, pp. 174–187.

❡ | PROBLEM SOLVING AND DISCUSSION ACTIVITIES

1. In what ways is the concept of sustainability related to the notion of carrying capacity? Is there concrete evidence of such a relationship?
2. Comment on the following statement by Barkham (1979 in Murphy, 1994, p.

282): "Carrying capacity is a phrase delightful in its simplicity, complex in its meaning, and difficult to define . . . ." Conduct a review of current literature to provide a justification for your comments.

3. How might the notion of carrying capacity contradict goals for maximizing growth? Should carrying capacity be applied in its strictest sense if, indeed, it would inhibit the growth of an area, especially an area characterized by sensitive natural and cultural resources?

4. Does a contradiciton exist between national parks and the pursuit of tourism? Draw upon the experience of at least three national parks located anywhere in the world to support your response.

5. It would appear that, despite the existence of regulations and legislation in protected areas, activities may still occur that degrade the environment and even the experiences of people using these areas. Why might this be the case? Is there anything that can be done to mitigate such problems? Cite specific examples of successful strategies and enforcement within national parks around the world.

6. What issues did the three Austrian provinces face in developing Hohe Tauern National Park? To what extent are these issues pertinent to the development and evolution of national parks in your region?

7. Comment on and justify your reaction to the following statements: (a) mass tourism is based on reckless, materialistic, and technological developments, a rejection of traditional ways of life, and acculturation to modernization and the various expressions of urbanization and (b) mass tourism has led to an impairment of the natural environments and traditional landscapes of tourist regions and, as a consequence, has also reduced the recreational value and the tourist appeal of regions.

8. It has been suggested that national park authorities should prohibit highly consumptive forms of resource utilization and should focus more on forms that stimulate a reflective and contemplative recreation. Do such forms of tourism exist? Elaborate and provide examples.

24

Understanding Visitor Experiences as a Basis for Product Development

ASEB GRID ANALYSIS AND THE BLACK COUNTRY MUSEUM IN THE WEST MIDLANDS OF ENGLAND

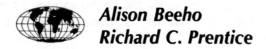

Alison Beeho
Richard C. Prentice

♪|KEY LEARNING POINTS

- Since the core of the tourism product is the experience it offers, attractions must pay more attention to offering an experience that satisfies visitors' needs, wants, and expectations.

- ASEB (activities, settings, experiences, beliefs) grid analysis is a new form of analysis that can be applied to address the experiential core of attractions. It provides a consumer-oriented approach to tourism product development.

- The traditional role of museums in Great Britain has changed from that of formal education to one wherein museums must now be seen by visitors as providing a participatory experience that is entertaining as well as educational. The nature of the experience will ultimately be affected by the interpretive methods adopted by attraction managers.

- Change must be viewed as continuous. Responding to visitor needs to provide a worthwhile experience that attracts and holds an audience, as well as encourages them to visit again, has become the basis for gaining a sustainable competitive edge, expecially in situations where the supply of museums or other attractions is growing faster than demand.

INTRODUCTION

This chapter introduces a new form of analysis, namely, ASEB grid analysis. The Black Country Museum in the West Midlands of England is used to illustrate the potential application of this form of analysis for the purpose of product development. ASEB grid analysis combines the elements of SWOT analysis (strengths, weaknesses, opportunities, threats) and the levels of the Manning–Haas–Driver–Brown demand hierarchy (activities, settings, experiences, benefits) and defines them conceptually as a grid or matrix.

SWOT analysis has proven useful as a tool in the strategic management of both not-for-profit and commercial organizations. ASEB grid analysis is proposed as a more effective consumer-oriented approach to marketing research within organizations that provide experiential products (e.g., museums). It emphasizes the experiences and benefits gained by visitors. These experiences and benefits are defined by museum visitors in their own words through qualitative in-depth interviews.

ASEB grid analysis is demonstrated through an examination of the experiences and benefits (or psychological outcomes) gained by visitors to the Black Country Museum, a museum that interprets social and industrial history. The case study investigates whether visitors gained the experiences and benefits they wanted or expected. Moreover, it examines whether museum staff's perceptions of the experiences and benefits gained through various site interpretation activities correspond to those actually sought or received by visitors. Optimizing visitor satisfaction levels by providing and maintaining the types of experiences that address the needs and wants of different museum visitors may be the only way that museums will be able to survive changing market forces and be able to retain, and even increase, visitor numbers in the future.

MUSEUMS AND THEIR CHANGING ROLES

Museums are popular tourist and leisure attractions throughout the world. There has been a rapid increase in the number of museums opened in Great Britain since the 1960s. Indeed, by 1990, there were almost 2500 museums in Great Britain, twice as many as in 1960. With increasing public interest in heritage,[1] culture, and history, there has also been unprecedented growth in the number of visits to museums. Approximately 58 percent of the British population visits a museum or art gallery at least once each year (Merriman, 1989). In 1993, the British Tourist Authority (BTA) recorded 79 million visits to museums and art galleries in Great Britain.

Museums have changed noticeably over the last three centuries. Until the sixteenth century, museums tended to comprise privately owned collections that were used by academics for research and studying. However, by the nineteenth century museums began to focus on making collections available to the public (Edson and Dean, 1994) and providing both education and inspiration for their audiences. The educational role of museums continues to change (Vergo, 1989). Contemporary museums interpret the past through the "preservation, articulation and exhibition of artifacts, as symbols of local importance and pride, and as places of education and entertainment" (Prince, 1990). However, they must provide pleasure and excitement in addition to factual information and education.

This change has generally been shaped by market forces and other external factors that have forced museums to adapt to the volatile needs of museum audiences (Edson and Dean, 1994). These factors include (1) economic pressures (i.e., the cost of maintaining collections with limited financial assistance), (2) societal changes (i.e., greater egalitarianism in access to culture and a more mobile society), (3) technological advances (e.g., the ability of television to convey information into people's homes, thereby diminishing the need to visit a museum), and (4) competition from other tourist attractions and leisure time activities. To increase visitation levels and enhance revenue, museums have had to broaden their visitor base and address more closely the needs of potential visitors.

Museum managers have recognized that museums exist to serve the public. Therfore, they have begun to acknowledge the importance of knowing who their visitors are and what they want when planning and designing exhibitions. During the 1980s, many museums in Britain began to offer visitors an involving experience of the past rather than just conventional glass cabinet displays of artifacts. This has led museums into the realm of *experiential consumption* (Lofman, 1991). An experience can be defined as "an event to be described in terms of a sensory, imaginal and affective complex" (Lofman, 1991). Therefore, the elements of experiential consumption include not only the setting, but also consumer thoughts, feelings, expressive behaviors, activities, evaluation, and stimulation through sensation.

Most people perceive their visit to a museum primarily as a social event and, increasingly, as entertainment (Yale, 1991). The delivery of entertaining experiences has been facilitated by the adoption of new technologies originating in North America. Increasingly museum visitors seek an "informed experience," rather than a formal educational trip (Herbert et al., 1989; Uzzell, 1989). It should not be assumed, however, that this will be the case for everyone. Museums must become more market-oriented as opposed to product-oriented (i.e., where the nature of the product is determined by the supply of collections or artifacts available). Market research should provide the basis for tailoring products to satisfy the specific needs, wants, and expectations of many types of actual and potential visitors. A market orientation can provide important insight into what experiences different types of visitors want, how they learn, why they enjoy some exhibits but avoid others, and what contributes to overall satisfaction (or dissatisfaction).

Museum visitors need to have their expectations met, and even raised. They also need to be captivated and to experience an element of surprise. In particular, they must experience opportunities for enrichment, satisfaction, and enjoyment, as well as derive value for money. Therefore, the role of the museum must include the following: (1) stimulating visitors' interests, helping them understand the resource being interpreted, and providing an experience that appeals to their emotions, imagination, and intellect (Middleton, 1990) and (2) providing an experience that is beneficial and encourages as many people of all ages and tastes as possible to visit again.

The modern museum's core product is the experience it provides (Goodall, 1993). Interpretative techniques play a critical role in the delivery of experiential products and, ultimately, in the benefits gained from a museum visit. Interpretation is essentially the process of "packaging and presenting history, by whatever means, to the consumer" (Ashworth, 1990). It involves attracting and holding the attention of visitors through entertainment and education.

Interpretative techniques include live interpretation (e.g., people dressed in period costume "bring the past to life"), dark rides (i.e., the visitor is transported through a scene), interactive displays, and other technology-based formats that create a "hands on" experience. The visitors' personal involvement in an exhibit is useful to encourage not only an understanding of the past, but also a questioning of its meaning for the present. For example, an objective of the Black Country Museum is to encourage ". . . visitors to 'step back in time' . . . to develop an interest not only in the history of the Black

Country, but also in the way people live and work today and in the future" (*Black Country Museum Visitor Guide*, 1994, p. 28).

The behavioral approach to leisure management is grounded in consumer behavior literature. For example, the expectancy theory developed in social psychology (Ajzen and Driver, 1992; Atkinson and Burch, 1972; Fishbein and Ajzen, 1975; Lawler, 1973) suggests that people engage in activities in specific settings to realize a group of psychological outcomes that are known, expected, and valued. People undertake leisure activities that meet certain goals or satisfy certain needs. Manning (1986) also stressed that most human behavior is goal-oriented, or aimed at need satisfaction. However, Stevens (1989) raised concern over museums' apparent neglect of the behavioral approach and questioned whether museum managers are "paying due regard to the needs, demands, aspirations, and sophistications of our visitors."

Indeed, visitor surveys have only recently been recognized as important decision-making tools influencing museum design (Merriman, 1991) and have generally been small scale, implemented with limited resources, and based on unsophisticated methodologies. They have tended to concentrate on a range of visitor characteristics (i.e., demographics and geographical location of visitors). Such research does little to advance the overall understanding of what motivates museum visiting or what contributes to visitor satisfaction.

ASEB GRID ANALYSIS: CONTEMPORARY PERSPECTIVES AND ISSUES

ASEB grid analysis is a new consumer-oriented management tool. Designed specifically to address issues arising from experiential consumption, it represents a refinement of conventional SWOT analysis.[2]

SWOT analysis provides management with the ability to develop strategies to balance controllable (usually internal) and uncontrollable (often external) factors (Holloway and Plant, 1992; Middleton, 1988). It does not, however, focus on visitor experiences and, therefore, tends to lack operational focus. ASEB grid analysis facilitates consumer or market-led product development and promotion at experiential attractions. It will become invaluable as museums and other tourist attractions seek to maintain visitor levels in the market circumstances previously described.

ASEB grid analysis focuses specifically on consumers and analyzes experiences using the visitors' own words and reactions. The grid also supplements the basic sociodemographic analysis that is commonly undertaken at attractions (Wertheim, 1994). Demographic data do not provide the insight into motivations and satisfaction which museum management requires to enhance visitor experiences and satisfaction levels.

ASEB grid analysis facilitates a more consumer-based approach to managing attractions by adding the levels of the Manning–Haas–Driver–Brown demand hierarchy to SWOT analysis. Manning (1986), Haas et al. (1980), and Prentice and Light (1994) extended the behavioral approach (i.e., that most human behavior is goal-oriented or aimed at need satisfaction) to recognize four levels of demand for outdoor recreation. As seen in Table 24.1, the hierarchy identifies demand for a particular leisure activity (Level 1) or the activities provided in a particular recreational setting (Level 2) and links these

TABLE 24.1
The Manning–Haas–Driver–Brown Sequential Hierachy of Demand

Level of Manning–Haas–Driver–Brown Hierarchy of Demand	Example from Manning (1986)	Example from Prentice (1993a)
Level 1: Activities	Wilderness hiking	Visiting heritage attractions
Level 2: Settings		
A. Environmental setting	Rugged terrain	Interesting and pleasurable viewing
B. Social setting	Few people	A place for a family day out
C. Managerial setting	No restrictions	Educational
Level 3: Experiences	Risk taking	Relaxing
	Challenge	Education/information
	Physical exercise	
Level 4: Benefits		
A. Personal	Enhanced self-esteem	Increased knowledge
B. Societal	Increased commitment to conservation	

with the experiences gained in that setting (Level 3) as well as with the ultimate benefits that flow from the satisfying experience (Level 4). In this way, the levels of demand can be ordered into a hierarchy that flows in terms of tangibility or abstractness.

Level 1 focuses on actual demand for specific activities such as wilderness hiking or visiting a museum. This level has been used by the present authors to review the activities undertaken by visitors, their motives, and their perceived satisfaction with the activities undertaken when visiting museums that interpret social and industrial history.

Level 2 comprises various environmental (e.g., a re-created Victorian village setting), social (e.g., a place for a nice family day out), and management (e.g., provision of educational information for visitors) settings in which activities take place, as well as the recreationist's expectations and satisfaction with the settings for the activity being pursued. As such, the setting is both objective and subjective. Since most activities are setting-dependent, activity and setting interact in determining the nature of the overall experience (Level 3) and, to some degree, the extent to which that experience is satisfying.

Experiences (Level 3) encompass what people consume when they undertake certain leisure activities in particular settings. They include satisfactions, motivations, or desired psychological outcomes (Manning, 1986; Prentice, 1993a; Prentice et al., 1993). Experiences are "the sum of a participant's mental, spiritual, physiological or other responses to a recreation engagement" (Driver, 1976). Typically, multiple experiences will be gained from participation in a particular leisure activity. At this level, visitors are asked about the type(s) of experience(s) the museum provided and what thoughts came into their minds or how they felt at particular exhibits.

Benefits or psychological outcomes (Level 4) refer to the ultimate value that people place on what they believe they have gained from participation in a certain leisure activity. These benefits include self-actualization, social bonding, physical fitness, stimulation, or nostalgia (Schreyer and Driver, 1989). Benefits may be personal or societal and are generally measured by reported satisfaction with a visit (Prentice, 1993b). Although

TABLE 24.2
ASEB Grid Analysis and Cell Identifiers

	Activities	Settings	Experiences	Benefits
Strengths	SA	SS	SE	SB
Weaknesses	WA	WS	WE	WB
Opportunities	OA	OS	OE	OB
Threats	TA	TS	TE	TB

benefits flow directly from experiences, they are distinct in that benefits can be spatially divorced from the museum site (i.e., visitors can take the benefits away with them and apply them to other domains of life). Equally, benefits need not be enduring and may need recharging through experiences offered by other activities.

ASEB grid analysis is defined conceptually as a matrix (see Table 24.2). Analysis is conducted by reference to each level of the Manning–Haas–Driver–Brown demand hierarchy in turn for each element of conventional SWOT analysis. Analysis is undertaken for each row by each column of the matrix, progressing sequentially from cell SA (assessment of the strengths of activities) to cell TB (assessment of the threats of benefits). Strengths and weaknesses of the activities, settings, experiences, and benefits are evaluated from a consumer perspective, as are opportunities and threats. Museum management can, therefore, assess visitor satisfaction with the experience(s) being provided and attempt to provide the types of experiences different visitors expect.

The Black Country Museum is one of the leading industrial heritage attractions in Great Britain. Using ASEB grid analysis, the experiences provided at the Black Country Museum can be compared directly with museums offering similar experiences (see Beeho and Prentice, 1995). Background relating to the Black Country Museum is outlined below, followed by highlights of a survey of visitors to the museum conducted by the authors.

THE BLACK COUNTRY MUSEUM: BACKGROUND

Locational Context and Historical Economic Development The Black Country Museum, an open-air museum, is located in Dudley in the West Midlands of England (see Figure 24.1), one of England's most densely populated conurbations, with major cities such as Birmingham and Wolverhampton within close proximity. Dudley itself had a total population of 304,615 persons (1991 Census). It experienced an average annual population growth of 2.4 percent between 1971 and 1991, but only of 0.4 percent since 1981. Dudley's unemployment rate was 8.9 percent (1991 census) compared to 14.6 percent in Birmingham (which had a population of 961,041 in 1991).

The Black Country region is generally not shown definitively on maps. It is an area of industrial activity recognized colloquially by its inhabitants. For the purpose of this case study, the Black Country covers an area of approximately 100 square miles (255

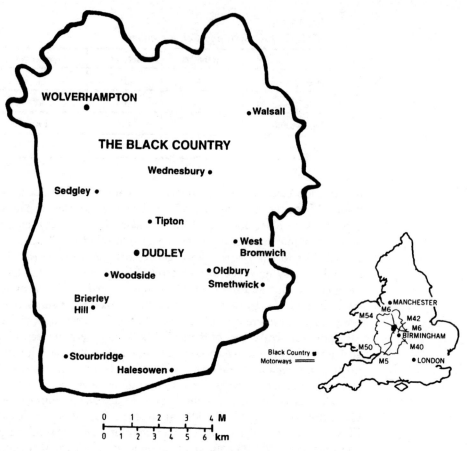

Figure 24.1
The Black Country region, West Midlands of England. (Base Map: Barnsby, 1980.)

square kilometers), and its boundaries are consistent with the area of the coalfield (or seams of coal) upon which it was developed. Originally, the area was based on the mining of coal and limestone and the working of iron, but today it is noted primarily for the manufacture of metal goods.

The title of the "Black Country" was given in the middle of the nineteenth century at a time when the Midlands was at the heart of Industrial Britain and when heavy industry and intensive mining changed the face of the land. Coal mining in large quantities turned the ground inside out, creating large expanses of dereliction and land subsidence. Thousands of industrial furnaces and chimneys filled the air with smoke and fire. In 1868, the area was described by the American consul in Birmingham as being "black by day and red by night." Hence, the region was named Black (Barnsby, 1980). Intensive industrial activity led to massive population growth in the region. In 1801, there were 97,242 people in the Black Country. By 1901, this had grown to 671,009, although the rate of growth slowed when the coalfield and mines became exhausted (from about 1851 to 1871).

Tourism in the The Black Country is a growing tourist destination attracting approximately two to three
Black Country million visitors every year (Black Country Tourism, personal communication, August
1995). Visitors originally consisted primarily of people on business or visiting friends and
relatives (VFR).[3] However, the resource base has changed considerably since 1986–1987
when new developments and a general "greening" of the area made the Black Country a
nicer place to visit. Heavy industrial areas have been demolished and landscaped, and
the development of hotel complexes has meant that more leisure visitors have been attracted and better catered to. The region is readily accessed by major motorway networks
(see Figure 24.1).

Tourism is a key element in the regeneration of the region and a catalyst for investment. Approximately 8500 people are employed in tourism in the Black Country. The
area offers a variety of attractions, including the Black Country Museum, Dudley Castle
and Zoo, Wolverhampton Art Gallery and Museum, Stourbridge Glass Industry (and
museum), Merryhill Shopping Centre, and several football stadiums that host various
events. The visitor base has been broadened as a result of international promotions, particularly in North America, in the 1990s.

The Black The idea to develop an open-air museum to interpret local social and industrial history
Country was conceived in 1952 by the Dudley Libraries Department. However, it was not until
Museum some 20 years later that the development was initiated by the "Friends" of the museum
and a steering committee comprising councillors and local industrialists.

The museum is positioned to be "for and about the people and industry of the Black
Country" (Walden, 1990). A 26–acre (10–hectare) site was developed in Dudley in 1976
to provide insight into the Black Country from the beginning of the eighteenth century.
The museum opened to the public in 1978, although only for a limited season. The
addition of new buildings and/or exhibits is continuous.

The museum has been managed by the Black Country Museum Trust Ltd. (an independent charitable trust company limited by guarantee) since 1975, but draws support
from both the public and private sectors. Dudley local authority provided the initial funds
to build the museum, but this was paid back through local funding sources (including
the West Midlands County Council) and federal grants (e.g., Derelict Land and Urban
Aid), European Regional Development Funds, Manpower Service Commission grants,
and funds from local companies and charitable trusts.

Authentic Black Country buildings were assembled to re-create a "living" village and
industrial community (see Figure 24.2). The museum is similar to many other heritage
attractions in that it is a contrived setting which is recognized as such by visitors (Goodall,
1993). The buildings provide the physical settings for displays made of the materials and
by the machinery and processes characteristic of the Black Country's role in Britain's
Industrial Revolution. Exhibits include a replica of the world's first steam engine, a recreation of a typical small Black Country coal mine, a canal trip to the underground
limestone quarry, and displays relating to other local industries including chain making,
nail making, a brass foundry, and an anchor forge. Visitors can see working machinery
and craftspeople who demonstrate traditional Black Country industrial processes.

The museum has a range of houses displaying interiors of different dates and social
classes. One cottage was moved to the site after having been declared unsuitable for
habitation due to land subsidence. The building now stands as a momento of how mining

THE MUSEUM SITE

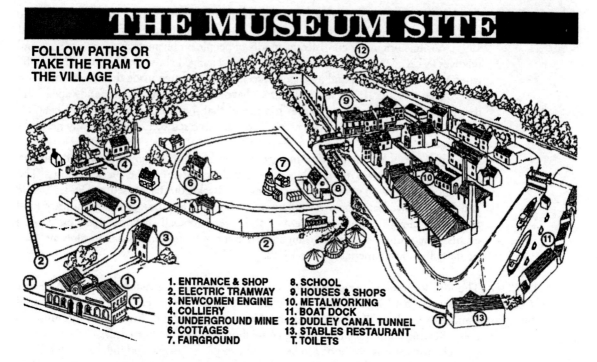

FOLLOW PATHS OR TAKE THE TRAM TO THE VILLAGE

1. ENTRANCE & SHOP
2. ELECTRIC TRAMWAY
3. NEWCOMEN ENGINE
4. COLLIERY
5. UNDERGROUND MINE
6. COTTAGES
7. FAIRGROUND
8. SCHOOL
9. HOUSES & SHOPS
10. METALWORKING
11. BOAT DOCK
12. DUDLEY CANAL TUNNEL
13. STABLES RESTAURANT
T. TOILETS

Figure 24.2
Site layout of the Black Country Museum located in Dudley in the West Midlands of England.

affected people's lives. A range of shops, a church, a public house, and a fairground are presented in a contrived village setting. Black Country trolley buses and trams are operated as well. Appropriately costumed individuals act as "talking labels" to explain the relevance of various buildings and exhibits to the development of the Black Country. Although these individuals do not role play (i.e., act out a specific character), their role is to use "live interpretation" to provide an enjoyable, informal, stimulating, educational, and interactive experience for visitors.

Annual visitation is approximately 270,000 persons. Similar museums such as the Ironbridge Gorge Museum in Shropshire and the more established North of England Open Air Museum in Beamish attract between 300,000 and 400,000 visitors annually. The most popular museum in Great Britain, the British Museum in London, received 5,896,692 visitors in 1994 (BTA, personal communication, August 1995). Half the visitors to the Black Country Museum come from within 20 miles (30 kilometers). School visits comprise one-third of total visits. About 10 percent are adult coach visitors. The split among visitor types has not changed noticeably, although school visits may have increased while the number of local visitors returning regularly may have decreased somewhat. Approximately 60 percent are first-time visitors.

ASEB GRID ANALYSIS AND THE BLACK COUNTRY MUSEUM

Overview of the Approach　ASEB grid analysis at the Black Country Museum was based primarily on semistructured qualitative interviews (i.e., visitors were asked open-ended questions so that experiences could be recorded in their own words; see Appendix 24.1). A convenient sample of 40 domestic tourists (defined as residents of the British Isles spending at least one night away from home) and 10 exhibit demonstrators was interviewed during July to September 1994. Each interview, conducted as visitors exited, lasted from 15 to 20 minutes.

These exploratory interviews were supplemented by direct observation of visitors to record their conversations and reactions to exhibits. The results of these research efforts were arranged into the cells of the ASEB grid as summarized in Table 24.3.

Applying the ASEB Grid to the Black Country Museum　STRENGTHS　Strengths include controllable factors that can be manipulated by the museum staff to provide a quality visit for many types of visitors. In turn, this should enhance efforts to build market share and maximize repeat visitation.

Strengths: Activities (SA)　The peak visitation level of 303,949 in 1990 suggests strong demand for this type of attraction. The Black Country Museum provides a multiattribute product that offers "something for everyone." Both children and adults may benefit from a trip to the museum. People who have personal links with the Black Country region visit to "see what life was like" and to obtain insight into local history.

Interviewees who visited similar attractions in the past two years (17 of the 40 interviewed), favorably compared the Black Country Museum with other similar museums [e.g., Blists Hill Open-Air Museum in Ironbridge (Shropshire) and Beamish (County Durham)]. In particular, the museum was thought to be interesting because of the mine and canal trip, which are not available at the neighboring Ironbridge Gorge Museum, for example. Some also commented on what they perceived to be an "authentic" village setting.

When asked about reasons for visiting, a substantial minority indicated that they had made an enjoyable previous visit. Repeat visitors were interested to see what changes or improvements had been made. Children, especially those who had made a previous visit to the museum with their schools, were a major influence on the decision to visit among a minority of visitors.

Visitors appear to have a very positive regard for the attraction. Approximately 83 percent of the 40 tourists stated that they would strongly recommend the museum to a friend or relative who was visiting the area, and the remainder said that they would possibly recommend it. Indeed, word-of-mouth communication is believed to have provoked some interest. Six stated that they had heard a lot about the museum and that this had given them their first incentive to visit. Those who came based on word-of-mouth referrals indicated that they were leaving feeling satisfied.

The visit is very much an informal experience (i.e., a "nice day out"). Almost all visitors enjoy wandering around at their own pace. Visitors liked the museum because it brought back memories (and, for some, was nostalgic) and because the site had been laid out in an esthetically pleasing manner. People believe that the trip will be enjoyable, especially if this was the case on a previous visit.

TABLE 24.3
ASEB Grid Analysis: The Black Country Museum in the West Midlands of England

	Activities	Settings	Experiences	Benefits
Strengths	Multiattribute product; Unique selling points; Generates repeat visits; Word-of-mouth referrals; High satisfaction levels	Pleasant setting; Visitor satisfaction; Educational, novel, reminiscent, authentic setting; Visitor–demonstrator interaction; Offers something "different"	Provides an enjoyable and educational experience; Emotional, reminiscent, provides insight into social/industrial history; Memory stimulation for people of whatever age or background; Management objectives achieved	Provides a range of benefits; Stimulates comparison with today, and is a good day out; Facilitates learning; Brings back fond memories; Benefical for young peopl; Benefits the wider society
Weaknesses	Declining visitor volume; Greatest decline in main summer period; Switch in markets; Activities offered need modification/expansion; Potential mismatch over visitor motivations	Not as much offered compared to competitors; More exhibits/activities need to be developed; Potential mismatch over sources of visitor satisfaction	Not as much variety and "life" compared with competitors; Visitor experience lacks characteristics of an industrial community; Chronology is not obvious, causing some confusion	Benefits are largely limited to those who have experienced the way of life presented
Opportunities[a]	Build on current strengths; Continually modify and add to existing exhibits/activities; Large available catchment area; Encourage school visits; Encourage repeat visits; Join forces with other local attractions	Build on exhibits that offer novelty/interaction; Attend to chronology issue; Bring museum village "to life"; Provide more factual information; Use a variety of interpretative techniques; Extend research activity	Build on strong experiential product; Expand interpretation of social and working lives of local people; Demonstrate more crafts and industrial processes; Interpret politics; Use a variety of interpretative techniques	Build on benefits that the museum offers to all types of visitors, and communicate these to potential visitors
Threats[b]	Possible market saturation, with possible finite number of museum visitors; Economic recession; Essentially a regional museum; Visitors may visit once and not return	Established competitors offer similar experiences; No immediate tourist market or infrastructure	Providing an experience based on memories; Traditional skills will die out; Experiences gained will lose authenticity as personal insight is lost; Restrictive cost and installation of interpretative media	Experiences may be difficult to understand (especially for younger people) which makes it hard for some people to benefit in the same way as people who have experienced the lifestyle presented

[a] Some strategies and tactics are included in this analysis.

[b] Some weaknesses are included in this analysis.

Strengths: Settings (SS) A main strength is the museum's *environmental setting*. The museum is perceived as offering a nice, quiet, clean, and pleasant environment. Visitors were also satisfied with the *social setting*, particularly aspects of the site that made them reminisce, raised their interest, exposed them to things that they had never seen before, educated them, gave them a feeling of being "a part of it all," or appeared authentic. Notably, reminiscence was not the sole or main response to the settings. Respondents favored aspects that related to them personally, as well as the novel settings of the coal mine and canal tunnels. They also reacted positively to the fact that there were no signs saying "do not touch."

The *managerial setting* is a "living" museum where visitors can become personally involved and immersed in the attraction. Visitors liked interacting with the demonstrators and enjoyed being able to see exhibits in actual working order. The visitor–demonstrator interaction established two-way communication that stimulated visitor interest and made people feel more comfortable. The museum was also reported as providing visitors with an opportunity to articulate and contextualize their life experiences, in addition to serving as an authoritative statement about the past.

Aspects of the museum liked most included the mine, village, canal trip, shops, and houses. Many liked the whole site. Other popular exhibits included the sweet shop, tram ride, school, and chemist. Visitors believed that the village and different exhibits were "authentic" representations of the past. A further strength was revealed by the staff interviews. Staff generally understood which aspects of the site were most enjoyable to visitors.

The coal mine (17 of the 40 interviewed) and canal trip (15 of the 40) were the most satisfying aspects of the site. This may highlight the importance of novelty. Taking a trip underground into a coal mine is something a majority of people have never done. More commonplace exhibits (i.e., the cottage, village, and shops) were less favored, although they formed a positive broader context from which the novel settings were viewed.

Overall, the setting may be seen as successful. Most visitors spent a longer time at the site than had been anticipated, which implies a high level of satisfaction, especially given that some were repeat visitors.

Strengths: Experiences (SE) The Black Country Museum appears to be providing both an enjoyable and an educational experience. The main experiences involved gaining an appreciation of past and present lifestyles and experiences (14 of the 40), were memory-related (14 respondents), or provided insight into social history (13 respondents). Hence, the museum offers memory stimuli as well as insights beyond the life experience of most visitors, regardless of their age and personal or regional background.

The research also revealed how visitors interpreted the period of time (e.g., their descriptions included "awful," "hard work," "terrible conditions," as well as more positive remarks such as "good times," "close community," "self-disciplined," and a life that was not so "rat-racy"). Many exhibits or objects within an exhibit brought back memories of the visitors' family, childhood, and/or industry (34 of 40).

A large minority of visitors felt nostalgic. However, a majority thought about the relative benefits of life today compared to the past (33 of the 40). Sympathy for the miners was a recurring feeling.

Ian Walden, present and founding director of the Black Country Museum, indicated the overall objective is to "preserve artifacts from the Black Country and to make people think about them" (personal communication, April 1995). It would appear that these objectives are being achieved. Visitors are encouraged to react and think about the exhibits, reflecting on nostalgia and personal memories as well as what happened in the Black Country.

Strengths: Benefits (SB)   The range of benefits gained is another strength. The most frequent benefit reported was being able to make comparisons to present-day life. Visitors gained an appreciation for the hardship endured in past lifestyles. This made them reflect upon and appreciate their present quality of life (13 of 40). Another frequently cited benefit was having a "good day out" (12 of 40). To this end, relaxation, having fun and enjoyment, the novelty provided by particular exhibits, being educated or gaining new knowledge, reflecting upon present-day experiences, and reminiscing about the past or a feeling of nostalgia were noted.

Interviews with exhibit demonstrators showed that they were aware of ways in which visitors were benefiting. However, staff believed that the two most frequent benefits gained by visitors were education or learning and reminiscing about the past. This differs to some extent from what the visitors reported. Only a minority of visitors reported that they benefited because they learned something new or because the experience had been educational. Although the museum does not refer to itself as an educational establishment, it provides a setting that facilitates learning. People believed that they benefited by having their interest captured and stimulated, although some reported that they were unable to take everything in during one visit and would have to return.

Similarly, in contrast to staff perceptions, the act of reminiscing was believed to be beneficial by only eight of the 40 tourists. Visitors were reminded of things they had forgotten—things they were able to talk to others about and which made them thankful for their lives today. These memories made them believe that the visit had been worthwhile.

Older respondents tended to believe that although the benefits for younger people could be immense, they may not be gained immediately. Most commented that hopefully the younger generation would reflect back on their visit and gain a new set of values. As such, the interaction between visitor and exhibit can be seen as beneficial beyond the individual to the wider society.

WEAKNESSES   Information about the weaknesses of the activities, settings, experiences, and benefits enables management to make more informed decisions. In essence, ASEB grid analysis focuses on potential mismatches between what is being provided and what the visitor actually wants.

Weaknesses: Activities (WA)   Visitation has dropped annually since 1990, although at a declining rate. The greatest decline (10 percent) occurred between 1990 and 1991. Total visitation between January and September 1994 was 24 percent below that evidenced in the same period in 1990. The peak summer period experienced the worst of this decline. Visitation in August 1994 was down 34 percent compared to August 1990, and July 1994 figures were 31 percent lower than those achieved in July 1990. Although the decline may be attributed in part to uncontrollable factors, visitors' perceptions of the weaknesses of the activities offered may provide some insight into the decline.

Some respondents who had visited similar attractions (e.g., Beamish or Blists Hill) believed that these sites offered more variety. Despite overall satisfaction, they suggested that the Black Country Museum needed further development to compete effectively with its major and longer established rivals. Some believed that history had been more effectively "brought to life" at other museum sites—that there were more sights, sounds, and smells at each exhibit at competitive attractions which provided a more realistic and lively experience.

Activities require continuous modification and expansion if market share is to be retained in an era characterized by both recession and more discriminating customer choice. Comparative research is necessary if analysis of the museum's market using the ASEB grid is to be effective.

As discussed earlier, interviews with exhibit demonstrators revealed a partial mismatch between staff and visitor perceptions of the reasons why tourists visit the museum. Such mismatches highlight important factors the museum has overlooked with regard to what visitors expect and, ultimately, their satisfaction. The main motives given by visitors included: (1) they wanted to return following a previous visit, (2) they had always wanted to visit, (3) they liked to visit this type of attraction, (4) they wanted a nice day out, or (5) they had been asked by their child. In contrast, demonstrators believed that visitors were coming for a nice day out, to relive memories, or for educational or nostalgic reasons.

With the exception of "a nice day out," these perceptions more accurately describe what visitors experience at the museum. There was no mention by visitors of motives such as nostalgia, reliving memories, being educated, or learning about a particular period of the past. In fact, many of the reasons for visiting were much more generalized than thought by staff, and could easily be transferred to another attraction or deferred until a later leisure opportunity.

Weaknesses: Settings (WS)   Only one respondent expressed disappointment with the museum site overall. This disappointment stemmed from comparisons made with a previous visit to Beamish. The expectation was that the Black Country Museum would have been on a much larger scale (e.g., although the quality of the houses was reported as good, the respondent expected to be able to see more streets, etc.).

Respondents generally believed that the Black Country Museum was not on as "grand a scale" and the exhibits were not as "polished" as at Beamish. Some visitors wanted to see more exhibits (e.g., a dentist, a bank, and methods of surgery), more rides in the fairground, more industrial processes, and more wet weather amenities.

Interviews with the staff revealed a different interpretation of weaknesses. One source of dissatisfaction noted by staff was that some visitors had not allowed enough time for their visit. A more fundamental mismatch between the perceptions of staff and visitors related to the interaction between visitors and demonstrators. Staff believed that visitor enjoyment was greatly enhanced through such interaction when, in fact, visitors are satisfied by (1) insights into the past beyond their life experiences, (2) memory stimulation (for those who are old enough to remember the past), (3) the esthetic environment, (4) the layout of the site, and (5) stimulation of personal and family interests. In other words, all three of the levels of settings identified in Table 24.1 provide a source of satisfaction. The demonstrators are only one part of the setting facilitating these experiences, and other aspects of the museum setting may need to be developed.

Weaknesses: Experiences (WE) As noted previously, some visitors believe that the Black Country Museum does not provide as much variety as other more established attractions. Although it is impossible to re-create total "authenticity" in a museum environment due to safety and pollution restrictions, there are no "real life" enactments at the museum. The Black Country Museum experience lacks characteristics associated with a thriving industrial community (i.e., the noise of heavy industry and smells such as factory smoke and domestic baking).

Moreover, many individual aspects of the museum can still be found in the industrial areas of Great Britain. Therefore, the "contrived" product of the museum partly competes with remnants of the "real" product. This is particularly so given that the museum does not focus on one particular period in time and chronology is not readily apparent. The period being interpreted at the museum could range from 1850 up to the 1950s. This could potentially result in a confusing visitor experience. Indeed, respondents made little or no reference to any particular period in time. They just referred in general to the "past" and the "present."

Weaknesses: Benefits (WB) The museum has one critical weakness in terms of visitor perceptions of the benefits gained. The main benefits are limited to those who have experienced the way of life being presented. Some younger people find it difficult to understand what is being interpreted because it represents a way of life that is outside their life experiences. Staff indicated that they have great difficulty in making younger people believe that people did once live like this. As the generations age, this weakness may become more apparent unless the settings are varied to counter it.

OPPORTUNITIES Opportunities, which originate from factors outside the direct control of the organization, present a positive situation or circumstance (e.g., through societal or economic trends, through technological improvements, or from competitive attractions). Strategies to capitalize on the opportunities must be developed. It should be noted that although many of the opportunities discussed below do not flow directly from the visitor interviews, the strategies are based on the research findings and assessment of the museum's strengths and weaknesses.

Opportunities: Activities (OA) The museum clearly has strengths to build on. However, to maintain novelty the museum must continuously extend the range of activities and exhibits. This can be expensive. Funding may be generated from external sources (e.g., if there were interest in using the museum as a film set) or a vigorous sponsorship campaign among private sector organizations interested in heritage attractions. Once achieved, awareness of new developments must be promoted among existing and prospective visitors.

The Black Country Museum's location in the heart of the West Midlands conurbation represents a major opportunity for market expansion. A large catchment area consisting of both residents and their visitors (VFR) exists within heavily populated centers such as Birmingham and Wolverhampton. In light of reduced visitor numbers, the museum should extend its marketing efforts to actively target adult residents of this area and their VFR guests, in particular those who are fairly affluent and have access to their own transportation. Senior citizens should also be targeted due to their available leisure time, their ability to relate to the period being interpreted, and in light of the increasing proportion of older people in the population.

Given that existing tourists seem to be reminiscing about the past in general and not the past of a particular area, the product must reflect a range of activities and experiences without losing its Black Country origins. The West Midlands is within reach of population centers in the southeast and southwest of England, as well as in parts of Wales and the North. Consideration should be given to extending marketing efforts to these areas and supplementing the museum's interpretation accordingly, principally to draw parallels with the pasts of these areas.

Since children influence family leisure decisions, school visits should continue to be encouraged during off-peak months to maintain overall attendance levels. In addition, incentives should be offered to enhance and maintain repeat visitation levels. Season tickets that encourage multiple visits at discounted rates each year could be considered, as could special events. Strategic alliances with local competitors to extend the range of experiences represent other possibilities. A consortium whose goal it is to attract more tourists to the West Midlands (in particular, the Black Country) or to establish cooperative marketing initiatives with other socioindustrial heritage attractions should be considered. This would help the Black Country Museum gain recognition and leverage marketing resources.

Opportunities: Settings (OS)   Visitors are becoming more discerning about their need for a museum visit that is enjoyable as well as educational—a visit in which they can become involved and even relive personal memories. Museums must heighten visitor satisfaction through providing the types of experiences expected. This can be achieved in part through improving the social and managerial settings.

Visitors wanted a wider variety of exhibits and more ways in which they could become involved in the exhibits. The most satisfying aspects were not necessarily within the direct experience or memories of the majority of visitors (i.e., the coal mine and the canal trip). Therefore, the museum should construct exhibits that increase the "novelty" factor. Suggestions included a 1920s cinema (already in construction phase), a police station, and more industries or trades (e.g., a blacksmith).

Given that satisfaction appears to vary with visitor type, the museum must offer "something for everyone," including education and fun for younger people and memory stimulation for older people. Domestic and industrial interests must not be overlooked. The period being interpreted also needs to be considered. Explicit reference to period can enhance the focus of museum promotions. Such theming may extend even to catering (e.g., visitors recommended the addition of an old-fashioned tea parlor, more ice cream vendors, and more picnic tables).

Participation by local school children, their teachers, and parents in role playing should be encouraged. Such educational activities can bring the village more to life and create more novelty and authenticity. Children and young persons could dress in period costume and attend school classes, enjoy themselves on the fairground rides, or play in the streets of the village with period toys (e.g., skipping ropes, playing hopscotch, and hooping). Similarly, volunteers wandering around in costume as "ghosts" of the past could potentially add to the missing dimensions of period.

The museum largely ignores conventional plaques and display boards as interpretative media. To counter reliance on demonstrators, more factual information could be provided, especially in exhibits and buildings not staffed by a demonstrator. Some respondents expressed a need for more signs and information panels or audiovisual displays to explain (especially to the younger generation) what happened and how things were done. A variety of interpretative media, including more conventional media, is required.

Such product development should be based on research that monitors visitor opinions, motivations, experiences, and the benefits gained. Research could also be used to assess the effectiveness of interpretation, reasons for not visiting, and visitor expectations prior to the actual visit.

Opportunities: Experiences (OE)   Building upon its strong experiential product, the museum could expand interpretation of the social and working lives of local people at whichever period is selected, possibly showing visitors what people would have done for relaxation or sports when they were not working. More crafts and industrial processes could also be demonstrated, and souvenirs should be available for sale. In addition, respondents believed that the politics of the period were understated. A setting depicting how people struggled in their daily lives and the political nature of a particular period (e.g., trade unions, role of Empire, Great Depression) could be created.

Depending upon available resources and suitability, a variety of interpretative techniques, including live reenactments, audiovisual displays, information boards, and interactive exhibits, should be considered. The learning experience could be made more "fun" to stimulate and capture the interest of children, and visitors could be given the chance to become more "involved" (e.g, by being encouraged to handle and use objects or even to be allowed to skip and play in the school yard).

Opportunities: Benefits (OB)   As discussed previously, the museum encourages people to reflect upon their present-day experiences and stimulates enjoyable reminiscing for those old enough to remember the past. Promotional efforts should emphasize the different benefits for different types and ages of visitors. The promotional message needs to persuade prospective visitors that the Black Country Museum can satisfy their individual needs. Particular attention must be given to younger people.

THREATS   Similar to opportunities, threats originate from factors that are outside the control of the organization. However, threats present factors that may have a negative effect or that may introduce a difficult situation to the operation of the organization. Once potential threats have been identified, the aim is to minimize the harmful effects by developing appropriate strategies based on consumer research to counteract any negative influences.

Threats: Activities (TA)   The BTA recorded the opening of 570 new museums in Great Britain between 1970 and 1988. The number of new museums opening each year remains consistent at just over 20. In contrast, visits to museums between 1976 and 1988 increased by only 12 percent (Middleton, 1990). This was followed in 1990 by economic recession.

Many museums in Great Britain have been witnessing declining visitor numbers since the economic recession began. In fact, approximately 38 percent of museums in the West Midlands area attributed declines in museum visitation to economic recession (BTA, personal communication, August 1995). Between 1992 and 1993, similar museums such as the Ironbridge Gorge Museum and New Lanark Visitor Centre in Scotland witnessed a downturn in visitor figures of 2 percent and 4 percent, respectively.

This raises the possibility of saturation in the market and also raises the thought that perhaps there is a finite number of museum visitors in a recessionary era. This creates particular problems for regional museums which may be compounded if people visit the museum and do not return because they are unaware of new developments or improvements. This threat cannot be removed until the British economy—especially that of the West Midlands—revives.

To mitigate these threats, the Black Country Museum must maximize visitor levels through building on and promoting experiences that satisfy each visitor type. For example, given that memory stimulation was one of the main experiences gained by visitors, an advertising campaign could be targeted at older visitors (individual, coach, and group) to encourage them to visit and "take a trip down memory lane."

Threats: Settings (TS)   A major threat is posed by competitive attractions that offer a similar visitor experience, but which have the advantages of having been established for a longer period, are larger, have wider recognition among the general public, and have an established market. Dudley is not an area where large numbers of people think of taking a holiday (unless visiting friends or relatives). Moreover, the immediate area around the museum site has limited tourism facilities, especially with regard to reasonably priced family accommodation.

To compete with more established attractions offering similar experiences, management must continue to provide satisfying experiences for all types of visitors. To attract more visitors from outside of the Dudley area, the Black Country Museum should actively target group organizers (e.g., coach operators and special interest groups such as transport enthusiasts) and the VFR market via special promotions. Efforts to maximize visitors from the main catchment areas must be maintained. Cooperative efforts to encourage development at the industry level are also believed to be critical.

Threats: Experiences (TE)   One very real challenge relates to the possibility that younger people will not have an enjoyable experience because their memories are too recent to be stimulated by the museum setting. This will be compounded as older generations disappear. Similarly, traditional crafts and skills will die out unless they are taught as part of a museum experience. The experiences to be gained will likely lose "authenticity" as personal insight is lost.

Alternatively, "authentic," dynamic, and stimulating visitor experiences can be created using technologically advanced interpretative techniques (e.g., dark rides, projected images, virtual reality). However, these techniques are costly and may be difficult to install given the nature and layout of the site [i.e., an open-air museum spread over 26 acres (10 hectares)]. On the other hand, although such techniques could detract from the authenticity of the buildings and artifacts, they could be used to provide "personal" insight by costumed models animated to relate "their" experience.

Threats: Benefits (TB)   Younger visitors have never experienced the lifestyle being interpreted at the Black Country Museum. This makes it difficult for them to benefit in the same way as older visitors. Consequently, the museum may need to offer exhibits depicting more recent times.

CONCLUSION

Based on the levels of the Manning–Haas–Driver–Brown hierarchy of demand and conventional SWOT analysis, ASEB grid analysis offers a more effective, consumer-oriented approach to tourism and leisure research that supplements conventional sociodemographic analyses. By focusing on the experiences and benefits derived, the analysis pays attention to what is actually being gained from a leisure activity and what visitors actually wanted and expected.

The analysis also facilitates the identification of possible contradictions in visitor experience. For example, although the Black Country Museum provoked the memories of some, its most popular components would appear to be those that do not relate to the life experiences of most visitors. ASEB grid analysis investigates whether the experiences gained correspond to what visitors wanted or expected. It also assesses whether the museum staff's beliefs about what they are offering are consistent with the experiences sought and received by visitors.

In an increasingly competitive marketplace, failure to deliver appropriate experiences and benefits can lead to visitor dissatisfaction and commercial failure. The modern museum, and other tourist attractions in general, must provide worthwhile experiences based on understanding visitor needs and motivations. ASEB grid analysis provides an effective method by which this may be planned and evaluated. By asking the consumer directly to relate their experiences and satisfaction, more informed product development and marketing decisions may be facilitated.

Although ASEB grid analysis is a qualitative technique, quantitative analysis using opinion scaling and similar techniques can be used to inform the ASEB grid. As such, the ASEB grid is versatile in terms of its application and is essentially a means of information analysis rather than a technique of data collection. Furthermore, the potential applicability of the ASEB grid is extensive and reaches beyond the hospitality and leisure industries (Babin et al., 1994).

ACKNOWLEDGMENTS

The authors would like to thank Mr. Ian Walden and staff at the Black Country Museum for their help and support throughout the research project.

NOTES

1. See Chapters 10, 11, and 25 for additional discussion regarding heritage tourism.
2. See Chapters 5, 6, 26, and 28 for additional discussion relating to strategic planning and SWOT analysis. SWOT analysis (1) examines potential strengths and weaknesses of a tourist attraction (i.e., how well the organization provides a tourism product) and (2) locates the organization in

terms of the wider market (i.e., how the organization operates in relation to external opportunities and threats, such as economic, political, or societal trends, and the actions of competitors).
3. See Chapter 26 for additional discussion of VFR tourism.

REFERENCES

Ajzen, I. and B.L. Driver. 1992. Application of the theory of planned behaviour to leisure choices, *Journal of Leisure Research*, 24, 207–224.

Ashworth, G. 1990. The historic sites of Groningen: which is sold to whom? In G. Ashworth and B. Goodall (eds.), *Marketing Tourism Places*. London: Routledge, pp. 138–155.

Atkinson, J.W. and D. Burch. 1972. *Motivation: The Dynamics of Action*. New York: John Wiley & Sons.

Babin, B.J., W.R. Darden, and M. Griffin. 1994. Work and/or fun: measuring hedonic and utilitarian shopping value, *Journal of Consumer Research*, 2, 644–656.

Barnsby, G.J. 1980. *Social Conditions in the Black Country, 1800—1900*. Wolverhampton: Integrated Publishing Services.

Beeho, A.J. and R.C. Prentice. 1995. Evaluating the experiences and benefits gained by tourists visiting a socio-industrial heritage museum: an application of ASEB grid analysis to Blists Hill Open-Air Museum, The Ironbridge Gorge Museum, United Kingdom. *Museum Management and Curatorship*, 14(3), 229–251.

Black Country Museum Guide (The). 1994. Pitkin Pictorials, Hants.

Driver, B. 1976. Quantification of outdoor recreationists' preferences. In B. Van der Smissen (ed.), *Research Camping and Environmental Education*, HPER Series, Vol. 11. PA: pp. 165–187.

Edson, G. and D. Dean. 1994. *The Handbook for Museums*. London: Routledge.

Fishbein, M. and I. Ajzen. 1975. *Beliefs, Attitude, Intention and Behaviour: An Introduction to Theory and Research*. Reading, MA: Addison–Wesley.

Goodall, B. 1993. Industrial heritage and tourism, *Built Environment*, 19(2), 93–104.

Haas, G.E., B.L. Driver, and P.J. Brown. 1980. Measuring wilderness experiences. In *Proceedings in the Wilderness Psychology Group*, New Hampshire, Durham, pp. 20–40.

Herbert, D.T., R.C. Prentice, and C.J. Thomas (eds.). 1989. *Heritage Sites: Strategies for Marketing and Development*. Aldershot: Avebury.

Holloway, C. and R.V. Plant. 1992. *Marketing for Tourism*, 2nd ed. Sydney: Pitman.

Lawler, E.E. 1973. *Motivations in Work Organisations*. Monterey, CA: Brooks-Cole.

Lofman, B. 1991. Elements of experiential consumption: an exploratory study, *Advances in Consumer Research*, 18, 729–733.

Manning, R.E. 1986. *Studies in Outdoor Recreation: A Review and Synthesis of the Social Science Literature in Outdoor Recreation*. Corvallis, OR: Oregon State University Press.

Merriman, N. 1989. The social basis of museum and heritage visiting. In S.M. Pearce (ed.), *Museum Studies in Material Culture*. Leicester: Leicester University Press, pp. 153–171.

Merriman, N. 1991. *Beyond the Glass Case: The Past, the Heritage and the Public in Britain*. Leicester: Leicester University Press.

Middleton, V.T.C. 1988. *Marketing in Travel and Tourism*. Oxford: Butterworth-Heinemann.

Middleton, V.T.C. 1990. *New Visions for Independent Museums in the U.K.* Chichester, West Sussex: Association of Independent Museums.

Prentice, R.C. 1993a. Motivations of the heritage consumer in the leisure market: an application of the Manning–Haas demand hierarchy, *Leisure Sciences*, 15(4), pp. 273–290.

Prentice, R.C. 1993b. *Tourism and Heritage Attractions.* London: Routledge.

Prentice, R.C. and D. Light. 1994. Current issues in interpretative provision at heritage sites. In A.V. Seaton (ed.), *Tourism, the State of the Art.* Chichester, West Sussex: John Wiley & Sons, pp. 204–221.

Prentice, R.C., S.F. Witt, and C. Hamer. 1993. The experience of industrial heritage: market overview and the case of black gold. *Built Environment,* 19(2), 137–146.

Prince, D.R. 1990. Factors influencing museum visits: an empirical evaluation of audience selection. *Museum Management and Curatorship,* 9(2), 149–168.

Schreyer, R. and B.L. Driver. 1989. The benefits of leisure. In E.L. Jackson and T.L. Burton (eds.), *Understanding Leisure and Recreation: Mapping the Past, Charting the Future.* State College, PA: Venture Publishing, pp. 385–420.

Stevens, T. 1989. The visitor—who cares?: interpretation and consumer relations. In D.L. Uzzell (ed.), *Heritage Interpretation, Vol. 2.: The Visitor Experience.* London: Belhaven Press, Chapter 12.

Uzzell, D.L. 1989. *Heritage Interpretation, Vol. 2: The Visitor Experience.* London: Belhaven Press.

Vergo, P. 1989. *The New Museology.* London: Reaktion Books.

Walden, Ian. 1990. The Black Country Museum: an integrated approach to the preservation of industrial history. In A *New Head of Steam: Industrial History in the Museum,* Proceedings from the Scottish Museum Council Conference on Industrial Museums, Glasgow, November, 37–40.

Wertheim, M.E. 1994. Market research for heritage attractions, *Journal of Vacation Marketing,* 1(1), 70–74.

Yale, P. 1991. *From Tourist Attractions to Heritage Tourism.* Huntingdon: ELM Publications.

∮ | PROBLEM SOLVING AND DISCUSSION ACTIVITIES

1. Identify the information requirements and process for undertaking (a) a comparable analysis and (b) a competitor analysis for the Black Country Museum or another museum in your region.

2. Consider the effectiveness of interpretative techniques and media at experiential attractions. How far should museum interpretation go in providing an "authentic" experience?

3. In large part, the discussion of opportunities and threats presented in this chapter focused on identifying strategies or tactics for overcoming weaknesses and/or capitalizing on strengths of the museum. What steps should the museum's managers take to ensure that they have a solid understanding of actual opportunities and threats before implementing specific strategies and/or tactics.

4. Prepare a draft of a marketing and development plan for the Black Country Museum based on the ASEB grid analysis, including identification and justification of priorities relating to both market and product development.

5. Compare the potential effectiveness of ASEB grid and conventional SWOT analyses in addressing different types of management problems.

6. Use the Manning–Haas–Driver–Brown demand hierarchy to explore the experiences and benefits that can be gained from visiting a heritage attraction in your

area. Do visitors at other types of heritage attractions receive experiences and benefits similar to those visiting socioindustrial heritage attractions such as the Black Country Museum?

7. Conduct an ASEB grid analysis at a tourist attraction in your area. Use Appendix 24.1 as a framework for consumer interviews. Provide a rationale for any changes you would make to this survey instrument.

8. One of the factors likely to affect future visitation at the Black Country Museum is the status of Dudley in the tourism marketplace. Identify steps that should be considered at the community or industry level to address this challenge.

APPENDIX 24.1: LIST OF QUESTIONS: IN-DEPTH VISITOR SURVEY, BLACK COUNTRY MUSEUM, DUDLEY, WEST MIDLANDS OF ENGLAND

1. Could you please explain why you decided to come here today? *(Why is that important?)*

2a. Did you like the museum site overall? *(Why? Which aspects did you like?)*

2b. Which aspect/part of the Black Country Museum did you find *most* satisfying? *(Why? In what ways was it satisfying? How did it make you feel?)*

3a. Can you please tell me in a few words what sort(s) of experience(s) the Black Country Museum has provided you with?

3b. Reflecting on your visit to the Black Country Museum today, which of the following phrases best describes the experience(s) that you received? Is that what you expected?
   A. The history of a particular industry
   B. How people used to live and work
   C. How things were made /the workings of an industrial process
   D. How technology has changed over the past century
   E. Entertainment /fun
   F. The history of the region
   G. Pleasant surroundings
   H. Insight into the restoration /conservation of buildings
   I. Other . . .

4a. I would like you to think of the most enjoyable exhibit/aspect of the site that you visited today. *(Name the exhibit /aspect of the site.)* Thinking of this exhibit/aspect, can you please tell me in a few words how you felt/what thoughts came to mind at that particular exhibit/aspect of the site?

4b. Could you please indicate from the following list, which phrase(s) best describes how you felt/what thoughts came to mind at that particular exhibit/aspect of the site?
   A. Sympathy for how the people used to live and work
   B. Appreciation of present-day quality of life
   C. Interest in the industrial processes of how things were made
   D. Impressed with how technology has changed over the last century
   E. An overall feeling of awe
   F. Made me think /reflect about life in the past
   G. Brought back memories

   H. I felt entertained/had fun
   I. Pleasure from being in pleasant surroundings
   J. Cultural pride/regional identity
   K. Other . . .

5a. How do you think you have benefited from coming here today? *(Why is it important to you that you gain . . . ?)* Think of the exhibit that satisfied you the most, what benefits did that provide?

5b. How do you think others in your party have benefited? *(Why is it important to you that they gain . . .)* What benefits do you think this particular type of attraction provides?

6. What changes would you make to the Black Country Museum to improve the experiences that visitors receive? *(Why is that important?)* What kind of experience would you like to have had today? What would have made your visit more satisfying?

7. Have you visited any other attractions like this in the past two years?
   If YES, which attraction(s) and how does it/they compare to the Black Country Museum?

8. Would you recommend this attraction to a friend or relative visiting the area?

9. Is there anything else which you would like to tell me about this attraction or your overall visit today?

25

Dinosaurs for Tourism

PICKET WIRE CANYON AND THE ROCKY MOUNTAIN PALEONTOLOGICAL TOURISM INITIATIVE, COLORADO, USA

 Robert M. O'Halloran

𝕲 | K E Y   L E A R N I N G   P O I N T S

- Natural heritage attractions are unique resources that are developed in the public eye. Therefore, decisions cannot be made in a vacuum. Involvement by residents of local communities, government agencies, and private sector representatives is vital.

- Partnerships involving public agencies and private business will become increasingly important and necessary as budgets tighten. Collaboration and cooperation to gain economies of scale is essential.

- In rural areas, infrastructure (e.g., transportation, water, sewage) and other services (e.g., food, interpretative services) are crucial to the development of paleontological tourism resources and to ensuring visitors have safe and enjoyable experiences.

- Visitors must be made aware of the fragile nature of the resource. Therefore, visitor ethics stressing the importance of low-impact use and interpretative services that provide educational opportunities concerning natural heritage sites are vital for sustainable tourism development.

INTRODUCTION

Protecting and conserving resources that provide tourism or recreation experiences creates challenges for the development and management of natural heritage areas. The Picket Wire Canyon in southeastern Colorado, a unique natural heritage site that reportedly has the longest dinosaur tracksite in the world (over 1300 visible tracks extending over one-quarter mile or 0.4 kilometers), is one example of an area that faced such a challenge.

In June 1991, Public Law 101–510, Section 2825 mandated the transfer of Picket Wire Canyon from the jurisdiction of the Secretary of the Army to the Secretary of Agriculture (United States Congress, 1991). The legislation also directed the agency to open the area for public recreation. The canyonlands are now part of the Comanche National

Grasslands. The problem for managers and planners is related to how the Picket Wire Canyon could be developed while protecting the resources and controlling development of this unique area.

This chapter provides an overview of how the development potential for a natural heritage site can be assessed while simultaneously recognizing the importance of preservation and conservation. The Picket Wire Dinosaur Tracksite is part of the Rocky Mountain Paleontological Tourism Initiative, a regional effort to develop and manage paleontological resources at natural heritage sites managed by the National Park Service (NPS), the Bureau of Land Management (BLM), and the United States Forest Service (USFS) in Colorado.

The natural heritage sites in this initiative form a triangular area in eastern Colorado comprising Florissant Fossil Beds National Monument (FNM) south of Colorado Springs, the Garden Park site for the Dinosaur Discovery Center near Canon City, and the Picket Wire Canyon near La Junta, Colorado. This triangle extends south from Florissant approximately 35 miles (56 kilometers) to Garden then east about 110 miles (177 kilometers) to the Picket Wire Canyon.

Data collected for this project focused on the Picket Wire Canyon as part of the Comanche National Grasslands of the US Forest Service, but they generally included other paleontological sites in Colorado, Nebraska, South Dakota, and Wyoming. Research included personal interviews with land management agency representatives (NPS, BLM, USFS), observations during interagency planning meetings, site inspections, and a review of the literature on tourism development, heritage tourism, recreational planning, and recent legislation on heritage sites. Interviews were also conducted with representatives of the National Park Service Partnership Program, the US Geological Survey, community officials, and potential partners from the private sector. Data and other information collected included visitor counts, site management plans, existing master plans, and operating plans from other natural heritage sites (e.g., Dinosaur National Monument in western Colorado and eastern Utah).

The Tourism/Recreation Opportunity Spectrum (T/ROS) and the Paleo/Partnership models are presented as tools to assist planning and decision making. These models provide the means to assess and classify natural heritage sites (T/ROS) as well as provide a framework for developing these sites (Paleo/Partner).

NATURAL HERITAGE TOURISM SITES AND HERITAGE PLANNING: CONTEMPORARY PERSPECTIVES AND ISSUES

Millar (1991) defined heritage[1] to include the natural, cultural, and built environments of an area. *Heritage tourism* comprises visits by persons from outside the host community that are motivated entirely or in part by interest in the natural and historical offerings of a community, region, group, or institution (Brown, 1993). Heritage tourism attempts to achieve a balance between public access, conservation, entertainment, education, visitor facilities, investment, and economic viability (Millar, 1991). Natural heritage tourism embodies a belief that one can learn something new and interesting from fossils and other artifacts from earlier eras and that the experience of viewing fossils and artifacts can be quite exciting (Behrensmeyer, 1994).

Traditionally, museums have been the places where fossils and objects of value to society are kept, cared for, and made available to the public (Behrensmeyer, 1994). Natural heritage tourism and recreation sites expand the museum concept by organizing physical landscapes as a type of outdoor museum. Regional cultural landscapes have become fertile ground for recognizing and developing heritage regions that incorporate historic, cultural, scenic, and recreational opportunities (Comp, 1993). In many natural heritage sites, the environment must be adapted to accommodate tourism and recreation experiences.

Local communities must be involved in the planning, use, and conservation of these resources.[2] Community involvement and interpretation encourage an awareness of, and pride in, the natural or cultural heritage of a community and enable the community to be proactive in promoting what it perceives to be unique (Millar, 1991).

Informed decision making for strategy formulation purposes requires access to quality information. Light and Prentice (1994) suggest that there is a deficiency of research coordinated at a regional level (i.e., mesoscale data) for tourism in general. Nonetheless, such data are especially crucial for the planning and marketing of natural heritage sites (Light and Prentice, 1994). An opportunity for strengthening data resources exists given the variety of expertise and experience among personnel at government agencies interested in natural heritage tourism, archaeology, and paleontology (i.e., the United States Forest Service, the Bureau of Land Management, the National Park Service, and the United States Geological Survey). An interagency effort has great potential for collecting and sharing these data.[3]

Light and Prentice (1994) also acknowledge the competitive nature of heritage tourism. Interpretation[4] is cited as being central to the success or failure of site development. To best interpret and develop these sites, they must first be classified for the type of tourism or recreation experience desired. A Tourism/Recreation Opportunity Spectrum (T/ROS) (USFS, 1994) conceptual framework can be used to classify sites for present and future use (see Figure 25.1).

The setting within the Picket Wire Canyon can be described as remote, pristine, and fragile. This setting provides opportunities for recreational activities (e.g., hiking, exploring, and biking) and educational activities (e.g., scientific exploration and general learning). The Picket Wire Canyon is classified as a semiprimitive site. There is little evidence of other users. Few on-site restrictions or controls exist, although public use of motorized vehicles is not permitted. Critical to the tourism experience afforded by the Picket Wire Canyon is the relative isolation from the sights and sounds of humans and a feeling of closeness to the outdoors in an environment that offers some challenge and risk (USFS, 1994).

The Paleo/Partnership model (see Figure 25.2) provides direction for shaping a partnership organization structure and action plan within natural heritage sites. Partnership goals should be to provide technical assistance for planning and design, including interpretive design and historic preservation for specific sites (National Park Service, 1994). In this case, the principal paleontological partners include the three natural heritage sites within the Rocky Mountain Paleontological Tourism Initiative. Site management issues and/or recommendations relevant at each step are outlined for the Picket Wire Dinosaur Tracksite and other attractions in the Comanche National Grasslands based on the site classification noted from the T/ROS.

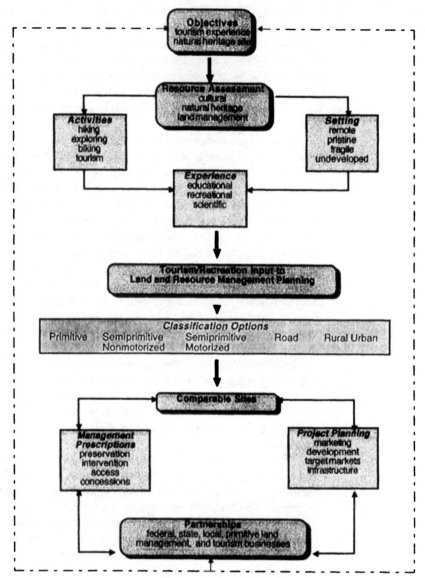

Figure 25.1
Tourism/recreation opportunity spectrum for the Rocky Mountain Paleontological Tourism Initiative: Picket Wire Canyon. (Adapted from the USFS ROS Users Guide, 1994. Courtesy of USDA, Forest Service.)

Step 1 identifies land management agency partners and other allied interests. In Step 2 the attractions and infrastructure for tourism development already in place as well as that which may be needed in the future are assessed. Step 3 conceptualizes what the tourism development will entail. It suggests that a balance between the type of experience planners and managers want to offer visitors and the wants and needs of the visitors is required.

Actual product development needs are identified in Step 4. The planning process must address issues pertaining to product type (e.g., theme park, hiking area, educational

Step 1:	Select a Balanced Partnership Organization
	USFS, NPS, USGS, Local & State Partners, Private Business?

Step 2:	Identify Community Attractions and Services
	a. Dinosaur Tracksite, Fossil Beds, Dinosaur Center, USAF Academy, Garden of the Gods, Royal Gorge, Bent's Old Fort
	b. Hiking, horseback riding, mountain biking, four-wheel-drive vehicles
	c. Hospitality infrastructure in Colorado Springs, Pueblo, Canon City, LaJunta
	d. Highway and road access

Step 3:	Visioning Process: Assessment
	a. Lack of awareness of the Picket Wire Resource
	b. Tourism development needs, staging areas
	c. Niche: longest dinosaur tracksite in the world; regional paleontological initiative
	d. Management; sustainable and responsible development

Step 4:	Product development
	Preservation, conservation, visitor ethics
	Water, sewage, food (carry in, carry out)
	Emergency needs
	Interpretation services: volunteers, concession operators

Step 5:	Marketing & Promotion
	Target Markets identified: schools, scientific research, recreationists, families
	Promotional efforts developed: soft sell, brochures, seminars, slow development, controlled access
	Concession efforts

Step 6:	Funding and Finance
	Concession agreements,'Friends' societies for fundraising
	Government funding: shrinking budgets, economic viability, use fees

Step 7:	Implementation and Evaluation
	Partnership management roles: Picket Wire is USFS land but needs to involve USGS, and needs US Department of Defense for access
	Cooperative management agreements

Figure 25.2
Application of the Paleo/Partnership model at Picket Wire Canyon. (Adapted from Bruns et al., 1994; Bruns and Stokowski, in press.)

outing, adventure tour). Other concerns addressed at this stage include whether it will be necessary to construct any facilities. Step 5 focuses on the identification of marketing and promotion strategies to be undertaken by the partners to achieve specific goals and objectives. Step 6 identifies the funding and possible financing sources for developing the site. Finally, implementation plans and evaluation strategies are delineated in Step 7.

As planning tools, both of these models provide managers with a framework for development. The first step, however, is to understand the site.

PICKET WIRE CANYON: LOCATIONAL CONTEXT AND BACKGROUND

Tourism Currently, each of the three sites in the Rocky Mountain Paleontological Tourism Initia-
Resources tive is considered to be a secondary tourist destination within Colorado. The primary
demand generators tend to be located near Florissant Fossil Beds National Monument
and include the United States Air Force Academy, Pikes Peak, the gambling town of
Cripple Creek, and the Garden of the Gods Park in Colorado Springs.

The Royal Gorge, which draws approximately 532,000 visitors annually, is located
close to the Garden Park site (Grenard, BLM, personal communication, 1994). A survey
conducted in the winter of 1989 and the fall of 1990 revealed that 76 percent of the
visitors to the Royal Gorge would also visit the planned Dinosaur Discovery Center in
the future (Grenard, personal communication, 1994).

The closest attractions or infrastructure to the Picket Wire site are Bent's Old Fort
and the cities of La Junta and Pueblo. Pueblo hosts the Colorado State Fair, which draws
more than one million visitors annually, thereby providing a base of potential visitors for
the Picket Wire Canyon.

Marketing and promoting Colorado attractions to include natural heritage sites
such as the Picket Wire Canyon will assist in the development of tourism resources
for all the sites. However, unless a comprehensive plan is devised to link attractions, the
natural heritage sites are likely to remain secondary destinations. If a plan is created
and a comprehensive historical/paleontological experience is provided, the region
could become a primary destination with a very positive economic impact on the
region.

Picket Wire Canyon possesses both natural and cultural heritage sites such as the
dinosaur tracksite, petroglyphs, archaeological sites, a ranch, and a Spanish church and
cemetery. These resources are important historical markers within the region. Fossil remains and artifacts trace the history of the area from the Jurassic period to the time when
Spanish explorers came to what is now Colorado. Spanish explorers in the late 1500s
continued the journey begun by Coronado 50 years earlier. While looking for gold, the
exploration groups encountered native populations. Many were killed or died on the trail.
Years later, the canyon was named *El Rio de Las Animas Perididas en Purgatorio*, or the
"River of Lost Souls," based on the remains of the explorers found at the site. A century
later, French trappers shortened the Spanish name to *Purgatoire*. American explorers
subsequently interpreted the French name to mean Picket Wire (USFS, 1993). The site
represents a cross section of early North American cultural and paleontological history,
thereby rendering it an important natural heritage resource.

The sustainability of the resources in the Picket Wire Canyon is a critical issue.
Although the tracksite is the world's largest continuously mapped assemblage of dinosaur
tracks, past fluvial erosion is believed to have destroyed a majority of the main footprint-
bearing bed (USFS, 1993). Heritage and paleontological resources also experienced some
damage during the years of Euro-American occupation, as well as from natural events
(USFS, 1993). People who left their marks on the canyon thousands of years ago will
not be back to update the petroglyphs or leave more grinding stones. The dinosaurs will
not be back to make more tracks. However, geologists and paleontologists believe that
there are many more unexposed tracks that are currently not in danger of being exhausted (Henry, personal communication, 1994).

To assist the preservation and conservation efforts of planners and managers, the tracksite and other resources should be recognized nationally and internationally by listing the Picket Wire Canyon as a national natural or heritage landmark or as a world heritage site (USFS, 1993). Such national or international designation would also mean that visitors would have easy access to the canyon.

Access and Topography
Access to Picket Wire Canyon is difficult because the roads, including the road leading from US Highway 50 to the main entrance, are poorly marked. From the meeting point outside the Picket Wire Canyon to the entrance of US Army land, the road is accessible only by four-wheel-drive vehicles. The land is rolling with many rocky and canyon areas. There is little shade, and temperatures can soar to 90°F or 100°F (32°C or 38°C) in the summer.

The legislation transferring management of the land from the Secretary of the Army (Department of Defense) to the Secretary of Agriculture (Department of Agriculture) stipulated that access to Picket Wire Canyon should be improved in a manner that does not interfere with the site mission (United States Congress, 1991). To date, this issue has not been fully resolved. Access to the resources through Minnie Canyon rather than through the currently utilized Withers and Iron Gate canyons is recommended by USFS officials due to the proximity of Minnie Canyon to the tracksite and other attractions (see Figures 25.3 and 25.4).

There is growing concern about the degradation of the tracksite, the church, and archaeological artifacts in the valley as the Picket Wire resources are made more accessible. According to Henry (US Geological Survey, personal communication, 1994), the dinosaur tracksite is threatened by the natural meandering of the Purgatory River. Solutions to this problem vary from creating an artificial track nearby to reinforcing the rock with rods or cement where it is threatened by erosion. However, using cement to change the course of the river or reinforce the banks of the existing river would be both temporary and damaging (Henry, personal communication, 1994). The implication is that nature will maintain a natural balance and that, as these tracks disappear, more will be uncovered upstream. To further complicate the issue, the Purgatory River may be designated as a "wild and scenic river." If such a designation is granted, rerouting or altering the path of the river may not be an option.

The maintenance and/or renewability of resources within the canyon remains a question. Nonetheless, its protection and conservation are important not only because of the resources available at Picket Wire Canyon, but also because of its linkages with other paleontological sites in the area.

Infrastructure
Current infrastructure (e.g., transportation, roads, and trails) must be considered before additional development can be realized. Paving access routes could pose a host of problems, including endangering the riparian zone at the base of the canyon. Infrastructure features such as utilities, water, power, waste treatment, and communications will need to be developed for expanded use. Currently, no formal decisions on the appropriate level of development have been made. Infrastructure decisions must be based on the needs of visitors. Knowing who these groups could be is important for development planning and decision making.

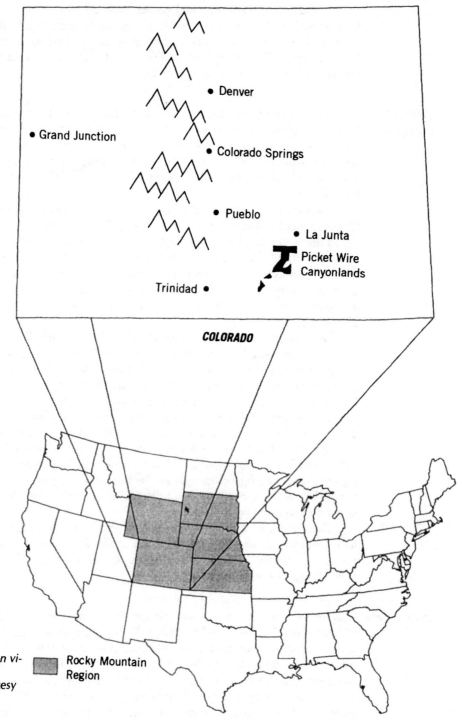

Figure 25.3
Picket Wire Canyon vicinity map. (From USFS, 1993. Courtesy of USDA, Forest Service.)

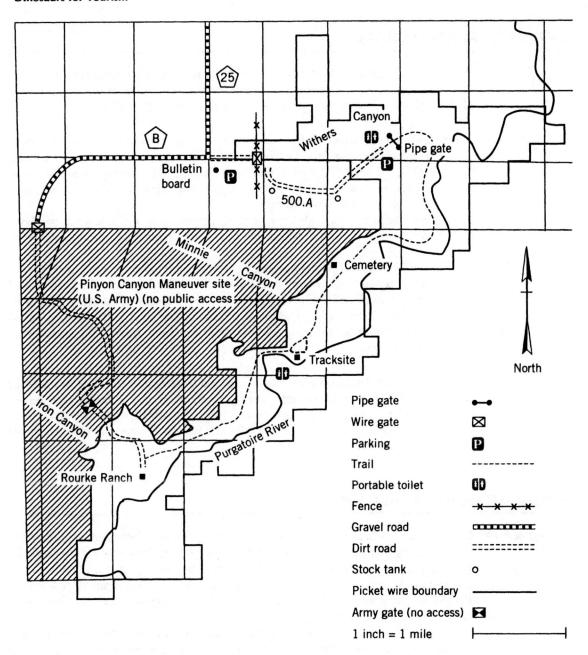

Figure 25.4
Picket Wire Canyonlands temporary hiking access. (From USFS, 1993. Courtesy of USDA, Forest Service.)

DEFINING TARGET MARKETS

Within natural heritage sites, it is critical that the target markets complement the sensitivities of the site. Therefore, a policy of controlled access is seen as being the most responsible form of management. Potential market segments include the following:

- *Educational institutions* (schools and universities) from surrounding locations in the triangular region that are within a three-hour drive of the site (e.g., La Junta, Pueblo, Trinidad, Colorado Springs, and Canon City). Drawing visitors from educational institutions is believed to be a good long-term investment for educating the public about natural heritage sites.
- *Scientific groups* (paleontologists, historians, geologists, archaeologists, and botanists) from government, higher education institutions, and private research interests.
- *Families and other people* who can be categorized into three travel groups: (1) day trips by people from within 50–200 miles (80–320 kilometers) of the site as well as pass-through traffic; (2) overnight stays; and (3) weekend or vacation trips made by residents from Pueblo, La Junta, Colorado Springs, and Canon City, as well as tourists driving on Interstate 25 from other locations within a three-hour drive (e.g., Denver).

Visitors could also be classified based on special interests and according to activity or trip purpose (e.g., nature photography, hiking, camping, cycling, painting, sightseeing). Whether visits are motivated by opportunities to visit a particular type of site (i.e., historic, prehistoric, cultural, or scenic) or to attend special shows or events should be noted when profiling markets.

PROPOSED DEVELOPMENT STRATEGIES

Staging Areas Staging areas, which serve as departure and parking points for visitors, are required. Currently, parking and access for the Picket Wire Canyon are located along the roadside. Any increase in visitation would necessitate a more formal staging area to ensure safety and security for visitors. One option is to locate an information center/staging area in Pueblo, one hour away. Other partners believe that the staging areas would best be located at the entrance to the canyon.

Staging sites would provide information about the dinosaurs, fossils, artifacts, and the ancient people that inhabited the land, as well as house a photographic display of all the attractions and castings of the tracks, thereby enhancing interpretation of the site's resources. Information centers located in the staging areas could also provide information about related sites.

Transportation Transportation in and out of the canyon for groups should be provided by subcontracting with a concessionaire. Concession guides, in conjunction with the USFS, could establish a carrying capacity[5] for the area, thereby limiting the number of visitors and controlling each expedition so that negative environmental impacts at the site are minimized. Trained guides could facilitate efforts to preserve, or at least conserve, the resources through on-site education.

Moreover, the use of concessionaires is a logical alternative for the USFS in light of significant budget cuts and staff reductions. Concessionaires could provide guided jeep, mountain bike, horseback, llama, and hiking tours. Concession operators could be selected based on criteria established by the Ecotourism Society that address the management practices of tour operators from an ecological or environmental perspective (Ecotourism Society, 1992).

Controlling Visitor Impact Rules and regulations for visitors could be posted on trail signs. Guides, volunteers, and Forest Service personnel should be authorized to enforce the rules and regulations. For individuals wanting to explore the area on their own, the current visitor permit system administered by the USFS could continue. This system would monitor the numbers of visitors on the site without a guide and would provide a means to respect the carrying capacity limits established for the area. Private visitors would register at the USFS office where they would pick up a permit and receive information on the area, rules and regulations, and the sensitivity of the resources. Controlling visitation requires achieving a balance between crowds and having a sufficient critical mass to render natural heritage development financially feasible.

Financing Natural Heritage Development The feasibility of developing the Picket Wire Canyon as a tourism and recreation resource depends on management's ability to engender a respect among the general public for the sensitivity and fragility of the unique natural environment. Funding through subcontractors could provide access, interpretation, and nonmonetary support. Scientific associations, geological and mining companies, local enterprises, universities, and schools represent important potential sources of economic support (through research and other educational activities). Creating awareness of the site is critical to facilitating the success of commercial interests. However, as alluded to earlier, a balance must be achieved between the number of visitors required to enhance the profitability of commercial ventures and the preservation and conservation goals of the natural heritage site.

Existing Facilities The canyon is isolated and there are few built structures. Indeed, the lack of facilities within the canyon presents a myriad of challenges (e.g., the difficulty of accessing assistance and providing care in an emergency situation and the lack of access to drinking water).

The Rourke Ranch, a former working ranch in the canyon which is now a historic site, has an energy supply, so some infrastructure is in place. However, toilet facilities are required at the ranch and dispersed throughout the canyon. Potable water must be brought in because it is currently not available inside the canyon. Conservation of the Rourke Ranch could be facilitated if it were converted to a visitor center. This would encourage interpretation and study of the paleontological and archaeological resources. However, this would only be practical if the currently used Iron Gate Canyon access is continued. The development of on-site information centers and use of existing facilities depend on the level of involvement of potential partners.

Partnership Programs

Comp (1993) indicated that recreational opportunities, historic sites, cultural institutions, and scenic and natural areas are essential elements of a heritage region. The USFS management plan identified a number of agencies that may jointly plan and develop the Picket Wire Canyon area. These included the National Park Service, the United States Fish and Wildlife Service, the Secretary of the Army, the Colorado Department of Natural Resources, and the Colorado State Historic Preservation Office (USFS, 1993). Additionally, the United States Geological Survey has evaluated much of the land in the canyon and has made plaster casts of the dinosaur tracks for further study.

There are a large number of other potential partners that could be excellent resources for interpretation, education, research, and funding, including local chambers of commerce, planning boards, "friends" organizations concerned with geology, paleontology, and archaeology, institutions such as the National Science Foundation, universities and schools, and organizations such as the National Historic Trust. Partnerships could also be forged with museums such as the Denver Natural History Museum and the Museum of Western Colorado to educate people about fossil and artifact collecting and the laws that govern such activity.

Although the notion of building a collaborative framework of support is not new, it encompasses some new ideas. Interest and assistance among citizens and local political groups, combined with government agency support, may not seem particularly remarkable. However, achieving a strong sense of cooperation among multiple counties, a variety of agencies and federal entities, state and federal politicians, and recreation and conservation groups would indeed be remarkable (Comp, 1993). With all these groups working together to educate and create awareness among the general public concerning paleontological and archaeological resources and the need to conserve and preserve natural heritage sites, the result could be a more environmentally sensitive and ethical visitor.

CONCLUSION

Development and public use of the Picket Wire Canyon can be advanced through evaluation of the site using the T/ROS as a tool to properly classify resources and subsequently develop an interagency management plan as described in the Paleo/Partnership model. The potential for development of natural heritage sites is immense. However, education and partnerships are key ingredients for effective development of paleontological heritage resources for tourism purposes.

By utilizing the conceptual models offered, the Picket Wire Canyon and other natural heritage tourism sites can be assessed and classified. Once classified, the goals and objectives for development of natural heritage tourism sites can be applied to the Paleo/Partnership model to guide planning and management of natural heritage sites.

ACKNOWLEDGMENTS

The author acknowledges the research efforts of the following students from the Graduate Tourism Program, School of Hotel, Restaurant, and Tourism Management, Daniels College of Business, University of Denver: L. Osius, J. Wheatley, A. Nyquist, D. San Ramon, and E. Frohlich.

NOTES

1. See Chapters 10 11, and 24 for additional discussion relating to heritage tourism.
2. See Chapters 5, 9, 11, 12, and 14–19 for additional discussion relating to community involvement and community-based tourism planning processes.
3. See Chapter 13 for additonal discussion regarding the importance of interagency cooperation and collaboration.
4. See Chapter 24 for additonal discussion relating to the role of interpretation in museum settings.
5. See Chapters 9, 22, and 23 for additional discussion relating to the use of carrying capacity and limits of acceptable change as management tools.

REFERENCES

Behrensmeyer, A. 1994. *Learning from Fossils: The Role of Museums in Understanding and Preserving Our Paleontological Heritage.* Paper presented at Partners in Paleontology: The Fourth Conference on Fossil Resources, October, Colorado Springs, Colorado.

Brown, K. 1993. Tourism trends for the 90s, *History News,* 48, 4–7.

Bruns, D., S. Richardson, and T. Sullivan. 1994. *Recreation-Tourism Community Partnerships for Sustainable Adventure Travel.* Paper prepared for the Fifth International Symposium on Society and Resource Management: Issues in Natural Resources Based Tourism, 9 June, Denver, Colorado.

Bruns, D. and P. Stokowski. In press. Sustaining opportunities to experience early American landscape. In *Nature and Human Spirit: Toward an Integrated Land Management Ethic,* section IV, Public Land Management Issues. Venture Press.

Comp, T.A. 1993. Heritage tourism comes of age, *History News,* 48(3), 9–12.

Ecotourism Society. 1992. *Responsible Travelers Fact Sheet.* Alexandria, Virginia.

Light, D. and R.C. Prentice. 1994. Market-based product development in heritage tourism, *Tourism Management,* 15(1), 27.

Millar, S. 1991. Heritage management for heritage tourism. In S. Medlik (ed.), *Managing Tourism.* Oxford, England: Butterworth–Heinemann, pp. 115–121.

National Park Service. 1994. *Dinosaur National Monument.* Washington, D.C.: United States Department of the Interior.

United States Congress. 1991. *Report to the Committees on Armed Services and Agriculture of the Senate and the House of Representatives.* June. Public Law 101–510, Section 2825.

United States Forest Service (USFS). 1993. *Picket Wire Canyonlands Interim Management Direction, Second Draft.* Comanche National Grassland, Pueblo, CO: United States Department of Agriculture.

United States Forest Service (USFS). 1994. *Recreation Opportunity Guide: Picket Wire Canyon.* Comanche National Grasslands, Pueblo, CO: United States Department of Agriculture.

✄ | PROBLEM SOLVING AND DISCUSSION ACTIVITIES

1. Identify a natural heritage site in or your near your area.
   a. Use the T/ROS as a guide to classify the site for existing and potential use.
   b. Use the Paleo/Partnership model to plan the management process for the site.
   c. What other attractions complement the natural heritage site? What attractions potentially compete with the site? Will demand for the area grow? If so, at

what pace? How might the natural heritage site penetrate the existing tourism market?

   d. Discuss and plan the use of existing facilities in this natural setting. What are the benefits and disadvantages of locating staging areas nearby or far away?

   e. Develop strategies to solicit partners who will contribute positively to the development of the site.

2. What is meant by "visitor ethics"? Develop a visitor code of ethics for the Picket Wire Canyon site or another natural heritage site.

3. To what extent are preservation and conservation compatible with multiple use of such resources? How should natural heritage sites be marketed?

4. What funding strategies are available to natural heritage attractions (such as the Picket Wire site) and nearby dependent communities? Investigate the strengths and weaknesses of alternative funding methods (i.e., entrance fees, fees for hiking permits, donations, fund raisers, sponsorships).

5. Outline the process you would use to determine carrying capacities within Picket Wire Canyon. What challenges might you face? How would you address these challenges?

26

Attracting the Invisible Tourist Market

VFR TOURISM IN ALBURY WODONGA, AUSTRALIA

 *Bob McKercher*

✤ | KEY LEARNING POINTS

- Consideration should be given to targeting nontraditional tourist markets in regional marketing plans. VFR travel represents a sizable market, yet it is often overlooked when developing strategic plans.
- One of the reasons why VFR travelers have not been studied in detail is that they are an "invisible market." Standard data collection techniques tend to miss the VFR segment. Therefore, there is a need to consider alternative methodologies to gain market information. Surveying residents about the friends and relatives who visit them represents an innovative and cost-effective means of gathering information about VFR travel.
- Timely and accurate market intelligence is required when developing strategic marketing plans. VFR travelers tend to exhibit travel patterns that are different from those of other tourists. Therefore, developing VFR marketing plans based on approaches that target other types of tourists will likely be ineffective.
- Local residents tend to be prolific hosts of visitors. They also influence the actions of their friends and relatives while in the area. Therefore, marketing strategies aimed at the VFR market should be targeted to residents, not visitors.

INTRODUCTION

VFR (visiting friends and relatives) travel is one of the most important, yet least examined, segments of the tourism industry. Although this market has not been targeted by most tourism authorities, it accounts for a sizable proportion of tourism activity in many destinations. This chapter examines the role that local government tourism agencies can play in attracting the VFR market to Albury Wodonga, a regional Australian community.

Residents of Albury Wodonga are prolific hosts of VFR travelers. In fact, VFR travel represents a potential A$50 million (US$36 million) for the region. However, the economic potential of the VFR market is not being realized because few VFR travelers visit the region's commercial tourist attractions. Moreover, hosts who play a significant role

509

in determining visitor activities do not believe that the region's commercial attractions are appealing.

The central question examined in this chapter is how local government tourism agencies can target the potentially lucrative, but elusive, VFR market. Before this question can be answered, a greater understanding of VFR travel to Albury Wodonga must be gained. An innovative methodology was developed to examine residents' involvement as hosts of VFR travelers and to obtain accurate and cost-effective market intelligence that could be used as input into the strategy formulation process.

This chapter highlights a number of key issues concerning tourism marketing and strategic planning: (1) The importance of VFR travel to the local tourism market mix is overviewed; (2) the role that local government tourism promotion agencies can play in tourism marketing is explored; (3) the importance of timely, accurate, and reliable market data to underpin the development of any marketing strategy is highlighted; and (4) an introduction to strategic marketing decision making is provided.

VISITING FRIENDS AND RELATIVES (VFR) TRAVEL: CONTEMPORARY PERSPECTIVES AND ISSUES

VFR travel is an important, though often ignored, component of tourism. It represents between 33 percent and 40 percent of all domestic tourism activity in countries such as Canada (Mill and Morrison, 1985), the United States (Gee, et al., 1989), and Australia (BTR, 1994). VFR travel is largely an inelastic form of tourism (Mill and Morrison, 1985) and tends not to be very sensitive to demand variations and seasonality (Bull, 1991). VFR travel is also typified by high levels of repeat visitation and, therefore, represents a stabilizing factor for many destinations given that tourism generally demonstrates high income and price elasticity, instability of demand, strong seasonality, and dramatic fluctuations in the popularity of specific destinations and products (Foster, 1985).

The motives and actions of VFR travelers are often different from other types of tourists. Hall (1995) suggests VFR travel is motivated by social reasons. Bull (1991) says that this form of travel is often driven by obligation. He adds that VFR trips satisfy "personal needs" and that this type of trip "is largely undertaken as an end in itself" (Bull, 1991, p. 28). VFR travel is characterized by above-average trip durations and a tendency for visitors to stay at a single destination. It is, therefore, an attractive market for destination areas that may lack dominant primary attractions.

Moreover, since these visitors usually do not use commercial accommodation, they are likely to have additional discretionary spending ability for other activities. While VFR visitors generally spend less per day than other tourists, a study conducted in the United Kingdom suggested that their expenditure levels may compare favorably with tourists staying in hotels if the area is well established as a tourist destination (Vaughan, 1986 in Ryan, 1991). As such, they represent a high potential market for attractions, shopping, and other activities.

To a large extent, VFR travel is an invisible tourism activity, the importance of which is rarely appreciated. Jackson (1990) illustrated that international VFR travel is substantially underreported. Indeed, only a small number of national tourism organizations (NTOs) specifically identify VFR travel as a distinct inbound tourist category. Likewise, some Australian and overseas domestic tourism statistics either exclude VFR travel or include it in the broader "pleasure travel" segment (NSWTC, 1993).

Jackson (1990) proposed that VFR travelers are not of great interest to tourism agencies because they generally do not use mainstream tourism facilities and do not necessarily respond to traditional promotional activities. Consequently, the development of marketing strategies to attract VFR travelers is hindered in Australia and elsewhere by the almost total lack of market knowledge about this important phenomenon.

THE ALBURY WODONGA REGION

Locational Context and Background Albury (New South Wales) and Wodonga (Victoria) are twin cities that straddle the New South Wales and Victorian borders on the Murray River in the foothills of the Victorian Alps (see Figure 26.1). The cities are located about 185 miles (300 kilometers) northeast of Melbourne and 375 miles (600 kilometers) southwest of Sydney. The capital of Australia, Canberra, is about a four-hour drive to the northeast. The twin cities, with a regional population of 92,000, form Australia's largest inland urban center that is not a capital city (AWDC, 1994). Like most cities that straddle state or provincial borders, some duplication of services and cross-border rivalries exist.

The area experiences a Mediterranean climate with cool, wet winters and dry, hot summers. Temperatures during the winter (June, July, and August) typically range from 28°F to 50°F (-2°C to 10°C). During the summer (December to March), the daily high is typically 95°F (35°C) or more. Pleasure travel peaks during the summer and autumn school holiday periods, and it troughs in late winter.

Traditionally, Albury Wodonga has been an important service center for the rural sector. In 1974, the twin cities were nominated as Australia's first National Growth Centre. This was part of an effort to decentralize the Australian economy and to stimulate rural development. The Commonwealth government formed the Albury Wodonga Development Corporation (AWDC) and funded substantial capital projects to enhance the region's attractiveness as an industrial base. Government departments, including the Australian Tax Office, relocated to the area and major manufacturers such as the Mars Corporation, Australian Newsprint Mills, and defense contractors established themselves in the region. Since then, the area's population has grown dramatically. Indeed, the AWDC estimates that 75 percent of the region's population in 1994 was born outside the area. This creates strong potential for VFR travel.

The region's economic climate is considered healthy for a regional community, although it is not as robust as that of Australia's capital city. Until the recession of the early 1990s, employment grew by about 5 percent per annum (AWDC statistics). Since then, growth levels have fluctuated marginally.

Organization of the Tourism Industry in Albury Wodonga Tourism promotion in the region is coordinated by Tourism Albury Wodonga (TAW), a committee of Albury City Council. It is funded jointly by the City of Albury and AWDC. The tourism industry provides about one-third of TAW's revenue, primarily through joint marketing initiatives. Wodonga Council funds the region's largest tourist information center. TAW is also responsible for the Albury Convention Bureau and, through Albury City Council, manages the Albury Convention and Performing Arts Centre and the pad-

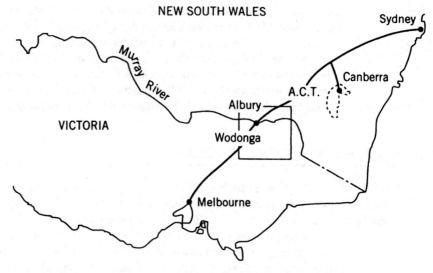

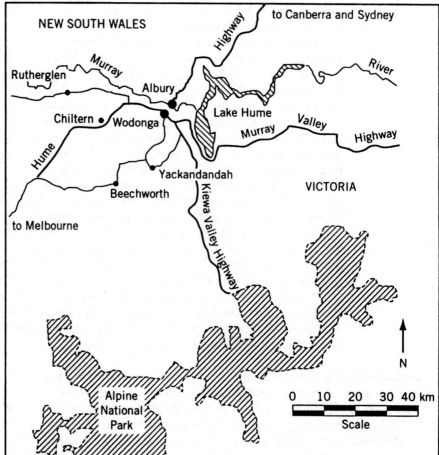

Figure 26.1
Albury Wodonga and
environs.

dle steamer, the P.S. Cumberoona. TAW is managed by a board comprising both local government officials and industry representatives. Various subcommittees report to the board, with the Marketing Committee being the most important.

The primary role of the local government organizations is to create awareness of the region as a tourist destination, while the private sector is normally responsible for the actual sale of tourism products. An exception involves the pursuit of major events (e.g., large conventions), where the local government organizations may actually close a sale. Designed to complement, not replace, the marketing activities of the private sector, many of the promotional activities coordinated by TAW are generic in nature and are targeted at creating a general awareness of, and desire to, travel to the area.

The success of local government marketing campaigns cannot be easily evaluated. Increases or decreases in visits to the area may be a function of factors lying outside the control of the region (e.g., legalized gambling in Victoria). Therefore, it is impossible to precisely attribute the rise or fall in tourist traffic to specific local government marketing campaigns. Consequently, local government tourism agencies may be accused of not being very effective.

Local tourism organizations also face the challenge of having to satisfy the competing, and often conflicting, interests of the local tourism industry and their political overlords. As a committee of Albury City Council, TAW must constantly justify its decision to promote the greater region when it is administered by only one city. Moreover, TAW is not immune to the emerging trend of downsizing and privatizing government activities. One local councillor, in particular, has been a vociferous advocate of dismantling and privatizing the organization.

Specific Issues Facing Tourism in Albury Wodonga

In early 1994, Colin Bransgrove, the executive director of TAW, was faced with the task of identifying strategies to improve the performance of the local tourism industry. The effects of the recent recession, liberalization of gaming laws in Victoria, deregulation of domestic air travel in Australia, and changing consumer tastes had all taken their toll on tourism in the Murray River area in general and Albury Wodonga in particular. Occupancy rates had fallen and attendance levels at the region's tourist attractions had declined. Encouraging results in the early months of 1994 suggested that the worst had passed. Visitor levels had begun to stabilize. Nonetheless, Mr. Bransgrove was under pressure, not only from the industry, but also from the board at TAW, to develop strategies to enhance industry performance.

The executive director was also searching for ways to improve tourism's appeal within the local community. Residents of Albury Wodonga were somewhat indifferent to tourism and essentially unaware of the benefits it brought to the region. Moreover, like residents of most other communities, they tended not to visit the region's "tourist" attractions, believing that they were of little interest to locals. As such, low attendance levels potentially jeopardized the profitability of many of the area's attractions. Two attractions in particular, the paddle steamer P.S. Cumberoona (see Figure 26.2) and the Ettamogah Pub (see Figure 26.3), an attraction based on an Australian cartoon icon, had suffered financial difficulties in the early 1990s. If the image of tourism could be improved, it was likely that attendance levels at these and other attractions might also improve.

Colin Bransgrove met with tourism management faculty from Charles Sturt University (CSU). Their discussions eventually focused on local residents and their involvement

Figure 26.2
The paddle steamer P.S. Cumberoona. (Courtesy of Hilary du Cros.)

in VFR travel. It was recognized that residents play a direct role in the tourism industry both as hosts of friends and relatives and as potential patrons of commercial tourist attractions. They also play an important indirect role in influencing the types of activities that visitors undertake. It was believed that if residents had positive images of their home community, they would encourage VFR travel. Conversely, if their impressions were negative, they could inhibit travel. Mr. Bransgrove stated:

> The VFR market is clearly a critical market for us, but we have never really developed any strategic approaches to target these people. What's more, we really know nothing about them, how big the market is, what people do, where they come from. . . . Better knowledge of the VFR market would help us develop an effective strategy. More effective tourism marketing activities targeted at local residents would allow us to capitalize on that strategy. Imagine marketing Albury Wodonga as a tourist destination to the residents of Albury Wodonga. I do not think it has ever been done before.

The case study described in this chapter emerged from those early conversations. Throughout 1994, TAW, with the help of CSU tourism management students and faculty, undertook a systematic examination of the VFR market with the ultimate goal of developing a marketing plan to capitalize on opportunities created by VFR travel. The target of this plan would not only be VFR visitors, but more importantly, the local residents who host friends and relatives. Mr. Bransgrove scheduled a meeting of the TAW Marketing Committee in late November 1994 to discuss the results of the study and to

Figure 26.3
The Ettamogah Pub.

begin to formulate a plan of action. The remaining sections of this chapter present an overview of tourism in the Albury Wodonga area as well as a summary of the project undertaken by faculty and students at CSU on behalf of TAW.

TOURISM IN ALBURY WODONGA

Attractions The Albury Wodonga area is a significant inland tourist destination, offering a wide array of natural, cultural, historic, and built attractions. The region's natural attractions are dominated by Lake Hume, the Murray River, and the Victorian and New South Wales (NSW) Alps. Lake Hume, an artificial lake built in the 1930s to provide water storage for irrigation and hydroelectric purposes, has become the focal point for many recreational activities. The lake, which is five times larger than Sydney Harbour, provides a venue for swimming, boating, and sailing activities. The Murray River, Australia's largest river, bisects the two cities. An extensive park system has been created along the shoreline in both Albury and Wodonga, and cycling paths have been developed along the river's flood plain and numerous billabongs.[1] The river itself is used for swimming and boating.

The Victorian Alps are located about one to one and a half hours south of the twin cities. They provide a focus for extensive tourism and recreational activity. Two of the state's three major downhill ski fields and their adjoining Alpine resort villages, Falls Creek and Mount Hotham, are located south of the city. These resort areas provide up to 10,000 beds of commercial accommodation and, in a good snow winter, welcome over

500,000 overnight visitors. Furthermore, the popular Alpine National Park (see Figure 26.4) provides cross-country skiing opportunities and, in the summer, offers bushwalking, horseback riding, and four-wheel driving.

The area is intricately linked to Australia's gold mining, winemaking, and bushranger past. Within a 20–mile (30–kilometer) radius of the twin cities are the important gold-mining towns of Beechworth (see Figure 26.5), Yackandandah, and Chiltern whose heritage townscapes have been preserved. The nearby community of Rutherglen, which is Australia's oldest winemaking area, produces world renowned fortified wines. The area was also home to Australia's most famous bushranger, Ned Kelly, who roamed through the area in the 1870s and, when finally apprehended, was imprisoned in Beechworth. The Kelly story is one of the core nineteenth-century Australian folklore legends, and Ned Kelly himself has become an Australian icon. Interestingly, Mick Jagger played Ned Kelly in a film produced in the early 1970s.

The area is also served by a number of built attractions. Until 1992, the tourism sector was dominated by the region's six large licensed clubs that offered poker machine or slot machine gambling to Victorians. Until then, gaming was illegal in Victoria but legal in New South Wales. Gambling-starved Victorians flooded across the Murray River to spend an estimated A$600 million (US$432 million) annually in border communities like Albury. The legalization of gambling and the opening of Victoria's casino in Melbourne in 1994 had a devastating effect on the rural clubs and the club-based tourism sector. Visitation levels in many border communities declined by 25 percent or more, affecting all sectors of the tourism industry. The clubs in Albury have not suffered as badly

Figure 26.4
Alpine National Park, Victoria.

Figure 26.5
Historic Beechworth.

as clubs in other locations. However, they have had to revise their marketing strategies to focus more on local residents and less on interstate tourists.

The area's other built attractions represent an odd amalgam of activities. The largest attraction in terms of visitor numbers is the Ettamogah Pub, a re-creation of a popular cartoon pub that has appeared in the magazine *The Post* for decades. Until the Ettamogah Pub was built, the most popular attraction was the Hume Weir Trout Farm, a fish farm/ tourist park. Frog Hollow Recreation and Tourist Park provides a range of recreational activities, including miniature golf, a maze, and croquet snooker.

The Ettamogah Sanctuary (see Figure 26.6) is a wildlife refuge for injured native animals that has been positioned as a tourist attraction since 1992. Finally, Albury commissioned the paddle steamer, the P.S. Cumberoona, as a bicentennial project in 1988 to re-create the bygone days when Albury was a major freshwater port transporting agricultural goods up and down the river. The paddle steamer operates short tours throughout the spring, summer, and autumn.

The built attractions have suffered from low patronage and low profitability in recent years. The Ettamogah Pub and its sister pub in Queensland went into receivership in 1993 before being sold. The P.S. Cumberoona has never operated at a profitable level, and it is now under pressure from the local council to run on a cost recovery basis or face decommissioning. The Aussie Land Adventure Park, a combined science/technology theme park, operated for less than two years before closing in 1992. Capturing the VFR market is believed to provide one avenue of economic stability for the region's attractions.

Figure 26.6
The Ettamogah Sanctuary.

Visitation VFR travel accounts for between 17 percent and 27 percent of all inbound travel to Australia (ATC, 1994; BTR, 1992), and about 47 percent of all domestic visitor-nights in Victoria and New South Wales (BTR, 1994). Developing accurate estimates of VFR travel for regional or transborder communities, however, is a much more difficult task. Tourism NSW includes Albury in its geographically large Murray Region that extends along the entire length of the state's southern border. However, it is likely that Albury experiences different patterns of tourist traffic compared to other parts of this region. As such, the statistics offer insight into likely visitation patterns and trends, but do not provide definitive travel data for Albury. Moreover, the Albury Wodonga region straddles the NSW/Victorian border. In the past, there has been a lack of comprehensive data gathered for the Victoria side of the region.

Available information suggests that proportionately less VFR tourism activity occurs in this region than elsewhere in NSW and Victoria, with estimates ranging from 25 percent to 29 percent of all trips (AWDC, 1988; CSU, 1991; NSWTC, 1992). A study conducted by the Victorian Tourist Commission during Easter 1985 reported that only 16 percent of travelers surveyed were visiting friends or relatives (VTC, 1985). By the same token, it is estimated that VFR travel to this area accounts for a lower proportion of total person-nights than elsewhere in southeastern Australia (CSU, 1991; NSWTC, 1992). Extrapolating NSW and Victorian state averages to the region suggests that only 38 percent of all visitor-nights are associated with VFR travel. The relative importance of hosts as a source of accommodation also appears to be declining (AWDC, 1988; NSWTC, 1990).

Accurate tourist visitation data for the twin cities is impossible to find, partly due to the imprecise nature of domestic tourism data collection methodologies and the lack of data for the Victorian side of the region. The New South Wales Tourism Commission (1993) has the most reliable figures. It estimates that in 1991–1992 about 370,000 overnight visitors generated 1.05 million person-nights in the area. The average length of stay was 2.8 nights, although a recent study of visitors to the Gateway Tourist Information Centre revealed that the median length of stay was 2.0 nights.

Tourists injected about A\$77 million (US\$55 million) into the local economy. The AWDC estimates that visitors spend about A\$150 million (US\$108 million) in the two-state region and create 3000 direct full-time equivalent jobs. It is possible, therefore, to estimate that over 700,000 overnight visitors come to the region each year and generate in excess of 2.0 million person-nights. Based on existing data, it is crudely estimated that about 190,000 VFR person-trips are taken to the Albury Wodonga region annually (27 percent share of all visits) and that 750,000 VFR person-nights are spent in residents' homes (37.5 percent of all visitor-nights).

Little research has been identified that examines the role the host plays in stimulating VFR travel and influencing VFR tourism activities. The author has identified only one such study (i.e., Nickerson and Bendix, 1991). Moreover, from an Albury Wodonga perspective, little attitudinal research has been conducted on the region's appeal as a tourist destination. An earlier study conducted by CSU faculty and students in 1990 attempted to provide some baseline data on the appeal of the region. Overnight visitors were asked about their perceptions of the area's attractions after having visited the region. Entertainment and recreation opportunities were the two most highly recommended features of the community. Its natural appeal, history, and local wineries rated highly. The Ettamogah Pub was mentioned by 5 percent of respondents, while shopping was mentioned by 2 percent of the sample (CSU, 1991).

Respondents were also asked to identify what should be promoted to optimize tourist visitation levels. The most frequently mentioned features were, in order, the landscape, local wineries, Lake Hume, recreation, the Murray River, licensed clubs and their poker machines, the pleasant climate, history, the Ettamogah Pub, and finally, the snowfields. Most notable is the relatively low importance placed on the area's built attractions.

OVERCOMING THE INFORMATION GAP: THE VFR STUDY

As indicated previously, although VFR travel is an important and potentially lucrative market for Albury Wodonga, remarkably little is known about VFR travel to the region, and even less is known about hosts' involvement in this activity. To overcome this information gap, a joint study was initiated by TAW and CSU tourism management students and faculty. As part of their assessable workload, third-year business management students conducted a series of telephone interviews with local residents about their family's involvement in VFR travel in March and April of 1994. A total of 225 households were surveyed, which represents a statistically reliable sample (at the 95 percent confidence level) of the estimated 25,000 households in the area.

The questionnaire was designed to elicit information about hosts' recent VFR experiences. Respondents were asked if friends or relatives had visited them during the 12 months to March 1994 and, if so, how many times. Respondents were then asked for details on the most recent visit by friends or relatives. The vast majority of these visits occurred during January to March 1994. As such, a seasonal bias is evident in the list of activities undertaken.

In a number of instances, the data were positively skewed (i.e., some large outlying numbers were reported). The impact of these outliers is to inflate the mean or average response for the sample. This can result in misleading conclusions being drawn about the region as a whole. To control for skew, the data have been analyzed using both median scores and trimmed means. Trimmed means exclude the largest and smallest 5 percent of responses when calculating the mean. Together, the two methods of estimating the impact of VFR travel provide a lower and upper boundary for the range of impacts in this area. Estimates based on median scores provide a conservative lower-end figure for VFR travel, while those based on trimmed means provide an upper estimate of the impact of this activity. In reality, the truth probably lies somewhere in between.

Highlights of the VFR Study The study revealed a number of important features about VFR travel (see Table 26.1). Other studies had significantly underrepresented the amount of VFR activity occurring in this area, but overestimated the length of stay. As a result, existing expenditure estimates are probably reliable. The study revealed that between 219,900 and 316,150 VFR person-trips were taken to Albury Wodonga from March 1993 to March 1994, a figure that is 25 percent to 80 percent higher than prevailing estimates. Importantly, however, rather than staying four or more nights, typical VFR travelers spent two to three nights in the region, indicating that most VFR activity occurs over weekend periods. Nonetheless, VFR visitors spent up to one million person-nights in Albury Wodonga in 1993–1994.

Holiday/pleasure was the most frequently cited trip purpose for VFR travel followed by family gatherings (e.g., weddings, birthdays, funerals, anniversaries, reunions). Family members were more than twice as likely to engage in VFR activity compared to friends, with siblings and their families accounting for the single largest travel group. The typical VFR party size was between two and three people. The travel party was twice as likely to be composed entirely of adults rather than to consist of adults traveling with children. Over 95 percent of VFR visitors stayed with other friends or family, or with their hosts in the region, suggesting little potential for the commercial accommodations

TABLE 26.1
Key Results of the Albury Wodonga VFR Survey[a]

Households participating in VFR travel in the Albury Wodonga area	87.6%
Number of visits per household per annum	Median: 5 Trimmed mean: 5.99
Estimated total number of person-trips taken to Albury Wodonga between March 1993 and March 1994	219,900 to 316,150
Estimated total person-nights spent in the region between March 1993 and March 1994	438,000 to 995,000
Estimated total expenditure by VFR visitors between March 1993 and March 1994 (millions)	A$21.4 to A$40.5
Estimated incremental expenditure incurred by residents when hosting friends and relatives between March 1993 and March 1994 (millions)	A$5.5 to A$11.3
Trip purpose	
Holiday/pleasure/for a visit	68.6%
Family gatherings	12.7%
Other	18.7%
Party Composition	
Family	64.3%
Friends	30.6%
Mix of family and friends	5.1%
Party size	Median: 2.00 Trimmed mean: 2.41
Length of stay	
One night	22.7%
Two to three nights	45.9%
Four or more nights	31.4%

[a] Number of households: 225.

sector to capitalize on this market. Almost 90 percent of all VFR visitors came from NSW, Victoria, or the Australian Capital Territory, with most driving six hours or less. A significant positive correlation was noted between distance traveled and length of stay.

The study revealed that residents of Albury Wodonga are prolific VFR hosts. Almost 88 percent of households surveyed welcomed friends or relatives in 1993–1994, with most of them hosting visitors on numerous occasions. Indeed, the median and trimmed mean number of visits recorded between March 1993 and March 1994 was five and six visits, respectively. Importantly, the study revealed that virtually all sectors of the community participate in this activity.

VFR travel to Albury is not affected by the hosts' age, family status, life stage, length of residency in the region, or place of birth. There was, however, a small but statistically significant inverse relationship between household income and participation in VFR travel. Hosts themselves incurred significant incremental expenses as a result of their friends or relatives coming to visit, estimated at A$25 (US$18) per VFR trip-night. These expenses resulted from food purchases, entertainment, petrol, entry fees, shopping, and gifts.

VFR Activities   Survey respondents were asked an open-ended question regarding the places visited or the activities undertaken during their most recent experience of hosting VFR guests. The results, (see Table 26.2), proved both enlightening for the region and disturbing for the owners and/or operators of the cities' built attractions.

Two important findings emerged. The first relates to the broad appeal of attractions located outside of Albury Wodonga to this market. Excluding shopping and various types

TABLE 26.2
Activities Undertaken During Most Recent Experience Hosting VFR Guests in Albury Wodonga[a]

Rank	Activity	Number of Mentions[b]	Percentage of Households
1	*Shopping*	64	32.5
2	Lake Hume	48	24.4
3	*Licensed clubs*	46	23.4
4	*Night clubs*	44	22.3
5	General sightseeing	43	21.8
6	Historic towns of Beechworth and Yackandandah	39	19.8
7	*Ettamogah Pub*	24	12.2
8	*Rutherglen wineries*	18	9.1
	Victorian Alps/foothills communities	18	9.1
10	Swimming	14	7.1
	Nothing in particular	14	7.1
12	Chiltern/Rutherglen	13	6.6
	Unspecified sports	13	6.6
14	*Lake Hume Trout Farm*	11	5.6
15	*Golfing*	9	4.6
16	*P.S. Cumberoona river cruise*	7	3.6
17	*Frog Hollow Tourist Attraction*	6	3.0
18	*Ettamogah Sanctuary*	5	2.5
19	Historic town of Jindera	4	2.0
20	Other sport	4	2.0
21	Other	2	1.0
Total		446	

[a] Number of households: 197.

[b] Multiple responses.

Note: Visits to built attractions are shown in italics.

of evening entertainment pursued in town, six of the top 10 activities undertaken or destinations visited were outside Albury Wodonga proper. It would appear that much of the appeal to the VFR tourist can be found in Lake Hume to the east, the historic gold-mining towns of Beechworth and Yackandandah to the south, the winegrowing region of Rutherglen and its associated historic gold-mining town of Chiltern to the west, and the Victorian Alpine area to the far south. Importantly, cultural attractions (i.e., art gallery, museums) were not mentioned by any respondent.

Second, with the exception of shopping and evening entertainment, built attractions, which ranked near the bottom of the list, appear to have limited appeal to the VFR market. Not including the Ettamogah Pub, which ranked seventh and was visited by 12 percent of households, built attractions were visited by between 2.5 percent and 5.6 percent of respondents. The apparent lack of desire to visit these facilities highlights a major marketing challenge for local tourist operators. The owners either have been unaware of the potential offered by the VFR market or have been unsuccessful in their marketing efforts aimed at local residents, who are the main decision makers when selecting weekend activities.

Participation in certain activities was influenced by the composition of the travel party and the demographic profile of the host. More than 60 percent of hosts who took their guests to night clubs were under 30 years of age. Friends as well as groups traveling without children, were far more likely to go to night clubs. Shopping was more likely to be undertaken when parents were visiting or when people were traveling with children than when siblings visited. Hosts were far more likely to take friends to Lake Hume than to take their parents. Travel parties comprising the hosts' parents and groups with children were most likely to tour historic towns.

Top of Mind Activities The challenge facing operators of built attractions was highlighted further when respondents were asked to identify the most appealing features of Albury Wodonga as a tourist destination (see Table 26.3). Again, four of the top five attractions were situated outside the city, with Lake Hume, the Alpine area, the wineries, and the historic towns dominating specified responses. Built attractions rated no higher than eighth.

These findings highlight a significant awareness problem that must be addressed by local tourism operators and TAW when promoting the region's tourism products to locals. In addition, the findings highlight the generally low perceived quality of many of these attractions. Rather than being seen as a hub from which day tours can be taken to outlying areas, it appears that many residents see the region as more of a doughnut, with Albury Wodonga as the hole in the middle and the broader region offering the edible outer dough.

Part of the awareness problem can be attributed to the inability of current marketing activities to reach local residents and, in particular, the failure of local tourist information guidebooks and brochures to reach residents. Although 80 percent of respondents believed that there was sufficient tourist information available, 89 percent indicated that they did not seek any information when planning their most recent visit by friends or relatives.

The task of promoting local tourist attractions to residents, and through them to VFR visitors, is complicated by the fact that although residents' awareness of the existence of

TABLE 26.3

Most Appealing Aspects of a Trip to Albury Wodonga and Environs[a]

Rank	Feature	Number of Mentions	Percentage of Households
1	Lake Hume	93	41.5
1	General/unspecified	93	41.5
3	Victorian Alps, including the ski fields	57	25.4
4	The city of Albury	30	13.4
5	Rutherglen wineries	29	12.9
6	Historic townships (Beechworth, Yackandandah and Chiltern)	25	11.2
7	Pleasant climate	19	8.5
8	*Licensed clubs*	15	6.7
9	*Ettamogah Pub*	10	4.5
10	*P.S. Cumberoona*	9	4.0
11	*Lake Hume Trout Farm*	6	2.7
12	*Golfing*	5	2.2
13	*Frog Hollow Tourist Attraction*	1	0.4

[a] Number of households: 224.

[b] Multiple responses.

Note: Built attractions are shown in italics.

built attractions is high, their knowledge of specific product offerings is low. Residents believe that they know all there is to know about these attractions and, therefore, do not want or feel the need for additional information. Promotional literature that might enhance product knowledge is thought to be irrelevant for local residents.

SWOT Analysis for VFR Travel The results of the study filled much of the information gap that existed and identified some key issues for consideration by the Marketing Committee. To complement these data, a SWOT analysis (strengths, weaknesses, opportunities, threats)[2] of the region's appeal to VFR tourists was also conducted (see Table 26.4).

Possible Initiatives The release of the VFR study coincided with the emergence of a number of initiatives that highlighted both the need for VFR tourist information and the opportunity to provide enhanced tourist services for local residents:

- The two largest private sector employers in the region contacted the city council requesting that a guidebook for new residents be developed focusing on local attractions, what is available, and how new residents can explore their new surroundings.

TABLE 26.4
SWOT Analysis of the Attractiveness of Albury Wodonga to VFR Travelers

Strengths	Weaknesses	Opportunities	Threats
A wide variety of activities and attractions to suit many tastes.	Lack of primary attractions and high-quality secondary attractions.	Regional population of 92,000.	Legalized gambling in Victoria and the opening of a casino in Melbourne will put greater pressure on the area's licensed clubs. They may not survive.
Tourism Albury Wodonga is recognized as one of the best regional tourism promotion organizations in Australia (winner of both the NSW and Victorian local government tourism organization in 1992 and 1995).	Some existing built attractions are struggling financially.	Close proximity to major population centers of Melbourne and Canberra (4 hours) and Sydney (6 hours).	The aftermath of the recession and the continued rural crisis may inhibit travel.
	Lack of knowledge of built attractions by residents, even though awareness of their existence is high.	Albury Wodonga is situated on the Hume Highway (the main highway between Melbourne and Sydney) and also enjoys good rail, bus, and air connections.	Climate is too hot in summer (35°C to 40°C), too cold and rainy in winter.
Regional attractions, such as Beechworth, Rutherglen, and Lake Hume are well known.	The perception among local residents that the built attractions are for visitors, not locals.	Large resident population not born in Albury Wodonga (75%).	
Residents have a positive opinion of the region (95.5% would recommend the area for a vacation).	Inability of tourist information to reach target audience.	Proximity to one of only two major downhill ski regions in Australia.	
Strong regional attractions.	Lack of information about the VFR market.	Growing population resulting in new VFR opportunities.	
	Lack of "local" tourist information for residents.	Growing industrial base resulting in many newcomers coming to the area.	
	Transborder issues hinder the collection and dissemination of tourist information.	Pleasant country atmosphere provides potential visitors with the opportunity to escape the city.	
	The potential impact of the negative images of the area residents may have.	Major expansions planned for the area's two universities.	
	Lack of awareness of tourist attractions by locals.	One of the few major freshwater destinations in Australia.	
		Pleasant climate in spring and autumn.	

- The board of TAW announced its intention to construct a mobile tourist information kiosk to be located in the heart of the city, creating a much-needed downtown venue for the distribution of tourist information.
- TAW's Marketing Committee, wanting to streamline tourism literature, supported the concept of creating a monthly "what's on" type of publication targeted at local residents outlining current events and attractions. This publication would complement the larger tourism publication aimed at visitors to the area that is produced twice yearly.
- The local newspaper, the *Border Mail*, announced that it was planning an advertising feature targeted at the holiday and VFR market for January when advertising purchases are normally low. TAW indicated a desire to assist with the editorial copy for this insert.

TAW also indicated that it was considering a range of other ideas to enhance the experience for residents and their visitors. Among the suggestions considered were the creation of walking trails throughout the city, publication of a local attractions map, more effective dissemination of information, and a greater presence at local trade shows targeting residents. In addition, some of its local television advertising began to target VFR visitors. New television advertisements aired locally for the P.S. Cumberoona ended with the line "the next time your friends or family come to visit, take them on the Cumberoona."

CONCLUSION: THE TASK

The bandwagon appeared to be rolling. Both TAW and the tourism industry were becoming more aware of the importance of the VFR market. Moreover, it was recognized that the best way to reach this potential A$50 million (US$36 million) market was through residents. The research demonstrated that residents typically welcomed friends or relatives five or six times each year and that they incurred substantial incremental expenses while their friends or family were visiting. Moreover, the study indicated that although residents play a critical role in influencing the activities of their visitors, they did not hold the local tourism product in high esteem. Furthermore, marketing efforts by commercial attractions were not reaching hosts. The industry recognized that increasing VFR traffic represented a cost-effective opportunity to increase patronage by residents and, therefore, profitability.

The study also illustrated the need for timely and accurate market information as the foundation for effective marketing strategies. Both TAW staff and tourism operators were surprised by the results. TAW staff did not have a strong appreciation of the importance of this market or of the role that residents played in the health of the local tourism industry. Most tourism operators naively assumed that they were receiving a substantial share of the VFR market. The low patronage rates were a shock to them. Now, though, they had some reliable market intelligence on which they could develop proactive strategies to address the problems.

A number of concerns, however, still perplexed Colin Bransgrove. While the market appeared attractive, he wondered how he could integrate a VFR marketing plan into the broader TAW marketing strategy. Moreover, he was unsure of the role that TAW, an organization charged with the task of bringing people to this area, should play in trying to convince residents to use their own facilities more. He was also uncertain of the role the tourism industry itself should play.

Two other important issues had not been addressed. The first was that no one had identified realistic goals and objectives for the VFR market. Could a marketing program increase use levels at local facilities by 5 percent or by 50 percent? Second, only A$3000 (US$2160) had been allocated to the VFR project and it was unlikely that further incremental funding would be provided. As such, any programs developed would have to be inexpensive to deliver and/or be coordinated with other promotional programs.

The TAW Marketing Committee was set to meet to discuss the final report on the study of VFR travel. The desired outcome of this meeting was to set the parameters for the development of a marketing plan aimed at VFR travelers and residents and then to develop such a plan. Ideally, the meeting would identify target goals and objectives as well as outline a range of activities that could be included in such a marketing plan. Colin Bransgrove was anxious to see how the meeting would go.

NOTES

1. A billabong is a channel from a river coming to a dead end or an oxbow lake.
2. See Chapters 5, 6, 24, and 28 for additional discussion relating to SWOT analysis.

REFERENCES

Australian Tourist Commission (ATC). 1994. *Tourism Pulse #26.* July. Sydney: ATC.

Albury Wodonga Development Corporation (AWDC). 1988. *Tourism in Albury Wodonga.* Albury, NSW: AWDC.

Albury Wodonga Development Corporation (AWDC). 1994. *Albury Wodonga Social Indicators: 1994 Update.* Albury, NSW: AWDC.

Bull, A. 1991. *The Economics of Travel and Tourism.* Sydney: Pitman.

Bureau of Tourism Research (BTR). 1992. *Australian Tourism Data Card,* Spring. Canberra: BTR.

Bureau of Tourism Research (BTR). 1994. *Domestic Tourism Monitor,* December Quarter 1993. Canberra: BTR.

Charles Sturt University (CSU). 1991. *Albury Wodonga Tourism Study.* Albury: CSU.

Foster, D. 1985. *Travel and Tourism Management.* London: Macmillan.

Gee, C.Y., J.C. Makens, and D.J.L. Choy. 1989. *The Travel Industry,* 2nd ed. New York: Van Nostrand Reinhold.

Hall, C.M. 1995. *Introduction to Tourism in Australia: Impacts, Planning and Development,* 2nd ed. Melbourne: Longman.

Jackson, R. 1990. VFR tourism: is it underestimated? *The Journal of Tourism Studies,* 1(2), 10–17.

Mill, R.C. and A.M. Morrison. 1985. *The Tourism System.* Englewood Cliffs, NJ: Prentice-Hall International.

New South Wales Tourism Commission (NSWTC). 1990. *Regional Tourism Trends in New South Wales–Murray Riverina.* Sydney: NSWTC.

New South Wales Tourism Commission (NSWTC). 1992. *Regional Tourism Trends in New South Wales–Murray Riverina.* Sydney: NSWTC.

New South Wales Tourism Commission (NSWTC). 1993. *Local Government Area Estimates of Visits, Visitor Nights and Tourist Expenditure, 1987/88–1991/92*. Sydney: NSWTC.

Nickerson N. and D. Bendix. 1991. A *New Look at* VFR. Proceedings of the Travel and Tourism Research Association 22nd Annual Conference. Salt Lake City, Utah: TTRA, pp. 373–379.

Ryan, C. 1991. *Recreational Tourism: A Social Science Perspective*. London: Routledge.

Victorian Tourism Commission (VTC). 1985. *Victorian Tourism Commission North–East Region Visitors Survey Quantitative Research Report*. Melbourne: VTC.

¶ | PROBLEM SOLVING AND DISCUSSION ACTIVITIES

1. Identify and discuss the key internal and exogenous issues that may affect the desire and ability of destination marketing organizations (such as convention and visitors bureaus, chambers of commerce, or state/provincial tourism ministries) to target the VFR market.

2. One of the themes of this chapter was the need for accurate and timely information when developing marketing strategies. Yet, the data presented in this chapter is by no means complete. Identify information gaps that are still evident, and discuss their implications for developing a marketing strategy to attract the VFR market.

3. A special meeting of the TAW Marketing Committee has been convened to discuss the issues presented in this case study. As chair of the meeting, Colin Bransgrove wants to achieve a set of specific outcomes that he can then take back to his staff for action. Identify and discuss the types of outcomes that Colin Bransgrove should achieve during this meeting.

4. Residents are key players in the region's tourism industry, yet they do not always seek, or feel the need to seek, tourist information. Discuss actions that could be developed to encourage greater awareness and use of local attractions among residents.

5. The local tourism industry is keen to improve its share of the VFR market. Using data presented in this chapter, calculate the increased levels of visitation and revenues that could accrue to the operators of built attractions if they could double their share of the VFR market. Then, discuss the potential advantages and risks of attracting this market, key strategies that might be considered by tourism operators, and how much money TAW should be willing to invest in incremental marketing activities. Admission fees (A$) for the attractions are as follows:

	Adults	Children	Family Pass
P.S. Cumberoona	$8	$4.50	$20
Frog Hollow	$6	$5	$20
Hume Weir Trout Farm	$5	$3	$16
Ettamogah Pub	Free	Free	Free
Ettamogah Sanctuary	$5	$2	Not applicable

6. The Marketing Committee is keen to develop a marketing strategy to attract the VFR market, but is working under a number of constraints, the least of which is its limited budget. Develop a marketing plan for TAW (or another tourism organization) to attract the VFR market. The plan should identify specific goals and objectives, include a concise situation analysis, propose strategies and tactical plans, outline costs, and identify control measures. When preparing this plan, identify where TAW (or the other tourism organization) should play a direct role in marketing, an indirect leadership/coordination role, and an even more distant role as a facilitator for private industry.

7. How much importance does your community or local/state/provincial government place on VFR travel? Interview key tourism and business leaders (including local tourism officers, senior management staff at commercial attractions, government officials, chamber of commerce staff, and others) to assess their perception of the importance of VFR tourism to the region. Prepare a brief report summarizing these findings.

8. Design a research methodology, including a survey instrument, to explore the importance of VFR tourism in your own community as well as residents' perceptions of the value of tourism to them.

27

Cultivating Markets for Economic Spin-offs

THE NIAGARA WINTER FESTIVAL OF LIGHTS, ONTARIO, CANADA

 *Laurel J. Reid*

¶ | K E Y   L E A R N I N G   P O I N T S

- Festivals must become more accountable to funding bodies and sponsors. Economic impact and return on investment potential must be demonstrated to both public and private sector investors. Evaluation and documentation of festival results provide feedback for future planning and development.

- Because of the accountability requirement, research is playing a more dominant role in helping to justify investments in festivals.

- A solid research program can help festivals reach the desired markets more efficiently and increase "high-yield" customers. Profiles of attendees must be generated on an ongoing basis to ensure that marketing efforts are targeted to more productive markets that are compatible with those served by festival sponsors.

- Community support is critical to the ongoing evolution of festivals. Therefore, the host community's attitudes and perceptions of the festival must be known.

INTRODUCTION

The Niagara Winter Festival of Lights (NWFL) is an internationally recognized light festival that has grown to be one of the largest of its kind in Canada. Based in Niagara Falls, Ontario, the NWFL began in 1982 as a community-driven initiative to increase tourism during the off-season. The festival features a dazzling array of light displays and events that are popular with both visitors and locals. Visitor numbers increase annually, partially due to positive publicity.

The provincial tourism ministry has designated the NWFL as one of Ontario's top 10 events. Moreover, the American Bus Association (ABA) named the festival to its prestigious *Top North American Events* list in 1994. This list features festivals that have strong market appeal for tour operators, offer high-quality visitor experiences, and exhibit effective management and marketing.

The NWFL provides an example of how research can strengthen marketing efforts and enhance economic value for sponsors and the community. This chapter demonstrates how marketing initiatives, marketing research, and economic impacts are linked to accountability and return on investment issues. First, the chapter discusses how and why these issues are relevant to festivals. A profile of tourism in the city of Niagara Falls, Ontario then offers a context for the subsequent description of the NWFL. A synopsis of the festival's history, organizational structure, facilities, and events sets the stage for examining marketing efforts. Finally, the role of marketing research and its relationship to sponsorship and other elements of the festival's marketing mix (promotion, distribution, pricing, and sponsorship) are presented.

FESTIVALS: CONTEMPORARY PERSPECTIVES AND ISSUES

Festivals Defined   Broadly defined, a *festival* is a celebration or display of a theme that occurs annually, or less frequently, to which the public is invited for a predetermined time (EPG, 1993; Getz, 1991a). Festivals typically are not housed in permanent fixed structures. The program may consist of several separate activities or events taking place in the same municipality or region. Community festivals generally use volunteer labor, are staged at one or more public venues, and are sponsored by local government and/or business or service organizations. These characteristics are believed to reflect "community ownership" of the event (Janiskee, 1994).

Festivals of all types are increasing around the world (Janiskee, 1994). Economic development, community development, and not-for-profit fundraising are among the main reasons for organizing, sponsoring, and marketing festivals (Smith and Getz, 1994). Recognizing that a balance between peak and off-season events is desirable, particularly if the festival aims to attract tourists, festivals are becoming more common year round (Janiskee, 1994).

Festivals generally focus on a theme: harvest/agriculture, ethnicity, commemoration, sports, culture, or the arts (EPG, 1993). For example, A *Taste of Chicago* in Illinois (USA) focuses on culture, and features Chicago's best dining, theater, music, museums, galleries, and other attractions. *The Edinburgh Fringe Festival* in Scotland highlights the visual and performing arts, including music, art, crafts, pageants, and other cultural attractions. The NWFL is a community festival themed around the magic of lights. Interestingly, a 1994 study of international festivals identified fireworks competitions, illuminated parades or festivals of light, and "First Night" celebrations (New Year's Eve celebrations) as growth areas (Smith and Getz, 1994), all three of which are integral components of the NWFL.

Community festivals often rely on outside funding. Consequently, accountability has become a principal focus of festivals in the 1990s. Increasingly, organizers are stressing the benefits as opposed to the costs associated with festivals. Management must be able to defend budgets and provide evidence to funding bodies and sponsors that festivals can be financially successful. Moreover, evaluation and documentation of festival results provide feedback for future planning and development.

Markets and Marketing Issues   Market intelligence is critical to festival growth, especially as sponsorships assume a greater role in supporting festival activities in the face of public sector budget constraints. Profiles of attendees must be generated on an ongoing basis to ensure that marketing efforts are targeted to more "productive" markets that are compatible with those served by festival sponsors. Particularly when tourists are targeted, organizers must attempt to attract "high-yield" visitors (i.e., those who stay longer than one day and, therefore, have higher expenditures).

Information on participation and satisfaction levels is essential (Robinson and Noel, 1991). Data on audience spending patterns are instrumental in assessing economic impacts. Research is also required to evaluate the success of marketing activities and to track visitor inquiries. Moreover, the proliferation of festivals and intense competition for consumer recreation time and dollars mean that festival product offerings must be regularly strengthened and differentiated. Product development decisions can be enhanced through understanding customer needs, wants, and perceptions.

Community support (as volunteers, participants, attendees, hosts of visitors) is critical to the ongoing evolution of festivals. Therefore, the host community's attitudes and perceptions of the festival must be known[1] (Blank, 1989; Murphy, 1985). Research can facilitate decisions relating to addressing negative attitudes, planning for future development, and devising marketing strategies (Ap, 1990).

The most common tool for profiling visitors is the survey. One critique of on-site surveys is the lack of systematic sampling which results in the selection of samples that are often not representative of the overall visitor mix (Getz, 1991a). The validity and reliability of information collected without the benefit of systematic sampling techniques may be questioned.

Despite these potential limitations, market research is important for establishing a targeted marketing program. Manipulation of the traditional marketing mix (product, promotion, distribution, and pricing), which gives a festival its "pull" based on understanding market profiles and preferences (i.e., product–market match), will help to ensure a festival's survival (Janiskee, 1994; Robinson and Noel, 1991).

Economic Impacts   The importance of establishing a festival's economic impact, along with the advantages and pitfalls of various approaches to assessing impacts, is well documented.[2] Undertaking economic impact studies generally coincides with the need to demonstrate the value of festivals to funding bodies. Economic impact assessments can have a strong effect on the future direction and growth of festivals. Reliable economic impact studies provide evidence of return on investment to public and corporate sponsors and, therefore, enhance the festival's ability to attract additional events, in-kind donations, committed officials, media sponsors, and community support (Peterson and Crayton, 1995).

Unfortunately, studies tend to exaggerate the net benefits of a festival through making inappropriate assumptions and overstating income and employment multipliers. Even when assessing the direct impacts, festival attendees are often unable to accurately recall the amount of money they spent. These limitations result in unreliable claims of impact assessment (Getz, 1991a, b).

Another question relates to the appropriateness of including resident spending in impact assessments. Incremental spending (i.e., additional revenue generated that would have been unlikely without the event) is a critical barometer of success. Some believe that resident spending should not be included, since residents would spend money anyway.

Festival organizers tend to focus on attendance at events. While such numbers may be meaningful from the perspective of providing indicators of exposure and reach for sponsors, they do not adequately reflect the economic spin-offs of a festival. Moreover, the reliability of attendance estimates, especially when admission to many events may be free, must be questioned. Emphasis must be shifted from volume of attendees to revenues generated (Getz, 1991b). This requires understanding the spending patterns of target markets.

Accountability and Sponsorship The trend toward establishing partnerships is increasing throughout the tourism industry, including the festival sector. Sponsors are usually considered as "partners" in the festival. Partnerships benefit all players due to improved festival development and the marketing and brand recognition enjoyed by both the festival and its sponsors (Smith and Getz, 1994).

Research can provide input into the formulation of strategies to retain existing sponsors and obtain new ones. Given increasing dependence on, and competition for, sponsorship revenue and related services, efforts to attract sponsors are becoming more professional. Festival organizers must demonstrate that sponsor participation is worthwhile, otherwise, sponsors are not likely to become, or stay, involved.

Sponsors seek information on audience size, market compatibility, and market exposure or reach (coverage). Other factors considered include (1) the festival's stature, (2) whether they (the sponsor) have exclusive rights, (3) links to distributors, (4) opportunities to sell products (spending patterns are useful for forecasting whether attendees may purchase sponsor-related products during the festival) and (4) long-term opportunities to enhance visibility and name recognition (Crompton, 1993, 1994). "Preferred supplier" agreements, where one or two sponsors are featured as key festival affiliates, are becoming more common (Smith and Getz, 1994) as a means to enhance brand awareness.

Festival and event organizers are enhancing their fundraising (often termed "development") skills in an attempt to reduce dependence on grants (Smith and Getz, 1994). Examples of initiatives conceived as supplementary revenue sources include miniature versions of the main events, theme parties, celebrity events, and membership sales. However, the success of these activities depends on sponsor support.

The links among research, marketing, economic impacts, sponsorship, and accountability are critical. Research helps delineate markets and facilitates the development of targeted marketing and promotional activities that result in the ability to leverage marketing dollars, especially if the "high-yield" attendee is targeted. Research can also help determine economic impacts and the return on investment to public and private sector investors and sponsors, thereby enhancing the potential of future fundraising efforts. These issues are examined below in the context of the NWFL.

THE NIAGARA WINTER FESTIVAL OF LIGHTS: LOCATIONAL CONTEXT AND BACKGROUND

The City of Niagara Falls, Ontario Niagara Falls, Ontario, which has a population of 76,500 people, is about half way between Toronto, Ontario and Buffalo, New York (about an hour's drive from each). Niagara Falls, New York is situated directly across the Niagara River. There are two sets of falls: Rainbow Falls on the American side of the Niagara River and Horseshoe Falls on the Canadian side (see Figure 27.1). The best vistas of both sets of falls are in Queen Victoria Park, Canada, which is owned and operated by the Niagara Parks Commission (NPC).[3]

Tourism in Niagara Falls, Ontario
The history of tourism in Niagara Falls dates back to the early nineteenth century. The opening of the Erie and Welland canals during the 1800s facilitated initial access to the Falls. When auto touring became popular after Word War I, attractions and accommodations sprang up in strip developments in the city, much of which survives today. By the late 1940s, the Falls drew 40,000 visitors per year. Tourism peaked from the 1950s to 1970s, but a recession in the early 1980s saw decreases in visitor numbers. In 1990–1991, with another tourism downturn across North America, several hotel properties in Niagara Falls, Ontario went bankrupt. The city now hosts an estimated 11–12 million local and international visitors annually (NPC, 1994).

The destination marketing function has predominantly been handled by the Niagara Falls Canada Visitor and Convention Bureau (VCB). In 1994, tourism marketing became the responsibility of a newly designated umbrella organization, Niagara Falls Tourism Inc. (NFTI). The VCB has retained information dissemination, customer service, and industry training functions. In 1994, NFTI received $831,000 (CAD)[4] from the city council, of which $380,000 (CAD), or 46 percent, went to the NWFL. The remaining $451,000 (CAD) was allocated to the VCB. An additional $1.2 million (CAD) was received from the private sector to coordinate marketing programs.

Almost half (45 percent) of the travel to Niagara Falls, Ontario and 52 percent of expenditures are generated during the summer (July to September). April to June account for 31 percent of visits and 26 percent of expenditures. The first and fourth quarters each generate about 10 percent of the visitors and expenditures. Visitors come from Ontario (47 percent), the United States (40 percent), and overseas (7 percent).

Only about 38 percent of trips made by Ontarians to Niagara Falls involve overnight stays (KPMG, 1994). Metropolitan Toronto generates the majority of Ontario-based trips followed by Southwestern Ontario dwellers living within 180 miles (290 kilometers). Lower-than-average per capita spending levels in Niagara Falls [about $74 (CAD) per visit, which is 30 percent below the provincial average] is a reflection of the average visitor's short length of stay (KPMG, 1994).

An estimated half-million motorcoach passengers visit Niagara Falls each year. Many also visit attractions located in other parts of the Niagara Region,[5] which boasts 13 of Ontario's top 30 attractions visited by motorcoaches, including the Niagara Winter Festival of Lights (KPMG, 1994).

NWFL: Be Here When the Nights Ignite!
EVOLUTION OF THE NWFL   Inspired by the American Festival of Lights in Niagara Falls, New York, which began in 1981, the Canadian NWFL was created as a parallel event in 1982. The two cities believed that they could work together to develop a major international celebration. The dual festivals have become a winter destination for people within a 180-mile (290-kilometer) radius of Niagara Falls. However, in terms of both events and visitation, the Canadian festival has developed to a greater degree than its American counterpart.

The NWFL, which is held over a 54–day period from mid-November to mid-January, draws over a million people annually. A dazzling array of sparkling displays line a 2-

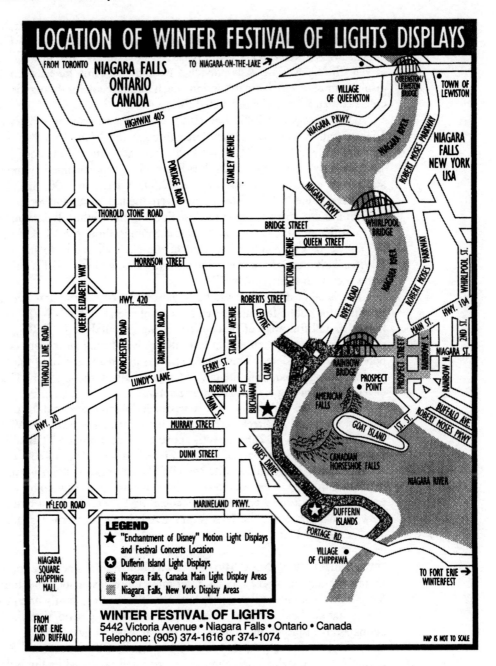

Figure 27.1
Festival of Lights location (program map). (Courtesy of Niagara Winter Festival of Lights.)

mile (3-kilometer) stretch of road in Queen Victoria Park, concentrated between the Rainbow Bridge and Dufferin Islands in Niagara Falls, Ontario (see Figure 27.1). Because admission to the Park is free, many visitors simply drive or walk through the park to view the lights. The Falls provide a majestic backdrop for between 40 and 50 light displays, most of which are in motion. Each display contains thousands of tiny lights and costs between $7,000 and $25,000 (CAD).

When it began in 1982, the festival received an operating subsidy from the city of Niagara Falls which was administered through the VCB. In 1983, this amounted to approximately $30,000 (CAD). By 1990, this had increased to about $130,000 (CAD). The total operating budget of the NWFL in 1990, supplemented by sponsorship support and private contributions, was about $500,000 (CAD). In 1990, the VCB attempted to divest itself of the NWFL. Major issues were the lack of support for the festival from the tourism industry (many properties close down in the winter), the stagnation of the product, and the ever-increasing financial commitment from the VCB. At the inception of the festival in 1982, only 15 percent of the city's allocation to the VCB went to the NWFL. This increased to over 39 percent in 1990, and the NWFL's allocation from the city was close to 46 percent by 1994.

The issue of divestiture was hotly debated by city councillors who argued that the benefit to the public far outweighed the cost of operating the NWFL. The VCB escaped having its full funding cut by council. However, funds were finally granted, with the proviso that it would continue to fund the festival during an interim period while other options were considered. This debate resulted in a reassessment of roles by major stakeholders. In particular, both the city of Niagara Falls, Ontario and NPC allocated staff to develop new funding and programming options.

In 1992, the NWFL became a separately incorporated not-for-profit organization with its own board of directors. However, financial support from the VCB continued. In June 1993, NWFL relocated directly across the street from the VCB and began independent operations. A summary of key NWFL facts is presented in Table 27.1.

The renewed commitment to the NWFL led to two partnership successes that ultimately contributed to festival growth. These involved participation by Walt Disney Company (Canada) Limited and Baton Broadcasting Systems (BBS), a nationwide television network that broadcasts the New Year's Eve celebration across Canada and provides a great deal of publicity.

NWFL ORIENTATION AND ACTIVITIES   Two of the festival's primary goals are to enhance tourism during the off-season and foster more tourism activity throughout the year. The focus is on the family. All major festival activities are free, family-oriented, nonalcoholic events that are held outdoors across from the Falls in Queen Victoria Park. Lights are permanently displayed throughout the festival. Special events complement the displays and take place throughout the two months, usually on the weekends. Some events such as the New Year's Eve celebration are funded and produced by the NWFL. Others are independently produced. Independent event producers enter into agreements to use the NWFL logo and promotion vehicles. Table 27.2 highlights events associated with the 1994 festival.

The first major event is the *Opening Ceremony* with live entertainment from Walt Disney World Resort, Florida, and Disney celebrities on hand to share in the festivities.

TABLE 27.1
Key Facts About the 1994 Festival of Lights

Organization

A not-for-profit corporation that generates its own operating revenue. Directors are appointed volunteers who do not receive compensation. The chair of the board liaises with staff. Staff also work in conjunction with the NPC, key employees of the city of Niagara Falls, the VCB, corporate sponsors, and members of the tourism and hospitality industry to coordinate event and marketing efforts.

Staff

A festival manager and permanent staff of one with additional full-time and temporary staff hired during the festival through federal job creation programs, as available. These positions include coordinators of special events, volunteer management, information distribution, on-site coordination, as well as a secretary/bookkeeper.

Volunteers

Approximately 300 at large, with most responsible to committees (see Figure 27.2).

Funding

Total 1994 festival revenue: $741,050 (CAD). 76% of revenue derived from grants; an additional 13% came from sponsors; the remaining 11% came from other sources.

Festival Slogan

Be Here When the Nights Ignite!

Festival Size

Fragmented counts estimate that more than 250,000 people and over 40 motorcoaches visited the first festival in 1982. Within two years, more than one million visitors traveled to Niagara Falls to experience the festival. Some sources say that numbers have continued to increase with the 1992 festival enjoying attendance of 2.4 million. Group traveler volumes have also increased dramatically with 5,436 motorcoaches visiting in 1992. These counts all appear to take into account pedestrian, automobile, and motorcoach passersby. The most reliable data estimates 1994 annual overnight visitor attendance at 174,390 with thousands of others who visit on a same-day basis (Dore and Patterson, 1994).

Venues/Sites

Most large events are held in Queen Victoria Park in the open air, along the Niagara Parkway opposite the Falls (see Figure 27.1). The site is owned and operated by the NPC. Events are produced by the NWFL with the permission of the NPC.

Major Events in 1994

Opening Ceremonies	Live Entertainment from Walt Disney World Resort,
New Years Eve Niagara Falls	Florida, *'Twas the Night Before Christmas*
Saturday Night Fireworks	Country Night
Candles in the Park	Festival Kid's Concert

Note: See Table 27.2 for event descriptions. All other events identified in Table 27.2 were separately produced and promoted as NWFL events as part of ongoing efforts to integrate tourism in the Niagara Region even though they were managed and funded independently.
(Courtesy of Niagara Winter Festival of Lights.)

TABLE 27.2
1994 Festival of Lights Calendar of Events

NOVEMBER 1994

Saturday/Sunday, November 12/13
Pre-Festival Fund raiser:"ART BY THE FALLS CHRISTMAS"
Arts and craft show sponsored by the Niagara Falls Rotary Sunrise Club.

Saturday, November 19
SANTA CLAUS PARADE
Marching bands, floats and Santa.

Saturday, November 19
OPENING CEREMONIES
Local dignitaries and special guests Mickey and Minnie Mouse. Fireworks display.

Saturday/Sunday, November 19/20
OPENING WEEKEND
"Mickey's 'Twas the Night Before Christmas," 25-minute show from Walt Disney World Resort, Florida. Tells the traditional Christmas story in musical form, featuring the Kids of the Kingdom, Mickey and Minnie Mouse, Goofy, Pluto, and others who perform a medley of classic Christmas songs. A great outdoor event in Queen Victoria Park.

Friday, November 25
FESTIVAL OF TREES
A fundraising competition of professionally decorated Christmas trees. Roman Court.

Saturday, November 26
MUSIC EXTRAVAGANZA SHOWCASE
Niagara Men's Chorus. Evening of music and comedy. Former Miss Canada emcees. Niagara Falls Secondary School. $10.00/ticket.

Saturday, November 26
HOLIDAY GALA
Evening of gourmet dining and dancing to the sounds of City Band at the Ameri-Canada Resort and Conference Center. Tickets $55.

Saturday, November 26
12th ANNUAL FESTIVAL OF LIGHTS MODERN SQUARE AND ROUND DANCE
Three rooms of dancing with three action callers. Stamford Collegiate.

DECEMBER 1994

Friday, December 2
NIAGARA-ON-THE-LAKE CHRISTMAS CANDLELIGHT STROLL
45-minute Victorian candlelight walk. Niagara-on-the-Lake. Events along Main Street.

Saturday, December 3
COUNTRY NIGHT ON THE MAIN STAGE
Queen Victoria Park, hosted by "Fun Bunch" from CHOW Radio. Country entertainment. Fireworks display.

Saturday/Sunday, December 3/4
11th ANNUAL FESTIVAL OF LIGHTS CHEERLEADING CHAMPIONSHIPS
St. Paul High School.

Saturday December 3
NIAGARA-ON-THE-LAKE CHRISTMAS EMPORIUM AND VICTORIAN CHRISTMAS

Sunday, December 4
6th ANNUAL FESTIVAL OF LIGHTS INVITATIONAL GYMNASTIC MEET
Mount Carmel Training Center.

Saturday, December 10
CANDLES IN THE PARK
Traditional family evening. Candlelight stroll through Queen Victoria Park. Christmas Carol Concert with Niagara Children's Chorus. Live Nativity scene by the Queensway Free-Methodist Church. Another Festival outdoor event.

Saturday, December 10
NIAGARA-ON-THE-LAKE CHRISTMAS PARADE

Saturday, December 10
BRIGHT'S LIGHTS UP A MYSTERY
Dinner in the cellars of Bright's Winery. Admission is $55 inclusive.

Friday, December 16
NIAGARA CONCERTS
Buffalo City Ballet presents the *Nutcracker*. Niagara Falls Secondary School Auditorium.

Saturday, December 17
CLAUDE HAGGERTY MAGIC SHOW
Master illusionist and his exotic cats perform a one-hour family show. Main stage in Queen Victoria Park.

Saturday/Sunday, December 17/18
NIAGARA SYMPHONY PRESENTS FOUR CONCERTS

Saturday, December 31
NEW YEAR'S EVE NIAGARA FALLS
Televised live by Baton Broadcasting Systems. Nonalcoholic, free, family celebration. Top entertainment. Fireworks. Show features Blue Rodeo, Ashley MacIsaac, Lisa Lougheed, Norman Foote, Harrison Kennedy, and Theresa Kelman.

JANUARY 1995

Friday/Saturday/Sunday, January 13/14/15
3rd INTERNATIONAL WINTER FESTIVAL OF LIGHTS INVITATIONAL GYMNASTICS MEET
Skyline Brock Hotel. Gymnasts

TABLE 27.2
(Continued)

from Ontario, Ohio, Pennsylvania, and New York.
Friday/Saturday/Sunday, January 13/14/15
WHEEL WORLD CAR SHOW
Three-day show. Cars from Canada and the USA. Some of the best customs, rods, and classics. Skylon Tower.

Saturday, January 14
FESTIVAL KIDS CONCERT
Sheraton Fallsview Hotel. World Champion double-dutch rope jumpers, the Lincoln Leapers. Children's entertainer Doug Barr and his Big Boy Band. Clowns and huggables. Only $2.50. Free for children under four years of age.

FORT ERIE WINTERFEST EVENTS

November 19, 1994–January 14, 1995
A VICTORIAN CHRISTMAS

Mildred M. Mahoney Dolls' House Gallery. Celebrate "A Victorian Christmas."
Saturday, November 26, 1994
SANTA CLAUS PARADE
Sponsored by the Chamber of Commerce.

OFFICIAL OPENING: The lighting of the lights with Town Crier.

FORT ERIE COMMUNITY CHORAL CHRISTMAS CONCERT

Saturday, December 3, 1994
HAY RIDES, MR. & MRS. CLAUS, ROAD RUNNER KIDDY TRAIN, CHILDREN'S ENTERTAINMENT

Saturday, December 10, 1994
CHAMBER OF COMMERCE LIGHTING AWARDS, SENIORS' TOUR OF CHRISTMAS LIGHTS & ROVING CAROLERS

Saturday, December 17, 1994
LIVE NATIVITY SCENE
Sponsored by Fort Erie Jaycees.

OTHER EVENTS TO ENJOY

Thursdays, Fridays, Saturdays, and Sundays
SENTINEL HORSE AND CARRIAGE RIDES

AND . . . nightly illumination of the Falls with thousands of sparkling lights. Light exhibits include 15 "Enchantment of Disney" motion light displays featuring famous Disney characters and themes as well as a "must see", the new Dufferin Island light displays.

FESTIVAL FIREWORKS SCHEDULE

Niagara Falls, Ontario
Saturday, November 1; Saturday, December 3; Saturday, December 31.

Note: All dollar amounts are expressed in Canadian dollars.
(Courtesy of Niagara Winter Festival of Lights.)

The *Enchantment of Disney* motion light displays, located near the main outdoor stage in Queen Victoria Park, feature familiar Disney figures and themes. Other major events include *New Year's Eve Niagara Falls* and *Country Night*. Select evenings feature fireworks extravaganzas over the Falls. Other events are staged at smaller venues, most of which draw near-capacity crowds. Most indoor events charge nominal admission fees.

NWFL ORGANIZATIONAL STRUCTURE AND STAFF   The NWFL structure was formalized for the first time in 1994. The governing body is a volunteer board of directors responsible for policy and decision making. Board members also act as committee chairpersons. A summary of each committee's role is provided in the festival's organizational chart (see Figure 27.2). There is also an advisory board that meets quarterly with the board of directors to discuss ideas for the festival.

The festival employs two full-time staff members, namely, the festival manager and the operations assistant. Since 1992, four additional temporary staff positions, funded through government job creation programs, have been created to help during peak operating times. As with most festivals, volunteers are an integral part of the NWFL (Getz, 1991a). A volunteer base of about 300 people performs a variety of tasks including staging, merchandising, office reception, and information distribution. The tourism/special

WINTER FESTIVAL OF LIGHTS

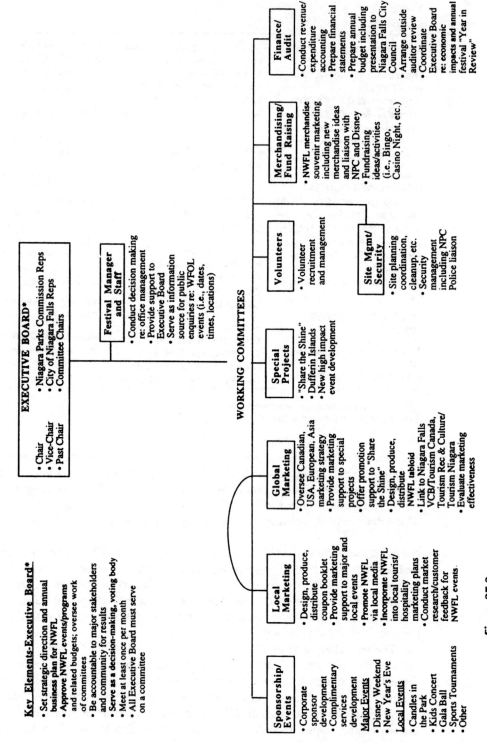

Key Elements-Executive Board*
- Set strategic direction and annual business plan for NWFL
- Approve NWFL events/programs and related budgets; oversee work of committees
- Be accountable to major stakeholders and community for results
- Serve as a decision-making, voting body
- Meet at least once per month
- All Executive Board must serve on a committee

EXECUTIVE BOARD*
- Chair
- Vice-Chair
- Past Chair
- Niagara Parks Commission Reps
- City of Niagara Falls Reps
- Committee Chairs

Festival Manager and Staff
- Conduct decision making re: office management
- Provide support to Executive Board
- Serve as information source for public enquiries re: WFOL events (i.e., dates, times, locations)

WORKING COMMITTEES

Sponsorship/Events
- Corporate sponsor development
- Complimentary services development

Major Events
- Disney Weekend
- New Year's Eve

Local Events
- Candles in the Park
- Kids Concert
- Gala Ball
- Sports Tournaments
- Other

Local Marketing
- Design, produce, distribute coupon booklet
- Provide marketing support to major and local events
- Promote NWFL via local media
- Incorporate NWFL into local tourist/hospitality marketing plans
- Conduct market research/customer feedback for NWFL events.

Global Marketing
- Oversee Canadian, USA, European, Asia marketing strategy
- Provide marketing support to special projects
- Offer promotion support to "Share the Shine"
- Design, produce, distribute NWFL tabloid
- Link to Niagara Falls VCB/Tourism Canada, Tourism Rec & Culture/ Tourism Niagara
- Evaluate marketing effectiveness

Special Projects
- "Share the Shine"
- Dufferin Islands
- New high impact event development

Volunteers
- Volunteer recruitment and management

Site Mgmt/ Security
- Site planning coordination, cleanup, etc.
- Security management including NPC Police liaison

Merchandising/ Fund Raising
- NWFL merchandise souvenir marketing including new merchandise ideas and liaison with NPC and Disney
- Fundraising ideas/activities (i.e., Bingo, Casino Night, etc.)

Finance/ Audit
- Conduct revenue/ expenditure accounting
- Prepare financial statements
- Prepare annual budget including presentation to Niagara Falls City Council
- Arrange outside auditor review
- Coordinate Executive Board re: economic impacts and annual festival "Year in Review"

Figure 27.2
Festival of Lights organizational chart.

events manager from the city of Niagara Falls, Ontario plays a key role in securing major sponsors and assists with the production of events.

Festival managers on both sides of the border communicate regularly. There is potential for joint promotions featuring the twin festivals and cities. However, actual collaboration is limited due to budget and human resource constraints as well as challenges created by the existence of multijurisdictional boundaries.

NWFL FUNDING SOURCES AND OPERATING BUDGET   Four major funding sources make the festival possible: (1) the city of Niagara Falls, Ontario (funds are channeled through NFTI), (2) the NPC, (3) corporate sponsors, and (4) local fundraising efforts. Support from these sources remained relatively stable between 1993 and 1994. The operating budget was about $740,000 (CAD) in both 1993 and 1994 (see Table 27.3). Revenues and expenditures are closely balanced so there is rarely a surplus. Percentage allocations from government grants, sponsors, and other revenue sources appear to be in line with those of other Canadian festivals where government grants range from 40 to 60 percent, sponsorship accounts for 13 to 27 percent, and other revenue sources make up the remainder (EPG, 1993; Getz, 1991a).

MARKET RESEARCH

The NWFL's market research system is in its development stage. Prior to 1993, little systematic research was conducted. Two major research initiatives—an economic impact study and a survey of community perceptions—are described below. Data from these studies provided benchmarks for future trends and represented the best available indicators of resident and visitor characteristics, their spending patterns, and satisfaction levels. It was believed that establishing the economic impact would help sustain and increase funding support.

Economic Impact Study   The economic impact study, which was conducted during the 1993 festival, focused on three populations: (1) festival visitors, (2) Niagara Region residents, and (3) Niagara Falls area businesses (Dore and Patterson, 1994). For the visitor survey, researchers distributed questionnaires at each event listed in the calendar of events using systematic intercept sampling over the length of each event, with the exception of three 10-minute intervals at the beginning, middle, and close of each event. During this time, researchers developed crowd estimates for their assigned area. Once this procedure was completed for each event, the area attendance counts were tabulated. Approximately 10,000 festival patrons were asked to complete and return self-administered mail questionnaires. An 18 percent response rate was achieved.

A telephone survey of 500 Niagara Falls and Niagara Region residents was also conducted to obtain demographic and direct expenditure information. The sample was contacted by telephone using stratified random sampling procedures based on names listed in the telephone directory. The response rate was 20 percent.

Finally, 170 businesses in the city were contacted by mail and asked to respond to a

TABLE 27.3

1994 Festival of Lights Statement of Revenue and Expenditures ($ Canadian)

	1993[a]	1994[a]
Revenue		
Public assistance		
City of Niagara Falls	$285,000	
Niagara Falls Canada VCB	95,000	
Niagara Falls Tourism Inc.[b]		$380,000
Tourism Canada grant[c]	82,770	
Region Niagara Tourist Council		5,000
Private sector		
Niagara Parks Commission	100,000	100,000
Corporate sponsors	102,000	135,000
Other revenue[d]	76,280	118,500
Total revenue	$741,050	$738,500
Expenses		
Office administration	$ 88,820	$117,900
Volunteer committee	1,500	2,500
Light displays	50,000	25,000
Events		
Event staging		127,500
Fireworks	15,000	
Opening ceremonies	39,500	
Disney Show	125,000	100,000
New Year's show	178,970	117,000
Kid's concert	17,070	
Candles in the park	4,000	
Miscellaneous events		20,000
Marketing		
Advertising/Printing	57,850	
Global print advertising		30,000
Lure brochure printing		16,500
Brochure distribution		2,000
Coupon book printing		12,000
Local print and radio		18,000
Tourism Canada (ads)	82,770	
Consulting	10,360	
Travel trade meetings	4,470	1,000
Joint marketing with US festival		1,000
Sponsorship development	36,160	93,000
Research	16,000	
Other	4,760	4,000
Section 25 expense		5,000
Merchandise/Fundraising		17,000
Site management/Security		29,000
Total expenses	$733,220	$738,400
Net income	$ 8,830	$ (100)

[a] Numbers have been rounded.

[b] In 1994, NFTI became the newly designated City DMO through which all city-designated tourism monies are channeled. It, in turn, provides funding to the VCB and the NWFL.

[c] One-time grant from Tourism Canada (now the Canadian Tourism Commission) provided for advertising.

[d] Includes fundraising efforts (bingo, holiday gala), merchandising (souvenirs concessions), cooperative coupon book revenues, and donations.

Source: Niagara Winter Festival of Lights.

self-administered mail/fax survey. While the visitor and resident surveys provided a good indication of the overall economic impact, the information provided by businesses assessed which businesses experienced changes in revenues and/or staff complements during the festival. A response rate of 35 percent was achieved.

The combined approaches established that the 1993 NWFL generated direct revenue of over $13.7 million (CAD) for the tourism and hospitality industries (see Table 27.4). This is important given that the NWFL invested $1.4 million (CAD) (cash plus donated services-in-kind) to mount the 1993 festival. When compared with direct revenues generated, this investment represents a benefit–cost ratio of approximately 9.8. These dollars were generated from approximately 175,000 festival *event-goers*. Visitor spending was concentrated in the accommodations and meals categories (see Table 27.5). Residents contribute little to the festival's overall economic impact. Indirect impacts were not included (Dore and Patterson, 1994).

Community Perceptions Survey Concurrently, festival organizers funded a Niagara Region resident survey to assess community perceptions and satisfaction levels (Reid, 1994). This telephone survey was conducted in February immediately following the 1993 festival. A systematic random sample of residents was drawn from the regional telephone directory. A total of 433 interviews was completed. Respondent demographics were compared to regional census data to ensure representativeness.

Approximately 68 percent of respondents had attended the NWFL at least once since 1989, with a majority attending every year. Attendance increased substantially over the five years prior to the study, leveling off in 1992 and 1993. There is high repeat visitation, suggesting that residents generally have positive attitudes about the festival. Most residents had attended at least four of the five previous festivals.

Virtually all attendees will drive or walk by the light displays (97 percent). The four most attended events were the Saturday Night Fireworks (19.2 percent), New Year's Eve Celebration (17.8 percent), Live Disney Shows (16.8 percent), and Opening Celebration (14.7 percent)—all events held in the park. Overall satisfaction levels were high. Resi-

TABLE 27.4

Geographic Visitor Segments and Direct Expenditures Attributable to the Festival of Lights ($ Canadian; n = 1800)

Visitor Group	Average Expenditure per Adult	Proportion of Total Visitors	Number of Visitors	Total Expenditures by Visitor Group
Southern Ontario	$ 65.05	61%	106,353	$ 6,918,295
United States	143.82	24%	41,884	6,018,004
Niagara Falls	10.13	12%	20,922	211,940
Northern Ontario	122.94	2%	3,487	428,692
Other visitors	93.48	1%	1,744	162,982
Totals		100%	174,390	$13,739,913

Note: Estimating the actual number of tourists requires several assumptions and data components. For a detailed discussion of methodological issues see Dore and Patterson (1994).

TABLE 27.5
Distribution of Visitor Expenditures

	All Visitors (%)	Southern Ontario (%)	United States (%)	Niagara Falls Residents (%)	Northern Ontario (%)	New Year's Eve Visitors[a] (%)
Total expenditures ($ CAD)[b]						
0–149	58.0	64.0	26.0	69.0	42.0	52.0
150–299	21.0	20.0	34.0	27.0	23.0	22.0
300–449	11.0	10.0	19.0	3.0	0.0	15.5
450–599	5.0	3.0	11.0	1.0	0.0	3.5
600+	5.0	3.0	10.0	0.0	35.0	7.0
Accommodations ($ CAD)						
0–99	67.5	70.5	43.9	—	65.4	63.5
100–199	19.2	18.5	31.5	—	15.4	18.0
200–299	8.6	8.5	14.8	—	0.0	12.0
300+	4.7	2.5	9.8	—	19.2	6.5
Meals ($ CAD)						
0–49	56.0	70.0	37.0	—	42.0	55.5
50–99	25.0	26.0	33.0	—	15.0	23.0
100–149	11.0	3.0	17.0	—	4.0	11.0
150–199	5.0	0.0	8.0	—	19.0	6.5
200+	3.0	1.0	5.0	—	20.0	4.0
Local transportation ($ CAD)						
0–49	94.0	95.3	89.0	—	73.0	93.5
50–99	4.4	3.8	8.0	—	12.0	4.5
100+	1.6	0.9	3.0	—	15.0	2.0
Other expenditures ($ CAD)[c]						
0–99	80.1	84.5	60.6	—	57.0	76.5
100–199	10.9	10.5	17.1	—	12.0	16.0
200–299	5.1	3.4	12.5	—	4.0	3.5
300+	3.9	1.6	9.8	—	27.0	4.0

[a] New Year's Eve figures are broken out separately to compare spending patterns with the festival as a whole.

[b] All figures are per party. Mean total expenditures per party: $190.48. Median: $63.89. Average per person expenditure per day is $75.54.

[c] Other expenditure includes souvenirs, personal services, and miscellaneous purchases.

Source: Dore and Patterson (1994).

dents viewed the festival as providing numerous and excellent entertainment opportunities for families. They also believed that public (municipal government) funding should prevail if the festival is to continue. Over half (58 percent) indicated that the festival had improved in the five preceding years. When asked about product improvements, "more lights" was cited by 28 percent, with "more events" and "improved parking" noted by about 10 percent each. Perceived benefits are that the festival brings tourism, provides entertainment, and generates revenue for the community. Residents are proud of the festival. Over 90 percent believed that it would be a loss if the NWFL ceased to exist.

VISITOR PROFILES AND TARGET MARKETS

NWFL visitor profiles were more clearly delineated as a result of the economic impact study. Southern Ontario, the United States, and Northern Ontario are the main visitor origins (see Table 27.6). This is consistent with general profiles of key geographic markets to the region. Geographically, a 180-mile (290-kilometer) radius has been identified as the primary target area for the Niagara Region and the NWFL. Included in this area are (1) Toronto, (2) other Southern Ontario, and (3) nearby American states (New York, Pennsylvania, Ohio, and Michigan). Secondary markets consist of the rest of Ontario, whereas tertiary markets include the rest of Canada and other nearby states.

Visitors to the NWFL are typically between 30 and 54 years, with a household income of $30,000 to $49,000 (CAD). They tend to travel to the festival in couples or groups by private vehicle. Parents with children comprise 40 percent of visitors, and those traveling with spouses or partners comprise 33 percent. Close to 80 percent come expressly for the purpose of attending the festival. Day trippers are in the majority (57 percent). Overnight visitors spend an average of $75.54 (CAD) per day [$190.48 (CAD) per party per trip]. While in Niagara Falls, over three-quarters dine in a restaurant and almost half shop for souvenirs (Dore and Patterson, 1994). Expenditures by day trippers are negligible.

These profiles have important implications for targeting and obtaining high-yield visitors. American visitors stay longer (almost half stay for two nights) and, therefore, tend to spend more on accommodations, meals, and other items than their Canadian counterparts. Increased marketing efforts should be directed at this geographic segment. The festival's objective of drawing visitors from nearby states is translating into strong economic gains from this market.

Regional attendees tend to be less lucrative but are still viewed as an important market. Regional festival-goers tend to be long-term residents of the region (10 years or more), with slightly more formal education than the general population. Almost one-quarter of respondents had friends and/or relatives from outside the Niagara Region who had attended the NWFL. About 60 percent of these friends and relatives stayed with residents, while 13 percent stayed in area accommodations. A majority of locals participated in other activities such as restaurant dining and shopping while attending the festival. Although the economic impact study showed that regional residents comprise only 20 percent of event attendees, the above evidence suggests that they have a role to play in influencing visits by friends and/or relatives to the region during the festival.[6]

THE MARKETING MIX

NWFL marketing activities have increased substantially since 1992, particularly as sponsors and partnerships develop and target markets are more accurately profiled. In 1994, the festival manager worked with two committees (local and global marketing committees; see Figure 27.2) to develop the overall marketing strategy. A consultant is hired periodi-

TABLE 27.6

Festival of Lights Visitor Profile (n = 1800)

	All Visitors (%)	Southern Ontario (%)	United States (%)	Niagara Falls Residents (%)	Northern Ontario (%)	New Year's Eve Only (%)
Percentage of all visitors[a]	100.0	61.0	24.0	12.0	2.0	NA[b]
Age (Years)						
15–19	2.7	3.0	2.0	7.0	8.0	4.5
20–29	15.8	18.0	10.0	13.0	23.0	17.0
30–39	32.3	33.0	30.0	40.0	23.0	38.0
40–54	34.9	35.0	37.0	23.0	38.0	31.0
55+	14.3	11.0	21.0	17.0	8.0	9.5
Income per household ($ CAD)						
29,999 or less	33.0	35.0	28.0	42.0	33.0	35.5
30,000–49,999	35.0	34.0	37.0	27.0	28.0	34.5
50,000–74,999	23.0	23.0	26.0	27.0	11.0	24.0
75,000–99,999	6.0	5.0	6.0	4.0	6.0	4.0
100,000+	3.0	3.0	3.0	0.0	22.0	2.0
Means ($ CAD)	$41,933	$40,758	$44,173	$37,307	$35,139	$40,075
Party type						
Alone	2.5	3.0	2.0	0.0	4.0	2.5
Parent(s) and child/Children	40.0	43.0	27.0	52.0	50.0	43.5
Spouse or partner	31.0	32.0	35.0	16.0	27.0	28.0
Friends	20.0	19.0	17.0	32.0	15.0	22.5
Tour group	4.0	1.0	14.0	0.0	4.0	3.0
Other family or relatives	2.5	2.0	5.0	0.0	0.0	0.5
Transportation						
Private vehicle	95.0	99.0	82.2	Not applicable	100.0	97.0
Bus or rail	4.8	1.0	16.3	Not applicable	0.0	3.0
Other	0.2	0.0	1.5	Not applicable	0.0	0.0
Length of stay						
Excursion/Day trip	57.0	64.5	19.0	Not applicable	38.0	57.0
1 Night	16.0	14.0	25.0	Not applicable	31.0	20.5
2 Nights	23.0	19.0	45.0	Not applicable	23.0	19.0
3+ Nights	4.0	2.5	11.0	Not applicable	8.0	3.5
Other activities						
Restaurant dining	78.4	76.4	84.9	43.3	100.0	83.0
Souvenir shopping	45.3	36.4	74.2	0.0	42.0	44.0
Live entertainment	41.0	40.6	38.3	70.0	50.0	100.0
Museum visit	24.3	21.3	33.7	13.3	27.0	18.0
Accommodation Type[c]						
Private home	58.9	64.8	28.0	Not applicable	19.0	62.5
Hotel or motel	39.6	34.4	70.0	Not applicable	62.0	35.0
Friends or relatives	1.1	0.6	1.0	Not applicable	15.0	2.0
Rented apartment	0.4	0.2	1.0	Not applicable	4.0	0.5

[a] Aggregate distribution of those who had preplanned to attend the Winter Festival of Lights; includes 0.6% who are other Canadians but not from the province of Ontario and 0.4% of visitors from outside North America such as overseas visitors.

[b] NA, not available.

[c] Accommodation type applies only to those visitors who stayed overnight.

Source: Dore and Patterson (1994).

cally to assist with designing advertisements. Gaining increased visibility among families is considered important to being positioned as a worthwhile attraction and drawing more overnight visitors.

The marketing budget, at about $178,000 (CAD) (including sponsorship development), represented about 24 percent of expenses in 1994. This is down from approximately 29 percent in 1993 due to the absence of a one-time grant provided by Tourism Canada[7] in 1993. The 1994 allocation, even excluding sponsorship development, compares favorably with an average of about $57,000 (CAD) spent per year for marketing by a cross section of other Ontario festivals and events (EPG, 1993). An overview of the festival's marketing mix, including specific marketing initiatives, is briefly presented below.

Promotion Most promotions are targeted at 30-to 45-year olds with families. This is consistent with the profile of the typical visitor. A formal media conference is held to launch the NWFL. Media personalities host many events to increase coverage. In addition, media releases highlighting each major event are sent to travel writers, magazines, and newspapers as well as radio and television stations within a 180-mile (290-kilometer) radius. Apart from sponsor development, also considered a form of promotion, the festival promotion mix includes advertising and publicity.

ADVERTISING The festival brochure and *Festival Magazine* (schedule of events) are the major vehicles used to promote the NWFL. In 1994, 300,000 of each were produced (included in the advertising expenses listed in Table 27.3). The *Festival Magazine* is presented in the form of a booklet. It is released close to the time of the festival and contains the schedule of events as well as a listing of special rates available. Cooperative advertising is used to offset the cost of producing the magazine. With the objective of obtaining higher-yield visitors, the *Festival Magazines* were distributed as newspaper inserts to selected homes (families in cities in Toronto, Southern Ontario, Upper New York state, Pennsylvania, Michigan, and Ohio), 62,000 went to Ontario travel information centers, 30,000 to Canadian Automobile Association (CAA) and American Automobile Association (AAA) offices, and 12,000 to Niagara Region convention delegates. The remainder were sent to people who made inquiries through the festival office, travel agents, Ontario toll-free numbers, and chambers of commerce within the primary geographic market area.

Radio commercials were produced, with costs largely absorbed "in kind" by broadcasters. Event radio advertising was aired locally on three Niagara Region stations. The total value of television and radio services received "in kind" was about $300,000 (CAD) in 1994. (Newspapers have always served as an important advertising vehicle, both locally and outside the region. Festival organizers also purchased magazine advertisements that reached a combined circulation of 2.6 million in Ontario and nearby states. In addition the festival is advertised on *Infovision*, (privately operated interactive touch-based computers located at tourist facilities throughout the Niagara Region). Posters are also produced.

PUBLICITY   Newspapers and word-of-mouth referrals are the predominant sources used to obtain festival information by residents (see Figure 27.3). Hence, positive publicity, particularly through newspaper coverage, is considered essential to generating excitement and interest in the festival, especially among area residents.

Based on information provided by the visitor profile, organizers are attempting to expand the festival's reach beyond the 180-mile (290-kilometer) market boundary to include nearby American states and Northern Ontario because these visitors tend to stay longer. Aggressive promotion beyond the Niagara Region did not begin until 1990. These efforts were advanced in 1993 when a five-year partnership was established with BBS, a Toronto-based television broadcaster affiliated with a national broadcasting system (CTV). This partnership yielded widespread complimentary television coverage. Approximately $0.5 million (CAD) in publicity is estimated to have been generated through broadcasting media in 1994 (e.g., the New Year's Eve show is rebroadcast across Canada on New Year's Day and several national television shows include segments on the festival before and throughout its duration).

Print publicity takes the form of editorial copy distributed to travel writers at major newspapers and magazines. Though newspapers and magazines located in the primary geographic area are the focus (e.g., Toronto, Buffalo, Rochester, Cleveland), publications as far away as Florida, Great Britain, and Japan have featured the festival. Travel writers are also sent media releases and invited to the NWFL.

Organizers track inquiries made through the festival's toll-free telephone number. In 1994, 67 percent of out-of-town requests for information were received on the toll-free line, while 32 percent came by mail. Independent requests by individuals were generated

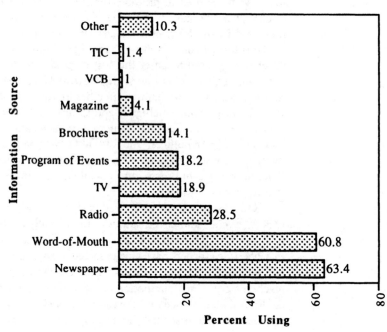

Figure 27.3
Information sources used by Niag-
ara Region residents.

through newspapers (56 percent), magazines (34 percent), and brochures (4 percent). Approximately 69 percent of tour operator requests for information came on the toll-free line, 23 percent by mail, and 7 percent by local telephone. Tour operator requests were generated through magazines (39 percent), brochures (26 percent), and newspapers (24 percent). Origins of tour operator inquiries were Michigan (40 percent), Ontario (23 percent), New York state (20 percent), Ohio (8 percent), and Pennsylvania (5 percent). Additional inquiries are made through the VCB, the Ontario tourism ministry, and area hotels.

Distribution   Niagara Falls has a highly developed inbound tour industry during the summer months. The focus of these tours has traditionally been on the Falls itself. Over 12,000 buses traveled through Queen Victoria Park to see the Falls in 1994 (NPC, 1994). Festival organizers are attempting to position the NWFL as a viable off-season alternative among tour operators. In 1993, the festival became a member of several tour associations because association membership and attending trade shows are believed to be critical, given budget limitations.

Due to human resource and budgetary constraints, NWFL participation in trade and consumer shows is undertaken in conjunction with the VCB. Direct mailings of festival brochures and programs are also sent to tour operators. Principal targets are tour companies within a 300-mile (480-kilometer) radius who already promote the festival and/or have made inquiries. It is difficult to track the success of these contacts. However, some hotels informally provide information to the NWFL about motorcoach operators.

Pricing   All major festival events are produced in Queen Victoria Park. Consequently, festival organizers must follow guidelines established by the NPC and present their plans for NPC approval. Although the NPC is committed to providing free access to the park, it has indicated a willingness to investigate the possibility for charging for some events.

Charging for events in Queen Victoria Park presents logistical challenges. Clearly, the cost of setting up a paid entry venue cannot exceed gate revenues. The resident survey found that almost 70 percent of respondents would not be adverse to paying a nominal fee for events [i.e. $2.00 (CAD)] (Reid, 1994). It is assumed that visitors would feel the same way. Although admissions revenue would likely contribute little to the overall economic impact of the festival, it would assist in generating operating funds.

No pricing strategy exists for group tours, mostly due to the "free" nature of many of the outdoor events. Independent hoteliers sell special packages to individuals (e.g., weekend packages) and select tour operators, but there has been no coordinated effort for tour package creation. This is consistent with other festivals and events in Ontario. Only about 33 percent offered group discounts as of 1993 (EPG, 1993) and only 3 percent offered commissions to the travel trade.

SPONSORSHIP

The festival's sponsorship goals are to leverage sponsor dollars and/or obtain in-kind marketing support. Corporate partners (or sponsors) are systematically targeted and approached with a formal proposal. Research is used to match sponsors with the festival's family image. Among its major sponsors [i.e., those who provide at least $5000 (CAD) in cash or through in-kind donations] are American Express, Baton Broadcasting Systems Ltd., Burger King, the Canadian Niagara Power Company, Kodak, Maid of the Mist, Mattel, McCain, Nestlé, Niagara Falls Hydro, the Niagara Region Tourist Council, Pizza Hut, and various hospitality and tourism enterprises in Niagara Falls.

Sponsorship packages are customized through negotiation to ensure that partners receive maximum value from their investment. Consistent with other festivals of this size, sponsor benefit packages typically include varying degrees of on-site promotion at specific events, promotional rights, product distribution rights, and employee involvement. These benefits are provided on a sliding scale, depending on sponsorship level. A formal agreement is signed but is left open to renegotiation should additional opportunities for sponsorship arise.

Long-term partnerships are encouraged in an attempt to yield more stable revenue sources and greater opportunities for sponsor image-building. Participant recall is becoming more of an issue among sponsors. Not only do they want their names to be seen and recognized by festival-goers, they also want customers to remember them (thus increasing the likelihood of product purchase).

Partnerships must be nurtured and cultivated. For instance, major sponsors are invited to events in Niagara Falls during the summer to keep lines of communication open and maintain contact. During the festival, potential sponsors and their families are invited to the Disney show, a family event. Major sponsors also receive invitations for an annual Sponsorship Weekend that includes sponsor family invitations and a Sponsor Appreciation Night.

MORE SPARKLE AND SHINE IN 1995 AND BEYOND

In response to the results of recent research initiatives and based on the experience gained during 1993 and 1994, a number of improvements were incorporated for the 1995 festival. The goal was to maintain and heighten satisfaction levels. Highlights of such modifications are presented below.

Product Offering and Event Programming

- Seven new light displays were added, including three new "Enchantment of Disney" motion light displays (18 in total as of 1995) and three additional motion displays contributed by local businesses. Some existing displays were relocated to give the festival a fresh look. To complement the surrounding landscape, nature theme displays continue to be added to Dufferin Islands.
- Four evenings of fireworks extravaganzas were scheduled (formerly there were three).
- Additional children's concerts were added between Christmas and New Year's Eve to strengthen the family image and broaden the appeal to children.
- The *Candles in the Park* candlelight stroll was changed to a candlelight Christmas carol concert to improve the focus of the event.
- Festival merchandise was streamlined. Items that did not sell well were elimi-

nated, popular items were improved, and a merchandise company was contracted to produce and distribute a merchandise line. Royalties were to be paid to the festival.

- Concession locations at major events were changed to service crowds more efficiently.
- A large screen was added during Opening Weekend and the live Disney shows to improve visibility for large crowds.
- Neighboring communities in the Niagara Region are establishing their own winter events schedules to complement NWFL offerings and make the region a more attractive winter destination (Fort Erie and Niagara-on-the-Lake have been the major players in this regard to date).

Promotion
- Maps were enhanced to more clearly delineate display areas on both sides of the border.
- Joint Canada/US promotion pieces were developed, including a joint calendar of events to encourage visitors to stay longer.
- An "ambassador campaign" was considered to enlist support from Niagara residents to encourage friends and relatives from outside the region to visit during the festival.
- The Canadian Tourism Commission (based on findings from the economic impact study) contributed $150,000 (CAD) to the VCB towards a cooperative marketing program aimed specifically at showcasing the NWFL to American markets. Matching funds from the private sector were raised to qualify for this funding.

Pricing
- A voluntary admission fee of $1 (CAD) was requested at all major events.

Sponsorship and Fundraising
- Results from the economic impact study were incorporated within sponsorhip collateral materials to highlight the benefits of participating in the NWFL.
- A new sponsor, the Ontario Lottery Corp. (OLC), formed a partnership with Brock University in St. Catharines and conducted on-site surveys at the New Year's Eve event.
- Convinced that the festival has a substantial impact on the economy, city officials channeled $380,000 (CAD) to the festival through NFTI. This sustained contribution is considered positive, particularly at a time when most organizations are experiencing reduced funding.
- BBS made a commitment to increase television promotion of NWFL events.
- A newly added National Hockey League exhibition game may become an annual event and, therefore, an additional source of revenue to help reduce dependency on grants and sponsors.
- Festival-sponsored motorcoach excursions to popular Toronto theater shows were consistently sold out.
- Smaller fundraising efforts (e.g., weekend barbecues) were coordinated to maintain a presence in the community throughout the year.

Organization   • In 1995, the VCB was reorganized and the NWFL became part of NFTI. The festival continues to operate independently with its own board of directors; however, several committees were eliminated. For instance, the local and global marketing committees were eliminated and marketing the NWFL became the responsibility of the NFTI marketing department.

Beyond 1995 Long-term planning is difficult given that a large part of NWFL's funds are awarded on an annual basis. This affects the ability of the NWFL to undertake long-term, high-cost initiatives such as concert site improvements. Key short-term initiatives for the period from 1996 to 1998 are to:

   • Further develop sponsorship and fundraising programs to increase the revenue base.
   • Conduct market research to more precisely identify homogeneous groups of high-yield tourists.
   • Market the festival and the Niagara Region throughout the year.
   • Raise community awareness about the benefits of the festival.
   • Encourage involvement by other regional municipalities.

Organizers realize that ways of estimating attendance must be refined to facilitate efforts to attract and sustain sponsorship. However, as noted earlier, revenue generated is often more important than actual visitor volume given the criteria used by the city and NPC when allocating funds.

CONCLUSION

This chapter has outlined the development of the Niagara Winter Festival of Lights and its marketing activities. A number of issues must be addressed with respect to festival offerings and markets to be served. The challenge is to design and implement research programs that will guide development and marketing efforts, including initiatives to generate higher-yield visitors who will stay longer and, therefore, spend more money in the region. Refined and systematic methods of research and evaluation are required on an ongoing basis. Knowledge of markets, their attendance levels, and their spending patterns makes festivals more accountable to sponsors and other funding bodies. The continued success of the Niagara Winter Festival of Lights depends on how well organizers respond to the challenges.

ACKNOWLEDGMENTS

Recognition must be given to the Niagara Winter Festival of Lights Board of Directors and Festival staff for their patience, support, assistance, and dedication to the NWFL. Special thanks go to the Festival Manager, Greg Bailey, and the 1994 Festival Chair, Ron Buffet.

NOTES

1. See Chapters 5, 9, 11, 12, and 14–19 for additional discussion of community attitudes and involvement in the tourism planning and development processes.

2. See *Festival Management and Event Tourism: An International Journal*, 2(1), 1994. The entire issue is devoted to this topic. Also see Chapter 12 of this book for an overview of approaches for conducting economic impact analyses.
3. The Niagara Parks Commission (NPC) is a self-funded agency of the Ontario provincial government. It maintains golf courses, restaurants, gift shops, campgrounds, flower gardens, marina facilities, and several attractions along the 32-mile (50-kilometer) Niagara Parkway. In effect, the NPC operates as a small city. Though NPC management works in close cooperation with Niagara Falls City Council, the NPC is not required to adhere to any municipal policy related to land use and, therefore, is able to plan and operate policy outside the city's jurisdiction.
4. At the time of writing $1.00 Canadian = US$0.72.
5. The Niagara Region comprises 12 municipalities and has a total population of 372,000. Key municipalities and their respective populations are St. Catharines (131,200), Niagara Falls (76,500), Welland (48,800), Fort Erie (27,100), Port Colborne (19,000), Lincoln (18,200), Thorold (18,000), Pelham (13,800), and Niagara-on-the-Lake (13,200).
6. See Chapter 26 for additional discussion relating to the role that local residents play in influencing the activities of VFR travelers.
7. Tourism Canada is now the Canadian Tourism Commission.

REFERENCES

Ap, J. 1990. Resident's perceptions research on the social impacts of tourism, *Annals of Tourism Research*, 17(4), 610–616.

Blank, U. 1989. *The Community Tourism Industry Imperative*. State College: Venture Publishing.

Crompton, J. 1993. Understanding a business organization's approach to entering a sponsorship partnership, *Festival Management and Event Tourism: An International Journal*, 1(3), 98–109.

Crompton, J. 1994. Benefits and risks associated with sponsorship of major events, *Festival Management and Event Tourism: An International Journal*, 2(2), 65–74.

Dore, M. and M. Patterson. 1994. *The Economic Impact of the Winter Festival of Lights, Niagara Falls, Ontario*. St. Catharines, Ontario: Brock University.

Economic Planning Group of Canada Ltd. (EPG). 1993. *Strategic Directions for the Planning, Development and Marketing of Ontario's Attractions, Festivals and Events, Vol. I: Summary Report*. Toronto: Government of Ontario.

Getz, D. 1991a. *Festivals, Special Events and Tourism*. New York: Van Nostrand Reinhold.

Getz, D. 1991b. Assessing the economic impact of festivals and events: research issues, *Journal of Applied Recreation Research*, 16(1), 61–77.

Janiskee, R. 1994. Some macro scale growth trends in America's community festival industry, *Festival Management and Event Tourism: An International Journal*, 2(1), 10–14.

KPMG (Consultants). 1994. *Marketing and Implementation Plan for Niagara Falls Tourism Inc.* Niagara Falls, Ontario: Niagara Falls Tourism Inc.

Murphy, P.E. 1985. *Tourism: A Community Approach*. New York: Methuen.

Niagara Parks Commission (NPC). 1994. *NPC Annual Visitor Statistics*. Niagara Falls, Ontario: NPC.

Peterson, K.I. and C. Crayton. 1995. The effect of an economic impact study on sponsorship development for a festival: a case study, *Festival Management and Event Tourism: An International Journal*, 2(3/4), 185–190.

Reid, L. 1994. *Niagara Winter Festival of Lights: Community Attitudes and Perceptions*. St. Catharines, Ontario: Brock University.

Robinson, A. and J.G. Noel. 1991. Research needs for festivals: a management perspective, *Journal of Applied Recreation Research*, 16(1), 78–88.

Smith, S.L.J. and D. Getz. 1994. *International Trends, Issues, and Case Studies in Festivals and Special Event Tourism*. Scottish Tourist Board. Waterloo, Ontario: Dauphin Associates.

∮ | PROBLEM SOLVING AND DISCUSSION ACTIVITIES

1. Which of the existing markets are most appropriate for the NWFL to target and why? Devise a marketing strategy that takes into account funding constraints and the organization's structural elements and associated responsibilities.

2. How may festival organizers enhance and promote the festival to tourists while retaining the community flavor and family feeling? Do you foresee any conflicts between engaging in wider promotional activities and retaining the community flavor? What compromises might be necessary in light of the goal to attract more high-yield visitors?

3. What products have the potential to be developed and/or enhanced based on the visitor profile and desire to attract more high-yield visitors? Why? Which activities and/or events are geared more to residents than tourists? How can these be improved to attract a broader geographic audience?

4. What steps can festival organizers take to attract more business from tour operators as well as enhance their relationships with the travel trade in general? To what extent is the goal of attracting more tour business consistent with the desire to attract a higher-yield visitor? What priority should such initiatives with the travel trade be accorded? Why?

5. How can the festival obtain the most current data relating to the demographic profiles and satisfaction levels of festival patrons within its current budget? What criteria/variables can be consistently applied over time to assess satisfaction levels of participants?

6. What funding avenues can realistically be pursued in the face of trends to decreased government backing? Evaluate the 1995 decision to charge voluntary admission fees to patrons at major festival events.

7. How might the festival best integrate marketing efforts with sponsor interests? What is the most effective way to maximize sponsorship dollars?

8. What criteria should be used to measure the festival's success on a continued basis? How can the NWFL ensure that it is able to satisfy such criteria?

9. Conduct an interview with management at a festival or event in your community to identify current issues, opportunities, and challenges this organization faces. Be sure to inquire about the role that research has played/will play in helping this organization capitalize on opportunities and mitigate challenges.

28

Planning for a Competitive Strategy in a Declining Industry

POSITIONING SPAIN'S ARNEDILLO SPA HOTEL

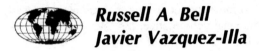

Russell A. Bell
Javier Vazquez-Illa

¶ | K E Y   L E A R N I N G   P O I N T S

- A consumer-oriented marketing plan must be the driving force in the planning process of any business. Successful planning requires that management have a clear understanding of where it wants to go and how it plans to get there, in both the short and the long term. Without a clear set of goals and objectives, the organization could become paralyzed.

- Planners cannot control the future, but they can develop strategies based on the anticipation of business trends that will allow the organization to be better prepared to respond to its target markets' changing needs.

- In the case of a declining business, if the decline can be reversed by some form of intervention, the company must make a tactical decision to continue its operation, search for a competitive strategy, and then devise and implement a contingency plan to allow a smooth transition from the previous position to the new one. An exceptionally rapid transition may result in a situation where the original target markets are prematurely eliminated before the new target markets have the opportunity to grow to a financially sustainable size.

- Operational considerations play a critical role in establishing a differentiated positioning for selected target markets.

INTRODUCTION

In the early 1990s, the Arnedillo Spa Hotel in Spain faced a decline in its market position. In response, the current generation of owners was forced to assume a greater role in the day-to-day operation of their facility and to devise both a short-term survival strategy and a long-term repositioning strategy. This chapter begins by reviewing the concept of planning as the centralized focus for a business strategy. This is followed by a detailed discussion of the Spanish spa industry, including comparisons with European and American spas.

The detailed situation review of the Arnedillo Spa is presented in the context of three major spa market paradigm shifts: (1) the emergence of the urban spa hotel, (2) the blending of spa and resort concepts, and (3) the emergence of new market segments.

STRATEGIC PLANNING AND COMPETITIVE STRATEGIES: CONTEMPORARY PERSPECTIVES AND ISSUES

Strategic Organizations must adopt clear and appropriate goals and objectives to ensure that their
Planning plans are ultimately successful. The driving force and focus for a strategic plan[1] is clearly the customer. Otherwise, any plan for financial performance, asset development, product–service features, and/or marketing will bear a high risk of failure.

Hiebing and Cooper (1993) suggest that marketing consists of (1) analyzing the market to determine insufficiently covered needs, (2) assigning those needs to a market segment, and (3) conceiving a strategy to target the chosen segment better than the competition. They (1993, p. 1) define the plan as "an arranged structure to guide this process."

Stevens et al. (1991) identify the four basic elements of a marketing plan as including the following: (1) a summary of the situation analysis (Where are we now?); (2) a set of objectives (Where do we want to go?); (3) a detailed strategy (How are we going to get there?); and (4) a set of procedures for monitoring results. They further emphasize the importance of planning by suggesting that "every study dealing with business failures uncovers the same basic problem whether it is called undercapitilization, poor location, or simply lack of managerial skills . . . all these problems have their root in poor planning" (1991, p. 4).

Makens (1988) also views the marketing plan as a road map that assists organizations in arriving at the desired destination on time and at a budgeted cost. The nature of the hotel industry—high fixed costs, heavy capitalization, and fixed locations—makes the need for planning, specifically at the strategic level, even more crucial. Mistakes from poor planning are difficult to remedy.

Planning involves not only doing things right, but also doing the right things. Planners cannot control the future, but they can develop strategies based on the anticipation of business trends that will allow the organization to be better prepared to respond to its target markets' changing needs.

The benefits of a marketing plan arise from the need to ensure future sales (Abbey, 1993). Planners must be able to detect the target markets' future needs and forge and implement the programs that will cater to those needs. Moreover, a strong marketing plan must identify appropriate strategies through conducting a SWOT analysis[2] (Nebel, 1991) (see Figure 28.1).

A hotel, such as the Arnedillo Spa Hotel in Spain, facing the situation presented in Quadrant 4 where internal weaknesses are compounded by threats in the external environment should resort to practical survival strategies. Management must understand the characteristics of the external environment and examine the internal environment to determine whether a tactical solution such as cutting costs to stay alive can be implemented while a turnaround strategy is being devised.

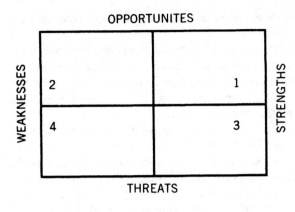

Figure 28.1
SWOT analysis quadrant.

Competitive Strategy Porter (1980) differentiates between companies in a terminal industry and companies that can still implement a successful competitive strategy in an industry in decline. The key point of differentiation is whether the decline can be reversed by some kind of intervention. Hence, understanding the process of industry evolution[3] and being able to predict a change of paradigm are of critical importance.

This view is supported by Levitt (1965), who reported that companies can affect the shape of their growth curves through product innovation and repositioning. He reinforced the importance of planning by recommending the adoption of a competitive strategy in the context of a plan that creates the framework for all the company's tactical actions.

If the business is to survive in the long term, it should adopt a contingency plan to cover the transition period between the previous positioning and the new one. An exceptionally rapid transition may bring about a situation where the new target markets have not grown to a financially sustainable size, while the previous target markets have been prematurely eliminated. The situation can become even more complicated when costly investments have been implemented.

Thus, the prescription for a declining company would be to (1) make a tactical decision to keep the company going, (2) search for a competitive strategy, and (3) devise and implement a contingency plan to allow a smooth transition from the previous position to the new one. Before discussing this process as it applies to the Arnedillo Spa, it is necessary to examine the historical evolution of the spa industry.

EVOLUTION OF THE SPA HOTEL CONCEPT: CONTEMPORARY PERSPECTIVES AND ISSUES

Early Spas Until World War II, a *spa* was a place where it was possible to practice what was commonly known as "taking the waters." Situated in attractive nature-oriented sites, spas were the primary alternatives available for the wealthy segment of society (the only ones who then had the resources to travel) to spend their vacations. To a large extent, spas derived part of their market appeal from a belief that spa treatments facilitated physical and mental rejuvenation. This was a significant factor at a time when medical science had not reached its current efficacy. Additionally, spa guests could engage in their favorite leisure habits, including gaming, attending horse races, or attending morning concerts in a nearby park.

After World War II, the spa sector experienced a significant decline in many countries due to an increase in competition from seaside resorts which capitalized on the growing popularity of beach vacations and improvements in medicine, especially the growth of antibiotics. In addition, traditional spa remedies for many ailments were considered antiscientific and more costly than receiving a prescription.

The decline was most severely felt in countries such as the United States, Canada, Spain, and Great Britain, where the belief in the effectiveness of spa treatments was rather weak. In some countries, however, the spa industry did not suffer decline because medical insurance systems (private and/or government) partially covered the costs of treatment at spas. This happened in countries such as France and Germany, where there was a strong historic belief in the value of spa treatments and where the medical profession had been closely connected to the management of spas.

During the 1960s and 1970s, North America witnessed the development of specialized kinds of spas (holistic, fitness, new age, beauty) which did not rely on the availability of hot springs for the delivery of services. Currently, a *spa hotel* may be broadly defined as a type of lodging where the main motivation for visiting is the availability of spa services, regardless of whether the customer is a fitness enthusiast, treatment follower, vacationer, or meeting attendee. This new definition has been implemented largely in North America, whereas European spas continue to be associated with the availability of a hot mineral spring or sea water. In North America, the concept of a spa is generally ascribed to resort destinations. With few exceptions, the urban spa hotel has not been widely adopted within the industry.

Spa Industry Performance Analysis   Only a few spas in North America are doing well (the average occupancy is around 40 percent). Those that have succeeded have attractive locations adjacent to metropolitan areas and strong programs. Orbeta-Heytens and Tabacchi (1994) identified some of the reasons the spa industry is doing poorly in the United States: 20 percent of potential customers think that spas are boring, 19 percent consider prices to be very high, 8 percent believe that spas do not appeal to families with small children, and 18 percent say that they do not go due to lack of time.

In Europe, the situation varies by country. Spa business accounts for about 50 percent of German tourism (Bywater, 1990). Health insurers subsidizing treatments and stays have played a major role in the development of German spas. However, the proportion of subsidized clients has dwindled from 23 percent in 1969 to 16 percent in 1989, indicating that although state and insurance reimbursements were key to the development of the sector, they no longer play a predominant role. Moreover, there is a constant increase in the number of people who stay at spa resorts, but who do not receive spa medical treatment.

While spa treatments in Italy had traditionally been subsidized, legislators are now trimming those subsidies as a result of the need to reduce budget deficits. With the exception of spas situated in the north that benefit from a share of the German market, these cutbacks have negatively affected Italian spas.

The spa industry in France has been very closely related to the medical profession. Although this has been a reason for success, it may also be a reason for the growing weakness of the spa sector. Most French spas are entirely dependent on state subsidies to operate profitably which is particularly troublesome at a time when budgetary cuts are common. In addition, medical control of spas has prevented them from attracting the fitness segment that has moved to thalassotherapy centers (sea water) due to the lack of attractive programs at traditional spas. *Les Dossiers de la Lettre Touristique (Produits cherchert marches, 1992)* emphasized that the thermal spa industry is growing at only 1 percent annually, while the thalassotherapy sector is growing at 6 percent per year.

Most spas in Spain have recently tried to appeal to the medical profession in an effort to gain support for thermal water-based treatments and to promote a growth strategy similar to that followed in France. In 1991, the Spa Association of Spain (ANET) developed a direct mail campaign targeted at the medical profession, particularly specialists in rheumatology, traumatology, and respiratory ailments. The results were disappointing, with no perceived increase in the market one year later.

The medical profession in Spain does not appear to believe in the validity of spa treatments for medical problems. Although hydrotherapy is widely applied in hospitals as a therapy to recover from trauma, most physicians question whether better results would be obtained by using mineral or thermal waters. Moreover, spa treatments are not studied in medical schools, and no scientific study has demonstrated the relationship between spa treatments and amelioration of a chronic illness. Consequently, efforts to convince the medical profession of the efficacy of these treatments seem destined to fail.

Limited efforts have been made to develop facilities and programs to attract fitness enthusiasts. Some Spanish spa owners believe that this strategy may bring about the end of the traditional spa sector, suggesting that they will lose their profile as health providers if fitness followers stay at spas. This would lead the spa industry to compete with any resort that offers hydrotherapy services.

Most spas in Spain have old structures that are in desperate need of renovation. To assist in the revamping of spas, the Spanish government implemented a social program that subsidizes stays and treatments for senior citizens. This has created a dangerous dependence on the state, especially given that the present government is cutting every aspect of the budget. In recent years, the state subsidies have remained flat. Hence, the bottom line of many spas has been affected due to inflation rates of between 5 and 6 percent. Under Spain's universal health system, spa treatments, as a general norm, are not subsidized by the government. Only cases that document in a scientific manner the validity of treatments are now considered for reimbursement.

It would appear that significant challenges loom for management of spa facilities in Europe, particularly in Spain where Arnédillo is located. A plan for repositioning in a declining industry is clearly required. First, however, it is critical to understand three significant paradigm shifts affecting the spa hotel industry.

Paradigm Shifts Affecting the Spa Hotel Industry

Paradigms establish boundaries and suggest ways to be successful within those boundaries. The spa industry in Europe worked for many years within the boundaries established by a strict concept of spas. The term "spa" itself is derived from the Latin *solus per aqua* (i.e., to get better through the water). Any therapy or service that questioned this premise was rejected. There were some establishments, however, that started to work around the limits of the paradigm through the creation of packages that combined medicine, tourism, and the development of American-style fitness programs. Those spas now seem to be the most successful (Bywater, 1990).

In the United States, although the concept of a spa was defined more broadly, emphasis on specialization led to spa development that attracted a narrow customer mix. The majority of American spas draw from only one or two market segments. This has proved to be a mistake due to the small size of the target markets. Additional mistakes have been made in underestimating the absence of other demand generators when assessing the feasibility of spa projects.

Many spas myopically continue to rely on tiny segments of adventure seekers, holistic health practitioners, or vegetarians. However, recent data, expert opinions, and health trends suggest that, whether in Europe or North America, the present paradigms governing the spa industry have prevented many operators from noticing broader trends affecting their businesses.

Three significant paradigm shifts are predicted to affect the hotel spa industry. First, the word "spa" will not necessarily be linked to rural or nonurban settings. New spa developments will tend to locate in urban settings and be linked with high-quality properties. Second, spas and resorts, whether in Europe or North America, are destined to become more alike. Finally, the business meetings segment is likely to become a primary target market. Each of these shifts is elaborated in the following discussion.

FIRST PARADIGM SHIFT: THE URBAN SPA HOTEL Increasingly, and especially in North America, there is evidence of a delinking of the spa destination from rural or nonurban settings to urban locales. Goegeon (1994) indicates that health-oriented amenities are the main reason for booking the Westin Hotel in Montreal (Canada) for most corporate clients, weekend travelers, and incentive trip winners. The hotel also targets the local market, which provides a substantial increase in revenue. The Westin offers programs that differ from the high-impact workouts of the 1980s and are more in line with the desire in the 1990s for balance and a little pampering (i.e., trying to bridge the gap between perspiration and relaxation). Westin management not only believes that the concept of an urban spa attached to a hotel will continue, but also believes that it will strengthen through the incorporation of more sophisticated and medically based approaches to stress management and relaxation.

Jennifer Tsonas, director of sales and marketing for the Peninsula (New York City, New York) (cited in Cassedy, 1994), stated that people make hotel choices based on the quality of the fitness centers. Similarly, managers from The Baltimore Hotel (Los Angeles, California) stress that the health club provides the property with a competitive edge. A hotel in San Francisco, the Lambourne, claims to be the first urban spa hotel in that city.

SECOND PARADIGM SHIFT: THE MERGER OF RESORT AND SPA DESTINATION CONCEPTS This trend has been emerging for several decades, to the point where differences between the conventional spa and the spa resort have become somewhat blurred. Traditionally, the spa constituted the main focus, and everything else was developed to support or reinforce spa programs. However, since the mid-1980s, spas have been incorporating facilities, services, and programs that traditionally were exclusively offered in resorts. This can be observed in many European countries where few spas today rely exclusively on hot springs. Programs for behavior modification common in American spas are spreading throughout the European industry (French thalassotherapy centers are an example). Although the attachment to water will likely remain a fundamental element for European spas, the paradigm shift may eventually prompt a broader concept for spas in Europe.

Similarly, some resorts have added facilities and services previously exclusive to spas (e.g., the PGA National Resort and Spa in Florida). At a spa resort, the spa does not have the preeminent role it plays in the traditional spa concept. The spa generally is added in an attempt to target more market segments or cater to the changing needs of the current segments.

THIRD PARADIGM SHIFT: A NEW PRIMARY TARGET MARKET   Spas in the United States have traditionally drawn most of their clients from the fitness segment. Married, career women in their forties are most likely to visit health spas (Withiam, 1993). In Europe, women also represent a sizable component of spa customers. However, in Europe, spa patrons are usually 60 years or older and typically suffer from some kind of rheumatic ailment. Nonetheless, the profile of the spa-goer in both North America and Europe is changing. Specifically, meeting planners are increasingly seeking spa resorts or urban retreats (urban spa hotels) to stage annual conventions. This trend is explained by several factors:

- *Impact on the bottom line*. Company directors are becoming aware that healthy employees lead to savings through less absenteeism.
- *Perception is reality*. A company that has meetings in a spa hotel is perceived to be a company that cares about its employees, thereby portraying a positive image to the potential market and society in general.
- *The general trend to healthier lifestyles*. Americans spent US$4.79 billion on health and natural foods in 1994, an increase of 14 percent over 1993. According to a Gallup poll, 69 percent of adults in the United States exercise weekly, up from 53 percent in 1985.

There are already examples to confirm this change. At PGA National Resort and Spa (Stone, 1994) where groups used to request such activities as shopping trips, they are now asking for spa services. At the Nob Hill Lambourne, there is a package called the "Ultimate Health Meeting."

It is believed that spa services provide a special ambience for business meetings that cannot be obtained at a conventional business hotel. Hence, it is conceivable that spa use may be enhanced by creating meeting packages that include spa services. Many people in the industry tend to agree that once conference attendees try spa services, they become repeat clients. To attract more of this market, "traditional" American spas must soften their strict policies regarding menus and exercise programs.

OVERVIEW OF THE SPA MARKET IN SPAIN

Size of the Current Market   Although the number of spa customers has increased significantly in the past few years, there are currently only about 190,000 customers who patronize the 50 spa resorts (4250 rooms that have been classified with at least one star and whose spa facilities fulfill a minimum of requirements) in Spain. Moreover, subsidized clients who pay the lowest price available account for most of the increase. Until the mid-1980s, there were fewer than 70,000 spa customers. The signing of a contract with the Ministry of Social Affairs and, to a lesser extent, the publicity generated due to this social program are believed to have been instrumental in increasing the figure to its current level.

The typical Spanish spa client is a senior citizen, usually a woman who, in 90 percent of the cases, lives in a nearby region. They are very loyal to one spa and usually go during the same season each year. According to ANET, just over 76 percent of the market goes to a spa for medical reasons (e.g., rheumatism or respiratory ailments). Within this segment of the market, which comprises senior citizens who stay 10–15 days, there are two main categories of spa patrons: (1) those who are subsidized by the government (55,000, or 38 percent) and (2) those who go on a private basis (90,000, or 62 percent).

People in the other major group (just under 24 percent of the total market, or 45,000 customers) have many different motivations for visiting a spa, although none of them follow medical treatments. Some are vacationers, whereas others are fitness enthusiasts, conference attendees, holistic health groups, or relatives who accompany others during their stay at the spa.

Spa hotel occupancy is around 70 percent. Social groups account for approximately 40 percent of rooms sold and 35 percent of total revenue. Given that the subsidization of spa treatments and stays will be limited in the future, spa hotels in Spain must seek to diversify their market base. Table 28.1 identifies potential target markets for spas in Spain.

TABLE 28.1
Potential Target Markets for Spain's Spas

Individual Leisure

Senior citizens who suffer from chronic ailments . . . white collar workers, couples, and singles who seek relaxation due to their intense daily work . . . fitness enthusiasts who may be attracted by a spa that has the facilities they normally use as well as water-based fitness facilities and appealing natural surroundings . . . followers of the healthy food trend who may be motivated by the possibility of combining healthy food with outdoor or indoor activities . . . people who want to lose weight and would benefit from the constant supervision available at a spa . . . vacationers, mainly families with children, who are seeking attractive natural surroundings and facilities and services for children . . . women who may be attracted by beauty-oriented services

Group Business

Conference attendees attracted by the appeal of "getting away from it all," water-based spa facilities, relaxation, and light exercise . . . incentive travelers who are attracted by a healthy and sophisticated product

Group Leisure

Adventure seekers organized by firms that specialize in staging resistance, sports, or thematic events in natural surroundings . . . holistic groups drawn by the opportunity to practice some of their techniques (e.g., yoga) in an isolated place . . . social groups comprised of retired people with chronic ailments subsidized by government . . . tour groups en route to a different destination or attracted by a demand generator other than the spa . . . institutions that have travel programs (e.g., savings banks in Spain)

Individual Business

Executives on business trips who stay at a spa because of its proximity to the city they are visiting and the availability of facilities for relaxation purposes

Strategies for the Spa Industry in Spain As a result of the current situation facing spa owners, three strategies are now being debated within the Spa Association of Spain: (1) strict medical specialization for all spas, (2) market diversification, and (3) stressing the hospitality dimension of spa properties.

Proponents of the first strategy advocate a strict medical specialization for all spas. The aim would be to have the public health system cover most of the spa users' expenses. Such a strategy would be driven by an inability to encourage new demand and would rely on attracting business from the market segment motivated by medical treatment. Although this is the most popular strategy among spa owners due to its economic implications, it is also the most unrealistic given historical reasons, budget considerations, medical beliefs, and the current situation in other European countries.

The second strategy recommends adapting to the new markets' needs in terms of services offered and length of stay. Diversification would be key. Each spa would focus on a few segments and develop its programs and services accordingly. In essence, this would entail adding new programs and services to the medical specialization proposed in the first alternative. The American model would be the pattern. Few spa owners favor this strategy due to fears of losing the existing market without gaining another one. Nonetheless, the diversification strategy would likely have positive effects on small and even medium-size properties.

The third strategy stresses the hospitality component of the properties. The spa would be the most critical factor in generating demand, although not the only one. Some refer to this as the "amenity spa" or the spa "à la carte." The advantage of this strategy, given the small size of existing spa segments, is that the spa would be able to work with a variety of segments. The disadvantages are that it would require a considerable investment in facilities, personnel, services, and advertising to reposition a specific property.

How the Arnedillo Spa Hotel is reacting to the current situation facing the spa industry in Spain is discussed below. Information presented comes largely from the perspective of one of the authors, Javier Vasquez-Illa, whose family owns the property.

SPAIN'S ARNEDILLO SPA HOTEL

History and Evolution Arnedillo Spa has been operated and owned by the present company since 1848. The company comprises two main family branches that have traditionally maintained a cooperative pact for the sake of the business. The spa was family-operated at the management level until the 1980s when the growth of the company allowed for the hiring of outside professionals in some executive positions such as the controller and personnel manager.

The hot spring was purchased by the founder of the company, Florencio Martínez de Pinillos, in 1847. Before moving to Arnedillo, he was the manager of Cestona, one of the then most important spas in Spain. At the time of purchase, the hot spring, which was owned by the town council and run by the people of Arnedillo, only targeted the local population. Most of the villagers worked in agriculture under very difficult circumstances due to the poverty of the soil and the mountainous country. The purchase of the spa prompted much needed economic development in the area based on the hot springs.

The consolidation phase of the business extended until World War I. The spa experienced its first golden age in the 1920s due to greater involvement of the owner in the management. The spa remained open during the Spanish Civil War, barely surviving the difficult years after the war. The beginning of industrial growth in Spain (late 1950s) coincided with the second golden age for the spa that extended into the mid-1970s. Throughout this time, the spa was open only during the summer season (June through October) due to a lack of demand during the rest of the year.

The purchase in 1986 of an additional hotel (El Olivar) situated close to the spa increased the spa staff and prompted the decision to lengthen the season in an attempt to increase cash flow to service the new mortgage. By 1991, the spa was operating throughout the year. This worsened an already declining trend in business performance. Moreover, the unexpected resignation (early retirement) of the Arnedillo Spa's general manager in the winter of 1992 left the company in a difficult position. His policy of constantly refurbishing the spa facilities and the two hotels of the Arnedillo Resort had given the company a solid reputation. During his tenure, the financial returns from the business had remained flat. Recently, these returns began to decline (see Table 28.2).

Facilities Arnedillo has two three-star hotels. The Hotel del Balneario has a capacity for 275 guests, while the capacity of the Hotel El Olivar is 100 persons. Each hotel has its own bar and restaurant. The newer hotel (El Olivar) has some conference rooms, although efforts to target this segment have not been very successful. There are two outdoor swimming pools (one of them heated with thermal water), a tennis court, a miniature golf course, and various terraces and garden areas. The spa is one of the biggest in Spain in terms of revenue and capacity. Most of the spa facilities are individual cabins which are used to provide thermal water and mud treatments for customers suffering from rheumatism. Steam baths are available to treat respiratory ailments.

The Arnedillo hotels are not the only ones in the area. There are two other one-star

TABLE 28.2
Balneario Arnedillo Income Statement: 1993 and 1994

	1994 (US$)	1993 (US$)
Net sales		
Hotel and food and beverage	2,537,219	2,189,833
Spa	1,745,455	1,563,637
Total sales	4,282,674	3,753,470
Undistributed operating expenses		
Cost of sales	845,674	831,686
Payroll	1,501,517	1,256,241
Employee benefits	564,710	470,161
Other operating expenses	900,804	545,840
Total operating expenses	3,812,705	3,103,928
Income before interest and depreciation	469,969	649,542
Interest	80,225	37,801
Depreciation	210,199	222,696
Income before taxes	179,545	389,045
Income tax	28,694	125,889
Net income	150,851	263,156

(Courtesy of Arnedillo Spa Hotel management.)

hotels with a capacity for 60 people each, as well as other accommodations in a lower category for a total of 50 people. These hotels cater to spa users who cannot afford the spa hotels' rates. Consequently, the spa is the ultimate beneficiary since these hotels' customers became spa clients.

Market Segments

The Arnedillo Spa attracts a diverse clientele. Characteristics of the various market segments are highlighted below.

GROUP LEISURE: SENIORS QUALIFYING FOR SOCIAL ASSISTANCE   These customers are 65 years or older, have relatively low incomes and education, and are retired. About 60 percent are female. They come from all over Spain, with a majority from Castilla (the largest region in Spain).

This market segment generates about 45 percent of rooms sold and about 30 percent of gross revenue at Arnedillo. They generally stay during the spa's low season at the Hotel del Balneario for two weeks and come in groups of 200 (which leaves part of the hotel for other clients who pay higher rates). They participate in excursions, parties, exercise classes, swimming, and other recreational activities. However, they are not heavy users of the bar facilities or services not included in the program. Arnedillo has increased the number of employees dedicated to this group.

These customers tend to suffer from ailments that can be treated with hydrotherapy and are usually referred by a doctor. The program is popular due to its quality. Indeed, spas in Spain are not able to meet the demand for more rooms to accommodate this market segment. A contract is signed between the spa and the Ministry of Social Affairs or another regional government agency that regulates the service provided—in particular, meals and the number of treatments provided. Each group includes two "disguised inspectors" whose final reports play a critical role in decisions to levy punitive measures against the spa if clauses are not fully respected.

When they arrive at the hotel they pay half the stipulated price. The government pays the remainder several months later. Prices have been frozen since 1993 as a result of budgetary cuts. Each client generates less than US$50 in revenue per day (services provided include accommodation in a double room with private bathroom, three meals with wine inclusive, daily treatment at the spa, and supervised activities). Although this group covers its variable costs, it does not cover its share of fixed costs. However, they make it possible for the bigger hotel to remain open during the low season, thereby avoiding an even greater loss.

GROUP LEISURE: SAVINGS BANKS PROGRAMS   Mostly between 50 and 68 years of age, this segment comprises clients of specific savings banks who have bought the vacation in Arnedillo through special prices negotiated by the banks. About 60 percent are female, with income and education levels that are higher than those of the former group. All of this segment comes from the Basque Country and Pamplona. The majority receives treatment for rheumatism. However, some whose age is between 30 and 50 come on weekends or for a few days for relaxation. Many of the younger clientele come with children, and thus babysitting services are part of the all-inclusive package. These guests tend to purchase more additional services than subsidized seniors.

Most of these customers stay at El Olivar Hotel during the low season. Although this segment is important to this hotel, it is rather insignificant for the company as a whole. In 1994, 1300 people stayed for an average of 12 nights each, thereby generating about 10 percent of total room-nights. They pay US$50 per day per person for the spa facilities plus an additional fee for the American meal plan (double room). This represents about 8 percent of the spa resort's total revenues. These rates do not entirely cover the fixed costs assigned to this group. The meal plan costs are critical in this respect.

There is intense competition for this segment because (1) financial institutions pay more and sooner than does the government and (2) they have a more attractive profile.

GROUP LEISURE: HOLISTIC HEALTH GROUPS   People within this segment range from 20 to 45 years of age. The majority are women. They tend to be stressed professionals, groups of friends seeking something different, or lonely men or women looking for companionship. Their income and education levels are generally high. Most of them come from the Basque Country, Rioja, Navarra, and Zaragoza. They spend most of the time in health sessions and are users of spa services. Visits by this group, which normally occur on weekends, are often organized by schools of yoga. Although the volume of business from this segment has been increasing, they accounted for less than 1 percent of rooms sold and revenue generated in 1994.

GROUP BUSINESS: CONFERENCES   This segment tends to comprise companies that traditionally held meetings or training sessions at resorts. Most conference delegates are males, aged 30 to 45, who occupy middle management positions. Most come from nearby regions, although parent companies are generally based in Madrid (see Figure 7.3). Conferences are held all year except for the month of August. This segment has evidenced continuous growth. However, although volume has increased, profits have not. The recent recession resulted in a more value-conscious conference consumer who was prepared to negotiate to receive the "best" rates. Notwithstanding, this is the most rewarding market in the group segment. In 1994, this group accounted for just under 2 percent of rooms sold and revenue generated.

GROUP BUSINESS: INCENTIVE TRAVEL   This group usually consists of salespeople, male or female aged 30 to 45, who come with their spouses and, often, with other people from the same company. They generally come from Madrid. They are heavy users of the spa services because everything is included in the price. They tend to display a more sophisticated lifestyle than the average spa client. As is the case in Spain in general, the incentive travel segment is fairly small and has evidenced only minimal increases since 1993. Most people who are awarded a trip prefer to go to the Canary Islands (see Figure 7.3). The addition of an indoor swimming pool and fitness center may generate more business from this segment in the future.

INDIVIDUAL LEISURE: SPA ENTHUSIASTS—SENIOR CITIZENS   Most of this segment comprises 60- to 70-year-olds who are either wealthy couples or, to a lesser extent, widows or single women who traditionally spend their vacations at spas. They tend to expect the same kind of service they have always received (i.e., same kind of room, same table at the restaurant, and even the same attendant at the spa). Many come with friends and are generally known by the management and employees. They have a strong faith in the effectiveness of treatments due to their own experience, and some of them have a tremendous influence on other guests and on management. They come from many different regions of Spain, although Madrid and the Basque Country are the primary origin areas. They enjoy sophisticated social activities—concerts, lectures, or full-service buffets by the pool—and disdain activities such as bingo.

This segment, which tends to visit in the summer, provides significant although declining revenue for the spa. It numbers approximately 2200 people per year who pay about US$110 per day per person all-inclusive. In 1994, they accounted for 27 percent of rooms sold, down from 31 percent in 1993 and 37 percent in 1992. Its contribution to revenue has also declined, from 51 percent in 1992 to 46 percent in 1993 and 45 percent in 1994.

INDIVIDUAL LEISURE: VACATIONERS—FAMILIES WITH CHILDREN   Typically young couples in their thirties, these are people who enjoy nature and the availability of outdoor activities. The majority prefers to stay at El Olivar in one of the junior suites or apartments that have a bedroom, a living room with a bed sofa, a private bathroom, and kitchen facilities. They make use of the hotel's babysitting services and are heavy users of the swimming pools. Most originate in the Basque Country.

This segment exhibits extreme seasonality, tending to come almost exclusively in the summer. There is, however, some growth in visits during long weekends throughout the year. Price is an element of concern. The volume of business from this segment has remained stable in the past few years due to price increases. They pay approximately US$90 for an apartment per day. In 1994, they accounted for less than 2 percent of rooms sold and revenue generated.

INDIVIDUAL LEISURE: COUPLES—RELAXATION PROGRAMS   This market comprises white collar workers in their late twenties to late forties who are attracted by the glamour of spa life. Many have very demanding jobs and, as a result, enjoy the opportunity to escape for a few days. They like the spa's relaxation facilities, especially the Roman Bath and its programs. They also like rambling in natural surroundings and wine tasting in the nearby wineries. Most come from the Basque Country and Madrid.

The advantage of this segment is that they tend to visit in any season, especially in fall and spring. The disadvantage is that their average stay is only two days (on weekends). Recently, a four-day program was implemented with positive results. This market is less price-sensitive than other segments due to their short stays and higher available income (most do not have children). Growth within this segment has been substantial. In 1994, they accounted for 9 percent of rooms sold, up from 7 percent in 1993 and 1 percent in 1992. They contributed about 11 percent of total revenue in 1994, compared to 9 percent in 1993 and 2 percent in 1992.

INDIVIDUAL LEISURE: FRIENDS—FITNESS ENTHUSIASTS   This segment has similar motivations as couples attracted by the relaxation programs. Originating primarily from the Basque Country and Madrid, they tend to demand more tailored services (e.g., private use of the spa's wine cellar for a party) than the relaxation segment.

The Decision-Making Environment

COMPETITION Similar to other Spanish spas, the majority of Arnedillo's clients come from within a 185-mile (300-kilometer) radius. Approximately 60 percent come from two regions, namely, Basque Country and Madrid. This increases to 75 percent in the individual leisure segment. Therefore, any spa within a 185-mile (300-kilometer) radius of Arnedillo which targets one or more similar segments can be considered to be a competitor. Arnedillo Spa has three primary competitors: Fitero (Navarra), Sicilia (Zaragoza), and Puente Viesgo (Cantabria). Spas that exclusively serve the subsidized government market are not considered to be competitors.

Fitero is the main competitor in the group leisure segment, specifically the savings bank program subsegment. It is also a competitor for senior citizens who are spa enthusiasts. Fitero does not target fitness enthusiasts.

Sicilia is only a competitor in the group leisure-savings bank program subsegment, where it has been developing an aggressive policy. It does not compete with Arnedillo in the individual leisure market due to its lower-quality facilities.

Puente Viesgo is a competitor in every segment except the "spa enthusiasts—senior citizens" subsegment. Puente Viesgo is not perceived as being suitable for rheumatism treatments because it does not have thermal waters. However, it is a serious competitor in the fitness enthusiasts subsegment and it is gaining market share at a rapid rate. Puente Viesgo is a relatively new entrant that can capitalize on its recently developed four-star facilities, exceptional location, and proximity (9 miles or 15 kilometers) to Santander, an urban tourist destination. Puente Viesgo is also beginning to outperform Arnedillo in the business segment.

LOCATION The area in which the resort is located is surrounded by rocky mountains with some vegetation. The temperature is warm most of the year, although the winter (and sometimes part of fall and spring) is cool (however, it is not cold enough to develop ski facilities). La Rioja (the province in which Arnedillo is located) is internationally known for its wines. It is considered to be a wealthy region of Spain, ranking second among all provinces in per capita purchasing power. Access has recently improved with the renovation of the local road that connects the spa with the main highway. This main highway links La Rioja with the Basque Country, the region where most of the spa clients reside.

PRICES Spa treatments at Arnedillo tend to be priced above industry averages. This is primarily because Arnedillo is the only spa in Spain that offers natural mud treatments. These treatments tend to be expensive because numerous employees are required to first transport the mud, then apply the mud to the spa users in individual cabins, and finally, clean and disinfect the area to allow another user to enter.

Hotel prices tend to follow the industry standards, and food and beverage prices are generally lower than the industry averages. The outgoing GM believed that, due to numerous restaurants in the nearby village, restaurant prices had to be kept low to sell a sufficient number of full-board plans. Although 80 percent of hotel clients made use of the in-house restaurants, this volume was not sufficient for the food and beverage area to be profitable.

PROMOTION Promotion of the spa was not seriously considered until the declining occupancy percentages led the board of directors to appoint a sales manager in 1988. Even so, the company culture did not change: word-of-mouth referrals were perceived as being most effective, and any expense for promotion was looked upon as being inefficient.

PEOPLE Labor problems began to emerge in the summer of 1993. Trade unions organized the company and found fertile ground to develop their strategies. Because there was no forecasting of occupancy, shifts were organized almost on a daily basis. Legislation on the maximum number of hours each worker could work per week was not respected by management. This was offset by paying higher wages than the average in the industry. However, employees had the feeling that they were always working, and the higher wages did not adequately compensate for this.

The majority of the employees live in accommodations in a separate area of each hotel. The previous general manager believed that the remote location made this necessary. In addition, the spa's reputation in the area for long working hours necessitated the hiring of workers from other parts of Spain.

POSITIONING The spa market had an image characterized as "elderly people seeking magic results for their chronic illnesses." For most people, a spa was the same as a sanitarium with deteriorated facilities and unfriendly service. The sales manager's attempts to change the spa's image were not very successful because decisions on new services and facilities were made without considering his opinion. Even his advertising proposals were not approved by the board of directors. In spite of these handicaps, he managed to obtain enough business to keep the hotels going during the low season, which gave him the reputation of being an efficient manager among some of the members of the board of directors.

FINANCE In March 1994, the sales manager was promoted to general manager. By this time, cash flow was not sufficient to cover short-term debts. Investments in the past 10 years had been made without regard to profits. Money was spent in the belief that somehow there was going to be a profit at the end of the year. This policy produced a situation where it was necessary to seek credit to pay the returns to the shareholders.

Considerable sums of money had been spent on refurbishing the spa to cater to the needs of the only market segment the company was actively targeting, namely, people suffering chronic ailments (especially rheumatism) who came on an individual basis or in groups. The only exception was the construction in 1993 of the Roman Bath, which clearly was targeted to new markets. The Roman Bath consisted of various small swimming pools, steam baths, and saunas at different temperatures for the users to go from one to another to relieve stress.

While still sales manager, the general manager had informed the board that the number of clients included in the rheumatism segment, specifically those who paid rack rates, was starting to decline. However, no action was taken by the board of directors.

Untouched for more than 20 years, the older and bigger 150–room hotel was in need of a profound rehabilitation. Most of the money had been invested in the renovation of spa facilities, the addition of new amenities such as the swimming pools, and the purchase of El Olivar. Table 28.3 presents comparative balance sheets for 1993 and 1994.

THE MEETING

In a meeting on June 1, 1994, the new general manager and his closest and newly appointed staff began to analyze the deteriorating situation. The remainder of this section presents dialogue from that meeting.

Resident manager: Customer complaints have increased, especially in the food and beverage area. We do not deliver the right service, and menus are also criticized. Our new fitness clients, the ones who come due to the opening of the Roman Bath, also complain. They enjoy the facility, but they do not like the food, the service, and the image of so many elderly people wandering about.

Spa area manager: I do not think it is just the fact of their mixing with elderly people. What they do not like is the appearance of these group clients who come subsidized by different institutions.

General manager: I can understand this. However, we need those groups to avoid closing our facilities during the low season.

TABLE 28.3
Balneario Arnedillo Balance Sheet: 1993 and 1994

	1994 (US$)	1993 (US$)
Property and equipment		
Land, buildings, and equipment	1,919,623	1,433,578
Leaseholds	47,952	837
Less accumulated depreciation and amortization	13,034	24,090
Net property and equipment	1,974,541	1,410,325
Current assets		
Inventories	189,068	0
Receivables	293,067	297,376
Cash	151,005	234,500
Total assets	2,607,681	1,942,201
Owner's equity		
Capital	452,046	452,046
Retained earnings	955,127	688,394
Long-term debt	681,452	203,129
Current liabilities	368,125	362,476
Total liabilities and owner's equity	2,607,681	1,942,201

(Courtesy of Arnedillo Spa Hotel management.)

TABLE 28.4
Problems at the Arnedillo Spa Hotel

Marketing Mix Element	Problems	Causes
People	Employees are not motivated and do not deliver good service	Poorly trained Poorly organized Feel they are working all the time because they live on the premises Weak reputation of the spa Lack of necessary skills Most are temporary labor
Product	Older hotel in need of renovation Most spa facilities focus on treatment followers	Cash flow invested in new hotel and spa Company has limited leverage capacity Lack of planning to anticipate future trends
Price	Prices in food and beverage are not high enough to cover costs Prices of the spa services are too high Group prices are too low	Intense competition in the area pushes the restaurant prices down High labor and material costs due to mud treatment Dependence on group business in low season
Place	Travel trade does not know the spa product	Travel trade is more interested in high-yield destinations
Promotion	The new spa services are not well known in the marketplace	Lack of communications strategy No advertising budget
Programming	Programs to target new and older segments are not developed	Lack of strategic thinking and marketing planning
Packaging	No yield management practices implemented to encourage demand through packages in the low demand periods	Lack of skills Lack of computer expertise
Partnership	The company philosophy favors short-term results above long-term position Liquidity problems Diminishing net income	Shareholders are used to receiving dividends under any circumstances No cash flow analysis before using the cash from operations for investment Sales from the main segment (treatment followers) are declining and sales from other segments do not compensate for the loss
Positioning	The general image of a spa is that of a pseudosanitarium Incompatibility of market segments	Spa industry in decline No communications effort (external or internal) to modify the image No consensus within industry on how to position spas Present spa segments are not large enough to disregard the less rewarding ones

Resident manager: However, it is clear that people who come to our resort attracted by the advertising campaign we are currently using may be a little disappointed to see that the young image transmitted by the advertisements does not correspond with reality.

General manager: I know. Something must be done to ensure that we are able to target different market segments and to create repeat customers. We need all of them, especially now that we are going through an awkward situation as far as our solvency is concerned. What can you tell us about this problem and also about personnel issues (questions directed to the controller and personnel manager)?

Controller: As far as our financial situation is concerned, I think we need to stop investing in the facilities. We need all of the economic resources to recuperate from what has become a tradition in this company—spending money before knowing the amount of profits to be generated.

General manager: But this could negatively affect our strategy of targeting new markets. The older hotel is not prepared to deal with new markets and, consequently, it needs to be thoroughly refurbished.

Controller: I know. I only want to stress the fact that if we do not control cash flows, we may end up in a very difficult economic situation.

Personnel manager: In relation to our employees, they seem to be lacking in motivation. They are complaining most of the time and, in many cases, they either do not have the necessary skills or do not want to learn. I have extremely difficult problems in dealing with the head waiter and the main restaurant's chef. They have been here for so many years they do not accept my authority.

The meeting was concluded when the general manager passed out a summary sheet that outlined the problems and their causes (see Table 28.4). The attendees agreed to meet in a week after studying the summary sheet to consider different solutions to the overwhelming problems.

NOTES

1. See Chapters 3–6 and 9 for additional discussion relating to strategic planning.
2. See Chapters 5, 6, 24, and 26 for additional discussion and examples of SWOT analysis.
3. See Chapters 2, 3, 5, and 7 for additional discussion relating to both the product life cycle and tourist area cycle of evolution concepts.

REFERENCES

Abbey, J.R. 1993. *Hospitality Sales and Advertising*, 2nd ed. East Lansing, MI: American Hotel and Motel Association.

Bywater, M. 1990. *Spas and Health Resorts in the EC*. EIU Travel & Tourism Analyst, No. 6, 52–57.

Cassedy, K. 1994. Oh so healthy, *Lodging*, 19(8), 90–93.

Goegeon, K. 1994. Urban renewal: the growth of the city spa, *Hotelier*, 6(5), 17–18.

Hiebing, R.G. and S.W. Cooper. 1993. *How to Write a Successful Marketing Plan*. Lincolnwood, IL: NTC Business Books.

Levitt, T. 1965. Exploit the product life cycle, *Harvard Business Review*, Nov./Dec., 81–94.

Makens, J. 1988. *Hotel Sales and Marketing Planbook*. Columbia, SC: Marion Clarence Publishing House.

Nebel, E.C. III. 1991. *Managing Hotels Effectively*. New York: Van Nostrand Reinhold.

Oberta-Heytens, A. and M.H. Tabacchi. 1994. Interational Spa and Fitness Association Directors Meeting, Spring.

Porter, M.E. 1980. *Competitive Strategy.* New York: The Free Press.

Produits cherchert marches, *Les Dossicro de la Lettre Touristique,* Supplement de la Lettre Touristique, Octobre 1992.

Stevens, R.E., D.L. Louden, and W.E. Warren. 1991. *Marketing Planning Guide.* Binghamton, NY: The Haworth Press.

Stone, J. 1994. Spas and "wellness"—Destinations showing healthy growth, *Meetings News,* 18(12), 40–41.

Withiam, G. 1993. Who goes to spas? *Cornell Hotel and Restaurant Quarterly,* 34(5), 13..

₰ | PROBLEM SOLVING AND DISCUSSION ACTIVITIES

1. Assume that you have been hired as a consultant to the Arnedillo Spa. Your task is to develop strategies to improve the performance and profitability of the spa. Answer the following questions sequentially as part of your report:
    a. What should be the agenda for the next staff meeting?
    b. What target market(s) should be the focus of future efforts and why? How will this address issues associated with both the compatibility and profitability of various segments?
    c. What short-term and long-term strategies should the management team adopt to survive? Justify your responses.
    d. Can the management team utilize intermediaries (the channel of distribution) more effectively?
    e. What should the general manager's primary focus of activity be for the next 12 months?
2. How spas in general are positioned in Spain will affect the Arnedillo Spa Hotel. If you were the general manager of the Arnedillo Spa Hotel, which of the three options outlined in this chapter would you encourage the Spanish spa industry to adopt? Why?
3. Identify a destination or other hospitality and tourism organization that was able to successfully implement a turnaround strategy to remove it from the decline stage of the life cycle. What tactics and strategies were implemented to execute the turnaround and avoid absolute decline?
4. How successful have spa hotels in urban settings been in your region? What factors have contributed to this success (or lack thereof)? How might these urban spa hotels prolong growth (or maturity) and avoid decline?
5. This chapter outlines three paradigm shifts affecting the spa sector. To what extent are these shifts evident in your region? Provide examples to justify your response.

Index

Lightning Source UK Ltd.
Milton Keynes UK
UKOW040854131011

180165UK00007B/65/P